WESTERN CIVILIZATION
VOLUME II

Early Modern Through the 20th Century

Seventh Edition

Editor

William Hughes
Essex Community College

William Hughes is a professor of history at Essex Community College in Baltimore County, Maryland. He received his A.B. from Franklin and Marshall College and his M.A. from the Pennsylvania State University. He continued graduate studies at the American University and the Pennsylvania State University. Professor Hughes is interested in cultural history, particularly the role of film and television in shaping and recording history. He researched this subject as a Younger Humanist Fellow of the National Endowment for the Humanities, and he was a participant in the Image as Artifact project of the American Historical Association. He is author of the chapter on film as evidence in *The Historian and Film* (Cambridge University Press) and has written articles, essays, and reviews for *The Journal of American History, The New Republic, The Nation, Film and History, American Film,* and *The Dictionary of American Biography*. Professor Hughes also serves as an associate editor for *American National Biography,* a twenty-volume reference work to be issued by Oxford University Press.

Cover illustration by Mike Eagle

Annual Editions
A Library of Information from the Public Press

The Dushkin Publishing Group, Inc.
Sluice Dock, Guilford, Connecticut 06437

The Annual Editions Series

Annual Editions is a series of over 55 volumes designed to provide the reader with convenient, low-cost access to a wide range of current, carefully selected articles from some of the most important magazines, newspapers, and journals published today. Annual Editions are updated on an annual basis through a continuous monitoring of over 300 periodical sources. All Annual Editions have a number of features designed to make them particularly useful, including topic guides, annotated tables of contents, unit overviews, and indexes. For the teacher using Annual Editions in the classroom, an Instructor's Resource Guide with test questions is available for each volume.

VOLUMES AVAILABLE

Africa
Aging
American Government
American History, Pre-Civil War
American History, Post-Civil War
Anthropology
Biology
Business Ethics
Canadian Politics
China
Commonwealth of Independent States
Comparative Politics
Computers in Education
Computers in Business
Computers in Society
Criminal Justice
Drugs, Society, and Behavior
Dying, Death, and Bereavement
Early Childhood Education
Economics
Educating Exceptional Children
Education
Educational Psychology
Environment
Geography
Global Issues
Health
Human Development
Human Resources
Human Sexuality
India and South Asia

International Business
Japan and the Pacific Rim
Latin America
Life Management
Macroeconomics
Management
Marketing
Marriage and Family
Microeconomics
Middle East and the Islamic World
Money and Banking
Nutrition
Personal Growth and Behavior
Physical Anthropology
Psychology
Public Administration
Race and Ethnic Relations
Social Problems
Sociology
State and Local Government
Third World
Urban Society
Violence and Terrorism
Western Civilization, Pre-Reformation
Western Civilization, Post-Reformation
Western Europe
World History, Pre-Modern
World History, Modern
World Politics

Library of Congress Cataloging in Publication Data
Main entry under title: Annual editions: Western civilization, vol. II: Early Modern Through the Twentieth Century.
    1. Civilization—Periodicals. 2. World history—Periodicals. Title: Western civilization, vol. II: Early Modern Through the Twentieth Century.
901.9'05   82–645823   ISBN 1–56134–218–1

Seventh Edition

Manufactured by The Banta Company, Harrisonburg, Virginia 22801

Printed on Recycled Paper

To the Reader

In publishing ANNUAL EDITIONS we recognize the enormous role played by the magazines, newspapers, and journals of the *public press* in providing current, first-rate educational information in a broad spectrum of interest areas. Within the articles, the best scientists, practitioners, researchers, and commentators draw issues into new perspective as accepted theories and viewpoints are called into account by new events, recent discoveries change old facts, and fresh debate breaks out over important controversies.

Many of the articles resulting from this enormous editorial effort are appropriate for students, researchers, and professionals seeking accurate, current material to help bridge the gap between principles and theories and the real world. These articles, however, become more useful for study when those of lasting value are carefully *collected, organized, indexed,* and *reproduced* in a *low-cost format,* which provides easy and permanent access when the material is needed. That is the role played by *Annual Editions.* Under the direction of each volume's *Editor,* who is an expert in the subject area, and with the guidance of an *Advisory Board,* we seek each year to provide in each *ANNUAL EDITION* a current, well-balanced, carefully selected collection of the best of the public press for your study and enjoyment. We think you'll find this volume useful, and we hope you'll take a moment to let us know what you think.

What exactly are we attempting to do when we set out to study Western civilization? The traditional course in Western civilization is a chronological survey of sequential stages in the development of European institutions and ideas, with a cursory look at Near Eastern antecedents and a side glance at the Americas and other places where westernization has occurred. So we move from the Greeks to the Romans to the medieval period and on to the modern era, itemizing the distinctive characteristics of each stage, as well as each period's relation to preceding and succeeding developments. Of course, in a survey so broad (usually advancing from Adam to the atom in two brief semesters) a certain superficiality seems inevitable. Key events whiz by as if viewed in a cyclorama; often there is little opportunity to absorb and digest the complex ideas that have shaped our culture. It is tempting to excuse these shortcomings as unavoidable. But to present a course on Western civilization that leaves students with only a jumble of events, names, dates, and places is to miss a marvelous opportunity. For the great promise of such a broad course of study is that it enables students to explore great turning points or shifts in the development of Western culture. Close analysis of these moments enable students to understand the dynamics of continuity and change over time. At best, the course can provide a coherent view of the Western tradition and offer opportunities for reflection about everything from forms of authority and religion to patterns of human behavior or the price of progress.

Of course, to focus exclusively on Western civilization is to ignore non-Western peoples and cultures. It hardly needs saying that Western history is not the only history that contemporary students should know. Yet it should be an essential part of what they learn, for it impossible to understand the modern world without some grounding in the basic patterns of the Western tradition.

As students become attuned to the distinctive traits of the West, they develop a sense of the dynamism of history. They begin to understand how ideas relate to social structures and social forces. They come to appreciate the nature and significance of conceptual innovation and recognize how values can infuse inquiry. More specifically, they can trace the evolution of Western ideas about nature, humankind, authority, and the gods, i.e., they learn *how* the West developed its distinctive character. And, as Reed Dasenbrock has observed, in an age that seeks greater multicultural understanding, there is much to be learned from "the fundamental multiculturalism of Western culture, the fact that it has been constructed out of a fusion of disparate and often conflicting cultural traditions."

Of course, the articles collected in this volume cannot deal with all of these matters, but by providing an alternative to the synthetic summaries of most textbooks, they can help students better understand the diverse traditions and processes that we label Western civilization. This book is like our history—unfinished, always in process. It will be revised biennially. Comments and criticism are welcome from all who use this book. To that end a postpaid article rating form is included at the back of the book. Please feel free to recommend articles that might improve the next edition. With your assistance, this anthology will continue to improve.

William Hughes
Editor

Contents

Unit
1

The Age of Power

Seven selections trace the evolution of political power in early modern times. Topics include the European state system, the emergence of British power, how the image makers cast the personage of Louis XIV, and the influence of John Locke on liberty.

To the Reader	**iv**
Topic Guide	**2**
Overview	**4**

1. **The Emergence of the Great Powers,** Gordon A. Craig and Alexander L. George, from *Force and Statecraft: Diplomatic Problems of Our Times,* Oxford University Press, 1983. **6**
   In 1600 Europe's greatest power complex was the old Holy Roman Empire, in league with Spain. By the eighteenth century, however, the *European system* was transformed so drastically that the *great powers* were Great Britain, France, Austria, Prussia, and Russia. How did such a shift occur? This essay traces the *evolution of the European state system* in early modern times.

2. **War, Money, and the English State,** John Brewer, from *The Sinews of Power,* Alfred A. Knopf, 1989. **12**
   England was a minor power in the great *wars* that ravaged Europe in the sixteenth and early-seventeenth centuries. But *European powers* soon came to fear and envy *Britain's military machine,* particularly its navy. John Brewer's introduction to his book on the topic explains the *institutional arrangements* and *economic strategies* that made England a major power.

3. **Competing Cousins: Anglo-Dutch Trade Rivalry,** Jonathan Israel, *History Today,* July 1988. **17**
   This article explores the rivalry between two great *naval powers.* It traces *Anglo-Dutch relations* "from commercial competition to open war and finally 'snarling alliance.'"

4. **The High Price of Sugar,** Susan Miller, *Newsweek,* Fall/Winter 1991. **22**
   In the *early-modern period,* the Atlantic formed the matrix for a new phase of Western civilization, one that combined European, American, and African elements. Central to this new system was the *triangular trade,* driven by Europe's demand for sugar and the sugar growers' reliance on *slave labor.* This article shows how the drive for profits transformed the Western world.

5. **The Fabrication of Louis XIV,** Peter Burke, *History Today,* February 1992. **25**
   Peter Burke explains how Louis XIV and his *image makers* exploited literature and the visual arts to enhance his power in France and his reputation in Europe.

6. **The 17th-Century 'Renaissance' in Russia,** Lindsey A. J. Hughes, *History Today,* February 1980. **29**
   This article, a survey of *western influences on Russian art and architecture,* demonstrates that *Peter the Great*'s program of westernization was not such a break from the past as has commonly been supposed.

7. **Locke and Liberty,** Maurice Cranston, *The Wilson Quarterly,* Winter 1986. **33**
   Unlike Thomas Hobbes, who built his political philosophy around the principles of order and authority, *John Locke* erected a system of political thought around liberty and private ownership of property. Reviewing Locke's life and thought, Maurice Cranston places the English philosopher's work in its political and intellectual context.

The concepts in bold italics are developed in the article. For further expansion please refer to the Topic Guide and the Index.

Unit 2

Rationalism, Enlightenment, and Revolution

Eleven articles discuss the impact of science, politics, music, economic thought, changing social attitudes, and the rights of women on the Age of Enlightenment.

Overview   **38**

8. **From Astronomy to Astrophysics,** James Trefil, *The Wilson Quarterly,* Summer 1987.   **40**
The *Copernican theory* invigorated the science of *astronomy,* setting in motion a chain reaction of discoveries by *Tycho Brahe, Johannes Kepler,* and *Isaac Newton* that transformed humanity's perception of the heavens—and ourselves. Today's astrophysicists use new *technologies* to further revise and enhance our cosmic vision.

9. **Newton's Madness,** Harold L. Klawans, from *Newton's Madness: Further Tales of Clinical Neurology,* Harper & Row, 1990.   **47**
Sir Isaac Newton was a universal genius who coinvented *calculus,* formulated three major *laws of mechanics,* articulated *theories of gravity and planetary motion,* and discovered the composition of white light. Twice during his life he suffered periods of prolonged psychotic behavior. Harold Klawans explores Newton's genius and his bouts with madness.

10. **Origins of Western Environmentalism,** Richard H. Grove, *Scientific American,* July 1992.   **51**
"The roots of Western *conservatism,*" says the author, "are at least 200 years old and grew in the tropics." This article traces the role of scientists in protecting the flora and fauna of Europe's new *colonies* in the tropics.

11. **The Birth of Public Opinion,** Anthony J. La Vopa, *The Wilson Quarterly,* Winter 1991.   **56**
The notion of *"public opinion"* was born during the eighteenth century. This article shows the connection between the *Age of Enlightenment* and the expression of a public with a defined will.

12. **The Commercialization of Childhood,** J. H. Plumb, *Horizon,* Autumn 1976.   **62**
A new attitude toward *children* emerged in England during the eighteenth century. It was a gentler and more sensitive approach, one that reflected a *change in social (and economic) attitudes.* Entrepreneurs soon developed imaginative products to exploit the emerging belief that children were shaped by their early environment.

13. **A Whole Subcontinent Was Picked Up Without Half Trying,** Pico Iyer, *Smithsonian,* January 1988.   **67**
India was the jewel of the *British Empire.* The ironic story of how the *East India Company* secured India for England is told here.

14. **The Godfather of the American Constitution,** Robert Wernick, *Smithsonian,* September 1989.   **75**
When James Madison and Alexander Hamilton advanced a new American instrument of government based on *checks and balances,* deliberation and choice, *separation of powers,* and wariness of human nature, they were following the lead of a French nobleman and man of letters. Robert Wernick traces *Baron de Montesquieu*'s life and his influence on the *Enlightenment* and the *American Constitution.*

The concepts in bold italics are developed in the article. For further expansion please refer to the Topic Guide and the Index.

15. **The French Revolution in the Minds of Men,** Maurice Cranston, *The Wilson Quarterly,* Summer 1989.   79

The French Revolution has had a dual existence. First there was the revolution of actual deeds and words. Then, says the author, there was the revolution as it "became inflated or distorted in the minds of later partisans." He describes the *myths of the French Revolution* and how such fabrications influenced later generations of revolutionaries.

16. **The Passion of Antoine Lavoisier,** Stephen Jay Gould, *Natural History,* June 1989.   83

Many people paid the price for the *French Revolution.* One of them was France's greatest scientist, Antoine Lavoisier. A child of the *Enlightenment* who favored some of the Revolution's early accomplishments, the famous chemist ran afoul of the *Committee of Public Safety* and its revolutionary tribunals. Stephen Jay Gould cites Lavoisier's accomplishments and ponders why in revolutionary times even a brilliant scientist is not immune from the political extremists.

17. **The First Feminist,** Shirley Tomkievicz, *Horizon,* Spring 1972.   88

Mary Wollstonecraft, author of *Vindication of the Rights of Women* (1792), cogently argued the case that the *ideals of the Enlightenment* and the *French Revolution* should be extended to *women.* This is her story.

18. **Gin and Georgian London,** Thomas Maples, *History Today,* March 1991.   93

After *Parliament* passed the *Gin Act of 1736,* riots broke out among the drinking poor of London. This article explains why the poor considered gin to be a precious friend and why the government felt obliged to control its use.

Overview   98

19. **Cottage Industry and the Factory System,** Duncan Bythell, *History Today,* April 1983.   100

The *Industrial Revolution* was one of the greatest discontinuities in history, or so it is widely believed. The popular notion of the origins of the *factory system* is that it cruelly uprooted the more humane system known as *cottage industry.* Duncan Bythell questions the conventional view in his assessment of the two *modes of production* and their impact on *social and economic conditions in England.*

20. **Sophie Germain,** Amy Dahan Dalmédico, *Scientific American,* December 1991.   107

Famous female mathematicians are a rarity. Sophie Germain's story shows us why. A talented and ambitious scientist and mathematician, Germain did highly original work in number theory and the theory of elasticity. But first she had to overcome the prejudices of family and colleagues.

Unit 3

Industry, Ideology, Nation-building, and Imperialism: The Nineteenth Century

Nine articles focus on the nineteenth century in the Western world. Topics include the working class, the Industrial Revolution, John Stuart Mill, and the expansion of Europe.

The concepts in bold italics are developed in the article. For further expansion please refer to the Topic Guide and the Index.

21. Engels in Manchester: Inventing the Proletariat, Gertrude Himmelfarb, *The American Scholar,* Autumn 1983.   **111**

Friedrich Engels, coauthor of the ***Communist Manifesto*** and patron of Karl Marx, wrote an influential study of ***working-class life*** in ***England.*** But was it an accurate description of the ***factory system,*** or was it colored by the author's ***communism***?

22. Samuel Smiles: The Gospel of Self-Help, Asa Briggs, *History Today,* May 1987.   **119**

In eighteenth-century America ***Benjamin Franklin*** was the prophet of ***self-help***; in nineteenth-century England it was Samuel Smiles. The latter's formula for ***success*** stressed the importance of role models, perseverance, and strenuous effort.

23. John Stuart Mill and Liberty, Maurice Cranston, *The Wilson Quarterly,* Winter 1987.   **125**

John Stuart Mill, the leading philosopher of Victorian England, reshaped the ideas of John Locke, David Hume, and others into classical ***liberalism.*** Still influential, Mill is read today for his defense of liberty. His ideas, says Maurice Cranston, "have contributed much to the debates of our own time about ***the freedom of dissenters, minorities, and women.***"

24. Giuseppe Garibaldi, Denis Mack Smith, *History Today,* August 1991.   **129**

Giuseppe Garibaldi was the hero of Italy's nineteenth-century quest for unification. Many tendencies of ***modern Italian politics*** have their origins in Garibaldi and his ***Red-Shirt movement.***

25. Sarah Bernhardt's Paris, Christopher Hibbert, *Mankind,* October 1982.   **134**

Through carefree times and through war and famine, for over half a century actress ***Sarah Bernhardt*** was at the center of the ***artistic and social life of Paris.*** The author's review of her colorful career provides a panorama of ***social and political change.***

26. 'The White Man's Burden'?: Imperial Wars in the 1890s, Lawrence James, *History Today,* August 1992.   **143**

Lawrence James surveys the racial theories, economic interests, and national rivalries that constituted nineteenth-century ***imperialism.***

27. Ecological Imperialism: The Biological Expansion of Europe, 900–1900, Alfred W. Crosby, *The Key Reporter,* Winter 1987-1988.   **149**

European emigrants and their descendants are scattered over many parts of the globe. By the end of the nineteenth century, they had established many neo-Europes that profoundly altered the world. But conventional accounts of European expansion have missed an important component—the ***ecological implications of imperialism***. This essay highlights a few of the changes wrought by the neo-Europeans.

The concepts in bold italics are developed in the article. For further expansion please refer to the Topic Guide and the Index.

Unit 4

Modernism and Total War: The Twentieth Century

Eleven selections discuss the evolution of the modern Western world, the Russian Revolution, the world wars, the Nazi state, the effects of Europe's loss of economic and political dominance in world affairs, and the 1991 revolution in Russia.

Overview   **152**

28. Sarajevo: The End of Innocence, Edmund Stillman, *Horizon,* Summer 1964.   **154**
Even after 50 years of explanations, it is difficult to understand why a political murder in a remote corner of the Balkans should have set off a war that changed Europe forever. This article provides another perspective on *the origins of the Great War.*

29. When the Red Storm Broke, William Harlan Hale, *American Heritage,* February 1961.   **158**
In 1917 the Allies hoped to keep Russia in the war against Germany, despite the collapse of the Romanov dynasty. This is the odd tale of America's futile and amateurish efforts to influence the *Russian Revolution.*

30. How the Modern Middle East Map Came to Be Drawn, David Fromkin, *Smithsonian,* May 1991.   **164**
The long-awaited collapse of the *Ottoman Empire* finally occurred in 1918. *World War I* and the *Arab uprising* paved the way for a new era in the Middle East. But it was the British, not the Arabs, who played the central role in reshaping the *geopolitics* of the region.

31. Remembering Mussolini, Charles F. Delzell, *The Wilson Quarterly,* Spring 1988.   **171**
Benito Mussolini won the praise of intellectuals, journalists, and statesmen for bringing order and unity to Italy during the early years of his *fascist regime.* In 1945, however, he and his mistress were executed; later, a mob in Milan mutilated the corpses. Here Charles Delzell chronicles the dictator's rise and fall.

32. Resistance of the Heart in Nazi Germany, Nathan Stoltzfus, *The Atlantic,* September 1992.   **178**
It is widely believed that it would have been useless and probably suicidal for Germans to have protested against the policies of *Hitler.* But Nathan Stoltzfus documents three instances of successful *opposition to Nazi programs.* He concludes that people must take responsibility for the conduct of their governments—even in brutal *totalitarian regimes.*

33. A People Under Terror: Italian Jews During World War II, Alexander Stille, *Dissent,* Fall 1991.   **183**
Italian fascism, unlike Hitler's fascist movement, did not rise to power on a program of *anti-Semitism.* In 1938, however, at the urging of his ally Hitler, Mussolini promulgated new *"racial laws"* directed against the Jews of Italy. This article shows what those decrees meant to the family of Enrico Di Veroli.

34. Night Witches, Snipers, and Laundresses, John Erickson, *History Today,* July 1990.   **187**
During World War II *women of the Soviet Union* were called upon to play many roles in the fight for survival against the German invaders. Their experiences are surveyed in this article.

The concepts in bold italics are developed in the article. For further expansion please refer to the Topic Guide and the Index.

35. 1945, Ryszard Kapuściński, *The New Republic,* January 27, 1986.   191

"Those who live through a war never free themselves from it." A Polish writer's memories of war are a reminder that *wartime heroism* is not confined to the battlefront. The civilian experience of *military conflict* is indelibly imprinted upon his memory. In this essay he recreates a wartime world of extreme tension and dread.

36. The War Europe Lost, Ronald Steel, *The New Republic,* October 6, 1979.   195

Unlike World War I, which was fought almost entirely in Europe, *the second war* was truly a world war, one that undermined the authority of the European states and broke their hold on the colonial world. Ronald Steel explains how and why the war reduced Europe's mastery over the world.

37. The August Revolution, Martin Malia, *The New York Review of Books,* September 26, 1991.   197

The Russian Revolution of August 1991 appears to have negated *the Russian Revolution of October 1917.* Thus, says the author (paraphrasing Marx), the Soviet experiment began in tragedy and ended in the hard-line communists' farcical attempts to hold on to power. This article by Martin Malia, an authority on the Soviet system, assesses the prospects of Boris Yeltsin's regime.

38. Facts on File, Paul Quinn-Judge, *The New Republic,* June 29. 1992.   204

In an attempt to discredit nearly 75 years of Communist Party dictatorship in *the Soviet Union,* Boris Yeltsin's new Russian regime released a series of important documents taken from the secret personal archives of party leaders. Among other things, they connect recent Soviet regimes with *international terrorism,* and they reveal a less flattering picture of *Mikhail Gorbachev* than the one typically promoted by Western journalists.

Unit 5

Conclusion: The Human Prospect

Seven articles examine how politics, war, economics, and culture affect the prospects of humankind.

Overview   206

39. Jihad vs. McWorld, Benjamin R. Barber, *The Atlantic,* March 1992.   208

This article explores two possible political futures, "both bleak, neither democratic." The first is a return to *tribalization,* an endless array of conflicts pitting culture against culture, ethnic group against ethnic group, religion against religion. The second is a single homogeneous *global network* "tied together by *technology, ecology, communications,* and *commerce."*

40. Europe's Muslims, Anthony Hartley, *The National Interest,* Winter 1990/91.   213

The controversy over Salman Rushdie's novel, *The Satanic Verses,* awakened the world to some of the *conflicts between Muslim and European values*—conflicts that may be intensified as the Muslim population of Europe grows. Anthony Hartley explores the status of Muslims in England, France, and Germany.

The concepts in bold italics are developed in the article. For further expansion please refer to the Topic Guide and the Index.

41. **World City-States of the Future,** Riccardo Petrella, *New Perspectives Quarterly,* Fall 1991.   **219**

The author, a futurist, anticipates that we are entering a *postnational* era that will be a high-tech version of *prenational* times. The new age will be dominated by "technologically highly developed city regions" linked by *"transnational* business firms that bypass the traditional *nation-state* framework."

42. **Global Boat People,** Andries Van Agt, *New Perspectives Quarterly,* Fall 1991.   **223**

Much of history has been the story of migrations. In our time, economic and political disturbances have combined with *mass communications* and the *transportation revolution* to create unprecedented *mass migrations* from the poorer to the richer parts of the world. Andries Van Agt analyzes the potential impact of this development.

43. **Return of the** *Volksgeist,* Isaiah Berlin, *New Perspectives Quarterly,* Fall 1991.   **226**

The *Enlightenment* advanced the principle of ·*cosmopolitanism,* the hope for a *universalist* culture based on widely accepted rational percepts. But eighteenth-century German poet and philosopher *Johann Gottfried Herder* promoted a counterideal: *nationalism.* It was Herder who argued that everyone needs to belong to a group, and every group needs a culture that is exclusively its own. Here Isaiah Berlin explores the relevance of Herder for our time.

44. **The Fall and Rise of French,** George Tombs and Angéline Fournier, *World Monitor,* May 1992.   **230**

Although European nations have lost nearly all their *colonies* since World War II, their languages remain entrenched in portions of the Third World. For instance, there are five times more French speakers in the world than 100 years ago. In the twenty-first century more than half of these will be in Africa. What does this say about the possibilities for a *global culture?*

45. **Whither Western Civilization?** Thomas Sowell, *Current,* September 1991.   **234**

The fate of Western civilization, says the author, "is intertwined with the fate of human beings around the world, whether they live in Western or non-Western societies." Thus, to understand the modern world it is essential to be aware of *the West's achievements and shortcomings.* But, says Thomas Sowell, the West should be judged by comparison to the achievements and shortcomings of other cultures and traditions, not by abstract standards of perfection.

Index   **241**
Article Review Form   **244**
Article Rating Form   **245**

The concepts in bold italics are developed in the article. For further expansion please refer to the Topic Guide and the Index.

Topic Guide

This topic guide suggests how the selections in this book relate to topics of traditional concern to students and professionals involved with the study of Western civilization. It can be very useful in locating articles that relate to each other for reading and research. The guide is arranged alphabetically according to topic. Articles may, of course, treat topics that do not appear in the topic guide. In turn, entries in the topic guide do not necessarily constitute a comprehensive listing of all the contents of each selection.

TOPIC AREA	TREATED AS AN ISSUE IN:	TOPIC AREA	TREATED AS AN ISSUE IN:
Art/Architecture	6. 17th-Century 'Renaissance' in Russia	Labor	19. Cottage Industry and the Factory System 21. Engels in Manchester
Business	3. Competing Cousins 4. High Price of Sugar 12. Commercialization of Childhood 19. Cottage Industry and the Factory System	Middle Class	22. Samuel Smiles
		Middle East	30. How the Modern Middle East Map Came to Be Drawn 39. Jihad vs. McWorld
Childhood	12. Commercialization of Childhood 35. 1945	Modernization	39. Jihad vs. McWorld 45. Whither Western Civilization?
Colonialism	10. Origins of Western Environmentalism 13. A Whole Subcontinent Was Picked Up 26. 'The White Man's Burden'? 44. Fall and Rise of French	Nationalism	24. Giuseppe Garibaldi 43. Return of the *Volksgeist*
		Nation-State	1. Emergence of the Great Powers 2. War, Money, and the English State 5. Fabrication of Louis XIV 41. World City-States of the Future
Democracy	11. Birth of Public Opinion		
Ecology	10. Origins of Western Environmentalism 27. Ecological Imperialism	Philosophy	7. Locke and Liberty 14. Godfather of the American Constitution 23. John Stuart Mill and Liberty 43. Return of the *Volksgeist*
Enlightenment	11. Birth of Public Opinion 12. Commercialization of Childhood 14. Godfather of the American Constitution 16. Passion of Antoine Lavoisier 17. First Feminist 43. Return of the *Volksgeist*	Politics/Authority	1. Emergence of the Great Powers 5. Fabrication of Louis XIV 31. Remembering Mussolini 32. Resistance of the Heart in Nazi Germany
Fascism	31. Remembering Mussolini 32. Resistance of the Heart in Nazi Germany 33. People Under Terror	Religion	6. 17th-Century 'Renaissance' in Russia 40. Europe's Muslims
Ideology	7. Locke and Liberty 21. Engels in Manchester 22. Samuel Smiles 23. John Stuart Mill and Liberty	Revolution	15. French Revolution in the Minds of Men 16. Passion of Antoine Lavoisier 29. When the Red Storm Broke 37. August Revolution
Industrial Revolution	19. Cottage Industry and the Factory System 21. Engels in Manchester	Science	8. From Astronomy to Astrophysics 9. Newton's Madness 20. Sophie Germain

TOPIC AREA	TREATED AS AN ISSUE IN:	TOPIC AREA	TREATED AS AN ISSUE IN:
Society	12. Commercialization of Childhood 18. Gin and Georgian London 19. Cottage Industry and the Factory System 35. 1945 40. Europe's Muslims 42. Global Boat People	**War (cont'd)**	34. Night Witches, Snipers, and Laundresses 35. 1945 36. War Europe Lost
Technology	39. Jihad vs. McWorld	**Westernization**	6. 17th-Century 'Renaissance' in Russia 39. Jihad vs. McWorld 45. Whither Western Civilization?
Totalitarianism	32. Resistance of the Heart in Nazi Germany 38. Facts on File	**Women**	17. First Feminist 20. Sophie Germain 34. Night Witches, Snipers, and Laundresses
War	1. Emergence of the Great Powers 2. War, Money, and the English State 3. Competing Cousins 28. Sarajevo: The End of Innocence 31. Remembering Mussolini	**Working Class**	18. Gin and Georgian London 19. Cottage Industry and the Factory System 21. Engels in Manchester

The Age of Power

The early modern period (c.1450-c.1700) was a time of profound change for Western civilization. During this epoch the medieval frame of reference gave way to a recognizably modern orientation. The old order had been simply, but rigidly, structured. There was little social or geographical mobility. Europe was relatively backward and isolated from much of the world. The economy was dominated by self-sufficient agriculture. Trade and cities did not flourish. There were few rewards for technological innovation. A person's life seemed more attuned to revela-

tion than to reason and science. The Church both inspired and delimited intellectual and artistic expression. Most people were prepared to subordinate their concerns to those of a higher order—whether religious or social. Carlo Cipolla, a distinguished European historian, has given us an interesting capsulization of the waning order: "People were few in number, small in stature, and lived short lives. Socially they were divided among those who fought and hunted, those who prayed and learned, and those who worked. Those who fought did it often in order to rob. Those who prayed and learned, learned little and prayed much and superstitiously. Those who worked were the greatest majority and were considered the lowest group of all."

That constricted world gradually gave way to the modern world. There is no absolute date that marks the separation, but elements of modernity were evident throughout Western civilization by the eighteenth century. In this context the late medieval, Renaissance, and Reformation periods were transitional. They linked the medieval to the modern. But what were the elements of this emergent modernity? Beginning with the economic foundation, an economy based on money and commerce overlaid the traditional agrarian system, thus creating a more fluid society. Urban life became increasingly important, allowing greater scope for personal expression. Modernity involved a state of mind, as well. Europeans of the early modern period were conscious that their way of life was different from that of their forebears. In addition, these moderns developed a different sense of time—for urban people, clock time superseded the natural rhythms of the changing seasons and the familiar cycle of planting and harvesting. As for the life of the mind, humanism, rationalism, and science began to take precedence over tradition—though not without a struggle. Protestantism presented yet another challenge to orthodoxy. And, as economic and political institutions evolved, new attitudes about power and authority emerged.

The early modern period is often called an Age of Power, primarily because the modern state, with its power to tax, conscript, subsidize, and coerce, was taking shape. Its growth was facilitated by the changing economic order, which made it possible for governments to acquire money in unprecedented amounts—to hire civil servants, raise armies, protect and encourage national enterprise, and expand their power to the national boundaries and beyond.

Power, in various early modern manifestations, is the subject of the articles assembled in this unit. "The Emergence of the Great Powers" surveys the shifting international balance of power during the seventeenth and eighteenth centuries. "War, Money, and the English State" explores relations among economy, society, and state in one country. "Competing Cousins" explores the Anglo-Dutch trade rivalry, and shows how natural political allies could be driven to war over economic conflicts. "The High Price of Sugar" describes the triangular trade and how the drive for profits and economic power transformed Western civilization into an Atlantic culture that combined European, American, and African elements. "The Fabrication of Louis XIV" explains how writers and painters were enlisted in the drive to enhance the reputation (and influence) of the "Sun King." "Locke and Liberty" covers the philosopher's attempts to formulate a "modern" philosophy of politics, one resting on liberty and property.

Looking Ahead: Challenge Questions

How did the modern international order evolve?

How could modern states, such as England, afford such heavy investments in their military establishments?

What accounts for the many shifts in Anglo-Dutch relations?

How extensive were the modernizing tendencies of the era? What, if any, impact did they have upon the remote sections of Europe, such as Russia?

What were the long-term consequences of the triangular trade?

What is it about John Locke's ideas that make them "modern"?

The Emergence of the Great Powers

Gordon A. Craig and Alexander L. George

I

Although the term *great power* was used in a treaty for the first time only in 1815, it had been part of the general political vocabulary since the middle of the eighteenth century and was generally understood to mean Great Britain, France, Austria, Prussia, and Russia. This would not have been true in the year 1600, when the term itself would have meant nothing and a ranking of the European states in terms of political weight and influence would not have included three of the countries just mentioned. In 1600, Russia, for instance, was a remote and ineffectual land, separated from Europe by the large territory that was called Poland-Lithuania with whose rulers it waged periodic territorial conflicts, as it did with the Ottoman Turks to the south; Prussia did not exist in its later sense but, as the Electorate of Brandenburg, lived a purely German existence, like Bavaria or Wurttemberg, with no European significance; and Great Britain, a country of some commercial importance, was not accorded primary political significance, although it had, in 1588, demonstrated its will and its capacity for self-defense in repelling the Spanish Armada. In 1600, it is fair to say that, politically, the strongest center in Europe was the old Holy Roman Empire, with its capital in Vienna and its alliances with Spain (one of the most formidable military powers in Europe) and the Catholic states of southern Germany—an empire inspired by a militant Catholicism that dreamed of restoring Charles V's claims of universal dominion. In comparison with Austria and Spain, France seemed destined to play a minor role in European politics, because of the state of internal anarchy and religious strife that followed the murder of Henri IV in 1610.

Why did this situation not persist? Or, to put it another way, why was the European system transformed so radically that the empire became an insignificant political force and the continent came in the eighteenth century to be dominated by Great Britain, France, Austria, Prussia, and Russia? The answer, of course, is war, or, rather more precisely, wars—a long series of religious and dynastic conflicts which raged intermittently from 1618 until 1721 and changed the rank order of European states by exhausting some and exalting others. As if bent upon supplying materials for the nineteenth-century Darwinians, the states mentioned above proved themselves in the grinding struggle of the seventeenth century to be the fittest, the ones best organized to meet the demands of protracted international competition.

The process of transformation began with the Thirty Years War, which stretched from 1618 to 1648. It is sometimes called the last of the religious wars, a description that is justified by the fact that it was motivated originally by the desire of the House of Habsburg and its Jesuit advisers to restore the Protestant parts of the empire to the true faith and because, in thirty years of fighting, the religious motive gave way to political considerations and, in the spreading of the conflict from its German center to embrace all of Europe, some governments, notably France, waged war against their own coreligionists for material reasons. For the states that initiated this wasting conflict, which before it was over had reduced the population of central Europe by at least a third, the war was an unmitigated disaster. The House of Habsburg was so debilitated by it that it lost the control it had formerly possessed over the German states, which meant that they became sovereign in their own right and that the empire now became a mere adjunct of the Austrian crown lands. Austria was, moreover, so weakened by the exertions and losses of that war that in the period after 1648 it had the greatest difficulty in protecting its eastern possessions from the depredations of the Turks and in 1683 was threatened with capture of Vienna by a Turkish army. Until this threat was contained, Austria ceased to be a potent factor in European affairs. At the same time, its strongest ally, Spain, had thrown away an infantry once judged to be the best in Europe in battles like that at Nordlingen in 1634, one of those victories that bleed a nation white. Spain's decline began not with the failure of the Armada, but with the terrible losses suffered in Germany and the Netherlands during the Thirty Years War.

In contrast, the states that profited from the war were the Netherlands, which completed the winning of its independence from Spain in the course of the war and became a commercial and financial center of major importance; the kingdom of Sweden, which under the leadership of Gustavus Adolphus, the Lion of the North, plunged into the conflict in 1630 and emerged as the strongest power in the Baltic region; and France, which entered the war formally in 1635 and came out of it as the most powerful state in western Europe.

It is perhaps no accident that these particular states were so successful, for they were excellent examples of the process that historians have described as the emergence of the modern state, the three principal characteristics of which were effective armed forces, an able bureaucracy, and a theory of state that restrained dynastic exuberance and defined political interest in practical terms. The seventeenth century saw the emergence of what came to be called *raison d'état* or *ragione di stato*—the idea that the state was more than its ruler and more than the expression of his wishes; that it transcended crown and land, prince and people; that it had its particular set of interests and a particular set of necessities based upon them; and that the art of government lay in recognizing those interests and necessities and acting in accordance with them, even if this might violate ordinary religious or ethical standards. The effective state must have the kind of servants who would interpret *raison d'état* wisely and the kind of material and physical resources necessary to implement it. In the first part of the seventeenth century, the Dutch, under leaders like Maurice of Nassau and Jan de Witt, the Swedes, under Gustavus Adolphus and Oxenstierna, and the French, under the inspired ministry of Richelieu, developed the administration and the forces and theoretical skills that exemplify this ideal of modern statehood. That they survived the rigors of the Thirty Years War was not an accident, but rather the result of the fact that they never lost sight of their objectives and never sought objectives that were in excess of their capabilities. Gustavus Adolphus doubtless brought his country into the Thirty Years War to save the cause of Protestantism when it was at a low ebb, but he never for a moment forgot the imperatives of national interest that impelled him to see the war also as a means of winning Swedish supremacy along the shore of the Baltic Sea. Cardinal Richelieu has been called the greatest public servant France ever had, but that title, as Sir George Clark has drily remarked, "was not achieved without many acts little fitting the character of a churchman." It was his clear recognition of France's needs and his absolute unconditionality in pursuing them that made him the most respected statesman of his age.

The Thirty Years War, then, brought a sensible change in the balance of forces in Europe, gravely weakening Austria, starting the irreversible decline of Spain, and bringing to the fore the most modern, best organized, and, if you will, most rationally motivated states: the Netherlands, Sweden, and France. This, however, was a somewhat misleading result, and the Netherlands was soon to yield its commercial and naval primacy to Great Britain (which had been paralyzed by civil conflict during the Thirty Years War), while Sweden, under a less

rational ruler, was to throw its great gains away.

The gains made by France were more substantial, so much so that in the second half of the century, in the heyday of Louis XIV, they became oppressive. For that ruler was intoxicated by the power that Richelieu and his successor Mazarin had brought to France, and he wished to enhance it. As he wrote in his memoirs:

The love of glory assuredly takes precedence over all other [passions] in my soul. . . . The hot blood of my youth and the violent desire I had to heighten my reputation instilled in me a strong passion for action. . . . *La Gloire,* when all is said and done, is not a mistress that one can ever neglect; nor can one be ever worthy of her slightest favors if one does not constantly long for fresh ones.

No one can say that Louis XIV was a man of small ambition. He dreamed in universal terms and sought to realize those dreams by a combination of diplomatic and military means. He maintained alliances with the Swedes in the north and the Turks in the south and thus prevented Russian interference while he placed his own candidate, Jan Sobieski, on the throne of Poland. His Turkish connection he used also to harry the eastern frontiers of Austria, and if he did not incite Kara Mustafa's expedition against Vienna in 1683, he knew of it. Austria's distractions enabled him to dabble freely in German politics. Bavaria and the Palatinate were bound to the French court by marriage, and almost all of the other German princes accepted subsidies at one time or another from France. It did not seem unlikely on one occasion that Louis would put himself or his son forward as candidate for Holy Roman emperor. The same method of infiltration was practiced in Italy, Portugal, and Spain, where the young king married a French princess and French ambassadors exerted so much influence in internal affairs that they succeeded in discrediting the strongest antagonist to French influence, Don Juan of Austria, the victor over the Turks at the battle of Lepanto. In addition to all of this, Louis sought to undermine the independence of the Netherlands and gave the English king Charles II a pension in order to reduce the possibility of British interference as he did so.

French influence was so great in Europe in the second half of the seventeenth

century that it threatened the independent development of other nations. This was particularly true, the German historian Leopold von Ranke was to write in the nineteenth century, because it

was supported by a preeminence in literature. Italian literature had already run its course, English literature had not yet risen to general significance, and German literature did not exist at that time. French literature, light, brilliant and animated, in strictly regulated but charming form, intelligible to everyone and yet of individual, national character was beginning to dominate Europe. . . . [It] completely corresponded to the state and helped the latter to attain its supremacy, Paris was the capital of Europe. She wielded a dominion as did no other city, over language, over custom, and particularly over the world of fashion and the ruling classes. Here was the center of the community of Europe.

The effect upon the cultural independence of other parts of Europe—and one cannot separate cultural independence from political will—was devastating. In Germany, the dependence upon French example was almost abject, and the writer Moscherosch commented bitterly about "our little Germans who trot to the French and have no heart of their own, no speech of their own; but French opinion is their opinion, French speech, food, drink, morals and deportment their speech, food, drink, morals and deportment whether they are good or bad."

But this kind of dominance was bound to invite resistance on the part of others, and out of that resistance combinations and alliances were bound to take place. And this indeed happened. In Ranke's words, "The concept of the European balance of power was developed in order that the union of many other states might resist the pretensions of the 'exorbitant' court, as it was called." This is a statement worth noting. The principle of the balance of power had been practiced in Machiavelli's time in the intermittent warfare between the city states of the Italian peninsula. Now it was being deliberately invoked as a principle of European statecraft, as a safeguard against universal domination. We shall have occasion to note the evolution and elaboration of this term in the eighteenth century and in the nineteenth, when it became one of the basic principles of the European system.

7

Opposition to France's universal pretensions centered first upon the Dutch, who were threatened most directly in a territorial sense by the French, and their gifted ruler, William III. But for their opposition to be successful, the Dutch needed strong allies, and they did not get them until the English had severed the connection that had existed between England and France under the later Stuarts and until Austria had modernized its administration and armed forces, contained the threat from the east, and regained the ability to play a role in the politics of central and western Europe. The Glorious Revolution of 1688 and the assumption of the English throne by the Dutch king moved England solidly into the anti-French camp. The repulse of the Turks at the gates of Vienna in 1683 marked the turning point in Austrian fortunes, and the brilliant campaigns of Eugene of Savoy in the subsequent period, which culminated in the smashing victory over the Turks at Zenta and the suppression of the Rakoczi revolt in Hungary, freed Austrian energies for collaboration in the containment of France. The last years of Louis XIV, therefore, were the years of the brilliant partnership of Henry Churchill, Duke of Marlborough, and Eugene of Savoy, a team that defeated a supposedly invulnerable French army at Blenheim in 1704, Ramillies in 1706, Oudenarde in 1708, and the bloody confrontation at Malplaquet in 1709.

These battles laid the basis for the Peace of Utrecht of 1713–1715, by which France was forced to recognize the results of the revolution in England, renounce the idea of a union of the French and Spanish thrones, surrender the Spanish Netherlands to Austria, raze the fortifications at Dunkirk, and hand important territories in America over to Great Britain. The broader significance of the settlement was that it restored an equilibrium of forces to western Europe and marked the return of Austria and the emergence of Britain as its supports. Indeed, the Peace of Utrecht was the first European treaty that specifically mentioned the balance of power. In the letters patent that accompanied Article VI of the treaty between Queen Anne and King Louis XIV, the French ruler noted that the Spanish renunciation of all rights to the throne of France was actuated by the hope of "obtaining a general Peace and securing the Tranquillity of *Europe* by a Ballance of Power," and the king of

Spain acknowledged the importance of "the Maxim of securing for ever the universal Good and Quiet of Europe, by an equal Weight of Power, so that many being united in one, the Ballance of the Equality desired, might not turn to the Advantage of one, and the Danger and Hazard of the rest."

Meanwhile, in northern Europe, France's ally Sweden was forced to yield its primacy to the rising powers of Russia and Prussia. This was due in part to the drain on Swedish resources caused by its participation in France's wars against the Dutch; but essentially the decline was caused, in the first instance, by the fact that Sweden had too many rivals for the position of supremacy in the Baltic area and, in the second, by the lack of perspective and restraint that characterized the policy of Gustavus Adolphus's most gifted successor, Charles XII. Sweden's most formidable rivals were Denmark, Poland, which in 1699 acquired an ambitious and unscrupulous new king in the person of Augustus the Strong of Saxony, and Russia, ruled since 1683 by a young and vigorous leader who was to gain the name Peter the Great. In 1700, Peter and Augustus made a pact to attack and despoil Sweden and persuaded Frederick of Denmark to join them in this enterprise. The Danes and the Saxons immediately invaded Sweden and to their considerable dismay were routed and driven from the country by armies led by the eighteen-year-old ruler, Charles XII. The Danes capitulated at once, and Charles without pause threw his army across the Baltic, fell upon Russian forces that were advancing on Narva, and, although his own forces were outnumbered five to one, dispersed, captured, or killed an army of forty thousand Russians. But brilliant victories are often the foundation of greater defeats. Charles now resolved to punish Augustus and plunged into the morass of Polish politics. It was his undoing. While he strove to control an intractable situation, an undertaking that occupied him for seven years, Peter was carrying through the reforms that were to bring Russia from its oriental past into the modern world. When his army was reorganized, he began a systematic conquest of the Swedish Baltic possessions. Charles responded, not with an attempt to retake those areas, but with an invasion of Russia—and this, like other later invasions, was defeated by winter and famine and ultimately by a lost battle, that of Pultawa in 1709, which

broke the power of Sweden and marked the emergence of Russia as its successor.

Sweden had another rival which was also gathering its forces in these years. This was Prussia. At the beginning of the seventeenth century, it had, as the Electorate of Brandenburg, been a mere collection of territories, mostly centered upon Berlin, but with bits and pieces on the Rhine and in East Prussia, and was rich neither in population nor resources. Its rulers, the Hohenzollerns, found it difficult to administer these lands or, in time of trouble, defend them; and during the Thirty Years War, Brandenburg was overrun with foreign armies and its population and substance depleted by famine and pestilence. Things did not begin to change until 1640, when Frederick William, the so-called Great Elector, assumed the throne. An uncompromising realist, he saw that if he was to have security in a dangerous world, he would have to create what he considered to be the sinews of independence: a centralized state with an efficient bureaucracy and a strong army. The last was the key to the whole. As he wrote in his political testament, "A ruler is treated with no consideration if he does not have troops of his own. It is these, thank God! that have made me *considerable* since the time I began to have them"—and in the course of his reign, after purging his force of unruly and incompetent elements, Frederick William rapidly built an efficient force of thirty thousand men, so efficient indeed that in 1675, during the Franco-Swedish war against the Dutch, it came to the aid of the Dutch by defeating the Swedes at Fehrbellin and subsequently driving them out of Pomerania. It was to administer this army that Frederick William laid the foundations of the soon famous Prussian bureaucracy; it was to support it that he encouraged the growth of a native textile industry; it was with its aid that he smashed the recalcitrant provincial diets and centralized the state. And finally it was this army that, by its participation after the Great Elector's death in the wars against Louis XIV and its steadiness under fire at Ramillies and Malplaquet, induced the European powers to recognize his successor Frederick I as king of Prussia.

Under Frederick, an extravagant and thoughtless man, the new kingdom threatened to outrun its resources. But the ruler who assumed the throne in 1715, Frederick William I, resumed the work begun by the Great Elector, restored Prussia's financial stability, and completed the centralization and modernization of the state apparatus by elaborating a body of law and statute that clarified rights and responsibilities for all subjects. He nationalized the officer corps of the army, improved its dress and weapons, wrote its first handbook of field regulations, prescribing manual exercises and tactical evolutions, and rapidly increased its size. When Frederick William took the throne after the lax rule of his predecessor, there were rumors of an impending coup by his neighbors, like that attempted against Sweden in 1700. That kind of talk soon died away as the king's work proceeded, and it is easy to see why. In the course of his reign, he increased the size of his military establishment to eighty-three thousand men, a figure that made Prussia's army the fourth largest in Europe, although the state ranked only tenth from the standpoint of territory and thirteenth in population.

Before the eighteenth century was far advanced, then, the threat of French universal dominance had been defeated, a balance of power existed in western Europe, and two new powers had emerged as partners of the older established ones. It was generally recognized that in terms of power and influence, the leading states in Europe were Britain, France, Austria, Russia, and probably Prussia. The doubts on the last score were soon to be removed; and these five powers were to be the ones that dominated European and world politics until 1914.

II

Something should be said at this point about diplomacy, for it was in the seventeenth and eighteenth centuries that it assumed its modern form. The use of envoys and emissaries to convey messages from one ruler to another probably goes back to the beginning of history; there are heralds in the *Iliad* and, in the second letter to the Church of Corinth, the Apostle Paul describes himself as an ambassador. But modern diplomacy as we know it had its origins in the Italian city states of the Renaissance period, and particularly in the republic of Venice and the states of Milan and Tuscany. In the fourteenth and fifteenth centuries, Venice was a great commercial power whose prosperity depended upon shrewd calculation of risks, accurate reports

upon conditions in foreign markets, and effective negotiation. Because it did so, Venice developed the first systemized diplomatic service known to history, a network of agents who pursued the interests of the republic with fidelity, with a realistic appraisal of risks, with freedom from sentimentality and illusion.

From Venice the new practice of systematic diplomacy was passed on to the states of central Italy which, because they were situated in a political arena that was characterized by incessant rivalry and coalition warfare, were always vulnerable to external threats and consequently put an even greater premium than the Venetians upon accurate information and skillful negotiation. The mainland cities soon considered diplomacy so useful that they began to establish permanent embassies abroad, a practice instituted by Milan and Mantua in the fifteenth century, while their political thinkers (like the Florentine Machiavelli) reflected upon the principles best calculated to make diplomacy effective and tried to codify rules of procedure and diplomatic immunity. This last development facilitated the transmission of the shared experience of the Italian cities to the rising nation states of the west that soon dwarfed Florence and Venice in magnitude and strength. Thus, when the great powers emerged in the seventeenth century, they already possessed a highly developed system of diplomacy based upon long experience. The employment of occasional missions to foreign courts had given way to the practice of maintaining permanent missions. While the ambassadors abroad represented their princes and communicated with them directly, their reports were studied in, and they received their instructions from, permanent, organized bureaus which were the first foreign offices. France led the way in this and was followed by most other states, and the establishment of a Foreign Ministry on the French model was one of Peter the Great's important reforms. The emergence of a single individual who was charged with the coordination of all foreign business and who represented his sovereign in the conduct of foreign affairs came a bit later, but by the beginning of the eighteenth century, the major powers all had such officials, who came to be known as foreign ministers or secretaries of state for foreign affairs.

From earliest times, an aura of intrigue, conspiracy, and disingenuousness surrounded the person of the diplomat,

and we have all heard the famous quip of Sir Henry Wotton, ambassador of James I to the court of Venice, who said that an ambassador was "an honest man sent to lie abroad for the good of his country." Moralists were always worried by this unsavory reputation, which they feared was deserved, and they sought to reform it by exhortation. In the fifteenth century, Bernard du Rosier, provost and later archbishop of Toulouse, wrote a treatise in which he argued that the business of an ambassador is peace, that ambassadors must labor for the common good, and that they should never be sent to stir up wars or internal dissensions; and in the nineteenth century, Sir Robert Peel the younger was to define diplomacy in general as "the great engine used by civilized society for the purpose of maintaining peace."

The realists always opposed this ethical emphasis. In the fifteenth century, in one of the first treatises on ambassadorial functions, Ermalao Barbaro wrote: "The first duty of an ambassador is exactly the same as that of any other servant of government: that is, to do, say, advise and think whatever may best serve the preservation and aggrandizement of his own state."

Seventeenth-century theorists were inclined to Barbaro's view. This was certainly the position of Abram de Wicquefort, who coined the definition of the diplomat as "an honorable spy," and who, in his own career, demonstrated that he did not take the adjectival qualification very seriously. A subject of Holland by birth, Wicquefort at various times in his checkered career performed diplomatic services for the courts of Brandenburg, Luneburg, and France as well as for his own country, and he had no scruples about serving as a double agent, a practice that eventually led to his imprisonment in a Dutch jail. It was here that he wrote his treatise *L'Ambassadeur et ses fonctions,* a work that was both an amusing commentary on the political morals of the baroque age and an incisive analysis of the art and practice of diplomacy.

Wicquefort was not abashed by the peccadilloes of his colleagues, which varied from financial peculation and sins of the flesh to crimes of violence. He took the line that in a corrupt age, one could not expect that embassies would be oases of virtue. Morality was, in any case, an irrelevant consideration in diplomacy; a country could afford to be served by bad men, but not by incompetent ones. Competence began with a clear understanding on the diplomat's part of the nature of his job and a willingness to accept the fact that it had nothing to do with personal gratification or self-aggrandizement. The ambassador's principal function, Wicquefort wrote, "consisted in maintaining effective communication between the two Princes, in delivering letters that his master writes to the Prince at whose court he resides, in soliciting answers to them, . . . in protecting his Master's subjects and conserving his interests." He must have the charm and cultivation that would enable him to ingratiate himself at the court to which he was accredited and the adroitness needed to ferret out information that would reveal threats to his master's interests or opportunities for advancing them. He must possess the ability to gauge the temperament and intelligence of those with whom he had to deal and to use this knowledge profitably in negotiation. "Ministers are but men and as such have their weaknesses, that is to say, their passions and interests, which the ambassador ought to know if he wishes to do honor to himself and his Master."

In pursuing this intelligence, the qualities he should cultivate most assiduously were *prudence* and *modération*. The former Wicquefort equated with caution and reflection, and also with the gifts of silence and indirection, the art of "making it appear that one is not interested in the things one desires the most." The diplomat who possessed prudence did not have to resort to mendacity or deceit or to *tromperies* or *artifices,* which were usually, in any case, counterproductive. *Modération* was the ability to curb one's temper and remain cool and phlegmatic in moments of tension. "Those spirits who are compounded of sulphur and saltpeter, whom the slightest spark can set afire, are easily capable of compromising affairs by their excitability, because it is so easy to put them in a rage or drive them to a fury, so that they don't know what they are doing." Diplomacy is a cold and rational business, in short, not to be practiced by the moralist, or the enthusiast, or the man with a low boiling point.

The same point was made in the most famous of the eighteenth-century essays on diplomacy, François de Callières's *On the Manner of Negotiating with Princes* (1716), in which persons interested in the career of diplomacy were advised to consider whether they were born with "the qualities necessary for success." These, the author wrote, included an observant mind, a spirit of application which refuses to be distracted by pleasures or frivolous amusements, a sound judgment which takes the measure of things, as they are, and which goes straight to its goal by the shortest and most neutral paths without wandering into useless refinements and subtleties which as a rule only succeed in repelling those with whom one is dealing.

Important also were the kind of penetration that is useful in discovering the thoughts of men, a fertility in expedients when difficulties arise, an equable humor and a patient temperament, and easy and agreeable manners. Above all, Callières observed, in a probably not unconscious echo of Wicquefort's insistence upon moderation, the diplomat must

have sufficient control over himself to resist the longing to speak before he has really thought what he shall say. He should not endeavour to gain the reputation of being able to reply immediately and without premeditation to every proposition which is made, and he should take a special care not to fall into the error of one famous foreign ambassador of our time who so loved an argument that each time he warmed up in controversy he revealed important secrets in order to support his opinion.

In his treatment of the art of negotiation, Callières drew from a wealth of experience to which Wicquefort could not pretend, for he was one of Louis XIV's most gifted diplomats and ended his career as head of the French delegation during the negotiations at Ryswick in 1697. It is interesting, in light of the heavy reliance upon lawyers in contemporary United States diplomacy (one thinks of President Eisenhower's secretary of state and President Reagan's national security adviser) and of the modern practice of negotiating in large gatherings, that Callières had no confidence in either of these preferences. The legal mind, he felt, was at once too narrow, too intent upon hair-splitting, and too contentious to be useful in a field where success, in the last analysis, was best assured by agreements that provided mutuality of advantage. As for large conferences—"vast concourses of ambassadors and envoys"—his view was that they were generally too clumsy to achieve anything very useful. Most successful conferences were the result of careful preliminary work by small groups of negotiators who hammered out the essential bases of agreement and secured approval for them from their governments before handing them over, for formal purposes, to the *omnium-gatherums* that were later celebrated in the history books.

Perhaps the most distinctive feature of Callières's treatise was the passion with which he argued that a nation's foreign relations should be conducted by persons trained for the task.

Diplomacy is a profession by itself which deserves the same preparation and assiduity of attention that men give to other recognized professions. . . . The diplomatic genius is born, not made. But there are many qualities which may be developed with practice, and the greatest part of the necessary knowledge can only be acquired, by constant application to the subject. In this sense, diplomacy is certainly a profession itself capable of occupying a man's whole career, and those who think to embark upon a diplomatic mission as a pleasant diversion from their common task only prepare disappointment for themselves and disaster for the cause which they serve.

These words represented not only a personal view but an acknowledgment of the requirements of the age. The states that emerged as recognizedly great powers in the course of the seventeenth and eighteenth centuries were the states that had modernized their governmental structure, mobilized their economic and other resources in a rational manner, built up effective and disciplined military establishments, and elaborated a professional civil service that administered state business in accordance with the principles of *raison d'état*. An indispensable part of that civil service was the Foreign Office and the diplomatic corps, which had the important task of formulating the foreign policy that protected and advanced the state's vital interests and of seeing that it was carried out.

BIBLIOGRAPHICAL ESSAY

For the general state of international relations before the eighteenth century, the following are useful: Marvin R. O'Connell, *The Counter-Reformation, 1559–1610* (New York, 1974); Carl J. Friedrich, *The Age of the Baroque, 1610–1660* (New York, 1952), a brilliant volume; C. V. Wedgwood, The *Thirty Years War* (London, 1938, and later editions); Frederick L. Nussbaum, *The Triumph of Science and Reason, 1660–1685*

(New York, 1953); and John B. Wolf, *The Emergence of the Great Powers, 1685–1715* (New York, 1951). On Austrian policy in the seventeenth century, see especially Max Braubach, *Prinz Eugen von Savoyen,* 5 vols. (Vienna, 1963–1965); on Prussian, Otto Hintze, *Die Hohenzollern und ihr Werk* (Berlin, 1915) and, brief but useful, Sidney B. Fay, *The Rise of Brandenburg-Prussia* (New York, 1937). A classical essay on great-power politics in the early modern period is Leopold von Ranke, *Die grossen Mächte,* which can be found in English translation in the appendix of Theodore von Laue, *Leopold Ranke: The Formative Years* (Princeton, 1950). The standard work on *raison d'état* is Friedrich Meinecke, *Die Idee der Staatsräsan,* 3rd ed. (Munich, 1963), translated by Douglas Scoff as *Machiavellianism* (New Haven, 1957).

On the origins and development of diplomacy, see D. P. Heatley, *Diplomacy and the Study of International Relations* (Oxford, 1919); Leon van der Essen, *La Diplomatie: Ses origines et son organisation* (Brussels, 1953); Ragnar Numelin, *Les origines de la diplomatie,* trans. from the Swedish by Jean-Louis Perret (Paris, 1943); and especially Heinrich Wildner, *Die Technik der Diplomatie: L'Art de négocier* (Vienna, 1959). Highly readable is Harold Nicolson, *Diplomacy,* 2nd ed. (London, 1950). An interesting comparative study is Adda B. Bozeman, *Politics and Culture in International History* (Princeton, 1960).

There is no modern edition of *L'amhassadeur et ses fonctions par Monsieur de Wicquefort* (Cologne, 1690); but Callières's classic of 1776 can be found: François de Callières, *On the Manner of Negotiating with Princes,* trans. A. F. Whyte (London, 1919, and later editions).

War, Money, and the English State

John Brewer

INTRODUCTION

'The hand that signed the paper felled a city;
Five sovereign fingers taxed the breath,
Doubled the globe of dead and halved a country;
These five kings did a King to death.'
Dylan Thomas,
Collected Poems, 1934–1952

From its modest beginnings as a peripheral power—a minor, infrequent almost inconsequential participant in the great wars that ravaged sixteenth and seventeenth-century Europe—Britain emerged in the late seventeenth and early eighteenth centuries as the military *Wunderkind* of the age. Dutch admirals learned to fear and then admire its navies, French generals reluctantly conferred respect on its officers and men, and Spanish governors trembled for the safety of their colonies and the sanctity of their trade. European armies, most notably those of Austria, Prussia and the minor German states, marched if not to the beat of British drums then to the colour of English money. Under the early Stuarts England had cut a puny military figure; by the reign of George III, Britain had become one of the heaviest weights in the balance of power in Europe. She had also acquired an empire of ample proportions and prodigious wealth. New England merchants, Southern planters, Caribbean slaves and Indian sepoys were subject to her authority. No sea was safe from British traders; even the Pacific and the Orient were beginning to feel the British presence. Thornhill's Painted Hall at the Naval Hospital at Greenwich (1717–25), with its extravagant depiction of Britain's military power, contained its share of wish fulfilment, but the allegorical presence of the four continents was not misleading: Britain was on the threshold of becoming a transcontinental power.

The extent of this transformation depends, of course, on the extent of the period one chooses. The change from the 1660s to the 1760s seems greater than those either from the 1650s to the 1750s or from the 1680s to the 1780s. The loss of the first British empire was even swifter than its acquisition. But we need to think not in decades but in larger epochs. The transformation of Britain into a major power in two or three generations is all the more striking when compared to the strategic and military history of the previous two hundred years. Ponder the question of how many English victories over continental powers you can name between the battles of Agincourt (1415) and Blenheim (1704). The most famous English soldier in the era between Henry v and Cromwell, Sir Philip Sidney, died at Zutphen (1586) in a futile action during a disastrous campaign. Nor will the obvious naval victories compensate for the poor showing of the nation's armies. Before the late seventeenth century spectacular naval victories never amounted to control of the oceans. Drake may have singed the King of Spain's beard, but he was incapable of cutting his throat. Aptly enough the *Sovereign of the Seas,* the pride of the seventeenth-century royal navy, had to be reduced in size because her three decks made her so unmanageable. Her effectiveness could not equal her pretensions. Only in 1763 did Britannia truly rule the waves, and by then she also controlled a lot more land.

There are several ways in which to explain this remarkable achievement. The most popular is implicitly patriotic and explicitly military, emphasizing the collective qualities of British redcoats and Jack Tars and the individual heroism of their leaders. To the former are normally ascribed those saturnine and English qualities of doggedness, tight-lipped determination and obduracy (though for some reason sailors are usually depicted as much less grim than soldiers), while to their officers are reserved those mercurial qualities of quick-wittedness, imagination and energy. Both, in their due proportion, are deemed valiant and brave. Seen in this light the history of Britain's military and strategic prowess resembles a gallery of eighteenth-century portraits in which the subjects, successful army and naval officers dressed in military regalia and touting swords, telescopes, maps and charts, occupy the foreground, while in the distance we observe some violent action fought by undifferentiated humankind. Marlborough, Cobham, Cumberland, Wolfe, Hawke, Anson, Vernon, Hervey and Rodney provide an exhibition of heroes, many of whom command more admiration today than they did in their own lifetimes.

Such an approach is not without its merits. For, though its rhetoric sometimes smacks of the *Boys' Own Paper* and tales of derring-do, it usually attends to the details of warfare—tactics and the conduct of battles—which, together with those quirks of fate which fascinated Tolstoy and infuriated Clausewitz, make up the substance of war and so often determine its outcome. Yet such accounts often lack a larger context. They are seen as part of the history of 'battles', or, in a more expansive version, of strategy, but remain disconcertingly separate from the overall history of a particular era.

A second interpretation of Britain's rise to power rejects the sanguinary glamour of battles and tactics, preferring to emphasize the economic and commercial roots of Britain's strategic advantage. There are at least two versions of the argument that Britain's aggrandizement was impelled by the powerful forces of commercial capitalism, the desire to increase profits and accumulate wealth. One is discreetly celebratory, the other overtly critical. The former points to Britain's commercial prowess and economic growth: the increase in output, the strength of her agricultural base, the abilities of overseas traders, the skills of her merchant marine and the wealth of her people. The latter draws our attention to the victims of British expansion: the costs incurred by the slaves, indentured servants and native peoples whose fate was inextricably bound up with the acquisition of new lands and the development of commodity markets.

At their worst these histories invoke 'the invisible hand' of the market as *the* explanation for all forms of behaviour, neglecting the complexities of culture and power. In their pessimistic version they can also reduce economic relations to an unmediated account of oppression and resistance. But the insights they offer are salutary. They remind us of the global context of Britain's newly acquired status and of the vital part—epitomized by the privatized imperialism of the East India Company—played by private initiative in the growth of wealth and empire. They underline the importance of economic and social resources—capital and labour, wealth and manpower—in enabling nations to become great powers. And some of this literature, especially the most eloquent and passionate writings, point to the stark contrast between the view from the metropolis and from its periphery. Englishmen may have prided themselves on their liberties and the rule of law, and praised the growth of commerce as a civilizing process, but authority was exercised very differently—often brutally and barbarously—in those distant lands and over those subject peoples which occupied the frontiers of commercial development.

Military heroics, economic growth and the global expansion of British enterprise all contributed to the changing international status of Britain. But to a very large degree they were accompanied by and depended upon a number of altogether less dramatic developments. Victory in battle relied in the first instance upon an adequate supply of men and munitions, which, in turn, depended upon sufficient money and proper organization—what modern military men call 'logistics' and sociologists dub 'infrastructure'. As seventeenth and eighteenth-century commentators knew, no amount of commercial skill, merchant shipping or national prosperity could secure the domination of trade routes or the protection of bases and colonies. These required troops and a navy, which in turn, required money and proper organization. Otherwise Britain might have fallen victim of what was recognized in the eighteenth century as the Dutch disease, a malady that prevented a nation enjoying unequalled individual prosperity and extraordinary commercial sophistication from remaining a state of great influence and power. Substantial economic resources were necessary to acquire the status of a major power; they were not, however, enough. Great states required both the economic wherewithal and the organizational means to deploy resources in the cause of national aggrandizement.

To illuminate the accomplishment of generals and admirals and cast light on the economy and commerce is, perhaps, to obscure or put unnecessarily into the shade those changes in government which made Britain's success possible. It is the aim of the following chapters to expose the hidden sinews which animated the British body politic, rendering it capable of those feats of strength which so impressed its allies and enemies. Though my account is very much concerned with war, it deals with bookkeeping not battles, with ink-stained fingers rather than bloody arms. Its focus is upon administration, on logistics and, above all, on the raising of money. Its heroes, if any there are, are clerks in offices. And its perspective is neither global nor from the periphery, but from Whitehall and Westminster, very much at the centre of the core.

Administrations thrive on routine. They abhor the stock in trade of the dramatist and the historian—change, disruption, violent action—aspiring to a ubiquity of sameness. Theirs is not only the quotidian: each day should be the same. But every administration creates friction in its attempt to impose order and structure on the entropic enterprise of collaborative human endeavour. It is precisely this tension between the desire for order and routine and the actualities of public conduct that creates the drama and conflict administrations are so eager to contain. The struggle for power and control may not have been fought out in the bright, sanguinary colours of battle nor on the large canvas of several continents but, no matter how contained or muted it might appear, its effects were far-reaching. The ability of government administrators to establish the routine by which revenues were collected, money raised and supply requisitioned could make the difference between victory and humiliation.

At the seat of dullness were the clerks. These pale and shadowy figures have never received their due. The eighteenth century saw an unprecedented expansion in the number of transcribers, copyists and record-keepers. A quick glance at the business accounts, financial records and government documents of this period attests to the prodigies of penmanship performed by men and women unaided by any mechanical means of duplication. Yet these clerks have no history. No group can ever have written so much and yet remained so anonymous. This is partly attributable to the difficulties of reconstructing their lives, but it is also the consequence of snobbery. The English revere the ownership of land and the tasks of manual labour; they have little time for pen-pushers, either clerical or intellectual.

What the clerks transcribed in the service of government—tax accounts, inventories of supplies, financial statutes, tables of revenue and trade, rules governing the borrowing of money and the purchase of equipment and supplies—is also not immediately accessible, for it requires a certain amount of technical knowledge. Modern readers, living in the era of the small investor and of media ever-attendant to the fate of stock-markets and rates of exchange, may have a better grasp of public and private finance than those eighteenth-century back-bench MPs who seemed incapable of understanding any money matter which could not be compared to the running of a landed estate. But they nevertheless confront a system, if such it can be called, whose technical complexities were considerable and whose practices, though superficially similar to those of today had their own distinctive logic.

Yet, for all these difficulties of tedium and technicalities (problems I hope to dispel), the chief reason why financiers and administrators have not received their fair share of attention, except in the most technical of scholarship, is because their importance does not accord with the conventional wisdom about the English/British state. It has long been a source of self-congratulation to the British liberal tradition that Britain was wise and politic enough to avoid the enormities of a 'strong state'. This view could scarcely be more fashionable in the present political climate, which seems intent on repudiating the political objectives and dismantling the administrative apparatus of the post-1945 era. Seen from the liberal perspective, the state intervention that was typical of British politics between 1945 and 1979 looks like a temporary diversion from the mainstream of the British political tradition. The eighteenth century on the other hand, exemplifies the weakness of central government. It is portrayed as a period when the powers of central government were devolved on the localities and diluted by a spoils system which provided income and office for the scions of the landed classes.

But there is another picture we can paint of the same era, the one depicted in this book. The late seventeenth and eighteenth centuries saw an astonishing transformation in British government, one which put muscle on the bones of the British body politic, increasing its endurance, strength and reach. Britain was able to shoulder an ever-more ponderous burden of military commitments thanks to a radical increase in taxation, the development of public deficit finance (a national debt) on an unprecedented scale, and the growth of a sizable public administration devoted to organizing the fiscal and military activities of the state. As a result the state cut a substantial figure, becoming the largest single actor in the economy. This was no minor adjustment in the scope and priorities of government; it was a major commitment of resources. Taxes rose to levels as high as any of those in Europe, matching those of many modern, underdeveloped states. Borrowing reached such heights that if eighteenth-century Britain had gone to the modern International Monetary Fund for a loan it would certainly have been shown the door. The creation of what I call 'the fiscal-military state' was the most important transformation in English government between the domestic reforms of the Tudors and the major administrative changes in the first half of the nineteenth century.

How are we to reconcile this view of an exceptionally active state with the liberal interpretation? Or are the two positions entirely incompatible? We should first notice that we are discussing two rather different aspects of government. States are Janus-faced: they look in, to the societies they rule, and out, to those other states with which they are so often locked in conflict. In the former instance the business of the state is usually that of maintaining public order and exercising public justice ('law and order'); government also probably takes responsibility for various forms of economic and social regulation. In the latter case, states compete with each other, employing either the peaceful means of diplomacy or the violent means of war. The liberal focus on the British state has resolutely concentrated its gaze on relations with the domestic polity. I want to draw attention to the state's international role, to its actions as a military and diplomatic power.

Perhaps, then, this is the answer to our conundrum. The British government was able to act effectively against its international enemies but was weak in its dealings with its own subjects. This dichotomy is neat, but raises more questions than it answers.

Political commentators in early modern Europe were haunted by the fear that changes in the character of warfare, particularly the emergence of large standing armies controlled by rulers, would enable monarchs and autocrats not only to subjugate their foes but to enslave their subjects. Liberty and the institutions which guaranteed such freedoms, notably parliaments and estates, could be swept away by brute force. Clearly seventeenth-century analysts—rather like twentieth-century sociologists—were sceptical of the view that a state's international standing and activities could be sharply separated from its power over civil society. They were right to be sceptical. Admittedly, before the mid-seventeenth century the chief beneficiaries of the growth of standing armies were not rulers but private entrepreneurs: money-lending and tax-gathering syndicates, military enterprisers who specialized in raising and leading troops. It was also possible to wage war by using conquest and tribute rather than domestic resources to fund hostilities. But by the mid-seventeenth century rulers were gaining control of the forces that marched in their name, and self-sustaining warfare—

the technique used by the Swedes in the seventeenth century and the Prussians in the eighteenth—was increasingly recognized as a hazardous, short-term solution because it could brook no check or setback. In the last resort states had to depend on domestic resources, in the form of money and men, and these were increasing under the direct control of monarchs and rulers.

The British were no exception. Indeed, judged by the criteria of the ability to take pounds out of people's pockets and to put soldiers in the field and sailors on the high seas, Britain was one of Europe's most powerful states, one which had acquired prodigious powers over its subjects. Whatever the situation when it came to the administration of law and order, in the fiscal-military sphere the state gained a hold as never before. This grip did not, however, become the stranglehold of autocracy, which raises, of course, the question of why Britain was able to enjoy the fruits of military prowess without the misfortunes of a *dirigiste* or despotic regime.

Before being seduced into that orgy of self-congratulation to which British historians are prone, we need to enter at least one qualification to the view that the British regime, for all its military effectiveness, was characterized by lightness of touch. The heavy-handedness of British rule increased the farther it extended beyond the metropolis. This may seem paradoxical, for British authority was much weaker outside England than within it. But it was for precisely this reason that the formal powers of British rule were so much greater farther afield. Coercive powers were required where tacit compliance was less assured. Subjects' rights were not the same on the banks of the Ohio, in Spanish Town or Dublin Castle as they were in London.

Yet, even in the metropolis, it was felt that liberties were under threat. Though the liberal view characterizes the eighteenth-century British state as conspicuous for its absence, this was not what most eighteenth-century commentators believed. They were obsessed by its growing presence. This anxiety is easy to understand. In the aftermath of the Glorious Revolution of 1688 the balance of political forces shifted decisively against those who had opposed or sought to limit Britain's role in international conflict. Britain plunged into a major, protracted struggle with Louis XIV's France.

The proponents of small government and limited warfare did not, however, surrender without a fight. On the contrary, they dug themselves in for a long struggle and, protected by the well-built fortifications of English constitutionalism, were able to conduct an effective war of containment. They fought to restrict the domestic effects of the fiscal-military state. And, although theirs was necessarily only a rearguard action, they enjoyed some success. The powers of the army over the civilian population were severely restricted, efforts to use civilian officers as a general 'police' rather than as tax gatherers were checked, and the bureaucracy's growth limited to those circumstances necessary for its successful operation.

The intensity of the struggle over the British state—about how it should be structured and what it should be allowed to do—is the most eloquent testimony that government had indeed undergone a radical transformation. But the protestations of those who opposed standing armies and big government were more than the mere symptoms of an important change; they became an integral part of Britain's institutional transformation. The war against the state helped to shape the changing contours of government: limited its scope, restricted its ambit and, through parliamentary scrutiny, rendered its institutions both more public and accountable.

Yet, paradoxically, this success made the fiscal-military state stronger rather than weaker, more effective rather than more impotent. Public scrutiny reduced speculation, parliamentary consent lent greater legitimacy to government action. Limited in scope, the state's powers were nevertheless exercised with telling effect.

This irony can best be understood if we reflect on what tend to be our rather naive and uncritical assumptions about what is meant by a 'strong' or 'weak' state. Too often strength is equated with size. But a large state apparatus is no necessary indication of a government's ability to perform such tasks as the collection of revenue or the maintenance of public order. Indeed, the opposite may prove true. In the hive that was the early modern European state there were often as many drones as workers; frequently as many sinecures as efficient offices. In short, big government is not always effective government.

A second solecism is that which fails to distinguish between what a state is entitled to do and what it can actually accomplish. To use the terminology of one distinguished social scientist, a regime may be strong in 'despotic power', entitled to dispense with its subjects' goods and liberties without legal restraint, but it may be weak in 'infrastructural power', lacking the organization to put its despotic power into effect. Conversely a state may be weak in 'despotic power' with strict limits on what it is entitled to do, but it may be strong on 'infrastructural power' capable of performing its limited tasks to telling effect.

To this distinction we need to add a consideration of the question of authority. The effective exercise of power is never merely a matter of logistics, a question of whether or not a state has the requisite bureaucracy or military cadres. States are not just centres of power; they are also sources of authority whose effectiveness depends on the degree of legitimacy that both regimes and their actions are able to command. Broadly speaking the less legitimacy, the greater the 'friction' produced by the conduct of the state and the more resources it has to devote to achieve the same effect.

The British fiscal-military state, as it emerged from the political and military battles that marked the struggle with Louis XIV, lacked many of the features we normally associate with a 'strong state', yet therein lay its effectiveness. The constraints on power meant that when it was exercised, it was exercised fully. As long as the fiscal-military state did not cross the bulwarks erected to protect civil society from militarization it was given its due. Yet it was watched with perpetual vigilance by those who, no matter how much they lauded its effectiveness against foreign foes, were deeply afraid of its intrusion into civil society.

The desire to restrict the political and military effects of war on the English polity, together with the almost total absence of hostilities on English soil, can give the impression that eighteenth-century wars were of little domestic consequence. Military action, after all, occurred far away beyond the horizon: in continental Europe (where foreign soldiers fought and died on Britain's behalf), in the colonies and on the quarterdecks of British battleships. Most of the military action was out of sight. It was not, however, out of mind. For the effects of war were never purely strategic,

nor were they confined to the scene of battle. They were felt on the home front, particularly on the economy.

War was an economic as well as military activity: its causes, conduct and consequences as much a matter of money as martial prowess. Nowhere in eighteenth-century Europe was this better understood than in Britain. As Casanova, visiting London shortly after the Seven Years War, discovered in his conversations with Augustus Hervey, the captor of Havana, the British viewed war as far more than a matter of honour. It was also a question of property and profit. The progress of hostilities was followed by many members of the public with an assiduity worthy of Tristram Shandy's Uncle Toby, but their interest was not in tactics or siege warfare but in the economic repercussions of war.

These were difficult to measure then and remain so today. Nevertheless most eighteenth-century commentators were sure that fluctuations in the fortunes of war and the conduct of peace affected the everyday conduct of economic life. Similarly they argued that the longer-term changes in the nature of government—the emergence of the fiscal-military state—had altered the balance of social forces in Britain by penalizing the landed classes, creating a new class of financier and laying a heavy burden of taxes on the ordinary consumer. For more than a generation the state was seen as one of the major agents of social and economic change.

These developments were not watched idly by interested parties. Changes in government produced new organizations in society at large. Special interest groups were formed. These new organisms, the offspring of a new environment created by an expanding state, sought to flourish, in evolutionary fashion, at the expense of other new species. Lobbies, trade organizations, groups of merchants and financiers fought or combined with one another to take advantage of the protection afforded by the greatest of economic creatures, the state. They struggled for access to the corridors of power, for information that would enable them to thwart, create or affect policy, and for the support of those parliamentarians who could hold the fiscal juggernaut in check. As their tactics grew more sophisticated they learned to transcend their sectionalism and to appeal beyond their self-interested ranks to the public at large. By the second half of the eighteenth century some of them had learned the value of parasitism, making the state, as Adam Smith pointed out, their host if not their hostage.

In this, narrowly defined commercial and trading interests were following a pattern that can be observed throughout the eighteenth century. When the fiscal-military state first emerged it enjoyed considerable autonomy and excited much hostility and confusion. But gradually a variety of social groups and interests reached an accommodation with it. Some, notably the 'landed interest', were much more successful than others in taking advantage of new circumstances, but none could afford the luxury of ignoring the remarkable changes in the British state which were the early eighteenth century's most distinctive feature. . . .

Competing Cousins
ANGLO-DUTCH TRADE RIVALRY

The fount of riches; the Harbour Office, Amsterdam, in a 1664 engraving.

***Jonathan Israel** charts the progress from commercial competition to open war and finally 'snarling alliance' of two assertive naval powers*

Jonathan Israel

The three bitter, hard-fought Anglo-Dutch Wars of the seventeenth century (1652–54; 1665–67; and 1672–74) constitute one of the very few major conflicts in Britain's history which can be ascribed in the main to commercial rivalry. Of course, dynastic, religious and other factors, sometimes downright xenophobia, played a sporadic part in shaping events. But, in essence, this vast seaborne conflict, fought out right around the globe, was about shipping and trade. The claim that the Anglo-Dutch wars of the seventeenth century were the outcome of 'commercial rivalry' is no doubt an old-fashioned commonplace of historical studies. But not all well-worn views are wrong.

But why did serious conflict between the Dutch and England break out only in the 1650s? This question has long perplexed historians. The Dutch, after all, first began to encroach seriously on English interests, especially in Russia and the Baltic, as far back as the 1590s. For it was at that time that the Dutch began to go beyond their traditional sphere of dominance—the bulk carrying traffic of northern Europe—and engross the world's 'rich trades'. This was largely the result

From *History Today*, July 1988, pp. 17-22. Reproduced by kind permission of History Today, Ltd., 83-84 Berwick Street, London W1V 3PJ, England.

of the upheavals of the 1580s in the southern Netherlands, and the closing of the River Scheldt, paralysing the trade of Antwerp, all of which caused a vast migration of textile and other industrial workers, of mercantile expertise, and of capital, to Amsterdam and other cities in Holland and Zealand. Around 1590, the Dutch became the first trading power in history equipped for hegemony over both the bulk and the rich trades.

The result was a prodigious explosion of Dutch maritime enterprise throughout the globe. Whereas until the 1590s, the Dutch controlled only the carrying of such commodities as grain, timber and salt in northern and western European waters, by 1609 they had achieved dominance over the East India spice trade, the Russia trade, the Arctic whale fishery, the Guinea gold trade, the distribution of sugar in Europe, and were threatening to take over most of the rest of the rich trades. Inevitably, the speed and impact of this Dutch break-through caused great unease and resentment not only in England but among the Hanseatic trading towns, the Portuguese, Danes, Venetians and others.

Briefly, during the second decade of the century, it seemed that the growing tension between England and the Dutch would lead directly to a major collision. The two nations were at loggerheads in the East Indies, in Russia, over the Spitsbergen whale fishery and also over the dyeing and finishing of England's cloth exports. But eventually, after several armed clashes, the tension eased off. Indeed, after 1621 in Europe, and 1623 in the East Indies, there was no longer any likelihood of serious confrontation for the forseeable future. England was still less competitive than the Dutch in shipping, finance, fishing and whaling, and several textile and other industrial processes and was still losing ground in her traditional northern markets. The improvement in the English mood was due to the fact that after 1621 when the Dutch-Spanish conflict resumed, England began to make rapid progress in a number of new markets. The essential cause of the sudden improvement in England's position was not so much, as is often claimed, England's neutrality in the Thirty Years' War as such, as the impact on the Dutch of the reimposition of the Spanish embargoes in 1621 and the resumption of the Spanish offensive against Dutch shipping. In fact, the improvement in Anglo-Dutch relations lasted precisely

as long as the Spanish embargoes and privateering campaign against the Dutch—until 1647.

From 1621 Dutch ships and goods were excluded from Spain until 1647 and from Portugal until that realm broke free of the Spanish Crown in December 1640. This was a heavy blow to the Dutch entrepôt in itself. But there was more. The heavy losses of Dutch shipping to the 'Dunkirkers' and to Spanish seapower generally, caused a sharp and sustained rise in Dutch freightage and insurance charges for European voyages which worked to the benefit of the previously less competitive English and Hanseatics. English gains in northern Europe were few, consisting in the main of the capture of the carrying of Baltic products to the Spanish Netherlands from which Dutch shipping was also excluded. The real gains were in the south. Between them, England and the Hanseatics now took over the bulk of the carrying trade between northern Europe and the Iberian Peninsula, while in the Mediterranean England captured sole hegemony over seaborne trade. For, as a result of the high freight charges, the Spanish embargoes and lack of access to Spanish silver which previously the Dutch had used to settle their balances in the Levant, the Dutch lost much of their trade with Italy and practically all their traffic [in] the Levant where—until 1621—they had been doing considerably better than the English.

The setbacks suffered by the Dutch at Spanish hands was arguably the decisive factor in English economic development in the 1630s and early 1640s. For it was the spectacular advances made by English trade in Flanders, Portugal, Spain, Italy and Turkey which saved England's cloth industries from what would otherwise have certainly been a period of catastrophic slump. For while England's cloth exports to her traditional markets in northern Europe fell off markedly during the Thirty Years' War, great quantities of English cloth—broadcloth as well as 'new draperies'—began to be sold after 1621, especially in Portugal, Spain, and Turkey.

Furthermore, the English East India Company was now provided with a secure market, sealed against the Dutch, for its pepper, spices, and indigo in southern Europe which abundantly compensated England for her total inability to challenge Dutch supremacy in selling East India commodities in France and

northern Europe outside Britain and Flanders.

Amid the prosperity of the 1630s and early 1640s, Englishmen were in no mood to ponder the true precariousness of their new-found hegemony in the commerce of southern Europe. Nevertheless, there were contemporaries who foresaw what would happen if and when Spain and the Dutch made peace. For the underlying reality was that the Dutch entrepôt still had many advantages over England as a general storehouse of commodities, in its vast shipping capacity and its financial institutions. Once the opportunity to challenge England's mastery of southern European markets and the Flanders trade arose, the Dutch merchant élite, with their unparalleled expertise and shipping resources could be expected to move back in with tremendous impetus. England was given a foretaste of what was to come when Portugal broke away from the Spanish crown late in 1640. Within a year or two there were more Dutch than English ships to be seen docking at Lisbon. This was unpleasant for English merchants used to a free hand in Portugal. But it was nothing compared with what was now about to happen.

Once Spain made peace with the Dutch, Dutch shipping was readmitted to the ports of Spain and Flanders, the embargoes on Dutch goods in the Spanish empire were lifted, the campaign of the Dunkirkers against Dutch shipping ceased, and the Genoese Republic ended its policy of importing from England, rather than from the Dutch entrepôt in deference to Spain, a major restructuring of European commerce was inevitable. Dutch shipping was bound to return to the ports of Spain, Flanders and Spanish southern Italy, as well as to Genoa, in large numbers. Dutch freight and insurance charges for voyages in European waters were bound to fall precipitately. Amsterdam's greater financial power, and the fact that interest rates were much lower in Holland than England, meant that the Dutch merchant élite would from now on have the edge over their English competitors in buying up the raw materials and fine goods of southern Europe. It is true that England was now too strongly entrenched in her new markets to be simply pushed to where she had been before 1621. But the blow when it fell was sudden, universal and, in some sectors of European trade, devastating.

Owing to reduced competitiveness in freightage, England lost ground in the north as well as in the south. Nor were these northern losses confined only to the carrying trade to Flanders. English and Scottish voyages through the Danish Sound declined every year between 1647 and 1652, despite the huge upsurge in demand for Baltic grain in western Europe at that time. Nevertheless, much the most serious losses were in southern Europe. Dutch ships returned in large numbers to Spanish, Italian and Ottoman ports squeezing England's recently flourishing southern carrying trade. Genoa turned from England to the Dutch entrepôt for its grain, timber and Baltic naval stores. In Spain, English merchants lost their dominance almost overnight. Where, for example, England overwhelmingly dominated the traffic in Spanish wools—the most valuable and esteemed wool in Europe—during the 1630s and early 1640s, by the end of the 1640s the lion's share of this important strand of commerce had been lost to the Dutch. Contemporary estimates place the Dutch share of this traffic, in 1650, at around 80 per cent. The Dutch breakthrough in Spanish wool and the Spanish market more generally not only stimulated an upsurge of fine cloth production in Holland and cut back sales of English cloth in Spain, it also, as an English contemporary noted with some exaggeration and typical resentment, led to the 'destruction of the vent of all fine cloths of English making both in Holland, France and the East lands', the latter being a reference to the Baltic. He might have added that it also provided the basis for the spectacular revival of the Dutch Levant trade which began in the late 1640s and seriously damaged England's commerce with the eastern Mediterranean.

After 1648, the Dutch world entrepôt entered a new phase in its development, the phase of its greatest impact on world trade. Many other trading nations besides England were adversely affected by the sudden post-1648 improvement in the competitive position of the Dutch in relation to their rivals. In particular, the Hanseatics and Danes lost heavily. But those powers were too weak to react. Only in the case of England was there a powerful backlash against this sudden further expansion of Dutch maritime, commercial and productive power. England had the power to react and her losses were simply too extensive to be accepted without a major and very aggressive response. By the end of the

1640s even southern European commodities earmarked for the English market itself, such as Zante currants, olive oil from Turkey and southern Italy and Canary wines, began pouring into England from the Dutch entrepôt instead of being shipped here, as before, from source on English vessels. The Navigation Act of 1651 was brought in specifically to deal with this new phenomenon. But while the Navigation Act did deal successfully with the post 1648 influx of southern European commodities into England, from Holland, there was nothing that Parliament could do, short of resorting to major force, to restore England's lost ascendancy in southern markets. Exactly the same was true of the Caribbean where improved Dutch competitiveness, combined with the royalist sympathies of the English colonists in Barbados and Surinam, had since the mid-1640s all but paralysed English trade.

The Navigation Act was a heavy blow to the Dutch entrepôt but not so serious as to have induced the United Provinces to go to war with England on that ground alone. What made war inevitable in the early 1650s was the increasingly aggressive attitude of the English towards Dutch shipping on the high seas. Already during 1650 a considerable number of Dutch vessels were brought into English ports on a variety of pretexts. Then, in 1651, the pressure was greatly stepped up. Between them, English licensed privateers and Parliament's navy that year seized a total of 140 Dutch ships in the North Sea, Channel and in the Caribbean. Harassment on such a scale seriously impeded the functioning of the Dutch world trading system. The Dutch tried negotiation but this did not work. They filled all Europe with complaints over English tyranny and violence on the high seas but this had no effect either. Another thirty Dutch ships were seized in January 1652 alone. The fact of the matter was either the Dutch state possessed the power to put a stop to the interference or Dutch world trade hegemony was at an end.

The mood of the Dutch leadership and public at the outset of the war of 1652–54 was decidedly grim. Parliament's navy had more and heavier 'first-rates' than the Dutch and was therefore markedly superior in firepower. Britain's shores lay astride the main Dutch sea-lanes and for the moment it was the Dutch merchant and fishing fleets which were the more vulnerable. From 1652 right down

to the end of the third war in 1674 England had the advantage in fire-power and made good use of it, winning nearly all the major battles in home waters. Again and again, the Dutch war fleet, gallantly though it fought, was shattered and dismasted at a faster rate than the English. In her sea-power, England proved to have the world's one and only effective weapon against Dutch world trade hegemony.

Yet England failed to break Dutch world trade supremacy. By a variety of means, political, strategic and financial the Dutch managed to neutralise the effects of English naval superiority so that at the conclusion of the three wars, in 1674, England had made no significant gains at Dutch expense except for New Amsterdam (New York), which at that time was considered less important than territories such as Surinam and Pulorun which the Dutch had captured from the English. Despite England's many and very real advantages in this vast maritime drama, a conflict which lasted a quarter of a century and was fought on every continent and sub-continent except Australia, Antarctica and Greenland, the whole business, from beginning to end, was an unmitigated failure from the English point of view.

The Dutch then won, or at any rate fought matters to a stalemate, despite losing most of the big battles. Indeed, there can be not the slightest doubt that despite her being the stronger sea-power, England inflicted considerably less damage on the Dutch entrepôt and world trading system during the third quarter of the seventeenth century than had Spain, with her embargoes and privateers, during the previous thirty years. But how is so astounding a paradox to be explained? One crucial element in the successful Dutch defence against the English onslaught was the dispersal of part of the Republic's slightly larger, if less powerful, war-fleet to distant parts so as to paralyse English shipping and trade away from the North Sea and Britain's home waters. In all three wars, the Dutch shut the English completely out of the Baltic. In the East Indies and the Persian Gulf English shipping was swept from the seas. In the first war, the Dutch swept the English from the Mediterranean and won an important battle off Livorno in March 1653 which is practically never mentioned in English history books. In the second war, too, the Dutch paralysed English Mediterranean trade. The second major element in the Dutch defence was their privateering war against English shipping. The English began by capturing many more Dutch merchant ships than *vice versa*. But this soon changed. In the second war the numbers were roughly equal but it was the Dutch who captured the more valuable prizes. This was bad enough from England's point of view but the real shock was what happened in the third war. When the third Anglo-Dutch war of 1672–74 began it seemed impossible that England could lose. Charles II declared war on the Republic in alliance with France, Cologne and Münster. The odds against the Dutch were simply overwhelming. English ministers expected to 'root the Dutch' entirely out of the Americas and make other vast gains besides. Yet again England gained nothing and was forced to settle both quickly and on humiliating terms.

By June 1672, the French and their German allies had overrun half the Republic and the Amsterdam Exchange was in the grip of a vast financial panic. All Europe gave the Dutch up for lost. In 1672–73, the States General ordered all merchant shipping and the fishing fleets to be kept in port, making tens of thousands of Dutch seamen and fishermen redundant. Yet this was precisely the key to the tremendous retaliation which was now unleashed against England and which made it impossible for Charles to go on with the war. For not only was there now nothing for English privateers

Substantial landing-raids on both sides of the North Sea were a feature of the Second Anglo-Dutch War; the Anglo-Dutch raid on the island of Terschiling in August 1666 (below) prompted de Ruyter's reprisal — the famous burning of the English fleet in the Medway.

to capture so that they soon disappeared from the seas but great numbers of redundant Dutch ships and seamen were available for privateering activity. The Dutch privateers of 1672 went out in packs and took up stations off the east coast of Britain, around the coasts of France, Portugal and Spain, off Virginia and New England and in the Caribbean. By December 1673 there were fifty Dutch privateers plying off the Iberian Peninsula alone—a pack of fourteen lying off Cadiz, eight off Portugal, and the rest in the Mediterranean, off Corunna and in the Bay of Biscay. From Italy to Massachusetts English ships were taken by the dozen and her merchant fleet thoroughly demoralised. A large Levant ship, The *Constantinople*, carrying cargo valued at £80,000 was 'shamefully taken' off Spain by a diminutive Zeelander carrying only twelve guns. Although national pride led to the whole

episode being suppressed in the collective memory in later times (so that it is never mentioned in modern books) this was certainly the greatest maritime disaster in Britain's history. Study of the surviving Dutch and English records shows that at the most conservative estimate 700 English vessels were captured and the real figure is almost certainly higher.

In the immediate aftermath, awareness of the scale of the losses removed all further appetite for struggle with the Dutch. The memory of it survived at any rate into the early eighteenth century. In 1712, when Anglo-Dutch tension again became so acute that there was open talk of war in London, Daniel Defoe reminded his countrymen that 'in the last war with the Dutch we lost 2,000 sail of ships great and small in the first year'. Defoe was exaggerating somewhat, but he was right that for England the war had been an immense disaster.

The Anglo-Dutch conflict of the seventeenth century came about owing to an overwhelming perception among Englishmen that the Dutch had 'miserably lessened us in all the trades of the world'. The answer, it had been expected, was England's superior fire-power. Yet, surprisingly perhaps, the Dutch managed to neutralise English naval superiority and to force England both to stop fighting, and equally important from the Dutch point of view, to stop harassing their shipping in peace time. And they achieved all this without making any concessions. The Anglo-Dutch struggle of 1652–74 was a stalemate which left the underlying causes of tension, at least in part, unresolved. Up to a point, the friction eased off owing to the rapid growth of English commerce, beginning in the 1660s, with regions such as the Caribbean, North America, West Africa, northern India and the Mediterranean. Nevertheless, down to the early eighteenth century, the Dutch remained the leading trading power in the Caribbean, West Africa, and India as well as in Europe and so much of the underlying friction continued.

The coming of William III, and the Glorious Revolution of 1688–89 did indeed transform the Anglo-Dutch relationship. From being enemies England and the Republic became allies presided over by the same prince and joined in a close military and naval partnership against France. The Anglo-Dutch partnership which was to figure prominently in world affairs for almost a century after

'A Description of Hogg-land' – a less than charitable English commentary of 1665 on the Dutch character.

1688 was based initially on a dynastic link and throughout on a perceived common need to check the rising power of France. Political objectives were always paramount in sustaining the coalition. Nevertheless, certain shared commercial and colonial goals also played a part. England and the United Provinces had a shared interest in trying to block the efforts of French mercantilist policy to promote French navigation and trade throughout the globe. For, by the 1680s the French were achieving considerable success in a number of key markets such as the Ottoman Levant, Spain and India. By 1720, France had replaced both England and the Dutch as the dominant trading power in the eastern Mediterranean.

The palpable threat posed by French mercantilism and its successes helped cement the Anglo-Dutch alliance into something solid and enduring. But we should not forget that much of the old underlying tension remained unresolved and continued to eat away at the edges of the alliance. Indeed, the underlying friction outlasted the alliance itself eventually to burst out afresh in the fourth Anglo-Dutch War of 1780–84. In European trade, there were constant wrangles, one of the most insistent stemming from the Dutch grip on the south Netherlands market after the allies conquered the area from the French during the War of the Spanish Succession (1702–13). 'We have conquered Flanders for them', complained Jonathan Swift, in a typical English anti-Dutch outburst of the time, 'and are in a worse condition as to our trade there than before the war began'. In

India where the Dutch continued to ply a larger traffic than the English down to the early eighteenth century a ceaseless cold war persisted. In the Indonesian Archipelago, the Dutch had resorted to strong-armed tactics to strip the English of much of their pepper trade with Java and Sumatra as recently as 1682–83 and the bad feeling lingered for long after that. Nor was the situation any different in Africa. Indeed, by 1700 the English had almost caught up with the Dutch in the Guinea gold trade and relations were worse than ever. 'It is most certain', noted Charles Davenant, 'that without regard to either peace or war at home, the Dutch West India Company and the Royal African Company have constantly maintained a sort of private war, the one against the other, for the empire of trade on the coast of Guinea.'

The Anglo-Dutch alliance lasted and, indeed, became one of the central realities of early modern world history. But it always remained a tense, uneasy arrangement, a 'snarling alliance' which filled the world with complaint and countercomplaint.

FOR FURTHER READING:

Charles Wilson, *Profit and Power. A Study of England and the Dutch Wars;* C.R. Boxer, *The Dutch Seaborne Empire, 1600–1800* (Hutchinson, 1977); Jonathan Israel, *The Dutch Republic and the Hispanic World, 1606–1661* (Oxford University Press, 1986); Simon Groenveld, 'The English Civil Wars as a Cause of the First Anglo-Dutch war, 1640–1652', *The Historical Journal*, xxx (1987); Jonathan Israel, *Dutch Primacy in World Trade, 1585–1740*.

The High Price of Sugar

To satisfy Europe's fondness for sweets, West Indian planters turned to Africa for plantation labor

Susan Miller

Right from the start, Columbus had a plan: to establish a sugar industry on Hispaniola much like the ones back home on the Canary and Madeira islands. So on his second voyage to the New World, he brought along several stalks of sugar cane. The Spanish hidalgos couldn't be bothered with the broiling, backbreaking task of growing and making the sweetener, so they forced the locals to do it for them. When the Indians started dropping from disease, the Spaniards turned to Africa. By the mid-16th century a nascent sugar industry completely dependent on black slave labor had taken hold in the Spanish Caribbean. The dramatic change on Hispaniola prompted a Spanish historian to write: "There are so many Negroes in this island, as a result of the sugar factories, that the land seems an effigy or an image of Ethiopia itself." Thus began a relationship between sugar production and African slavery that was to dominate Caribbean life for nearly four centuries.

This relationship had already existed in the Old World for hundreds of years. The first reference to sugar dates back to 350 B.C., with the report that people in India were eating rice pudding with milk and sugar and sipping drinks flavored with the sweetener. A little later, in 327 B.C., Alexander the Great's general, Nearchus, sailing from the mouth of the Indus River to the Euphrates, asserted that "a reed in India brings forth honey without the help of bees, from which an intoxicating drink is made though the plant bears no fruit." But not until about A.D. 500 is there unmistakable written evidence of sugar *making;* the technology didn't spread westward until the Moorish invasion of Europe in the seventh century. Sugar, according to anthropologist Sidney Mintz, followed the Koran.

The first Africans were enslaved soon afterward. Mintz reports that a slave revolt involving thousands of East African laborers took place in the Tigris-Euphrates delta as early as the mid-ninth century. Slavery grew more important as European crusaders seized the sugar plantations of the eastern Mediterranean from their Arab predecessors. By the 15th century, African slaves supplied the labor for the Spanish and Portuguese plantations on the Atlantic islands off the coast of Africa. To the Spanish way of thinking, then, African slaves were the logical solution to the labor shortages in the New World.

While Spaniards in the Caribbean were the first to produce and export sugar, their pioneering efforts were soon outstripped by developments on the American mainland. Sugar cane prospered in the Spanish territories of Mexico, Paraguay and Peru. By 1526, the Portuguese had begun shipping sugar from Brazil to Lisbon in commercial quantities.

By the end of the 17th century, the British had also established stakes in the Caribbean, and slavery became an integral part of their newly settled colonies almost from the start. Dutch traders, who had a foothold in Brazil, first introduced sugar making to English colonists on the island of Barbados in the 1630s. From humble beginnings, the British sugar industry spread north to the Leeward Islands, where it soon wrought a social, economic and political transformation so sweeping and rapid that historians have called it the Sugar Revolution. "England fought the most, conquered the most colonies, imported the most slaves and went furthest and fastest in creating a plantation system," writes Mintz in "Sweetness and Power." In 1655, when Britain conquered Jamaica—an island nearly 30 times the size of Barbados—she came to dominate the north European sugar trade.

The sugar industry was a messy business. Planters, clearing huge tracts of forested land, devastated the environment. In 1690, trees covered more than two thirds of the British colony of Antigua. By 1751 planters had stripped every acre suitable for cultivation. Antiguan John Luffman, writing in 1786, observed that even the largest hills were "clothed with the luxuriant verdure of the sugar cane to their very summits." The rapid deforestation only heightened the region's propensity for drought and erosion.

It was also extremely lucrative. In the 18th century, Antigua rivaled Barbados as one of the leading producers in the Caribbean, although neither could compete with Jamaica or French Saint Domingue (Haiti). "Barbados, in one period, and Antigua, in another, were producing more wealth than the entire North American continent," says Conrad Goodwin, an anthropologist who (along with geographer Lydia Pulsipher) has spent more than a decade excavating and studying sugar plantations on Antigua and the neighboring island of Montserrat.

The production of sugar—from holing, planting and harvesting to crushing, boiling and curing—depended on a large work force. To meet the demand for labor, Antiguan planters imported tens of thousands of slaves from Africa. In 1678 there were 2,308 whites and 2,172 blacks on the island. By the mid-18th century, Antigua's population had grown to nearly 40,000, and blacks outnumbered whites 10 to 1. David Barry Gaspar, an historian at Duke University, speculates that the ratio of blacks to whites would have been even higher if thousands hadn't committed suicide or died as the result of accidents, disease, poor diet, hard labor and mistreatment at the hands of their masters. "Because of the general oppressive environment of slavery, the slave population was not self-reproducing," says Gaspar. Their ranks had to be constantly replenished with imports from Africa.

A slave's life was grim beyond our capacity to imagine and sometimes beyond their capacity to endure. The workday was endless, and beatings were common for the smallest infraction. Mary Prince, a slave who lived on a number of different Caribbean islands in the early 19th century, describes her treatment by one particularly cruel owner: "To strip me naked—to hang me up by the wrists and lay my flesh open with the cow-skin, was an ordinary punishment for even a slight offence."

The conditions on plantations drove some slaves to suicide and infanticide. Others fought back with insubordination, malingering and feigned illnesses. Running away was virtually impossible since by the mid-18th century the forests had been cleared and most of the smaller islands afforded no place to hide. But, as recent scholars have begun to see, the slaves were often resourceful in adapting to their plight. "I'm not saying that slavery wasn't bad, because it was," says Pulsipher. "But slaves were not just victims. We should give them credit for being able to seize a bad situation and make the best of it."

On most plantations slaves managed to carve out a degree of autonomy by insisting on certain rights, such as a weekly day off and the right to sell, at Sunday market, food they had grown in their own gardens. "One of the forms of both accommodation and resistance, especially on Montserrat, was through these slave gardens up in the hills," says Goodwin. "Because they could escape white eyes, these gardens had connotations of freedom and self-worth. But the gardens were also advantageous to slave owners because they relieved them of some of the responsibility of supplying food to slaves."

Sunday, market day, had little religious significance for slaves who, at least in the early years, didn't attend church. Because slavery did not square with their religious teachings, Anglican planters had little interest in converting their labor force. It was not until the late 1700s, when the Moravians and Methodists arrived and opened their doors to slaves,

that Sunday became important as a day of worship. In the meantime, they quietly practiced the religious traditions they had brought over from Africa. Islam had some influence, but it's not known how much.

But even after the introduction of Christianity, Sunday remained one of the few days that slaves found free time to enjoy themselves. John Luffman offered this description of a musical afternoon. "Negroes are very fond of the discordant notes of the banjar and the hollow sound of the toombah . . . The banjar is the invention of and was brought here by the African Negroes, who are most expert in the performance thereon, which are principally their own country tunes. To this music I have seen 100 or more dancing at a time . . . The principal dancing time is on Sunday afternoons, when the great market is over. In fact, Sunday is their day of trade, their day of relaxation, their day of pleasure, and may be called the Negroes' holiday."

Slaves seized an opportunity that was given them by the western European calendar and, quickly and entrepreneurially, started the markets. "Slaves used this time to socialize, reaffirm cultural links, meet their mates and sell whatever it was they had for sale: the baskets they'd woven, the food they'd made or the vegetables they'd grown. It was a time to improve their economic status, in small but significant ways."

In excavating Galways Plantation on Montserrat, Pulsipher and Goodwin unearthed an unusual abundance of artifacts from the plantation's slave village, including imported porcelain dishes, clay pipes, buttons, clothing fasteners, beads and coins. "These people were into a material culture," says Pulsipher. "Our theory is that their wealth was a result of their gardens up on the hillsides." Judging by the artifacts, Goodwin suspects slaves on Galways Plantation possessed maybe twice the material wealth of slaves on typical plantations in the southern United States.

In other parts of the Caribbean, however, slaves were not so fortunate. On Antigua, slaves had trouble finding space to plant their gardens because nearly every acre was in cane. Despite laws ordering slave owners to provide plantations with provision grounds, many wouldn't spare the land to ensure that slaves were adequately fed.

Throughout the Caribbean, sugar plantations were a curious blend of farm-

ing and factory work because so much of the industrial processing of the sugar was carried out on the spot. Mintz has dubbed the plantations "precocious cases of industrialization," and even the planters themselves recognized their industrial elements. In "An Essay Upon Plantership," Samuel Martin, an Antiguan planter writing in 1773, described the plantation as a machine with many moving parts: if one part broke, the machine broke. "Even that early, labor was very important, filling many cogs in the machine," says Goodwin.

The "sugar" cycle began in August or September, when the laborers prepared the fields for planting. Slaves, wielding hoes under a mercilessly hot sun, dug holes about five or six inches deep and about five feet square, into which they placed cane cuttings, covered them with a layer of mold and prayed for rain. The slaves tended the new cane shoots as they grew; the crop was harvested, one field at a time, 15 months later.

When it came to the harvest, timing was everything. As soon as the sugar cane was ripe it had to be cut and ground, often within 24 hours to keep it from spoiling. Black overseers, called drivers, would stand behind a line of slaves, crack their whips and give the order to start cutting. From the break of dawn until after dusk, the slaves toiled in the hot, sticky fields—cutting the cane, gathering up the stalks, stripping off the leaves and loading the 100-pound bundles onto ox carts bound for the mill. The pace was so frenzied that pregnant women were sometimes obliged to give birth in the field and then continue working.

For the slaves who fed the mill, the work was less physically demanding but posed different dangers. The feeders, as they were called, were liable, especially when tired, to get their fingers caught between the vertical rollers that crushed the cane. A watchman stood ready with a hatchet to sever an arm before it could be drawn into the machine. As terrible as this must have been, the alternative was worse. The rollers couldn't be stopped by flipping a switch. "If the limb wasn't chopped off, the slave would be crushed to death," says Goodwin.

The boilermen had a less exacting but hotter and heavier task. Juice from the sugar cane would enter the boiling house by a pipe that ran from the mill, and workers would siphon it into a great copper basin. After several hours of boiling and skimming, the slaves would ladle the steamy liquid into a number of successively smaller coppers until it was ready to crystallize. The sugar was then cooled, packed into barrels and rolled into the curing room. Holes were drilled in the bottoms of the barrels, allowing the molasses to drain into separate containers.

Laboring in temperatures above 100 degrees, the boilermen often worked through the night, and the darkness increased the likelihood of serious burns from the scalding, sugary liquid. But because their job required a high degree of knowledge and skill, the boilermen were among the most valued slaves on the plantation.

Slaves used the molasses and skimmings from the boiling house to make rum. Water, molasses, yeast and lees were combined in a fermenting cistern and left for a week to 10 days. The fermented liquid was distilled into rum and decanted in wooden barrels. The rum, as well as sugar and molasses, was stored in a warehouse until a ship arrived to carry it either to Europe or to one of the North American colonies.

In the 17th century, there emerged two so-called triangles of trade. The first and most famous of these linked Europe to Africa and the West Indies. European goods, such as trinkets, arms, gunpowder and gin, were exchanged for slaves in West Africa. The slaves were shipped to the West Indies and sold for sugar, coffee, indigo and other tropical products, which were then sent to the European mother country. The second triangle wasn't vital to world trade until the mid-18th century. In this scenario, New England merchants shipped rum to Africa, exchanged the rum for slaves and sailed to the West Indies, where they sold the slaves, bought molasses for rummaking and returned home.

As several scholars have pointed out, trade was not limited to these two triangles; more often than not, it moved in several directions. "Some of the trade did actually flow in legal channels as it was supposed to do, within a single imperial system," notes Philip D. Curtin, author of "The Rise and Fall of the Plantation Complex." "Much of it flowed outside those channels."

The sugar industry—so prosperous for nearly two centuries—had started to decline by the mid-19th century. Several factors contributed to its downward spiral: emancipation of the slaves, falling sugar prices and the development of alternative sweeteners. Still, on some islands—Puerto Rico, Barbados, Cuba and the Dominican Republic—sugar remains the main export today. On Antigua, the only reminders of the sugar heyday are the ruins of countless plantations, the Cavalier rum factory (which must import its molasses from the Dominican Republic) and a population that traces its roots to Africa. On Antigua, as with so many islands, one monoculture has simply been exchanged for another: tourism is now virtually the only industry.

Despite the changes wrought by 500 years of contact with the Old World, the people of the West Indies have managed to build a vibrant culture, mixing European elements with those of Africa and the Americas. In the British West Indies, for example, cricket.has long been the most popular sport. Before a recent match between Montserrat and Antigua, the Montserratian team, which hadn't won a game all season, performed an old African rite to increase its chances: rising at dawn, they gathered on the playing field and started dancing . . . to drive away the evil spirits.

The Fabrication of Louis XIV

Peter Burke *looks at how images and the image-makers made the Sun King appear as the larger-than-life 'top ruler' of 17th-century Europe.*

Peter Burke

Peter Burke is Reader in Cultural History at Cambridge University and Fellow of Emmanuel College.

In the seventeenth century, European governments devoted more attention to the public image of the ruler than at any time since the later Roman empire. Among these governments, it was the French who were the most concerned with the ways in which the king was represented (despite considerable competition from the Habsburgs, especially Philip IV). The most elaborate and self-conscious attempts at projecting a favourable image of the ruler were those made by a group of officials, artists and men of letters (or women of letters, notably Mademoiselle de Scudery) in the reign of Louis XIV, especially in the period of his personal rule, which lasted for more than half a century (1661–1715), allowing historians to observe changes over the long term.

The official attention paid to the royal image makes it appropriate to analyse representations of Louis, as more recent propaganda has often been analysed, in terms of who says what to whom, through what channels and codes, in what settings and with what intentions and effects. The absence from their vocabulary of modern terms such as 'propaganda' or 'ideology' does not imply that viewers and listeners of this period were unaware of attempts at persuasion. Seventeenth-century schools paid a good deal of attention to rhetoric, while the place of the phrase 'public opinion' was taken by one of the king's favourite terms, 'glory'. The term 'propaganda' is all the more appropriate because the government was concerned not only to present the king in a heroic light but also

to spread official interpretations of specific events of the reign.

To begin with the channels and codes, the media of the seventeenth century. The co-existence of traditional media with new ones and their constant interaction is a striking feature of the system. Among the traditional media, ritual surely takes pride of place, from the everyday rituals such as the royal *lever,* in which Louis was handed his clothes by leading noblemen, to special occasions like 'touching for the king's evil', practised since the Middle Ages and still performed by Louis two or three times a year. This was no mere survival, for as the great French historian Marc Bloch pointed out in the 1920s, the recorded numbers of sick people touched by kings of France actually increased in the seventeenth century. Louis touched as many as 2,000 sick people on occasion. Foreign visitors have left vivid descriptions of these rituals, snapshots of the court of the Sun King.

What these snapshots do not reveal, however, are the changes that took place in the rituals over more than half a century. Louis is associated with Versailles, but he only made this palace his main residence in 1682. It is likely that his everyday life was increasingly ritualised in the course of the reign. Why? The traditional explanation is a political one—that the upper nobility were encouraged, if not compelled, to come to court in order to cut them off from their local power bases. The court therefore had to be made glamorous. However, the historian should beware of too cynically utilitarian an interpretation of the system as if Louis and his advisers were standing outside it. It is extremely likely that they felt the glamour too.

Ritual is the oldest stratum in the archaeology of the royal image. In the

second place comes architecture. The construction of magnificent buildings, especially palaces, as symbols of a new régime was traditional enough. However, Versailles was much grander than earlier French palaces, and it had a more complex iconography, centred on the sun. The Louvre was also rebuilt 'to make people respect the king and leave them with an impression of his power'. This phrase comes from a memorandum by Jean-Baptiste Colbert, a key document showing that the minister (who combined the posts of Superintendent of Finance and Superintendent of the King's Works) regarded architecture as a powerful means of impression management.

There was also a Renaissance stratum in the media available to Louis XIV. For example, the court ballet (the French equivalent to the Stuart masque) often carried a political message. Louis XIV used to dance in ballets in his younger days, especially in the role of Apollo, or the sun, wearing for the purpose a special golden wig. In the second place, there was the state portrait, a genre which had developed in the sixteenth century (from Holbein's Henry VIII to Titian's Charles V). It was normal for monarchs to commission a few such portraits. In the case of Louis XIV, however, some 300 have survived, suggesting unusual concern with his image. Indeed, the king must have spent a significant part of his life sitting to painters. Like Charles V, Louis also commissioned 'war artists' to follow him on campaign and record his achievements on the spot.

The free-standing statue was another Renaissance genre. Early modern rulers were frequently represented in this way, usually on horseback. What was new in the reign of Louis XIV was the scale of the operation. During what has been called the 'statue campaign' of the 1680s,

From *History Today*, February 1992, pp. 24-30. Reproduced by kind permission of History Today, Ltd., 83-84 Berwick Street, London W1V 3PJ, England.

a series of nearly twenty statues of the king, were commissioned for public squares in Paris (Place Louis-le-Grand, Place des Victoires) and in provincial towns; Aix, Angers, Arles, Besancon, Bordeaux, Caen, Dijon, Grenoble, Le Havre, Limoges, Lyons, Marseilles, Montpellier, Pau, Poitiers, Rennes, Tours and Troyes. Free-standing permanent triumphal arches were also erected in Paris and the provinces, for the first time since the decline of the Roman empire.

Particularly effective, however, was the official use of media which could be reproduced mechanically—tapestries (made at the state factory of the Gobelins); medals; and printed texts and images. Sixteenth-century rulers often issued twenty or thirty medals to commemorate the major events of their reigns, but Louis struck more than 300, telling what contemporaries called 'the story of the king' in bronze.

Print had also been exploited to some degree by Renaissance monarchs, but was used on a much grander scale by Louis XIV. For example, the visual image of the king was widely diffused by means of engravings. About 700 different engravings of Louis have survived. The medals too were engraved and the engravings grouped into an official 'medallic history' of the reign. An official newspaper, the *Gazette de France* (founded in 1631) issued reports twice a week on the actions of the king. The government also commissioned poems in praise of Louis and histories of his reign, encouraging Racine to abandon the theatre, and Boileau poetry, in order to celebrate the king's deeds in prose. Like the artists, Boileau and Racine were also invited to accompany Louis on campaign.

It is time to move from the media to the message. Of course the sheer size of Versailles, or some of the statues, was a message in itself, but there are more precise communications to be decoded. The visual image of the king was a stereotyped image, a kind of identikit Louis, and an image which was enhanced in the traditional manner. Louis was not a tall man, and the contrast between his physical height and what might be called his 'social height' was carefully camouflaged. Costume helped create the king (as Thackeray once demonstrated in a cruel cartoon). Seventeenth-century decorum did not allow ordinary clothes in representations of royalty, so Louis was portrayed in his coronation robes or in Roman armour

(but wearing a modern wig). He might appear as a god, usually Apollo or Jupiter but occasionally as Neptune. In these images he is normally surrounded by dignified or dignity-giving properties such as curtains, columns, orb, sceptre, sword, chariot, and trophies. Female personifications of Victory and Fame frequently stand or hover nearby, while various human figures are represented in attitudes of submission—defeated enemies, cowering captives, and so on. Monsters are often trampled underfoot, the hydra of heresy, for example, or the three-headed dog Cerberus, the heads in this case signifying the Triple Alliance of Louis' enemies, the Empire, Britain and the Netherlands.

Louis was described by means of a standard list of epithets. He was (in English alphabetical order), august, conquering, enlightened, generous, god-given, heroic, illustrious, immortal, invincible, just, magnanimous, pious, triumphant and wise. In a word, he was 'great', an adjective officially adopted in 1671. Indeed, LOUIS LE GRAND was generally written in capital letters even in a text in lower case. Readers, viewers and listeners were also regularly informed that Louis was accessible to his subjects, the protector of arts and letters, the extinguisher of heresy, the restorer of the laws, the extender of the frontiers, the second founder of the state and the most powerful monarch of the universe.

In literature, as in the visual arts, the image of the king was associated with that of heroes from the past. Louis was variously presented as a new Augustus (finding Paris brick and leaving it marble), a new Alexander (the young king's favourite comparison), a new Charlemagne, a new Constantine, a new St Louis. Apart from these mortals, the king was compared to Hercules, to Neptune, to Jupiter, and more especially to Apollo and the sun.

Such grandiose comparisons are not easy for historians from a twentieth-century democratic culture to swallow. It is easy—too easy—for us to dismiss them as empty formalities or to accuse their authors of servility. It is necessary to remember that panegyric of this kind was traditional (a classical tradition revived at the Renaissance), and also that the genre could be used (as it was on occasion by Boileau and Racine) to transmit other messages—to advise the king while appearing only to praise him.

It is also interesting to see the increasing use of new techniques of presentation, notably of statistics ('political arithmetic' as contemporaries called it). For example, a medal struck to commemorate the revocation of the Edict of Nantes carries the inscription, *Vicies Centena Millia Calvinianorum Ad Ecclesiam Revocatam* (Two Million Calvinists brought back to the Church). Another medal is inscribed 'Forty Towns on the Rhine captured in a Single Month'. The effect is not unlike that of headlines in a twentieth-century newspaper.

These rather general eulogies of the king were accompanied by many more specific messages. The history of the reign was presented, in the words of an official historian (as it happens, Racine), as 'an unbroken series of marvels'. More or less the same series of marvels recurs in the official newspapers, in the tapestries produced at the royal factory of the Gobelins, in the decoration of the state apartments at Versailles (directed by Charles Le Brun), and in the so-called 'medallic history' of the reign.

On the international front, we see, again and again, the diplomatic defeat of Spain in the contest for precedence, the conquest of Franche-Comté, the crossing of the Rhine and the invasion of the Dutch Republic, the humiliation of Genoa, etc. On the domestic front, there is the issuing of a law-code, the embellishment of Paris, the restoration of military discipline, and the re-establishment of religious unity—at least outwardly—by the Revocation of the Edict of Nantes in 1685.

Examples of what modern media analysts call the 'pseudo-event' and the 'non-event' can also be found. An engraving was published in 1671 showing an official visit of the king to the Academy of Sciences, a visit which had not actually taken place. On the other hand, a medal struck to commemorate the devastation of Heidelberg in 1689 was not included in the official medallic history. Once again the term 'impression management' seems to be in order.

Who then, was sending these messages? Who was speaking through the rituals, the statues, the poems and so on? Do we hear the voices of individual artists alone or was there someone telling them what to say? Was it Louis himself? The image of the king presented in his so-called 'memoirs' describes him as taking every political decision and as being concerned with the welfare of his subjects in every detail. However, we happen to know that Louis was not responsible for his own image. He did not even write these memoirs—they were ghosted by a team of collaborators. As for the creation of the king's public image, it was supervised by a leading minister, the previously mentioned Colbert, who functioned for some twenty years as what we might call a minister for propaganda.

Not long after taking his place at the side of the young king, Colbert can be found corresponding with a writer and critic, Chapelain, about the best way to ensure the king's glory. Chapelain's confidential reports on the French literary scene have survived, a fascinating assessment of the aesthetic, moral and political merits and faults of the leading writers of the time. Chapelain also recommended the use of visual media such as medals, pyramids, columns, equestrian statues, triumphal arches, and so on. As Superintendent of the King's Works, Colbert was well placed to act on this advice, and so he did. He spent a good deal of public money on artistic and literary patronage.

This kind of patronage was traditional by the seventeenth century, but the scale was grander than usual, as we have seen, and in any case Colbert went further. Like the good bureaucrat he was, he wanted an organised, institutionalised system, and so he set up what was known as the 'little academy', a small group of men of letters (including Charles Perrault, better known today as the author of *Little Red Riding Hood*) who met at his house twice weekly to advise on the king's public image, vetting other people's projects and devising some of their own, notably inscriptions for medals. Academies of Science (1666), Architecture (1671) and Music (1672) were also founded (the Academy of Painting and the Académie Française were already in existence by this time). I do not mean to suggest that the aim of these foundations was purely cosmetic, to put a good face on Louis and his regime. It might be more exact to call Colbert 'Minister for the Arts' rather than Minister for Propaganda. All the same, he was concerned to get what political return he could for Louis out of the money that was spent.

For whose benefit, to convince whom, was this money spent? Not (I think) for the majority of the king's subjects, the 20 million Frenchmen and women of the period. In this respect the propaganda for Louis is quite unlike that for twentieth-

century rulers. His media was not mass media. The royal memoirs, or better, reflections on the art of government, were written for an audience of one, the Dauphin, and was never intended for publication. The flattering verses by Corneille, Racine, and many lesser poets were addressed in the first instance to the king and read aloud to him, although they were circulated more widely later.

The rituals, festivals and ballets may resemble television in their glitter and glamour and their simultaneous appeal to eye and ear, but unlike today's media they were designed for a minority of privileged viewers, the court. All Parisians had an opportunity to see the major processions, arches of triumph and other monuments, but only a few would have been able to decode the iconography and the Latin inscriptions. After all, France in this period was a culture of restricted literacy, in which 75 per cent of brides and grooms in the years 1686–90 were unable to sign their names to the marriage registers.

I believe that the broadcasters of information about Louis were trying to reach three audiences in particular. In the first place, a high-status domestic audience, who may be conveniently described in a standard phrase of the time as the court and the city, *la cour et la ville*. In the second place, foreign courts. Hence ambassadors were invited to the festivals at Versailles and presented with medals, tapestries, royal portraits and so on. One reason for preferring Latin inscriptions to French was their international currency. In the third place, odd as it may seem now, the broadcasters were trying to reach us, or more exactly, posterity as they envisaged it. Hence monuments were built to last, official histories written, and medals buried in the foundations of buildings such as the new Louvre or the Observatory.

What kind of reception did these images receive and how successful were they in presenting Louis to these audiences? There is obviously no way of measuring the effects of all this propaganda, but at least a few reactions can be cited. On the positive side, the king's rivals and enemies were sufficiently impressed to imitate some of his methods. William III had his own medallic history, the emperor, Leopold, built Schönbrunn as a Viennese Versailles, while Peter the Great founded an official newspaper on the model of the *Gazette,* a tapestry

factory on the model of the Gobelins, and an Academy of Sciences on the model of the Académie des Sciences. At home, it is not difficult to find examples of private individuals, like the Duc de Feuillade, who took the initiative in raising monuments to the king's glory.

On the negative side, there is evidence of a vocal minority of dissenters. For the French Protestants, for example, Louis was not Augustus or Constantine but Pharaoh or Nero. It is likely that some of the attempts to glorify Louis were counter-productive, notably the statue on Place des Victoires which was frequently condemned as blasphemous for its inscription, *'To the Immortal Man'*, and for the lamps burning before it, as if before a holy image. The statue was indeed a gift to the counter-propagandists, to English, Dutch and German writers of pamphlets against Louis, especially in the last twenty-five years of the reign. The Dutch were particularly adept in parodying the official propaganda for Louis. On one occasion they reprinted one of the medallic histories of the reign and slipped into it five plates of satirical medals. Home-made satires on Louis were also in circulation in manuscript, especially in the later years of the reign.

To view this enterprise of image-making in perspective, it is of course necessary to look at changes during Louis' reign, as well as to examine the place of the reign in developments over the long-term. Like other parts of Europe, from Spain to Sweden, seventeenth-century France was a society in which power was increasingly centralised. There was consequently a greater need than before for a magnificent symbol of centrality. Hence the attention paid to the images of rulers such as Philip IV of Spain and Louis XIII of France. Louis defined himself by comparison to these rulers, his father-in-law and his father respectively, imitating them in order to surpass them. Philip IV was the planet king, Louis the sun. Philip had a Hall of Mirrors in his palace at Madrid, Louis a still more splendid one at Versailles. The Spanish court was famous for its ritualised formality, but Louis made the rituals of Versailles still more elaborate. At the same time his representations emphasised his accessibility to his subjects, in contrast to the remoteness of Philip IV. Louis' style might be described as midway between the stiff Spanish manner and the more demotic style of other seventeenth-century kings, notably Gustav Adolf of

Sweden, who liked to speak to his subjects in the marketplace.

Centralisation had its price. In the course of the century, there was a dramatic increase in the demands which the government made on the people, both for money and for recruits to the army. These demands were frequently resisted; small-scale rebellions were common. The higher nobility resented the way in which the king ruled without consulting them.

The regime was consequently in need of legitimation. However, in the course of the seventeenth century the French monarchy went through what may be called a 'legitimation crises' or a 'crisis of representations'. The increasing acceptance of the Cartesian universe, in other words the image of the world as a vast machine, encouraged scepticism about the efficacity of the royal touch and about the analogy between Louis XIV and the sun. There was a dramatic contrast between the ardent young monarch of the 1660s and 1670s, who campaigned in person and was generally victorious, and the old man who sat in Versailles receiving news of French defeats.

All these difficulties needed to be camouflaged by the media. It is surely no accident that the statue campaign dates from the mid-1680s, or that most of the 300-odd medals as well as the two medallic histories were produced in the latter half of the reign. The increasing amount of time, energy and money poured into the representations of Louis XIV may therefore be interpreted as a response to the increasingly acute problems faced by the regime. As the political scientist Harold Lasswell once wrote, 'A well-established ideology perpetuates itself with little planned propaganda . . . When thought is taken about ways and means of sowing conviction, conviction has already languished'.

FOR FURTHER READING

F. Bluche, *Louis XIV,* (English translation, London 1990); M. Jones, *Medals of the Sun King* (British Library pamphlet, 1979); J. Klaits, *Printed Propaganda under Louis XIV* (Princeton, 1976); L. Marin, *The Portrait of the King* (English translation, New York 1988); J. Walton, *Louis XIV's Versailles* (New York, 1986).

The 17th-Century 'Renaissance' in Russia

Lindsey A. J. Hughes

Russian culture underwent a series of changes in the seventeenth century that some historians have described as a delayed 'Renaissance' that preceded the dramatic Westernisation of his country by Peter the Great. Echoes of Western art and culture had, of course, reached Russia long since: for example, elements of classical antiquity inherited from Byzantium; a style akin to Romanesque to be found in the architecture of the twelfth century; and the late fifteenth- and early sixteenth-century Kremlin cathedrals and palaces built by Italians. But a number of factors, not least the 250-year long Mongol occupation and adherence to the Orthodox faith, had served to isolate Russia from the mainstreams of European culture. The result was that at the beginning of the seventeenth century Muscovy not only lagged behind the West in intellectual and scientific matters, but also had a more limited repertoire of art forms, most of which were harnessed to the service of the Church. This is not to underrate the achievements of Old Russian craftsmen, who made objects of great beauty, nor to overlook the indigenous folk tradition in wooden architecture and applied art, but merely to point to a state of affairs that increasingly conflicted with Russia's efforts to learn much needed military and technical skills from the West.

Changes in Russian art began not so much with the overt importation of Western devices as with the fossilisation of traditional forms. One senses this most clearly in the numerous mid-seventeenth-century churches, built after the centuries-old pattern of a cube capped by one or five domes, but with the builder's imagination lavished on the exterior decoration of carved brickwork, limestone and ceramics. Byzantine forms were frequently retained as mere tokens, as, for example, in domes of solid brick, rising from the roof with no connection to the interior. But now domestic and ecclesiastical buildings began to receive an increasingly uniform treatment, their facades divided into storeys by window surrounds, cornices and half-columns of Western-inspired design. In the 1680s a style by the name of Moscow or 'Naryshkin' Baroque appeared. Alongside conventional Orthodox church designs, symmetrically planned and decorated in Western style, there appeared novel centrally-planned churches composed of one or more towers of receding octagons. The decorative features of Moscow Baroque, including carved and stepped gables, 'strap-work' ornamentation, ornate window surrounds, portals and columns based on the Classical orders, have been traced to such diverse sources as the Ukraine, Byelorussia, Poland, the Low Countries, Germany and Italy.

In religious painting one observes, alongside a tendency towards intricate decorativeness and complex compositions, a more realistic approach to the depiction of the human face and body, nature and architecture. New genres appeared, including portraiture from live models, secular murals and canvasses for interior decoration, and precise engraving for architectural and other purposes. Parallel developments are found in literature, with the growing popularity of secular tales and the beginnings of poetry and drama. If one also takes into account an increase in the importation and translation of foreign secular books and the establishment of Russia's first seat of higher learning, the Moscow Academy, in 1687, it is not hard to see how the term 'Renaissance' might have some limited application to this period of Russia's cultural history, even in the absence of any clear awareness of the rediscovery of antiquity.

These and other developments can be attributed to a number of events and circumstances which served simultaneously to bring Muscovy closer to the West and to weaken old traditions and prejudices. The curtain raiser to the century, the Time of Troubles, which concluded with the election of Mikhail Romanov as Tsar in 1613, and had seen the country invaded by Poles and Swedes, underlined Russia's military backwardness. In the words of S. F. Platonov: 'The Time of Troubles showed the need for close contact with the West and the need for armies equipped and trained on Western lines.' Military needs were to set the tone of 'borrowing' for the century. In the classic formula of S. M. Soloviev, 'the new had to appear in the guise of directly useful objects . . . with craftsmanship'; but Russians could scarcely avoid the less tangible aspects of Western life, 'like children tricked into learning by toys'.

A further step along the path to secularisation was marked by the mid-century schism in the Russian Orthodox Church, when many of the faithful—the Old Believers—were alienated by Patriarch Nikon's reforms of Church texts and ritual, instituted in 1653 and aimed at restoring it to the original Byzantine model. In addition to weakening the Church's internal unity, the preparation of the reforms and the subsequent schism obliged the authorities to use the services of theologians, translators and teachers from the clergy of Muscovy's better educated Orthodox neighbours, notably the Ukraine and Byelorussia. Fear of the 'Latin and Lutheran' West also confirmed the Church in its efforts to improve its educational standards.

A third significant event was the annexation of the previously Polish ruled Left-Bank Ukraine to Muscovy in 1654, Kiev itself being temporarily secured in 1667 and in perpetuity from 1686. Political and religious contacts with this and other polonised regions formed an important element in seventeenth-century Westernisation.

It is against this general background, in a century which also saw intensified diplomatic ties with most Western states, that one notes a steady flow of foreign personnel into Muscovy, amongst them merchants, who had visited the country since the arrival of the English in 1553 and had established permanent colonies and warehouses in a number of towns.

1. THE AGE OF POWER

Some of them served the tsars as special agents, travelling abroad to recruit mercenaries and craftsmen, while others were licensed to set up manufactures, such as the Dutchman Andrew Vinius's Tula ironworks (1632), Johann van Sveden's Moscow paper mills (1660s), which employed 'the best masters of paper making from the German lands', and the textile mills set up by Paullson and Tabert in the 1680s. In 1687 another Dutchman, Daniel Hartmann, was granted special trading rights because since 1655 he had brought to Russia 'many fine wares, medicines and many kinds of weapon for infantry and cavalry at lower prices than ever before'. There was a growing demand for 'fine wares' of Western origin in court circles. Palaces and mansions, previously sparsely furnished, were adorned with furniture, mirrors, clocks, painted fabrics, portraits and prints of foreign origin or inspiration.

Increasingly the demand for such goods was met not only by importers but by foreign craftsmen on the spot. In 1679 Jacob Reutenfels, an envoy from Tuscany, remarked on the rising standards of Muscovite workmanship, which were achieved 'thanks to their dealings with foreigners, which become freer with every day'. But Frenchman Foy de la Neuville, visiting Moscow in 1689, remarked: 'Without the Germans, who are in Moscow in great numbers, they would be able to do nothing.'

One group of foreign experts whose skills were in great demand were architects, although the government's practical orientation meant that it was fortifications experts and civil engineers rather than exponents of palace and church building whose services were sought. This policy of employing foreign architects began with Tsar Mikhail summoning foreigners to reconstruct city walls and fortifications in the 1620s and continued to the end of the century when Peter I engaged engineers from Brandenburg to fortify Azov in 1696. Some foreigners were employed on less mundane projects. For example, in 1624–25, the Englishman Christopher Galloway built the fanciful upper section of the Kremlin Spassky tower and installed a clock, much to the delight of the royal family. At about the same time one John Taller or Taylor, presumed to have been an Englishman, carried out restoration work on some of the Kremlin churches, and in 1660–62 the Swedish 'engineer' Gustav Dekentin provided interior designs for a royal dining hall 'in the new

foreign manner'. The first stone bridge over the Moskva River, built in about 1687, has been attributed to a 'Polish monk' and a handful of other buildings may tentatively be attributed to foreign authorship, but in general it appears that until Peter I's reign the overall design and construction of buildings remained in the hands of native masters. This is confirmed by the hybrid design of most seventeenth-century Russian buildings that, even when highly Westernised in decoration, can rarely be traced directly to foreign prototypes.

Large numbers of craftsmen came to Russia from the Polish-Lithuanian borderlands, especially during the Russo-Polish Wars of 1654–67. In 1672 a special district of Moscow—the *meshchanskaya sloboda*—was allocated to these mainly Byelorussian foreigners and housed a number of petty traders and craftsmen. The most influential group was initially employed on two of Patriarch Nikon's grandiose buildings schemes—the Iversky Monastery on Lake Valdai and the Monastery of the Resurrection at New Jerusalem, begun in 1654 and 1656 respectively. The latter was intended as a symbol of both Nikon's own prestige and the power of the Orthodox Church, both soon to be undermined by the patriarch's personal downfall and the schism. In 1666 seventeen Byelorussian craftsmen, including six carpenters and five tile-makers, were transferred from New Jerusalem to the royal workshops in Moscow. These two bands of craftsmen, together with other fellow-countrymen, brought new artistic devices to Muscovy, the former specialising in a distinctive form of high relief Baroque carving, the latter in glazed ceramics that had been employed at New Jerusalem in the construction of Baroque window surrounds, portals and

iconostases. In 1681 the woodcarver Klim Mikhailov became head of the 'carving and joinery' section of the Tsar's main workshop, the Armoury. In 1667–68 he and other Byelorussians prepared decorative carving for the new wooden royal palace at Kolomenskoe and later produced a number of wooden iconostases, or icon stands, of which at least one survives, dated 1683–85, in the main cathedral of the Novodevichy Convent. It is possible that the architectural components of icon stands—carved and twisted columns, profiled cornices—influenced the carved stone decoration of Moscow Baroque.

By the middle of the century the Moscow Armoury comprised a complex of workshops producing not only small arms but also a wide range of useful and decorative objects for the royal household. It has been described as a seventeenth-century Russian 'Academy of Arts'. Amongst its finest products were icons, many of them painted in the new manner. The best known painter of the Armoury school was Simon Ushakov (1626–86), whose works departed from old stylised conventions in their naturalistic treatment of the human face, use of light, shade and, to a lesser degree, perspective and realistic depiction of nature and objects. The main features of Ushakov's style can be seen in his 'Old Testament Trinity' (1671). Alongside icon painters, the Armoury employed secular artists, who worked on the interior decoration of palaces, portraits, engravings, banners, etc. In 1687–88 there were twenty-seven icon painters and forty secular artists. Some, like Ushakov who was also an accomplished engraver and portrait painter, worked in both genres. There are records of a number of foreign artists employed in the Tsar's service, including the Dutchman Hans Dieters, who arrived in 1642, and his fellow-countryman Daniel Wuchters who, in a petition of 1667, described his skills as 'the art of painting portraits and biblical themes in life size . . . and diplomatic pictures on canvas'. In 1670, Peter Engels, a 'master of perspective' from Hamburg, came to Moscow and was hired for court projects. It is to these and other foreign artists, most of whom took pupils, that we may attribute the new interest in portrait painting in court circles, a genre hitherto frowned upon, if not specifically banned, by the Church. Those seventeenth-century personages who had their portraits painted or engraved included Tsars Aleksei (1645–76) and Fedor (1676–82), Tsarevna Sophia, regent from 1682–89, ministers of foreign affairs A. S. Matveev and Prince Vasily Golitsyn and Patriarchs Nikon and Joachim.

Apart from the tutelage of foreign artists, it is possible to trace new devices in art and architecture to foreign graphic material. One well-attested source is the illustrated *Piscator* Bible in its 1650 and 1674 Amsterdam editions, copies of which were owned by Armoury employees. Modified copies of its late Renaissance engravings are found in a number of seventeenth-century church frescoes. Foreign prints and broadsheets were brought into Muscovy by merchants and sold in the streets of Moscow and other towns. The Church authorities were highly suspicious of such prints and in 1674 Patriarch Joachim tried to ban their sale, complaining that merchants 'buy paper prints of German origin and sell these prints which are made by the German heretics, Lutherans and Calvinists, according to their own damned persuasion, crudely and wrongly'.

The first published translation of a Western architectural manual—Vignola's *Rules of the Five Orders of Architecture*—appeared only in 1709, but Muscovite libraries acquired a number of works on architecture and allied subjects. In 1637, for example, the Cannonmakers' Chancellery, which employed foreigners, sent several architectural works to the royal library. The collections of Tsar Aleksei, Tsar Feodor and Patriarch Nikon contained several titles on architecture, atlases and illustrated descriptions of foreign states and cities. Both the Armoury and the Pharmacy owned foreign books, but the most impressive repository was the Ambassadorial Chancellery, which amassed a large collection for the use of its staff. Sixteen works in French, Italian and German on architecture, carving, landscape gardening and fountains were acquired from the exiled director of the Chancellery, A. S. Matveev, in 1677, whilst further titles on palace and civic architecture were added in 1682–83. The Chancellery had its own workshops for the production of charters and manuscripts and its own architectural team.

Another source of influence was the Moscow Foreign or 'German' Colony which, apart from housing a number of hired men and their families from the Protestant states of Europe, also provided an interesting example of European town-planning. Founded in 1652,

the colony was indicative of the growing numbers of foreign personnel, who hither-to had resided in the heart of the city, and of continuing attempts to isolate their 'harmful' influence. Bernard Tanner, who visited Moscow with a Polish delegation in 1678, reported that the inhabitants 'kept everything as neat and orderly as in German towns, quite unlike the Muscovite practice. They have built many houses, which are made with economy and skill'. By the late 1680s, when it was described by the Jesuit Georgius David, the colony appeared 'more handsome than other districts . . . It contains many fine stone mansions which the German and Dutch merchants have lately built as their residences.' By the time Hendrik de Witt made his engraving at the beginning of the eighteenth century, many of the buildings were of stone and included some of the most imposing palaces in Moscow, like the one built for Peter I's favourite, Franz Lefort, in 1697–98. There were Protestant churches in the colony, including those of the 'old' and 'new' Lutheran communities built in 1684 and 1694–95 respectively. There was no question, however, of Muscovites being introduced to Catholic Baroque through the colony as Catholics were not granted permission to erect a church until the very end of the century; nor, indeed, was the direct borrowing of non-Orthodox ecclesiastical designs to be expected. The official view was that the churches of 'heretics' were 'vile'. 'It is not seemly that either stone or wooden Latin or Lutheran churches should be built in the Muscovite state . . . Such heretical Lutheran or Latin buildings are profane and vile . . . an abomination of desolation on the sacred soil of the Holy Russian land', runs a tract of the 1680s, attributed to arch-conservative Patriarch Joachim of Moscow. The fact that the secular authorities tolerated such 'abominations', albeit safely tucked away in the Foreign Colony, shows how the needs of the State overrode the strictures of the Church. As is well known, the young Peter had no scruples about frequenting the colony and even his father Tsar Aleksei had applied to one of the colony's pastors for help in putting on the first court theatricals in the 1670s.

Seventeenth-century Russians acquired their knowledge of the West more from contacts at home than from travel abroad. The long and hazardous journey, official formalities and restrictions and simple fear of the unknown ensured that, until a

number were forced to do so by Peter, few Muscovites ventured into Western Europe. With the exception of journeys to the Ukraine and Byelorussia, there is no evidence that Russian architects and craftsmen went abroad in pursuit of their careers. A number of potential patrons did, however, and it is interesting to record the comments of Tsar Aleksei's English physician Samuel Collins (1671), who writes:

'Since His Majesty has been in Poland and seen the manner of the Princes' houses there and ghess'd at the mode of their Kings, his thoughts are advanc'd and he begins to model his court and edifices more stately, to furnish his rooms with tapestry and to contrive houses of pleasure abroad.'

Aleksei had visited the Polish-ruled towns of Smolensk, Vilna, Polotsk, Vitebsk and others during the campaign of 1654–56 and subsequently Polish influence, mainly through the medium of Byelorussia, was evident in the interior and exterior decoration of new and refurbished palaces and in the output of the Armoury. Aleksei employed a Byelorussian churchman and writer, Simeon Polotsky, as court poet and tutor to his children.

Many diplomatic missions visited the West during the seventeenth century and, although there is little direct evidence of artistic borrowing via this route and frustratingly little in the way of diaries, travel accounts and personal letters, some impressions of Western art were recorded. A visit to Denmark in 1621 prompted the priest Ivan Shevelev to compose a 'Treatise on the Lutherans', in which he expressed disapproval of the worldly appearance of Danish churches decorated with military trophies and 'indecent' statues and paintings, 'the nakedness of the bodies bedecked with gold and silver and their secret places lasciviously and shamelessly exposed'. The realistic nude failed to gain currency in seventeenth-century Muscovy. Ambassador Vasily Likhachev, who visited Italy in 1659, was more favourably impressed. He thought the architecture of Leghorn 'very fine' and Florence 'wonderfully built with very lofty palaces'. Standard impressions recur in official reports of this kind; for example, Muscovites were amazed by the size of many buildings in the West, impressed by the predominance of stone edifices and intrigued by fountains and other mechanical curiosities. The far more numerous accounts written by foreign travellers to Russia are equally informative. Few failed to be impressed by the quantity of churches and their colourful interiors, but most were struck by the apparent uniformity of Byzantine patterns, lack of sophistication in the fine arts and, in particular, the low levels of science and learning. Adam Olearius from Holstein, who made several visits to Russia in the 1630s–40s, writes: 'They have images painted with oil upon wood, wretchedly coloured and ill-proportioned.' Jacob Reutenfels wrote: 'The churches are shown respect by all, for they are for the most part tall and elegantly built, but they cannot in any respect compare with our own for size and magnificence.' Georg Schleissing, who came to Russia with a delegation from Brandenburg in 1684, remarked disparagingly that there was as little comparison between Russian 'palaces' and those of Rome, Florence and Venice as 'between a fly and an elephant'.

Foreigners for the most part remained unaware of the changes taking place in seventeenth-century Russian culture, but in Russia itself leading churchmen were alive to the dangers of innovation. The Church authorities and Old Believers alike feared the 'cunning' of the West, its concern for legality, form and reason as opposed to intuitive Orthodox 'wisdom'. In the words of the Old Believer leader, Archpriest Avvakum, burnt at the stake in 1682: 'Even though I am untutored in words, yet I have wisdom, untutored in rhetoric and philosophy, yet I have the wisdom of Christ within me.' Avvakum complained that painters depicted Christ 'with a plump face, curly hair, fat arms and muscles, thick fingers and likewise thick lips and altogether make him look like a German, big-bellied and fat, except that no sword is painted on his hip'. Nikon himself personally destroyed icons that were too innovatory, commanding that they be painted 'according to the ancient tradition', and his successor Joachim warned that icons 'should be made according to the ancient Greek traditions and not from seductive Latin and German pictures'.

It is no coincidence that defence of these new trends came from the Armoury. Simon Ushakov himself produced a tract on icon-painting in which he compared art to the reflective properties of a mirror. His fellow painter Josif Vladimirov in a tract written c. 1665–66 appealed for better craftsmanship and a more positive attitude towards foreign art: 'How can you claim that only Russians are allowed to paint icons and that only Russian icon-painting may be revered whilst that of other lands should be neither kept nor honoured? When we see the image of Christ or the Mother of God printed or painted with great skill, be it by our own or by foreign artists, our eyes are filled with great love and joy.'

A similarly positive attitude towards foreign culture can be observed in a number of high-ranking Muscovites, whose patronage of the arts went beyond the customary commissioning of chapels and acquisition of religious objects. One such was Prince Vasily Vasilievich Golitsyn (1643–1714), head of the Ambassadorial Chancellery and the leading statesman of the regency of Peter's half-sister Sophia (1682–89). Golitsyn was well educated for his time and knew Latin and Polish. He was described by the Russian historian Klyuchevsky as a 'fervent admirer of the West' who abandoned 'many of the sacred traditions of Russian antiquity'. His Moscow mansion and adjoining church were in the Moscow Baroque style. Inside the rooms were fitted out with rich furnishings, mirrors, portraits and engravings of foreign origin and there was a large collection of foreign secular books. We can only speculate on the direct sources of Golitsyn's taste. As Chancellor, he was in constant contact with foreigners and, although he never visited the West, his service in the Ukraine from 1676–81 would have introduced him to that region's more Westernised culture. Under Golitsyn the Ambassadorial Chancellery had its own workshops that produced diplomatic charters, engravings and architectural projects.

Golitsyn's patroness Sophia herself commissioned a number of buildings in the Moscow Baroque style, including new churches and residences in the Novodevichy Convent. The Church of the Transfiguration (1687–88) is an intriguing example of the transitional style, conventionally five-domed but decorated with a harmonious framework of Classical columns and window surrounds, whilst the contemporaneous Church of the Assumption was modelled on a Ukrainian design. Another of Sophia's Ukrainian-inspired buildings was the Church of Prince Josaphat (1688) on the royal estate at Izmailovo, with three towers placed from west to east. In an engraving of the princess, dated c. 1687, the usual Orthodox trappings of stylised royal portraits are supplemented by seven Virtues represented by Classical figures.

Other patrons receptive to Western art forms include A. S. Matveev, the boyar, Bogdan Khitrovo, who directed the Armoury from 1654–80, a number of Peter's maternal relatives, the Naryshkins, who commissioned Moscow Baroque churches, Peter's sister Natalia and Prince Boris Golitsyn. Western innovations were adopted or perceived only by a small élite, confined to court, government and church circles, yet this does not detract from their significance; one of the criticisms levelled by historians against the more consciously Westernised culture of the eighteenth century is that it, too, was a veneer, under which old traditions, illiteracy and superstition survived almost unscathed. The difference is that in the seventeenth century one is still dealing with sporadic influence rather than with the systematic imitation and large-scale importation of craftsmen adopted by Peter and his successors. In Peter's reign Westernisation found its expression in secular culture—the civic buildings of St. Petersburg, portraits and engravings of Russia's military and naval exploits and of the Tsar in military attire, triumphal arches—whereas in the seventeenth century Western-inspired devices were applied mainly to religious objects—such as churches, icons, frescoes, iconostases. It has been argued, notably by the nineteenth-century Slavophiles, that seventeenth-century Westernisation was a more 'natural' process than Peter's violent changes, but it is as futile to speculate on probable developments without the intervention of Peter as to ponder the growth of Russian Western-style democratic institutions without the Bolsheviks. All that can be said is that Peter's reforms were not as unheralded nor such a revolutionary break with an uneducated and inward-looking past as has sometimes been suggested.

NOTES ON FURTHER READING

G. H. Hamilton, *The Art and Architecture of Russia*, 2nd edn., Penguin (Harmondsworth, 1977) and J. H. Billington, *The Icon and the Axe*, Weidenfeld and Nicolson (London, 1966). Lindsay A. J. Hughes, 'Western Graphic Material as a source of Moscow Baroque Architecture', *Slavonic and East European Review*, IV, 1977, 433–43 and 'The Moscow Armoury and innovations in 17th-century Muscovite art', *Canadian-American Slavic Studies*.

Locke and Liberty

As an articulate champion of liberty and toleration, of common sense and healthy measure in all things, England's John Locke (1632–1704) became in many respects the guiding spirit for America's Founding Fathers. His perception that personal freedom requires the private ownership of property remains a cornerstone of American political thought. Nonetheless, Locke is a hazy figure to most Americans, even as they approach the 1987 bicentennial of the Constitution, which embraces many of his ideas. Here, Maurice Cranston *reviews the man's life and work.*

Maurice Cranston

Maurice Cranston, 65, a former Wilson Center Guest Scholar, is professor of political science at the London School of Economics. Born in London, he was educated in England at St. Catherine's College and Oxford. His books include John Stuart Mill *(1965),* Jean-Jacques, The Early Life and Work of Jean-Jacques Rousseau, 1712–54 *(1982), and the reissued* John Locke: A Biography.

Among the philosophers of the modern world, John Locke has always been held in especially high regard in America. His influence on the Founding Fathers exceeded that of any other thinker. And the characteristically American attitude toward politics—indeed, toward life—can still be thought of as "Lockean," with its deep attachment to the rule of law, to equal rights to life, liberty, and property, to work and enterprise, to religious toleration, to science, progress, and pragmatism.

Like the Founders, Locke had participated in a revolution—the bloodless Glorious Revolution of 1688–89, in which the English overthrew the despotic King James II to install the constitutional monarchy of William and Mary and confirm Parliament's supremacy. Locke had justified that rebellion in his writings with arguments against "unjust and unlawful force," arguments that were cited as no less powerful in the American Colonies during the 1770s.

Earlier philosophers had theories about justice, order, authority, and peace. Locke was the first to build a system around *liberty*.

Locke's chief works—*An Essay Concerning Human Understanding, Two Treatises of Government,* and his first *Letter Concerning Toleration,* all published in London in 1689–90—spoke in terms that Thomas Jefferson, James Madison, and other Americans recognized. Men were created equal by God and endowed by Him with natural rights; the earth was given by God to men to cultivate by their own endeavors, so that each could earn a right to property ("the chief end" of society) by the application of his labor to the improvement of nature. In the New World, Locke's message received a warmer welcome than in crowded, feudal Europe.

The practical men who led the American Revolution and wrote the Constitution and the Bill of Rights recognized Locke as a Christian, like themselves, who had discarded nonessential dogmas and yet retained a pious faith in the Creator and in the Puritan virtues of probity and industry. Other European philosophers influenced the Framers' thinking: Montesquieu (1689–1755) contributed a republican element and Jean-Jacques Rousseau (1712–78) a democratic element, neither present in the constitutional–monarchist system of Locke. But the French philosophers, though they worked in a field prepared by Locke, did not have his hold on the American mind.

But who *was* John Locke?

Paintings, including a 1672 portrait by John Greenhill that Locke admired, show a tall, lean, and handsome man with a dimpled chin and large, dark, languorous eyes. He had asthma; one of his teachers, the great medical scientist Thomas Sydenham, urged him to rest much to conserve the "needful heat." A contemporary at Oxford called him a "turbulent spirit, clamorous and never contented," who

could be "prating and troublesome." The earl of Shaftesbury, his long-time patron, thought him a "genius."

So, apparently, did Locke. His self-esteem shows in the understated Latin epitaph he wrote for himself before he died at age 73. The plaque at the Essex church where he was buried describes him as merely a scholar "contented with his modest lot," who "devoted his studies wholly to the pursuit of truth."

Locke was never a candid man. He had an almost Gothic love of mystery. A Tory spy once wrote that at Oxford Locke "lives a very cunning unintelligible life"; he was often absent, but "no one knows whither he goes." In his letters and notebooks, he used ciphers and a shorthand system modified for purposes of concealment. Yet a picture emerges from these and other sources: Locke was one of the most adept, compelling, and idiosyncratic "new men" to rise in what he called "this great Bedlam," 17th-century England.

John Locke was born on August 29, 1632, at Wrington in Somerset in the west of England, where modern commerce first began to challenge the old medieval order. His grandfather, Nicholas Locke, was a successful clothier. His less prosperous father, John Locke, was a lawyer and clerk to the local magistrates. His mother came from a family of tanners; she was 35 when her first child, the future philosopher, was born; her husband was only 26. The baby was baptized by Samuel Crook, a leading Puritan intellectual, and brought up in an atmosphere of Calvinist austerity and discipline.

England was Bedlam partly because of

tension between the arrogant, authoritarian, and High Anglican King Charles and the increasingly assertive and Puritan House of Commons. In 1642, when Locke was 10 years old, the Civil War began between the Royalist forces (the Cavaliers) and the Parliamentary army (the Roundheads). The struggle was religious and social as well as political. The ultimately victorious Parliamentarians tended to be drawn not from the traditionalists of the Church of England and the leaders of feudal society, but from the Calvinists and Puritans, men from England's "new class" of rising merchants.

Among these were Locke's Devonshire cousins, named King, who rose swiftly from the trade of grocers to that of lawyers, and then via Parliament to the nobility itself. Young John, too, would benefit from England's great upheaval.

During the Civil War, his father was made a captain of Parliamentary Horse by Alexander Popham, a rich local magistrate turned Roundhead colonel. Popham became fond of his captain's son. When Westminster, the country's best boarding school, was taken over by Parliament, Popham found a place there for the boy.

That was the *first* stroke of fortune that would assist Locke's rise from the lower- to the upper-middle class—a group whose aspirations he may have reflected when, as a political philosopher, he gave the right to property first priority among the rights of man.

At Westminster, Locke was influenced by headmaster Richard Busby, a Royalist whom the Parliamentary governors had imprudently allowed to remain in charge of the school. By the time Locke won a scholarship to Oxford's premier college, Christ Church, which he entered at age 20, he was well ready to react against the rule of the Puritan "saints" at the university.* By 27, Locke had become a right-wing monarchist; by 1661, when he was 29, and the Restoration had put the deposed king's son Charles II on the throne, Locke's political views were close to those of the conservative thinker of the previous generation, Thomas Hobbes.

---

*The Oxford routine was still medieval. Undergraduates had to rise at 5:00 A.M. to attend chapel, and do four hours' work in Hall before supper at noon. Conversations with tutors, and among students in Hall, had to be in Latin. Students had to hear at least two sermons a day, and visit their tutors nightly "to hear private prayers and to give an account of the time spent that day."

In a pamphlet Locke wrote at that time, he said that no one had more "veneration for authority than I." Having been born in a political "storm" that had "lasted almost hitherto," he had been led by the calm that the Restoration brought to value "obedience."

By his early 30s, Locke was less interested in politics than in medicine, a new subject at Oxford. During the summer of 1666, he chanced to perform a small medical service for a student's father, Anthony Ashley Cooper, the future earl of Shaftesbury and leader of the Whig party, champion of the rights of Parliament over the Crown.† Even then Shaftesbury, a wealthy Presbyterian, was a vocal political "liberal," the chief foe of measures designed by the Anglican majority to curb the freedom of religious Nonconformists. If Locke had not already come over to Shaftesbury's views, the earl must soon have pulled him across the last few hurdles.

At 35, Locke went to live at Shaftesbury's London house as his physician. After he saved the earl from the threat of a cyst of the liver, Shaftesbury decided that Locke was too talented to be spending his time on medicine alone, and work of other kinds was found for him. Thus began Locke's 15-year association with a powerful patron.

Gradually, Locke discovered his true gifts. First he became a philosopher. At Oxford he had been bored with the medieval Aristotelian philosophy still taught there. Reading French rationalist René Descartes first opened his eyes to the "new philosophy" that was providing the underpinnings of modern empirical science. Discussions with Shaftesbury and other friends led him to begin writing early drafts of the *Essay Concerning Human Understanding,* his masterpiece on epistemology, the study of how we know what we know.

Shaftesbury, short, ugly, and vain, shared Locke's interest in philosophy and science. He was pragmatic: Though anti-Catholic, he thought that religious toleration would help unite the nation, the better to pursue the kind of commercial imperialism that was proving so profitable for the seafaring Dutch.

---

† The name Whig seems to have come from *Whiggamore,* a term for "horse thief" used by 17th-century Anglicans or "Tories" to express scorn for Scottish Presbyterians.

Charles II, though he favored toleration primarily for the sake of Catholic recusants, agreed with Shaftesbury. In 1672, the king made Shaftesbury his chief minister, lord high chancellor. But the two soon fell out. Shaftesbury came to believe that England's main rival in trade and her potential enemy was not Holland but France, while Charles II remained strongly pro-French. Ousted as the king's minister, Shaftesbury became his leading adversary.

Later, when Charles II refused to deny his brother, a professed Catholic, the right to succeed him as James II, Shaftesbury tried to get the House of Commons to make the succession illegal. The people, he said, had a right to say who should rule. When Charles resisted, Shaftesbury called on his allies to rebel. The plot was nipped, and in 1682 the earl fled to Holland, where he soon died.

Locke, too, went to Amsterdam. One year later he was expelled *in absentia* from his "studentship" at Oxford by the king's command. The next summer, after Charles II's death and James's accession to the throne, the duke of Monmouth led a failed rebellion against the new king. Locke, named by the government as one of Monmouth's agents in Holland, went into hiding as "Dr. van der Linden."

Locke's friends in Holland included many of those who plotted with the Dutch prince William of Orange to topple James II, who was indeed deposed in 1688. We do not know how deeply Locke was involved, only that he returned to London in 1689 with William's wife Mary, the new English queen.

These were the events behind Locke's most famous works.

By the time the *Two Treatises of Government* appeared, Englishmen had come round to Shaftesbury's view: They justified deposing James II not just because he advanced Catholicism, but also because he had tried to be an absolute monarch like France's Louis XIV. In his preface, Locke said that he hoped the *Two Treatises* would help "justify the title of King William to rule us." But he did most of the writing when Charles II was king. Then, the question of whether a people had the right to rebel against their ruler was not a backward-looking moral issue but a forward-looking moral challenge.

Thomas Hobbes wrote *Leviathan* (1651) to provide new reasons for men to obey kings. In the *Two Treatises,* Locke used Hobbes's "social contract" to justify revolt against despots.

Locke's 'Shattered and Giddy' England

The tremors that rocked John Locke's times echo in his letters. England's fissures—between Crown and Parliament, Anglicans and Dissenters, aristocrats and achievers, rich and poor—had left a "shattered and giddy nation," he wrote at age 27. Few men "enjoy the privilege of being sober."

During the century before Locke's birth in 1632, England's population almost doubled, topping five million in 1540. But with growth came several woes: rising prices, falling "real" wages, and poor harvests and frequent famines caused by a miniature global ice age that lasted from about 1550 to 1700. While England was a naval power, as the 1588 defeat of the Spanish Armada had shown, the Dutch were far ahead in turning maritime prowess to profit.

BUT BUSINESS WAS becoming important: Retail shops created by a new breed of merchant began to replace the old market fairs. Abroad, firms chartered by the Crown traded English woolens and African slaves for West Indian molasses and sugar and American fish and timber; the East India Company (est. 1600) dealt in textiles and tea. Commerce had not (yet) remade England; if Locke's home county, Somerset, prospered from new industries (notably clothing), it was also plagued by such poverty that people, wrote one chronicler, "hanged themselves from want." But, slowly, medieval England was becoming the mercantile nation that, by the 18th century, would create the British Empire.

Authority was eroding. The Roman Catholic Church's supremacy had been broken by the Protestantism that had arrived via Martin Luther's Germany and Huldrych Zwingli's and John Calvin's Switzerland, and by King Henry VIII'S 1534 creation of the Church of England. And while the peerage was still dominant, the expanding landed gentry and the new commercial class now had to be heard. By the early 17th century, as historian Lawrence Stone has noted, "respectful subservience [to aristocracy] was breaking down."

King Charles I (1625–49), was besieged by troubles. Suspected by his Protestant subjects of "popish" leanings, he waged an unpopular war in Europe and, later, failed to secure Parliament's support in his effort to quash rebellion in Scotland, leading to the Civil War in 1542. The pro-Parliament Roundheads tended to be Calvinists (Presbyterians), Puritans, or Protestant Nonconformists— the rising merchants and the gentry. The royalist Cavaliers were High Church or Catholic aristocrats. The 1648 triumph of the Parliamentary Army under (among others) the ardent Puritan, Oliver Cromwell, was to an extent a victory—and not the final one—of the "new" middle-class England. Soon after, the English did what most Europeans then considered unthinkable: They beheaded their king and established a commonwealth.

Within five years, Cromwell assumed absolute power. His Protectorate was austere. Fancy dress, amusements such as alehouses and horseraces, and lively arts such as theater were discouraged. The Puritan zealots who controlled Oxford, wrote one of Locke's contemporaries, enjoyed "laughing at a man in a cassock or canonical coat." They would "tipple" in their chambers, but would not enter taverns or permit such diversions as "Maypoles, Morrises [folk dances], Whitsun ales, nay, scarce wakes." So unpopular were Puritan efforts to impose moral discipline that most Englishmen joined Locke in hailing the Restoration of Charles II in 1660. But the monarchy would never be the same. After Charles's successor, James II, was deposed, William and Mary became England's first constitutional monarchs. Merriment returned to everyday life. At Oxford, nearly 400 taverns flourished, as did, said one critic, "easy manners, unmorality, loose language, disrespect."

WHILE PROTESTANTISM—particularly Puritanism—played a large role in 17th-century politics, its influence went further. In the arts, it infused the epic poem *Paradise Lost* (1667), John Milton's eloquent attempt to "justify God's ways to man." In science, the mental traits fostered by Protestantism—independence, individualism, skepticism of authority—were central.

Early in the century Francis Bacon had called for close scrutiny of the natural world, for the adoption of the experimental method, and for an inductive style of reasoning. Among those who heeded him were Isaac Newton, Robert Boyle, and William Harvey, the pioneering anatomist. All helped dispose of scholasticism, the medieval system of inquiry that proceeded, in Aristotelian style, by deduction from untestable assumptions. The "new science" that they espoused encouraged a radical reconsideration of all areas of thought—in political theory, in economics, and in philosophy itself. It was, of course, an upheaval to which Locke himself made vital contributions.

Hobbes's social contract united men, whom he viewed as natural enemies, in a civil society with a common purpose. Locke did not see men as enemies. He took a Christian view. He argued that men were subject, even in a state of nature, to natural law, which was ultimately God's law made known to men through the voice of reason.

Hobbes's theory had simplicity: Either you are ruled or you are not ruled, either you have obedience or you have liberty, either you have security and fetters or you have chaos and danger. Neither condition is ideal, said Hobbes, but the worst government was better than none at all.

The Lockean analysis was less pessimistic.

Locke believed that men could be both ruled and free. While subject to natural law, men also had natural rights— notably rights to life, liberty, and property. These rights were retained when men contracted to form political societies. Instead of surrendering their freedom to a sovereign, as Hobbes suggested, men had merely *entrusted* power to a ruler. In return for justice and mutual security, they had agreed to obey their rulers, on condition that their natural rights were respected. Natural rights, being derived from natural law, were rooted in something higher than the edicts of princes, namely the edicts of God. They were "inalienable."

Locke's "right to revolution"—to reject a ruler who failed to respect natural rights—thus derived not only from the social contract but also from the supremacy of God's law to man's. People who might have misunderstood, or been unimpressed by, the social contract in abstract philosophy could appreciate the principle that God's law is higher than that of kings. And while Locke based his politics on religion, his was not the astringent faith of the Catholics or of Calvin, but that watered-down Christianity later known as Modernism.*

Locke's writing during his stay in Holland included a travel journal. It revealed how he would visit some great cathedral or chateau, but then take an interest only in working out the exact dimensions. He detested ceremonies and show, which he thought irrational and wasteful, and was pleased to find that one of the best Dutch universities had nondescript architecture. It proved "that knowledge depends not on the stateliness of buildings, etc."

"Knowledge" is the key word. Locke's philistinism was no aberration. He wanted to get away from the imagination, from the vague glamour of medieval things, from unthinking adherence to tradition, from enthusiasm, mysticism, and glory; away from all private, visionary insights and down to the plain, demonstrable facts. This was central to his mission as a philosopher and reformer. His antipathy to poetry and imaginative artists was coupled with scorn for ivory-tower scholars who talk "with but one sort of men and read but one sort of books." They "canton out to themselves a little Goshen in the intellectual world where the light shines. . . . but will not venture out into the great ocean of knowledge."

Locke's venturing made him a polymath, but he was in no sense a smatterer. True, his expertness was not equal in all the subjects he chose to study. Compared to his friends, chemist Robert Boyle and

*Locke rejected original sin. He maintained in *The Reasonableness of Christianity* (1695) that Christ had come into the world not to redeem wrongdoing man, but to bring immortality to the righteous. Locke, a professed Anglican, here argued like a Unitarian, though he felt that word conjured up the unpopular image of a skeptical dissenter.

Sir Isaac Newton, the great physicist, he was an amateurish scientist. His knowledge of the Scriptures was questionable. Although he wrote influential essays on monetary policy, he could not appreciate the subtlety of other economists. But what was important in Locke's case was not his versatility, but that each department of knowledge was related in his mind to all the others.

In the *Essay Concerning Human Understanding,* Locke says in the opening "Epistle" that in an age of such "master builders" as Boyle, Sydenham, and "the incomparable Mr. Newton" it is "ambition enough to be employed as an underlaborer in clearing the ground a little and removing some of the rubbish that lies in the way of knowledge." Locke did much more than that: The *Essay* provides the first modern philosophy of science.

A recurrent word in the work is a Cartesian one, "idea." Locke's usage is curious. He does not merely say that we have ideas in our minds when we think; he says that we have ideas in our minds when we see, hear, smell, taste, or feel. The core of his epistemology is the notion that we perceive not *things* but ideas that are derived in part from objects in the external world, yet also depend to some extent on our own minds for their existence.

The *Essay* attacks the established view that certain ideas are innate. Locke's belief is that we are born in total ignorance, and that even our theoretical ideas of identity, quantity, and substance are derived from experience. A child gets ideas of black and white, of sweet and bitter, *before* he gets an idea of abstract principles, such as identity or impossibility. "The senses at first let in particular ideas, and furnish the yet empty cabinet." Then the mind abstracts theoretical ideas, and so "comes to be furnished with ideas and language, the materials about which to exercise its discursive faculty."

In Locke's account, man is imprisoned in a sort of diving bell. He receives some signals from without and some from within his apparatus, but having no means of knowing which if any come from outside, he cannot test the signals' authenticity. Thus man cannot have any certain knowledge of the external world. He must settle for *probable* knowledge.

Locke's general philosophy has obvious implications for a theory of morals. The traditional view was that

some sort of moral knowledge was innate. Locke thought otherwise. What God had given men was a faculty of reason and a sentiment of self-love. Reason combined with self-love produced morality. Reason could discern the principles of ethics, or natural law, and self-love should lead men to obey them.

Locke wrote in one of his notebooks that "it is a man's proper business to seek happiness and avoid misery. Happiness consists in what delights and contents the mind, misery is what disturbs, discomposes or torments it." He would "make it my business to seek satisfaction and delight and avoid uneasiness and disquiet." But he knew that "if I prefer a short pleasure to a lasting one, it is plain I cross my own happiness."

For Locke, in other words, Christian ethics was natural ethics. The teaching of the New Testament was a means to an end—happiness in this life and the next. The reason for doing what the Gospel demanded about loving one's neighbor, etc., was not just that Jesus said it. By doing these things one promoted one's happiness; men were impelled by their natural self-love to desire it.

Wrongdoing was thus for Locke a sign of ignorance or folly. People did not always realize that long-term happiness could usually only he bought at the cost of short-term pleasure. If people were prudent and reflective, not moved by the winds of impulse and emotion, they would have what they most desired.

The preface to the English edition of the first *Letter Concerning Toleration* says, "Absolute Liberty, just and true Liberty, equal and impartial Liberty is the thing we stand in need of." Many people assumed these words to be Locke's; Lord King, a relative, made them an epigraph in a Locke biography. In fact, they were the words of the translator of Locke's original Latin, William Popple.

Locke did *not* believe in absolute liberty, any more than he believed in absolute knowledge. He thought the way to achieve as much as possible of both was to face the fact that they were limited and then to see what the limitations were. As he did with knowledge in the *Essay,* Locke focused on the liberty that men cannot have, to show the liberty they can achieve. The limits are set by the need to protect the life, property, and freedom of each individual from others, and from the society's common enemies. No other limits need be borne, or *should* be.

Locke set men on the road to the greatest possible liberty by the method he used to set them on the road to the greatest knowledge—teaching the impossibility of the absolute.

Locke guarded his anonymity with elaborate care. The *Essay,* which made him famous throughout Europe in his own time, was one of the few works that appeared under his own name. Most were published anonymously. When an English translation of the first *Letter Concerning Toleration* was issued in London, Locke protested that it had happened "without my privity."

Some of his secrecy stemmed from his days of hiding in Holland, some was for fun, some plainly neurotic. Some added a needed touch of romance to his relations with his women friends.

While Locke never married, he sought female affection and courted a formidable lot of professors' bluestocking daughters. Once, when he was 27, his father wrote to him of a Somerset widow who was "young, childless, handsome, with £200 per annum and £1,000 in her purse," but Locke would not settle down. His closest relationship with *any* person developed in 1682, when Locke, then 50, met Damaris Cudworth, the 24-year-old daughter of a Cambridge philosopher. They exchanged verses and love letters (signed "Philander" and "Philoclea"); he called her his "governess," a role that he was oddly fond of inviting his women friends to assume. Yet no union resulted, although the two were to remain close, even years after she married a nobleman and became Lady Masham.

Locke, as he wrote to an old friend, considered "marriage and death so very nearly the same thing."

Locke was careful with money. His detailed accounts show that during his 30s he had a modest income of about £240 a year from rental property in Somerset, in addition to stipends from Christ Church and profits from investments.* Once, when going abroad, he asked an uncle not to let his tenants

know, "for perhaps that may make them more slack to pay their rents."

Locke's attentiveness to important people brought him not only lodgings—he had no home, being always the guest of various admirers—but job offers as well. He was once the Crown's secretary of presentations, a £300-a-year job involving ecclesiastical matters. He refused an ambassadorship in Germany, saying that the duties there more befitted someone who could "drink his share" than "the soberest man" in England. Shaftesbury made him secretary of the Lords Proprietors of Carolina, in which role he advertised for settlers (people who could behave "peaceably" and not use their "liberty" for "licentiousness") and helped write a constitution for the colony.†

In his mid-60s, Locke became the dominant member of a new Board of Trade. Though the post paid £1,000 a year, Locke complained to a friend: "What have I to do with the bustle of public affairs while sliding under the burdens of age and infirmity?"

Among other things, Locke's board made linen-making the "general trade" of Ireland (partly to keep the Irish out of England's wool business). When pauperism became an issue, Locke argued that the problem was not "scarcity of provision or want of employment," but indiscipline and "corruption of manners, virtue, and industry." He urged (unsuccessfully) new laws for the "suppression of begging drones." Healthy men between 14 and 50 caught seeking alms should serve three years on navy ships "under strict discipline at soldier's pay." Boys and girls under 14 should be "soundly whipped."

Lady Masham explained that Locke was "compassionate," but "his charity was always directed to encourage working, laborious, industrious people, and not to relieve idle beggars, to whom he never gave anything." He thought them wastrels, and "waste of anything he could not bear to see."

Locke was 68 before he retired, to the Masham country house, to spend his last years writing a commentary on the New Testament.

Although Locke has sometimes been dismissed as an ideologue of the age of bourgeois revolutions, he is in many respects the 17th-century thinker whose teaching is most relevant to the concerns of our own time. During the 19th century, that great age of nationalism and imperialism, Locke's individualism seemed narrow and dated. But in the presence of the kind of despotic and totalitarian regimes that have emerged during the 20th century, Locke's defense of the rights of man has taken on a new immediacy. During World War I, Woodrow Wilson looked to Locke to justify the use of force against tyranny. When World War II posed an even more intense challenge to democracy, Winston Churchill proclaimed the aim of victory in Lockean terms, as "the enthronement of human rights."

Numerous declarations and covenants of human rights have since expressed the principles through which the West has sought to formulate its demand for freedom under law. That is something we have claimed not only for our fellow citizens, but (as Locke did) for all men—not an ideal of perfect justice, but a minimal standard to which any government can fairly be called upon to conform. We no longer expect every nation to govern itself as democratically as we do ourselves, but we do demand that they all respect human rights, and we can still look to Locke for the classic formulation of the philosophy that informs that demand.

Modern opinion has often sought to add to assertions of the rights of individuals, pleas for the rights of groups, economic, ethnic, racial, regional, or whatever. But again, that was anticipated by Locke when he argued for the toleration of dissidents and minorities. In his time, religious persecution was at issue; in ours it is political. But persecution as such has not changed its character, and the case for toleration that Locke worked out 300 years ago is no less pertinent today than it was then. It is, if anything, more urgent, since progress has made persecution more common, efficient, and cruel.

The "storm" of change in which Locke was born continues. So, remarkably, does the value of his ideas on how to deal with change, maintaining the maximum liberty and justice for all.

---

*Though no plunger, Locke did speculate with some success (as Shaftesbury had) in the slave trade and in sugar plantations in the Bahamas. He wrote at least some books for money, among them a volume on French grape and olive cultivation (something good has "come out of France"). The estate he left, worth close to £20,000, was no fortune, but not a pittance either.

---

† Rejecting a "numerous democracy," the document prescribed legislative power balanced between citizenry and a local aristocracy; freemen had to "acknowledge a God." Locke received membership in the Carolina aristocracy and some land, But the colonists, who began arriving in 1659, repudiated the Lords Proprietors; the aristocracy was never created, and Locke's land appears to have yielded no rent.

Rationalism, Enlightenment, and Revolution

This unit explores facets of the Age of Reason (the seventeenth century) and the Enlightenment (the eighteenth century). These two phases of the Western tradition had much in common; both placed their faith in science and reason, both believed in progress, and both were skeptical about much of the cultural baggage inherited from earlier periods. Yet each century marked a distinctive stage in the spread of rationalism. In the seventeenth century a few advanced thinkers (Locke and Descartes, for example) attempted to resolve the major philosophical problems of knowledge, i.e., to develop a theoretical basis for rationalism. The eighteenth century saw in the works of Kant and Hume a continuation of that theoretical enterprise, but there was a new development as well: Voltaire, Diderot, and others campaigned to popularize science, reason, the principles of criticism, and the spirit of toleration. Increasingly, the critical attitudes engendered by rationalism and empiricism in the seventeenth century were brought to bear upon familiar beliefs and practices in the eighteenth century.

Several articles in this unit show the advance of critical reason. Science, the model for many of the new intellectual attitudes, is treated in "From Astronomy to Astrophysics," "Origins of Western Environmentalism," and "Newton's Madness." "The First Feminist" reviews Mary Wollstonecraft's arguments for "enlightened" treatment of women, while "The Commercialization of Childhood" explores the Enlightenment's impact upon child rearing. "The Birth of Public Opinion" shows the connection between the Enlightenment and the new emphasis on the public will. "The Godfather of the American Constitution" demonstrates how the ideals of the Enlightenment influenced the Founding Fathers of a new nation across the Atlantic.

The new attitudes often were troublesome, even revolutionary. During the seventeenth and eighteenth centuries no tradition seemed safe from criticism. Even the Bible was scrutinized for contradictions and faulty logic. Universities and salons became intellectual battlegrounds where advocates of the ancient classics (only recently restored and returned to favor by Renaissance humanists) confronted the stalwarts of modernity. But the struggle went beyond a mere battle of the books. Powerful religious and political institutions were subjected to the test of reason and were usually found wanting. The goal was to reorganize society on a rational or enlightened basis and to develop a new morality based on reason, not authority.

Of course, rationalism was not confined to the seventeenth and eighteenth centuries, as any reader of Aristotle or Aquinas can attest. Nor did the influence of the irrational disappear during the Age of Reason. The period, after all, witnessed a great European witch craze and a millenarian movement in England. And those who doubt that atavistic attitudes could surface among the rationalists need only explore Newton's interest in alchemy and Pascal's mysticism. As for the Enlightenment, many have questioned how deeply its ideals and reforms penetrated eighteenth-century society. "Gin and Georgian London" shows us that the drinking poor stubbornly resisted the enlightened legislation passed by Parliament on their behalf. And at the level of high politics, we are hardly surprised to learn that the so-called enlightened despots of the Continent stopped short of instituting reforms that might have diminished their authority. Modern rationalism did not cause the great powers to reign in their ambitions, as the international rivalries of the period demonstrate. And while the doctrines of the Enlightenment may be enshrined in the noblest expressions of the French Revolution, that great upheaval also witnessed mass executions and systematic efforts to suppress freedom of expression. The excesses of the Revolution are exemplified by the senseless execution of France's most brilliant scientist (see Stephen Jay Gould's article, "The Passion of Antoine Lavoisier"). The long-range impact of

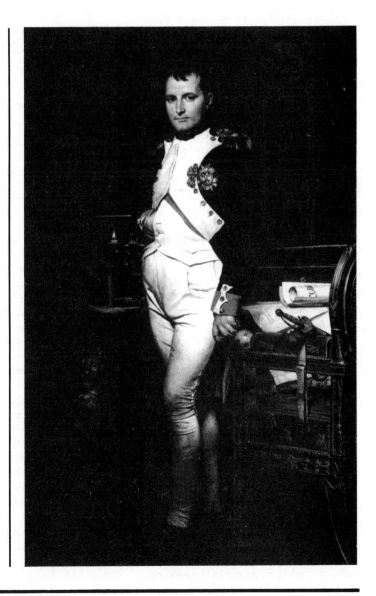

the revolution is treated in "The French Revolution in the Minds of Men," where Maurice Cranston writes about the upheaval as it "became inflated or distorted in the minds of later partisans." Still, as Herbert Muller has written, the Enlightenment "not only diffused knowledge but set up public standards of truth. Its principles were aboveboard, freely accessible to all men, and not dependent upon intuitive, mystical, or received truth."

In our century, with its mass atrocities, world wars, and nuclear weapons, it is difficult to sustain the Enlightenment's faith in reason. But even before our recent disillusionment, rationalism provoked a powerful reaction—romanticism. In contrast to the rationalists, romantics trusted emotions and distrusted intellect; they viewed nature not so much as a repository of scientific laws, but as a source of inspiration and beauty; they were preoccupied with self-discovery, not social reform; and often they drew upon the medieval experience for their images and models. It lives on in our modern programs of mass education and social uplift, which is to say that it is embodied in contemporary liberalism and that its prospects are precarious.

Looking Ahead: Challenge Questions

What were the major advances in astronomy made by Copernicus, Brahe, Kepler, Galileo, and Newton? How do their methods and results compare to the work of modern astrophysicists?

How deeply did rationalism penetrate the lives of ordinary seventeenth- and eighteenth-century Europeans?

In what ways did the Enlightenment influence American political institutions?

How did new views of human nature affect eighteenth-century attitudes about womanhood and childhood?

How did it happen that France's greatest scientist was victimized by the French Revolution?

What impact did cheap gin have upon Georgian London?

From Astronomy to Astrophysics

James Trefil

James S. Trefil, is professor of physics at the University of Virginia. Born in Chicago, Illinois, he received a B.S. (1960) from the University of Illinois, a B.A. and an M.A. (1962) from Oxford University, and an M.S. (1964) and a Ph.D. (1966) from Stanford University. He is the author of Meditations at Ten Thousand Feet *(1986).*

Nicolaus Copernicus (1473–1543) was a Pole, a churchman, an intellectual recluse, and a somewhat enigmatic figure. Much is unknown about him, yet he sparked a scientific revolution that powerfully influenced the subsequent five centuries. Today, looking back at his life and work, it is difficult to comprehend the magnitude of the Copernican Revolution, how momentous a change it really was for 16th-century Europe. But altering civilized man's view of the cosmos is exactly what he did.

Guided by his uncle, a Roman Catholic bishop, Copernicus was elected to a position as canon (business manager) at the Cathedral of Frauenburg in his native Poland. He traveled widely, studied in Italy, and was a model scholar and churchman. From roughly 1512 on, he developed a scheme of a planetary system in which the planets moved and the Sun stood still. He confided his manuscript to a printer only in 1540, at age 67. As the story goes, he received a copy of his published book on the day he died, three years later.

The book, *On the Revolutions of the Celestial Spheres,* is an odd mixture of revolutionary and traditional ideas. Since Claudius Ptolemy (circa A.D. 100–178), the ancient Greek astronomer who advocated a geocentric model of the universe,

Even in medieval Europe, skywatchers developed elaborate systems for interpreting groups of stars. At left, an early 16th-century artist portrays a relationship between parts of the human body and the zodiac.

Europeans had envisioned the Sun, stars, and planets embedded in concentric spheres around the Earth, with God, in effect, cranking the mechanism from the outside.

Copernicus realized that the daily motion of the stars across the sky resulted from the Earth's rotation, and that the complex motions of planets were the natural effect of their movement around the Sun. His system, of course, was not identical to the modern one. To account for the true planetary orbits, Copernicus had to put his planets on epicycles (small circles centered on the rims of larger ones). The centers of the larger circles lay not in the Sun, but at a point in space between the Sun and the Earth. Even if it could not be proved, his view had an immense allure for adventuresome minds.

Copernicus's scheme was only somewhat simpler than Ptolemy's, but it prompted astronomy students (at least from 1543 on) to realize that they could question traditional wisdom. Human reason was freeing itself from burdens of the past—another major step for Europeans who had just experienced the throes of the Reformation, Martin Luther's break with the monolithic authoritarianism of Rome.

Another consequence of the Copernican system—one often overlooked—is that it expanded mankind's concept of the universe. Formerly, with a seemingly stationary Earth, the realm of the stars lay just beyond Saturn's orbit; the entire universe seemed only as big as the solar system. But with Earth orbiting the Sun, the stars had to be far away to appear stationary. In one fell swoop, Copernicus moved the Earth from the center and set it moving in a new heaven of wider horizons. He and Christopher Columbus were contemporaries. Each man revealed a new world to Europe—but Copernicus was charting a realm whose outer boundaries have yet to be discovered.

Reprinted from *The Wilson Quarterly*, Summer 1987, pp. 50-63. From **Space, Time, Infinity** by James S. Trefil. © 1985 Smithsonian Institute. Published by Pantheon Books, Random House. Reprinted by permission.

As it happened, *On the Revolutions of the Celestial Spheres* spread quickly throughout Europe, encountering far less ecclesiastical opposition than Galileo would later face. For one thing, Copernicus was well connected in the church. For another, the unsigned preface of his book presents the Copernican system as a mathematical exercise, not necessarily a statement about the real world. This pretension left plenty of maneuver room for theologians and scholars.

Among Copernicus's readers was the Danish nobleman Tycho Brahe (1546–1601), who had a lifelong obsession with measuring the heavens accurately. During the 16th century, observation was not much more accurate than it had been during the time of Ptolemy. Tycho, born before the invention of the telescope, pushed the accuracy of naked-eye astronomy to its limit. He built astronomical instruments, such as a huge brass quadrant and a four-cubit sextant, to reduce

errors associated with reading small scales. He compensated for the expansion and shrinkage of his brass instruments due to temperature changes, devising tables to correct for these effects. He even built an underground observatory to reduce wind vibrations.

In part, the quest for precision grew out of the desire to distinguish between the Copernican and Ptolemaic systems, and because people of the mid-16th century had witnessed some unusual events

Going Back to Stonehenge

Today most people take the sky for granted. Not so the ancients. They used the sky as clock, calendar, navigational aid, and oracle.

Among the oldest observatories, according to British astronomer Gerald S. Hawkins, is Stonehenge—a series of concentric circles, marked by large stones, standing on a plain near Salisbury, England. In 1963, Hawkins argued that Stonehenge enabled skywatchers, perhaps as early as 3100 B.C., to mark the solstices (when viewed correctly, the Sun rises over a 35-ton Heel Stone), the lunar cycles, and eclipses. Similar ruins stand around the world, in places as disparate as Scotland, Kenya, and the central United States.

Cro-Magnon people were probably the first humans to note the stars. Animal bones with markings that correspond to lunar phases, dated 9,000 to 30,000 years old, have been found in Europe. Between 3000 B.C. and 2000 B.C., Babylonians in Mesopotamia devised the first systematic calendar, based on 235 lunar months (29.5 days apiece) in 19 solar years. Between 1646 and 1626 B.C., they made the first detailed astronomical records, and later (circa 400 B.C.) used mathematics to predict celestial events. They were astrologers too. Atop immense, stepped, mud-brick towers, such

as the ziggurat of Ur in southeastern Iraq (construction began in 2100 b.c.), Babylonian priests prayed to the Moon god Nanna-Sin while surveying stars.

Ancient Egyptians also were stargazers. Many of their great monuments—such as the Great Pyramid of Cheops and the temple at Karnak—are aligned with key positions of the Sun, Moon, and stars. Yet, despite Egypt's creation of a "modern" calendar (12 30-day months, plus five extra days), the Babylonians surpassed the Egyptians in astronomical sophistication.

The Greeks were the first scientists, not only recording celestial motion but wondering why stars and planets moved along particular paths. They sought physical rather than religious explanations. Thales of Miletus (circa 585 B.C.) predicted eclipses; Pythagoras (circa 580–500 B.C.) and his school deduced that the Earth is round, and Eratosthenes of Cyrene (circa 276–194 B.C.) devised a method for measuring its circumference at the equator—250,000 stadia (the width of a stadium, 607 feet), a figure quite close to the actual 24,902 miles. By the second century A.D., Claudius Ptolemy summarized four centuries of Greek astronomy in his treatise *Almagest*. As early as 720 B.C., Chinese astronomers kept watch for "portentous" events: eclipses, comets,

meteors, planetary alignments. But their observations were not "scientific"; they tended simply to record, not analyze, unusual phenomena.

In Central America, circa 1000 A.D., Mayan astronomers on the Yucatan Peninsula constructed an observatory, the Caracol of Chichén Itsá. It demonstrates in its architecture alone—through alignments with certain stars and planets—a knowledge of solstices, lunar cycles, and the motions of the Morning and Evening Star (Venus). Their astronomical records, detailed on the bark leaves of an almanac called the Dresden Codex (it is now in a Dresden museum), reveal great sophistication: They calculated the length of a 365-day solar year, a 29.5 day lunar cycle, and the cycles of Venus within minutes of their true periods.

Throughout North America, Indian tribes, too, practiced astronomy. Atop Medicine Mountain, in Wyoming's Bighorn Range, lies a circular arrangement of "loaf-sized" rocks. This "medicine wheel," in which 28 35-foot-long lines of rocks, seemingly spokes, reach out from a central hub to a surrounding circle of rocks, is believed to have been used for astronomical purposes Similarly, the Hohokam Indian structure at Casa Grande near Phoenix, Arizona, contains 14 windowlike openings, eight of which are aligned with the rising and setting Sun during solstices and equinoxes. Other Sun-marking sites exist at Chaco Canyon, New Mexico, and Hovenweep, Utah. And, at Caholkia, Illinois, the American "woodhenge"—concentric circles comprised of 49 poles, with the largest circle measuring 410 feet across—is thought to have been a tool for measuring solstices and equinoxes, and possibly to predict eclipses.

The Mayan Caracol of Chichén Itzá, as it may have appeared circa 1000 A.D.

in the heavens. On November 11, 1572, for instance, a new star appeared in the constellation of Cassiopeia—so bright that during the next month it could be seen in daylight. Repairing to his beautifully crafted instruments, Tycho took a series of readings. He established beyond a doubt that the object (now called Tycho's supernova) moved less than the most distant planet in the sky and was therefore beyond the sphere of the stars. This feat established the 25-year-old Dane as one of Europe's premier astronomers.

So impressed was King Frederick II of Denmark that he installed Tycho on the Baltic island of Hven and provided the money to construct the world's largest astronomical observatory. There Tycho built instruments and gathered data unprecedented in both volume and accuracy.

All was well, until Tycho ran afoul of Frederick's successor, Christian IV, over a number of issues—such as whether or not Tycho had the right to throw peasants into his private dungeon. So the astronomer packed up his data, instruments, and court jester, and quit Hven for the court of Emperor Rudolf II in Prague.

TYCHO'S UNDOING

All told, Tycho lived an unusual life. At an early age, he was kidnapped by his wealthy and childless uncle Jorgen, who raised him in a castle in Tostrup. Sent to the University of Copenhagen to study jurisprudence, Tycho—profoundly impressed by an eclipse of the Sun in 1560—instead spent his time studying the stars. Prone to emotional outbursts, at the age of 20 he dueled a fellow student over the question of who was a better mathematician. During the battle, Tycho lost a piece of his nose and had to wear a gold alloy prosthesis. Even his death was bizarre. At a banquet attended by much of Prague's nobility, he partook copiously of Bohemian beer. Not wishing to appear impolite—so the story goes—he ate and drank without excusing himself. Bladder stones may have been his undoing; he fell into a fever that night and died 11 days later.

Tycho's data tables went to an impecunious Austrian mathematician he had hired after his arrival in Prague—Johannes Kepler.

Kepler (1571–1630) was a mystic by nature. But, when confronted with all the

17th-century Chinese skywatchers at the Imperial Observatory observed the stars with astronomical instruments, some imported from Europe.

data that Tycho had collected over a lifetime, he felt compelled to question some of his basic assumptions. Instead of trying to force Tycho's data into preconceived patterns, Kepler returned to the basics and considered which shapes best described the motions of the known planets.

GALILEO AS MARTYR

Kepler's results are stated in what are now known as Kepler's first and second laws of planetary motion. The first law says that a planet's orbit assumes the shape of an ellipse—rather than a circle—with the Sun at one focus; the second law indicates that planets move faster when near the Sun than they do when farther away. In other words, as a planet passes near to the Sun it "swings around," speeding up as it does so.

Kepler published these two laws in 1609. A third and final law was published in 1619, relating the length of a planet's "year" to its distance from the Sun. Thus it became possible to shed excess conceptual baggage that scientists had developed to justify a false notion, namely, that celestial objects move along circular orbits.

Following the observational work of Copernicus, Tycho, and Kepler, Galileo Galilei (1564–1642) was the first to study the sky through a telescope.

Ironically, Galileo is one of those men in history who is famous for the wrong reasons. Because of his notorious trial in

1633 by the Roman Inquisition he has, perhaps undeservedly, become enshrined as a "martyr of science." Legend has it that he stood alone as a champion of the heliocentric universe against the forces of dogmatism and authority. This is unfortunate, because Galileo did many other things during his lifetime that were worthy of lasting fame. He was, for example, the founder of modern experimental physics. He also made the first break with naked-eye astronomy by starting a systematic study of the heavens with a telescope. He was largely responsible for bringing the ideas of Copernicus to the attention of the intellectual community of 17th-century Europe. It was this seemingly heretical activity, of course, that eventually caused him to draw the attention of the Inquisition.

The son of a musician in Pisa, Galileo studied at the local university and embarked on a career teaching mathematics. As the story goes, his early interest in physics is associated with observations conducted at the Pisa cathedral. He noted that a cathedral lamp required the same amount of time to complete a swing no matter how wide the range of the swing. Later, Galileo suggested that this principle could be used to develop a pendulum clock. His studies of physics and mathematics helped him to win a position in the Medici court in Florence in 1610.

While in Venice in 1609, Galileo learned of the recent invention of the telescope in the United Netherlands. He devised a superior lensmaking technique and produced a telescope capable of magnifying an image 32 times. It was an immense step forward. Astronomers could thereupon examine the heavens with more than the power of the unaided human eye. He opened a window on the cosmos and was not slow to exploit it.

During the years after the building of his telescope, Galileo and others saw many new things. Mountains loomed on the Moon where no mountains were supposed to be. The apparently unblemished

Sun had spots. Venus was seen to go through phases as does the Moon. Galileo observed the four largest moons of Jupiter and caught a hint of Saturn's rings. As has happened ever since, whenever a new window on the sky is opened, the first glimpse shows an undreamed-of richness and complexity.

Why were these discoveries so important? The first two—lunar mountains and sunspots—showed that the Greek ideal of heavenly perfection was incorrect. Also,

the fact that Venus could be observed to pass through Moonlike phases proved that at least one other planet orbited the Sun. And Jupiter's four moons belied the assumption that everything orbited Earth. These facts had enormous psychological impact during the 17th century.

ENTER NEWTON

Galileo announced the first of these findings in his book *The Starry Messen-*

New Efforts in Astronomy

Since the discovery in 1932 that radio waves emanate from the Milky Way's center, astronomers have been scanning the "invisible" universe. That task requires special instruments. Because only visible light, radio waves, and some infrared radiation can penetrate the atmosphere, special devices are sent into space aboard satellites. Below, some details about the latest efforts to analyze specific kinds of electromagnetic radiation:

• RADIO WAVES (wavelength: one millimeter to 10 meters): The first radio telescope—a bowl-shaped antenna measuring 9.4 meters across—was built in Illinois in 1937. Today, "interferometry"—a computerized system that merges signals from an array of radio telescopes—allows astronomers to simulate one enormous dish. The Very Large Array in New Mexico synchronizes 27 radio telescopes to form images equivalent to those of one 24-kilometer dish. Currently, the National Science Foundation is building the Very Long Baseline Array; with 10 antennas spanning Hawaii to St. Croix, its "baseline" will measure 7,500 kilometers.

• INFRARED RADIATION (wave-

length: one micron to one millimeter): Infrared radiation carries crucial data about star and planet formation. NASA's Kuiper Airborne Observatory, a 0.9 meter telescope aloft at 41,000 feet, has charted infrared sources since 1975. More impressive, the joint U.S.–Dutch–British Infrared Astronomical Satellite mapped more than 250,000 sources during 1983. On the drawing board for the 1990s are two space-based observatories: NASA's $600 million Shuttle Infrared Telescope Facility and the European Space Agency's Infrared Space Observatory.

• VISIBLE LIGHT (wavelength: 300 nanometers to one micron): Delayed because of space shuttle troubles, NASA's $1.5 billion Hubble Space Telescope awaits launch in 1988. Its 2.4-meter telescope will capture visible, infrared, and ultraviolet radiation, detecting objects 50 times fainter and seven times farther away than those detectable by Earth's best telescopes. Still, ground-based observatories with larger apertures remain important in spectral analysis. By the mid-1990s, Hawaii may house two giant optical telescopes; the $87 million Keck Telescope, using a honeycomb design,

will join 36 mirrors into a single 10-meter mirror, while the proposed $125 million National New Technology Telescope will achieve a 15-meter aperture—the world's largest.

• ULTRAVIOLET RADIATION (wavelength: 10–300 nanometers). The first ultraviolet telescopes were hoisted aloft on high-altitude balloons. Today, the International Ultraviolet Explorer, a U.S.–European satellite launched in 1978, examines radiation from intergalactic matter and the outer layers of stars. Soon, NASA's Extreme Ultraviolet Explorer, now being developed, will study high-energy ultraviolet rays, so far uncharted.

• X-RAYS (wavelength: .01–10 nanometers). So energetic are x-rays that studying them requires a unique telescope design: cylindrical mirrors to deflect x-rays into focus. Between 1978 and 1981, the orbiting Einstein Observatory satellite used this method (as did its European counterpart, Exosat) to collect data on pulsars, neutron stars, and galactic nuclei. The latest x-ray space observatory is Japan's Astro-C, launched in February 1987 (approximate cost: $40 million). By 1995, NASA hopes to place in orbit the Advanced X-Ray Astrophysics Facility, a $1 billion telescope 100 times more sensitive than the Einstein Observatory.

• GAMMA RAYS (wavelength: less than .01 nanometers): Gamma rays are more energetic than x-rays, and difficult to measure. Thus the European gamma ray observatory, Cos-B, took seven years (1975–82) to make a gamma ray chart of the sky. In 1990, NASA plans to launch a $500 million space-based Gamma Ray Observatory, 10 times more sensitive than Cos-B, which will carry instruments supplied by the United States and Germany.

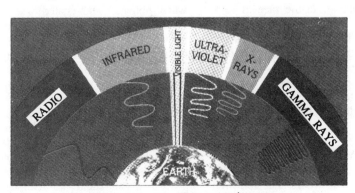

A schematic diagram of the electromagnetic spectrum.

ger. He called Jupiter's satellites the Sidera Medici (Medicean Stars), attempting to flatter his hoped-for patrons, the Medici family. The ploy worked. He received support from Florence, and today those satellites are called the Galilean Moons.

Furthermore, the maestro had a way with words, writing—unlike Copernicus and Kepler—in the vernacular, Italian in this case. Through his writings, Copernican ideas spread throughout Europe. Galileo's trial did not curb the spread of these ideas—indeed, its only effect was to guarantee that the center of astronomical studies would move across the Alps to the Protestant countries of Europe and eventually to England.

In the same year that Galileo died, 1642, Isaac Newton was born. It is a coincidence, of course, but one that symbolizes the continuity of the development of scientific ideas about the universe during the 17th century.

The scientific revolution of the 17th century culminated in the work of Isaac Newton, who developed a view of the universe still held today. His most important contribution to astronomy is the law of universal gravitation, which states that any two objects in the universe will experience a force of attraction proportional to their masses and to the distance between them. The laws that Kepler deduced from Tycho's data can also be derived from Newton's work.

In later years, a legend grew about how Newton realized that one gravitational law governed the entire universe. The part that sticks in the public fancy is the fall of an apple in an orchard.

To understand Newton's insight in that orchard, one must remember that, until his time, the science of astronomy and the science of mechanics (which dealt with the motions of things on Earth) were totally separated. No one had yet connected the stately turning of the planets with the fall of an apple on Earth. Newton's gift to humanity was to show that such artificial distinctions do not hold in nature—that the universe is a single, seamless web, and that the forces guiding the Moon also cause apples to fall.

To demonstrate the unity of the gravitational force, Newton imagined what would happen if a cannon were placed on a mountaintop, firing successive projectiles, with an increase in the charge of each shot. Eventually, with just enough gunpowder, the cannonball would fly around the world, overcoming gravity's downward pull and maintaining a constant altitude.

This hypothetical missile, he concluded, was behaving like the Moon, or any other satellite. In his own words, "[I] compared the force requisite to keep the Moon in her Orb with the force of gravity at the surface of the Earth, and found them to answer pretty nearly." In effect, Newton had seen that the Moon and the Earth continually fall toward each other, offset by their orbital motion. With this realization, any simple distinction between terrestrial and celestial science—a notion accepted since ancient Greece—crumbled. Using calculus, a method that he originated, Newton worked out the planets' orbits and demonstrated that they followed Kepler's laws.

His vision of the solar system in perpetual motion led naturally to a model of the universe resembling a geared clock. Once the solar system had been created, its future history lay ordained. But a debate ensued along these lines: mathematician G. W. Leibniz argued that God had made an automated universe; theologian Samuel Clarke contended that God was continually adjusting the works. Either way, the Creator had more leisure than with Ptolemy's system, which ascribed to God (or appointed angels) the turning of cranks. Newton believed that God created a mechanistic universe and then fine-tuned the machinery while it operated.

It is difficult to overemphasize the importance of this new scientific movement, and of Newton's place as its prime mover. He completed the work begun by Copernicus and his successors.

In fact, the Newtonian Synthesis gave rise to another powerful idea: Events anywhere in the universe can be studied in laboratories on Earth. And, if nature's laws are constant, then all events of the past—right back to the creation of the universe—are accessible to investigation.

It is comforting, in the face of such advances in scientific knowledge, to reflect on how it all started. An obscure Polish scholar was able to set in motion a scientific revolution capped by, of all things, a view of space and time based on an inspired interpretation of a fallen apple in an English orchard.

ON TO MOUNT PALOMAR

During the 200 years that followed Newton's discovery of the workings of the solar system, astronomers developed two improved tools. First, bigger, and sometimes better, telescopes allowed astronomers to collect more light from objects farther away. And second, improved theoretical tools, based on calculus and Newton's laws, enabled scientists to analyze (and therefore predict) the behavior of more complex celestial phenomena. The delicate interplay of instrumental and theoretical advances was like a waltz through history—first one partner would lead, then the other.

Galileo turned a primitive telescope toward the heavens. But to go beyond Galileo, it was necessary to build better telescopes. This was no easy task.

Newton saw no future in the type of telescope used by Galileo. Called the refractor, it uses a series of lenses to collect and focus incoming light. Unfortunately, it also suffers from a defect known as "chromatic aberration," in which colored fringes appear around an image's edges. Consequently, Newton built a telescope without lenses. Such a *reflector* telescope uses curved mirrors, made of polished metal, to focus light at the back of the instrument. However, his first models had little more power than did Galileo's refractor.

By the mid-18th century, techniques for fashioning mirrors from metal had been perfected. By the 20th century, mirrors were ground from glass and then coated with reflective metal. Today, such highly efficient light collectors are the workhorses of astronomy. The most famous (and most productive) of these giants is the 200-inch telescope located at the Hale Observatory on Mount Palomar near San Diego, California.

Completed in 1948, Hale's main mirror is 17 feet (five meters) across and weighs 14.5 tons. Technicians ground away more than five tons of glass from the original 20-ton disk to form a concave surface, which became reflective when polished and coated with a thin layer of aluminum. To construct the immense disk, molten Pyrex glass was poured into a form, then allowed to cool for eight months to keep the glass from cracking.

The telescope itself is so big that at one time an astronomer sat inside it to observe the stars. Today, however, a computer monitors observations. It is so well balanced that an electric motor no more powerful than one found in a food processor can rotate it. Although the Soviets now have a larger optical telescope operating in the Caucasus Mountains, technical troubles have limited its usefulness.

Improved telescope designs enabled astronomers to expand their inventory of the solar system. William Herschel (1738–1822), born in Germany, was a musician-turned-astronomer who lived in England during the 18th century. He built his own reflecting telescopes because he could not afford to buy one made by craftsmen. Believing that studying the heavens was one way to peer into the mind of God, Herschel set out to catalogue everything in the sky.

FINDING NEPTUNE

On March 13, 1781, Herschel observed a fuzzy object, hitherto unknown. His telescope allowed him to see that this new object was not just a point (as most stars appear), but something with an extended structure. Since the object moved against a background of fixed stars, it had to be a planet or a comet. And, given that 2,000 years of skywatching had turned up only six planets, European astronomers looked carefully before concluding that Herschel really had found another planet—one located too far from the Sun to be seen by the naked eye. It was christened Uranus, and became the first planet discovered in modern times.

Astronomers throughout Europe worked to chart its orbit. It quickly became apparent that applying Newton's law of gravitation to the new planet did not give a correct description of its path in the sky. Working independently, an English and a French astronomer came to the same conclusion. In 1845, John Couch Adams and Urbain-Jean-Joseph Le Verrier showed that this orbital discrepancy could be explained if there were yet another planet beyond Uranus. On September 23, 1846, astronomers in Berlin saw it—the planet we now call Neptune.

While the discovery of Uranus depended on the development of better telescopes, the discovery of Neptune depended on the ability of theoreticians to predict the orbit of the new planet. In fact, once told of its general location, observers at Berlin took less than one night to pinpoint Neptune. The ninth planet, Pluto, was also found through computation and observation.

About the same time that Herschel was expanding our perception of the solar system, the return of a comet in 1758 as predicted served to provide dramatic confirmation of the clockwork universe developed by Newton. In 1682, Edmund Halley (1656–1742) had observed a large comet approach the Sun and swing away. Looking at historical records, he found that a bright comet with roughly the same orbit had appeared in 1531 and 1607. Using Newton's laws and the positions of the planets, Halley calculated the orbit of the comet and predicted that it would again be near the Sun in 1758. Its appearance, on Christmas Day of that year, provided a major verification of Newton's description of the universe.

With telescopes and satellites routinely probing the farthest reaches of the universe, one would expect few surprises in the relatively mundane study of our own neighborhood in space. Not so. In 1978, scientists at the U.S. Naval Observatory in Flagstaff, Arizona, obtained high-grade photographs of Pluto, showing that the planet has a moon. It was christened Charon, after the boatman charged with conducting souls of the dead to the underworld, Pluto's realm. This discovery allowed astronomers to estimate the mass of Pluto, a value insufficient to explain all of the vagaries of the orbits of Neptune and Uranus. Thus, there still may be pages to be written in the story of the solar system—a possible 10th planet.

SEEING THE SPECTRUM

Beyond our own star system lie other stars, perhaps with their own planets. From a science concerned with determining *where* stars and planets are, the new discoveries changed the focus of astronomy to the question of *what* they are. A new science, astrophysics, emerged as a complement to astronomy. It seeks to reveal the nature of the stars through an understanding of the laws of physics.

The basis for this new departure in man's view of the heavens was a famous experiment by Isaac Newton. He noted that a glass prism held up to a beam of sunlight broke the light into its constituent colors—a "spectrum" of sunlight.

For a long time, this peculiar property of light was merely a nuisance to lens-makers. Then, in 1802, physician William Hyde Wollaston found narrow bands of missing color in the spectrum of sunlight. By 1814, a physicist, Joseph von Fraushofer, made the first map of these lines, which now bear his name. Their origin remained a mystery until 1859, when Gustav Kirchhoff, working with Robert Bunsen at Heidelberg, showed that the lines were caused by familiar chemical elements in the Sun's outer atmosphere that absorb certain wavelengths of light.

Such "spectral analysis" works something like this: Each kind of element (e.g., hydrogen, nitrogen), when pushed to an "excited" state, emits a unique spectrum of light—a kind of atomic fingerprint. In fact, burning an element gives off a specific "emission spectrum," while passing light *through* an element causes certain colors to be absorbed, creating an "absorption spectrum." The correspondence between atoms and their unique spectra is daily evident: A neon light glows red; sodium-vapor street lamps emit yellow light; mercury-vapor lamps are bluish-white. Each element has its own colors.

Discovering this connection between atoms and light was enormously important. As early as 1868, bright lines were observed in the Sun's spectrum—lines that had no counterpart in any known element on Earth. Scientists concluded that a new element was present on the Sun, one that they named helium (from the Greek word for Sun, *helios*).

There was, as far as anyone could tell, no helium on the Earth. In 1895, however, helium was discovered in certain uranium-bearing minerals. Once again, it turned out that the Earth was not as different from the rest of the universe as some people had thought.

From these early days, the technique of identifying chemicals by their light spectra has penetrated every corner of modern technology. Spectroscopy is today used in industrial quality control (to monitor the presence of impurities), in medicine (to identify substances taken from the body), and in many other areas where one must determine the chemical constituents of materials. It even figures in courtroom dramas, where substances identified by this sort of analysis are accepted as legal evidence.

Once scientists had proven that known elements make up the Sun and other stars, another question arose: How could the stars shine so brightly for so long? Astrophysicists had calculated that, even if the Sun were made of pure anthracite coal, it could have shone for only 20,000 years—instead of the 4.5 billion years so far.

Throughout the last decades of the 19th century, scientists tried to determine the Sun's fuel source. The answer came from a completely unexpected quarter—the study of radioactive materials. By the 1930s, a number of things had become clear: First, certain nuclear processes alter the weight of atoms; second, the weight change is related to energy by means of Einstein's famous formula, $E = mc^2$. Arthur (later Sir Arthur) Eddington, working in England during the 1920s, had suggested that the conversion of mass to energy might be the process that provided the Sun's energy. But no one knew enough about nuclear physics at that time to consider Eddington's suggestion as anything more than an educated guess.

In fact, the Sun shines through a fusion process in which lighter elements are transmuted into heavier ones, liberating energy. Detailed knowledge of this phenomenon grew out of a small conference held in Washington, D.C., in April 1938. The gathering had aimed to unite astrophysicists and nuclear physicists. The former knew about stellar structure; the latter understood something of the reactions taking place in stars. The interchange must have been extraordinarily effective: Shortly thereafter Hans Bethe of Cornell University worked out the earliest model of fusion in stars.

The theory was so successful that Bethe was awarded a Nobel Prize for physics in 1967. His idea of nuclear reactions in our Sun allowed scientists to begin to understand the very fires of creation.

Newton's Madness

Madness in great ones must not unwatched go.
—Shakespeare *Hamlet*

We are all born mad. Some remain so.
—Samuel Beckett, *Waiting for Godot*

Harold L. Klawans, M.D.

Sir Isaac Newton is one of the few scientists in the history of Western civilization whose reputation is universal and whose name is synonymous with genius. Newton, Aristotle, Einstein—I doubt if there are many others. Newton lived from 1642 to 1727. Today he is considered to have been a natural philosopher. He was actually a physicist and mathematician and, with the possible exception of Albert Einstein, he may well have been the most original and influential theorist in the history of science. His list of accomplishments is impressive:

1. The coinvention of calculus. Working independently, Newton and Gottfried Wilhelm Leibniz both "invented," or discovered, calculus.
2. The discovery of the three laws of mechanics (Newton's laws) which transformed the entire field of physics.
3. The formulation of the law of gravity.
4. The discovery of the composition of white light.
5. The formulation of a theory of planetary motion.

The list does not end there, but my purpose here is not to investigate the mind of Sir Isaac Newton and the influence of that mind on Western civilization. Rather, it is to explore the nature and cause of Newton's madness and its effect on Newton the man and Newton the scientist. For Newton became mad. Not permanently deranged, but twice during his life, he suffered periods of prolonged abnormal behavior, bordering on psychosis. His madness was of his own doing, and it was a malady that did not leave him unscathed.

The first episode of his madness lasted through most of 1677 and 1678, while the second began in 1693. The former is not as well documented in contemporary records, for it came at a time in his career when he was not yet a public figure. Newton's symptoms of "madness" began at about the time of his first scientific publication concerning his theory of the composition of white light. Newton himself considered this work to be "the oddest if not the most considerable detection which has hitherto been made in operations of Nature." His paper was not immediately accepted by the entire scientific community and Newton's reactions to the criticisms of this work were not the logical reactions of a finely tuned genius. Newton scholar Richard S. Westfall studied these responses and suggested that Newton's behavior showed definite signs of abnormality. Westfall was particularly struck by Newton's correspondence with a critic named John Lucas:

> The correspondence dragged on until 1678, when a final shriek of rage from Newton, apparently accompanied by a complete nervous breakdown, was followed by silence. The death of his mother the following year completed his isolation. For six years he withdrew from intellectual commerce, except when others initiated a correspondence, which he always broke off as soon as possible.

It was not until 1684 that Newton once again began to seek the company of others and to interact with fellow scientists.

Although most studies of Newton's life have passed over this first instance of altered behavior, it is generally acknowledged in both the historical and scientific communities that in the years 1692 and 1693, Newton underwent a period of severe emotional and mental disturbance. This entire episode has always had about it something of an air of mystery. The first biography of Newton, published in London and Paris in 1728, the year after Newton's death, was written by a Frenchman named Bernard Le Bovier de Fontenelle, who was the permanent secretary of the Academie Royale des Sciences. Le Bovier de Fontenelle based his work largely on information and material given to him by John Conduitt. Conduitt was married to Newton's niece and had spent many years and much energy collecting materials for a projected biography of Newton that he intended to write but that he never undertook. Whatever he gave to Fontenelle contained no reference to any mental disorder suffered by Newton. Either Conduitt was ignorant of this episode or he knew of it but decided to suppress it—the latter being far more likely. Fontenelle's biography was widely read and, since it was based on contemporary source material, it became the primary foundation of virtually all subsequent studies of Newton's life. For the next hundred years, no biographies even hinted at the possibility of a mental illness.

In 1820, this viewpoint began to change. In that year, the French astronomer Jean Baptiste Biot wrote a sketch of Newton for the *Biographie Universelle*, in which he stated that in 1693, Newton suffered what Biot termed a "derangement of the intellect," during which his "reason" was abnormal.

Much of the proof that this "derangement of the intellect" actually took place became readily available only in 1961 when Volume 3 of Newton's correspondence, covering the years 1688 through 1694, was finally published. Most accounts of Newton's illness have dated its onset to late 1693. However, a careful study of his correspondence reveals definite signs of emotional stress beginning at least eighteen months earlier. On January 26, 1692, Newton, who was then living in Cambridge, complained to John Locke that his old and hitherto completely loyal friend, Charles Montague, had been false to him, and that he, Newton, was "done with him." The same distrust is revealed in other letters written at the same time.

Whether the conflicts that Newton experienced in his relationship with Montague, Locke, and others were real or imaginary, we have no way of proving, but since numerous relationships were similarly affected at the same time, the odds are that the problem originated in Newton's mind or behavior. For the next eighteen months, the letters reveal nothing out of the ordinary.

Beginning on May 30, 1693, there is a period of three and a half months of silence, during which we have no record of any letter either received or written by Newton. The silence was finally interrupted by correspondence in which he exhibited the peculiar sensitivity that had been present during the early months of the previous years, but in a far more intensified form. Newton sent the following strange letter to the famous diarist Samuel Pepys on September 13, 1693:

Sir,

Some time after Mr. Millington had delivered your message, he pressed me to see you the next time I went to London. I was averse; but upon his pressing consented, before I considered what I did, for I am extremely troubled at the embroilment I am in, and have neither ate nor slept well this twelve month, nor have my former consistency of mind. I never designed to get anything by your interest, nor by King James's favour, but am now sensible that I must withdraw from your acquaintance, and see neither you nor the rest of my friends any more, if I may but leave them quietly. I beg your pardon for saying I would see you again, and rest your most humble and most obedient servant,

Is. Newton

The same year, Newton wrote to Locke: "being of the opinion that you endeavoured to embroil me with women and by other means I was so much affected with it as that when one told me that you were sickly and would not live I answered twere better you were dead. I desire you to forgive me this uncharitableness." Both Pepys and Locke recognized that Newton's mind was deranged, and in other letters it is clear that his memory was also impaired.

These symptoms are reminiscent of those of his first episode of madness, which also resulted in Newton's withdrawing from society: suspiciousness of others, accusations, and withdrawal.

What, in fact, caused these two breakdowns?

Did Newton have a recurring psychosis—such as manic depressive affective disorder—with two separate and distinct psychotic breaks? Or were there specific factors in his life that precipitated each of these periods of psychological maladjustment?

Most of Newton's twentieth-century biographers have focused on the latter and have suggested a staggering number of hypotheses to explain the precipitation of one or the other of these episodes:

1. The shock of his mother's death. This hypothesis is all very Freudian. Unfortunately, Mrs. Newton died in 1679, too late to account for the first episode and too early for the second.
2. A fire that destroyed some important papers.
3. Failure to obtain a desired administrative post in London.
4. Exhaustion following the writing of his *Principia.*
5. Religious fervor.
6. Local problems with the university at Cambridge.

The list goes on and on. I will attempt neither to document them all nor to refute them one by one. Instead, I will invoke what I sometimes call "Baker's law." Baker's law is a law that I have propounded out of one of A. B. Baker's irrascible bedside pronouncements. A. B. Baker, one of the leading figures of American neurology in the middle third of this century, was primarily responsible for the founding of the American Academy of Neurology, which has, in fewer than forty years, become the leading force in American and world neurology, and one of the founders of *Neurology,* the first American medical journal dedicated solely to the field. He was also the chairman of neurology at the University of Minnesota, where I began my formal training in neurology.

Abe Baker was a clinician who shot from the hip. During a typical teaching session, one of my fellow first-year residents was presenting a patient who had a confusional psychosis. After telling Abe about the entire medical history of this patient and the results of the physical examination, this poor, unsuspecting resident then began to recount the patient's psychiatric history. Abe would have none of it. He exploded. A psychiatric history is a waste of time, he said. No neurologist should ever take one. Everybody has psychiatric problems. The whole world is crazy, so are all its inhabitants. The question is not if a patient has a psychiatric problem. The question is whether the patient has a neurologic problem that can account for his or her behavior. That is a neurologic question and has to be evaluated on neurologic grounds, not on psychiatric ones. A psychiatric history is irrelevant.

Thus, Baker's law: The entire neurologic issue is whether the patient has a neurologic disease or not. All else is mere commentary.

Did Newton have a neurologic problem that could account for his psychosis? If he did, his mother's death is irrelevant. If not, then his mother's death is a subject for psychiatrists to debate.

What evidence is there that Newton could have had a neurologic disorder? From his correspondence, a list of his signs and symptoms, both neurologic and psychiatric, can easily be compiled. They include

1. Severe insomnia
2. Extreme sensitivity in personal relations
3. Loss of appetite
4. Delusions of persecution
5. Memory difficulties
6. Some overall decrease in mental acuity

This is certainly the type of behavioral manifestation that can be seen in a variety of diffuse processes that cause mild (neurologically speaking) alteration in the function of both hemispheres of the brain. It is a neurologic rule of thumb that generalized behavioral symptoms such as these are usually related to diffuse or generalized dysfunction of the entire brain, that is, both halves, rather than just disease in a single location. Diseases that affect a single site in the brain, in contrast, cause symptoms that are related specifically to the normal function carried out by that location: weakness, speech difficulty, and loss of vision.

Because behaviors like memory, concentration, intellect, and judgment are not localized in one spot, they are more likely to become deranged in mild diffuse diseases that insult the brain generally without singling out any one specific locus.

A neurologic cause is, therefore, plausible as an explanation for Newton's odd behavior. But what cause? In recent years, two separate scientific reports have suggested that Newton's madness was caused by chronic mercury poisoning and that the poisoning was self-induced, a product of Newton's interest in alchemy.

Two English scientists named Spargo and Pounds conducted a careful examination of the records of Newton's chemical experiments. Newton had shown an interest in alchemy and chemistry and had even purchased a variety of apparatuses and chemicals as early as 1669. His last dated chemical experiments were carried out in February 1696, not long before he left Cambridge and moved to London. During his many years in Cambridge, Newton carried out several hundred chemical experiments, of which only a small number were specifically dated. However, from those that are dated, it is clear that Newton ran many of his experiments shortly before the first signs of each of his episodes of "madness." Newton made use of a wide variety of materials in his chemical research, including nonmetallic materials, such as sulfur, "sal armoniak" (ammonium chloride), and sulfuric and nitric acids, and metals, such as antimony, mercury, iron, tin, bismuth, lead, "arsnick," and copper, as well as many of their ores. Metals tended to play a prominent role in virtually all Newton's experiments, and mercury in particular was a major component in many of his studies.

In many of his experiments, Newton heated metals, their ores, or their salts to convert them into a volatile form. He would often heat these substances in open vessels, breathing in the fumes and tasting the formed products. Some of these experiments were simple and took little time, while others were complex and extended over many hours or, in a few cases, even days. While conducting research, Newton regularly slept in his laboratory by the same fire, which did not go out for weeks on end. Since most of the volatized metal fumes would have settled back into the fire only to be volatilized again, this clearly exposed him to an additional risk of metallic poisoning.

Newton conducted a number of alchemical experiments in December 1692 and January 1693, in which he used antimony, antimony ore, and a "mercurial water of lead," which was probably a lead amalgam. In these experiments a saltlike substance appeared in the neck of the retort. After reporting the taste of this substance under two conditions, he then continued: "I held it to ye side of ye flame of candle and it did not take flame as [sulphur] would do but yet fumed away and ye fumes made the side of ye flame look blue."

Information about Newton's working habits in chemistry is also found in the recollections of his assistant, Humphrey Newton:

He very rarely went to bed till two or three of the clock, sometimes not until five or six, lying about four or five hours, especially at spring or the fall of the leaf, at which time he would employ about six weeks in his laboratory, the fire scarcely going out either night or day, he sitting up, one night as I did another, till he had finished his chemical experiments, in the performance of which he was the most accurate, strict, exact. What his aim might be I was not able to penetrate into, but his pains, his diligence at those set times made me think he aimed at something beyond the reach of human art or industry.

About six weeks at spring, and six in the fall, the fire in the elaboratory scarcely went out, which was well furnished with chemical materials as bodies, receivers, heads, crucibles, etc., which was (sic) made very little use of, the crucibles excepted, in which he fused his metals: he would sometimes, tho' seldom, look into an old mouldy book which lay in his elaboratory, I think it was titled Agricola de metallis, the transmuting of metals being his chief design.

Tasting mercury compounds and breathing the fumes of its various salts is highly hazardous. Metallic fumes are one of the most efficient ways of introducing an excessive amount of a metal into the body, since they enter the lungs and are quickly absorbed. It was at this point that Newton began to suffer from poor digestion and insomnia. It is even possible that Newton himself identified the cause of his symptoms as exposure to the quicksilver (mercury) vapors. After all, its effects had been known to alchemical writers for centuries before Newton, and Newton was quite familiar with their writings. In the following passage, Newton hints at the correct diagnosis of his malady:

The last winter by sleeping too often by my fire I got into an ill habit of sleeping and a distemper which this summer has been epidemical put me further out of order, so that when I wrote to you I had not slept an hour a night for a fortnight together and for five nights together not a wink. I remember I wrote to you but what I said of your book I remember not. if you please to send me a transcript of that passage I will give you an account of it if I can.

Obviously, Newton was exposed to metallic mercury in 1692–93. Was that also the case in 1676? The answer is yes. The experiments he performed in connection with his study of "optiks" often involved significant exposure to mercury vapors, and during the period 1676–79 he also began a period of intense study of alchemy.

The exposure is proved. Newton was at risk for mercury poisoning. But does mercury poisoning cause madness?

In his 1964 textbook on mercury poisoning, *The Toxicity of Mercury and Its Compounds* (Amsterdam: Elsevier), Peter Bidstrup supplied the following description of chronic mercury poisoning: "Nervous irritability, tendency to blush easily, and a history—often best obtained from friends or members of the family— of change of temperament, a tendency to avoid meeting friends and unexplained outbursts of temper."

This description certainly reminds us of Newton. Of course, the initial symptoms of mercury poisoning differ from patient to patient. In 1893, the great English neurologist William R. Gowers investigated the syndrome of chronic mercury poisoning and pointed out that it often begins with irritability and difficulty with concentration, followed by insomnia and finally by hallucinations and maniacal excitement. There is frequently a compelling, overwhelming timidness; a shyness of strangers; an embarrassment about the illness; discouragement and apathy about all aspects of life (but not despair); a loss of self-confidence; a loss of joie de vivre progressing to depression; and finally, a loss of memory.

The key to suspecting that a patient undergoing such a personality change has a neurologic disorder is the appearance of neurologic signs and symptoms. In mercury poisoning, the most common of these is a tremor.

And Newton had a tremor: His handwriting in 1692–93 became tremulous, while before and afterward, it was firm and precise.

We are now two-thirds of the way to diagnosis.

1. Newton had sufficient exposure.
2. Newton had a clinical picture that is consistent with mercury poisoning, including neurologic findings.

But what good is a hypothesis unless it can be tested? Not much. It is the last step that is critical in reaching a diagnosis. Is there any way to prove that Newton actually had a toxic amount of mercury in his body?

Spargo and Pounds did just that. Today, we often diagnose mercury poisoning by measuring the amount of mercury present in the urine, the blood, or the hair. Obviously, the first two cannot be evaluated for Newton, but Spargo and Pounds were able to locate several locks of his hair. In them they found clear evidence of excessive amounts of mercury.

Abe was right: Baker's law at work. The diagnosis could have been made on neurologic grounds, without the need of taking a psychiatric history.

What happened to Newton following his second episode of madness?

In 1696, Newton moved to London and became master of the mint, leaving Cambridge—and alchemy—behind him. During his London years, he enjoyed both power and worldly success. His position at the mint assured a comfortable social and economic status, and he was an active and able administrator.

After the death of Robert Hooke, the great microscopist, in 1703, Newton was elected president of the Royal Society and was annually reelected to this post until his death. In 1704, he published his second major work, the *Opticks,* based entirely on work completed decades before. In 1705, he was knighted by Queen Anne who, according to Conduitt, believed that it was her good fortune to have lived at the same time as, and to have known, so great a man. In London, "he reigned as the most famous man of his age, of Europe, and—as his powers gradually waned and his affability increased—perhaps of all time, so it seemed to his contemporaries" (Conduitt). In the more than 30 years that he lived in London, after leaving Cambridge, his illness (insomnia, loss of appetite, loss of memory, melancholia, delusions of persecution, and possibly trembling of the hands, as seen in his writing) appears to have been for the most part forgotten. But he never recovered his former level of function, spoke little in company, and was rather languid in his look and manner.

Although his creative years had passed, Newton continued to exercise a profound influence on the development of science. In effect, the Royal Society was his instrument, and he played it to his personal advantage. His tenure as president has been described as tyrannical and autocratic, and his control over the lives and careers of younger disciples was all but absolute. Newton could not abide contradiction or controversy and marshaled all the forces at his command in his various disputes. In his battle with Leibniz over who had priority in the discovery of calculus, Newton enlisted younger men to fight his war of words, while behind the lines he secretly directed charge and countercharge. In the end, the actions of the society were little more than extensions of Newton's will, and until his death he dominated all science without rival.

Looking over his entire career, it seems likely that his two episodes of mercury poisoning left their scars. His

recovery was probably not complete, and Newton was left less overwhelmingly brilliant than he had once been, and tainted by a paranoid, hypersensitive streak.

This cannot be proved, nor can it be disproved.

But it fits the facts.

To me the most impressive part of this tale is not the fact that Newton developed mercury poisoning; after all, his exposure to mercury was significant. Nor is it the fact that scientific sleuthing done two hundred years after Newton's death has been able to find evidence that he did indeed suffer from mental aberrations due to his mercury exposure. It is the fact that despite these episodes of prolonged toxicity to his brain, he still retained sufficient intellectual capacity to remain the greatest intellect of his age.

AUTHOR'S NOTE

The fact that mercury poisoning causes madness has long been suspected, and by the late nineteenth century it was part of general medical knowledge. In those times mercury was used in the felt-hat industry as a "carrot" or stiffening agent, and the most characteristic symptom of its workers was a tremor called "Hatters" shakes in the United Kingdom and Danbury Shakes in the United States. Since this condition was often accompanied by mental aberrations, Lewis Carroll based his character the Mad Hatter in *Alice in Wonderland* on a hatter whose madness was caused by mercury poisoning.

The two scientific articles that identified mercury poisoning as the cause of Newton's madness are these:

1. I. W. Johnson and M. L. Wolbarsht, "Mercury Poisoning: A Probable Cause of Isaac Newton's Physical and Mental Ills." *Notes Records of the Royal Society of London* 34 (1979): 1–9.
2. P. E. Spargo and C. A. Pounds, "Newton's 'Derangement of the Intellect': A New Light on an Old Problem." *Notes Records of the Royal Society of London* 34 (1979): 11–32.

The scientific analysis given here is based primarily on their discoveries. (The quotations from Newton's correspondence come from these secondary sources.) The best discussion of Newton's first mental crisis was presented by Robert F. Westfall (*Isis* 57 [1966]: 299–307).

A. B. Baker died in 1988. An obituary summarizing his contributions to neurology was published in *Neurology* (38 [1988]: 456). It makes no mention of Baker's law.

Origins of Western Environmentalism

Strategies to preserve nature arose as newly colonialized tropical lands were exploited in the 17th and 18th centuries. Scientists played an important role in this burgeoning concern

Richard H. Grove

Richard H. Grove has traveled to the Caribbean, South Africa, India and Mauritius, among other places, to study the history of environmental concerns. He holds degrees in geography from the University of Oxford, in conservation biology from University College, London, and in history from the University of Cambridge. Grove, who has worked as a consultant for several organizations, including Friends of the Earth, runs the Global Environmental History Unit at Cambridge. He is a lecturer in environmental history at Churchill College and a research associate at the National Institute of Science, Technology and Development in New Delhi.

Widespread misgivings about the effects of economic activity on the environment can seem a uniquely modern preoccupation—the re-

sult of industrialization, an expanding population and a science sophisticated enough to trace cause and effect. Theodore Roosevelt's pride, the U.S. Forest Service, and the myriad nature refuges established in England by naturalist Nathaniel Charles Rothschild are remembered more as attempts to preserve unspoiled nature than as responses to worries about impending environmental doom.

In truth, the roots of Western conservationism are at least 200 years old and grew in the tropics. Arising in a search for utopia, European-based environmentalism first took shape in the mid-18th century. At that time, colonial enterprise began to clash with Romantic idealism and with scientific findings.

The setting for this conflict was the threatened ecology of tropical islands and lands, from the Caribbean Sea to Asia. In London, Paris and other imperial capitals, these islands became allegories for the world at large. The power of this metaphor and the simultaneous

emergence of a community of professional natural scientists spurred governments to protect the environment.

The image of an untouched tropical island had long been associated with a Western vision of utopia. In the *Divine Comedy,* for example, Dante Alighieri set earthly paradise in a southern ocean. During the 15th and 16th centuries, voyages by Christopher Columbus and Ferdinand Magellan gave Europe its first glimpse of such islands.

As growing international trade extended Europe's commercial reach, it permitted "exploitation" of these sites for more philosophical needs. Exotic lands were seen as symbols for idealized landscapes: Edens, Arcadias or New Jerusalems. Eventually, as the large, uncharted terrains of India, Africa and America were explored, all wilderness became vulnerable to colonialization by an ever expanding myth.

During the 17th century, the full flowering of what could be called the Edenic island discourse led to the realization that European colonial rule could be environmentally destructive. Agriculture and the harvesting of timber, minerals and game by the government-run Dutch, British and French East India companies began to destroy idyllic terrain. The work of some contemporary artists communicated the extent of this degradation to Europeans. Drawings of Mauritius in 1677, for instance, forcefully depicted the stark reality of felled ebony forests. A coherent awareness of the ecological impact of capitalism and colonial rule began to emerge.

This insight was inextricably linked to the growing social leverage and often radical agenda of the scientific lobby of the time. During the late 17th and early 18th centuries, the urgent need to understand unfamiliar floras, faunas and geologies for commercial purposes attracted many scientists into employment with the trading companies.

These scientists, almost all of whom were medical surgeons or custodians of the early colonial botanical gardens, were an essential part of the administrative machinery of the East India companies. Hendrik B. Oldenland was a case in point: he served as curator of the botanical garden, doctor, town engineer and superintendent of roads for the Dutch Cape Colony in South Africa.

As companies extended territorial acquisitions, the associated research community grew proportionately. By 1838 more than 800 surgeons were employed by the British East India Company in India and in the East Indies. As time passed, increasingly complex administrative and technical demands were made on these highly educated and often independent-minded employees.

By the 19th century academies and scientific societies were established throughout the new territories. These institutions made it easy for scientists to communicate and debate their observations of the changes wrought by imperialism. Environmental theories and an ever growing flood of information about natural history and ethnology were diffused through meetings and publications. Thus, at the same time as it had promoted large-scale ecological change, the colonial enterprise had also created a coterie of men—and some women—predisposed to rigorous analytic thinking about the processes of ecological change and the need for land control.

One of the first places where science

spurred conservation was Mauritius. Although initially visited by the Portuguese, this island in the Indian Ocean was claimed by the Dutch in 1598; it fell under French rule in 1721 and thereafter became directly associated with the utopic visions of Romanticism and French physiocracy, an economic philosophy based on the "laws of nature" and the methods of Isaac Newton.

The first Dutch settlers were not conservationists. By the time they left, Mauritius's vast hardwood forests were largely depleted in areas easily accessible from the coast. As a result, zealous anticapitalist French reformers attempted to forestall further deforestation. Mauritius became the site for some of the earliest experiments in conservation.

These initiatives were carried out by scientists who, characteristically, were followers of Jean-Jacques Rousseau and the rigorous empiricism associated with the French Enlightenment. They viewed responsible stewardship of the environment as an aesthetic and moral priority as well as a matter of economic necessity. On Mauritius, these men—including Philibert Commerson, Pierre Poivre and Jacques Henri Bernardin de St. Pierre—wished to construct a just society, uncorrupted by absolutist France.

The strategies of these scientists were founded on an awareness of the potentially global impact of modern economic activity. Commerson, a botanist trained by Linnaeus, had been the royal botanist accompanying Louis Antoine de Bougainville on his voyage around the world. Commerson's wife, Jeanne Baret, traveled with him, becoming the first woman to circumnavigate the globe. (She accomplished this feat by starting the trip disguised as a manservant.) As a result of this journey, she inspired her husband, the most experienced botanist of the 18th century, to take a post as state botanist on Mauritius in 1768.

Bernardin de St. Pierre, an engineer who joined Commerson on Mauritius, was shocked by the deforestation he witnessed on his arrival. Yet he also believed he had found an unequaled harmony between people and nature in Mauritius, a harmony celebrated in his novel *Paul et Virginie,* one of the first French Romantic novels. Bernardin de St. Pierre felt that the preservation of this harmony demanded rigorous protection of natural resources.

Commerson and Bernardin de St. Pierre in turn stirred the climatic and

economic anxieties of Poivre, who had been appointed governor of Mauritius in 1767. An adherent of physiocracy, Poivre believed scientific knowledge should be applied to land management. Originally a Jesuit missionary, he had studied Indian and Chinese forestry and horticultural methods and had been greatly influenced by the botanical gardens and forest protection methods he had observed in the Dutch-run Cape Colony.

In the course of trying to acquire useful medical plants in India, the Dutch learned that their own classification methods were less sophisticated and efficient than the medicobotanical systems of an Indian caste—the Ezhava—from Malabar. Hendrik Adrian van Rheede Tot Drakenstein, who promoted forest conservation in the Cape Colony, organized a translation of the Ezhava texts into Latin. The resulting 12 volumes were published in Amsterdam as the *Hortus Malabaricus,* the garden of Malabar. These books formed the basis of all subsequent European classifications of South and Southeast Asian plants. Recognition of the superiority of the Ezhava system accounted for the first protection of trees and plants by the Dutch.

Although it may have been novel in a Western context, the protection of natural resources has been promoted since time immemorial. This recognition is especially significant today as researchers and others increasingly turn to native peoples for an understanding of the medicinal value of tropical plants or to small-scale efforts to stem desertification. Indigenous strategies have successfully combated soil erosion and deforestation in precolonial East Africa, the Cape Verde Islands, the Kingdom of Ghana and Mauryan India, as well as in the early colonial empires of China and Venice. As early as 450 B.C., for example, Artaxerxes I attempted to restrict cutting Lebanese cedar.

But the central, innovative aspect of French conservationism on Mauritius was the perceived relation between deforestation and local climatic change. A 1769 ordinance incorporated several stipulations prompted by this understanding: 25 percent of all landholdings were to be kept as forest, particularly on steep mountain slopes, to prevent soil erosion; all denuded areas were to be reforested; and all forests within 200 yards of water were to be protected. Eight years later a fully staffed forest service was set up. And in 1803 clearing of forest was forbidden higher than one third up a mountainside.

The early laws were not confined to forests. Pollution of water by effluent from indigo factories and sugar mills engendered more laws in 1791. In 1798 regulations were introduced to control vital but diminishing fish stocks.

The English were quick to imitate the example of the French policy in Mauritius. Again, these efforts were brought about by scientists, this time in the West Indies and in the Caribbean as well as, later, in India. In Tobago, an island in the eastern Caribbean, the work of Stephen Hales and Soame Jenyns was especially important. Hales, a plant physiologist who lived from 1677 to 1761, pioneered the study of transpiration, root pressure, the circulation of sap and the relation between green plants and the atmosphere. His friend Jenyns was the member of parliament for Cambridge and one of the Lords Commissioners for Trade and Plantations, the group that was responsible for settling Tobago.

Using techniques pioneered by Newton, Hales established a clear link between the atmosphere and plant processes. His experiments suggested a causal relation between trees and rainfall. Hales and his colleagues warned against the dangers of deforestation. Citing the examples of Jamaica and Barbados, where clearing for massive plantations had led to extensive soil erosion, Hales urged Jenyns and the Lords Commissioners to protect forests.

As a result, in 1764 forest reserves were established on Tobago. On land settlement maps these areas, which covered about 20 percent of the island, were marked as "reserved in wood for rains." Rain reserves were a revolutionary concept. They still exist today, although somewhat enlarged, as the oldest reserves of their kind in the world.

Similar measures were enacted on the West Indian island of St. Vincent in 1791. The Kings Hill Forest Act also protected the forests for climatic reasons. This piece of legislation was inspired by Alexander Anderson, the curator of the St. Vincent Botanic Garden—the first such garden to be founded in the Western Hemisphere. Anderson, like his French colleagues in Mauritius, was attracted by visions of utopian landscapes peopled by noble savages. By procuring protection of the St. Vincent forests, he hoped to prevent extinctions of species, protect

the climate and preserve the island's idyllic quality. In practice, however, this vision was shattered. During the 1790s, the indigenous Carib people were uprooted and the culture stamped out.

The policies developed on Mauritius, Tobago and St. Vincent eventually provided the justification and practical models for the forest planting and protection systems that developed in India after 1847. Until then, it seems that concerns about environmental change had been delayed by the vastness of the subcontinent, which concealed the impact of soil erosion and deforestation.

The roots of environmentalism in India were strongly reinforced by the writings of Alexander von Humboldt, the famous German geographer and explorer. He promulgated a new ecological concept of the relation between people and the natural world: that of the fundamental interrelation of humankind and other forces in the cosmos. His ideas, which drew extensively from the holistic thinking of Hindu philosophers, presented a scientifically reasoned interpretation of the threat posed by unrestrained human activities.

Humboldt's views influenced some of the scientists working for the British East India Company. These men were receptive to a way of thinking that related deforestation, water supply, famine, climate and disease in a coherent fashion. Humboldt based his theories on detailed observations carried out over several years, supplemented by historical records of the level of Lake Valencia in Venezuela.

Several Scottish scientists, including Alexander Gibson, Edward Balfour and Hugh F. C. Cleghorn, became enthusiastic proselytizers of the conservationist message. They advocated establishing a forest system in India that was unequaled in scale. In an 1852 report, they warned that a failure to set up an extensive forest system would result in ecological and social disaster.

The study took a global approach, drawing on evidence and scientific papers from all over the world. Its authors argued that rapid deforestation might cause severe rainfall decline, reduced runoff and ultimately famine. They pointed to widespread deforestation and ensuing soil erosion on the southwestern coast of India, the Malabar Coast.

Their message struck at the heart of the British East India Company's con-

cerns: revenue. The destruction in Malabar had caused commercially important harbors to silt up and become useless. This experience provided early evidence of what might happen in the absence of a state conservation program. (It should be mentioned that early warnings about deforestation in India came as much from indigenous rulers as from scientists. In 1830 the Rajah of Nilumbur alerted the governor of Bombay to the serious consequences of felling too many trees.)

The researchers' activities proved highly alarming to the British East India Company. Officials grasped the association between deforestation and famine fairly quickly, fearful as they always were of agrarian economic failure and social unrest. Unfortunately, it required an initial famine for scientists to gain credibility in the eyes of the government. Only then did the state take measures to protect the environment.

In India, periods of serious drought between 1835 and 1839, in the early 1860s and between 1877 and 1878 were all rapidly followed by state programs to strengthen forest protection. The forest conservation system set up in India, which was based in part on the Mauritius experience, later provided the model for most of the state conservation systems in Southeast Asia, Australia and Africa and, later, in North America.

Drought prompted environmental policy in other colonies as well. John Croumbie Brown, a pioneer of conservation in the Cape Colony, secured government agreement to conserve forests and prevent burning of grasslands only after the drought of 1862–1863 wreaked havoc on settler agriculture.

The South African drought of 1862, the worst ever recorded, had implications that extended far beyond conservation policies in Africa. It encouraged the development of an entire school of desiccationist theory that related the colonial experience to the world at large for the first time. Many scientists became convinced that most of the semiarid tropics were becoming arid as a result of colonial deforestation, an idea that has been confirmed by recent study.

Theories of widespread climatic change acquired further credibility in March 1865, when a paper by James Fox Wilson was presented at the Royal Geographical Society in London. The report, "On the progressing desiccation of the Orange River in

Southern Africa," made a strong case. Wilson, a naturalist, believed that the Orange River was becoming deprived of moisture and that the Kalahari Desert was expanding. He attributed the desiccation to the "reckless burning of timber and the burning of pasture over many generations by natives."

Present at Wilson's lecture was the explorer David Livingstone. He vehemently disagreed, asserting that rainfall had declined because of natural geophysical phenomena. Another speaker, Sir Francis Galton, a cousin of Charles Darwin, believed the introduction of cheap axes into Africa by Europeans had promoted excessive deforestation and consequent drought. Yet another member of the audience, Colonel George Balfour of the Indian Army—brother to Edward—sounded a more caustic note. Rainfall decline in India, he asserted, was caused principally by the European community, including the plantation owners.

Balfour argued that countermeasures were necessary. He said he had been informed that the government of Trinidad had prohibited cutting trees near the capital in order to ensure a supply of rain. Balfour was quick to point out that in precolonial times it had been the practice of Indians to sink wells and "plant topes of trees" to encourage water retention. In 1866, in another Royal Geographical Society discussion, Balfour cited the example of Mauritius, where "the Government had passed laws to prevent the cutting down of trees, and the result has been to secure an abundant supply of rainfall." Thus, the debate about climatic change had become international in scope by the mid-1860s. Detailed research raising the possibility that the very composition of the atmosphere might be changing reinforced the concerns.

Such views, which presaged contemporary fears about global warming, found early advocacy in the writings of J. Spotswood Wilson. He presented a paper in 1858 to the British Association for the Advancement of Science on the "general and gradual desiccation of the earth and atmosphere." Upheaval of land, destruction of forests and waste by irrigation were not sufficient to explain the available facts on climatic change, Wilson stated in his paper. Instead, he believed, the cause lay in the changing proportions of oxygen and carbonic acid in the atmosphere. Wilson argued that their respective states were connected with the relative rates of their production

and absorption by the animal and vegetable kingdom. This paper probably helped to influence the ideas of debaters at the Royal Geographical Society several years later.

Wilson concluded with a dismal set of remarks. Changes in the atmosphere were "in the usual course of geological changes, slowly approaching a state in which it will be impossible for man to continue as an inhabitant. . . . As inferior races preceded man and enjoyed existence before the earth has arrived at a state suitable to his constitution, it is more probable that others will succeed him when the conditions necessary for his existence have passed away."

Raising the specter of human extinction as a consequence of climatic change was a shocking psychological development in 1858. Yet it was consistent with fears that had been developing among the international scientific community for a long time. The concept of species rarity and the possibility of extinction had existed since the mid-17th century, when the scope of Western biological knowledge began to embrace the tropical world.

The demise of the auroch, a form of wild cattle, in 1627 in Poland and of the dodo in the 1670s in Mauritius had made a considerable impact. In 1680 the Polish government had set aside large areas of forest where hunting was prohibited. The contemporary survival of the wisent, or European bison, is attributed to this isolated effort. And in 1713 attempts were made to prevent the demise of redwood trees on the South Atlantic island of St. Helena.

The publication in the early 1830s by Charles Lyell of the *Principles of Geology* gave firm foundation to the confused awareness of extinction already shared by some East India Company scientists. The book questioned the permanence of species and laid the basis for modern understanding of geological change. Lyell questioned the ideas presented in Genesis, overturning notions about the speed of environmental processes. Paradoxically, this discussion emphasized the apparent helplessness of humanity in the face of environmental change.

Other scientists were probing these ideas as well. In the 1840s Ernest Dieffenbach chronicled the fauna of Mauritius, New Zealand and the Chatham Islands, which lie off the coast of Chile. He too became acutely aware of the

potential for further rapid extinction if European economic activity spread. Indeed, a paleontologist named Hugh Edwin Strickland, who understood the threat because of his work on the dodo and other vanished birds of the Mascarenes (Mauritius and Réunion islands), suggested that all of New Zealand be made a nature reserve.

The publication of *The Origin of Species* by Darwin in 1859 placed extinction in the dynamic context of natural selection. His theory served to sharpen the predicament of colonial scientists, many of whom were already aware of the part played by humans in hastening the demise of certain species.

A central part of the response to the existential havoc created by *Origin* served to fuel efforts to enact state conservation legislation. For instance, Cleghorn, who was the first inspector general of the Madras Forest Department, which was set up in 1856, stated that uncontrolled deforestation would both cause the loss of valuable species and prevent botanists from assembling evidence for evolution. (He was aware that such arguments might not carry great weight with government, and so he chose to emphasize the more obvious economic hazards of climatic change and resource depletion.)

Origin made protection a more valid concept in the eyes of the government. Indeed, between 1860 and 1870, a flurry of protectionist legislation was enacted in Britain and its colonies. Once again the galvanizing force was an island colony: Tasmania. A comprehensive law designed to protect indigenous Tasmanian birds was introduced in 1860, supported principally by an amateur naturalist, J. Morton Allport.

Other territories rapidly followed suit. By 1865 the colonial legislatures of Natal in South Africa and Victoria in Australia introduced laws to protect several animals and birds. Somewhat belatedly, in 1868, the U.K. introduced its first measures to protect birds. Significantly, the architect of the British measure was Alfred Newton, a frequent correspondent with Allport and the first prominent scientist to recognize the validity of Darwin's theory. Such early measures to protect species, all closely connected to opinions of Lyell and Darwin, offered a symbolic as well as practical opportunity to try to reassert control over a process of environmental degradation that was now understood as global.

By the mid-19th century long-established anxieties about artificially induced climatic change and the loss of species had reached a climax. The spread of Western economic development, initially through colonial expansion, was increasingly seen by more perceptive scientists as eventually threatening the survival of humanity.

If a single lesson can be drawn from the early history of conservation, it is that states will act to prevent environmental degradation only when their economic interests are shown to be directly threatened. Philosophical ideas, science, indigenous knowledge and people and species are, unfortunately, not enough to precipitate such decisions. Time and again, from the 1850s onward, some scientists have discovered that the prospect of artificially induced climatic change, with the full weight of its implications, was one of the few effective instruments that could persuade governments of the extent of an environmental crisis.

Our contemporary understanding of the threat to the global environment is thus a reassertion of ideas that reached maturity over a century ago. It is to be regretted that it has taken so long for the warnings of early scientists to be taken seriously.

FURTHER READING

TRACES ON THE RHODIAN SHORE: NATURE AND CULTURE IN WESTERN THOUGHT FROM ANCIENT TIMES TO THE END OF THE EIGHTEENTH CENTURY. Clarence J. Glacken. University of California Press, 1967.

SCOTTISH MISSIONARIES, EVANGELICAL DISCOURSES AND THE ORIGINS OF CONSERVATION THINKING IN SOUTHERN AFRICA, 1820–1900. Richard Grove in *Journal of Southern African Studies,* Vol. 15, No. 2, pages 163–187; January 1989.

COLONIAL CONSERVATION, ECOLOGICAL HEGEMONY AND POPULAR RESISTANCE: TOWARDS A GLOBAL SYNTHESIS. Richard H. Grove in *Imperialism and the Natural World.* Edited by John M. MacKenzie. University of Manchester Press, 1990.

The Birth of Public Opinion

The rule of public opinion is now taken more or less for granted. Presidents consult the polls before announcing new policies; legislators invoke their constituents' desires to justify their votes; television network executives worship the Nielsen ratings. This idea of a public with a defined will that can be expressed is a relatively modern one, born of the Age of Enlightenment. But what we think of as "public opinion" means something far different from what it did in the 18th century. Historian Anthony La Vopa *examines how the idea has changed.*

Anthony J. La Vopa

Anthony J. La Vopa, a former Wilson Center Fellow, is professor of history at North Carolina State University. Born in New York City, he received a B.A. from Boston College (1967) and a Ph.D. from Cornell University (1976). He is the author of Prussian Schoolteachers: Profession & Office, 1763–1848 *(1980) and* Grace, Talent, and Merit: Poor Students, Clerical Careers and Professional Ideology in Eighteenth-Century Germany *(1988).*

In the liberal democracies of the West, and in a growing number of other nations, the "public" and its "opinion" are fixtures of modern life. Indeed, it is hard to imagine how culture and politics ever managed without them. The highbrow poet, the pulp novelist, the classical musician, the rock star, the avante-garde filmmaker, the director of TV sit-coms: All of these producers of "culture" need an image of the "public" and its expected reaction, whether they aim to please or to antagonize their audience. Without a "public," government has no way of entering into a dialogue with society; it relies instead on a barrage of propaganda. Unable to express its opinion publicly, society has no way (short of the threat of violent upheaval) of making government responsive to its changing needs.

The ancient *polis,* of course, had its public forum and its *vox populi.* But "public opinion" is, as historians measure such things, a recent innovation. It was in the course of the 18th century that "public" joined "opinion" in a new pairing—and the result was a dramatic change in the meaning of the latter word. At the beginning of the 18th century, "opinion" had generally connoted blinkered vision and fickleness, in contrast to the unchanging universality of Truth. By the end of the century, opinion in its "public" guise was endowed with a rational objectivity. Public opinion was the authoritative judgment of a collective conscience, the ruling of a tribunal to which even the state was subject. It was to be confused neither with blind adherence to traditional authority nor with the mob loyalty that modern political demagoguery seemed to command.

The timing of this semantic shift was no accident. The 18th century was the Age of Enlightenment in Europe, and "public opinion" was one of its characteristic products. It was not simply that the "public," in the ideal, embodied the Enlightenment's aspiration to construct a truly rational polity, able to criticize itself objectively. The new pairing distilled the values, aspirations, and misgivings of the educated and propertied elite that gave the Enlightenment its social profile.

As historian Keith Baker and several other scholars have demonstrated, "public opinion" exercised its strongest appeal and exhibited its ironies most dramatically in *ancien regime* France. That, too, is no accident. As the sacred authority of the Bourbon monarchy was eroded beyond recovery, the need for a secular replacement—a single, undivided source of political legitimacy—seemed increasingly urgent. An arena of open political conflict was forming, but to many Frenchmen it seemed to portend chaos rather than progress. Hence the duality that marked 18th-century appeals to public opinion everywhere in continental Europe and the Anglo-American world was heightened in France. "Public opinion" *did* loom as a workable alternative to traditional authority, and in that sense it was eminently modern from birth. And yet there is also a sense in which the concept, in its original state of innocence, was an antidote to the onset of modern politics. In our own era, as politics takes the form of photo opportunities and sound bites, that antidote can seem at once all the more appealing and all the less likely to work.

Who appealed to the tribunal of public opinion in the 18th century? A complete list would include Voltaire, Immanuel Kant, Denis Diderot, and other familiar figures from the Enlightenment's pantheon, but it would also take us deep into the lower tiers of thinkers. By the close of the 18th century, reverence for the public's judgment had become obligatory among progressive clergymen as well as among the skeptics who dismissed Christianity as mere "superstition." It was shared—or at least seemed to be shared—by opposing camps of scholars; by novelists and by their critics; by government ministers and by opposition journalists.

Whether "public opinion" was already a "preponderant force" in Europe by the 1780s, as playwright Louis-Sébastien Mercier claimed at the time, is open to question. The historical record leaves no doubt, however, that the concept was gaining currency and winning credibility. It became credible in part because an actual "public" was forming. Historians are now in a position to explain this phenomenon, since they have ceased to approach the Enlightenment simply as a March of Ideas and have studied it as a process of social communication and social change. Public opinion—in the broadest sense of the term—was an intricate circuit of writing, reading, and talking. Its jurisdiction lay within the expanding universe of print. Full-fledged membership in the true "public"—the "enlightened" tribunal—required a measure of affluence and education that the majority of Europeans, including many of the literate, did not enjoy. Within that limitation, however the public was to be found in microcosm wherever men gathered to discuss the ideas circulated in print. Its locales ranged from elegant salons to modest coffee houses. It might be said, in fact, that a network of "enlightened" communities, peopled by only a few thousand souls, invented public opinion as a way of talking about and validating itself.

This is also a way of saying, of course, that the tribunal of public opinion was a weapon in the Enlightenment's large arsenal of abstractions. It figures as such in Voltaire's campaign against Christian intolerance; in the mounting attacks on royal despotism and aristocratic corruption in France; in the rationales of reform-minded government officials throughout Europe; in the efforts to liberate literature and the arts from conventional rules. The point is not that public opinion was an empty abstraction from the start but that it was so appealing precisely because it was a highly serviceable fiction.

Napoleon once remarked that "Cannon killed feudalism," but "ink will kill modern society." The 18th-century men of letters were more likely to observe that ink—or, more precisely, printer's ink—was *creating* modern society. Its most obvious creation was "the public."

This is not to suggest that print was being produced on a modern scale. Until the steam engine was harnessed to move-able type in the early 19th century, there was little improvement in the hand-operated wooden press Johann Gutenberg had invented in 1450. Even if the technology had been better, the market for print would have remained pitifully small by modern commercial standards. The majority of the European population still lacked the excess cash and the sophisticated reading skills that most books and periodicals required. In 1785 the Netherlands' *Gazette de Leyde,* a French-language newspaper with a press run of just over 4,000, was one of the most widely read in Europe.

And yet historians speak of an 18th-century "revolution" in print, and not simply because the century witnessed a proliferation of printing shops, booksellers, reading clubs, and circulating libraries. On the eve of the French Revolution print offered Europeans far more information, a much greater variety of ideas, and incomparably more entertainment than it had offered a century earlier. In most educated homes reading was no longer primarily an act of religious devotion; the Bible and the devotional tract had been displaced by the novel and the entertaining journal. Government had become a newsworthy subject, and often an object of controversy, in a variety of newspapers available along the main commercial and postal routes.

The demand for print was growing, though it remained narrowly restricted by modern standards. In aristocratic circles "pedantry" still provoked disdain but illiteracy had become an embarrassment. If reading had become a habit among the well-born, there was a veritable craving for print among the much larger population Samuel Johnson classified as "that middle race . . . who read for pleasure or accomplishment." Bourgeois government officials, clergymen, lawyers and other professionals, merchants, affluent artisans, and shopkeepers—these educated and propertied commoners, along with their wives and children, were the typical consumers in the new print market.

If alarmed government officials and clerics had had their way, the range of consumer choices would have been considerably narrower. Even in "absolutist" France, however, official censorship was held in check by its own inconsistencies and the behind-the-scenes mediation of liberal-minded officials. The royal law courts (the *parlement*) in Paris still ordered the hangman to burn books publicly,

and among the works consumed by the flames were Voltaire's *Philosophical Letters* (1734) and Jean Jacques Rousseau's *Emile* (1762). But these acts of official censure likely whetted the reading public's appetite for risqué literature, and in any case they were not necessarily followed by a royal ban. Many publishers—the publication of the last 10 volumes of the *Encyclopédie* may offer the most striking example—simply sidestepped the director of the Library and his small army of censors by not applying for the royal *privilége.* More often the government allowed questionable material to pass through the quasi-legal loophole of "tacit" permission. Even that was not required for legal briefs. In the scandal trials of the 1780s barristers used these briefs to portray their clients as hapless victims of aristocratic arrogance and royal despotism. Printed in thousands of copies, these *memoires* did much to create the impression that the entire establishment was hopelessly corrupt.

There was also a heavy flow of illegal literature, most of which was supplied by Dutch and Swiss publishers on the borders of the Bourbon kingdom. Contraband in print was smuggled in crates past bribed customs officials, or hidden in men's breeches and under women's skirts. French booksellers tempted their customers with anti-Christian tracts and with pornography; with pamphlets detailing the sufferings of dissident writers in royal dungeons; with scabrous "libels" of prominent figures in the royal family, at court, and in the government. *Les Fastes de Louis XV* (1782) was perhaps the most widely read clandestine book in France on the eve of the Revolution. It included a lurid inventory of the depravities of Madame du Barry, the court mistress of Louis XV, who, in the words of its anonymous author "had ascended in one leap from the brothel to the throne."

The modern "public" owed its origins and its growth to this cornucopia of print. In its broadest contours, however, the new public was as much a product of talk as it was of reading. As print entered symbiosis with new kinds of conversation in new social settings, it produced myriad ripple effects that cannot be measured by press runs and sales figures. Novel-reading, for example, was central to a new kind of domestic privacy in many educated bourgeois households.

Among the bestsellers were epistolary novels such as Samuel Richardson's *Pamela* (1741) and Rousseau's *La Nouvelle Héloise* (1761), which spun their plots around the joys and perils of courtship and marital life and were well-suited to filling the idle hours of mothers and daughters. Even when such novels were not read aloud in the family circle, as they often were, they helped create a new, emotion-charged language of family intimacy.

As the bourgeois family circumscribed its private space, developing its own moral standards, it also examined itself obsessively in the printed pages of the novel. This self-examination was critical to the emergence of a modern public. It helps explain, in fact, why the public eventually assumed a critical posture towards government.

By the early 18th century, reading and conversation were nourishing each other in a variety of new public and quasi-public spaces. These spaces formed as the center of public life shifted from the royal courts of Europe to the cities, and as pedigrees and titles ceased to be the exclusive requirements for admission. Versailles and the courts modeled on it embodied the principle that the king was the only "public" figure, since his person was the single and indivisible source of all public authority. Royal splendor radiated outward through a court aristocracy displaying itself in relentless rounds of ceremony and theatrical festivity.

Since the early 17th century, Paris had witnessed the emergence of a new kind of public society that would eventually displace Versailles. Originally an overwhelmingly aristocratic milieu, it called itself "the world" (*le monde*) as a way of saying that it encompassed everyone who counted. *Le monde* gathered regularly in the capital's salons, under the guidance of highborn women in need of amusement and intellectual sustenance. In the highly mannered conversational art of the salon, gossip and scandal shaded naturally into literary discussion. In the 18th century, as the market for literature expanded, *le monde* opened its doors to the well-known as well as to the well-born and to the well-heeled. For the bourgeois man of letters regular appearances on the salon circuit, perhaps at the cost of literary effort, had become a requirement of literary celebrity.

By the mid-18th century the salon was one of several European institutions that brought together noblemen and educated and propertied commoners in new rituals of sociability and intellectual exchange. The royal academies founded in the 17th century by Louis XIV in Paris had counterparts throughout provincial France. The "academicians" were appointed from the ranks of the educated bourgeoisie and the clergy as well as from the office-holding aristocracy. While their public ceremonies paid homage to the monarchy, they formed what one member in Dijon called a "republic" of "citizen-spirits" behind closed doors. The monarchy had no reason to question this arrangement; by promoting a frank exchange of ideas, the academies were able to clarify vital public issues. The same purpose was served by the academies' many essay contests, which were open to all men of wit and literary talent. The typical winner may have been a mediocrity mouthing conventional wisdom, but there were stunning exceptions. In 1750 the Dijon Academy awarded first prize to a watchmaker's son and former vagabond named Jean Jacques Rousseau. A misfit in *le monde*, paralyzed in the face of salon politesse and wit, Rousseau had used the occasion of the essay contest to launch his attack on the falseness of modern civilization.

Most European universities suffered by comparison with the new academies. Stereotyped as bastions of tradition-bound, boorish pedantry, they were crowded with obscure commoners who survived hand-to-mouth while preparing for the clergy. They were not the kind of places aristocratic scions were likely to visit on the Grand Tour. But several universities were anything but academic ghettos. Tounis College in Edinburgh entered the 18th century as little more than a stodgy Presbyterian seminary, but in the middle decades of the century, under the leadership of the town council and several reform-minded professors, it introduced a modern curriculum in the liberal arts. The new offerings catered to sons of gentlemen as well as to future clergymen, since they blended a "godliness" free of zealotry with the urbane "politeness" that the weekly *Spectator* had begun to propagate from London several decades earlier. Thanks to its university, Edinburgh, a provincial city in London's orbit, became known as a modern Athens.

On the continent, the closest equivalent was the Georg-August University of Göttingen, founded by the Hanoverian government in 1737. Attracting first-rate scholars with its generous salaries and well-endowed library, and frowning on the theological polemics that soured life at other universities, the Georg Augusta was soon an innovative center in the fields of law, politics, history, and classical studies. Again commoners mixed with noblemen, who came to Göttingen from across Europe to groom themselves for government service or simply for a life of leisured refinement. In the space of a few decades a sleepy provincial town became one of the intellectual entrepôts of Europe.

Another refuge from social convention was the new "brotherhood" of Freemasonry, which crossed the Channel from London in the 1730s and spread across the urban landscape of France and the German states. Outside the lodge "brothers" might face each other across the barriers of rank and wealth, or might find themselves on opposite sides of volatile confessional and "political" issues. But within its artificially segregated space they could shed their social skins and inherited prejudices and discuss ideas (or at least some ideas) as one "human being" to another.

If Freemasonry formed a micro-public, it was also paradoxically a cult movement that shut out the public at large. More typical of the new sociability was the coffee house. In the course of the 18th century, as coffee drinking became a daily habit for millions of Europeans, the café became a fixture of urban life. London may have remained the world's caffeine capital, but Vienna, with 48 coffee houses by 1770, was a formidable rival. The visitor to any provincial capital, court town, or university town could expect to find at least one or two such establishments. Most did not aspire to the elegance of Vienna's Café Milani, whose mirrored hallways, marble facades, and chandeliers were reminiscent of Versailles. Instead they offered an atmosphere of intimacy to be found nowhere else outside the home. Friends and colleagues could gather regularly to enjoy a cup of coffee or tea, perhaps accompanied by a pastry; to play cards or billiards; to read the newspapers and other periodicals; to discuss the affairs of the day.

"You can meet half the world in Richter's café," Friedrich Schiller observed from Leipzig in 1785. This was still an exclusive "world," requiring affluence and leisure, but it was far more open than the Parisian salons of a century earlier. The openness and the informality made for intense, sometimes volatile discussion of the latest novel or review, of changes in government policy, of rumors of war and prospects for peace. The vibrant coffee house, a German observer remarked with understandable exaggeration, was a "political stock exchange where the most daring and clever heads from all social stations gather."

Ironically, women were not among the assembled heads, just as they were largely absent from the academies, the lodges, and the university lecture halls. As the presiding figures at salons, and as authors and readers of fiction, women had played a critical role in the formation of a "public." But political scientist Joan Landes is probably correct in arguing that, the more bourgeois the public became, the less room and tolerance it had for women. Bourgeois resentment of aristocratic privilege often focused on the intellectual pretensions and the political intrigues of high-born salon women. The *salonnière* became the foil to the ideal wife and mother, who shunned public life in the conviction that her "natural" role was to rear her children and to support her husband with modest intellectual companionship at home. If the novel kept women involved in the literary public as readers, it also directed their search for self-fulfillment to an idealized world of domestic happiness, insulated from the hurly-burly of professional life and politics.

This fictional dichotomy at once reflected and sanctioned a new kind of social segregation. As educated men found a refuge from the rigors of public life in the new domesticity, they found a respite from domesticity in their lodges, their clubs, and their coffee houses.

But while the 18th-century public had its visible locales, there was also a sense in which it remained invisible. To some, its invisibility was the key to its power. The true public had to have a single will or conscience, and that evoked something greater than a mere aggregate of institutions or communities. This is not to say that the public was a fiction; there *was* a circuitry of written and spoken words out there, and somehow something called "opinion" formed in it and flowed through it.

When authors appealed to this invisible tribunal of public opinion, however, they were evoking an *ideal* rather than a

measurable force. It requires a strenuous leap of historical imagination to grasp the ideal in its original state of innocence and to make sense of expectations that may seem hopelessly naive today.

At the core of the ideal was the principle of "publicity." Today this term makes us think of the corporate PR person, with smokescreens of apparent candor, or of *paparazzi* appealing to the public's "right to know" as their cameras follow celebrities into bedrooms. What struck 18th-century observers was not the abuse of publicity in an open society, but its vast potential to open up a closed society. In old-regime Europe, secrecy was one of the guiding principles of life. Government set an example by regarding the practice of statecraft as an *arcanum,* a secret expertise that ordinary subjects were not in a position to understand and had no right to know. When the French *parlements* began to "go public" by publishing their remonstrances, the Crown stubbornly insisted that it alone decided what was fit for public consumption. England was considered an excessively open polity by French standards, but until at least the 1770s London newspapers risked prosecution when they published reports on the debates of the House of Commons.

Government policy reflected the tenacity of traditional norms. In the political arena formed by the ruler's court, intrigue was the stuff of politics; behind the court's elaborate facade of public ceremony, ministers competed with courtiers and mistresses to win favor and to carry the day. In their very different social settings, guilds of skilled craftsmen jealously guarded trade secrets.

"Publicity" meant a new openness, with its promise of a new civic spirit. The expectation was not, of course, that closed governments would suddenly throw open their doors to public scrutiny. Government would follow the example of society, as people became more transparent to each other in all walks of life. In the intricate pecking order of old-regime corporatism, everyone was expected to command the authority and render the deference appropriate to his station. Confined to their social personae, people never interacted simply as persons or, in 18th-century parlance, in the purity of their shared "humanity." It was this kind of purely human communication that Masonic lodges aspired to achieve, and that the 18th-century cult of friendship idealized.

Print had even greater potential to effect the same egalitarian transparency. Print did not bring author and reader face to face, and that was its paradoxical advantage. Its, impersonality made for a kind of "human" intimacy, free of domination and subservience, that face-to-face social relations rarely admitted. Eighteenth-century authors were fond of evoking this paradox; the faceless mass of readers were, or at least could be, their "friends" and their "confidantes."

With its call for public scrutiny and, at a deeper level, its new spirit of open and egalitarian exchange, the Enlightenment developed a strikingly modern strategy for reform. If government was to be accountable to public opinion, it had to be open to the public gaze. If abuses were to be remedied, they had to be brought to the light of day and discussed without inhibition in the public forum. All this sounds sensible enough, but we are likely to be brought up short by the 18th-century corollary: that the new openness would somehow generate a moral consensus about the direction reform ought to take. In our age of election polls and marketing surveys, the "public" tends to break down into groups with "interests" and corresponding "opinions," some coalescing into larger coalitions, others colliding head-on. Public opinion is a statistical aggregate, not the judgment of a single ethical voice.

There was a strain of 18th-century thought that regarded the pursuit of self-interest as a positive force for change, although it saw the individual, and not the group, as its proper agent. It was precisely because public opinion promised to transcend self-interest, however, that it was hailed as the moral arbiter for the entire society and polity. Inspired by their roseate image of Periclean Athens and the Roman Republic, 18th-century rationalists sought a modern collective expression of the classical ideal of civic virtue. Now that "each citizen is able to speak to the entire nation through the medium of print," the French Academy was informed by one of its new members in 1755, "the men of letters are for a dispersed public what the orators of Rome and Athens were in the midst of an assembled public."

In a rational society, public goals would be established by men who had an unobstructed view of the public welfare and hence could form disinterested judgments. Their consensus was, to be sure, an "opinion," which was to say that it was less than a definitive grasp of Truth. If the consensus was nonetheless authoritative, that was because the myriad judgments that constituted it had been made in splendid moral isolation. The crux of the matter—the axiomatic assumption—was that public opinion ought to be grounded in, and ought to draw its moral force from, the inviolable privacy of the individual conscience.

Like the ancient assembly, public discussion in print was a collective enterprise; but, as the German philosopher Christian Garve (1742-1798) reminded his readers, in the end each member of the public "must judge for himself," as though from a position of unconditional moral autonomy. The point was not simply that open coercion was intolerable; even subtler forms of power—the authority of tradition, for example, or the seductive force of rhetoric—threatened to violate the purity of this ideal.

The formation of public opinion was seen as a process of purification. As the warring "passions" were strained out, the authoritative consensus of "reason" emerged.

We tend to smile patronizingly at the naiveté of this expectation. The assumption of a universal "reason" seems highly dubious in the light of modern cultural relativism and philosophical agnosticism, and in any case the need for consensus now seems less urgent. The ascendancy of interest-group politics, after all, has not shattered most Western polities; nor has a .pluralistic culture, with its incessant clash of opinions, torn them apart.

To reform-minded men in the 18th century, however, the term "interests" often evoked caste prejudices and the abuse of legal privileges. Group self-interest meant corporate selfishness, which seemed incompatible with rational progress. The prospect of open conflict raised the specter of chaos, probably in the form of civil war. In the 16th and 17th centuries, Europeans had been plagued by religious war between Catholics and Protestants (as in France, the Netherlands, and Germany) and between a Protestant Establishment and radical dissenters (as in England). Skeptical rationalists wanted to tame religious beliefs by reducing them to one more species of "opinion," but they were acutely aware that in matters of faith, opinions easily hardened into prejudices.

The 18th century was "an age of *enlightenment,*" Immanuel Kant reminded his readers in 1784, but it was not "an *enlightened* age." There was ample reason to fear that religious fanaticism and intolerance were alive and well. In England and Germany, Protestantism proved receptive to Enlightenment rationalism, but it also spawned movements like Pietism and Methodism, which sought to rekindle the evangelical fire. In France, Jansenism had similar aspirations, as its cult of miracles and the ecstasies of its "convulsionaries" demonstrated. As late as 1766, following an unsuccessful appeal to the *parlement* in Paris, the young Chevalier de la Barre was tortured, beheaded, and burned on suspicion of having mutilated crucifixes. The case prompted one of Voltaire's most impassioned appeals to "the public."

In modern democracies, political parties are supposed to play a central role in generating public opinion. But most 18th-century observers would have agreed with Christian Garve that "public opinion ceases to exist as soon as parties occur." The spirit of "party" meant fierce loyalty to a "particular" cause, without regard for the common welfare, and the history of sectarian fanaticism left no doubt that that spirit was pernicious. This was the lesson that accompanied the application of the word "party" to an emerging arena of modern political conflict. Political partisanship joined religious zealotry as a threat to the reasoned, tolerant consensus that public opinion promised to articulate.

Both varieties of "party" threatened to fracture the body politic—or, as Garve might have put it, both kinds of opinion were incompatible with a truly public opinion. Whether the leader was a religious zealot or a political demagogue, he won the blind following of the "mob" rather than the reasoned consent of autonomous individuals. In both cases mass mobilization was a kind of contagion, an epidemic of "enthusiasm." And in both cases "enthusiasm" meant the kind of self-delusion that precluded rational judgment. The religious enthusiast mistook his neurotic obsessions for the voice of the Lord. Likewise, the political enthusiast mistook his "metaphysical" fantasies for universal truths about man and his "natural" rights.

By the eve of the French Revolution, the tribunal of public opinion was expected to fill a plethora of needs, and it was beginning to register the tensions among them. When the public censured the authoritarian government, the tunnel-visioned corporatism, and the over-zealous confessionalism of the old regime, it was the voice of a modern polity in the making. But public opinion also promised to preclude new, secular outbreaks of the party spirit. In that capacity it was an antidote to modernity, embodying the rationalist's fear that the polity was entering a chronic condition of partisan conflict. Even as French critics of the monarchy assumed an openly confrontational stance, they sought to dispel the specter of open contestation with their appeals to an authoritative consensus. Still "absolutist" in theory, the government had little choice but to respond in kind.

The final irony is that public opinion had become a kind of absolute in its own right. Precisely because the public will was no longer embodied in the person of the king, it had to find expression in a collective unity. It expressed itself in "opinion," and not in the transcendent truths that religious believers claimed to find in Revelation or in the depths of their own souls. But as a collective conscience hovering above mere "interests," and as a consensus purified of passions, public opinion had its own claim to transcendence.

T he "people of intellect govern, because in the long run they form public opinion, which sooner or later subjugates or reverses every kind of despotism." This dictum was published by the royal historiographer of France in 1767, but it would not have been a bad guess to attribute it to a Czech intellectual celebrating the recent Velvet Revolution. When we speak of the former East Bloc countries joining (or returning to) the "free" West, we mean, among other things, that their governments have at last abandoned the pretext of embodying the Will of the Proletariat and have become accountable to public opinion.

As the recent thaw in Eastern Europe advanced, in fact, some historians had the eerie feeling that they were listening to a telescoped replay of an 18th-century script. Once again intellectuals were orchestrating a verbal assault on authoritarian government, often couched in the morally charged languages of fiction and philosophy. There was the same evocation of the public as a collective conscience, of public opinion as the record of its judgment, and of the principle of openness, or publicity, as the crux of reform. We seemed to have entered a time warp and to have recovered the original innocence invested in the concept of public opinion.

But the script has also been telescoped in another sense. The former Stalinist satellites are leaping headlong into the world of political parties, election campaigns, interest-group politics, and mass marketing. As they make the leap, vaulting optimism gives way to skepticism and the apotheosis of public opinion is muted, if not repudiated. Indeed, East European intellectuals find themselves fighting off a mood of bitter disillusionment as their political revolutions, along with their literary renaissance, are threatened by the allure of Western-style commercialism and by the withering attention of the electronic media.

Mass education and mass literacy, radio and television, modern advertising and electioneering: All have contributed to the fact that the modern public is a far cry from the 18th-century ideal. Despite the continuity of language, the opinion now measured incessantly in surveys and polls cannot be "public" in the 18th-century sense; as the invisible will has become the measureable aggregate, the concept has lost its original promise of moral invincibility. In a process that 18th-century rationalists would have regarded as self-contradictory, public opinion breaks down into a melee of *opinions,* and endless argument among claimants

for the allegiance of the real public. One hopes for a clear numerical majority, not an authoritative consensus.

To judge by historical experience since the 18th century, all this does not necessarily spell doom for the Eastern European experiments. The problem may lie with a kind of purism in the original ideal—an aversion to the uncontrollable messiness of pluralistic conflict and mass participation. Those who still indulge in such purism may set themselves up for a plunge into disillusionment. Only those who can reconcile themselves to the fact that public opinion does not produce a pure consensus of reason will be able to navigate democratic politics successfully.

In 18th-century Europe, the onset of disillusionment was gradual, but it gained pace at the end of the century. "Friends of the Revolution," Garve wrote some time in the mid-1790s, "take refuge in public opinion as a *Qualitas occulta* that explains everything—or as a higher power that can excuse everything." Garve had in mind the orators and journalists who had justified mob violence and the Terror in revolutionary France. Others had already observed that the expanding market for print was a mixed blessing for *belles lettres*. If it created a reading public, it also threatened to reduce literature to one more trivial commodity and to leave authors at the mercy of fickle consumers in search of effortless entertainment.

In its 18th-century apotheosis, public

opinion was the voice of an educated and propertied elite. Faced with the Revolution's surge of democratic politics, and with the egalitarian momentum of an increasingly commercialized print market, the elite began to justify certain kinds of exclusion within the promise of openness. The sexual division of labor might exclude women from active participation in the new public, but how [to] justify the continued exclusion of the broad mass of men? How could a part— the educated and propertied part—claim to speak credibly for the whole? Why were some people more capable of disinterested judgment than others? There were many answers, all justifying an elite's claim to speak with an authoritative voice. Authority now lay in the broad vision afforded by property ownership and education; in the professional's expert judgment on issues the "lay" public could not judge; in the literary critic's mission to guard "standards" against the onslaught of trash.

Public opinion would remain a court of appeal, but the size and composition of the jury had become a contentious issue. Public opinion may still evoke an ideal of rational consensus, but it turns out that the ideal itself is not exempt from political conflict or indeed from the struggle for profit. The new Eastern European democracies are learning this lesson very fast, though they have reminded us that, at least for a moment, public opinion can be the voice of conscience.

The Commercialization of Childhood

In eighteenth-century England, picture books, playthings, and educational gimcracks became a thriving business: a trend that has continued from that time to this

J. H. Plumb

A new attitude toward children developed in England during the eighteenth century, an attitude that spread as easily to Boston, New York, and Philadelphia as it did to Birmingham, Leeds, and Glasgow. It was a gentler and more sensitive approach to children, one that was part of a wider change in social attitudes: a growing belief that nature was inherently good, not evil, and what evil there was derived from man and his institutions. The dominant attitude toward children in the seventeenth century had been autocratic, even ferocious: "The new borne babe," Richard Allestree wrote in 1658, "is full of the stains and pollutions of sin which it inherits from our first parents through their loins."

From birth, English children were constrained. They spent their first months, sometimes a year, bound tightly in swaddling clothes. Their common lot was fierce parental discipline. Even a man of such warm and kindly nature as Samuel Pepys thought nothing of beating his fifteen-year-old maid with a broomstick and locking her up for the night in his cellar, or whipping his boy-servant, or boxing his clerk's ears. Of two hundred manuals on child rearing prior to 1700, only three, those by Plutarch, Matteo Palmieri, and Jacopo Sadoleto, did not recommend that fathers beat their children.

In 1693 John Locke finally gave expression to what was clearly a new and more liberal attitude toward child rearing and education in *Some Thoughts Con-*cerning Education*. This was by far his most popular book; it was reprinted nineteen times before 1761 and was as well known in America as in England. Locke believed in arousing the child's interest in education by a system of esteem for those who did well, and shame for those who were reluctant to learn. He disapproved of the time-honored method of flogging boys into learning, a sentiment that was already widespread but to which his authority gave added force. He was equally opposed to bribing the child to work through material rewards: "The *Rewards* and *Punishments* then, whereby we should keep Children in order, *are* quite of another kind; and of that force, that when we can get them once to work, the Business, I think, is done, and the Difficulty is over. *Esteem* and *Disgrace* are, of all others, the most powerful Incentives to the Mind, when once it is brought to relish them. If you can once get into Children a Love of Credit, and an Apprehension of Shame and Disgrace, you have put into them the true Principle." As well as arguing for a more liberal attitude toward the child, Locke also pleaded for a broader curriculum in schools. He believed education should fit man for society as well as equip him with learning; hence he pressed for lessons not only in drawing but also in French. He opposed teaching languages by a rigid grounding in grammar and urged that Latin be taught by the direct method, as it would had it been a living language.

After Locke, education of children increasingly became social rather than religious. Greater emphasis was placed on its usefulness in the child's future life in society. Although a knowledge of the classics was still regarded as the mark of a gentleman, more and more small schools, run for a profit, provided a far more practical education—in bookkeeping, penmanship, the English language, foreign languages, mathematics, navigation, surveying, geography, and the use of globes. It was this type of education, not the grammar schools, that flourished vigorously in the eighteenth century.

By 1740, and perhaps before, children were no longer regarded as sprigs of old Adam, whose wills had to be broken by the rod. Nor was education regarded as a genteel accomplishment; boys and girls were being educated in order to play effective and successful roles in an aggressive commercial society. And because commercial opportunities everywhere abounded, parents were willing to invest, as never before, in the education of their children. Naturally enough this had a profound influence on the production of children's books.

Books by which children could be taught had existed from the first days of printing—alphabets, grammars, and the like—but few were designed specifically for children. Authors and publishers made very little attempt to entice the young mind with attractive and compelling illustrations and typography. It should be remembered that fairy stories, ballads, riddles, and fables were intended as much for adults as for children. Indeed, Aesop was not specifically adapted for children in England until 1692, when Sir Roger L'Estrange produced his edition.

The late seventeenth and early eighteenth centuries saw the beginnings of new attitudes toward children's literature and methods of learning to read. In 1694, "J. G." published *A Play-book for children, to allure them to read as soon as they can speak plain. Composed of small pages, on purpose not to tire children, and printed with a fair and pleasant letter. The matter and method plainer and easier than any yet extant,* which was, for once, a true statement in a blurb. The author states in his preface that he wished to "decoy Children into reading." The book has wide margins and large type; its language is simple and concrete and mostly within the compass of a child's experience. It did well enough to be reprinted in 1703, by which time a few other authors, noticeably William Ronksley, were attempting to find methods and materials more suitable for very young children.

Ronksley believed in teaching by verse according to the meter of the Psalms—first week, words of one syllable, the next week words of two syllables, and so on. And he used jokes, riddles, and proverbs to sugar his pills. Even so, his and other innovative children's books of Queen Anne's reign were designed, quite obviously, to be chanted, to be learned by the ear rather than by the eye. They were meant more for teachers and parents to teach with than for a child to enjoy. Similar books were slow to appear, and it is not until the 1740's that the change in style of children's literature becomes marked. The entrepreneurial noses of Thomas Boreman and John Newbery twitched and scented a market for books written specifically for children that would be simple to produce and enticing to the eye. Of course, it was not quite as simple as that. Children do not buy books; adults do.

So the new children's literature was designed to attract adults, to project an image of those virtues that parents wished to inculcate in their offspring, as well as to beguile the child. By their simplicity, these alphabet and reading books also strengthened parent's confidence in their ability to teach their children to read at home. The new children's literature was aimed at the young, but only through the refraction of the approving parental eye.

By the 1740's and 1750's the market was there, ready to be exploited, and no man was quicker to seize the opportunity than John Newbery, whose *Little Pretty Pocket-Book,* published in 1744, captured the public imagination. Until the early nineteenth century Newbery's family continued to produce quantities of children's literature. Each decade the number of titles grew, and the most popular books were reprinted over and over again. The range was exceptional—from simple books for reading, writing, and arithmetic to *The Newtonian System of Philosophy Adapted to the Capacities of young Gentlemen and Ladies . . . Lectures read to the Lilliputian Society by Tom Telescope.*

The latter book is crystal-clear and the examples are exceptionally apposite. Its attitudes toward the universe, humanity, philosophy, and the natural sciences would have drawn cheers from the Encyclopedists. It is not only a brilliantly produced book for adolescent children, but it also gives us a novel insight into how the ideas of the Enlightenment were being disseminated through society. How ideas are transformed into social attitudes is a most complex problem, and social historians have almost all neglected the influence of children's literature in changing the climate of ideas. *Tom Telescope* therefore deserves a closer study.

There are six lectures. The first is on matter and motion, quite brilliantly explained. The second deals with the universe, particularly the solar system, and also with the velocity of light. Tom Telescope then moves on to atmosphere and meteors, and to mountains, particularly volcanoes, and earthquakes, and to rivers and the sea. Minerals, vegetables, and animals follow, and the final lecture is on the natural philosophy of man—his senses, the nature of his understanding, and the origin of ideas, with a great deal of optics, including the prism, and a section on pleasure and pain. The book is relatively brief—only 125 pages—but is wide-ranging, giving a simple outline of the most advanced attitudes toward the universe and man's place in it. God is present through his works and also as the divine wisdom that reason, if pursued, will ultimately reveal to mankind.

The philosophic attitude is purely Lockian, as the science is entirely Newtonian. "All our ideas, therefore," says Tom Telescope, "are obtained either by *sensation* or *reflection,* that is to say, by means of our five senses, as *seeing, hearing, smelling, tasting,* and *touching,* or by the *operations of the mind* [upon them]."

Although packed with lucid scientific information, the book has many asides, allegories, and stories that plead for a compassionate humanity, particularly toward animals. Tom's plea is based on the new attitude that cruelty to animals is improper. Cruelty between animals is necessary to sustain the animal world; hence cruelty, in this aspect, is a part of divine wisdom. But necessity alone permits human cruelty toward animals in the shape of killing and eating. Wanton cruelty is reprehensible, particularly to young animals and, above all, young birds. Most detestable of all is the taking or destruction of eggs (a common theme in eighteenth-century children's books).

Tom has no patience, however, with those who put kindness to animals before that to their fellow men. Tom's lecture reminds his hostess, Lady Caroline, of her neighbor Sir Thomas, whom young Tom has seen treat animals well if they please, "but rave, at the same time, in a merciless manner, at poor children who were shivering at his gate, and send them away empty handed." Another neighbor, Sir William, "is also of the same disposition; he will not sell a horse, that is declining, for fear he should fall into the hands of a master who might treat him with cruelty; but he is largely concerned in the slave trade (which, I think, is carried on by none but *we good Christians,* to the dishonour of our *coelestial Master*) and makes no difficulty of separating the husband from the wife, the parents from the children, and all of them . . . from their native country, to be sold in a foreign market, like so many horses, and often to the most merciless of the human race." Kindness to animals, yes, but greater kindness to human beings is the burden of Tom's final lecture.

Tom Telescope had an extraordinary success. Within a few weeks of its publication in 1761, it was on sale in Norwich and was being advertised there in the newspapers. A new edition was required in 1762, a third edition in 1766, and a fourth in 1770. All together there were at least ten editions by 1800. It is difficult, however, to be in any way certain of the size of these editions. Newbery printed fifteen hundred copies of his juvenile edition of Dr. Johnson's *Idler;* but there were editions of ten thousand for his very popular *Little Pretty Pocket-Book.* Doubtless the editions of *Tom Telescope* varied, the second probably much larger than the first, which, following Newbery's usual practice, would be small to test the market. By conservative estimate, the book probably enjoyed a sale of twenty-five to thirty thousand copies between 1760 and 1800, but the number could be far higher. Hence Lockian and Newtonian ideas, combined with a compassionate humanity, were being widely disseminated among the middle-class young.

Newbery's success with *Tom Telescope* did not go unnoticed, and the range of books on science designed for children grew. *A Museum,* published about 1750 and containing essays on natural history and the solar system, had run to fifteen editions by 1800. The Reverend Samuel Ward completed twelve such volumes on *The Modern System of Natural History* in 1776. In the same year, *Mr. Telltruth's Natural History of Birds and of Animals* was written for very young children—it too was full of reasonableness of nature. And it cost only sixpence. In 1800 one publisher advertised thirty-eight books for children, covering the arts and sciences; of these, fifteen were scientific and only two dealt with religion. Geography, history, and the classics were rapidly adapted to the needs of juvenile readers.

Newbery and other publishers also produced quantities of moral tales, more beloved, one suspects, by parents than by children. Through Edward Augustus Kendall, the Newberys produced new types of fables, derived from the ballad of Cock Robin, in which birds develop human attributes, converse freely among themselves, and offer their own criticisms of human failure and shortcomings. Kendall wrote *The Swallow, The Wren, The Canary, The Sparrow;* and their themes are simple—cruelty to birds, taking eggs, breaking up nests, and caging finches are the marks of an evil boy. Cruelty is wicked, humane behavior laudable. Charity and benevolence will not only make a child happy but bring him the proper social rewards.

A similar burden is echoed in the potted biographies of eminent children and in the examples of historic characters held up for the edification of youth. The themes of most of them are avoidance of cruelty, violence, brutality, and the development of innocent virtues like obedience, sensitivity, a love of nature, and therefore of reason, which naturally leads to industry, benevolence, and compassion. Nothing was regarded as more edifying than the death of a model child.

Augustus Francis Emilian, perhaps the most nauseating boy in all children's literature, takes twelve pages to die in *Juvenile Biography,* a translation of an eighteenth-century French novel. After being on the point of death for more than thirty-six hours, Emilian rallies sufficiently at the last moment to say, although with painful effort, "What grieves me most is to quit you Mamma, as well as not to have lived long enough to be useful to my country." Not surprisingly, "At these immortal words a rattling in the throat stifled the half-articulated words." However, death did not come for another page and a half.

Even in the enlightened eighteenth century, there continued a savage, macabre streak in attitudes toward children. (Corpse viewing—practiced at Wesley's school at Kingswood—was thought of as salutary.) Yet, the desire to entertain, delight, and instruct children had disguised, if not obliterated, much of the heavy moralizing. Between 1780 and 1800, though, the moral note gets stronger. Mrs. Sarah Trimmer was the most formidable of children's writers at that time, and Mrs. Trimmer was not light of heart. The works of Mrs. Trimmer and Mrs. Anna Barbauld, another gentlewoman who produced countless instructive and moralistic tales, covered the shelves of the Newbery bookstore when Charles Lamb and his sister Mary went there in 1802. Lamb, himself a writer of children's stories, wrote indignantly to Samuel Taylor Coleridge: " 'Goody Two Shoes' is almost out of print. Mrs. Barbauld's stuff has banished all the old classics of the nursery; and the shopman at Newbery's hardly deigned to reach them off an old exploded corner of a shelf, when Mary asked for them. Mrs. B.'s and Mrs. Trimmer's nonsense lay in piles about. Knowledge insignificant and vapid as Mrs. B.'s books convey, it seems, must come to a child in the *shape* of *knowledge,* and his empty noddle must be turned with conceit of his own powers when he has learnt that a Horse is an animal, and Billy is better than a Horse, and such like; instead of that beautiful Interest in wild tales which made the child a man, while all the time he suspected himself to be no bigger than a child . . . Think what you would have been now, if instead of being fed with Tales and old wives' fables in childhood, you had been crammed with geography and natural history!"

Nevertheless, the contrast in the range of what was available for children between, say, 1700 and 1800, is vivid. By 1800 there was no subject, scientific or literary, that did not have a specialized literature designed for children—often beautifully and realistically illustrated, at times by such distinguished book illustrators as Thomas Bewick. The simpler textbooks—for reading, writing, and arithmetic—were carefully designed, with large lettering, appropriate illustration, and a small amount of print on a large page; and there were books for very young children, such as *A Pretty Plaything for Children.* Novels specifically written about children for children began with *Sandford and Merton,* by Thomas Day. And the arts, as well as letters, were catered to—Master Michael Angelo's *The Drawing School for Little Masters and Misses* appeared in 1773, and there were books designed to teach children the first steps in music. As with adult books of the same era, less prosperous children could buy their books a part at a time. Nor was it necessary to buy the books; they could be borrowed. By 1810, there was a well-established juvenile library at 157 New Bond Street. Some owners of circulating libraries even maintained a special section for children.

As well as becoming far more plentiful, children's books also became cheaper. John Newbery used every type of gimmick to extend his market. With the *Little Pretty Pocket-Book* he offered—for an extra twopence—a ball for the son or a pincushion for the daughter. He used new types of binding that did not stain, and he even tried giving a book away when the purchaser bought the binding. He advertised his books in every possible way—rarely did a parent finish one of his books without finding in the text a recommendation to read others. He sensed that there was a huge market ready for exploitation, and he was right.

Within twenty years children's books were a thriving part of the Newcastle printer's trade; indeed, educational books attracted a very large number of provincial printers in the late eighteenth century, for they were well aware of the hunger of shopkeepers, tradesmen, and artisans for education, not only for themselves, but also, and most emphatically, for their children. The printers of Philadelphia did not lag behind those of the English provinces; they were some of the earliest in the field of children's literature outside London. In 1768 Shorhawk and Anderton, principally a firm of druggists, advertised "a very great choice of books adapted for the instruction and amusement of all the little masters and mistresses in America." (John Newbery was also the proprietor of the famous Dr. James's Fever Powder, which he plugged remorselessly in his books: the relationship between the marketing of children's books and patent medicines was always close.)

By 1800 children's books had become very cheap; those costing a penny were plentiful, and this was at a time when books in general, because of inflation, had increased in price by 25 per cent. Nevertheless, Oliver and Boyd of Edinburgh turned them out by the score under the title of *Jack Dandy's Delight.* They published forty at sixpence, twenty-six at twopence, forty at one penny, and forty at a halfpenny. The penny books were well printed and delightfully illustrated. Only the poorest families of unskilled laborers could not afford a halfpenny. Like Thomas Paine's *The Rights of Man,* children's literature was within the range of the industrious working class, and particularly of those families whose social ambition had been stirred by the growing opportunities of a new industrialized society—more and more parents were willing to make sacrifices to secure them for their children. Middle-class parents had begun to buy children's books in quantity.

From 1700 onward, the intellectual and cultural horizons of the middle-class child, and of the lower-middle-class child, had broadened vastly. There was an air of modernity about a great deal of his reading, a sense that he belonged to a new and exciting world. The same was true of a child's education, both the formal, so long as grammar school was avoided, and the informal. Itinerant lecturers in science, usually accompanied by complex electrical apparatuses, were exceptionally popular. Although their courses were mainly for adults, more often than not they offered cheap tickets for children. Indeed, this became a common practice for public amusements that were also partly educational.

The range and variety of such amusements may be demonstrated by looking at what was available at Leeds, a prospering industrial and commercial city of Yorkshire, during the summer months of 1773. In April families at Leeds were regaled by Mr. Manuel of Turin with his display of automatons, including an Indian lady in her chariot moving around the table at ten miles an hour and the "Grand Turk, in the Seraglio dress, who walks about the table smoking his pipe in a surprising manner." All the automatons, of course, were accompanied by mechanical musical instruments.

After Mr. Manuel, Mr. Pitt arrived with his principal marvel, a self-moving phaeton that traveled at six miles an hour, climbed hills, and started and stopped with the touch of a finger. He also brought along his electrifying machine, his camera obscura, his miraculous door that opened inside, outside, left, or right by the turn of a key. All this for one shilling. The phaeton either wore out, broke down, or proved too expensive to move, for it was dropped by Pitt, who continued for some years to travel the Midland circuit of Nottingham, Leicester, Coventry, and so on, but only with his scientific apparatus. Quite obviously he made a tolerable living from his traveling show.

On August 10 the attraction at Leeds was geographic, as a model of the city and suburbs of Paris arrived at the town hall. It covered eighteen square feet and was extremely elaborate. Viewing began at nine in the morning and closed at eight in the evening. In September a spectacular, double-column advertisement with woodcuts announced the arrival of Astley's circus, with prices as usual, at a shilling for front seats, sixpence for back, but Astley warned that boys trying to climb in would be taken care of by guards. He also brought along with him his famous "Chronoscope," an apparatus for measuring the velocity of projectiles.

The emphasis was on marvels, curiosities, usually mechanical or optical ones, that were new and remarkable. Hence children were given a keen sense of a new, developing, and changing world in which mechanical ingenuity and electricity and science in general played an active part—a totally different cultural atmosphere from the one their grandparents had lived in. Their cultural horizons, too, were widened by the availability of music to listen to in festivals and concerts, the cheapness of musical instruments, and the plentiful supply of music teachers. Art materials were to be found in every provincial town, and so were drawing masters, who taught in the home as well as in the school. Prints of old masters and modern artists were a commonplace of life. Visually, it was a far more exciting age for children than ever before.

Through most of these amusement, however, ran the theme of self-improvement and self-education. The same is true of indoor games as well as outdoor excursions. Playing cards had long been used to inculcate knowledge—largely geographic, historical, and classical. One of the earliest packs, from about 1700, taught carving lessons—hearts for joints of meat, diamonds for poultry, clubs for fish, and spades for meat pies. But more often than not these were imports, usually from France. The eighteenth century witnessed a rapid increase in English education playing cards, so that almost every variety of knowledge or educational entertainment could be found imprinted on their faces. The majority of booksellers, provincial as well as metropolitan, stocked them. Some cards were designed for the education of adults, or at least adolescents, but there were packs, very simply designed, for young children so they could play and learn at the same time. One pack, for example, taught the first steps in music.

After playing cards, one of the earliest educational games to be developed was the jigsaw puzzle, seemingly an English invention by the printer-bookseller and young entrepreneur John Spilsbury, who in 1762 produced dissected maps for the teaching of geography. These enjoyed an immediate, perhaps a phenomenal, success, and by the mid-1760's Spilsbury had thirty different jigsaw maps for sale. Unfortunately he died young—in his twenties—but what he had launched quickly proliferated, not only in the teaching of history, geography, and morals, but also purely for fun, though even these puzzles tended to have a moral message of self-improvement.

The principal publisher of educational games became John Wallis, whose firm began to flourish in the 1780's and lasted until 1847, during which time it dominated the field of educational games, some of which were extremely complex. In the seventeenth century, Pierre du Val had used gambling games, with painted boards and dice, to teach geography and history; indeed, it has been said that Louis XIV learned his lessons this way, for the French court and aristocracy of the seventeenth century had no inhibitions about children gambling. In England the first dice game played on a painted board for instruction seems to have been invented by John Jefferys in 1759. His game was called A Journey through Europe, or The Play of Geography, and the players moved along a marked route according to the throw of their dice. This proved very popular and spawned a host of similar games, some of extreme complexity, such as Walker's Geographical Pastime exhibiting a Complete Voyage Round the World in Two Hemispheres, which must have taken hours to play. There were also card games, often employing a rebus, which were extremely popular for teaching spelling, extending the vocabulary, and quickening the wits.

By the early nineteenth century, in spite of the novelist Maria Edgeworth's fulminations about their uselessness, almost as many kinds of educational toys were available as there are today. There were complex mechanical toys—water mills, printing presses, looms—which could be assembled and made to work. There were cheap inflatable globes, complicated perspective views, and toy theatres with movable scenery and actors, on which whole plays could be acted and reacted from the scripts provided. There were scientific toys, camera obscuras and the like, made cheaply for children. By that time, too, there were large quantities of toys on the market whose educational value was present, if secondary—Noah's arks, animal farms, soldiers and forts of every variety for the potential soldier, and of course, dolls and doll houses. These varied from the extremely

cheap—cutouts in paper with brightly colored interchangeable clothes—to elaborate models with wax or earthenware faces, jointed bodies, and complete wardrobes. And in London there were, by 1800 at least, two shops that specialized in making rocking horses. In 1730 there had been no specialized toy shops of any kind, whereas by 1780 toy shops abounded, and by 1820 the trade in toys, as in children's literature, had become very large indeed.

Children, in a sense, had become luxury objects upon which their parents were willing to spend larger and larger sums of money, not only for their education but also for their entertainment and amusement. Indeed, by the second half of the eighteenth century, the most advanced radicals had become deeply concerned by the growing indulgence of parents toward their children, particularly the waste of money on useless toys. Maria Edgeworth denounced dolls and doll houses, had no use for rocking horses, and strongly disapproved of stuffed lambs, squeaky pigs and cuckoos, and all simple action toys. She was for a pencil and plain paper, for toys that led to physical exercise—hoops, tops, and battledores—and for a pair of scissors and paper for a girl to cut out her fancies

with. Later, boys should be given models of instruments used by manufacturers—spinning wheels, looms, paper mills, and the like. The interest in Maria Edgeworth's long discussion of toys lies in the huge variety that obviously abounded in the 1790's—a variety not as extensive, of course, as today's, but reflecting our world rather than the world of seventeenth-century England.

Whatever the attitudes of parents, or of educational reformers, children had become a trade, a field of commercial enterprise for the sharp-eyed entrepreneur. The competition was fiercest, the ingenuity greatest, in children's literature and in indoor games that taught as well as amused. Both fields were remarkably inventive, and their most important feature was that they encouraged teaching in the home. They were so skillfully designed, so beautifully illustrated, that they gave confidence to parents as well as children by the ease with which they could be used. Ease of comprehension was as important as the delight of the contents, and books that combined both had an enduring success generation after generation. The most permanent effect of this revolution in children's literature was to marry text and illustration. Like all true marriages, that has proved indissoluble.

A Whole Subcontinent Was Picked Up Without Half Trying

The East India Company went to India not to conquer, but to trade, yet it ended by acquiring a jewel for Victoria's crown

Pico Iyer

The author, born of Indian parents, went to Eton and Oxford. He wrote last on the Assassins (Smithsonian, October 1985). He has written Video Night in Kathmandu, *published by Knopf.*

Images of the British raj in India are everywhere of late. On television re-runs, the divided rulers of Paul Scott's *Jewel in the Crown* sip their tea in scented hill stations and swap idle gossip in the palaces of local princes. At movie houses, we can savor all the hot intensities that blast a decorous English visitor the moment she steps ashore after *A Passage to India,* to be engulfed in a whirlwind of mendicants, elephants, snake charmers and crowds. In New York, British director Peter Brook's nine-hour production of an ancient Hindu epic poem, *The Mahabharata,* has lately been playing to packed houses and considerable critical praise. Best-selling books

like *Freedom at Midnight* re-create the struggle of two great cultures, mighty opposites with a twinned destiny, as they set about trying to disentangle themselves and their feelings before the Partition of 1947. Across the country, strolling visitors marveled a few years ago at all the silken saris and bright turbans of the Festival of India (SMITHSONIAN, June 1985) and, even more, at the exotic world they evoke: the bejeweled splendor of the Mogul courts; dusty, teeming streets; and all the dilemmas confronting the imperial British as they sought to bring Western ideas of order to one of the wildest and most complex lands on Earth.

Behind all the glamour and the glory, however, lies one of history's mischievous ironies. For the raj, which did not begin until 1858 when the British government officially took over India from a private trading company was in fact only the final act in a long, crooked and partly accidental drama. Much of the British empire, in fact, was acquired, according to a celebrated phrase, "in a fit of absence of mind."

When the London merchants of what became the East India Company first sent ships to the East in 1601, they were not bound for India at all but for the Spice Islands of the Dutch East Indies, and the English traders who set foot on the subcontinent a little later actually sought to avoid conquest. Directors back in London kept telling them that conquest would only cut into profits. "All war is so contrary to our interest," they reminded field employees in 1681, "that we cannot too often inculcate to you our strictest aversion thereunto."

But India was still part of the fading Mogul empire, which a century earlier had brought Muslim administrators and conquerors. Just to protect its ability to do business in a land already riddled with fierce animosities, the company found itself forced to defend trading posts with hired soldiers. Before long, the posts became cities (Calcutta, Bombay, Madras) and their soldier garrisons, small private armies. As assets and responsibilities mounted, the merchants, who had come out as supplicants bearing gifts to local princes for an inside track on trade, gradually became soldiers, and then became local rulers themselves.

By the time the company was disbanded in 1858, hardly more than a thousand British officers controlled India, an area the size of Europe in which 200 million people—about a quarter of them Muslim, but a majority Hindu—spoke more than 200 different languages. By then, the company had carried home such Indian terms as "bungalow," "verandah," "punch," "dungarees" and "pyjamas." They had also imported back to Britain many pukka (first class) habits such as smoking cigars, playing polo and taking showers. Most of all, they had laid the foundations for, and forced the British government to get involved in, what was about to become the most ambitious, and the most anguished, empire in modern history.

The East India Company was originally conceived in September 1599, when a group of London merchants resolved to raise £30,000 for sending ships to the East to collect silks, spices and jewels "upon a purely mercantile bottom." On the last day of the 16th century, Queen Elizabeth I gave her blessing and five British vessels set sail for what is now known as Indonesia. Upon arrival, they found the Dutch far from eager to share their profits. The British therefore turned back to India's west coast, dropping anchor near Surat in 1608, and Sir William Hawkins proceeded to the impe-rial Mogul court in Agra to seek permission to set up a trading post. But the Portuguese, who had staked some claims on the subcontinent when Vasco da Gama landed in 1498, proved quite as reluctant as the Dutch were to part with their monopoly.

TRADING REQUESTS, BACKED UP BY FORCE

As the Mogul emperor dithered about giving permissions and the Portuguese connived, the British took to backing up their local requests with threats of force. By 1639, English traders were established on the east coast, too, leasing for £600 a year a harborless beach just five miles long and one mile wide, which they christened Fort St. George (later Madras). In 1661 they picked up another site when, for a paltry annual rent of £10, King Charles II handed over a barren island called Bombay, which had been part of his dowry from Catherine of Braganza. A generation later, after some skirmishes, the company gained permission to set up shop in a stinking mudflat in Bengal; it quickly developed into Fort William (Calcutta, now a city of ten million, grew up around it).

The India that these British traders came to do business in was a thoroughly bewildering place, a vast expanse of land filled with millions of peasants ruled by a small number of princes—mostly Muslim—with power derived from a court whose opulence could put any in Europe to shame. The Moguls, a band of intruders of Mongolian, Turkish and Persian origin, had formally established their empire in India in 1526; by the time the British arrived, they ruled most of northern India save for a few fiefdoms still controlled by tribute-paying Hindu rajas. Though ruthless, the Moguls had cultivated tastes, especially for Persian-style gardens, poems and miniatures.

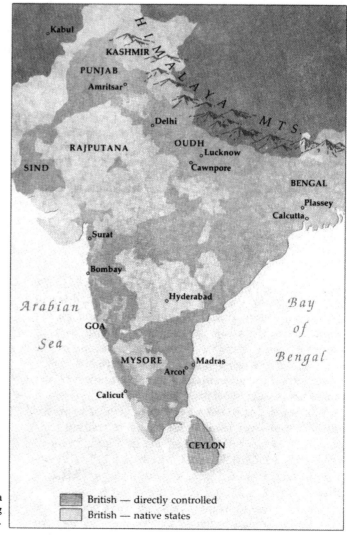

By mid-19th century, British controlled almost all of India either directly or through alliances with partially self-ruling "native states" run by rajas.

British — directly controlled
British — native states

The young emperor Jahangir, for example, boasted of slaughtering 17,000 animals and nearly 14,000 birds, yet he was a great patron of the arts. His successor, Shah Jahan, secured his throne by murdering rivals, yet he was also the romantic who built an exquisite shrine, the Taj Mahal, to the memory of a beloved wife.

Jahangir's father, Akbar, the greatest Mogul emperor, prudently married Hindu princesses, observed Hindu festivals and even placed Hindus in high office. Thus, even those he displaced were inclined to see him not as the head of a Muslim state, but simply as the Muslim head of a nonpartisan India. When Akbar died in 1605, however, the court degenerated into a series of vicious successional struggles animated by an operating principle known as *takht ya takhta* (throne or coffin). Aurangzeb, whose 49-year rule began in 1658, applied special taxes to Hindus and reputedly demolished Hindu temples, sowing the seeds of the furious Hindu-Muslim animosities that would shadow British India till the end and that

poison relations between India and Pakistan to this day.

Against this turbulent background, the British were free to ply their trade as they wished, selling silver and devices like clocks and firearms in return for cotton, spices, silk, indigo, jewels and opium. Before long the East India Company was one of the largest employers in London. In India, its major settlements developed into self-sufficient communities, with forts, warehouses, residents and even their own law courts. To defend these "civil servants," each of the trading posts also kept a company of "military servants."

The highest authority in each company settlement was a Governor-in-Council (the Governor of Madras from 1687–92 was one Elihu Yale, who a bit later bequeathed his fortune to help found a small college in New Haven) and these officials developed a taste for the regal extravagance of local potentates. By 1700, the Governor of Bombay would emerge from his private quarters only in

palanquined splendor, attended by 40 servants and preceded by underlings waving silver wands. Each course at dinner was announced by a fanfare of trumpets, and some state dinners ran to 600 different dishes.

Most junior employees, later known as griffins, arrived in India expecting to earn just £10 a year as "writers," or clerks. In anticipation of becoming factors or merchants, however, they took out loans and basked in affluence inconceivable at home. The day's work was generally confined to the hours between 9 A.M. and noon: the rest of the day was given over to eating, napping, gambling, drinking—and more drinking. During long, sweltering evenings, they smoked hookahs, sometimes loaded with opium, and were pleasantly distracted at titillating nautch dances.

If the rewards of a posting to India were high, the risks were higher. "Two monsoons are the age of a man" ran a gloomy company saying, and many a company man did not survive his first six

Carrying on the customs of the Mogul rulers, British hunted tigers from the backs of elephants, although letting the great beasts trample and gore the hunting trophies was a rare and grisly experience.

Naughty nautch parties featured food, drink, sweet music and sometimes debauchery, since many dancing girls were also prostitutes. When more Englishwomen began arriving, such pleasures, as easy racial mixing, sharply declined.

months of punishing heat and dust. If he were not laid low by malaria, cholera or smallpox, he was likely to be undone by such exotic threats as snakebite, heatstroke, jungle fever or local dancing girls. None of this was helped, of course, by amateur doctors who thought the best cure for cholera was a red-hot iron on the heel. Small wonder that Bombay became known as the "burying ground of the English."

As the Mogul empire began to collapse, a host of contenders swarmed into the vacuum. In 1789, Nadir Shah of Persia marched on Delhi, slaughtered many of its people and carried its treasures, including the Peacock Throne, back to Tehran. The Afghans, too, made intermittent raids from the northwest, and the Marathas, a predatory band of horsemen, were carving sizable chunks out of the middle of the empire. And for all the company's attempts to discourage interloping, more and more free-lance adventurers kept flocking in from Europe, equipped with forged trading passes and a hunger for a quick killing.

The threat that most unsettled the English, however, came from the French, who in the 1750s were engaged in a

global war with Britain. In 1746, the French boldly seized Madras and in 1750 their Governor, Joseph François Dupleix, ingeniously set about hiring and training native troops, known as sepoys. Dressed in smart uniforms and transformed into soldiers, these men became the envy of local princes, who were soon turning over tracts of land in exchange for French-trained sepoys. In this way France came to control a large part of southern India. The British cause seemed doomed—until a suggestion arose from a moody young man who had come over as a clerk just seven years before: Why not create a counterforce of sepoys and seize the provincial capital of Arcot, which was under French control? Then, with a vastly outnumbered force of 500 and three small field guns, Robert Clive (page 71) made good on his plan, and the French challenge in India was effectively stifled.

Hardly had the British begun to catch their breath than another threat emerged up the coast, where the new nawab of Bengal, Siraj-ud-Daula, attacked Calcutta. Leading 80,000 foot soldiers, 20,000 horsemen and 400 trained elephants

against a crumbling and ill-fortified garrison defended by scarcely 200 men, he took Fort William without much difficulty. That night, the European captives were locked up in a brig known as the Black Hole, an 18-by-14-foot room with a door on one side and, on the other, a small iron-barred window leading onto a verandah. The stifling air and crush of bodies in the room were compounded by the sweltering summer heat. When morning broke on June 21, 1756, the cell was packed with corpses.

Many scholars today believe that early claims made for the Black Hole of Calcutta—describing 128 dead out of 146—may have been inflated by a factor of three. Even so, the British could hardly fail to be psychologically chilled and outraged by an episode that dramatized all their worst fears of dark suffocation. Two British captives were said to have survived only by sucking the sweat off their shirts. Sixteen-year-old Mary Carey was rumored to have stayed alive—while her husband, her mother and her 10-year-old sister all died—by drinking her own tears.

One year after the Black Hole, Clive sailed up the coast from Madras and led

800 troops and roughly 2,000 sepoys against a force of more than 50,000 at Plassey. There, defying the odds again, he routed Sirajud-Daula. He also defied company rules by playing politician and installing as the new nawab an elderly Mogul general named Mir Jafar. By now, the crumbling Mogul empire was in no position to resist; indeed, in 1765, the emperor actually made Clive his dewan (revenue collector) for the whole state of Bengal. Thus the company found itself controlling one of the richest provinces in the land, source of almost two-thirds of all Britain's imports from Asia.

After the takeover of Bengal, relations between the British and the natives changed radically. Company merchants were now free to roam the province, helping themselves to the fruits of the land through joint ventures with Indian partners. Suddenly they were in a position to expect presents themselves. They could not only live with the local rulers, they could live like them, too.

With their "Honorable Masters" nine months' passage and 7,000 miles away, the company men, unsupervised and uncircumscribed, began "shaking the pagoda tree" to their heart's content. Clive was given £211,500 by the nawab he had installed and, 18 months later, another grant assuring him of £27,000 a year for life—at a time when a gentleman in England could live well on £800 a year. Even that much was perhaps Clive's due. But one Mr. Watts was rewarded for his bravery at Plassey with £117,000. Another British merchant was given a very profitable saltworks complete with a staff of 13,000 workers. Still another set up his own mint. Even so, for every British fortune made, ten native fortunes were accumulated.

As news of such profligate doings reached London, the city was scandalized. But every young man wanted a position in India, and company panjandrums in England, no strangers to corruption themselves, were soon accepting £2,000 or more in bribes to secure them such positions. "Animated with all the avarice of age and all the impetuosity of youth," Edmund Burke would tell assembled members of Parliament, traders "roll in one after another; wave after wave; and there is nothing before the eyes of the native but an endless hopeless prospect of new birds of prey and passage."

Most outrageous of all to many in the British squirearchy was that once they

Fiercest Englishman in India, Robert Clive won crucial battles, went home filthy rich but unhappy.

got back home, the self-appointed nawabs—nabobs, as the corrupted term had it—were beginning to overturn Britain's age-old social structure. Clive, for example, had gone to India the unpromising son of a penurious country gentleman. By the time he returned in 1760, he was the equivalent of a millionaire and a local hero rich enough to repair his family home, buy another nearby, purchase an estate in Ireland and snap up a house in London's fashionable Berkeley Square. Just for good measure, he also helped himself to a "rotten borough" seat in Parliament. Yet the company was sinking toward bankruptcy. In 1773, the directors had to appeal to the Bank of England for a £1.4 million loan.

Though the government granted the loan, it made an attempt to curb the company's authority. Under the Regulating Act of 1778, all business in India was to be overseen by a Governor General in Calcutta, who would put an end to both "private trade" and those infamous "presents." Eleven years later, Parliament established a six-man Board of

Control, including two members of Parliament, to sit above the company directors. This was the first step that would eventually lead to the raj, the period of official British government control.

Warren Hastings (page 72), the first Governor General, could not have been further removed from the idle and indulgent nabobs: even as de facto ruler of British India from 1772–85, he rode eight miles each day before breakfast, drank nothing stronger than tea, took cold baths and turned in at 10 every night. Under the Governor General's highly principled eye, extracurricular profits were quickly cut down, earned salaries somewhat increased.

More than just instilling a new sense of discipline, Hastings brought a sense of civility. He was an educated man, schooled in Persian and Bengali and firmly convinced that the company should treat local customs with respect. He skillfully persuaded Indian princes to form alliances with the company, and under his influence scholars introduced the rest of the world to India's fascinating cultures.

To support this approach, he began importing a new kind of British official, young men willing to study local languages and traditions, more devoted to king and country than to self. In time, such types became the backbone of the body that would be the brightest creation of the British raj: the Indian Civil Service.

More and more men streamed into the subcontinent: not just *boxwallah* traders now, but soldiers, scholars and sophisticated young administrators. And as they tried to make themselves at home in alien land, the newcomers laid the foundations of that closed society of splendor and heartache that would later so fascinate E. M. Forster and Paul Scott. For where the rough-and-ready merchants of old had lived like local princelings, the new arrivals preferred to live like well-heeled Britons. Tom-toms were gradually replaced by fife-and-drum corps, curries by English dishes and local clothes by the latest (or almost latest) London fashions. Country houses complete with tidy gardens began to spring up along the Hooghly River in Calcutta. Places like the Bread and Cheese Bungalow, the Jockey Club and Eden Gardens began to crop up around the City of Palaces. The city of Calcutta came to resemble a sweet-and-sour Bath.

Each morning before the heat of midday, in this imported version of England intensified and exaggerated by its distance from home, the entire beau monde would travel en masse to the local racecourse, and every day at dusk would take the air in carriages along the Embankment. Days would pass in one long round of social calls and afternoon naps, evenings in card games, recitals, balls and dinner parties (complete with sherbet: ice from Maine was delivered by sailing vessel). Musical entertainments like *The Poor Soldier* began to be staged at local theaters, with farces bravely attempted in which women's roles were taken by "awkward giants with splay feet, gruff voices and black beards." Before long, even that last deficiency was being taken care of: each October, shiploads of eligible young women began arriving with the cooler weather in what later came to be known as the Fishing Fleet; each spring, a few Returned Empties sadly took the long, unmarried journey home.

British-Indian society still shone with an air of gilded gentility. Silken canopies graced the private boxes at Calcutta theaters, while palanquins with golden bells

and embroidered curtains were carried down St. Thomas Road. One typical bachelor in Calcutta in the 1780s kept 63 servants. Even a man at war did not consider relinquishing his sense of privilege: a captain going to battle in 1780 was generally accompanied by a steward, a cook, a "boy," a horsekeeper, a grass cutter, a washerman and, of course, a mistress. He also had to bring along at least 15 coolies to transport his tent and large bed, camp stools, folding table, maybe six trunkfuls of tableware, cases of wine, a hamper of live poultry, a goat and, not surprisingly, an extra tent for supplies.

HYDER ALI AND TIPU SULTAN

Such extravagance and eccentricity were hardly confined to the British side, of course. Against them were arrayed colorful adversaries like Hyder Ali and his son Tipu Sultan, who in the 1760s seized control of the predominantly Hindu state of Mysore and proceeded to run it as their own private fiefdom. For decades, father and son were a constant menace to the British presence in the south, now and then setting fire to the country houses on the outskirts of Madras and

leading their mercenary *lootywallahs* on one pillaging expedition after another.

Not far away, the British faced another kind of resistance from courtly Muhammad Ali, whom they had installed as nawab of Arcot. Though constantly entwined in shady deals and entangled in ceaseless financial wrangles, the tall and dignified gentleman somehow contrived to live like a king for 50 years. Each day, palanquins filled with Europeans determined to collect money owed would line up outside his Chepauk Palace in Madras; each night, the same men could be seen retreating, still unpaid but thoroughly won over by his apologies and charming ways. At his death, the Ali left behind outstanding debts of more than £30 million.

As the 18th century drew to a close, British India became more and more divided by its own distinctive caste system and plagued by scurrilous gossip and social rivalry. The first great victim of snobbery was, ironically enough, Hastings. In spite of—or maybe because of—his success in bringing some order to India, the Governor General was challenged by jealous rivals and in 1787, after returning to London, he faced impeachment charges in effect blaming him for everything that had gone wrong in

First Governor General, Warren Hastings tried to reform British rule and was slandered for his trouble.

India. After a spectacular, protracted trial he was acquitted. Lord Cornwallis, the patrician soldier who had surrendered to George Washington at Yorktown just five years earlier, was sent to India as a replacement. To some degree, Cornwallis extended his predecessor's program of moral reform, establishing auditors to oversee expenses, enforcing an absolute distinction between those who governed and those who traded. Yet he had few of Hastings' wide sympathies: summarily removing from high office in Calcutta every native but one, he sought to stamp out the threat of corruption by attacking the spirit of cooperation.

Lord Wellesley, who took over as Governor General in 1798, was quite another sort of imperial aristocrat. Realizing that his overseers at home were preoccupied with the threat from Napoleon, and rationalizing his assertiveness by pointing to the French march into Egypt in 1798, he briskly set about extending British authority. His troops defeated Tipu Sultan, trounced the long-troublesome Marathas and annexed Indian territory left and right by pressing permanent alliances on local princes. By the time he was recalled in 1805, the grip of the British could be felt across the entire subcontinent.

That year, Wellesley, without the knowledge of the directors back home, set up in Calcutta a kind of Oxbridge-on-the-Hooghly named Fort William College. Here young Englishmen were to learn such languages as Arabic, Persian, Urdu and Sanskrit while cultivating a deeper understanding of local traditions. Thus Wellesley came to embody both the main strains, imperialism and Orientalism, that would compete for preeminence throughout the raj. The company was in control of much of India; now it had to decide whether to treat the place as treasure chest, military base, branch office or incipient independent nation. As the British set about "improving" India, for better and for worse, they were driven partly by their arrogant sense of rectitude, partly by an earnest sense of duty, the mixed feelings that would give the raj its tragic, bittersweet tang.

Through it all, the company was more and more supervised by Parliament. In 1813, despite a renewed charter, it was stripped of its Indian trading monopoly. Twenty years later, the company was again allowed to survive, but its assets were liquidated, its ships dispersed and

its directors left with little power. At the same time, Indians were allowed to hold increasingly higher administrative posts.

Yet for all its diminishing power, the last 50 years of the East India Company's presence in India in some respects marked a kind of golden age. This was due in large part to a group of thoughtful Englishmen who saw themselves as guardians of a fledgling state and who were committed to preparing the Indians for eventual self-government. The Britons' duty, according to one of them, Mountstuart Elphinstone, was "to prevent people making laws for [India] until they see whether it wants them."

Typical of the best of these men was Charles Metcalfe, of Eton and Fort William College, a solitary and introspective soul who first proved his mettle at 23 when he was sent to deal with Maharaja Ranjit Singh. Famous for his harem, his opium addiction and his possession of the Koh-i-noor diamond, the one-eyed Singh had established a powerful kingdom among the warlike Sikhs, which was guarded by a well-trained army led by European mercenaries. Yet somehow, in an unexpected development that was to become one of the most moving and oft-repeated features of the raj, the British scholar and the flamboyant Indian chieftain struck up a friendship and they sealed it with a treaty of mutual respect.

In recognition of this diplomatic coup, Metcalfe was made Resident at Delhi at the tender age of 27, which meant he presided over an area half the size of Britain. By encouraging agriculture, Metcalfe virtually quadrupled revenues in only six years; more important, perhaps, he abolished the slave trade and outlawed capital punishment, at a time when the former was still going strong in the United States and the latter was often still the lot of a 40-shilling thief in Britain. "Our dominion in India is by conquest," Metcalfe wrote. "It is naturally disgusting to the inhabitants and can only be maintained by military force. It is our positive duty to render them justice, to respect and protect their rights."

While such men sought to nurture Indian culture, another group steadfastly believed that Britain had a very different kind of moral mission in India—to rescue the locals from the darkness of heathen superstition. No longer were Hinduism and Islam merely regarded as strange and distasteful; now they were seen as positively immoral. Even William Wilberforce, Britain's leading crusader

against slavery, told Parliament in 1818 that he hoped to see the subcontinent "exchange its dark and bloody superstition for the genial influence of Christian light and truth."

RITUAL MURDER AND SELF-IMMOLATION

Both conflicting impulses came together in one of the last of the company's great Governors General, William Bentinck, who was determined to promote British interests, but only by increasing Indian happiness. After canvassing the opinions of Hindus, he outlawed the custom of suttee, whereby Hindu widows were required to fling themselves upon their husband's funeral pyre. Perhaps the most urgent challenge Bentinck faced was the rising threat of thuggee, the practice of ritual murder that by the 1820s was claiming some 20,000 victims a year. Working in small groups, the Thugs (our word originated here) would fall in with travelers and journey by their side for days or even weeks at a time, often under the pretext of protecting them. Then one night, when the moment was right, the Thugs would suddenly fall upon their companions and strangle them with consecrated bandanas before flinging them into graves as offerings to Kali, goddess of destruction. More than 40 Thug groups existed in India—one man alone boasted 719 murders—until Bentinck, through a system of informers, brought them to justice.

As the British came to govern more and more of India, they developed an even stronger feeling of racial superiority, the spirit of paternalism carrying not only concern but all the condescension that the word can imply. The increased separation of the races had been intensified by the growing presence of upper-class British women on the subcontinent. Women led more insulated lives than their husbands and, rarely seeing the locals, were apt to fear or disdain them. By now, therefore, Indians were no longer sharing nautch parties with their British neighbors and company men were no longer paying courtesy calls on local maharajas. The view of many memsahibs was sadly reflected in the dismissive judgment of one Mrs. Graham, circa 1809, in her *Journal of a Residence in India:* "These [Indian] people, if they have the virtues of slaves, have their vices also. They are cunning and incapable of truth; they disregard the imputation of lying and perjury and would consider it folly not to practise them for their own interest."

For their part, many Indians were increasingly alarmed by all this. Their outrage was hardly soothed when the British responded to a humiliating defeat in the First Afghan War and the disastrous retreat from Kabul with a flurry of saber-rattling and territorial acquisition. In 1848 they annexed the Punjab. In 1856 they took over the large, corrupt and troubled province of Oudh. And they continued to show less and less respect for local customs.

In 1857, native grievances flared up in one dramatic blaze. The final explosion was sparked by a relatively small charge: the introduction of a new kind of Enfield rifle, whose cartridges, it was rumored, had to be greased not with wax and vegetable oil, as before, but with animal fat. The British were sensitive to the fact that no Hindu would touch cow's fat and no Muslim would touch pig's fat; some-

how, though, their orders granting permission to use vegetable oil either got confused or distorted. When 85 sepoys were thrown into jail for refusing to accept the new cartridges, their enraged comrades stormed the prison and the whole blood-crazed mob set to murdering every foreign man, woman or child they could lay hands on.

While a few pockets of the country got caught up in the bedlam of the mutiny, most parts remained fairly calm. Nobody, however, could ignore the tales of atrocities on both sides. Perhaps the most famous event was the sepoy siege of Lucknow. At Cawnpore (now Kanpur), hundreds of European women and children surrendered on guarantee of safe passage—and all were promptly and brutally slaughtered. In response, the British staged mass hangings and bayoneted mutinous sepoys on sight. Near Amritsar, the incident of the Black Hole was horribly repeated, and reversed, as one Major Cooper executed 287 captives, only to find that another 45 had died of suffoca-

tion in the tiny police station to which he had committed them. After five months of bloodshed, when the mutiny was put down by the British and loyal Indian troops, the government of Great Britain took over all responsibility from the British East India Company.

Commerce now formally gave way to empire. And despite the protestation of one of its chief executives, John Stuart Mill, the company that had been signed into being by Queen Elizabeth I was now signed into extinction by Queen Victoria. Its army was reorganized into the Indian Army; its Governor General, Lord Canning, became the first Viceroy of India. Thus began the last act of a drama that would culminate 90 years later in Gandhi's campaign of nonviolent resistance and in Paul Scott's heart-torn figures stranded in an imperial twilight. By the time India gained independence in 1947, it was hard for anyone to recall that the whole adventure had begun almost 350 years before with a group of merchants in search of nothing more than a "quiet trade."

The Godfather of the American Constitution

Montesquieu, a French baron with radical ideas, bequeathed us our 'checks and balances'

Robert Wernick

Mr. Wernick, a regular contributor, wrote about Philippe Egalité and the French Revolution.

First novels are often erotic and almost always autobiographical. *The Persian Letters,* one of the earliest and most famous of European novels, published anonymously in Amsterdam and a runaway best-seller of the 1720s, is a bit of both.

Its author, Charles-Louis de Secondat, Baron de La Brède, Baron de Montesquieu, winegrower and man of letters, nobleman and philosopher of liberty, is having the 300th anniversary of his birth celebrated this year. By a happy coincidence this is also the 200th anniversary of the convening of the first Federal Congress empowered under the new American Constitution. Curiously enough, we began to exist as a nation upon the adoption of a Constitution drawn up by men who knew Montesquieu's political views practically by heart and regarded him as an oracle.

The young man who brought out *The Persian Letters* in 1721 was a long way from being an oracle, but the cast of his character was already formed. He was bright, irreverent and fascinated by the ever-changing spectacle of 18th-century life. The novel consists of a stream of imaginary letters flowing back and forth between Persia and Paris. Two young Persian noblemen, Usbek and Rica, have gone abroad to observe the exotic customs of the Europeans, which gives the author a chance to poke a good deal of fun at the laws and morals, doctors and lawyers and society ladies of Paris that flourished during the reign of Louis XIV, the "Sun King"—all seen through the bemused yet coolly rational eyes of complete outsiders.

Their letters, describing the odd and irrational ways of the West, are matched by letters written by wives and eunuchs of the harem back in Ispahan. Of course, the missives from home reveal a life far more odd and irrational than anything Usbek and Rica are lampooning abroad. Usbek, the mild-mannered Persian gentleman visiting Paris salons, is a despot in his own harem, with power of life and death over a number of women who are allowed to see no other man and who have no function in life except to satisfy their husband's every whim. While the master spends months, and finally, years, sending them sprightly letters about the manners of the infidels, the women pour out on paper their repressed sensuality, their peevish jealousies and resentments and childish tantrums. From a safe distance Usbek tries to calm them down. The book ends melodramatically when Roxana, the most cherished of Usbek's wives, is caught in bed with a lover, declares her independence and kills herself.

In real life Montesquieu never had the bad taste to imitate literature. No suicide, in fact no display of violent emotion of any kind, was to mar his well-regulated existence. Passion rather bored him. One person in love, he observed, was very much like any other, while the world of ideas was full of infinite variety. He took a cool, distant view of his own as well as other people's behavior. His wide-ranging studies had taught him that the same actions can take on very different aspects at different times and in different places.

Like Usbek, he was an aristocrat who never really had to worry about where the money was coming from. He had forebears in both the sworded nobility (*noblesse d'épée*) and the gowned nobility (*noblesse de robe*), those high-born, black-frocked men who, from the 15th century until the revolution, dispensed the laws of France from seats in the regional *parlements* of the kingdom. Despite their name, the *parlements* had little in common with the English Parliament. They were primarily law courts, and a seat in any one of them—like most administrative posts in the French government of the ancien régime—was a commodity that could be passed on by inheritance, as Montesquieu's uncle did to him, or sold to the highest suitable bidder, as Montesquieu himself would do at age 36 when he got tired of his official duties and needed a little extra cash.

As a great landowner and a *parlementaire,* Montesquieu accepted the privileges and prejudices of his class. He knew the limitations of the *parlements,* but he defended them on the grounds that a man who had put out a good deal of money to get a government office was more apt to show independent judgment than one appointed by the king and serving at the royal whim.

From a 20th-century standpoint, his private life looks more like Usbek's than perhaps he would have appreciated. His profitable marriage with a Protestant woman, only a year before his uncle's death, made Montesquieu extremely rich. Although he appreciated his wife (she was a first-rate housekeeper and bookkeeper), he paid as little attention to her as possible. She remained devoted to him, competently managing the chateau and vineyards of La Brède while he traveled, visiting the leading intellectual figures of England, Germany and Italy, or kept up a fashionable bachelor's establishment in Paris. He had a number of affairs with ladies of quality, some of them stormy—but never stormy enough to disturb the equilibrium of his life. The most important thing about an affair, Montesquieu said, was to know how to break it off cleanly once the thrill was gone.

At La Brède, he said affectionately, Nature wore her bathrobe, and he regularly went back to enjoy the place at grape-picking season, staying until he had overseen arrangements for selling his wine to discriminating customers all over Europe. He had three children, including a daughter Denise, of whom he was very fond. But noble lineages are not built on fondness. When it became clear that his only son was not going to have a male heir, he married off Denise, much against her will, to a third cousin twice her age. He was a dull creature, but the match would perpetuate the name and keep the property in the family.

What Montesquieu really considered important, however, was study and the play of ideas, mostly to be found in Paris when he was free of all his family affairs. This was the great age of witty but serious conversation, a perpetual play of give-and-take among the finest minds in Europe. Though his ideas had his own personal coloring, they generally reflected the intellectual climate of the day. This was the dawn of the Enlightenment, and a radical and self-confident group of thinkers, known as philosophes, were proposing nothing less than tearing down the structure of ideas on which European civilization had rested for centuries and putting a new one in its place.

They had grown up in a world in which it was assumed that chaos could best be kept at bay if speech, thought, trade and faith were regulated by the central authority of church and state. In the face of all that, the philosophes preached about freedom of thought and speech, equality under the law, separation of church and state, religious toleration, representative government, public education, individual rights—liberties that the Western world now takes for granted, as if they had always existed as part of the human heritage.

Eighteenth-century intellectual activity in France was typically conducted in a *salon,* where a society hostess would regularly invite a group of congenial people for food and civilized talk. Like the cocktail party, its much-debased modern derivative, the salon provided an opportunity for exchanging gossip, for amatory intrigue, for pulling delicate political strings. Its main function, however, was to stimulate freewheeling discussion of new and provocative ideas. In the salon of an expert hostess like Julie de Lespinasse, the guests were "so well assorted that they were in harmony like the strings of an instrument in the hands of a skilled tuner."

Whenever he visited a new town, Montesquieu liked to climb up a high tower and get a good overall look at the place, then come down and examine different parts of it at leisure. He approached intellectual problems in rather the same way. This was the Age of Reason, before specialists and experts had taken over everything, and a well-educated man might still claim all knowledge as his province. Montesquieu presented to the Academy of Bordeaux learned papers on such heterogeneous subjects as Echoes, the Transparency of Objects, and the Uses of the Kidney Glands. He made an Olympian survey of general principles, then leaped down among the details, following them with no fixed plan, much as they might come up in the course of a brisk conversation with such philosophes as Helvétius and Voltaire, in the salon of Madame de Tencin or Madame Geoffrin.

This was not an efficient method of studying the physical sciences, but it was suited perfectly to the loose-jointed masterpiece on which he spent 15 years or so of his life—and to which he was still adding variations when he lay old and blind and dying in his library at La Brède. This work is *L'Esprit des Lois* (*The Spirit of the Laws*) whose more than 600 chapters are grouped in 31 books. Completed in 1743 and published in 1748, it is one of the most influential works of all time, a treatise celebrated enough to have a big city street named after it: Bordeaux's Boulevard de l'Esprit des Lois. *L'Esprit* is a grab bag of general principles and particular observations, with a theory of government, and many reflections on ancient and modern history. Montesquieu also commented on the influence of climate on national character and wrote an outline

of what (a hundred years later) would receive the name of sociology. The section that had the most impact on America dealt with the separation of powers (legislative, executive and judicial), drawn from his conversations in England with Viscount Bolingbroke.

Montesquieu began with the then highly radical premise that laws are not the result of a divine revelation to Moses or Lycurgus or any other of the traditional lawgivers of antiquity, but a natural evolution out of everything that influences the life of a country, including climate, soil, habit, tradition, history, religion and even how the inhabitants make their living. A rational man, he said, could study these matters the way Newton had studied the natural world, and use the knowledge to adjust the laws of his country in the direction of greater liberty for all. As two of Montesquieu's most avid American readers, James Madison and Alexander Hamilton, put it in the *Federalist* papers, men were now capable of "establishing good government from reflection and choice," instead of having to "depend for their political constitutions on accident and force."

Madison and Hamilton were babes in arms when *The Spirit of the Laws* appeared in 1748. Great Britain's colonies in North America were just that, part of the British empire and proud of it. They would soon help the mother country fight a great war against French colonists and their Indian allies to the north and west. Nevertheless, it was in these English colonies that some of Montesquieu's notions took deepest root.

When Americans began to grow restive under the distant rule of England, Montesquieu's writings provided them with a framework of ideas into which they could fit their grievances and their aspirations. In England, Bolingbroke had taught Montesquieu to dislike statesman Robert Walpole's tight hold on the Colonies in the reigns of George I and George II. Now the Colonists used Montesquieu to strengthen resistance to George III.

They believed that their rights were guaranteed by the constitution of England, but there was no written constitution of England they could appeal to. The English constitution was, and still is, an unwritten fundamental consensus of the proper rules of governing for the British nation. In fact, in 1748 there had never been a nation anywhere in the world with a written constitution. But, as a great admirer of the English, Montesquieu recognized that in England something new had evolved. It was "neither a classical republic nor a feudal monarchy," as Professor Judith Shklar put it in a paper read at a symposium on Montesquieu held in Washington, D.C. last spring, "but a liberal state, with a representative government, separation of powers, and judicial enforcement of personal rights. By explicating this new order so succinctly and clearly, Montesquieu in effect wrote out a new English constitution that was the equivalent of a first draft available to future constitution-makers."

The blueprint Montesquieu furnished Americans had two important features, both from the wonderworking *Spirit of the Laws,* Book XI, Chapters 3 and 6. One important idea was the definition he gave to "liberty," that watchword of the American Revolution. "Liberty is the right of doing whatever the law permits." To Americans, in 1776 or 1989, that meant a law-abiding citizen "had the right to be left alone." Chapter 6 gave American Constitution writers their holy writ. But, Montesquieu added, a man's sense of liberty is related to his feeling of personal safety. "In order to have this liberty, it is requisite the government be so constituted as one man need not be afraid of another."

England had such a government, Montesquieu believed, and its great virtue was a separation of the civil authority into three branches that did not overlap. "When the legislative and executive powers are united in the same person, or in the same body of magistrates, there can be no liberty. . . . Again, there is no liberty, if the power of judging be not separated from the legislative and executive powers." Nearly all the 55 lawyers and planters who served in the Federal Convention of 1787 took this lesson to heart.

At the Convention, James Madison cited Montesquieu as his authority for insisting on the separation of the executive, legislative and judicial powers in the new government, forerunner of the celebrated system of checks and balances we use today. The man more than any other responsible for our Constitution (SMITHSONIAN, September 1987), Madison also used the words of Chapter 6 as the text for his sermon on the separation-of-powers principle in his influential *Federalist* 47.

Madison encountered Montesquieu at Princeton under the guidance of Presi-

dent Witherspoon. Several other members of the Convention that drew up the Constitution in Philadelphia in the summer of 1787 had studied *The Spirit of the Laws* under Witherspoon, too. So thoroughly did he drill the subject into his pupils that, 20 years after leaving college, Madison could still quote whole paragraphs from memory. Madison, in effect, also used Montesquieu as a straw man, when he exploded Montesquieu's idea that republics are unstable and can exist only in a confined area—like England—with a homogeneous population. Not so, said Madison, on the Convention floor and later in his *Federalist* 10. In a small state or territory a majority could act in concert "and execute their plans of oppression." But in an extended republic such as the United States, he insisted, the large number of parties made such collusion almost impossible. "In the extent and proper structure of the Union"—a republic that would be 1,300 miles long and 1,000 miles wide—"we behold a republican remedy for the diseases most incident to republican government."

Significantly, even when Madison tried to convince his fellow delegates that, contrary to Montesquieu, the very diversity of the 13 states insured that no one group or interest would come to dominate, he did so by appealing to another of Montesquieu's precepts—the spirit of practical moderation. Montesquieu favored compromise and adjustment. Just as did the lawyers and planters of the Convention in Philadelphia, who no longer had a revolution to win but needed to set up a system that would work, he hated extremes.

Because Montesquieu had only limited faith in the goodness of human nature, he reasoned that anyone who possessed power would be likely to increase it, and the only way to stop him was by a system of rival powers, a view that the Founding Fathers, fearful alike of the tyranny by the many or the few, thoroughly subscribed to. "The oracle who is always consulted and cited on this subject," said Madison, "is the celebrated Montesquieu. If he be not the author of this invaluable precept in the science of politics, he has the merit at least of displaying and recommending it most effectually to the attention of mankind."

Montesquieu always had his eye on the matter of fact. His ideas might be revolu-

tionary, but he was never a revolutionary himself. Freedom was something that grew gradually out of the history of a country, not something that could be imposed by one group of people on another. If he had lived long enough to hear Rousseau talk about the necessity of forcing men to be free, or Saint-Just proclaim that a "republic consists in the extermination of everything that opposes it," Montesquieu would have thought he was dealing with madmen.

"Political liberty," he wrote, "consists in security; or, at least, in the opinion that we enjoy security." Modern critics of U.S. Supreme Court decisions that seem to give accused persons too many rights might ponder Montesquieu's belief that "It is on . . . the goodness of criminal laws that the liberty of all subjects principally depends." Montesquieu had no illusions that men left to themselves would automatically strive for the betterment of the human race. His historical studies had taught him how efficient and long-lasting a despotism, based on pure terror and violence, could be. He would have put no faith at all in the pronouncement of another French nobleman who played a major role in the Enlightenment, Jefferson's friend and idol, the Marquis de Condorcet, who predicted that "the moment will arrive when the sun will shine on none but free men."

Condorcet was a much deeper and more original thinker than Montesquieu. A mathematical genius and a man of great generosity of spirit and breadth of vision, Condorcet had every quality except common sense. He hated Montesquieu's idea of the separation of powers because it muddied the pure radiance of his idea of universal liberty. All power to the people, Condorcet declared, and forget all this nonsense about checks and balances, which can only frustrate the people's will. Montesquieu could have told him (and he did, in Book V, Chapter 11) that if you start with direct rule by the people you are likely to end up with a concentration of despotic power that is far worse than any king's.

The French Revolution of 1789 began, true to Montesquieu's legacy, in a spirit of reform, but it was soon taken over by extremists. In the name of liberty and the people, a few hundred members of the Parisian Jacobin Club seized power and (among other things) proceeded to condemn Condorcet to death for having opinions different from their own.

Condorcet spent the last months of his life in hiding from Robespierre's bloodhounds, writing a voluminous work to prove by rigorous logic that the human mind was infinitely perfectible. One day, famished and exhausted, he stumbled into a roadside inn and ordered an omelet. When they asked him how many eggs he wanted in it, he didn't know what to say—a marquis, even an impoverished marquis like Condorcet, would never have had any reason to be inside a kitchen—and he answered at random, "Twelve." Marked out at once as a suspicious character, he spent the next two nights in jail and escaped the guillotine through death by poison or a heart attack.

Montesquieu, the winegrower who had to deal every year with the unforgiving necessities of soil, climate and human perverseness, always knew how many eggs went into his omelets. Once he had been to the top of his tower, he liked to come down and feel the earth under his feet. He had no use for the kind of philosopher who deals only with abstract generalities.

It was that solid, down-to-earth feeling which made Montesquieu's ideas so congenial to the Madisons and Hamiltons, who were trying to deal with the intractable materials of local selfish interests and build them into a united commonwealth. And that is why this suave, quietly ironic, long-nosed French nobleman became, in effect, the godfather of the United States of America.

The French Revolution in the Minds of Men

Maurice Cranston

Maurice Cranston, a former Wilson Center Guest Scholar, is professor of political science at the London School of Economics. Born in London, he was educated at St. Catherine's College and Oxford University. His books include John Stuart Mill *(1965),* Jean-Jacques: The Early Life and Work of Jean-Jacques Rousseau, 1712–54 *1982, and* John Locke: A Biography *(1985).*

On July 14, 1989—Bastille Day— political and cultural leaders of every ideological persuasion assembled in Paris to celebrate the bicentennial of the French Revolution. Was there something strange about their unanimous applause? All subsequent major revolutions, such as those that took place in Russia and China, remain controversial today. But the French Revolution, which served as the direct or indirect model for these later upheavals, now passes for an innocuous occasion which anyone, Marxist or monarchist, can join in celebrating.

Was this proof only of the anaesthetizing power of time, that two centuries could turn the French Revolution into a museum piece, an exhibition acceptable to all viewers, even to a descendent of the old Bourbon monarchs? Or is there something about the French Revolution itself that, from its beginning, sets it apart from later revolutions?

The *tricouleur,* the *Marseillaise,* the monumental paintings of David—all celebrate a series of connected events, alternately joyous and grim, which make up the real, historical French Revolution. But there is another French Revolution, one which emerged only after the tumultuous days were over and the events and deeds became inflated or distorted in the minds of later partisans. This is the French Revolution as myth, and it is in many ways the more important of the two.

It is so, one could argue, because the myth, and not the reality, inspired the scores of revolutions that were to come. The actors of the French Revolution, announcing their principles on behalf of all mankind, clearly intended their deeds to have a mythic dimension. They wanted to inspire others to follow their example. Consider the Declaration of the Rights of Man, passed in August of 1789. At no point does it refer to the specific conditions or laws of France. Instead, it speaks in grand universals, as if it were the voice of mankind itself. Replete with terms like citizen, liberty, the sacred rights of man, the common good, the document provides the lexicon for all future revolutions.

By contrast, the earlier revolutionary models which stirred the French in 1789 to act—the English Revolution of 1688 and the American Revolution of 1776— had been essentially political events, limited in scope and conservative in objectives. The English revolutionists claimed to restore the liberty that the despotic James II had destroyed; the American revolutionaries made the kindred claim that they were only defending their rights against tyrannical measures introduced by George III. Neither revolution sought to change society.

The French Revolution, however, sought to do exactly that. Indeed, to many of the more zealous French revolutionaries, the central aim was the creation of a new man—or at least the liberation of pristine man, in all his natural goodness and simplicity, from the cruel and corrupting prison of the traditional social order.

It is easy to see how this grandiose vision of the Revolution's purpose went hand-in-hand with the emergence of Romanticism. The great Romantic poets and philosophers encouraged people throughout the West to believe that imagination could triumph over custom and tradition, that everything was possible given the will to achieve it. In the early 1790s, the young William Wordsworth expressed the common enthusiasm for the seemingly brave and limitless new world of the Revolution:

> France standing on the top of golden hours, And human nature seeming born again.

Here we encounter one of the many differences between reality and myth. The reality of the French Revolution, as Tocqueville maintained, was prepared by the rationalist philosophers of the 18th-century Enlightenment, by Voltaire, Diderot, Helvétius, d'Alembert, and Holbach no less than by Rousseau. Its myth, however, was perpetuated during the 19th century by Romantic poets such as Byron, Victor Hugo and Hölderlin. Byron in his life and in his poetry bore witness to that romanticized revolutionary idealism, fighting and then dying as he did to help the Greeks throw off the Turkish yoke and set up a free state of their own.

The grandeur of its lofty aims made the French Revolution all the more attractive to succeeding generations of revolutionaries, real and would-be; the violence added theatrical glamor. The guillotine—itself an invention of gruesome fascination—together with the exalted status of its victims, many of them royal, noble, or political celebrities, made the Terror as thrilling as it was alarming. The wars which broke out in 1793, when France declared war on Great Britain, Holland, and Spain, were fought not by professional soldiers but by conscripts, ordinary men who were expected to "know what they fought for and love what they know." These wars were thought of as wars of liberation. It hardly mattered that Napoleon turned out to be an imperialist conqueror no better than Alexander or Caesar; he was still a *people's* emperor.

If historians of the French Revolution are unanimous about any one point, it is this: that the Revolution brought the people into French political life. To say that it introduced "democracy" would be to say too much. Although popular suffrage in varying degrees was instituted as the revolution unfolded, no fully democratic system was set up. But popular support came to be recognized as the only basis for legitimating the national government. Even the new despotism of Napoleon had to rest on a plebiscitary authority. These plebiscites, which allowed voters only to ratify decisions already made, denied popular sovereignty in fact while paying tribute to it in theory. (The vote for the Constitution which made Napoleon emperor in 1804—3,500,000 *for* versus 2,500 *against*—hardly suggests a vigorous democracy.)

But if Napoleon's government was not democratic, it was obviously populistic. The people did not rule themselves, but they approved of the man who ruled them. The end of Napoleon's empire in 1815, which was also in a sense the end of the historical French Revolution, could only be brought about by the intervention of foreign armies.

Those foreign armies could place a king on the throne of France, as they did with Louis XVIII in 1815, but they could not restore the principle of royal sovereignty in the hearts of the French people. They simply put a lid on forces which would break out in another revolution 15 years later, this time not only in France but in other parts of the Western world.

The French Revolution had turned the French into a republican people. Even when they chose a king—Louis-Philippe—to lead that revolution of 1830, he was more of a republican prince than a royal sovereign in the traditional mold. Louis-Philippe, the "Citizen King," had to recognize, as part of his office, "the sovereignty of the nation." And what kind of sovereign is it, one may ask, who has to submit to the sovereignty of the nation? The answer must clearly be, one who is king neither by grace of God nor birth nor lawful inheritance but only through the will of the people, who are thus his electors and not his subjects.

The "sovereignty of the nation" was a new and powerful idea, a revolutionary idea, in the 19th century. At the philosophical level, it is usually ascribed, with some justification, to the teaching of Jean-Jacques Rousseau, whom Edmund Burke, Alexis de Tocqueville, and many lesser commentators considered the ideologue of the French Revolution. What Rousseau did was to separate the concept of *sovereignty,* which he said should be kept by the people in their own hands, from the concept of *government,* which he urged the people to entrust to carefully chosen elites, their moral and intellectual superiors. Rousseau held that neither hereditary kings nor aristocrats could be considered superiors of this kind. Rousseau was uncompromisingly republican. To him a republic could be based only on the collective will of citizens who contracted to live together under laws that they themselves enacted. "My argument," Rousseau wrote in *The Social Contract,* "is that sovereignty, being nothing other than the exercise of the general will, can never be alienated; and the sovereign, which is simply a collective being, cannot be represented by anyone but itself—power may be delegated, but the will cannot be."

The sheer size of France, however, with a population in 1789 of some 26 million people, precluded the transformation of the French kingdom into the sort of direct democracy that Rousseau—a native Swiss—envisaged. Still, the Americans had very recently proved that a nation need not be as small as a city-state for a republican constitution to work. And as an inspiration to the average Frenchman, the American Revolution was no less important than the writings of Rousseau.

The American Revolution thus became a model for France, despite its conservative elements. Moreover, the American Revolution later served as a model for others largely because its principles were "translated" and universalized by the French Revolution. In Latin America, the Spanish and Portuguese colonies could not directly follow the American example and indict their monarchs for unlawfully violating their rights; Spain and Portugal, unlike England, recognized no such rights. But following the example of the French Revolution, Latin Americans like Simón Bolivar and José de San Martin were able to appeal to abstract or universal

principles. To describe Bolivia's new constitution in 1826, Simón Bolivar used the same universal and idealistic catchwords which the French had patented 37 years before: "In this constitution," Bolivar announced, "you will find united all the guarantees of permanency and liberty, of equality and order." If the South American republics sometimes seemed to run short on republican liberty and equality, the concept of royal or imperial sovereignty was nonetheless banished forever from American shores. The short reign of Maximilian of Austria as Emperor of Mexico (1864–1867) provided a brief and melancholy epilogue to such ideas of sovereignty in the New World.

Even in the Old World, royal and aristocratic governments were on the defensive. In 1815, the Congress of Vienna, under Prince Metternich of Austria's guidance, attempted to erase the memory of the Revolution and restore Europe to what it had been before 1789. Yet only five years after the Congress, Metternich wrote to the Russian tsar, Alexander I, admitting, "The governments, having lost their balance, are frightened, intimidated, and thrown into confusion."

The French Revolution had permanently destroyed the mystique on which traditional regimes were based. No king could indisputably claim that he ruled by divine right; nor could lords and bishops assume that their own interests and the national interests coincided. After the French Revolution, commoners, the hitherto silent majority of ordinary underprivileged people, asserted the right to have opinions of their own—and to make them known. For once the ideas of liberty, democracy, and the rights of men had been extracted from philosophers' treatises and put on the agenda of political action—which is what the French Revolution with its "universal principles" did—there could be no security for any regime which set itself against those ideals.

In old history textbooks one can still find the interpretation of the French Revolution first advanced by Jules Michelet and Jean Jaurès and other left-wing historians who explained the Revolution as one abolishing feudalism and advancing bourgeois capitalist society. While few historians still view the Revolution this way, the Michelet interpretation was widespread during the 19th century, and its currency prompted many an aspiring Robespierre to "complete" the revolution.

Completing the revolution meant overthrowing the bourgeoisie in favor of the working class, just as the bourgeoisie had supposedly overthrown the feudal aristocracy in 1789. The convulsive year of 1848 was marked in Europe by several revolutions which attempted to complete the work of 1789. Their leaders all looked back to the French Revolution for their "historic justification." Tocqueville observed of these revolutionaries that their "imitation [of 1789] was so manifest that it concealed the terrible originality of the facts; I continually had the impression they were engaged in play-acting the French Revolution far more than continuing it."

If the 19th century was, as many historians describe it, the "century of revolutions," it was so largely because the French Revolution had provided the model. As it turns out, the existence of a proper model has proved to be a more decisive prod to revolution than economic crisis, political unrest, or even the agitations of young revolutionaries.

Indeed, the role of professional revolutionaries seems negligible in the preparation of most revolutions. Revolutionaries often watched and analyzed the political and social disintegration around them, but they were seldom in a position to direct it. Usually, as Hannah Arendt observed, "revolution broke out and liberated, as it were, the professional revolutionists from wherever they happened to be—from jail, or from the coffee house, or from the library." Tocqueville made a similar observation about the revolutionaries of 1848: The French monarchy fell "before rather than beneath the blows of the victors, who were as astonished at their triumph as were the vanquished at their defeat."

Disturbances which during the 18th century would hardly have proven so incendiary ignited one revolution after another during the 19th century. They did so because now there existed a revolutionary model for responding to crises. During the 1790s, revolutionaries outside of France such as Toussaint L'Ouverture in Haiti and Wolfe Tone in Ireland tried simply to import the French Revolution, with its ideals of nationalism, equality and republicanism, and adapt it to local conditions. And well into the 19th century, most revolutionaries continued to focus their eyes not on the future but on the past—on what the French during the 1790s had done in roughly similar circumstances.

To be sure, the French Revolution possessed different and even contradictory meanings, differences which reflect the various stages of the historical Revolution. The ideals and leaders of each stage inspired a particular type of later revolutionary. The revolutionary men of 1789–91, including the Marquis de Lafayette, inspired liberal and aristocratic revolutionaries. Their ideal was a quasi-British constitutional monarchy and suffrage based on property qualifications. The revolutionaries of 1830–32 realized this liberal vision in France and Belgium.

The Girondins and moderate Jacobins of 1792–93 became the model for lower-middle-class and intellectual revolutionaries whose political goal was a democratic republic and usually some form of a "welfare state." The French Revolution of 1848, with its emphasis on universal manhood suffrage, and the state's obligation to provide jobs for all citizens, initially embodied their vision of society.

A third type of revolutionary, the extremists of 1793–94 such as Robespierre and Gracchus Babeuf, inspired later working-class and socialist revolutionaries.

A reactionary such as Prince Metternich would hardly have distinguished among these three types of revolutionaries. But a later observer, Karl Marx, did. Seeing that the nationalist revolutions of his time ignored the socialist-radical strain of the French Revolution, he came to deplore its influence on later revolutionaries.

Marx, who by 1848 was already active in communist politics, condemned what he considered the confusion of understanding in most of these revolutionary movements. An emotional yearning to reenact the dramas of 1789–1815 seemed to him to stand in the way of a successful revolutionary strategy. In a letter to a friend in September, 1870, Marx wrote: "The tragedy of the French, and of the working class as a whole, is that they are trapped in their memories of momentous events. We need to see an end, once and for all, to this reactionary cult of the past."

Vladimir Ilyich Lenin had no such reservations. He passed up no rhetorical opportunity to present his Russian Bolsheviks as the heirs of the French revolutionary tradition and the Russian Revolution of 1917 as a reenactment of France's Revolution of 1789. Lenin went so far as to call his Bolshevik faction "the Jacobins of contemporary Social-Democracy."

It is not difficult to understand Lenin's motives. Throughout the 19th century, most of the successful revolutions in Europe and Latin America had been nationalist revolutions. (Indeed, when the revolutionary German liberals of 1848 issued their Declaration of Rights, they ascribed those rights to German *Volk* as a whole and not to private persons.) But the example of the French Revolution suggested that a revolution could be more than just a matter of nationalism. Taking the example of the French Revolution under the fanatical Robespierre, one could argue, as Lenin did, that the true goal of revolution was to alter the way people lived together, socially and economically.

Yet, as we know, Lenin looked back upon a century when attempts at radical social revolutions had been ultimately and uniformly abortive. The French Revolution of 1848, which removed the "liberal" King Louis-Philippe, briefly gave greater power to the working class. During its most promising days, the anarchist Pierre-Joseph Proudhon (1809–1865) even accepted a seat in the legislative chamber. But the coup d'état of Napoleon III in 1851 soon brought an end to all this. The communist movement, which Marx described as a specter haunting Europe, produced no more tangible results than most specters do. Before World War I, Marx was notably less influential as a theoretician than were the champions of "revolutionary socialism" such as Proudhon and Ferdinand Lassalle (1825–1864) who persuaded the workers that their interests would be better served by reform and democratic process than by revolution.

It was World War I which put revolutionary socialism back on the agenda again. The "war to end all wars" gave Lenin the opportunity to persuade the world that the French Revolution could be repeated as a communist revolution in, of all places, Russia. Not only did the upheavals of war play into his hands but the ideology and propaganda adopted by the Allied powers in World War I did so as well. When their early military campaigns went badly, the Allies attempted to make the war more popular, and the enormous casualties more tolerable, by declaring their cause to be a war for "liberty." In the name of liberty, Great Britain, France, and the United States encouraged the subject nations of the German, Austrian and Turkish empires to throw off the imperial yoke.

2. RATIONALISM, ENLIGHTENMENT, AND REVOLUTION

But in championing national liberty, the Allies were guilty of hypocrisy. Neither Great Britain nor France had any intention of permitting nationalist revolutions within their own empires or those of any neutral power. But Lenin was able to catch them in the trap of their own contradictions.

By declaring to the world that the Bolshevik seizure of power in 1917 was a reenactment of the French Revolution, he was able to attach to his regime all those strong, if mixed, emotions which the French Revolution had kindled in the outside world from 1789 on. In symbolic ways, both large and small—such as naming one of their first naval ships *Marat,* after the French revolutionary leader—the early Soviets underscored their connection with the earlier revolution. The attempts of the Allied powers to send in troops to save Tsarist Russia from the Bolsheviks was immediately seen by a war-weary world as a reactionary, counter-revolutionary "White Terror," and public opinion soon put an end to that intervention.

After 1917, the Soviet Union's self-image became less that of a revolutionary regime and more that of a well-established socialist empire. This transition unexpectedly enabled its adherents at last to obey Marx's injunction to abolish the cult of the revolutionary past and to fix their eyes on the present. The idea of revolution thus passed from the left to the ultra-left, to Stalin and Trotsky and, later, to Mao Zedong and his Cultural Revolution in China.

Yet even during the extreme phase of the Cultural Revolution, Mao still evinced his debt to the French Revolution, a debt which he shares with the later "Third World" revolutionaries. Whenever a revolutionary leader, from Ho Chi Minh and Frantz Fanon to Fidel Castro and Daniel Ortega, speaks of a new man, or of restructuring a whole society, or of creating a new human order, one hears again the ideas and assumptions first sounded on the political stage during the French Revolution.

In fact, there can be no doubt that a "cultural revolution" is what Robespierre set afoot in France, and what, if he had lived, he would have tried to bring to completion. As a disciple of Rousseau, he truly believed that existing culture had corrupted modern man in all classes of society, and that an entirely new culture was necessary if men were to recover their natural goodness. The new religious institutions which Robespierre introduced—the cult of the Supreme Being and the worship of Truth at the altar of Reason, as well as the new patriotic festivals to replace the religious holidays—were all intended to be part of what can only be called a cultural revolution. Robespierre did not believe that political, social, and economic changes alone, however radical, would enable men to achieve their full humanity.

But while the ideals and the language of the cultural revolution sound nobler than those of the political revolution, such elevation of thought seems only to authorize greater cruelty in action. Robespierre's domination of the French Revolution lasted for only a short period, from April 1793 until July 1794, when he himself died under the same guillotine which he had used to execute his former friends and supposed enemies. Moderation was restored to the French Revolution after his execution by the least idealistic of its participants—a cynical Talleyrand, pusillanimous Sieyès, and a crudely ambitious Napoleon. Likewise, moderation was restored to the Chinese Revolution by the Chinese admirers of Richard Nixon. Yet while moderation had been restored to the real historical French Revolution, the inevitability of the return to "normalcy" was often conveniently ignored by later revolutionaries.

And what of France itself? At first glance, all the major subsequent "dates" of French history seem to be in a revolutionary tradition or at least of revolutionary magnitude—1830 (Louis-Philippe); 1848 (the Second Republic); 1852 (the Second Empire); 1871 (the Third Republic); 1940 (the Vichy French State); 1945 (the Fourth Republic); 1958 (the Fifth Republic). Yet these headline dates, all suggesting recurrent tumult, may be misleading: France has not been wracked by major upheavals nor by social earthquakes that left the structure of society unrecognizable, as Russia and China were after their revolutions. Continuity may be the most striking feature in French life. Robert and Barbara Anderson's *Bus Stop to Paris* (1965) showed how a village not more than 10 miles from Paris remained unaffected year after year by all the great rumblings in the capital. Are we dealing with a revolution whose myth is all out of proportion to the facts?

Tocqueville, that most dependable of all political analysts, offers an answer:

The major change effected by the Bourbon kings during the 17th and 18th centuries was the increasing centralization of France and the creation of a strong bureaucracy to administer it. This bureaucracy, in effect, ruled France then and has continued to rule it through every social upheaval and behind every facade of constitutional change. This bureaucracy has provided stability and continuity through the ups and downs of political fortune. The French Revolution and Napoleon, far from making an abrupt break with the past, continued and even accelerated the tendency toward bureaucratic centralization.

Tocqueville almost broached saying that the French Revolution never happened, that the events not only looked theatrical but were theatrical: The French could afford to have as many revolutions as they pleased, because no matter what laws they enacted, or what persons they placed in their legislative and executive offices, the same civil servants, the functionaries, the members of *l'Administration,* would remain in command.

How many revolutions can the historian cite as having left the people better off at the end than they were at the beginning? Unfortunately the discrepancy between its myth and its reality may have made the French Revolution a deceptive model for other nations to imitate. The myth treated society like a neutral, ahistorical protoplasm from which old corrupt institutions could be extracted and into which new rules for human interaction could be inserted at will. The reality was that France, with its unusually strong state bureaucracy, could withstand the shocks and traumas of radical constitutional upheaval.

In modern history, revolution often seems a luxury that only privileged peoples such as the French and the Americans and the English can afford. Less fortunate peoples, from the Russians in 1918 to the Cambodians in 1975, on whom the burden of the established regimes weighed more cruelly, have often enacted their revolutions with catastrophic results. It is perhaps one of the harsher ironies of history that, since the defeat of Napoleon in 1815, the more a country appears to need a revolution, the less likely it will be able to accomplish one successfully.

The Passion of Antoine Lavoisier

With its revolution, France founded a rational republic and lost a great scientist

Stephen Jay Gould

Stephen Jay Gould teaches biology, geology, and the history of science at Harvard University.

Galileo and Lavoisier have more in common than their brilliance. Both men are focal points in a cardinal legend about the life of intellectuals—the conflict of lonely and revolutionary genius with state power. Both stories are apocryphal, however inspiring. Yet they only exaggerate, or encapsulate in the epitome of a bon mot, an essential theme in the history of thinking and its impact upon society.

Galileo, on his knees before the Inquisition, abjures his heretical belief that the earth revolves around a central sun. Yet, as he rises, brave Galileo, faithful to the highest truth of factuality, addresses a stage whisper to the world: *eppur se muove*—nevertheless, it does move. Lavoisier, before the revolutionary tribunal during the Reign of Terror in 1794, accepts the inevitable verdict of death, but asks for a week or two to finish some experiments. Coffinhal, the young judge who has sealed his doom, denies his request, stating, "La république n'a pas besoin de savants" (the Republic does not need scientists).

Coffinhal said no such thing, although the sentiments are not inconsistent with emotions unleashed in those frightening and all too frequent political episodes so well characterized by Marc Antony in his lamentation over Caesar: "O judgment! thou are fled to brutish beasts, And men have lost their reason." Lavoisier, who had been under arrest for months, was engaged in no experiments at the time. Moreover, as we shall see, the charges leading to his execution bore no relationship to his scientific work.

But if Coffinhal's chilling remark is apocryphal, the second most famous quotation surrounding the death of Lavoisier is accurate and well attested. The great mathematician Joseph Louis Lagrange, upon hearing the news about his friend Lavoisier, remarked bitterly: "It took them only an instant to cut off that head, but France may not produce another like it in a century."

I feel some need to participate in the worldwide outpouring of essays to commemorate the 200th anniversary of the French Revolution. Next month, on July 14, unparalleled displays of fireworks will mark the bicentenary of the fall of the Bastille. Nonetheless, and with no desire to put a damper on such pyrotechnics, I must write about the flip side of this initial liberation, the most troubling scientific story of the Revolution—the execution of Antoine Lavoisier in 1794.

The revolution had been born in hope and expansiveness. At the height of enthusiasm for new beginnings, the revolutionary government suppressed the old calendar, and started time all over again, with year I beginning on September 22, 1792, at the founding of the French republic. The months would no longer bear names of Roman gods or emperors, but would record the natural passage of seasons—as in *brumaire* (foggy), *ventose* (windy), *germinal* (budding), and to replace parts of July and August, originally named for two despotic Caesars, *thermidor.* Measures would be rationalized, decimalized, and based on earthly physics, with the meter defined as one ten-millionth of a quarter meridian from pole to equator. The metric system is our enduring legacy of this revolutionary spirit, and Lavoisier himself was the guiding force in devising the new weights and measures.

But initial optimism soon unraveled under the realities of internal dissension and external pressure (the powerful monarchists of Europe were, to say the least, concerned lest republican ideas spread by export or example). Governments tumbled one after the other, and Dr. Guillotin's machine, invented to make execution more humane, became a symbol of terror by sheer frequency of public use. Louis XVI was beheaded in January, 1793 (year one of the republic). Power shifted from the Girondins to the Montagnards, as the Terror reached its height and the war with Austria and Prussia continued. Finally, as so often happens, the architect of the terror, Robespierre himself, paid his visit to Dr. Guillotin's device, and the cycle played itself out. A few years later, in 1804, Napoleon was crowned as emperor, and the First Republic ended. Poor Lavoisier had been caught in the midst of the cycle, dying for his former role as tax collector on May 8, 1794, less than three months before the fall of Robespierre on July 27 (9 Thermidor, year II).

Old ideals often persist in vestigial forms of address and writing, long after their disappearance in practice. I was reminded of this phenomenon when I acquired, a few months ago, a copy of the opening and closing addresses for the course in zoology at the Muséum d'Histoire naturelle of Paris for 1801-2. The democratic fervor of the revolution had faded, and Napoleon had already staged his *coup d'etat* of 18 Brumaire (November 9, 1799), emerging as emperor de facto, although not crowned until 1804.

2. RATIONALISM, ENLIGHTENMENT, AND REVOLUTION

Nonetheless, the author of these addresses, who would soon resume his full name Bernard-Germain-Etienne de la Ville-sur-Illon, comte de Lacépède, is identified on the title page only as C^en Lacépède (for *citoyen,* or "citizen"—the democratic form adopted by the revolution to abolish all distinctions of address). The long list of honors and memberships, printed in small type below Lacépède's name, is almost a parody on the ancient forms; for instead of the old affiliations that always included "member of the royal academy of this or that" and "counsellor to the king or count of here or there," Lacépède's titles are rigorously egalitarian—including "one of the professors at the museum of natural history," and member of the society of pharmacists of Paris, and of agriculture of Agen. As for the year of publication, we have to know the history detailed above—for the publisher's date is given, at the bottom, only as "l'an IX de la République."

Lacépède was one of the great natural historians in the golden age of French zoology during the late eighteenth and early nineteenth century. His name may be overshadowed in retrospect by the illustrious quartet of Buffon, Lamarck, Saint-Hilaire and Cuvier, but Lacépède—who was chosen by Buffon to complete his life's work, the multivolumed *Histoire naturelle*—deserves a place with these men, for all were *citoyens* of comparable merit. Although Lacépède supported the revolution in its moderate first phases, his noble title bred suspicion and he went into internal exile during the Terror. But the fall of Robespierre prompted his return to Paris, where his former colleagues persuaded the government to establish a special chair for him at the Muséum, as zoologist for reptiles and fishes.

By tradition, his opening and closing addresses for the zoology course at the Muséum were published in pamphlet form each year. The opening address for year IX, "Sur l'histoire des races ou principales variétés de l'espèce humaine" (On the history of races and principal varieties of the human species), is a typical statement of the liberality and optimism of Enlightenment thought. The races, we learn, may differ in current accomplishments, but all are capable of greater and equal achievement, and all can progress.

But the bloom of hope had been withered by the Terror. Progress, Lacépède asserts, is not guaranteed, but is possible only if untrammeled by the dark side of human venality. Memories of dire consequences for unpopular thoughts must have been fresh, for Lacépède cloaked his criticisms of revolutionary excesses in careful speech and foreign attribution. Ostensibly, he was only describing the evils of the Indian caste system in a passage that must be read as a lament about the Reign of Terror:

> Hypocritical ambition, . . . abusing the credibility of the multitude, has conserved the ferocity of the savage state in the midst of the virtues of civilization. . . . After having reigned by terror [*regné par la terreur*], submitting even monarchs to their authority, they reserved the domain of science and art to themselves [a reference, no doubt, to the suppression of the independent academies by the revolutionary government in 1793, when Lacépède lost his first post at the Muséum], and surrounded themselves with a veil of mystery that only they could lift.

At the end of his address, Lacépède returns to the familiar theme of political excesses and makes a point, by no means original of course, that I regard as the central structural tragedy of the nature of any complex system, including organisms and social institutions—the crushing asymmetry between the need for slow and painstaking construction and the potential for almost instantaneous destruction:

> Thus, the passage from the semisavage state to civilization occurs through a great number of insensible stages, and requires an immense amount of time. In moving slowly through these successive stages, man fights painfully against his habits; he also battles with nature as he climbs, with great effort, up the long and perilous path. But it is not the same with the loss of the civilized state; that is almost sudden. In this morbid fall, man is thrown down by all his ancient tendencies; he struggles no longer, he gives up, he does not battle obstacles, he abandons himself to the burdens that surround him. Centuries are needed to nurture the tree of science and make it grow, but one blow from the hatchet of destruction cuts it down.

The chilling final line, a gloss on Lagrange's famous statement about the death of Lavoisier, inspired me to write about the founder of modern chemistry, and to think a bit more about the tragic asymmetry of creation and destruction.

Antoine-Laurent Lavoisier, born in 1743, belonged to the nobility through a title purchased by his father (standard practice for boosting the royal treasury during the *ancien régime*). As a leading liberal and rationalist of the Enlightenment (a movement that attracted much of the nobility, including many wealthy intellectuals who had purchased their titles to rise from the bourgeoisie), Lavoisier fitted an astounding array of social and scientific services into a life cut short by the headsman at age fifty-one.

We know him best today as the chief founder of modern chemistry. The textbook one-liners describe him as the discoverer (or at least the namer) of oxygen, the man who (though anticipated by Henry Cavendish in England) recognized water as a compound of the gases hydrogen and oxygen, and who correctly described combustion, not as the liberation of a hypothetical substance called phlogiston, but as the combination of burning material with oxygen. But we can surely epitomize his contribution more accurately by stating that Lavoisier set the basis for modern chemistry by recognizing the nature of elements and compounds—by finally dethroning the ancient taxonomy of air, water, earth, and fire as indivisible elements; by identifying gas, liquid, and solid as states of aggregation for a single substance subjected to different degrees of heat; and by developing quantitative methods of defining and identifying true elements. Such a brief statement can only rank as a caricature of Lavoisier's scientific achievements, but this essay treats his other life in social service, and I must move on.

Lavoisier, no shrinking violet in the game of self-promotion, openly spoke of his new chemistry as "a revolution." He even published his major manifesto, *Traité élémentaire de chimie,* in 1789, starting date of the other revolution that would seal his fate.

Lavoisier, liberal child of the Enlightenment, was no opponent of the political revolution, at least in its early days. He supported the idea of a constitutional monarchy, and joined the most moderate of the revolutionary societies, the Club of '89. He served as an alternate delegate in the States General, took his turn as a *citoyen* at guard duty, and led several studies and commissions vital to the success of the revolution—including a long stint as *régisseur des poudres* (director of gunpowder, where his brilliant successes produced the best stock in Europe, thus providing substantial help in France's war against Austria and Prussia), work on financing the revolution by *assignats* (paper money backed largely by confiscated church lands), and service on the commission of weights and measures that formulated the metric system. Lavoisier rendered these services to all governments, including the most radical, right to his death, even hoping at the end that his crucial work on weights and measures might save his life. Why, then, did Lavoisier end up in two pieces on the *place de la Révolution* (long ago renamed, in pleasant newspeak, *place de la Concorde*)?

The fateful move had been made in 1768, when Lavoisier joined the infamous Ferme Générale, or Tax Farm. If you regard the IRS as a less than benevolent institution, just consider taxation under the *ancien régime* and count your blessings. Taxation was regressive with a vengeance, as the nobility and clergy were entirely exempt, and poor people supplied the bulk of the royal treasury through tariffs on the movement of goods across provincial boundaries, fees for entering the city of Paris, and taxes on such goods as tobacco and salt. (The hated *gabelle,* or "salt tax," was applied at iniquitously differing rates from region to region, and was levied not on actual consumption but on presumed usage—thus, in effect, forcing each family to buy a certain quantity of taxed salt each year.)

Moreover, the ·government did not collect taxes directly, They set the rates and then leased (for six-year periods) the privilege of collecting taxes to a private finance company, the Ferme Générale. The Tax Farm operated for profit like any other private business. If they managed to collect more than the government levy, they kept the balance; if they failed to reach the quota, they took the loss. The system was not only oppressive in principle; it was also corrupt. Several shares in the Tax Farm were paid for no work as favors or bribes; many courtiers, even the King himself, were direct beneficiaries. Nonetheless, Lavoisier chose this enterprise for the primary investment of his family fortune, and he became, as members of the firm were called, a *fermier-général,* or "farmer-general."

(Incidentally, since I first read the sad story of Lavoisier some twenty-five years ago, I have been amused by the term farmer-general, for it conjures up a pleasantly rustic image of a country yokel, dressed in his Osh Kosh b'Gosh overalls, and chewing on a stalk of hay while trying to collect the *gabelle.* But I have just learned from the *Oxford English Dictionary* that my image is not only wrong, but entirely backward. A farm, defined as a piece of agricultural land, is a derivative term. In usage dating to Chaucer, a farm, from the medieval Latin *firma,* "fixed payment," is "a fixed yearly sum accepted from a person as a composition for taxes or other moneys which he is empowered to collect." By extension, to farm is to lease anything for a fixed rent. Since most leases applied to land, agricultural plots become "farms," with the first use in this sense traced only to the sixteenth century; the leasers of such land then became "farmers." Thus, our modern phrase "farming out" records the original use, and has no agricultural connotation. And Lavoisier was a farmer-general in the true sense, with no mitigating image of bucolic innocence.)

I do not understand why Lavoisier chose the Ferme Générale for his investment, and then worked so assiduously in his role as tax farmer. He was surely among the most scrupulous and fair-minded of the farmers, and might be justifiably called a reformer. (He opposed the overwatering of tobacco, a monopoly product of the Ferme, and he did, at least in later years, advocate taxation upon all, including the radical idea that nobles might pay as well.) But he took his profits, and he provoked no extensive campaign for reform as the money rolled in. The standard biographies, all too hagiographical, tend to argue that he regarded the Ferme as an investment that would combine greatest safety and return with minimal expenditure of effort—all done to secure a maximum of time for his beloved scientific work. But I do not see how this explanation can hold. Lavoisier, with his characteristic energy, plunged into the work of the Ferme, traveling all over the country, for example, to inspect the tobacco industry. I rather suspect that Lavoisier, like most modern businessmen, simply jumped at a good and legal investment without asking too many ethical questions.

But the golden calf of one season becomes the shattered idol of another. The farmers-general were roundly hated, in part for genuine corruption and ini-

quity, in part because tax collectors are always scapegoated, especially when the national treasury is bankrupt and the people are starving. Lavoisier's position was particularly precarious. As a scheme to prevent the loss of taxes from widespread smuggling of goods into Paris, Lavoisier advocated the building of a wall around the city. Much to Lavoisier's distress, the project, financed largely (and involuntarily) through taxes levied upon the people of Paris, became something of a boondoggle, as millions were spent on fancy ornamental gates. Parisians blamed the wall for keeping in fetid air and spreading disease. The militant republican Jean-Paul Marat began a campaign of vilification against Lavoisier that only ended when Charlotte Corday stabbed him to death in his bath. Marat had written several works in science and had hoped for election to the Royal Academy, then run by Lavoisier. But Lavoisier had exposed the emptiness of Marat's work. Marat fumed, bided his time, and waited for the season when patriotism would become a good refuge for scoundrels. In January 1791, he launched his attack in *l'Ami du Peuple* (the Friend of the People):

> I denounce you, Coryphaeus of charlatans, Sieur Lavoisier [coryphaeus, meaning highest, is the leader of the chorus in a classical Greek drama] Farmer-general, Commissioner of Gunpowders. . . . Just to think that this contemptible little man who enjoys an income of forty thousand livres has no other claim to fame than that of having put Paris in prison with a wall costing the poor thirty millions. . . . Would to heaven he had been strung up to the nearest lamppost.

The breaching of the wall by the citizens of Paris on July 12, 1789, was the prelude to the fall of the Bastille two days later.

Lavoisier began to worry very early in the cycle. Less than seven months after the fall of the Bastille, he wrote to his old friend Benjamin Franklin:

> After telling you about what is happening in chemistry, it would be well to give you news of our Revolution. . . . Moderate-minded people, who have kept cool heads during the general excitement, think that events have carried us too far . . . we greatly regret your absence from France at this time;

you would have been our guide and you would have marked out for us the limits beyond which we ought not to go.

But these limits were breached, just as Lavoisier's wall had fallen, and he could read the handwriting on the remnants. The Ferme Générale was suppressed in 1791, and Lavoisier played no further role in the complex sorting out of the farmers' accounts. He tried to keep his nose clean with socially useful work on weights and measures and public education. But time was running out for the farmers-general. The treasury was bankrupt, and many thought (quite incorrectly) that the iniquitously hoarded wealth of the farmers-general could replenish the nation. The farmers were too good a scapegoat to resist; they were arrested en masse in November 1793, commanded to put their accounts in order and to reimburse the nation for any ill-gotten gains.

The presumed offenses of the farmers-general were not capital under revolutionary law, and they hoped initially to win their personal freedom, even though their wealth and possessions might be confiscated. But they had the misfortune to be in the wrong place (jail) at the worst time (as the Terror intensified). Eventually, capital charges of counter-revolutionary activities were drummed up, and in a mock trial lasting only part of a day, the farmers-general were condemned to the guillotine.

Lavoisier's influential friends might have saved him, but none dared (or cared) to speak. The Terror was not so inexorable and efficient as tradition holds. Fourteen of the farmers-general managed to evade arrest, and one was saved as a result of the intervention of Robespierre. Madame Lavoisier, who lived to a ripe old age, marrying and divorcing Count Rumford, and reestablishing one of the liveliest salons in Paris, never allowed any of these men over her doorstep again. One courageous (but uninfluential) group offered brave support in Lavoisier's last hours. A deputation from the Lycée des Arts came to the prison to honor Lavoisier and crown him with a wreath. We read in the minutes of that organization: "Brought to Lavoisier in irons, the consolation of friendship . . . to crown the head about to go under the ax."

It is a peculiar attribute of human courage that when no option remains but

death, criteria of judgment shift to the manner of dying. Chronicles of the revolution are filled with stories about who died with dignity—and who went screaming to the knife. Antoine Lavoisier died well. He wrote a last letter to his cousin, in apparent calm, not without humor, and with an intellectual's faith in the supreme importance of mind.

I have had a fairly long life, above all a very happy one, and I think that I shall be remembered with some regrets and perhaps leave some reputation behind me. What more could I ask? The events in which I am involved will probably save me from the troubles of old age. I shall die in full possession of my faculties.

Lavoisier's rehabilitation came almost as quickly as his death. In 1795, the Lycée des Arts held a first public memorial service, with Lagrange himself offering the eulogy and unveiling a bust of Lavoisier inscribed with the words: "Victim of tyranny, respected friend of the arts, he continues to live; through genius he still serves humanity." Lavoisier's spirit continued to inspire, but his head, once filled with great thoughts as numerous as the unwritten symphonies of Mozart, lay severed in a common grave.

Many people try to put a happy interpretation upon Lagrange's observation about the asymmetry of painstaking creation and instantaneous destruction. The collapse of systems, they argue, may be a prerequisite to any future episode of creativity—and the antidote, therefore, to stagnation. Taking the longest view, for example, mass extinctions do break up stable ecosystems and provoke episodes of novelty further down the evolutionary road. We would not be here today if the death of dinosaurs had not cleared some space for the burgeoning of mammals.

I have no objection to this argument in its proper temporal perspective. If you choose a telescope and wish to peer into an evolutionary future millions of years away, then a current episode of destruction may be read as an ultimate spur. But if you care for the here and now, which is (after all) the only time we feel and have, then massive extinction is only a sadness and an opportunity lost forever. I have heard people argue that our current wave of extinctions should not inspire concern because the earth will eventually recover, as so oft before, and perhaps with

pleasant novelty. But what can a conjecture about ten million years from now possibly mean to our lives—especially since we have the power to blow our planet up long before then, and rather little prospect, in any case, of surviving so long ourselves (since few vertebrate species live for ten million years).

The argument of the "long view" may be correct in some meaninglessly abstract sense, but it represents a fundamental mistake in categories and time scales. Our only legitimate long view extends to our children and our children's children's children—hundreds or a few thousands of years down the road. If we let the slaughter continue, they will share a bleak world with rats, dogs, cockroaches, pigeons, and mosquitoes. A potential recovery millions of years later has no meaning at our appropriate scale. Similarly, others could do the unfinished work of Lavoisier, if not so elegantly; and political revolution did spur science into some interesting channels. But how can this mitigate the tragedy of Lavoisier? He was one of the most brilliant men ever to grace our history, and he died at the height of his powers and health. He had work to do, and he was not guilty.

My title, "The Passion of Antoine Lavoisier," is a double-entendre. The modern meaning of *passion,* "overmastering zeal or enthusiasm," is a latecomer. The word entered our language from the Latin verb for suffering, particularly for suffering physical pain. The Saint Matthew and Saint John Passions of J. S. Bach are musical dramas about the suffering of Jesus on the cross. This essay, therefore, focuses upon the final and literal passion of Lavoisier. (Anyone who has ever been disappointed in love— that is, all of us—will understand the intimate connection between the two meanings of passion.)

But I also wanted to emphasize Lavoisier's passion in the modern meaning. For this supremely organized man— farmer-general; commissioner of gunpowder; wall builder; reformer of prisons, hospitals, and schools; legislative representative for the nobility of Blois; father of the metric system; servant on a hundred government committees—really had but one passion amidst this burden of activities for a thousand lifetimes. Lavoisier loved science more than anything else. He awoke at six in the morning and worked on science until eight, then again at night from seven until ten. He devoted one full day a week to scientific experiments and called it his *jour de bonheur* (day of happiness). The letters and reports of his last year are painful to read, for Lavoisier never abandoned his passion—his conviction that reason and science must guide any just and effective social order. But those who received his pleas, and held power over him, had heard the different drummer of despotism.

Lavoisier was right in the deepest, almost holy, way. His passion harnessed feeling to the service of reason; another kind of passion was the price. Reason cannot save us and can even persecute us in the wrong hands; but we have no hope of salvation without reason. The world is too complex, too intransigent; we cannot bend it to our simple will. Bernard Lacépède was probably thinking of Lavoisier when he wrote a closing flourish following his passage on the great asymmetry of slow creation and sudden destruction:

Ah! Never forget that we can only stave off that fatal degradation if we unite the liberal arts, which embody the sacred fire of sensibility, with the sciences and the useful arts, without which the celestial light of reason will disappear.

The Republic needs scientists.

The First Feminist

In 1792 Mary Wollstonecraft wrote a book to prove that her sex was as intelligent as the other: thus did feminism come into the world. Right on, Ms. Mary!

Shirley Tomkievicz

The first person—male or female—to speak at any length and to any effect about woman's rights was Mary Wollstonecraft. In 1792, when her *Vindication of the Rights of Woman* appeared, Mary was a beautiful spinster of thirty-three who had made a successful career for herself in the publishing world of London. This accomplishment was rare enough for a woman in that day. Her manifesto, at once impassioned and learned, was an achievement of real originality. The book electrified the reading public and made Mary famous. The core of its argument is simple: "I wish to see women neither heroines nor brutes; but reasonable creatures," Mary wrote. This ancestress of the Women's Liberation Movement did not demand day-care centers or an end to women's traditional role as wife and mother, nor did she call anyone a chauvinist pig. The happiest period of Mary's own life was when she was married and awaiting the birth of her second child. And the greatest delight she ever knew was in her first child, an illegitimate daughter. Mary's feminism may not appear today to be the hard-core revolutionary variety, but she did live, for a time, a scandalous and unconventional life—"emancipated," it is called by those who have never tried it. The essence of her thought, however, is simply that a woman's mind is as good as a man's.

Not many intelligent men could be found to dispute this proposition today, at least not in mixed company. In Mary's time, to speak of *anybody's* rights, let alone woman's rights, was a radical act. In England, as in other nations, "rights" were an entity belonging to the govern-ment. The common run of mankind had little access to what we now call "human rights." As an example of British justice in the late eighteenth century, the law cited two hundred different capital crimes, among them shoplifting. An accused man was not entitled to counsel. A child could be tried and hanged as soon as an adult. The right to vote existed, certainly, but because of unjust apportionment, it had come to mean little. In the United States some of these abuses had been corrected—but the rights of man did not extend past the color bar and the masculine gender was intentional. In the land of Washington and Jefferson, as in the land of George III, human rights were a new idea and woman's rights were not even an issue.

In France, in 1792, a Revolution in the name of equality was in full course, and woman's rights had at least been alluded to. The Revolutionary government drew up plans for female education—to the age of eight. "The education of the women should always be relative to the men," Rousseau had written in *Emile*. "To please, to be useful to us, to make us love and esteem them, to educate us when young, and take care of us when grown up, to advise, to console us, to render our lives easy and agreeable; these are the duties of women at all times, and what they should be taught in their infancy." And, less prettily, "Women have, or ought to have, but little liberty."

Rousseau would have found little cause for complaint in eighteenth-century England. An Englishwoman had almost the same civil status as an American slave. Thomas Hardy, a hundred years hence, was to base a novel on the idea of a man casually selling his wife and daughter at public auction. Obviously this was not a common occurrence, but neither is it wholly implausible. In 1792, and later, a woman could not own property, nor keep any earned wages. All that she possessed belonged to her husband. She could not divorce him, but he could divorce her and take her children. There was no law to say she could not grow up illiterate or be beaten every day.

Such was the legal and moral climate in which Mary Wollstonecraft lived. She was born in London in the spring of 1759, the second child and first daughter of Edward Wollstonecraft, a prosperous weaver. Two more daughters and two more sons were eventually born into the family, making six children in all. Before they had all arrived, Mr. Wollstonecraft came into an inheritance and decided to move his family to the country and become a gentleman farmer. But this plan failed. His money dwindled, and he began drinking heavily. His wife turned into a terrified wraith whose only interest was her eldest son, Edward. Only he escaped the beatings and abuse that his father dealt out regularly to every other household member, from Mrs. Wollstonecraft to the family dog. As often happens in large and disordered families, the eldest sister had to assume the role of mother and scullery maid. Mary was a bright, strong child, determined not to be broken, and she undertook her task energetically, defying her father when he was violent and keeping her younger brothers and sisters in hand. Clearly, Mary held the household together, and in so doing forfeited her own childhood. This experience left her with an everlasting gloomy streak, and was a strong factor in making her a reformer.

At some point in Mary's childhood, another injustice was visited upon her, though so commonplace for the time that she can hardly have felt the sting. Her elder brother was sent away to be educated, and the younger children were left to learn their letters as best they could. The family now frequently changed lodgings, but from her ninth to her fifteenth year Mary went to a day school, where she had the only formal training of her life. Fortunately, this included French and composition, and somewhere Mary learned to read critically and widely. These skills, together with her curiosity and determination, were really all she needed. The *Vindication* is in some parts long-winded, ill-punctuated, and simply full of hot air, but it is the work of a well-informed mind.

Feminists—and Mary would gladly have claimed the title—inevitably, even deservedly, get bad notices. The term calls up an image of relentless battle-axes: "thin college ladies with eye-glasses, no-nonsense features, mouths thin as bologna slicers, a babe in one arm, a hatchet in the other, grey eyes bright with balefire," as Norman Mailer feelingly envisions his antagonists in the Women's Liberation Movement. He has conjured up all the horrid elements: the lips with a cutting edge, the baby immaculately conceived (one is forced to conclude), the lethal weapon tightly clutched, the desiccating college degree, the joylessness. Hanging miasmally over the tableau is the suspicion of a deformed sexuality. Are these girls man-haters, or worse? Mary Wollstonecraft, as the first of her line, has had each of these scarlet letters (except the B.A.) stitched upon her bosom. Yet she conformed very little to the hateful stereotype. In at least one respect, however, she would have chilled Mailer's bones. Having spent her childhood as an adult, Mary reached the age of nineteen in a state of complete joylessness. She was later to quit the role, but for now she wore the garb of a martyr.

Her early twenties were spent in this elderly frame of mind. First she went out as companion to an old lady living at Bath, and was released from this servitude only by a call to nurse the dying Mrs. Wollstonecraft. Then the family broke up entirely, though the younger sisters continued off and on to be dependent on Mary. The family of Mary's dearest friend, Fanny Blood, invited her

to come and stay with them; the two girls made a small living doing sewing and handicrafts, and Mary dreamed of starting a primary school. Eventually, in a pleasant village called Newington Green, this plan materialized and prospered. But Fanny Blood in the meantime had married and moved to Lisbon. She wanted Mary to come and nurse her through the birth of her first child. Mary reached Lisbon just in time to see her friend die of childbed fever, and returned home just in time to find that her sisters, in whose care the flourishing little school had been left, had lost all but two pupils.

Mary made up her mind to die. "My constitution is impaired, I hope I shan't live long," she wrote to a friend in February, 1786. Under this almost habitual grief, however, Mary was gaining some new sense of herself. Newington Green, apart from offering her a brief success as a schoolmistress, had brought her some acquaintance in the world of letters, most important among them, Joseph Johnson, an intelligent and successful London publisher in search of new writers. Debt-ridden and penniless, Mary set aside her impaired constitution and wrote her first book, probably in the space of a week. Johnson bought it for ten guineas and published it. Called *Thoughts on the Education of Daughters,* it went unnoticed, and the ten guineas was soon spent. Mary had to find work. She accepted a position as governess in the house of Lord and Lady Kingsborough in the north of Ireland.

Mary's letters from Ireland to her sisters and to Joseph Johnson are so filled with Gothic gloom, so stained with tears, that one cannot keep from laughing at them. "I entered the great gates with the same kind of feeling I should have if I was going to the Bastille," she wrote upon entering Kingsborough Castle in the fall of 1786. Mary was now twenty-seven. Her most recent biographer, Margaret George, believes that Mary was not really suffering so much as she was having literary fantasies. In private she was furiously at work on a novel entitled, not very artfully, *Mary, A Fiction.* This is the story of a young lady of immense sensibilities who closely resembles Mary except that she has wealthy parents, a neglectful bridegroom, and an attractive lover. The title and fantasizing contents are precisely what a scribbler of thirteen might se-

cretly concoct. Somehow Mary was embarking on her adolescence—with all its daydreams—fifteen years after the usual date. Mary's experience in Kingsborough Castle was a fruitful one, for all her complaints. In the summer of 1787 she lost her post as governess and set off for London with her novel. Not only did Johnson accept it for publication, he offered her a regular job as editor and translator and helped her find a place to live.

Thus, aged twenty-eight, Mary put aside her doleful persona as the martyred, set-upon elder sister. How different she is now, jauntily writing from London to her sisters: "Mr. Johnson . . . assures me that if I exert my talents in writing I may support myself in a comfortable way. I am then going to be the first of a new genus . . ." Now Mary discovered the sweetness of financial independence earned by interesting work. She had her own apartment. She was often invited to Mr. Johnson's dinner parties, usually as the only female guest among all the most interesting men in London: Joseph Priestley, Thomas Paine, Henry Fuseli, William Blake, Thomas Christie, William Godwin—all of them up-and-coming scientists or poets or painters or philosophers, bound together by left-wing political views. Moreover, Mary was successful in her own writing as well as in editorial work. Her *Original Stories for Children* went into three editions and was illustrated by Blake. Johnson and his friend Thomas Christie had started a magazine called the *Analytical Review,* to which Mary became a regular contributor.

But—lest anyone imagine an elegantly dressed Mary presiding flirtatiously at Johnson's dinner table—her social accomplishments were rather behind her professional ones. Johnson's circle looked upon her as one of the boys. "Wollstonecraft" is what William Godwin calls her in his diary. One of her later detractors reported that she was at this time a "philosophic sloven," in a dreadful old dress and beaver hat, "with her hair hanging lank about her shoulders." Mary had yet to arrive at her final incarnation, but the new identity was imminent, if achieved by an odd route. Edmund Burke had recently published his *Reflections on the Revolution in France,* and the book had enraged Mary. The statesman who so readily supported the quest for liberty in the American colonies had his doubts about events in France.

2. RATIONALISM, ENLIGHTENMENT, AND REVOLUTION

Mary's reply to Burke, *A Vindication of the Rights of Men,* astounded London, partly because she was hitherto unknown, partly because it was good. Mary proved to be an excellent polemicist, and she had written in anger. She accused Burke, the erstwhile champion of liberty, of being "the champion of property." "Man preys on man," said she, "and you mourn for the idle tapestry that decorated a gothic pile and the dronish bell that summoned the fat priest to prayer." The book sold well. Mary moved into a better apartment and bought some pretty dresses—no farthingales, of course, but some of the revolutionary new "classical" gowns. She put her auburn hair up in a loose knot. Her days as a philosophic sloven were over.

Vindication of the Rights of Woman was her next work. In its current edition it runs to 250-odd pages; Mary wrote it in six weeks. *Vindication* is no prose masterpiece, but it has never failed to arouse its audience, in one way or another. Horace Walpole unintentionally set the style for the book's foes. Writing to his friend Hannah More in August, 1792, he referred to Thomas Paine and to Mary as "philosophizing serpents" and was "glad to hear you have not read the tract of the last mentioned writer. I would not look at it." Neither would many another of Mary's assailants, the most virulent of whom, Ferdinand Lundberg, surfaced at the late date of 1947 with a tract of his own, *Modern Woman, the Lost Sex.* Savagely misogynistic as it is, this book was hailed in its time as "the best book yet to be written about women." Lundberg calls Mary the Karl Marx of the feminist movement, and the *Vindication* a "fateful book," to which "the tenets of feminism, which have undergone no change to our day, may be traced." Very well, but then, recounting Mary's life with the maximum possible number of errors per line, he warns us that she was "an extreme neurotic of a compulsive type" who "wanted to turn on men and injure them." In one respect, at least, Mr. Lundberg hits the mark: he blames Mary for starting women in the pernicious habit of wanting an education. In the nineteenth century, he relates, English and American feminists were hard at work. "Following Mary Wollstonecraft's prescription, they made a considerable point about acquiring a higher education." This is precisely Mary's prescription, and the most dangerous idea in her fateful book.

"Men complain and with reason, of the follies and caprices of our Sex," she writes in Chapter 1. "Behold, I should answer, the natural effect of ignorance." Women, she thinks, are usually so mindless as to be scarcely fit for their roles as wives and mothers. Nevertheless, she believes this state not to be part of the feminine nature, but the result of an equally mindless oppression, as demoralizing for men as for women. If a woman's basic mission is as a wife and mother, need she be an illiterate slave for this?

The heart of the work is Mary's attack on Rousseau. In *Emile* Rousseau had set forth some refreshing new ideas for the education of little boys. But women, he decreed, are tools for pleasure, creatures too base for moral or political or educational privilege. Mary recognized that this view was destined to shut half the human race out of all hope for political freedom. *Vindication* is a plea that the "rights of men" ought to mean the "rights of humanity." The human right that she held highest was the right to have a mind and think with it. Virginia Woolf, who lived through a time of feminist activity, thought that the *Vindication* was a work so true "as to seem to contain nothing new." Its originality, she wrote, rather too optimistically, had become a commonplace.

Vindication went quickly into a second edition. Mary's name was soon known all over Europe. But as she savored her fame—and she did savor it—she found that the edge was wearing off and that she was rather lonely. So far as anyone knows, Mary had reached this point in her life without ever having had a love affair. Johnson was the only man she was close to, and he was, as she wrote him, "A father, or a brother—you have been both to me." Mary was often now in the company of the Swiss painter Henry Fuseli, and suddenly she developed what she thought was a Platonic passion in his direction. He rebuffed her, and in the winter of 1792 she went to Paris, partly to escape her embarrassment but also because she wanted to observe the workings of the Revolution firsthand.

Soon after her arrival, as she collected notes for the history of the Revolution she hoped to write, Mary saw Louis XVI, "sitting in a hackney coach . . . going to meet death." Back in her room that evening, she wrote

to Mr. Johnson of seeing "eyes glare through a glass door opposite my chair and bloody hands shook at me . . . I am going to bed and for the first time in my life, I cannot put out the candle." As the weeks went on, Edmund Burke's implacable critic began to lose her faith in the brave new world. "The aristocracy of birth is levelled to the ground, only to make room for that of riches," she wrote. By February France and England were at war, and British subjects classified as enemy aliens.

Though many Englishmen were arrested, Mary and a large English colony stayed on. One day in spring, some friends presented her to an attractive American, newly arrived in Paris, Gilbert Imlay. Probably about four years Mary's senior, Imlay, a former officer in the Continental Army, was an explorer and adventurer. He came to France seeking to finance a scheme for seizing Spanish lands in the Mississippi valley. This "natural and unaffected creature," as Mary was later to describe him, was probably the social lion of the moment, for he was also the author of a best-selling novel called *The Emigrants,* a farfetched account of life and love in the American wilderness. He and Mary soon became lovers. They were a seemingly perfect pair. Imlay must have been pleased with his famous catch, and—dear, liberated girl that she was—Mary did not insist upon marriage. Rather the contrary. But fearing that she was in danger as an Englishwoman, he registered her at the American embassy as his wife.

Blood was literally running in the Paris streets now, so Mary settled down by herself in a cottage at Neuilly. Imlay spent his days in town, working out various plans. The Mississippi expedition came to nothing, and he decided to stay in France and go into the import-export business, part of his imports being gunpowder and other war goods run from Scandinavia through the English blockade. In the evenings he would ride out to the cottage. By now it was summer, and Mary, who spent the days writing, would often stroll up the road to meet him, carrying a basket of freshly-gathered grapes.

A note she wrote Imlay that summer shows exactly what her feelings for him were: "You can scarcely imagine with what pleasure I anticipate the day when we are to begin almost to live together; and you would smile to hear how many plans of employment I have in my head, now that I am confident that my heart has found peace . . ." Soon she was pregnant. She and Imlay moved into Paris. He promised to take her to America, where they would settle down on a farm and raise six children. But business called Imlay to Le Havre, and his stay lengthened ominously into weeks.

Imlay's letters to Mary have not survived, and without them it is hard to gauge what sort of man he was and what he really thought of his adoring mistress. Her biographers like to make him out a cad, a philistine, not half good enough for Mary. Perhaps; yet the two must have had something in common. His novel, unreadable though it is now, shows that he shared her political views, including her feminist ones. He may never have been serious about the farm in America, but he was a miserably long time deciding to leave Mary alone. Though they were separated during the early months of her pregnancy, he finally did bring her to Le Havre, and continued to live with her there until the child was born and for some six months afterward. The baby arrived in May, 1794, a healthy little girl, whom Mary named Fanny after her old friend. Mary was proud that her delivery had been easy, and as for Fanny, Mary loved her instantly. "My little Girl," she wrote to a friend, "begins to suck so manfully that her father reckons saucily on her writing the second part of the Rights of Woman." Mary's joy in this child illuminates almost every letter she wrote henceforth.

Fanny's father was the chief recipient of these letters with all the details of the baby's life. To Mary's despair, she and Imlay hardly ever lived together again. A year went by; Imlay was now in London and Mary in France. She offered to break it off, but mysteriously, he could not let go. In the last bitter phase of their involvement, after she had joined him in London at his behest, he even sent her—as "Mrs. Imlay"—on a complicated business errand to the Scandinavian countries. Returning to London, Mary discovered that he was living with another woman. By now half crazy with humiliation, Mary chose a dark night and threw herself in the Thames. She was nearly dead when two rivermen pulled her from the water.

Though this desperate incident was almost the end of Mary, at least it was the end of the Imlay episode. He sent a doctor to care for her, but they rarely met again. Since Mary had no money, she set about providing for herself and Fanny in the way she knew. The faithful Johnson had already brought out Volume I of her history of the French Revolution. Now she set to work editing and revising her *Letters Written during a Short Residence in Sweden, Norway, and Denmark,* a kind of thoughtful travelogue. The book was well received and widely translated.

And it also revived the memory of Mary Wollstonecraft in the mind of an old acquaintance, William Godwin. As the author of the treatise *Political Justice,* he was now as famous a philosophizing serpent as Mary and was widely admired and hated as a "freethinker." He came to call on Mary. They became friends and then lovers. Early in 1797 Mary was again pregnant. William Godwin was an avowed atheist who had publicly denounced the very institution of marriage. On March 29, 1797, he nevertheless went peaceably to church with Mary and made her his wife.

The Godwins were happy together, however William's theories may have been outraged. He adored his small stepdaughter and took pride in his brilliant wife. Awaiting the birth of her child throughout the summer, Mary worked on a new novel and made plans for a book on "the management of infants"—it would have been the first "Dr. Spock." She expected to have another easy delivery and promised to come downstairs to dinner the day following. But when labor began, on August 30, it proved to be long and agonizing. A daughter, named Mary Wollstonecraft, was born; ten days later, the mother died.

Occasionally, when a gifted writer dies young, one can feel, as in the example of Shelley, that perhaps he had at any rate accomplished his best work. But so recently had Mary come into her full intellectual and emotional growth that her death at the age of thirty-eight is bleak indeed. There is no knowing what Mary might have accomplished now that she enjoyed domestic stability. Perhaps she might have achieved little or nothing further as a writer. But she might have been able to protect her daughters from some part of the sadness that overtook them; for as things turned out, both Fanny and Mary were to sacrifice themselves.

Fanny grew up to be a shy young girl, required to feel grateful for the roof over her head, overshadowed by her prettier half sister, Mary. Godwin in due course married a formidable widow named Mrs. Clairmont, who brought her own daughter into the house—the Claire Clairmont who grew up to become Byron's mistress and the mother of his daughter Allegra. Over the years Godwin turned into a hypocrite and a miser who nevertheless continued to pose as the great liberal of the day. Percy Bysshe Shelley, born the same year that the *Vindication of the Rights of Woman* was published, came to be a devoted admirer of Mary Wollstonecraft's writing. As a young man he therefore came with his wife to call upon Godwin. What he really sought, however, were Mary's daughters—because they were her daughters. First he approached Fanny, but later changed his mind. Mary Godwin was then sixteen, the perfect potential soul mate for a man whose needs for soul mates knew no bounds. They conducted their courtship in the most up-to-the-minute romantic style: beneath a tree near her mother's grave they read aloud to each other from the *Vindication.* Soon they eloped, having pledged their "troth" in the cemetery. Godwin, the celebrated freethinker, was enraged. To make matters worse, Claire Clairmont had run off to Switzerland with them.

Not long afterward Fanny, too, ran away. She went to an inn in a distant town and drank a fatal dose of laudanum. It has traditionally been said that unrequited love for Shelley drove her to this pass, but there is no evidence one way or the other. One suicide that can more justly be laid at Shelley's door is that of his first wife, which occurred a month after Fanny's and which at any rate left him free to wed his mistress, Mary Godwin. Wife or mistress, she had to endure poverty, ostracism, and Percy's constant infidelities. But now at last her father could, and did, boast to his relations that he was father-in-law to a baronet's son. "Oh, philosophy!" as Mary Godwin Shelley remarked.

If in practice Shelley was merely a womanizer, on paper he was a convinced feminist. He had learned this creed from Mary Wollstonecraft. Through his verse Mary's ideas began to be disseminated. They were one part of that vast tidal wave of political, social, and artistic revolution that arose in the late eighteenth century, the romantic movement. But because of Mary's unconventional way of life, her name fell into disrepute during the nineteenth century, and her book failed to exert its rightful influence on the development of feminism. Emma Willard and other pioneers of the early Victorian period indignantly refused to claim Mary as their forebear. Elizabeth Cady Stanton and Lucretia Mott were mercifully less strait-laced on the subject. In 1889, when Mrs. Stanton and Susan B. Anthony published their *History of Woman Suffrage,* they dedicated the book to Mary. Though Mary Wollstonecraft can in no sense be said to have founded the woman's rights movement, she was, by the late nineteenth century, recognized as its inspiration, and the *Vindication* was vindicated for the highly original work it was, a landmark in the history of society.

Gin and Georgian London

The production of gin was actively encouraged in Britain during the Restoration period, but its increasing grip on the London poor had disastrous effects for the following century. Thomas Maples *examines the gin problem and what it took to stem the flow.*

Thomas Maples

Thomas Maples is a farmer and free-lance journalist, and former student of history at Athens State College, Alabama.

Henry Fielding was correct in his comparison of ancient Greeks with the gin-soaked London masses of early eighteenth-century England. The reckless abandonment with which a large sector of the poor pursued the evil spirit gin, affected not only each individual's life, but changed the social and economic complexion of early London.

'Genievie', or the shortened form, gin, was first produced by Franascus de la Boe of Holland in the mid 1600s. It was not until the final stages of the seventeenth century that gin was introduced to the people of London. This occurred when British soldiers returned from war on the European continent and brought the new-found discovery with them. Up to the 1680s the exportation of gin by Holland was small. After the British got a taste of the drink, exports to England rose to over ten million gallons in the late 1680s.

At the start of the eighteenth century, gin was not among the popular beverages consumed by the people of London. During this time, beer was the favourite of the working class with an estimated brewery of over eleven million barrels.

In order to establish the production of gin and promote the spirit to the English commoners, Charles I formed a company and gave it exclusive rights to distill and manufacture gin and vinegar in the cities of London and Westminster. This venture proved to be highly unprofitable for the investors because the English distillery was much too small to produce enough gin. The spirit did not become popular among the large masses of poor until later measures were taken.

Although the first legal attempt to benefit gin production failed to materialise, a further-reaching turn of events thrust gin into the forefront in 1689. In this year, the British government strictly prohibited the importation of *any* spirituous liquors from foreign countries. They also opened up the distilling trade to any and all British citizens, who paid a duty to manufacture these beverages.

These new laws were enacted in part because of hostility towards France, and secondly to help balance trade by encouraging British distillers to produce cheap English spirits from cheap English corn in unlimited quantities. To further appease the distillers and encourage production, no licence was required to produce and retail gin as was required with the alehouses.

At the time, the cheapness of gin was a result of a conscious economic programme. The distilling industry received special favours from government officials because the distillation of gin boosted the agricultural economy through the use of the plentiful supply of grain.

The land-owners were able to take advantage of this new marketing avenue for the corn by becoming informal partners with the distilling industry, thus ensuring an ample amount of grain to be used to produce spirituous liquors. Finally, there was a ready market for cheap, available gin among the masses of poor people who lived in London. The social and economic implications, caused indirectly by the mass consumption of gin in later years, was not considered at the start. The importation restriction of 1689 was designed merely to benefit 'everyone' in England.

Although the catalyst for 'gin madness' occurred in 1689, it took until the 1720s for the evil to spread unchecked through the London masses. The city at this time was in great uproar. It was a hustling, growing London that offered both opportunity and despair to its inhabitants. The people of the city were involved in various brutal and degrading pastimes. Social pleasures such as cock-fighting, hare-hunting, bull- and bear-baiting and the drinking of gin were common during this period.

In fact, drinking gin was considered one of life's earthly pleasures for men. Such notable officials as Sir Robert Walpole and John Wilkes considered the drinking of gin to be a normal diversion. Walpole received his taste for wine at an early age because his father thought it was wrong for young Robert to witness the intoxication of his father while himself remaining sober. Walpole carried this taste for hard-drinking into his later years in public office. It was this general lack of concern among the upper and middle classes as to the harmful effects of alcoholism that helped instill the use of alcohol so deeply among the poor.

From *History Today,* March 1991, pp. 42-47. Reproduced by kind permission of History Today, Ltd., 83-84 Berwick Street, London W1V 3PJ, England.

In early eighteenth-century England, the poor of London had an especially difficult time making a living. Lack of work and grim social and living conditions, caused many to turn to violence, crime, prostitution and gin as a means of escape from their hopeless situations.

Of all the so-called 'social' pleasures of the times, gin was the most accessible. It was within everyone's reach. Throughout London every fifth house catered to gin in some manner. Numerous 'dram' or 'gin' shops were selling the devilish spirit for practically nothing. Taverns boldly advertised 'drunk for a penny, dead drunk for two pence and straw for nothing'. Gin was sold at the smallest monetary amount so that everyone was able to become intoxicated when they wished.

Although the social pleasures remained and no thought was given to sober living, the realistic issue of drinking gin came sharply into focus in the late 1720s. Sober facts such as a higher prevalence of violent crimes among the poor, increased death-rates and declining birth-rates were among the consequences due to the poisonous alcohol. In the first half of the eighteenth century the population of London remained static between one million and one and a half million people. However, during this same period the records from the *London Bills of Mortality* (the records of burials and baptisms kept by the company of parish clerks) showed three burials for every two baptisms. These statistics did not

In spite of this cartoon (above), the Gin Act of 1736 did not signify the burial of 'Madame Geneva'. Walpole, who introduced the Act, was already the subject of satire, for his increasing dependence on excise duties (right). He had hoped to boost government coffers still further with revenue from the new licencing laws, but neither this, nor an end to the alcohol problem, was achieved by the Act.

change until the end of the eighteenth century when birthrates became higher than death rates.

Taking all this into account, Parliament initially acted in 1729 to curtail gin consumption. The government imposed a licence of £20 on retailers and a tax of two shillings a gallon on cheap liquor. This act was not enforced strictly. In 1733, the Act of 1729 was repealed by Sir Robert Walpole because of pressure from vested interest groups. Wheat-growers and other agricultural leaders protested that sales of agricultural products were diminished greatly because of the resulting fall in consumption.

The onslaught of drunkenness which followed the repeal of the Act of 1729 soon reached epic proportions. In 1735 over 5.3 million gallons of gin were consumed by the people of London. The vested interest groups that forced the earlier repeal could not overcome the now seemingly everyday horrors that accompanied this new round of drunkenness.

The Gin Act of 1736 originated from a petition to Parliament from the Middlesex justices, who wanted action taken to curb the excessive sale of cheap liquors. Only then did Walpole and his ministry begin to start to work on a bill limiting gin sales.

Walpole answered his critics in 1736 by proposing a bill prepared by himself and Sir Joseph Jekyll, Master of the Rolls. This bill served a two-fold purpose. Not only would the sale of gin be strictly prohibited without a licence, but the taxes collected from the shop owners would help increase government revenue. The Gin Act of 1736 passed through Parliament unopposed on May 20th, although it did have silent critics. William Pulteney, a political opponent of Walpole, thought that only through total prohibition would gin consumption be halted. He kept his views silent however, because of fear of political repercussions from the distilling industry and other segments of the middle and upper classes.

The Gin Act of 1736 was directed towards stopping the supplies of gin to the small shop owners, taxing the liquor out of existence. The Act stated that all retailers were to pay a duty of twenty shillings per gallon on all spirits sold and that all alehouses, vendors and brandy-shops were to purchase annually a licence costing £50.

Because of these higher taxes on gin, the vested groups which were affected tried to force a repeal of the Act as they had successfully accomplished in 1729. Letters and pamphlets were distributed to distillers and retailers urging them virtually to ignore the new Act. Gin shop owners covered their tavern signs in black to commemorate the demise of 'Mother Gin'.

Riots erupted in several areas of London throughout 1736 and 1737 because the drinking poor did not want to lose their precious 'friend'. The masses did not understand why years of acceptable traditions had suddenly become inappropriate. In addition, it was felt that the growing number of government informers, motivated by a £50 reward, were causing harm to the retail of gin. As Lord Chol-

(Left) The demon drink causing tempers to fray, an engraving from a contemporary edition of Henry Fielding's *Tom Jones*, and (right) the author himself. Fielding was especially concerned with Parliament's reticence in tackling alcoholism in London, which he perceived was 'by no means . . . a spiritual offence alone'.

mondeley stated in a debate in the House of Lords:

> The people discovered that without informers, the new law was without operation; and the informers were therefore, persecuted by them without mercy, and without remission, till at last no man would venture to provoke the resentment of the populace for the reward to which information entitled him.

All of these actions taken by the masses and vested interest groups had some effect on Walpole's decision to repeal the Act of 1736 but, in fact, the Gin Act of 1736 was doomed from the beginning. The Act failed because the law was impossible to enforce. Distillers and retailers ignored the law and formed so called 'speakeasies', never slowing down business. The small dram shop owners, who were poor themselves, did not have enough money to buy licences and pay taxes thus the government could not collect on the money due. In addition, it was impossible for the commissioners of excise to 'discover all the petty dealers' and spirituous liquors continued to be sold in 'small obscure shops and at the corners of the streets.' When Walpole fell from power a short time later, gin consumption was reaching its zenith.

The next attempt to halt gin drinking occurred in 1743 when a more moderate bill was presented to Parliament. This bill was aimed towards checking, rather than totally prohibiting the sale of the spirituous liquors. In this bill, the duties per gallon were to be lowered from twenty shillings to a few pence and the purchase price of a licence reduced from £50 to twenty shillings. However, only taverns and shop owners who were previously licenced by the Justices of the Peace were to be granted permission to sell the spirituous liquors.

This Gin Act of 1743 passed Parliament, though only after a long and heated debate in the House of Lords. The Bishop of Oxford opposed the bill vigorously, because he felt that 'the liberty of selling liquors, which are allowed to be equally injurious to health and virtue, will by this law become general and boundless'. The bishop further added that he could 'discover no reason for doubting that the purchasers will be multiplied by increasing the numbers of the vendors, and the increase of the sale of distilled spirits, and the propagation of all klnds of wickedness are the same'.

Lord Talbot was in agreement with the Bishop of Oxford and he said that 'in-

'Drunk for a penny, dead drunk for two pence'. The gin problem of eighteenth-century London was reflected in a decrease in birth-rate and a rise in death-rate. The problem was not confined to this century, however, as Cruickshank's engraving of 1829 reveals.

stead, therefore, of promoting a practice so evidently detrimental to society, let us begin our opposition by rejecting this bill'. Although the bill had its opponents, the Act became law by a vote of fifty-seven members in favour, to thirty-eight members opposed.

In retrospect, this enactment was moderately successful when compared to its predecessors. Gin sales declined and distillation was curbed. It was this decrease in sales that prompted distillers to pressure Parliament into amending the Act. In 1747, Parliament gave in to the pressure and amended the law of 1743 by allowing distillers to sell gin at the retail shops upon purchase of an annual licence.

The amendment proved disastrous, as gin consumption again increased dramatically. By 1750, Londoners were consuming over eleven million gallons of gin a year, and the city again was in despair. It was not until another piece of legislation, prompted by protests from notable figures, that gin sales slowed down.

Two of the most famous and outspoken critics of gin were Henry Fielding and William Hogarth. Through Fielding's writings and Hogarth's paintings the realities of the 'poison' gin, were brought to the attention of the people.

Hogarth's depiction of everyday life among the London poor in 'Gin Lane' painted a realistic and horrifying account of the evils of gin, from the stupefied

seller of ballads, to the drunken woman lying on the steps in a euphoric coma.

Fielding contributed to the attack on gin by publishing the first constructive examination of crime in London. In *An Inquiry into the Causes of the Late Increase of Robbers, etc.,* he placed the major cause of crime in London on gin consumption and drunkenness amongst the poorer masses. Fielding stated that drunkenness was 'a vice by no means to be construed as a spiritual offence alone, since so many temporal mischiefs arise from it: amongst which are very frequently robbery, and murder itself.' He continued that:

> Wretches are often brought before me, charged with theft and robbery, whom I am forced to confine before they are in a condition to be examined; and when they have afterwards become sober, I have plainly perceived from the state of the case, that the *Gin* alone was the cause of the transgression.

Fielding was not only concerned about crime and gin in eighteenth-century London but also with the lack of commitment on the part of Parliament to help solve the problem. He was further adamant concerning the obsolete laws with which many members in Parliament were aligning themselves:

> What physicians tell us of the animal functions will hold true when applied to laws; both by long disuse lose all

their elasticity and force. Forward habits grow on men, as they do on children, by long indulgence; nor will either submit easily to correction in matters where they have been accustomed to act at their pleasure.

Because of the issues raised by Fielding and Hogarth, the ministry of Henry Pelham attacked the gin trade viciously. The so-called Tippling Act of 1751 started gin's demise. This enactment disallowed distillers from selling gin at the retail level or to any unlicenced vendor. Only persons licenced by the government were allowed to retail gin and licences were limited to innkeepers, victuallers and vendors who paid a duty of £10 rent for their establishments. Furthermore, strength was given to the Act by providing that debts of less than £1 were not recoverable under the law. This made the small buyer less attractive to the distillers.

Punishment for violators was severe. For the second offence, the accused was imprisoned and whipped repeatedly. The third transgression resulted in transportation. These new laws resulted in the elimination of the small gin shop owners and left the distribution of gin to responsible distillers and retailers.

This final Gin Act in 1751 caused the amount of gin consumed to drop from eight million gallons in the early 1750s to less than two million gallons in 1760. The effects of gin on eighteenth-century London were without a doubt, the greatest social and economic enemy of the period. Gin affected more lives, both directly and indirectly, than any war or other episode in eighteenth-century England.

From the years 1720–50, gin's presence among the London lower class was devastating. The harm it incurred was reflected in the sharp increase in death-rates, the decline in birth-rates, the frequency of violent crimes, and the quality of life suffered bitterly.

Because government leaders and the people did not realise the brutal consequences of gin, no precautions were taken to guard against its infiltration. By 1720, gin was deeply embedded into London society and the later attempts by Parliament to remove the vice proved extremely difficult. When Parliament finally did enact legislation, the results were disastrous. The Gin Acts of 1729, 1736 and 1743 were either too difficult to enforce effectively or were not enforced at all.

In the earlier Acts, Parliament was more interested in protecting the various interest groups, than in curbing gin sales. Only through the conscious efforts of such men as William Hogarth, Henry Fielding and Henry Pelham did the flow of gin slow to a trickle in the 1750s. With the tougher laws enacted in 1751, the role that gin played in London society was greatly diminished. Only when the small dram shops were forced out of business, was the period known throughout London as 'gin madness' able to take its place in eighteenth-century English history.

FOR FURTHER READING:

William Thomas Laprade, *Public Opinion and Politics in Eighteenth-Century England.* (Westport, Connecticut: Greenwood Press, 1971); Dorothy Marshall, *Dr. Johnson's London.* (New York: John Wiley & Sons, Inc., 1968); Peter Quennell, *Hogarth's Progress.* (New York: The Viking Press, 1956); George Rudé, *Hanoverian London 1714–1808.* (University of California Press, 1971); H. T. Dickinson, 'Walpole and His Critics', *History Today* (June 1972); John Styles, 'Crime in Eighteenth Century England', *History Today* (March 1988).

Industry, Ideology, Nation-building, and Imperialism: The Nineteenth Century

The early years of the nineteenth century were marked by the interplay of powerful countervailing forces. The French Revolution and industrialization provided the impetus for political, economic, and social changes in Western civilization. The ideals of the French Revolution remained alive in France and inspired political movements in other parts of Europe as well. Industrialization brought material progress for millions, particularly the burgeoning middle class, but often at the expense of the great mass of unskilled workers who were victims of the low-paying, impersonal factory system. Shifting demographic patterns created additional pressures for change. It had taken all of Europe's history to have reached a population of 180 million in 1800. Then, in the nineteenth century, Europe's population doubled, causing major migrations on the continent, typically from the countryside to the cities, and sending waves of emigrants to America, Australia, and elsewhere. By 1919 about 200 million Europeans had settled elsewhere.

But forces of continuity were at work also. Notwithstanding the impact of industrialism, much of Europe remained agrarian, dependent upon the labor of peasants. Christianity remained the dominant religion and, for the moment, the institution of monarchy retained the loyalty of those who wanted to preserve an orderly society. In addition, millions of Europeans, having experienced more than enough turbulence during the French Revolution and Napoleonic era, were willing to embrace even the most reactionary regimes if they could guarantee peace and stability.

The interplay of tradition and change raised vital new issues and generated fundamental conflicts in politics and thought. Of necessity the terms of political discourse were redefined. The century was an age of ideologies: conservatism, with its distrust of untested innovations and its deep commitment to order and tradition; liberalism, with its faith in reason, technique, and progress (usually measured in material terms); various forms of socialism, from revolutionary to utopian, each with its promise of equality and economic justice for the downtrodden working class; and nationalism, with its stirring demand, at once unifying and divisive, that the nationalities of the world should be autonomous. Even Darwinism, the great scientific paradigm of the era, was misappropriated for political purposes. Transformed into Social Darwinism, it was used to justify the dominance of Western nations over their colonies. Popular misconceptions of evolution also reinforced prevailing notions of male supremacy.

In sum, the nineteenth century, for those who enjoyed economic and political status, was the epitome of human progress. For the rest, many of whom shared the materialist outlook of their "betters," it was a time to struggle for a fair share of the fruits of progress.

Several articles in this unit explore the dynamics of change in the nineteenth century. Economic forces and related ideologies are covered in "Engels in Manchester" and "Samuel Smiles: The Gospel of Self-Help." That social change did not always bring opportunities for women, even those who were educated and from relatively well-off families, is a theme of the article "Sophie Germain." That piece should be read in conjunction with the article on Sarah Bernhardt, which gives a somewhat different perspective on what a woman could accomplish in the nineteenth century. Maurice Cranston's article on John Stuart Mill treats a wider range of issues associated with liberty and liberalism in nineteenth-century England. Denis Mack Smith's profile of Giuseppe Garibaldi offers some insights on nation-building in Italy, while "The White Man's Burden" takes up the topic of European imperialism during the 1890s. "Ecological Imperialism" examines long-term biological aspects of European expansion.

Looking Ahead: Challenge Questions

Samuel Smiles, Friedrich Engels, and John Stuart Mill were eminent Victorians, yet their perceptions of nineteenth-century England varied greatly. What were their responses to the great issues of their age and how can we account for the differences?

What, if anything, do the careers of Sophie Germain and Sarah Bernhardt reveal about the place of women in France during the nineteenth century?

What were Giuseppe Garibaldi's contributions to the unification of Italy?

What was meant by "the white man's burden," and what role did this theme play in late-nineteenth-century imperialism?

Unit 3

Cottage Industry and the Factory System

Duncan Bythell

AT THE CENTRE OF MOST PEOPLE'S picture of Britain's industrial revolution in the nineteenth century stands the dark, satanic mill, where an exploited and dispirited army of men, women and children is engaged for starvation wages in a seemingly endless round of drudgery: the pace of their labour is determined by the persistent pulse of the steam engine and accompanied by the ceaseless clanking of machines; and the sole beneficiary of their efforts is the grasping, tyrannical, licentious factory master, pilloried by Charles Dickens in that loud-mouthed hypocrite and philistine, Mr. Bounderby. Crude and exaggerated though this image is, it depicts very clearly the main features of the pattern of production which became widespread in the manufacturing industries, not only of Britain, but also of the other advanced countries, by the end of the nineteenth century. For it highlights the emergence of the factory, where hundreds labour together under one roof and one direction, as the normal type of work-unit; it stresses the new importance of complex machine-technology in the process of production; and it emphasises that, because ownership of these machines, of the building which houses them and the engine which drives them, rests with the private capitalist, there exists an unbridgeable gulf between him and his property-less wage-earning employees.

This system of production, which is usually assumed to have been pioneered and rapidly adopted in Britain's textile industries around the end of the eighteenth century, did not, of course, emerge in a wholly non-industrial world. The popular picture suggests that it replaced – or rather, brutally displaced –

an earlier type of organisation, variously referred to as 'the domestic system', the 'outwork system', or simply as 'cottage industry', which differed totally from the factory system. Whereas the latter concentrates workers under one roof in an increasingly urban enviroment, the former disperses employment into the homes of the workers, most of whom live in the countryside. Although the modern mill is filled with the factory master's costly machinery, the domestic workshop houses simple and traditional hand-tools – the spinner's wheel, the weaver's loom, the curdwainer's bench, the nail-maker's forge, and the seamstress' humble pins and needles – which actually belong to the worker. And whilst the factory system implies clear class division, with the wage-earner firmly subordinated to, and perpetually at odds with, his employer, the domestic system gives the head of the household an independent, quasi-managerial status, which enables him to control his own time and to direct, in a 'natural' fatherly way, the efforts of his family team.

The unspoken assumption is that, in the undisciplined, fulfilling, and relatively classless world of cottage industry, the common man was certainly happier, even if he was materially worse off, than his grandson. Only in the last desperate phase, when the dwindling band of domestic handworkers found themselves competing hopelessly against the new generation of factory machine-minders, is the idyllic image tarnished; and the haunting picture of the doomed handloom weaver, striving in his cellar to match the output of his wife and children who have been forced into the factory, reinforces the notion that, between old and new systems, there is nothing but contrast, conflict, and competition.

Any concept of historical change based on snapshots taken on separate occasions tends to emphasise differences and discontinuities. In the caricature of the domestic and factory systems just presented, they appear to be completely antithetical. Yet on closer examination, the story of most industries which 'modernised' in the course of the nineteenth century is full of important elements of *continuity* and *complementarity* between the factory and the pre-factory stages of their development; and it is on these two dimensions, rather than on the stark contrasts suggested by the traditional stereotype, that I want to focus attention.

Let us consider continuity first. A number of historians have recently suggested that the existence of the domestic system of production in such industries as textiles was one of the main features

Factory spinning

 From *History Today*, April 1983, pp. 17-23. History Today, 83-84 Berwick Street, London W1V 3PJ. Reprinted by permission.

distinguishing the pre-industrial economies of Europe from the Third World countries of today; and although they prefer the abstract concept of 'proto industrialisation' to the well-established and perfectly adequate term 'domestic system', they are essentially claiming that the industrial revolutions of the nineteenth century could not have taken place without the prior development of a form of production which, in their view, was to provide both the capital and the labour needed for modern industrial development.

In making this claim, proponents of the theory of 'proto industry' are drawing attention to one of the most important, but often misunderstood, features of the classic domestic system – the fact that it already showed a clear distinction between the capitalists who controlled it and the wage-earners who depended upon it for their livelihood. For the domestic system, no less than the factory system which replaced it, was a method of mass-production which enabled wealthy merchant-manufacturers to supply not only textile fabrics, but also items as diverse as ready-made clothes, hosiery, boots and shoes, and hardware, to distant markets at home and abroad. In order to do so, they, like the factory masters who followed them, bought the appropriate raw materials and hired wage-labour to convert them into finished products. The pay roll of some of these merchant-manufacturers could run into many hundreds: in the late 1830s, for example, Dixons of Carlisle, cotton manufacturers, employed 3,500 handloom weavers scattered over the border counties of England and Scotland and in Ulster; a decade or so later, Wards of Belper, hosiers, provided work for some 4,000 knitting frames in the counties of Derbyshire, Nottinghamshire, and Leicestershire; and as late as the 1870s, Eliza Tinsley and Co. put out work to 2,000 domestic nail- and chain-makers in the west Midlands.

To service and co-ordinate such large and scattered forces required an elaborate system of communication and control in which the key figures were the agents – variously known as 'putters-out', 'bagmen', and 'foggers' – who were the equivalents of the modern supervisor or shop-floor manager. Certainly, the workers whom these great men employed generally owned their own tools, although in the case of an elaborate piece of machinery like the knitting frame they often had to hire it; and most of them worked on their own premises – although, again, it was by no means rare for the individual weaver, knitter, or nail-maker to rent space and tools in another man's shop. But except in a few minor rural trades like straw-plaiting and lace-making in the south and east Midlands, they neither provided their own raw materials, nor had they any interest in marketing the goods they helped to make. They were, in short, wage-earners who happened to own some of the tools of their trade. But the trade in which they worked was organised by capitalists; and far from making goods to sell to local customers, they were often, all unknowing, supplying the wants of West Indian slaves and North American frontiersmen.

The crux of the argument about continuity between domestic and factory systems of mass-production turns on whether it was actually the case that the firms which set up the first modern factories in a particular industry were already active in it on a putting-out basis, and whether the last generation of domestic workers transformed themselves into the new race of factory hands. Of course, no one is maintaining that continuity was direct and complete in every single industry or region where such a transition occurred: indeed, there were areas such as East Anglia or the Cotswolds where the change-over simply did not take place, and where a once important industry gradually vanished as the old domestic system dwindled and died. But where 'modernisation' did happen in traditional outwork industries in the course of the nineteenth century, as it did in the textile industries of Lancashire and Yorkshire and in the hosiery trade of the east Midlands, historians seem to be agreed that it was existing firms which played a leading role, albeit cautiously and belatedly in some instances, in setting-up the factory system and in embodying some of their capital in buildings and machines; in other words the fortunes made, and the expertise in marketing and managing acquired, in the old system of production were important in enabling the new system to develop.

There is less agreement, however, as to how far the existing hand-workers in any particular industry really did shift over to the factory. The theory of 'proto industry' suggests that the domestic system had created a country-dwelling but landless proletariat in many ways at odds with the traditional rural society around them: they had only a minimal involvement in the agrarian economy, and were therefore rootless and prone to migration; they possessed manual skills irrelevant to farming activities; and as wage-earners, they were obliged to respond to the pressures and the opportunities of a market economy in which the price of survival was adaptability. In terms of both work-skills and mental outlook, that is to say, they were already well-equipped to form the first generation of the modern industrial labour force.

But did this actually happen? The traditional picture suggests not, because it depicts a stubborn refusal to come to terms with changed circumstances and, indeed, a downright hostility to 'machinery' which, in the Luddite movement of 1811-16 in the Midlands and the various outbreaks of loom-smashing in Lancashire and elsewhere, sometimes erupted in violence. Clearly, the worker's readiness to change with the times depended partly on age, and partly on opportunity. Case studies based on census returns for Lancashire weaving villages during the crucial phase of transition in the middle of the nineteenth century suggest that, once a powerloom shed had been started locally, the younger married men were ready enough to take work in it, but that the elderly were either reluctant to do so, or were debarred by the employer, and therefore stuck to the handloom. But until there was a mill virtually on the spot, most of these villagers believed they had little option but to stick to the handloom, and for want of other opportunity they continued to bring their children up to it. Probably the most important strand of continuity in the labour force was in fact provided by the children of the last generation of hand-workers: by and large, a trade dies out because it stopped recruiting sometime before; and the demise of occupations like handloom weaving was finally assured when families were willing and able to put their offspring into something different, instead of forcing them to follow automatically in father's footsteps.

By highlighting the division between capital and labour which characterised the domestic no less than the factory system of production, and by considering the continuity which this engendered, the new theory of 'proto industry' has pinpointed certain popular misconceptions about the nature of cottage industry. First of all, it must be clear that when economic historians refer to 'outwork' or 'cottage industry' they are *not* talking about a world where each family simply makes manufactured goods for its own use – although in even the most advanced societies elements of the home-made and the do-it-yourself survive. Nor are they discussing the self-employed craftsman or genuine artisan – the village shoe-maker and tailor, or the more sophisticated urban wig-maker or cabinet-maker – who produced and sold 'one-off' goods directly to the order of their local customers, and whose successors are still to be found in some parts of the modern economy. Indeed – and this is a second error which needs to be corrected – in the strict sense they are not dealing with 'skill' or 'craft' at all. As a method of mass-production, the greater part of cottage industry involved the

The weaver at his domestic hand loom (above) contrasts sharply with work on a factory power loom (below).

making of plain, simple, inexpensive goods by hands which, although they became more nimble and adept with experience, had neither needed nor received much initial training. Weaving heavy woollens and hammering nails and chains required a certain strength; but weaving plain calico, knitting coarse stockings, sewing buttons on shirts, plaiting straw, and sticking matchboxes together with glue called for neither brain nor brawn. A seven-year apprenticeship to learn the 'mysteries' of most domestic industries was unnecessary, when the work merely involved the monotonous repetition of a few simple

movements of the fingers; and because the work was unskilled and undemanding it was considered particularly suitable for women and children. Domestic industry, like factory industry, involved the worker in much mindless drudgery; the chief difference was that, in working at home with hand-tools, the wage-earner could go at his or her own pace, instead of having to keep up with the steam engine.

Thirdly, just as we need to abandon the notion that the domestic system was all about skilled craftsmen, so we must reject the idea that it was predominantly about 'men' at all. One of the advantages

which the old terms 'domestic system' and 'cottage industry' have over 'proto industry' is that they suggest an important feature which old-style mass-production shared with the early textile mills: a domestic or cottage workshop called on the efforts of housewife, grandparents, and children of both sexes, as well as those of the household's head. Thus the average weaving or knitting family would run two or three looms or frames, and in addition would operate any ancillary machinery needed to prepare or finish the work. Because it worked as a team, the domestic work unit could also practice division of labour, so that each member could specialise on just one stage in the sequence of production. Like any other family business, a workshop involved in the domestic system was a collective enterprise to which all contributed who could: and only when the household included no children old enough to do even the simplest tasks did it depend for its income on what a man could earn by his own unaided efforts. Because the capitalist-controlled outwork industries made particular use of women's and children's labour in this way, female workers were generally in a clear majority in the work force; and in the mass-production section of the needlework trades, where outwork remained particularly important until late in the nineteenth century, and which included men's tailoring and shirt-making as well as dress-making and lace stitching, the preponderance of women was especially striking.

Fourthly, we must not imagine that, in a capitalist controlled industrial system such as outwork was, relations between masters and operatives were marked by much sweetness and light. Since the main tie between them was the cash nexus, disputes about wages could be frequent and bitter. Most employers in the industries which used the domestic system operated in a tough competitive environment, and their likely reaction to a spell of bad trading conditions would be to cut the piece-rates they paid their workers. Most of the scattered rural outworkers were disorganised and docile, and could offer little, if any, resistance; and in any case, for women and children a pittance was deemed better than no work at all. But the adult men – especially those who lived in the towns, and did the better-class work which needed more strength or skill – were another matter. They had a clear conception of the work and wages proper for a man, and they were better able to take collective action against underpaying masters and weak-willed blacklegs who broke the conventional rules.

As a result, at different times in the late eighteenth and early nineteenth centuries, fierce strikes broke out in such towns as Manchester, Coventry, Barnsley and Norwich, major centres of handloom weaving; among the urban framework knitters of Nottingham and Leicester; and among the nail-makers of the Black Country. At a time when

formal trade unionism was a shadowy affair, and in difficult political and economic circumstances, some at least of Britain's industrial outworkers played their part in sustaining patterns of collective bargaining which, *faute de mieux,* sometimes involved great violence; whilst the support these disgruntled men gave to the various campaigns for parliamentary reform between the 1790s and the 1850s has been frequently noted by historians.

Once we have abandoned such misconceptions about the nature of the domestic system as it had come to exist

by the end of the eighteenth century, it is easier to see the similarities and the points of continuity between it and the factory system which was eventually and gradually to supersede it. And when we realise that the domestic system, far from being some prehistoric monster which expired when the first cotton factory was built, actually expanded and persisted in many industries and regions until well into the second half of the nineteenth century, we become aware, not only that the two types of mass-production overlapped in time, but also that they complemented each other,

(Above left) The Domestic Rope Maker; from *The Book of Trades,* 1804. (Above right) Making ropes by Huddart's Machinery.
(Below left) An outworker making pins at home: (below right) a needle pointer at work in a factory in Redditch, Worcester.

rather than competed. The textile industries usually occupy the forefront of any discussion of the domestic and factory systems; and in view of their wide geographic dispersal, their rapid expansion, and the hundreds of thousands they had come to employ by the late eighteenth century, this is entirely appropriate. But because, starting with the spinning branch of the British cotton industry in the 1770s, it was in these industries that the complete triumph of the factory system was achieved earliest, attention has been deflected from the many other trades – particularly shoe-making, clothing, and some branches of hardware – where the domestic system actually became more, rather than less, important. For although the first half of the nineteenth century saw the disappearance into the factory first of spinning and then of weaving in Lancashire and Yorkshire, it also witnessed the expansion of mass-production by outwork methods in the ready-made clothing trades and in the boot and shoe industries. And apart from the fact that these growing industries increased output by traditional rather than modern methods, there were other, less expansionary trades – such as Midlands hosiery and Black Country nail-making – which remained fossilised at the 'domestic' stage of development until well after 1850. In addition, the latter part of the nineteenth century actually saw a number of new, small-scale manufactures, such as paperbag and cardboard-box making, establish themselves as cottage industries. Thus, if outwork had more or less disappeared from the staple textile industries by the 1850s, it was more firmly entrenched than ever in and around many of the industrial towns of the Midlands and the south of England, and, above all, in what were to become known as the 'sweated trades' of London. Why was this?

The pioneering experience of the textile industries suggests some of the answers. Contrary to popular belief, even in the cotton industry, the transition from the domestic to the factory system was a slow, piecemeal affair, which took three generations; and in wool, linen and silk, the process was even more protracted. The reason was simple: the first power-driven machines of the 1770s revolutionised *spinning* only; and by making it possible to produce thread on a scale and at a price which would have been inconceivable in the days of the spinning wheel, they simply created a good deal more work for a great many more work-

ers – in this case, the weavers – at the next stage in the production process. And so long as enough extra weavers could be found at wages the employers were prepared to pay, there was no need to think of replacing the handloom with some labour-saving device, as yet uninvented. Thus between 1780 and 1820, the growth of spinning factories marched *pari passu* with a vast increase in the number of handloom weavers' shops; and technical progress in one section of the industry merely led to the multiplication of traditional handwork in associated sections.

The Croppers of the West Riding of Yorkshire were much involved in the machine-wrecking Luddite movement of 1812.

The same thing was to happen in other industries later: when lace-making was mechanised in Nottingham from the 1820s, there was a consequent increase in the amount of stitching, finishing and mending for hand-sewers in their homes; when machines were first used to cut out the components of a stock-sized shoe or coat, they made more unskilled assembly work for domestic workers; and even when the sewing machine had transformed the traditional needlework trades, it did not necessarily drive them out of the home into the factory, because, as a compact, hand-powered, and relatively inexpensive tool, it could be used in a domestic workshop as effectively as in a large factory. In all these ways, factory and domestic systems often co-existed and complemented each other in a given industry. Since it was rarely either possible or necessary for new techniques to be

introduced simultaneously at every stage in the process of manufacture, flexible combinations of centralised factory work at one stage, and cottage industry at the next, were perfectly practicable.

There was often a regional dimension to the co-existence of these two types of mass-production, and it was here that elements of competition emerged between them. In the classic case of cotton weaving, for example, the handloom survived as the dominant machine in some parts of Lancashire for almost a generation after it had largely given way to the powerloom in others: in large towns such as Stockport, Oldham and Blackburn, factory production was taken up in the 1820s by manufacturers who already operated spinning mills; but it made little progress in the small towns and villages of north-east Lancashire, such as Padiham, Colne and Haggate before the 1840s. In part, this reflected local differences in the availability of labour and capital, for the more remote rural areas were richer in the former than in the latter. But independent of such regional differences, there was also a qualitative side to this 'staggered' adoption of the powerloom, because the early, clumsy factory looms could cope better with the plain types of cloth than with fancy or patterned goods. Other industries were later to show similar disparities in the rate at which different districts and sections adopted new techniques: for example, the boot and shoe industry of Leicester

Merchants in the Cloth Hall, Leeds in 1814. Merchants used cottage industries as a method of mass-production to supply their buyers.

cheap, unskilled, and unorganised labour. So long as he could find enough workers who had no choice but to take his work at the wages he was prepared to offer – no matter how low these might be – he could meet his production targets and reap his expected profits. From the late eighteenth to the late nineteenth centuries, there were many regions of Britain which could provide just such supplies of labour: a high and sustained rate of population increase, together with the greater commercialisation of agriculture, tended to create pools of unemployed or under-employed workers in many rural areas; and in so far as these impoverished country people moved off to the towns in search of more work and better wages, they often merely added to the chaos and confusion in the unskilled urban labour markets.

But what kept the domestic system alive after the mid-nineteenth century more than anything else was the continued availability – long after most adult men had deserted these low paid, dead-end jobs – of female and child labour: incapable of collective self-defence, and often deliberately ignored by their better organised menfolk; accustomed to regarding any earnings, however minute, as a worthwhile contribution to family income; and often only able to work on a part-time or casual basis – they were ideal for many employers' purposes. And in a perverse way, because it thrived on family labour, the domestic system actually helped to perpetuate its own labour force: because cottage industry, by enabling the whole household to earn, acted as a great inducement to early marriages and large families, and thus contributed to the 'population explosion' which was so important a feature of Britain's industrial revolution.

Because labour could be much cheaper in one part of the country than in another, an old-fashioned employer who stuck to outwork could still hope to compete with his more ambitious and enterprising fellows elsewhere who had switched over to factory production. Only in the last quarter of the nineteenth century did a combination of new circumstances – including rural depopulation, compulsory schooling (which both kept young children out of the labour market and widened their horizons), rising real incomes (which made small supplementary earnings less essential to a family), and more 'chivalrous' male

seems to have relied more on factory production and less on outwork than did that of Northampton in the second half of the nineteenth century; whilst in the 1890s, cottage industry was more apparent in the ready-made clothing trade of London than in that of Leeds.

In short, the domestic system of mass-production in British industry took a long time a-dying during the nineteenth century. It might expand in one trade at the very time that it was contracting in another; in some industries, it could enjoy a harmonious co-existence with factory production for many years, whilst elsewhere it might struggle on in arduous competition for a generation or more. Why was this? How could this technically primitive form of large-scale production remain viable for so long in important parts of the world's first industrial economy?

To find the answer, we must try to fathom the minds of the entrepreneurs in the different industries, as they calculated how best, in a complex and competitive world, to get their goods to market with least cost and least trouble to themselves. A manufacturer who had grown up with the domestic system as the dominant mode of production in his trade would need strong inducements to abandon it, because under normal circumstances it offered him many advantages. If his employees provided their

own tools and workrooms, he himself was spared the need to tie up his own capital in bricks and mortar and in machinery; and in times of periodic trade depression or slack seasonal demand – and most of these industries were subject to one or other of these risks, if not, indeed, to both of them – it was the worker, not his employer, who suffered when plant and equipment were standing idle. It was not that these great merchant-manufacturers lacked capital – indeed it required remarkably little fixed capital in most of these industries to build or rent a small factory and fill it with new or second-hand machinery; nor was it generally the case that appropriate new techniques were not available – the time-lag between invention and adoption of a new machine is a recurrent feature in many of these trades; it was rather the case that their capital under the domestic system was embodied in unused raw materials, goods 'in the make', and stocks in the warehouse.

Nevertheless, because it involved more sophisticated machinery, the application of power, and the construction of large, purpose-built work premises, the factory system of production was capital-intensive, rather than labour-intensive. By contrast, what an employer had to rely on to keep cottage industry viable was an abundance of

Gathering Teasels in the West Riding of Yorkshire, an aquatint after George Walker. Teasels are still used to raise the nap on woollen cloth.

(Below) *The Preemer Boy,* 1814; aquatint after George Walker. 'Preeming' is detaching, with an iron comb, the bits of wool on the teasel.

only stay in business if they themselves adopted American methods of production. Both the cotton manufacturers of the 1820s and the boot and shoe manufacturers of the 1890s had to overcome strong opposition from workers still suspicious of machinery and still attached (in spite of the precarious economic position in which it left them) to the domestic system: but once the entrepreneurs in any industry had concluded, for whatever reasons, that the disadvantages of cottage industry outweighed the benefits, its days were numbered.

From the worker's point of view, even if we forget the caricature, the dark satanic mill offered an uninviting prospect; but it is hard to escape the conclusion that the domestic system was in many ways even less agreeable. Even where cottage workers were not directly competing with factory workers – and I have suggested that it would be wrong to put too much emphasis on this side of the story - most of them were poorly paid, and likely to be alternately overworked and under-employed. Worst of all, they were subject to all kinds of abuses, not only from employers and their agents, but often from heads of households and fathers of families who connived, however reluctantly, in the exploitation of their own wives and children. Men may have been unwilling to accept the separation of home and workplace which the gradual replacement of the domestic system by the factory system involved: but in its long-term implications for family life, it was probably one of the most beneficial, as well as one of the most fundamental, of all the changes brought about by the industrial revolution.

attitudes towards women as workers – help gradually to eliminate some of the sources of cheap labour and thus undermine one of the domestic system's chief props.

Changes in market conditions, as well as the increasing difficulty of finding suitable labour, could also be instrumental in persuading entrepreneurs to abandon old-style mass-production in favour of the factory. When, for example, attractive new export markets opened up

for the English cotton industry in Latin America in the early 1820s, Lancashire manufacturers knew that they would be better able to increase output by introducing powerlooms than by seeking out more handloom weavers at higher wages; and when, more than two generations later, British boot and shoe manufacturers were faced with an 'invasion' of their own home market by cheap mass-produced, factory-made American imports, they recognised that they could

FOR FURTHER READING:
D. Bythell, *The Sweated Trades* (Batsford, 1978); J. L. and B. Hammond, *The Skilled Labourer* (London, 1919); G. Stedman Jones, *Outcast London* (Oxford University Press, 1971); P. Kriedte, H. Medick and J. Schlumbohm, *Industrialization before Industrialization* (Cambridge University Press, 1981); D. Levine, *Family Formation in an Age of Nascent Capitalism* (Academic Press, 1977); J. M. Prest, *The Industrial Revolution in Coventry* (Oxford University Press, 1960); E. P. Thompson, *The Making of the English Working Class* (Gollancz, 1963; Penguin Books).

Sophie Germain

*An extraordinary mathematician, she struggled against the prejudices
of 19th-century French society to produce enduring work in number theory
and the theory of elasticity*

Amy Dahan Dalmédico

*Amy Dahan Dalmédico is a member of
the staff at the Centre National de la
Recherche Scientifique and a lecturer at
the École Polytechnique. This article has
been translated and adapted from a story
that first appeared in* Pour la Science, *the
French edition of* Scientific American.

Can you name a famous female mathematician? I would wager that you cannot. But you should first think of Hypatia of Alexandria. Her contemporaries praised her work in mathematics, although none of it survives. Perhaps her writings were destroyed by the Christian monks who stoned her to death in 415 for her pagan beliefs. More than 1,300 years later there was the Marquise de Châtelet, who translated Sir Isaac Newton's *Principia Mathematica* into French. In 1750 the Italian scholar Maria Gaetana Agnesi, known for her achievements in differential calculus, became the first woman professor of mathematics.

Like Hypatia, the Marquise and Agnesi, Sophie Germain fought fiercely against the prejudices of her family, friends and co-workers to become an accomplished mathematician. Germain possessed exceptional talents, great ambition and an undistracted passion for science. She taught herself mathematics and physics and produced original work in number theory and the theory of elasticity. Despite these accomplishments, Germain has still not received the recognition she deserves.

Sophie Germain was born in Paris on April 1, 1776, a decade before the French Revolution and a century after the Scientific Revolution. The laws of Newton governed the cosmos, while the decrees of Louis XVI ruled France. Germain supported political change and advanced the cause of mathematics and physics, and she would fight most fiercely to break the barriers that kept women out of science.

Her father, Ambroise-François Germain, focused his attention on the French Revolution. Ambroise belonged to the society of liberal, educated bourgeoisie. The Germain family had been merchants for generations, and they were comfortable financially. To protect his interest, Ambroise served as an elected deputy of the third estate of the Constituent Assembly of 1789.

At the age of 13, Sophie was described as shy and awkward. She felt her family was obsessed with money and politics, and she took refuge in her father's library, where her intellectual development began. She tutored herself in mathematics by reading every book she could find. Just as she could not understand her parents' interest in politics, they could not grasp her love of mathematics. They thought her interest was astonishing for her age and incongruous with her sex.

The Italian mathematician G. T. Libri-Carrucci—who later became Germain's friend—recounted how the young woman overcame her parents' insistence that she abandon her interest in mathematics. While the family slept, she would study by candlelight. On winter nights when the ink froze in the well, she would read, wrapped in blankets. Her determination outlasted the will of her parents. And despite her "strange" interests, her father supported her financially throughout her life. Germain neither married nor obtained a professional position that could sustain her.

Germain enjoyed reading about Archimedes in the *History of Mathematics,* by Jean-Etienne Montucla. She identified with Archimedes' struggle to continue his research in the midst of the Roman invasion of Syracuse. She progressed from Etienne Bezout's treatise on arithmetic to the works of Newton and the Swiss mathematician Leonhard Euler.

Relatives, friends and educators paid little attention to the interests and talents of young Sophie. They saw little purpose in engaging the mind of a girl from a middle-class family.

Germain was 19 when the Ecole Polytechnique was founded. She obtained the lecture notes for many courses, including analysis taught by Joseph-Louis Lagrange and chemistry by Antoine-François Fourcroy. During one session, Lagrange asked his students to evaluate the course. Fearing her opinions would be ignored, Germain submitted her comments under the name of a former student, Antoine-August Le Blanc. (It is not known whether Le Blanc gave his consent.)

Germain's education in science was extremely unusual for a woman of her social status. During the 18th century, science was taught to some aristocratic women through popularized accounts written specifically for them. The books revealed only enough science to allow a woman to chat about the subject at social events. Francesco Algarotti wrote one of the most notable books of this genre: *Sir Isaac Newton's Philosophy Explain'd for the Use of the Ladies.*

Algarotti believed women were interested only in gallantry and love, and so he tried to teach physics while catering to those interests. His book revolves around a dialogue between a marquise and her interlocutor. In one scene the interlocutor teaches the inverse square law. He explains that the force of gravity—or the intensity of light—decreases in proportion to the inverse square of the distance between the object and the observer. The marquise replies that she is familiar with the concept. "I cannot help thinking . . . that this proportion in the squares of the distances of places . . . is observed even in love. Thus after eight days absence love becomes sixty four times less than it was the first day." Such digressions fill the pages of the book and obscure the few passages that explain physics rigorously.

Germain had no tolerance for such frivolous literature. She was enraged by Joseph-Jérôme Lalande when he implied that she would not be able to understand the work of Pierre-Simon Laplace until she read Lalande's book *Astronomy for Ladies*. Germain made it known publicly that she would not speak to Lalande again.

Her education was disorganized and haphazard. She was granted meetings with Lagrange and several other scientists. Some challenged her with small problems. But Germain yearned for professional training. She was never given the opportunity.

Germain was isolated not only from the community of male scientists but also from the society of educated women. Her social status did not allow her to converse with aristocratic women. Furthermore, she was not related to a male scientist who could introduce her ideas on her behalf—a strategy that worked for the Duchess of Gotta and Madame Lalande.

Germain may also have contributed to her own isolation. She avoided social encounters simply because of modesty and shyness. She believed, like the encyclopedists whom she had read, that her contributions to science would stand the tests of time and social prejudice on their own.

Germain was left outside the scientific community during a period when it was attracting more members, organizing more institutions and encouraging more collaboration than ever before. She was no longer studying in the cold, but she would have to climb an icy wall to gain recognition for her work.

At the turn of the 19th century, Germain found some of her greatest opportunities in the field of number theory. Her first professional contacts, Lagrange and Adrien-Marie Legendre, were both very interested in the subject and encouraged her to learn it.

Over several years she developed a thorough understanding of the complicated methods presented in *Disquisitiones Arithmeticae* by the German mathematician Carl Friedrich Gauss. Excited by the book, Germain wrote him a dozen letters between 1804 and 1809. She signed the letters with the pseudonym "Le Blanc" because she feared "the ridicule associated with being a female scholar."

In her first letter to Gauss, Germain discusses Fermat's equation, namely,

$$x^n + y^n = z^n$$

where x, y, z and n are integers. Pierre de Fermat believed he could prove that the equation cannot be solved if n is greater than 2. To this day, this conjecture, which is known as Fermat's last theorem, has not been proved [see "Fermat's Last Theorem," by Harold M. Edwards; SCIENTIFIC AMERICAN, October 1978].

Germain discovered that Fermat's equation cannot be solved if n is equal to $p-1$, where p is a prime number of the form $8k + 7$. (For example, if k equals 2, then p is a prime number, namely, 23, and n equals 22.) Germain explained her proof to Gauss and remarked: "Unfortunately, the depth of my intellect does not equal the voracity of my appetite, and I feel a kind of temerity in troubling a man of genius when I have no other claim to his attention than an admiration necessarily shared by all his readers."

Gauss responded: "I am delighted that arithmetic has found in you so able a friend. Your new proof . . .is very fine, although it seems to be an isolated case and cannot be applied to other numbers."

In 1806 Germain relayed a message to Gauss through Joseph-Marie Pernety, an army commander who was her friend. Germain was concerned for Gauss's safety as Napoleon I had recently conquered most of Prussia. She told Pernety she feared Gauss might suffer the same fate as Archimedes, who was killed by the Romans. Pernety sent a messenger to report that Gauss was well but that the mathematician did not know Sophie Germain. In her next letter to Gauss, Germain—alias Le Blanc—revealed her true identity.

Gauss was surprised and delighted, "A woman because of her sex and our prejudices encounters infinitely more obstacles than a man in familiarizing herself with complicated problems. Yet when she overcomes these barriers and penetrates that which is most hidden, she undoubtedly possesses the most noble courage, extraordinary talent and superior genius." Gauss was sincere in his praise of Germain as revealed in letters to the German astronomer Heinrich W. M. Olbers.

In 1808 Germain wrote to Gauss, describing what would be her most brilliant work in number theory. Germain proved that if x, y and z are integers and if

$$x^5 + y^5 = z^5$$

then either x, y or z must be divisible by 5. Germain's theorem is a major step toward proving Fermat's last theorem for the case where n equals 5.

Gauss never commented on Germain's theorem. He had recently become professor of astronomy at the University of Göttingen, and he set aside his work in number theory. He became consumed with professional and personal problems.

For the most part, Germain's theorem remained unknown. In 1823 Legendre mentions it in a paper in which he describes his proof of Fermat's last theorem for the case where n is 5. (In 1676 Bernard Frénicle de Bessy had proved the case where n is 4; in 1738 Euler had found the solution for n equals 3.) Germain's theorem was the most important result related to Fermat's last theorem from 1738, until the contributions of Ernst E. Kummer in 1840.

Sophie Germain depended on Gauss to guide her research in number theory. When their correspondence ceased, she searched for new problems and new mentors. In 1809 she found a challenge that would inspire some of her finest work. She strove to explain the classic experiments of Ernst F. F. Chladni, a German physicist who was investigating the vibrations of elastic plates.

In his experiments, Chladni poured fine sand on top of a glass plate. He then rubbed a bow against the plate, causing a vibration. The sand bounced away from regions that vibrated and collected at "nodes," places that remained still. Within seconds, the plate was covered with a series of sandy curves. The patterns were symmetric and spectacular: circles, stars and other geometric figures [*see illustration*]. The character of the pattern depended on the shape of the plate, the position of the supports and the frequency of the vibration.

On a visit to Paris in 1808, Chladni presented his experiments before 60 mathematicians and physicists of the First Class of the Institute of France, a section of the French Academy of Science. Chladni's demonstrations so astounded the scientists that they asked him to repeat his demonstration before Napoleon. The Emperor was impressed, and he agreed that the First Class should award a medal of one kilogram of gold to anyone who could devise a theory that explained Chladni's experiments. In 1809 the First Class announced the contest and set a deadline of two years for all entries.

Germain seized this opportunity. For more than a decade, she would attempt to devise a theory of elasticity. She would compete or collaborate with some of the most eminent mathematicians and physicists. She would feel proud to contribute to a subject that explored the frontier of 19th-century science.

Nevertheless, Germain would remain a stranger in the world of science. Etiquette demanded that she obtain a letter of invitation each time she wished to visit an institution. Her host was required to provide transportation and escorts. These formalities restricted her freedom to discuss topics with scientists. Consequently, she had many difficulties in leaping from the field of number theory to the subject of elasticity.

To prepare herself for a theory of vibrations, she turned to texts such as Lagrange's *Analytical Mechanics* and Euler's essays on the vibrations of elastic rods. Germain tried to explain the behavior of elastic plates by applying the methods that Euler had used. Euler had suggested that a force applied to a rod is counteracted by an internal force of elasticity. He claimed that the force of elasticity at any point along the rod is proportional to the curvature of the rod. Euler's essays inspired Germain to invent a similar hypothesis. She proposed that at any point on a surface, the force of elasticity is proportional to the sum of the major curvatures of the surface at that point. The major curvatures are the maximum and minimum values of curvature out of all the curves formed when planes cut through the surface perpendicularly.

In 1811 Germain was the only entrant in the contest, but her work did not win the award. She had not derived her hypothesis from principles of physics nor could she have done so at the time,

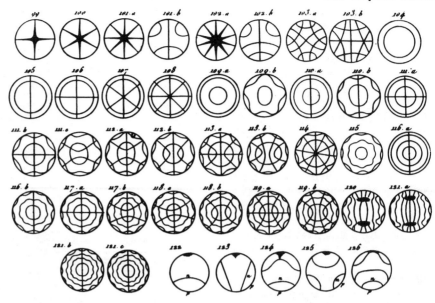

CHLADNI'S FIGURES are formed when a surface covered with sand is struck so that it vibrates. The sand collects along lines where the vibrations are weakest. Sophie Germain was a major contributor to the mathematical theory that explains the figures. The illustration above was reproduced from the 1809 edition of *Traité d'Acoustique,* by Ernst F. F. Chladni.

because she lacked knowledge of analysis and the calculus of variations.

But her work did spark new insights. Lagrange, who was one of the judges of the contest, corrected the errors in Germain's calculations and came up with an equation that he believed might describe Chladni's patterns. Lagrange deduced that if z is the amplitude of the vibration and if z is small, then

$$\frac{d^2z}{dt^2} + k^2 \left[\frac{d^4z}{dx^2} + \frac{d^4z}{dy^2} + \frac{d^4z}{dx^2dy^2} \right] = 0$$

where t is time, k is a constant and x and y represent points on the surface.

By 1811 the First Class extended the contest deadline by two years, and again Germain submitted the only entry. She demonstrated that Lagrange's equation did yield Chladni's patterns in several simple cases. But she could not devise a satisfactory derivation of Lagrange's equation from physical principles. For this work, she received honorable mention from the First Class.

At about the same time, Simeon-Denis Poisson began to invade Germain's intellectual territory. He would become her chief rival. In stark contrast to Germain's experience, Poisson approached the subject of elasticity with all the resources available to a 19th-century scientist.

Poisson entered the Ecole Polytechnique in 1798 at the age of 17. Lagrange and Laplace noticed his talents in prob-

lem solving and abstraction. With the support of Laplace, Poisson moved easily through the ranks of academia. He became a professor at the Ecole Polytechnique and at the Faculty of Sciences in Paris. He frequented the famous Société d'Arcueil, where some of the most distinguished scientists came to discuss and perform novel experiments. Laplace and Claude-Louis Berthollet led the society, and Poisson was its mathematical adviser. In 1812 Poisson, who had entered the heart of the scientific community, was elected to the First Class.

Poisson sought to explain the vibrations of elastic plates by applying the Newtonian model of physics. He began with the idea that a plate consists of molecules that mutually repel and attract one another. He then made what may have seemed like a set of plausible assumptions. He derived a very complicated formula and, by simplifying it, arrived at Lagrange's equation. By modern standards, Poisson's assumptions seem absurd, and he was successful in his derivation of Lagrange's equation only because he had been aware of the work of Germain and Lagrange.

In 1814 Poisson published his article on elastic plates. As a member of the First Class, he was ineligible to compete for the prize. But many of his peers believed Poisson had found a theory that explained the physical mechanisms of Chladni's patterns. The prize was not retired, however.

"I have greatly regretted not knowing the paper of Poisson," Germain wrote in 1815 in an essay on elasticity. "I spent time, precious to me, waiting for the publication." In this paper, she attacked Poisson's approach while trying to propose her own explanation. Germain postulated that the force of elasticity is proportional to the applied force, which in turn is related to the deformation of the surface. The force at one point is proportional to the sum of all curvatures through that point. She then showed that the sum of all curvatures is related to the sum of the maximum and minimum curvatures. Finally, she derived Lagrange's equation from the sum of major curvatures.

This essay became Germain's third entry in the contest whose judges were at that time, Legendre, Laplace and Poisson. They could not accept her postulate that the effect—the deformation—is necessarily proportional to the cause, that is, the applied force. Indeed, decades would pass before an explanation was found. With this reservation, the judges awarded Germain the prize of the First Class. Germain did not attend the award ceremony. Perhaps she thought the judges did not fully appreciate her work, or perhaps she simply did not want to appear in public.

To Germain, the award represented formal recognition of her competence. It gave her authority and confidence. But the scientific community did not show the respect that seemed due to her. Poisson sent a laconic and formal acknowledgment of her work. He avoided any serious discussion with her and ignored her in public. A few years earlier she had viewed herself as an inferior novice in the company of giants. Now she felt no admiration for her colleagues.

Her spirits were soon lifted by a new friendship with Jean-Baptiste-Joseph Fourier. Germain and Fourier both suffered in their careers because of their rivalry with Poisson, and they shared a dislike of him. Through Fourier's efforts, Germain began participating in the activities of the Parisian scientific community. She attended sessions of the Academy of Sciences and was the first woman who was not the wife of a member to do so.

In the 1820s she began an ambitious research project to refine her proofs and contributions to number theory. She and Legendre worked on the project as equal collaborators. She also published a review of her theory of elasticity. She

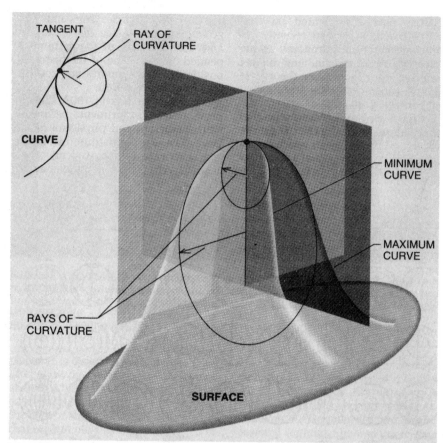

CONCEPT OF CURVATURE was fundamental to Sophie Germain's work on the theory of elasticity. A curve can be closely approximated, at any point, by a circle that shares a tangent with the curve at that point. The curvature is equal to the inverse of the length of the ray that runs from the center of the circle to the point of tangency. For a surface, the curvature at a point is related to the curvature of the curves formed by the intersection of the surface with planes perpendicular to the surface at that point. Out of all such curves, the one that has the greatest curvature and the one that has the least are known as principal curves.

became interested in various scientific fields and socialized with the intellectual elite. Her curiosity and her charm were appreciated by all.

Although Germain certainly produced work worthy of a degree, she never received one. In 1830 Gauss failed to persuade the University of Göttingen to award her the title of *doctor honoris causa*.

After battling breast cancer for two years, Sophie Germain died on June 27, 1831, at the age of 55. She is described on her death certificate as *rentere*, which translates as "a person of private means" but which has the connotation of "an independent woman."

Before her death, she outlined a philosophical essay, which she never finished. It was published posthumously as *General Considerations on Sciences and Letters*. In the essay, she tried to identify the intellectual process in all human activities. She believed the intellectual universe is filled with analogies. The human spirit recognizes these analogies, which then leads to the discovery of natural phenomena and the laws of the universe. We should recognize the analogies between the life of Sophie Germain and our own, and they should lead us to strive for excellence in the face of prejudice.

FURTHER READING

"Examen Des Principes Qui Peuvent Conduire à La Connaissance Des Lois De L'Equilibre Et Du Mouvement Des Solides Elastiques." Sophie Germain in *Annales de Chimie et de Physique*, Series 2, Vol. 38, pages 123–131; 1828.

Sophie Germain: An Essay In The History Of The Theory Of Elasticity. Louis L. Bucciarelli and Nancy Dworsky. D. Reidel Publishing Company, 1980.

"Mécanique Et Théorie Des Surfaces: Les Travaux De Sophie Germain." Amy Dahan-Dalmédico in *Historia Mathematica*, Vol. 14, No. 4, pages 347–365; November 1987.

"Étude Des Méthodes Et Des "Styles" De Mathématisation: La Science Et L'Elasticité." Amy Dahan Dalmédico in *Sciences à l'Epoque de la Révolution.* Paris, Librairie Blanchard, 1988.

In the figure, labels read: TANGENT, RAY OF CURVATURE, CURVE, MINIMUM CURVE, MAXIMUM CURVE, RAYS OF CURVATURE, SURFACE.

Engels in Manchester

Inventing the Proletariat

Gertrude Himmelfarb

Gertrude Himmelfarb is Distinguished Professor of History at the Graduate School of the City University of New York. She is the author of several books, including On Liberty and Liberalism: The Case of John Stuart Mill. *This essay is adapted from her volume,* The Idea of Poverty: England in the Early Industrial Age, *published by Knopf.*

Friedrich Engels, writing in 1845, described Chartism as only one manifestation of the "social war" that was being waged in England, a war that was bound to issue in a full-scale revolution. And this not in the remote future but within a few years, following the economic crisis he predicted for 1846–47, or the one after that in 1852–53.

> The proletarians, driven to despair, will seize the torch which Stephens [the Chartist] has preached to them; the vengeance of the people will come down with a wrath of which the rage of 1793 gives no true idea. The war of the poor against the rich will be the bloodiest ever waged. Even the union of a part of the bourgeoisie with the proletariat, even a general reform of the bourgeoisie, would not help matters. . . . The revolution must come; it is already too late to bring about a peaceful solution.

Nothing could now prevent the revolution. All that could be hoped for was some mitigation of the violence, and that would depend on the "development" of the proletariat. "In proportion, as the proletariat absorbs socialistic and communistic elements, will the revolution diminish in bloodshed, revenge, and savagery," noted Engels.

In most commentaries on Engels's book, *The Condition of the Working Class in England,* this scenario of revolution has been dismissed as a *folie de jeunesse,* a youthful excess of zeal that was surely mistaken, at least in its timing, but that did not seriously affect the substance of the book or the subject denoted by the title. Engels himself was so little discomfited by the patent failure of this prediction that, in supervising the English edition almost half a century later, he let stand the whole of this passage (and others to the same effect), noting only that he had been right in predicting the repeal of the Corn Laws.

Questions have been raised about the accuracy of Engels's citation of documents and the accuracy of the documents themselves, about the bias in his selection of sources and the bias in the sources themselves, about the representativeness of his examples and the validity of his generalizations. But there is another question that is no less important. To what extent was his account of the condition of the English working class shaped by his prognosis of social war and revolution? He himself claimed that the class struggle and revolution were the logical, necessary consequences of the total impoverishment of the proletariat—its "immiseration" in the language of later Marxism. One may well be wary of an ostensibly descriptive or empirical account of the condition of the English working class that so neatly confirmed Engels's ideological predispositions. This does not necessarily invalidate his account; it may be that his ideology was firmly rooted in the actuality. It does, however, mean that the whole of the historical record has to be examined: the reports, articles, and books cited by Engels, his personal observations and reflections, and another set of sources he did not cite or make explicit—the ideas he brought with him to his study of the English working class. To raise this issue is not to subject him to any special or invidious kind of examination. It is only to take seriously ideas he himself took seriously. In the preface to the English edition written many years later, he observed that the book revealed the "stamp of his youth," "traces of the descent of modern Socialism from one of its ancestors, German philosophy"—by which he meant that he had not yet emancipated himself from the philosophy and politics of Young Hegelianism.

Die Lage der arbeitenden Klasse in England was published in Leipzig in 1845; the first English language edition appeared in 1887 in America, and in 1892 in England, under the title *The Condition of the Working Class in England in 1844.* The date in the English title reminds us that almost half a century intervened between the book's original publication and its first appearance in England, a period during which the book was known only in Germany (and mainly in the German radical movement) and not at all in the country that was the object of its concern (except perhaps among the small group of German émigrés in London). Whatever else may be said about it—as social reportage, ideological polemic, literary text, psycho-biographical revelation, or "semiotic" exercise—Engels's book was not, in the context of early Victorian England, a contemporary document in the way that Carlyle's or Cobbett's writings were. It was contemporary in the sense of being contemporaneous with the period it was describing. But it had no public resonance, no echoes in public opinion, no part in the shaping of the public consciousness. Later, to be sure, the book did enter the public domain, at a time, not by accident, when English socialism finally emerged as an important force. It has since become so much a part of the historical record, of the consciousness of historians if not of contemporaries, that it has been accused of unduly dominating that record. For this reason as well as its intrinsic interest—as a picture of the English working classes seen through the eyes of a German radical newly resident in England—*The Condition of the Working Class in England* is a fascinating historical document.

Engels was twenty-two years old when he arrived in Manchester in November 1842 to join a textile firm in which his father was a partner. He remained in England for twenty-one months and started his book after his return to Germany in September 1844; it was completed by March and published in May. These bare facts are suggestive enough, although they hardly begin to tell the story. By the time the young man came to England, he had been initiated into the various factions of German radicalism known collectively as Young (or Left) Hegelianism, had met the leading figures in that movement (Wilhelm Weitling, Moses Hess, Bruno and Heinrich Bauer, Arnold Ruge, and Karl Marx), had published articles on various subjects (including an attack on the mill owners of his own town, of which his father was one), and had become a regular contributor to the radical journal, the *Rheinische Zeitung.* Before leaving for England he paid two visits to Cologne to meet with the staff of the *Zeitung.* On one occasion he was coolly received by the newly appointed editor, Karl Marx, who disapproved of his association with the "Freien" sect in Berlin, the extremist faction led by the Bauers and Ruge. Another editor, Moses Hess, befriended him and engaged him in long discussions. "We spoke about current questions," Hess wrote to a friend several months later, "and he, an Anno I revolutionary, departed from me an enthusiastic communist." Those "current questions" must have included England, for Hess had just published his book, *Die europäische Triarchie,* describing the three stages in the history of human emancipation: the German Reformation that he identified with religious freedom, the French Revolution with political freedom, and a future English revolution with social freedom.

When Engels arrived in England it was as a confirmed communist and an avowed revolutionary. His first weeks were spent in London, and either then or on a subsequent visit he met the German colony of exiled revolutionaries, members of the League of the Just who had been implicated in the Blanquist uprising in Paris in 1839; they were, he later explained, the first "proletarian revolutionaries" he had met. During his first week in London he wrote three articles for the *Rheinische Zeitung,* one of which assured his German readers that the inherent "contradictions" in the English economy could be resolved only by revolution. No sooner had he installed himself in Manchester than he sent off an article entitled "The Condition of the Working Class in England," which opened by asserting that that condition was becoming "daily more precarious, in spite of the fact that unemployment had recently decreased and the English worker was generally in a far better state than the German or French worker.

> The worker there (in Germany and France) earns just enough to allow him to live on bread and potatoes; he is lucky if he can buy meat once a week. Here he eats beef every day and gets a more nourishing joint for his money than the richest man in Germany. He drinks tea twice a day and still has enough money left over to be able to drink a glass of porter at midday and brandy and water in the evening. This is how most of the Manchester workers live who work a twelve-hour day.

This affluence, however, was temporary for the smallest fluctuation of trade would throw thousands out of work, and a major depression was in the offing.

In the following months, in the spare time left him from business, Engels managed to write a series of articles for a German émigré magazine in Zurich (the *Rheinische Zeitung* having ceased publication), other articles for the Owenite *New Moral World* and the Chartist *Northern Star,* and a long essay, "Outlines of a Critique of Political Economy," for the *Deutsch-Französische Jahrbücher* edited by Marx and Ruge in Paris. When the Soviet translator of the "Critique" later commented on the lingering traces of "ethical 'philosophical' communism" and "abstract principles of universal morals and humaneness," he had in mind such passages as that on the private ownership of land: "To make land an object of huckstering . . . was the last step towards making oneself an object of huckstering. It was and is to this very day an immorality surpassed only by the immorality of self-alienation." For the most part, however, the "Critique" was an impassioned but not notably "philosophical" or moralistic analysis, using the language and concepts of political economy—wealth, value, price, capital, rent, wages—to criticize the system of private property that the political economists took for granted. That system, Engels argued, was destined to collapse as a result of its inherent contradictions. Competition would lead to monopoly and the centralization of property; economic crises would become more acute and widespread; the world would be divided into capitalists and workers and eventually with the impoverishment of the small capitalists, into millionaires and paupers; wages would decline to the point where the worker received "only the very barest necessities, the mere means of subsistence"; and the final crisis would result in the abolition of private property and the "total transformation of social conditions." (Fifteen years later Marx, in his own *Critique of Political Economy,* paid tribute to Engels's "brilliant outline" that anticipated his own in so many respects.)

The final words of Engels's essay read like an advertisement for *The Condition of the Working Class in England.* Having raised the question of machinery and the factory system, Engels explained that that subject was beyond the scope of the present essay. "Besides," he added, "I hope to have an early opportunity to expound in detail the despicable immorality of this system, and to expose mercilessly the economist's hypocrisy which here appears in all its brazenness." The allusion was to the book he was planning on the political and economic state of England, with a chapter or two on the working class. He published two articles on that subject in yet another German émigré magazine in the summer of 1844. That same summer, returning from England, Engels stopped off in Paris to meet the exiled revolutionaries assembled there, including Karl Marx. That visit marked the beginning of a lifelong friendship and collaboration between the two men. It may also have been then, perhaps on the advice of Marx, that Engels decided to devote the whole of his forthcoming book to the English working class.

Returning to his home in Barmen in the Rhineland, Engels immersed himself in the books and newspapers he had brought with him from England—not, however, to the exclusion of political activities. He joined Hess in founding a new radical periodical, helped organize a working-class society, addressed two public meetings in which he explained why the continued expansion and impoverishment of the proletariat would lead to a social revolution "in a very short time," continued to write for the *New Moral World* and various German radical publications, and contributed his small part to *The Holy Family* (Marx's polemic against the Bauers and Stirner)—all this during the six or seven months in which he also wrote the 300-odd-page *Condition of the Working Class in England.* It was a prodigious accomplishment, testifying to his extraordinary intellectual vitality and his total political commitment.

Even if one were unaware of the ideological background of *The Condition of the Working Class in England,* one could not fail to see in it a good deal more than a descriptive account of that "condition." At the very least it included an analysis of the system responsible for that condition, a moral critique of both the condition and the system, and a prognosis of the development of the system and its eventual destruction by those who suffered so grievously under it. In a letter to Marx written soon after he started work on the book, Engels explained that he was drawing up a "bill of indictment" against the English bourgeoisie and, by the same token, against the German bourgeoisie.

I shall present the English with a fine bill of indictment. I accuse the English bourgeoisie before the entire world of murder, robbery and all sorts of other crimes on a mass scale, and am writing an English preface which I shall have printed separately and shall send to the English party leaders, literary men and Members of Parliament. Those fellows will have to remember me. Moreover, it is a matter of course that while I hit the bay I also mean to strike the donkey, namely the German bourgeoisie, of whom I say clearly enough that it is just as bad as the English, only not so courageous, consistent and adept in sweat-shop methods.

In the book itself Engels was entirely candid about his purpose, at least in respect to the English. In the preface addressed to "the Working Classes of Great Britain," he identified himself with the workers in the struggle against their "oppressors," and throughout the book he spoke of the middle classes as "murderers," the social order as a systematic form of "social murder," and the class struggle as a form of "social war."

The bill of indictment consisted of descriptions, episodes, and statistics culled from parliamentary reports, newspapers, books, and pamphlets, supplemented by Engels's own observations and judgments. The effect was a picture of desperate, hopeless misery: workers dying of starvation or so malnourished and enfeebled as to be on the verge of death, fifty thousand homeless people wandering the streets of London and millions more crowded into the meanest, foulest slums, all of them clothed in rags, exposed to the damp and cold, their bodies sickly, crippled, stunted, deformed. The moral state of these unfortunates was no less appalling, as they drowned their sorrows in drink, vented their rage in crime and violence, and lost themselves in the only indulgence left to them, sexual licentiousness. As misery and vice was the refrain of Malthus's work, so degradation and demoralization was the refrain of Engels's.

Occasionally, Engels raised the issue that has exercised his critics: Was the condition he described the extreme or the average condition of the working class? What part of the working class was in that state of destitution, degradation, and demoralization? In the course of one chapter, caustically entitled "The Great Towns," he estimated that one-tenth of the workers were utterly degraded, that 12 percent lived in the foulest cellars, and that "the average is much nearer the worst cases than the best"—the "worst" having just been described as "bitter want, reaching even homelessness and death by starvation." Potentially every worker was in that worst condition. "Every proletarian, everyone, without exception, is exposed to a similar fate without any fault of his own and in spite of every possible effort."

It could be said that Engels's portrait was so stark because the reality itself was stark. He had arrived in Manchester, the worst of all industrial towns—"the shock city of the age," as Asa Briggs has aptly called it—at the worst of all times, in the midst of the most severe economic depression in half a century. Even then, however, as he himself reported in the first of his newspaper articles from Manchester, less than 10 percent of the workers were unemployed, and those who were employed could afford a quantity and quality of meat and drink that would have been the envy of the German or French worker. Engels did not reproduce that passage, or anything like it, in his book, but he could have done so without any logical inconsistency (although it would have detracted from the prevailing impression of gloom). For the point was not so much the actual, existential condition of the worker as his essential and potential condition, the condition that was his simply by virtue of his being a "proletarian," a member of the propertyless class. It was this state of propertylessness that doomed the worker to the "worst" condition even if, for the moment, he seemed to be in a "better" or "best" condition. In this sense the question of percentages and averages was irrelevant, since it was the extreme, not the average, that was the essential condition of the whole of the working class.

In the same sense, every aspect of the worker's being, his moral and intellectual as much as his economic and physical condition, was in that extreme state. One might have expected a bourgeois reformer like Edwin Chadwick to speak of the working class as a "race" so thoroughly degraded and demoralized that it "must really have reached the lowest stage of humanity," or to describe dwellings in which "only a physically degenerate race, robbed of all humanity degraded, reduced morally and intellectually to bestiality could feel comfortable and at home." It was, in fact, from Chadwick and his kind—J. P. Kay (later Kay-Shuttleworth), Peter Gaskell, Nassau Senior, and other "bourgeois" reformers, critics, and investigators—that Engels took his material. He went further than they did, however, because his purpose was different. They wanted to arouse the consciousness and conscience (and perhaps the fears as well) of the middle classes in order to promote specific reforms. Engels wanted to portray the workers in that condition of destitution and degradation which was a prelude not to reform but to revolution, a revolution to restore the humanity that the present system denied to them.

There was no hidden agenda here, no secret strategy. Engels was quite explicit about the revolutionary implications of his account. Again and again he interrupted his description of the vile state of the workers to hold out the promise of redemption, the redemption that would come, not as the result of rebellion, but in the very act of rebellion. The impulse to rebel was the saving grace, the one glimmer of humanity in an otherwise dehumanized race.

There is, therefore, no cause for surprise if the workers, treated as brutes, actually become such; or if they can maintain their consciousness of manhood only by cherishing the most glowing hatred, the most unbroken inward rebellion against the bourgeoisie in power. They are men so long only as they burn with wrath against the reigning class. They become brutes the moment they bend in patience under the yoke, and merely strive to make life endurable while abandoning the effort to break the yoke.

. . . How can such a sentence [to the division of labor] help degrading a human being to the level of a brute? Once more the worker must choose, must either surrender himself to his fate, become a "good" workman, heed "faithfully" the interest of the bourgeoisie, in which case he most certainly becomes a brute, or else he must rebel, fight for his manhood to the last, and this he can only do in the fight against the bourgeoisie.

To every point the same message came through: the condition of brutality was the precondition for change, the only kind of change that was of any consequence—revolution. "The Great Towns" opened with a memorable description of hordes of people crowded together, streaming past one another, yet brutally indifferent to and entirely separated from one another. It was an altogether repulsive sight, repugnant to human nature itself. "This isolation of the individual, this narrow self-seeking, is the fundamental principle of our society elsewhere, [and] it is nowhere so shamelessly barefaced, so self-conscious as just there in the crowding of the great city." The "dissolution of mankind into nomads" reminded Engels of the recent book by Max Stirner, the most anarchistic of the Young Hegelians, who described all of society and capitalist society preeminently as a "war of each against all." In this atomistic, ferociously competitive world, everyone looked upon everyone else as an object to be used and exploited, and the capitalists, being the strongest, were able to seize everything for themselves, leaving the mass of the poor with the barest means of existence. But these same cities, the breeding places of misery and vice, were also—and here Engels parted from Stirner—the "birthplaces of the labor movements." Were it not for the cities, the workers, isolated and exploited as individuals, would have been slower in coming to a consciousness of their oppression, of their class interests and class identity. Thus the cities aggravated the social problem and,

by aggravating it, helped solve it; they were the disease and the remedy. "The great cities have transformed the disease of the social body, which appears in chronic form in the country into an acute one, and so made manifest its real nature and the means of curing it."

Industrialism had the same dual aspect. It stupefied the worker by limiting him to a single process in the division of labor, enslaved him by the tyrannical discipline of the factory, dehumanized him by reducing him to a machine, a "chattel" to be used and discarded as his employer saw fit—but it was also the means of his salvation. The most highly industrialized part of the economy produced the most intelligent and energetic workers who were in the forefront of the labor movement and of the class struggle. Even those workers who were not so intelligent, whose "mental state" was as enfeebled as their physical condition, who were more ignorant than the working classes of Spain and Italy—even they, by sheer force of "necessity," came to know their own interests and to know them to be implacably opposed to the bourgeoisie. Similarly the immigration from Ireland, which had the immediate effect of degrading and barbarizing the English workers, also "deepened the chasm between workers and bourgeoisie, and hastened the approaching crisis."

In each case the disease contained within itself its own antidote. Since the antidote matured only as the disease did, the disease had to run its course before the antidote became effective. As in a grave sickness where the fate of the patient was determined by the final, violent crisis, so the social disease had to await its crisis. The only difference was that the English nation, unlike an individual patient, could not die. "And as the English nation cannot succumb under the final crisis, but must go forth from it, born again, rejuvenated, we can but rejoice over everything which accelerates the course of the disease." (This was later to be known as the "worse is better" principle, the principle that makes reactionaries preferable to reformers—"reformists," as Marxists called them—and, in one famous instance, Nazis preferable to Social Democrats.)

When Engels authorized the translation and publication of *The Condition of the Working Class in England* in 1887, in the midst of another economic crisis, he believed the book to be as relevant and urgent as ever. The timing of the revolu-

tion may have been inexplicably delayed, but the revolution itself was still on the agenda of history. From the perspective of "mature Marxism," Engels's work was a case study of capitalism *in extremis,* the existential confirmation of the scenario outlined in the *Communist Manifesto* and elaborated in *Capital.*

To be sure, there were deviations, some traces of "German philosophy," which gave it the "stamp of his youth." Engels's own example of that vestigial idealistic philosophy was the passage: "Communism is a question of humanity and not of the workers alone. . . . Communism stands above the strife between bourgeoisie and proletariat." He might also have cited the image of the city as the "dissolution of mankind"; or the portrait of the worker deprived of his "humanity" and "manhood," forced to rebel in order to assert himself as a "human being"; or, the Feuerbachian "generic" or "species" man in the preface addressed to the "Working Classes of Great Britain":

I found you to be more than mere *Englishmen,* members of a single isolated nation, I found you to be *Men,* members of the great and universal family of Mankind, who know their interest and that of all the human race to be the same. And as such, as members of this Family of "One and Indivisible" Mankind, as Human Beings in the most emphatical meaning of the word, as such I, and many others on the Continent, hail your progress in every direction and wish you speedy success.

Apart from these occasional idealistic effusions, as he later thought them, and some unfortunate predictions, Engels had good reason to be pleased with the *Condition,* for it gave every appearance of corroborating the *Manifesto* both in its general thesis and in its details. The pauperization of the English working class appeared here, as in the *Manifesto,* as the necessary precondition for the historical process that would inevitably lead to revolution. And in the *Condition,* again as in the *Manifesto,* material impoverishment was accompanied by a moral degradation that ensured the total alienation of the working class. Although the word "alienation" did not appear in the *Condition* (or for that matter in the *Manifesto,* except to deride the "True Socialists" who still talked of the "alienation of humanity"), it was a thoroughly alienated working class Engels described, a class alienated from "generic" humanity as well as from bourgeois society and culture.

Like the proletariat in the *Manifesto,* which was utterly divorced from bourgeois family relations, national character, law, morality and religion, the English working class in the *Condition* was a "race wholly apart" in just these respects. "The workers speak other dialects, have other thoughts and ideals, other customs and moral principles, a different religion and other politics than those of the bourgeoisie." In some ways the workers were more humane than the bourgeoisie, friendlier, more generous, less greedy, less bigoted. But it was their less agreeable traits Engels dwelt on at much greater length and in starker detail: drunkenness, brutality, licentiousness, and criminality. To be sure, there was an explanation for each of these. They drank themselves into a state of bestiality and engaged in hideous sexual practices because these were the only pleasures they had. They stole and committed crimes because they were starving and desperate. They were irreligious for the same reason that they were illiterate, because the bourgeoisie totally ignored their education save for the futile attempt to inculcate the incomprehensible dogmas of conventional religion. Their families were destroyed by the factories and by filthy, crowded homes devoid of any domestic comfort. Where the family was not "wholly dissolved," it was "turned upside down," with the wife working and the unemployed husband at home, a situation that "unsexes the man and takes from the woman all womanliness." In addition to the sexual promiscuity among the workers themselves, the women were at the mercy of their employers, who enjoyed the traditional privilege of the master over the slave, the *jus primae noctis*—except that the employer could choose to exercise that right at any time.

The working class and the bourgeoisie were thus "two radically dissimilar nations, as unlike as difference of race could make them." They were different as much by will as by circumstance. The rejection by the working class of bourgeois morality and culture was an expression of defiance, a conscious or unconscious act of rebellion. Crime was a form of "social war," a war that the bourgeoisie had been waging against the proletariat and that the proletariat was now turning against their exploiters. Stealing was more than a means of

staving off hunger, it was a "primitive form of protest," a denial of the "sacredness of property," an assertion by the worker of "contempt for the existing social order" and of opposition to the "whole conditions of his life." The "surplus population" that roamed the streets, begging, stealing, and murdering, was engaged in the same social war: "He among the 'surplus' who has courage and passion enough openly to resist society to reply with declared war upon the bourgeoisie to the disguised war which the bourgeoisie wages against him, goes forth to rob, plunder, murder, and burn!" These violations of the law were the evidence of a society "already in a state of visible dissolution," the prelude to that "universal outburst" whose symptoms were ordinary crimes. Atheism was another form of that social war. Echoing Marx's essay "On the Jewish Question" published the previous year, Engels equated religion with the worship of money. "Money is the god of this world; the bourgeois takes the proletarian's money from him and so makes a practical atheist of him." That atheism announced to the world that the proletariat no longer respected the "sacredness and power of the earthly God" and was prepared to "disregard all social order."

If the working class and bourgeoisie were "radically dissimilar," so were the modern working class and the preindustrial workers. Engels's account of the latter recalls the ambiguous passage in the *Manifesto* about the "feudal, patriarchal, idyllic relations" that had been "pitilessly torn asunder," leaving nothing but "naked self-interest" and "callous 'cash-payment.' " The *Condition* enlarged upon that idyllic preindustrial state.

So the workers vegetated throughout a passably comfortable existence, leading a righteous and peaceful life in all piety and probity; and their material position was far better than that of their successors. They did not need to overwork; they did no more than they chose to do, and yet earned what they needed. They had leisure for healthful work in garden or field, work which, in itself, was recreation for them, and they could take part besides in the recreations and games of their neighbours, and all these games—bowling, cricket, football, etc., contributed to their physical health and vigour. They were, for the most part, strong, well-built people, in whose physique little or no

difference from that of their peasant neighbours was discoverable. Their children grew up in the fresh country air, and, if they could help their parents at work, it was only occasionally; while of eight or twelve hours of work for them there was no question.

Engels continued in this vein, rhapsodizing about those "respectable" workers who had a "stake in the country," who were good husbands and fathers, drank no more than was good for them, mingled happily with the yeomanry and had a comfortable "patriarchal relation" with their "natural superior," the squire. Their children enjoyed the same natural relationship with their fathers; working at home, and raised in "obedience and the fear of God," they grew up in "idyllic simplicity and intimacy with their playmates." (This moral regimen did not preclude the practice of premarital intercourse, but since it was invariably followed by marriage, that "made everything good.")

The idyll went on for several hundred words before the fatal flaw emerged. Just as in the *Manifesto* where the "feudal, patriarchal, idyllic relations" were shortly exposed as the "idiocy of rural life," so in the *Condition* that comfortable, respectable, patriarchal existence suddenly appeared, in mid-paragraph, to be a life "not worthy of human beings." Spared the violent fluctuations of the industrial cycle, the workers were also spared all mental and political activity. "Comfortable in their silent vegetation," they were intellectually dead, aware only of their petty, private concerns, and ignorant of the "mighty movement which, beyond their horizons, was sweeping through mankind." In truth, they were not human beings; they were merely "toiling machines in the service of the few aristocrats who had guided history down to that time." It was only when the industrial revolution roused them out of that happy life, making them "machines pure and simple," that they were forced to "think and demand a position worthy of men," and thus were drawn into the "whirl of history."

This portrait of the happy, healthy, moral, if mentally torpid preindustrial worker has been criticized by some historians as the familiar myth of the Golden Age, and defended by others on the ground that that age was indeed golden compared with that which followed. The controversy, however important in its own terms, is largely irrelevant to Engels. For here, even more than in the rest of his book, he was concerned not so much with the actual condition of the preindustrial workers as with their role in his historical schema; and in that schema these workers had no role. If Engels's account of them seems mythical and unhistorical, it is because they themselves were unhistorical, which is to say prehistorical—prehistorical from the perspective of the revolution that would bring them on the stage of history and make them the leading actors in history, the agents of the "dissolution" of society and the "transformation" of mankind.

It is no accident that the *Condition* was one of the first occasions when the phrase "industrial revolution" was used, not once but repeatedly, and with the full force of a revolutionary event. The industrial revolution was for Engels the decisive "historical moment," the beginning of the expansion and concentration of the means of production which led to contradictions and crises. It was also then that the working class started its descent into pauperism and degradation which left it no choice but to rebel. The preindustrial workers, by contrast, were not "ripe for revolution" because the economy was not ripe for revolution. Spared the misery that was a precondition of revolution, they were healthy, happy, and comfortable; spared the self-consciousness that would have made them rebellious, they were apathetic and torpid. They had precisely the qualities required of them in a drama in which their only role was to exist and survive. Like a nation without a history, they were happy—and boring.

In the preface to the German edition of his book, Engels explained that a "knowledge of proletarian conditions" was necessary to provide a "solid ground for socialist theories," and that only in England did these conditions exist "in their classical form and in their perfection." *The Condition of the Working Class in England* was meant to give that solid, empirical "ground" for Marxist theory. All the essential ingredients were there: the preindustrial workers in a comfortable, unconscious, unrevolutionary state; the modern proletariat pauperized and degraded, reduced to a "slavery" worse than the serfdom of old, totally alienated from bourgeois morality and culture; the "lower middle class" impoverished and forced down into the ranks of the proletariat; society divided into two irreconcilable classes; the bourgeoisie, the "ruling class," exercising the "power of the State"; the increasing concentration of industry, wealth, property, and population; the increasing intensity of economic crises, misery, and "social war"; and finally the "violent revolution, which cannot fail to take place." Although no one of these propositions was novel in England at the time, the totality was. And it was the totality that added up to an ideology significantly different from the prevalent modes of English radicalism and significantly similar to that of the *Communist Manifesto.*

A distinctive and crucial part of this ideology was its vocabulary—"proletariat" most notably. The word was not invented by Marx or Engels. Derived from the Latin *proles* (offspring), it originally referred to the lowest class of Roman citizen who served the state only by producing children. In one variation or another (as an adjective, or in the French form of *prolétaires*), it was used in England from at least the seventeenth century to describe either the ancient populace or the contemporary "rabble." In its modern meaning, applied to the working classes as a whole, it began to appear in Germany in the mid-1830s and was popularized in 1840 by Pierre Joseph Proudhon's *Qu'est-ce que la propriété?* and in 1842 by Lorenz von Stein's *Der Sozialismus und Communismus des heutigen Frankreichs.* (Unlike Proudhon, Stein was a conservative who was as wary of the proletariat as of socialism or communism.) By the time Engels wrote the *Condition,* "proletariat" was part of the vocabulary of French and German Socialists—but not of English radicals.

Engels himself was fully aware of the alien connotation of "proletariat." The original preface to the *Condition,* written in English and intended for distribution to members of parliament and English literary men, was couched in the familiar English vocabulary. It was entitled "To the Working Classes of Great Britain," its salutation read "Working Men!" and the text itself referred to "working men." The German preface, however, which followed the English one, started by speaking of the condition of the "working class," went on in the next sentence to "proletarian conditions," and in the following paragraph to the "English proletariat"—all on the first page—and concluded with some comments on terminology.

I have used the word *Mittelklasse* all along in the sense of the English word *middle-class* (or *middle-classes,* as is said almost always). . . . Similarly, I have continually used the expressions working men (*Arbeiter*) and proletarians, working class, propertyless class and proletariat as equivalents.

The opening words of the book established the significance of the term. "The history of the proletariat in England," Engels explained, dated from the second half of the eighteenth century with the invention of the steam engine and textile machinery. These inventions gave rise to an "industrial revolution, a revolution which altered the whole civil society." England was the "classic soil" of this revolution and, therefore, "the classic land of its chief product also, the proletariat." The preindustrial worker, the handweaver working at home, had been "no proletarian." With the appearance of the spinning jenny the class of farm weavers merged with the new class of weavers who lived entirely upon wages, had no property and so became "working men, proletarians." At the same time, the propertyless, wage-earning agricultural laborers became an "agricultural proletariat." The proletariat was fully developed only in England because only there were both industry and agriculture transformed by the industrial revolution. "The industrial revolution is of the same importance for England as the political revolution for France, and the philosophical revolution for Germany." It was decisive for the development of the economy and even more for the development of the proletariat. "The mightiest result of this industrial transformation is the English proletariat."

Engels prided himself on the fact that his was the first book to deal with "*all* the workers." And so it did, all workers being subsumed under the category of the proletariat. The "industrial proletariat," the "mining proletariat," and the "agricultural proletariat" shared the crucial characteristic of being propertyless. By the same token, the propertied classes—the middle class and landed aristocracy—belonged to the single class of the "bourgeoisie": "In speaking of the bourgeoisie I include the so-called aristocracy."

This condition of propertylessness proletarianized the workers and then, by the logic of capitalist development, pauperized them. Contemporaries (and historians) might object that not all workers were impoverished, that the navvy or artisan was in a far better state than the agricultural laborer, and the factory worker better off than the handloom weaver. Engels recognized these differences but regarded them as ultimately inconsequential. If some workers were not actually currently impoverished, they were so essentially and potentially. They were a single class characterized by a single condition; the propertylessness that defined them as the proletariat pauperized them and revolutionized them. That single "class" and "condition" were reflected in the singular title. It was probably out of deference to English usage that Engels chose to call his book *The Condition of the Working Class* rather than *The Condition of the Proletariat.* But he could not have adopted the more familiar "working classes," "poor," or "people" without doing violence to his thesis.

The idea of poverty that emerged from the book was implicit in the word "proletariat." It was total, unrelieved poverty, a poverty that extended itself to every realm of life—cultural, moral, and intellectual as much as material—a poverty that created a class so different as to constitute a different "race." The poverty of the proletariat was quantitatively different from the poverty of the old poor: the preindustrial poor were less impoverished, less hardworking, less miserable. And it was qualitatively different, creating a new consciousness, a new identity and a new historical role. This is what impressed Lenin when he read the *Condition:* "Engels was the *first* to say that the proletariat is *not only* a suffering class; that it is, in fact, the disgraceful economic condition of the proletariat that drives it irresistibly forward and compels it to fight for its ultimate emancipation. And the fighting proletariat *will help itself.*"

Engels was not, in fact, the first to say that. Stein made it the crucial difference between the "proletariat" and the "poor." There had always been poor, he said. What was new and dangerous, was the proletariat: "dangerous in respect of its numbers and its often tested courage; dangerous in respect of its consciousness of unity; dangerous in respect of its feeling that only through revolution can its aims be reached, its plans accomplished." This dangerousness, which made the proletariat so perilous to Stein, was a source of pride and hope to the Young Hegelians. When they distinguished between the proletariat and the poor, it was precisely

the size and courage of the new class, its unity, self-consciousness, and above all, revolutionary character that made it superior to the old poor, that made it a historical class endowed with the highest historical mission.

In his "Introduction to the Critique of Hegel's *Philosophy of Right,*" published early in 1844, Marx described the proletariat (in a passage now regarded as the classic expression of Feuerbachian "humanism") as "a class of civil society which is not a class of civil society, an estate which is the dissolution of all estates, a sphere which has a universal character by its universal suffering." Less well known but equally notable was the next paragraph in which the "artificially *impoverished*" proletariat was contrasted to the "*naturally arising poor*"; the latter, impoverished by nature and natural circumstances, would be gradually absorbed into the larger class that was impoverished by the artificial institution of private property. In *The Holy Family,* the following year, the proletariat retained some of that generic, humanistic character—"the abstraction of all humanity"—while acquiring a more historical, deterministic character, for it was driven to revolt against the inhuman conditions of its life by "absolutely imperative *need*—the practical expression of necessity," the necessity to abolish private property in order to "abolish" itself. "It is not a question of what this or that proletarian, or even the whole proletariat, at the moment *regards* as its aim. It is a question of what the *proletariat* is, and what, in accordance with this *being,* it will historically be compelled to do." By 1847 Marx was attacking Proudhon, who had been one of the first to popularize the idea of the proletariat as well as the idea of property as "theft," for not appreciating the revolutionary nature of poverty, for seeing "in poverty nothing but poverty, without seeing in it the revolutionary subversive side, which will overthrow the old society." At the same time Engels, in the credo he drew up for the Communist League (parts of which were incorporated in the *Communist Manifesto*), explained the difference between the old poor and the new proletariat.

Poor folk and working classes have always existed. The working classes have also for the most part been poor. But such poor, such workers as are living under conditions indicated above, hence proletarians, have not always

existed, any more than free and unbridled competition has always existed.

It was this new idea of poverty that pervaded the *Condition*—a poverty qualitatively different from the old, just as the proletariat was qualitatively different from the poor. In his commentary on Engels's book, Steven Marcus has suggested a psychoanalytic distinction between poor, on the one hand, and "working class" or "proletariat," on the other. Inspired by Erik Erikson's observation that young Gandhi's interest in "the poor" rather than in "labor" was a symptom of what Gandhi himself had called his "mother complex," Marcus applied this distinction to Engels.

As a boy, he [Engels] had often given his little savings to "the poor." As a young man, he has now decided in more ways than one actively to throw his lot in with labor, with the working class or proletariàt. The difference between an identification with "the poor" and an identification with the "working class" represents, among many other things, the measure in which an idealistic and rebellious young man could appreciate for himself a traditional historical masculine identity and maintain that identity even in the role of insurrection against the world in which it was grounded.

Whatever credibility one assigns to this feminine–masculine dichotomy, it is interesting that "poor" should be taken to connote an attitude of passivity or acquiescence, and "working class" or "proletariat" an attitude of rebelliousness. This much, at least, is consistent with the Marxist interpretation.

What was unique about the *Condition,* distinguishing it from everything else Marx and Engels wrote at this time or later, was the fact that here the proletariat was something more than a historical abstraction, a logical category subsumed under a larger historical schema, a "world-historical" class furthering the "world-historical" movement of communism. Instead of the usual abstract, universal proletariat, Engels described a specifically English proletariat, located in real towns and villages, living in real cottages and cellars, working at real jobs, participating in real events, suffering real hardships, and indulging in real vices. All this was attested to by real newspapers, books, parliamentary reports, and personal observations. Contemporaries may not have known Engels's proletariat under that name and might have disputed his descriptions, generalizations, and predictions. But they would have recognized the names of the towns and villages, the views of back streets and houses, the scenes of riots and demonstrations, the titles of newspapers and royal commissions, the identities of politicians and writers. And they would have responded (as readers still respond) to the emotive force of the book, the dramatic evocation of misery and the powerful sense of outrage. Almost twenty years later, rereading the *Condition* in preparation for the writing of *Capital,*

Marx confessed to Engels that it made him feel his advancing years.

How freshly and passionately, with what bold anticipations and no learned and scientific doubts, the thing is still dealt with here! And the very illusion that the result itself will leap into the daylight of history tomorrow or the day after gives the whole thing a warmth and jovial humour—compared to which the later "gray in gray" makes a damned unpleasant contrast.

That passion and boldness, the illusion that his predictions would "leap into the daylight of history tomorrow or the day after," came in no small part from the powerful ideology Engels imposed on the actuality of history. His English proletariat was the "world-historical" proletariat writ small, a miniature version of the universal phenomenon. If the English working classes never carried out Engels's prediction of revolution, it was for the same reason that they resisted the label "proletariat"—resisted in fact the whole of the historical schema that would have made them what Lenin was pleased to call a "fighting proletariat."

Samuel Smiles: The Gospel of Self-Help

Victorian Britain's prophet of honest toil was far from being the crudely complacent reactionary, as he has sometimes been caricatured.

Asa Briggs

Asa Briggs is Provost of Worcester College, Oxford, and author of The BBC, The First Fifty Years *(Oxford University Press, 1985).*

Self-help was one of the favourite mid-Victorian virtues. Relying on yourself was preferred morally—and economically—to depending on others. It was an expression of character even when it did not ensure—even, indeed, when it did not offer—a means of success. It also had social implications of a general kind. The progressive development of society ultimately depended, it was argued, not on collective action or on parliamentary legislation but on the prevalence of practices of self-help.

All these points were made succinctly and eloquently, but none of them originally or exclusively, by Samuel Smiles whose *Self-Help* appeared in one of the golden years of mid-Victorian Britain, 1859, the year that also saw the publication of John Stuart Mill's *Essay on Liberty* and Charles Darwin's *The Origin of Species*. Mill examined the attractions of individuality as well as the restraints on individualism: Darwin explored struggle as well as evolution, or rather explained evolution in terms of struggle. Neither thinker escaped attack. Smiles by contrast was not looking for argument and counter-argument. He believed that he was expounding not something that was new or controversial but something that was old and profoundly true, a gospel, not a thesis; and that behind that gospel was a still more basic gospel, the gospel of work.

Smiles did not claim that all his contemporaries practised self-help. He rather extolled the virtues of self-help as part of an 'old fashioned' but 'wholesome' lesson in morality. It was more 'natural,' he admitted, to be 'prodigal' than to be thrifty, more easy to be dependent than independent. What he was saying had been said by the wisest of men before him: it reflected 'experience, example and foresight'. 'Heaven helps them who help themselves.'

As far as individuals were concerned, Smiles was anxious to insist on the value of perseverance, a favourite word of one of his heroes, George Stephenson. 'Nothing that is of real worth,' he insisted, 'can be achieved without courageous working. Man owes his growth chiefly to that active striving of the will, that encounter with difficulty, which he calls effort; and it is astonishing to find how often results apparently impracticable are then made possible.' As far as society was concerned, 'national progress was the sum of individual industry, energy and uprightness' as 'national decay' was of 'individual idleness, selfishness and vice. What we are accustomed to decry as great social evils will, for the most part, be found to be but the outgrowth of man's perverted life.' 'The spirit of self-help is the root of all genuine growth in the individual; and exhibited in the lives of many, it constitutes the true source of national vigour and strength. Help from without is often enfeebling in its effects, but help from within invariably invigorates. Whatever is done for men and classes to a certain extent takes away the stimulus and necessity of doing for themselves; and where men are subjected to over-guidance and over-government, the inevitable tendency is to render them comparatively helpless.'

Smiles adopted the phrase *Self-Help*, which proved to be very difficult to translate into other languages, from a lecture by the American reformer and prophet, R. W. Emerson, delivered in 1841; and while Smiles' own book first appeared in 1859, its contents had first been delivered by Smiles in lectures to Leeds working men fourteen years before—one year, indeed, before the passing of the repeal of the corn laws. While the book belonged unmistakably to mid-Victorian Britain, the message, therefore, was an early-Victorian transatlantic message, delivered in years not of relative social harmony in Britain but of social conflict. The point is of crucial importance in any discussion of Victorian values in the 1980s. Smiles emerged not from a conservative but from a radical background, the background of Chartism, and the Anti-Corn Law League. He was not encouraging Leeds working men to be quiescent or deferential but to be active and informed. Richard Cobden was one of his heroes. Another was the radical Joseph Hume, and both figured prominently in *Self-Help*. Smiles knew them both personally, and in a letter to Cobden in 1841 he had described the extension of the suffrage as 'the key to all great changes, whose object is to elevate the condition of the masses.'

Smiles' direct political involvement was limited, however, after the 1840s, and he settled down during the next decade to the more complacent view, which he expressed in 1852, that 'as men grow older and wiser they find a little of good in everything . . . they begin to find out that truth and patriotism are not confined to any particular cliques or parties or factions.' Indeed, he moved well

From *History Today*, May 1987, pp. 37-43. Reproduced by kind permission of History Today, Ltd., 83-84 Berwick Street, London W1V 3PJ, England.

to the right of Cobden, and by the late-Victorian years, when new political causes, radical or socialist of which he disapproved were being canvassed, what he had had to say had come to sound 'conservative', as it has done to late-twentieth-century defenders of 'Victorian values'.

Yet there is a difference in the response. Whereas late-Victorian rebels attacked Smiles for his cheerful economics, claiming—unfairly—that he was interested only in individual advancement reflected in material success, late-twentieth-century defenders have praised him primarily for his hard economic realism. In particular, Sir Keith Joseph, himself writing from a Leeds vantage point, in the introduction to a new and abridged edition of *Self-Help* (1986), has set out to rehabilitate Smilesian trust in the *entrepreneur* and 'the virtues that

make him what he is'. While describing *Self-Help* as 'deeply expressive of the spirit of its own times', he does not note that these were changing times and that modes of economic organisation and responses to 'entrepreneurship' were very different by 1904, the year when Smiles died, from what they had been when *Self-Help* was published.

Smiles was born not in Leeds but in Haddington, a few miles east of Edinburgh, seven years before the birth of Queen Victoria, and he took a medical degree from Edinburgh University. His first book was called *Physical Education: or the Nurture and Management of*

Upward mobility — this 1861 cartoon shows a 'Lancashire working-man living rent free in his own home', the fruits of diligence and temperance.

Children, and was published in 1838, the year he moved to Leeds. There is an evident Scottish strain in his writing before and after, although curiously it is less apparent in *Physical Education* than in some of his other work. It was, after all, Robert Bruce who had had attributed to him the motto 'if at first you don't succeed, try, try, try again', and Calvin who had provided Scotsmen with a religion which made the most of austerity and vocation.

In more modern times Thomas Carlyle, born seventeen years before Smiles, had described life as 'a scene of toil, of effort, of appointed work', and had extolled 'the man who works' in the warmest language: 'welcome, thou art ours; our care shall be of thee'. The mill-owner economist, W. R. Greg, writing one year after the publication of *Self-Help,* praised Carlyle above all others for 'preaching

upon the duty and dignity of work, with an eloquence which has often made the idle shake off their idleness and the frivolous feel ashamed of their frivolity. He has proclaimed, in tones that have stirred many hearts, that in toil, however humble, if honest and hearty, lies our true worth and felicity here below'.

Smiles himself took as one of his examples of perseverance in *Self-Help* Carlyle's prodigious effort to rewrite the first volume of his *French Revolution* after a maid had used the manuscript to light the kitchen and parlour fires: 'he had no draft, and was compelled to rake up from his memory facts, ideas and expressions, which had long been dismissed'. No one could have appreciated this experience more than Smiles who was a prodigious writer who followed up *Self-Help* with many volumes, including three related works *Character* (1871), *Thrift* (1875) and *Duty* (1880). He also produced a history of his publisher, John Murray and 'his friends' in 1891.

Self-Help was full of anecdotes. Essentially it was a case-book drawing its material, including some of its most apposite quotations, from personal biographies. 'Our great forefathers still live among us in the records of our lives', he claimed, again very much as Carlyle had always claimed. 'They still sit by us at table, and hold us by the hand'. There was more than a touch of Victorian hero worship here. Yet Smiles always broadened the range to include the humble as well as the great, extending the range as far as he possibly could in his *Life and Labour* (1887). Biographies offered demonstrations of 'what men can be, and what they can do' whatever their station. 'A book containing the life of a true man is full of precious seed. It is still a living voice'. And much as he made his own living out of books, Smiles maintained that living examples were far more potent as influences than examples on paper. His book *Thrift* took as its motto a phrase from Carlyle 'Not what I have, but what I do is my kingdom'. He might have chosen instead Emerson's motto, 'The importance of man as man . . . is the highest truth'.

Smiles himself was a lively phrasemaker, interlacing his anecdotes, which by themselves were memorable and well set out, with short phrases that linger in the mind—'he who never made a mistake never made a discovery'; 'the tortoise in the right road will beat a racer in the wrong'; 'the nation comes from the nur-

sery'. Such phrases bind together the whole text of *Self-Help* which is far more readable—as it is pertinent—today than the verse of Martin Tupper's *Proverbial Philosophy* (1838), the popularity of which (on both sides of the Atlantic) reached its peak during the 1850s. It is far more readable too than most of the many other Victorian books designed to inspire young men like the anonymous *Success in Life* (1852), the original idea of which had been suggested by 'an American publication', perhaps John Todd's *Hints Addressed to the Young Men of the United States* (1845), which included one chapter on 'industry and economy' and another on 'self-government and the heart'. Smiles himself acknowledged a debt to G. L. Craik's *Pursuit of Knowledge under Difficulties* (1831), published by Charles Knight who specialised in diffusing knowledge. Indeed, he had been so inspired by it, Smiles wrote, that he learnt some of its key passages by heart.

The transatlantic element in the self-help literature demands a study of differences as well as of influences. There were to be many American 'success' books aiming, as Smiles aimed, at large audiences, some of the first of which were influenced, as Smiles was, by the cult of phrenology. The later line of descent can be traced through books, which move from phrenology to popular psychology, like J. C. Ransom's *The Successful Man in his Manifold Relations with Life* (1887), A. E. Lyon's *The Self-Starter* (1924), Dale Carnegie's *How to Win Friends and Influence People* (1936), C. E. Poppleston's *Every Man a Winner* (1936) and Norman Vincent Peale's *The Power of Positive Thinking* (1955). Yet many of these authors are slick where Smiles was sturdy, and consoling where he was inspiring. Few would have had much sympathy either with Smiles' attack on 'smatter knowledge'. Such 'short-cuts', he explained, as learning French or Latin in 'twelve lessons' or 'without a master', were 'good for nothing'. The would-be learner was more to blame than the teacher, for he resembled 'the lady of fashion who engaged a master to teach her on condition that he did not plague her with verbs and particles'.

One American with whom Smiles has sometimes been compared is Horatio Alger (1832–99) after whom a twentieth-century American business award was named. In his own lifetime Alger's sales were spectacular, though his books took

the form of stories rather than biographies or homilies. *Ragged Dick* was one title, *Upward and Onward* another. The *genre* has been well described as 'rags to riches stories', although the twentieth-century award was endowed more generally to honour a person who had 'climbed the ladder of success through toil and diligence and responsible applications of his talents to whatever tasks were his'.

There are as many myths about 'Holy Horatio' as Alger himself propounded. In fact, he allowed a far bigger place to luck (sponsors appearing by magic at the right time and place) than Smiles ever could have done, and he grossly simplified the nineteenth-century social context, particularly the city context, in which poor people found or failed to find their chances. As the late-nineteenth-century American institutional economist, Richard T. Ely, put it neatly, 'if you tell a single concrete workman on the Baltimore and Ohio Railroad that he may get to be president of the company, it is not demonstrable that you have told him what is not true, although it is within bounds to say that he is far more likely to be killed by a stroke of lightning.'

Smiles was less concerned with social 'mobility' than with mental and physical 'effort', but he, too, could be accused of living in a land of myth when he exclaimed that 'energy accomplishes more than genius'. It was a favourite mid-Victorian statement, however, which implied a contrast between what was happening then and what had happened before, and between what was happening in Britain and what was happening elsewhere. By stating it so simply Smiles actually did influence *entrepreneurs,* few of whom depended on great intellects or on deep and systematic study. William Lever, for example, fittingly born in 1851, was given a copy of *Self-Help* by his father on his sixteenth birthday, and treasured it so much that he in turn gave copies to young men he employed in his works at Port Sunlight. On the front page of one such copy the words are inscribed, 'It is impossible for me to say how much I owe to the fact that in my early youth I obtained a copy of Smiles' *Self-Help.*'

Andrew Carnegie (1835–1919) would have made no such comment. Yet his own biography not only proclaimed many Smilesian virtues, but might well have provided the basis for an Alger true story. Carnegie was born in a tiny weaver's cottage at Dunfermline, and he had his first real break in life when he became a messenger boy in a Pittsburgh telegraph office at a salary of $2.50 a week. In 1901, when he had sold his steel business for $480 million, he became the richest man in the world. 'It's a God's mercy I was born a Scotsman,' he declared in a remark that might have appealed to Smiles, 'for I do not see how I could ever have been contented to be anything else.'

The testimonials Smiles himself received from readers of his books often came from people very differently placed from Lever or Carnegie. Thus, a working man in Exeter told him that his books had 'instructed and helped him greatly' and that he wished 'every working man would read them through and through and ponder them well'; a surgeon in Blackheath declared that *Self-Help* had given 'fresh energy and hopefulness to his career'; and an emigrant to New Zealand exclaimed that self-help had 'been the cause of an entire alteration in my life, and I thank God that I read it. I am now devoted to study and hard work, and I mean to rise, both as regards my moral and intellectual life. I only wish I could see the man who wrote the book and thank him from my heart'.

There was at least one late-Victorian socialist, a man who was himself capable of inspiring 'the millions', who was deeply impressed by Smiles. Robert Blatchford, pioneer of *Merrie England,* wrote an essay on *Self-Help* after Smiles' popularity had passed its peak in which he condemned fellow-socialists who spoke mockingly of Smiles as 'an arch-Philistine' and of his books as 'the apotheosis of respectability, gigmanity and selfish grab'. Blatchford himself considered Smiles 'a most charming and honest writer', and thought *Self-Help* 'one of the most delightful and invigorating books it has been my happy fortune to meet with'. He paid tribute to Smiles' indifference to worldly titles, honour and wealth, and declared that the perusal of *Self-Help* had often forced him 'to industry, for very shame'.

The prolific rationalist writer Grant Allen, a leading spokesman of the late-Victorian revolt, took a very similar view. In a little book published in 1884 called *Biographies of Working Men* he asserted his debt to Smiles and made explicit what many of Smiles' critics then and since failed to see in Smiles' work. 'It is the object of this volume', Grant Allen began, 'to set forth the lives of

working men, who through industry, perseverance and high principle, have raised themselves by their own exertions from humble beginnings. Raised themselves! Yes, but to what? Not merely, let us hope, to wealth and position, nor merely to worldly respect and high office, but to some conspicuous field of real usefulness to their fellow men.' Smiles made the same point in *Self-Help*. He would not have shared Allen's view, however, which brings out clearly the difference between the mood of the 1850s and the 1880s, that 'so long as our present social arrangements exist . . . the vast mass of men will necessarily remain workers to the last, [and] no attempt to raise individual working men above their own class into the professional or mercantile classes can ever greatly benefit the working classes as a whole'.

Nonetheless, on certain social matters, Smiles had often expressed radical views. Like many people trained as doctors he was deeply concerned with public health. As Mary Mack has pointed out, Jeremy Bentham had used medicine as a source of *analogy* for the understanding of morals and legislation, and Smiles, who as a young man met Edwin Chadwick and Dr Southwood Smith, Bent-

ham's disciples, never believed that the environment should be left uncontrolled if it threatened the private health not only of the deprived but of people and power and influence. Smiles supported measures, too, to deal with the adulteration of food. Drawing a distinction between economic and social *laissez-faire*—and he was not alone in this—he was fully aware of the presence in mid-Victorian society not only of Adam Smith's beneficent invisible hand but of a 'terrible Nobody'. Indeed, Charles Dickens could not have written more forcefully than Smiles did:

> When typhus or cholera breaks out, they tell us that Nobody is to blame. That terrible Nobody! How much he has to answer for. More mischief is done by Nobody than by all the world besides. Nobody adulterates our food. Nobody poisons us with bad drink . . . Nobody leaves towns undrained. Nobody fills jails, penitentiaries, and convict stations. Nobody makes poachers, thieves, and drunkards. Nobody has a theory too—a dreadful theory. It is embodied in two words: laissez-faire— let alone. When people are poisoned with plaster of Paris mixed with flour, 'let alone' is the remedy . . . Let those who can, find out when they are

A 'Punch' cartoon of 1858 attacking the adulteration of food — one of the areas where Smiles decidedly did not believe in the principle of laissez-faire.

cheated: *caveat emptor.* When people live in foul dwellings, let them alone, let wretchedness do its work; do not interfere with death.

Like many other believers in economic *laissez-faire* Smiles was prepared to use the machinery of the law to provide a framework for dealing with abuses:

Laws may do too much . . . but the abuse of a thing is no proper argument against its use in cases where its employment is urgently called for.

Throughout the whole of his life Smiles was far too active a Victorian to believe that *vis inertiae* was the same thing as *laissez-faire.* Nor was he ever tempted, as many Americans were, into the entanglements of social Darwinism. There is no reference to Herbert Spencer in his *Autobiography,* which appeared in 1905, one year after his death, and only one reference to Darwin. One of the lecturers he had heard at Edinburgh, he observed *en passant,* had already expounded very similar views 'or at all events had heralded his approach'.

There was another subject which fascinated Smiles and which he believed required very positive state intervention—national education. He had forcefully urged the need for a national system in Leeds in 1850, and he paid tribute in his *Autobiography* to W. E. Forster, MP for neighbouring Bradford, who 'by a rare union of tact, wisdom and commonsense, introduced and carried his measure [the 1870 Education Act] for the long-wished education of the English people. It embodied nearly all that the National Public School Association had so fruitlessly demanded years before'.

In pressing for nationally provided primary education in Leeds in 1850 and later, Smiles had been drawn into controversy with Edward Baines, editor of the *Leeds Mercury* and one of the most vociferous advocates, then and in 1870, of education managed by voluntary agencies and not by the state. In the course of a continuing controversy Smiles had no doubts about his own position. There were no analogies between education and free trade in commodities, he pointed out:

The classes who the most require education are precisely those who do not seek it. It is amongst the utterly uneducated that the least demand exists. In the case of bread it is very different. The consumer wants it, knows he wants it, and will give every present consideration for it.

A further false analogy, he thought, was that between education and the freedom of the press:

Nobody proposes to establish newspapers for everybody, supported by the government, and the want of such a Press is not felt. But let it be shown that it is of as much importance to the interests of society that everybody should have a newspaper as that everybody should be educated, and then the analogy may be admitted . . . but not till then.

It was through his philosophy of education that Smiles blurred any divisions that others might have made between 'self-help' for the individual and 'mutual self-help' for the group. He always attached even more importance to adult— or continuing—education than to school education, necessary though the latter was. The process which started at school had to be followed through: 'the highest culture is not obtained from teacher when at school or college, so much as by our ever diligent self-education when we have become men.' Such education could

be fostered in groups like the group of young working men he had addressed in Leeds. There were possibilities of other forms of 'mutual self-help' also, for example friendly societies. Indeed, in *Thrift* Smiles made as much as he could of the mutual insurance principle. He could never have been accused of neglecting 'welfare', provided that it did not lead to dependence.

The Smiles message was not merely a transatlantic one. It made its way round the world, sometimes to the most unlikely places. It was translated into Dutch and French, Danish and German, Arabic and Turkish, 'several of the native languages of India' (in the words of a happy publisher) and Japanese. Victorian values, it was implied, were universal values, and there was confidence in their power to change societies. The Japanese, in particular, treasured it, and many of them continue to treasure it. 'The English work forms an octavo of moderate size,' *The Times* wrote; 'in Japanese it is expanded into a book of fifteen hundred pages.' This was no handicap to its sale, for it seemed as useful as looms and steam engines. In Latin America the Mayor of Buenos Aires is said to have compared Smiles with Rousseau and to

The doctrine of 'honest toil' could have a radical cutting-edge, as in this 1858 'Punch' cartoon of the working man 'enlightening' the 'superior' (but idle) classes.

have added 'Alexander the Great slept with his Homer, Demosthenes and Thucydides, and every notable man of the times should have at hand the social gospel'.

The universalism was restricted, however, although it went with the universalism of steam power and railways, in particular. Smiles had become secretary of a railway company in 1845 and he wrote *The Life of George Stephenson* two years before *Self-Help*. Nonetheless, he ended *Self-Help* with a chapter which introduced a word which was at least as difficult to translate from English into other languages as 'self-help' itself—the word 'gentleman'. Hippolyte Taine, convinced that the three syllables 'gentleman' summed up the whole history of English society, felt that the syllables expressed all the distinctive features of the English upper-class—a large private income, a considerable household of servants, habits of ease and luxury and good manners, but it also implied qualities of heart and character. Smiles, however, felt that:

> For Englishmen a real 'gentleman' is a truly noble man, a man worthy to command, a disinterested man of integrity, capable of exposing, even sacrificing himself for those he leads; not only a man of honour, but a conscientious man, in whom generous instincts have been confirmed by right thinking and who, acting rightly by nature, acts even more rightly from good principles.

Taine's reference to Mrs Craik's novel *John Halifax, Gentleman* (1856) is a practical illustration of the extension of the old ideal of the gentleman in a new nineteenth-century society. He might have referred instead to the last pages of *Self-Help*, where Smiles chose a 'grand old name' to express the kind of character he most wanted to see in action. Smiles drew out the 'grand old name' of the gentleman from its upper-class context. It had no connection with riches and rank, he argued, but with moral worth.

The equipoise of society rested on such ideological balances as well as on the balance of interests. From the 1870s onwards, however, both kinds of balance broke down. Britain was never again the same.

FOR FURTHER READING:

Samuel Smiles, *Self-Help* (first edition 1853, Penguin Books with an introduction by Keith Joseph, 1986); Asa Briggs, *Victorian People* (Penguin Books, 1985); Grant Allen, *Biographies of Working men* (1884); J. Burnett, editor, *Useful Toil: Autobiographies of Working people from the 1820s–1920s* (Penguin Books, 1974); T. Travers, *Samuel Smiles and the Pursuit of Success in Victorian Britain* (Canadian Historical Association, 1971); M. D. Stephens and G. W. Roderick, *Samuel Smiles and Nineteenth-Century Self-Help in Education* (Nottingham Studies, 1983).

John Stuart Mill and Liberty

The leading philosopher of mid-Victorian England, John Stuart Mill (1806–73), claimed an "ability and willingness to learn from everybody." This was not necessarily a celebrated man's ritual, if becoming, modesty. In Mill's mind, the ideas of earlier thinkers—e.g., John Locke, David Hume, Jeremy Bentham, his own father James Mill—were transformed over the years into classical liberalism, the idea that society is best served by maximum personal freedoms and minimal government. Recent scholarship, as Maurice Cranston *relates, has provided new insight into the life of the philosopher who may have learned "from everybody," but was driven to heed some more than others.*

Maurice Cranston

Maurice Cranston, 67, a former Wilson Center Guest Scholar, is professor of political science at the London School of Economics. Born in London, he was educated at St. Catherine's College and Oxford University. His books include John Stuart Mill *(1965),* Jean-Jacques, The Early Life and Work of Jean-Jacques Rousseau, 1712–54 *(1982), and* John Locke: A Biography *(1985).*

John Stuart Mill has held the attention of the reading public of the Western world longer than any other 19th-century philosopher, with the notable exception of Karl Marx.

Each man is known as theorist of one central idea. Marx is read by his admirers as a champion of equality. Mill is read for his words on liberty, words that have contributed much to the debates of our own time about the freedom of dissenters, minorities, and women. He was always controversial. William Gladstone, the great Liberal Party leader, disapproved of Mill's ideas, and refused to attend his funeral. Yet he called him "the Saint of Rationalism."

John Stuart Mill was born in his father's comfortable London home in 1806, a time when the Industrial Revolution was already beginning to transform England into a prospering urban nation with a rising middle class, whose leaders' concerns included how to govern and improve such a rapidly changing society. James Mill, a strict disciplinarian who had risen from humble origins to become a senior civil servant with the East India Company, was by then a noted historian, economist, and philosopher. He was an advocate of Jeremy Bentham's utilitarianism, which held that all issues of right and wrong could be settled by measuring the amount of pleasure or pain that might be caused by any private action or public policy.

James Mill did not send his eldest child to any school; he taught him at home following a strenuous plan of education devised by himself and Bentham to produce the perfect utilitarian. John learned both Greek and Latin before he was nine years old. Religion was excluded from his upbringing.

Mill's education was completed early—and early, too, appeared his oddly coexisting streaks of conformism and rigorous independence. At age 17, he was earning his living as a clerk in the India office where his father worked. During that year he published his first article—in *The Westminster Review,* the leading English literary journal—and also made his debut as a radical reformer, spending two nights in jail for distributing pamphlets recommending contraceptive techniques as a solution to the problem of poverty in Britain.

At age 20—as he recalled in his *Autobiography,* published after his death in 1873—Mill suffered a depression, from which he recovered by reading poetry. Through Wordsworth and others he discovered romanticism, which challenged the rationalistic philosophy that had been so carefully inculcated in him. "I did not lose . . . sight," he wrote, of "that part of the truth which I had seen before." But "I thought that it had consequences which required to be corrected, by joining other kinds of cultivation with it."

Mill aimed at working out a new system of philosophy combining the virtues of rationalism with those of romanticism. But how to reconcile two schools of seemingly opposed thought? The rational solution, Mill decided, could only be to revise logic itself. Mill's chief contribution to this endeavor was his *System of Logic* (1843), which he began at age 24. That it took him 13 years to finish the work was closely related to Mill's less than rational personal life.

Mill was afflicted by a deep sense of loneliness. Once, at the age of 23, he wrote to a friend of his longing for a "perfect friendship." Soon after he started on his *Logic* essay, Mill met a handsome, intelligent, and imperious young woman named Harriet Taylor. He fell in love with her, and she with him. But Harriet happened to be married—to John Taylor, a prosperous wholesale druggist with a house in London and a country place. She was also the mother of two small children (soon to be joined by a third).

Even so, during the 19 years before the druggist's death in 1849 enabled them to marry, she and Mill kept constant company.

Alternately reckless and furtive, they behaved as if they were lovers, something they always denied. And yet it was a strangely guilt-ridden relationship. Harriet set up house on her own in rural Blackheath and traveled on the Continent with Mill. They remained, in Harriet's word, *Seelenfreunden* ("soul mates"), because, Mill said, they did not wish to hurt her husband. Mill seems not to have guessed that Mr. Taylor might be as much wounded by the appearance of adultery as by its reality. Nevertheless, Mill, in nervous anger, broke with both his friends and his relatives to lead a rather solitary life with Harriet at Blackheath.

Her hold over his thinking was considerable. If her situation with Mill was a "romantic" one, a triumph of love over convention, her views were not Wordsworthian at all. They were closer to those of the Enlightenment—rationalistic, utilitarian, and radical. Hence, paradoxically, she reinforced on Mill the influence of his father, and not that of the poets.

One example of her influence on Mill is his *Principles of Political Economy,* a long and not conspicuously original book, which debuted in 1848 when Mill was 42. It was originally dedicated to "Mrs. John Taylor," from whom, Mill wrote, he first grasped many of the book's ideas. After John Taylor's death, and their marriage nearly two years later in 1851, Mill took to describing each of his works as a "joint-production" with Harriet. He even spoke of his wife as "the inspirer, and in part the author, of all that is best in my writings." Mill's contemporaries took these tributes as polite hyperbole, but recent scholarship on his manuscripts confirms her larger role.

For instance, in the first edition of *Political Economy,* Mill accepted David Ricardo's theory of value, which focuses on the amount of labor invested in the manufacture of a product. Mill also accepted the Malthusian doctrine that any improvement in the condition of the poor will be negated by the growth of population (although Mill's remedy for over-

population is not Thomas Malthus's "moral restraint," but contraceptive devices). And Mill endorsed Adam Smith's teaching against the state's intervention in the nation's economic life, arguing that England was already sufficiently burdened with taxes. Economic well-being, he said, required the spur of competition.

When, within a year, a second edition appeared, an essential part of the thesis was reversed. Harriet, who had been won over to the Left by the antimonarchical revolts that shook France and other Continental countries in 1848, pressed Mill to delete criticisms of socialism and communism. Thus, Mill first dismissed proposals for communal property ownership as "almost too chimerical to be reasoned with." In the new edition, these ideas became "the most valuable elements of human improvement now existing."

Harriet's influence is most significant in Mill's best-known work, *On Liberty,* published in 1859, not long after her death. It is not simply a defense of freedom in the liberal tradition of John Milton and John Locke; it outlines a conception that differs with their ideas, and, strikingly, with Mill's other writings.

For example, Mill described *On Liberty* as a "kind of philosophic textbook of a single truth." This truth was that "the sole end for which mankind are warranted, individually or collectively, in interfering with the liberty of action of any of their number, is self-protection." Elsewhere, Mill attacked the notion of building on a "single truth" in politics; he had criticized the French philosopher Auguste Comte for seeing only one point of view "when there are many others equally essential."

In a later work, *Utilitarianism* (1863), his best-known work on ethics, Mill saw liberty as a part of man's "social state," at once "so natural, so necessary, and so habitual to man, that (except at rare times) he never conceives himself otherwise than as a member of a body." In *On Liberty,* society is the enemy.

The essay is very much a plea for something that both Mill and Harriet felt strongly about: the freedom of the isolated person standing outside of and apart from the social body. Whereas earlier liberal philosophers, such as John Locke, had depicted freedom as something to be secured against the constraints of governments or the state, Mill

represents freedom as something to be secured primarily against the constraints of other people. Mill does not say much about political rulers; he dwells on the domination of the individual by unwritten laws, conventional ideas, social rules, and public opinion. "When society is itself the tyrant"—over the individuals it comprises—its tyranny is worse than "many kinds of political oppression." A need exists for protection against society's tendency to impose, "by other means than civil penalties, its own ideas and practices as rules of conduct on those who dissent from them."

We need to remember that Mill wrote *On Liberty* at a time and place when the constraints of the state were few and those of society were many, and, often, onerous. Victorian England was not the land of the despotic Stuart kings, where the liberty Locke pleaded for was mainly a right endangered by political interference. Mill's Victorian contemporaries were seldom oppressed by government, which was minimal (the 1851 census counted fewer than 75,000 public employees, compared with 932,000 in France in 1846). But nearly all individuals were constantly pressured by neighbors, employers, husbands, and fathers, who were dominated in turn by taboos and conventions governing a host of matters—courtship, dress, recreation, use of the Sabbath, and much else.

If Mill felt these constraints keenly, and Harriet even more so, he took care in presenting his case, so it should not seem to be the romantic protest of an alienated individual against a bourgeois environment. He argued as coldly and logically as possible.

There are, he suggested, three possibilities to consider when deciding if men should have freedom of opinion and expression. First, the opinion in question may be true, in which case it is plainly right that it should be published. Second, the opinion may be false; it would still be good for it to be published, because truth gains vigor from being challenged and vindicated. (A true belief that is never challenged becomes a dead maxim, which everyone repeats and nobody thinks about.) Third, the opinion may be partly true and partly false. Again Mill argued for expression, on the ground that the exercise of disentangling the false from the true would help to correct errors.

Since these exhaust the possibilities, Mill concluded, it must always be right to grant liberty of opinion and expression.

"If all mankind minus one were of one opinion, and only one person were of the contrary opinion," Mill wrote, "mankind would be no more justified in silencing that one person, than he, if he had the power, would be justified in silencing mankind." The "peculiar evil" of silencing one opinion is that it robs "the human race; posterity as well as the existing generation; those who dissent from the opinion still more than those who hold it."

Discussing freedom of action, Mill staked out even more dangerous ground, again under Harriet's sway. Mill rejected the Christian teaching that men are born in sin and that the self must be denied. He asserted his belief in the goodness—and the *potential* goodness—of man. While he conceded that there was sometimes a need for self-denial in putting public happiness before private happiness, Mill emphasized the value of self-expression. Far from accepting the doctrine of the depravity of man, he suggested that it is chiefly through the cultivation of their individuality that "human beings"—and it is to be noted that he uses that term rather than "men"—become "noble and beautiful object[s] of contemplation."

He pleaded for personality, variety, even eccentricity. "In this age the mere example of non-conformity, the mere refusal to bend the knee to custom, is itself a service." Eccentricity rises where "strength of character" abounds. "The amount of eccentricity in a society has generally been proportional to the amount of genius, mental vigour and moral courage which it contains."

Yet Mill was not advocating unbridled self-expression, or unlimited freedom. Indeed, he said at the beginning of *On Liberty* that his task was to set out exactly what the limits of freedom were. His conclusion: One man's right to liberty of action stops at the point where it might injure or curb the freedom of another man. "The only purpose for which power can be rightfully exercised over any member of a civilized community, against his will, is to prevent harm to others." Otherwise every adult should be allowed to do as he likes.

But supposing, the critic might ask, that what a man likes to do is wrong? Surely he should not then be allowed to

do it? Surely the important thing is not that men should do what they want to do but what they *ought* to do? And might it not be the duty of society to help men do what they ought to do?

Mill did not shirk these questions. Take alcoholism, for instance.

Britain's 19th-century prohibitionists viewed drunkenness as a social evil, which could be remedied by enforced abstinence. Mill denied that prohibition would uphold morality. If there was no temptation to overcome, he pleaded, there would be no virtue in overcoming temptation. Morality lies in choosing the better and rejecting the worse. No option, no morality. There would be no scope for character development in a society that closed its bars and brothels, making vice impossible. Mill did not deny that drink did harm. Yet his remedy was not to curb liberty, but to promote responsible behavior by spreading enlightenment.

It may be that Mill was too optimistic about the power of enlightenment to educate people, too confident about the capacity of men to better themselves morally. And yet, one must not overstate his optimism. His concern for freedom for self-improvement was essentially a concern for those individuals who *chose* to improve themselves. He did not think that the majority had yet developed that capacity. This was why the majority was, in his eyes, the chief enemy of the individual's liberty.

Mill was a liberal, but not a democrat. Of all tyrannies, he dreaded most the "tyranny of the majority." When Mill thought of freedom, he had in mind the rights of minorities—for example, Irish Catholics, West Indian blacks, and, above all, the minority that was a numerical majority, women. In two tracts, *The Enfranchisement of Women* (1851) and *The Subjection of Women* (1869), he made a remarkable contribution to the literature of feminism, though neither essay had much impact until years later.

Harriet surely inspired these writings. But what is singular about them is that they do not demand, in the manner of most feminist writing, equality for women. Rather, Mill argues for the *liberty* of women, which is linked with the liberty of men. He does not urge that women should be freed from the domination of men, but that women as well as men should be freed from the rule of custom, habit, and tradition, which holds both sexes in bondage.

Women's rights" are claimed—for instance, the right to own property or to vote in parliamentary elections. Yet these are not claimed as natural rights or ends in themselves, but as elements of a wider program of human emancipation, in which women's interests are seen as identical to men's. In *Considerations On Representative Government* (1861), Mill rejected the idea of "Mr. [John] Bright and his school of democrats" that a vote was any man's or woman's right. A vote, Mill argued, was a trust. It should be exercised only by responsible people, male or female. Mill recommended that educated persons be allowed plural votes, to give their voice the added weight it deserved. He suggested that proportional representation be introduced into parliamentary elections, not because it was more democratic, but to provide better for the representation of minorities.

Mill believed that the day would come when the demand for universal suffrage would prove irresistible. The answer, he thought, would be to reform the tax system so that "every grown person in the community" should become a taxpayer. He did not want a system of voting "like that of New York," which enabled people who paid no taxes to vote for levies on people who did.*

Mill also urged preparation for universal suffrage via immediate universal education. His belief in the saving powers of enlightenment led him to favor the enlargement of the state's powers to counteract the pressures of society. He agreed that the state had the right to interfere with the freedom of the family in forcing children to go to school. Since children are excluded from the class of people for whom freedom is demanded in *On Liberty,* his proposal for compulsory education (which began, at the primary level, in 1880) is not, in itself, inconsistent with his principles. But his plea for the control

---

*Various qualifications (e.g., property ownership, taxpayer status) kept British voter rolls low during the 19th century. Mill, as a Liberal M.P., tried but failed to amend the Reform Bill of 1867 to allow women to vote in national elections. In 1918, Parliament enfranchised all men over age 21 and women over 30 who could (or had husbands who could) vote in local elections. Women were finally welcomed at the polls on the same terms as men only in 1928—nine years after U.S. women got the vote, 16 years before French women did.

of marriage and childbearing cannot escape that criticism. He asks not only for laws that would "forbid marriage unless the parties can show that they have the means for supporting a family," he also invites society to step in where the laws are ineffective, so that an improvident marriage shall become a subject of social stigma.

It was precisely because Mill set such a high value on intellectual and general culture that he mistrusted those who lacked it. He scorned the proletariat. The English working classes, he wrote, "are in conduct the most disorderly, debauched, and unruly, and least respectable and trustworthy of any nation whatsoever." He was, therefore, anxious to ensure that universal suffrage did not raise the status of the people in any more than a nominal sense. "The people ought to be the masters," he wrote, "but they are masters who must employ servants more skillful than themselves." He even proposed that institutions be set up to ensure a "standing opposition to the will of the majority."

Mill detested the idea of the nation being ruled by nobles or by the rich. But he did favor rule by another elite—professional administrators, civil servants, and bureaucrats like himself and his colleagues at the India office, who were responsible for governing millions on the subcontinent.

"There is a radical difference," he wrote, "between controlling the business of government and actually doing it." He wanted the controlling to be done by Parliament and a representative body of taxpayers, and the actual governing to be done by specialists, with a "commission of legislation" (also composed of specialists) to draft measures on which Parliament would be invited to vote.

Ordinary people "do not need political rights in order that they may govern, but in order that they may not be misgoverned."

When Harriet died in 1858, at Avignon, France, Mill wrote to Louis Blanc, the French socialist, that England had lost its "greatest mind." Mill's grief was intense, but short-lived. His health, frail throughout his years with Harriet, improved. During their seven years of marriage, he had published little. He emerged from his long seclusion, during which he had earned the reputation of a misanthrope, to become a popular figure in London intellectual society.

In 1865, at age 59, Mill was invited to stand for Parliament as a Liberal Party candidate in London's Westminster district. He said he would do so if it was understood that his only object in the House of Commons would be to promote the ideas expressed in his writings and that no further pledges were demanded of him.

As a campaigner, Mill did not promise to be a crowd-pleaser. At one of his election meetings, the novelist Thomas Hardy—a distant relation of Harriet's—described him standing "bareheaded," with "his vast pale brow, so thin-skinned as to show the blue veins, sloped back like a stretching upland," conveying "to the observer a curious sense of perilous exposure."

Yet Mill had blunt-spoken charm. Once he held a meeting for working people—who had no vote, but, Mill thought, possessed as much right as the middle classes to see and hear their representative. Mill's foes exhumed all the harsh words he had ever written about the proletariat. A man carrying a placard saying that the lower classes, "though mostly habitual liars, are ashamed of lying," asked Mill if he had written those words. Said Mill: "I did." After a pause, the workers cheered. Their leader told Mill that they appreciated his candor. Mill soon found he had more power to sway such a crowd than any other Liberal M.P. except William Gladstone.

In his *Autobiography*, Mill recalls the time when a Tory government sent police to break up a meeting of workingmen in Hyde Park. The men, says Mill, "showed a determination to make another attempt at meeting in the Park, to which many of them would probably have come armed; the Government made military preparations to resist the attempt, and something very serious seemed impending." Mill decided to address the workers' meeting. "I told them that a proceeding which would certainly produce a collision with the military could only be justifiable on two conditions; if the position of affairs had become such that a revolution was desirable, and if they thought themselves able to accomplish one. To this argument, after considerable discussion, they at last yielded."

In Parliament, Mill upheld workers' right of assembly and backed working-class candidates. In general, Mill argued for progressive causes in the Commons. He tried to save the lives of some Irish nationalists condemned for fomenting rebellion. He led a campaign against Governor Edward Eyre of Jamaica, who had arrested and hanged more than 30 black rebels. He fought for prostitutes' civil liberties, imperiled by a Contagious Diseases Act, and gave speeches (invariably to a derisive audience) in favor of women's suffrage.

But Mill was not always progressive. He distanced himself from the men he called "philanthropists" on, for instance, the abolition of capital punishment. In 1868, he spoke in the Commons for retention of the death penalty for murder, with his arguments drawn from his utilitarian theory of morals.

The threat of death, he said, was uniquely powerful as a deterrent, more likely than any other form of punishment to diminish the number of murders. Since the general goal of public policy should be to minimize pain, such deterrence should be paramount. Second, Mill argued that a quick death on the gallows was less painful in fact than a lingering death in prison (even though the fear of such a death had a greater power to deter criminals); execution was thus less cruel than life imprisonment. Mill did not imagine that even the "philanthropists" would be so foolish as to advocate any punishment for murder less severe than a life sentence without parole.

Mill's support for capital punishment was popular, but some of his other views were too advanced for even Westminster's enlightened 19th-century bourgeoisie. His support for contraception and divorce, his association with union leaders, and above all his feminism, cost him re-election in 1868. When he lost his Commons seat, he went to Avignon; there, near the cemetery where Harriet was buried, he bought a house, which he furnished with items from the hotel room in which she had died.

Five years later, at age 66, Mill died at Avignon.

Before he left London, Mill had become a close friend of a fellow parliamentarian, Viscount Amberley, who shared his ideas and continued to champion them. Shortly before he died, Mill became the agnostic's equivalent of a godfather to the Amberleys' infant son. Said Lady Amberley: "There is no one whose steps I would rather see a boy of mine following." The child's name was Bertrand Russell.

Giuseppe Garibaldi

Infrequently does a historian acquire the reputation of synonymity with the history of the country he or she has studied, but Denis Mack Smith *has accomplished this fact with his work and writing on Italy. This is a portrait of Italy's hero of the risorgimento in which the author deftly combines an assessment of the achievement with all the colour of Garibaldi's personal idiosyncracies.*

Denis Mack Smith

Giuseppe Garibaldi is one of the great men of the nineteenth century. He was a remarkably successful admiral and general. He was the very prototype of patriotic hero, but also a great internationalist, and later in life one of the pioneers of Italian socialism. Connecting all his activities was the fact that he was a liberator by profession, a man who spent his life fighting for oppressed peoples wherever he found them, however naive his analysis of oppression. Whatever he did, moreover, was done always with passionate conviction and boundless enthusiasm, and this makes his character the more striking and attractive.

Garibaldi's career was dazzlingly full of colour and incident; but behind the public personality was someone of simple good nature and amiability, a lovable and fascinating person of transparent honesty whom men would obey unhesitatingly and for whom many were glad to die. In his time he was probably the most widely known and loved figure in the world. He appealed directly to the common people, just because he himself was the embodiment of the common man: as a radical democrat and humanitarian he believed above all else in liberty and social justice. Yet, at the same time, he was quite exceptional in character, a real individual and non-conformist, whether in his religion, his clothes, his personal habits, or in the events of his extraordinary life.

Tough cookie; a heroic image of Garibaldi at Caprera, the remote island to which he eventually retired, having played a major role in steering Italy towards unification.

From *History Today,* August 1991, pp. 20-26. Reproduced by kind permission of History Today, Ltd., 83-84 Berwick Street, London W1V 3PJ, England.

Garibaldi lived from 1807 to 1882. He was born in Napoleonic France, and all his life, like Cavour, spoke Italian imperfectly. By trade he followed his father and became a sea-captain. He knew the Black Sea and also the China seas. He served in ships of Italy and France, and also of the United States and Peru, and even for a time with the Bey of Tunis; and he also captained the first screw-propelled steamer to fly the Italian flag. Twice in his life he was a schoolmaster, at Constantinople and Montevideo. Once at least he was a commercial traveller, and once he worked in a candle factory on Staten Island. He married three times. For several years he was engaged to a wealthy and talented Englishwoman, and subsequently he proposed unsuccessfully to another. In the course of his various wanderings he claimed British as well as United States citizenship; sat as an elected deputy in the French assembly; and was offered a command by Lincoln in the American civil war. In sum, it was a more than ordinarily variegated and dramatic life, and this provided a fitting back-cloth for his flamboyant character.

Garibaldi first became a household name with his defence of Rome in 1849. Before then, however, and this is most important for understanding his temperament and influence, he had been for half his adult life a guerrilla leader in the political bear-garden of Brazil and Argentina. When he returned from South America to Europe he brought back a novel and successful type of warfare. A few irregulars, by breaking the accepted conventions of war, could acquire a high nuisance-value in foreign-occupied Italy.

The South American influence is seen in the gaucho costume that Garibaldi carried to the end of his life—the cloak or poncho, and the red shirt which came from the slaughter houses of Buenos Aires. Following the gaucho example, his Italian armies were able to live in hostile territory by lassoing stray animals and barbecueing them in the open. The hard democracy of the pampas, furthermore, had taught Garibaldi to treat all men as equals, and many Italians were subsequently to learn through him a new freedom of behaviour, to give up obsequious habits of hand-kissing and caste apparel and deferential forms of speech. Italy also learnt by the same means a dangerous praxis of government, one not without analogues in Italian history but which had been developed to a fine art in a land where the caudillo and the pronun-

ciamento were accepted as normal.

Garibaldi came back to Europe with a confirmed love of fighting. He never was able to resist the call of battle, especially where honour was to be plucked or people delivered. All too easily he convinced himself that he was fighting for humanity and liberty in general. From earliest boyhood his actions and day-dreams show his fixation on becoming a hero and making the world a freer and healthier place. Surprisingly unambitious himself, he offered his services alternately to king and republic, to one caudillo after another, even on one occasion to the Pope. Such a simple soul inevitably became the catspaw of more selfish and less idealistic factions, in Italy as in Uruguay and the Rio Grande. Himself a man of complete integrity, he was also credulously quixotic, a romantic Arthurian knight who rushed in to support some causes which later he had reason to regret.

Garibaldi's importance in the history of Italy is firstly as a soldier, and secondly as a patriotic legend. At a time when statesmen were silent and impotent, he, with a single-minded and simple-minded belief in victory, had the brute courage to act; and it was the kind of action that ennobled his country, publicised her grievances and potentialities, and cheered and emboldened the laggards and the sceptics among his countrymen.

For example, in 1848, with only a few score men, he dared to take on the might of Austria in a private war. In 1849 his defence of the Roman republic kept liberal Europe breathless with admiration, and proved that some Italians at least knew what to fight for and loved what they knew. His retreat from Rome subsequently furnished an abundance of martyrs to feed the cult of patriotism, and gave Italy her one risorgimento heroine in the South American creole, Anita. These feats were enough to make him celebrated. But eleven years later, in 1860, Garibaldi on his own initiative set off with a thousand men for Sicily, and in a few months conquered almost half of Italy; only to hand it over without fuss to his great enemy Cavour, and return voluntarily, a king-maker, into humble private life.

Compared with this quite extraordinary achievement, his other military exploits were not so momentous. It is true that in the Austrian wars of 1859 and 1866, though very poorly equipped by the government, he proved himself the

only Italian general who had enough skill and character to earn the respect of his opponents. But he failed in three separate attempts at a march on Rome, and the jealousy of the regular army, coupled with the strong personal and political dislike of almost all Italian statesmen, contrived to make him henceforward an isolated figure.

When present politics merged into past history, Garibaldi's importance in the risorgimento was to be deliberately played down by the Establishment. The army disliked him for his outstanding military success, the Church for his heresies, Cavour and the deputies for his political insubordination, the middle classes for his threat of social revolution. Even Mazzini broke with him over his obstinate disobedience and individualism. The official historians of Italy, therefore, in their subsequent effort to develop a justification for the triumph of Piedmont and conservatism, made him out to be unserious as a character, and merely marginal in his contribution to victory.

Nor did he himself leave much reliable documentary evidence in his wake for the benefit of later historians. His several versions of autobiography were fanciful—one was written in hendecasyllabic verse—and sometimes even contradictory. There were no close disciples to annotate his every movement, and his letters were those of an extrovert who obstinately spoke of other things than his own mental processes. The guerrilla armies upon whom his fame depended inevitably melted away and left no archives; and, in any case, his battles had been mostly impromptu combinations without any prearranged plan that could be re-created. Hence the romantic legends on the one hand, and official denigration on the other, both equally untrustworthy.

Yet Garibaldi it was, along with Mazzini, who succeeded in accustoming the rest of Europe to the idea of an Italian nation, and he it was who forced Cavour to go faster and further than seemed possible or desirable on any rational analysis. It was his uncritical and unshakeable confidence in unification that finally converted the sceptical statesmen in Turin, and his constant refusal to count the cost brought about almost the only military victories in the saga of national rebirth. He had discovered the secret of inspiring untrained volunteers with an enthusiasm that moved mountains and frontiers. Along with Gordon he is the supreme leader of irregulars in partisan warfare. Through him the common people were won over to a cause that might otherwise have seemed in their eyes remote and profitless; or at least he helped to obscure their vision of what was happening until they were too late to intervene and stop it.

If Garibaldi was mistrusted by the new ruling classes of Italy whom he had helped into power, it was partly because he remained this type of popular hero. His main backers, apart from certain radical financiers such as Adriano Lemmi and the armament firm of Ansaldo, were not politicians but ordinary people whose imagination was fired by his panache and his genuine altruism. The illiterates who voted uncomprehendingly for Italy in the plebiscites often did so because told that this was to support 'Don Peppino' or 'Galubardu'. The concept of Italy for these people was at best a vague abstraction, at worst a meaningless word.

The risorgimento, like all revolutions, was the work of a small, perhaps very small, minority. Again and again Garibaldi had to lament that Neapolitans, Venetians and Romans in turn stirred hardly a finger to 'liberate' themselves from 'foreign' or priestly rule. His volunteers were mostly made up of townsmen from the north, with a nucleus of simple adventurers; they were chiefly professional men and students hoping to avoid their examinations. Often he bewailed this unpromisingly narrow basis of recruitment. The peasants who formed the great majority of Italians, though personally moved by his heroism in adversity, were usually neutral or hostile. His army was sometimes treated as a band of brigands. Villages could bar their gates against him; the local inhabitants often refused him information while acting as unofficial spies for the Austrian soldiery; and he even found some who made no concealment of welcoming a return to Austrian rule.

The fact was that admiration for Garibaldi's person seldom went with any desire to share the hardships which he undertook on the nation's behalf. 'The Italians have too much individual egoism and too little love of their country,' he complained:—'this hermaphrodite generation of Italians whom I have so often tried to ennoble, little though they deserve it.' Patriotism certainly existed, but it was really strong only among remarkable individuals. Usually it was a generalised, rhetorical feeling, skin-deep, and falsified by other sentiments. Noisy patriotic demonstrations could thus be a compensation, making amends for earlier frigidity. In particular, the widespread—but quite exceptional—popular insurrection in Sicily was partly a mere grudge-war against the Neapolitan overlords, partly a peasants' revolt that cut across politics and had nothing to do with patriotic feeling.

As soon as Garibaldi was in retirement, and once he too, like the separatists and peasants in Sicily, was in opposition to the new Italy which they had together helped into existence, he became the natural focus of many of these same discontents, the natural outlet and expression of a general disillusionment. When the romantic cult of Garibaldi grew up in the collective subconscious, it was in part a boost for national morale during a period of disappointment. His exploits were to be sometimes exaggerated in compensation for the dreary

Two *Punch* cartoons satirise Garibaldi's dealings with Victor Emmanuel and Pope Pius IX. Preferring royal dictatorship to a parliamentary system, Garibaldi in his relationship with the monarch, showed none of the hostility he felt towards the Catholic faith.

showing made by the national army between 1848 and 1866. A legend appeared, compounded by romantic story-tellers such as Dumas who liked a good tale as much as the truth.

In this phase of his life Garibaldi became a kind of idealised symbol of the millennium, a sanctified representative of that different and more glorious national revolution which should have taken place but had not. In Naples and Sicily he had been credited with magic powers; and in the more sober north women held up their children for him to bless, even for him to baptise. Garibaldi's image replaced that of God in many a humble peasant's cabin, and his haircut *alla nazzarena* helped this illusion. Prostrate with arthritis, he was carried in solemn procession through the streets of Milan and Palermo, and it seemed like the catafalque of a miracle-working saint.

Abroad, too, he was the object of an extravagant adulation. When injured by a bullet in 1862, twenty-three surgeons from all over the world were sent to see him by zealous enthusiasts. Passionate love-letters arrived secretly from wives of members of both House of Commons and House of Lords, and Cavour knew what he was doing when he slyly sent authenticated locks of the hero's hair to London for distribution to the faithful. Garibaldi's daughter religiously kept even his nail clippings, and a host of relics was preserved for the edification of those who came on pilgrimage in the weekly packet-boat to Caprera.

The 1860s found this ex-dictator of the Two Sicilies in more or less continual opposition, and this did much to weaken popular allegiance to the state and so store up dangers for the future. Naturally he resented that his project for an Italian revolution had been obstructed by the politicians and then captured and drastically watered down. As long ago as the 1830s he had fled into exile after being condemned to death by the king's government. Again, after his retreat from Rome, he had been arrested and exiled for another four years. Three times subsequently did the national army move against him to stop his conquest of Rome, and in one engagement they crippled him for life. But this made him only yet more of a popular hero, and unprecedented mass ovations misled his not very subtle or critical mind into dangerous deeds of insubordination. Laconic communiques were issued from Caprera criticising various aspects of government policy. Parliament he condemned as the seat of corruption and gerrymandering, as a rubber stamp for ministerial autocracy, a fraud designed by the clever lawyers who specialised in oratorical dexterity and corridor intrigue. 'Give us battles, not liberties,' was his cry to the king; for behind 'liberties' he discerned a contrivance by parliament to prefer an oligarchy of wealth and intellect at the expense of the common people.

What made this attitude particularly dangerous was that Garibaldi understood from the king that he might rely on royal support in subverting the normal constitutional government of the country. Sometimes he was even positively encouraged to rebel, and this led directly to his tragic wounding at Aspromonte. Victor Emanuel engaged in private political activity behind the backs of all of his successive Prime Ministers, just as he commonly appointed or dismissed them without any reference to parliament; and in such monarchical irresponsibility is the key to many involved moments in modern Italian history.

For example, the king came to blows frequently with Cavour over the morals and politics of the Court; whereas on the other hand, Garibaldi was someone he could appreciate—a bluff, frank, soldierly man, with a firm sense of loyalty and without the subtle finesse and secondary aims of a politician. Garibaldi was always genuine, and what he said rang true, even if it was silly; whereas Cavour and his successors were guileful and dissembling almost from habit. Moreover, they used parliament to control the king, while Garibaldi on the contrary preferred a royal dictatorship over parliament. Cavour was not only too much a civilian for Victor Emmanuel, who liked people in uniform; he was also too clever; and the king had his own reasons for preferring character to intelligence.

This secret royal favour, when combined with Garibaldi's own lack of brains, his recklessness, his urge towards action and his great popular following, made him a person of great but irresponsible power. The United States Minister wrote back to his government in 1861 that, 'though but a solitary and private individual, he is at this moment, in and of himself, one of the great Powers of the world.' Garibaldi's political views are therefore of peculiar interest.

The first point to be made is that he was too simple and guileless to understand more than the surface of politics. Florence Nightingale, one of his great admirers, was shocked on meeting him to find that he understood very little indeed of the causes he so ardently professed. He was a convinced republican, but also fought for the monarchy; he believed in dictatorship, but all his life fought for freedom and against despotism; he was a bellicose patriot, but also adhered to a pacifist internationalism.

And yet in some convictions he never wavered, for instance in his antipathy to the Catholic faith and his attachment to democracy. He always believed in a wider suffrage and in free and universal education. Unlike the twentieth-century Garibaldians, he thought it criminal folly for a poor country such as Italy to acquire overseas colonies and spend so much on armaments. Repeatedly he addressed memoranda to the Great Powers on the abolition of war and on the means of creating through international arbitration a United States of Europe. For he was a patriot with a difference. 'If Italy ever in her turn threatened the independence of neighbour states, I should regretfully but surely be on the side of the oppressed.' Such a statement would have astonished some of his later disciples.

Garibaldi's combination of idealism and simple good sense can also be traced in his notions on social reform; for here he spoke with genuine knowledge and feeling. By heredity, environment and temperament, he understood the masses as Cavour and Mazzini never did, and if others had shared his understanding, Italy might have been a more stable and tranquil place today. He believed prophetically that 'the great future of Italy lies with her working classes,' and hence that their emancipation and education was an urgent task. Proudly he called himself a socialist; but his socialism was of the heart not of the head; it was based not on class-war but on easing the tension between capital and labour. Though disapproved of by Marx, this sentiment nevertheless was to become an important strand within the Italian socialist movement.

Another trend inside the Italian Left has been towards authoritarianism, and this too goes back to Garibaldi. His own favourite type of warfare had accustomed him to the need for quick and unchallenged decisions, and his preference for autocratic methods became instinctive. Among his volunteers the penalty for disobedience was instant death; and we are told that he would shoot a man without stopping to take the cigar from his mouth.

In politics his aim was always freedom, but people might have to be forced to be free. Whenever he possessed civil authority he chose to be a dictator, and he was hailed as *Duce* by the mob when he appeared on numberless balconies. Too unambitious, unintelligent and uncorrupted to play the Mussolini himself, he advocated a royal dictatorship. Government needed the *fasces*—he employed the very word. And the deputies should be packed off home as a corrupting and disabling element; for Cavour seemed to be setting up a pseudo-constitutional government like that of Louis Napoleon, in which liberty was only a sham. Garibaldi's impatience here with Italian parliamentarism was excessive. He sensed the disease, but was not the man to devise an adequate remedy. Yet in partial explanation it may be remembered that, in 1922, many of the liberals who claimed to inherit from Cavour were also to invoke the *fasces* against a corrupt and anarchical parliamentary regime.

G. M. Trevelyan admirably describes that great moment when the hero of two worlds stepped down from his autocratic position at Naples and retired to a lonely island off Sardinia. For a long time he had been an admirer of Robinson Crusoe, and at Caprera he too could exist free from the intrigue and misgovernment that he thought were ruining his country. Caprera was a barren granite outcrop where he could live a simple life independent of the social obligations and political involvements he so much disliked; and there, not far from that other romantic island of Montecristo, he spent most of his declining days, surrounded by his legitimate and illegitimate children.

With difficulty he built up a farm in this unlikely spot, helped by heavy subventions from his admirers all over the world. His affairs were always entangled, for he was a bad administrator and the farm was singularly unprofitable. But his needs were few. He himself, when in health, would milk the cows. He washed his own shirts, and rarely possessed more than one change of clothing. He had trained himself to cut a coat and trousers by eye. For food he was self-sufficient. Increasingly he became a vegetarian, though to go shooting and spearing fish remained almost his favourite pastime.

He also read books—his small library included Shakespeare, Byron, Plutarch, La Fontaine, Voltaire, Arthur Young on agriculture, and other English books on navigation, agriculture and the art of war. And he wrote too, partly to try to earn his living, partly to stir up the younger generation to emulation of great deeds. The three novels he wrote are dull and absurd to a degree, and his poems are often embarrassing; but he had a genuine love of roughly improvised verse such as may still be found here and there among the Italian peasantry.

Garibaldi died at Caprera in 1882. Always unconventional, he had enjoined his wife to place his body on a pyre of aromatic wood, and to burn him under the open sky in the same pagan, hygienic way he had lived. But the dignitaries of Rome, whom he had always execrated alive, would not be done out of a good funeral, and were revenged on him dead. They argued, as an added touch of irony, that burning would offend people's religious sensibilities. So he was incongruously buried in the presence of dukes and ministers. The world had the last word against him.

His own last word was a Political Testament. To his children and friends he bequeathed his love for liberty and truth. He explicitly condemned the Catholic priesthood and the Mazzinians as the great national enemies. And again he recommended his countrymen to select the most honest man in Italy and make him a temporary dictator. Only when Italians were more educated to liberty, and their country was less threatened from outside and in, should dictatorial rule give way to a regular republican government. Here, in brief, was a neat abstract of the lessons learnt by a simple-minded but strong-hearted soldier during a lifetime of devotion to an ideal.

Sarah Bernhardt's Paris

Christopher Hibbert

Christopher Hibbert is a prize-winning British author of more than 30 books of history, military history and biography. They include The Days of the French Revolution; The Great Mutiny: India 1857; Versailles; The Court of St. James's; The House of the Medici; Disraeli and His World; *and biographies of Charles I, George IV and Edward VII.*

In the summer of 1862 an astonishingly thin young girl with a pale face, frizzy reddish hair, intense blue eyes and a prominent nose stood on the corner of the Rue Duphet and the Rue St. Honore in Paris looking at the yellow playbills which were pasted up to advertise forthcoming productions at the Theatre Francais. *Iphigenie by Jean Racine,* one of these playbills announced, *For the Debut of Mademoiselle Sarah Bernhardt.* "I have no idea how long I stood there, fascinated by the letters of my name," she recorded years later. "But I remember that it seemed to me as though every person who stopped to read the poster looked at me afterwards."

Sarah Bernhardt was then just eighteen. Her mother, a beautiful woman of Jewish Dutch descent, had once been a milliner and was now a highly successful courtesan with an apartment in the Rue St. Honore where, so it was said, attractive women of her calling could command a hundred thousand francs a month and enjoy the use of two carriages and the services of a footman and a chef. Certainly Julie Bernhardt lived well, and in her comfortable apartment received a succession of generous friends, protectors and lovers, bankers and noblemen, musicians and writers. They included the Italian composer Gioacchino Rossini, who had settled in Paris some years before, Alexandre Dumas, the prodigal, exuberant author of *The Three Musketeers,* who believed that in fiction as in

life the two most important ingredients were "*l'action et l'amour,*" and Charles Auguste-Louis-Joseph, Duc de Morny, the half-brother of the Emperor Napoleon III whose *coup d'etat* he had helped to engineer.

Napoleon III had been born in Paris in 1808, the third son of a younger brother of Napoleon I. Adventurer and idealist—though with his waxed moustache and half-closed eyes, looking, as Theophile Gautier said, "more like a ringmaster who has been sacked for getting drunk"—he believed himself to be a man of destiny, bound to follow his star. After the overthrow of the Orleans monarchy in 1848 he was elected Prince President of the Second Republic, and four years later, following the *coup d'etat* by which he forcibly dissolved the *Assemblee Nationale Legislative,* he was proclaimed Emperor. Since then, with the help of Baron Haussmann, Prefet de la Seine, he had been transforming Paris, intent not only upon freeing the fine monuments of the past from the jumble of buildings that enclosed them on every side, and upon creating a modern dazzling *ville lumiere* with wide, gaslit boulevards and magnificent perspectives, but also upon ensuring that it became a capital city which artillery could overawe with clear fields of fire against revolutionary mobs.

Under Haussmann's ruthless direction pavements were torn up and narrow streets demolished; grandiose apartment blocks took the place of huddled houses whose poor occupants were forced out into the suburbs. Five hundred miles of water mains were laid, over 200 miles of sewers; more than 30,000 gas lamps replaced the ancient lanterns; railway stations were constructed close to the heart of the city. Imposing new thoroughfares were driven through the gardens of the Luxembourg Palace; the Boulevard de Sebastopol made its way through a populous district beside the cast-iron and

glass food markets known as Les Halles; the Boulevard Haussmann pushed east from the Place de l'Etoile; the Boulevards Saint-Germain and St. Michel and the Rue de Rennes appeared on the Left Bank. The Ile de la Cite was transformed and its greatest pride, Notre-Dame, restored under the direction of Eugene-Emmanuel Violet-le-Duc. The Tuileries and the Cour Carree were joined by a new gallery along a lengthened Rue de Rivoli. The Bois de Boulogne was laid out with artificial lakes and carriage drives. In 1861 the foundation stone of a vast opera house, which was to occupy almost three acres, was laid to the north of the Boulevard des Italiens; and here, after fourteen years' work, Charles Garnier's extravagant edifice, decorated with 33 varieties of marble and the works of 73 sculptors, was opened at last, a fitting tribute to the pomp and opulent display of the Second Empire.

In this prosperous and rapidly changing city of 1,825,000 people, the cosmopolitan capital of the world, the working day of the poor began as those more fortunate were going to bed after a night of pleasure. Before dawn *chiffonniers* appeared with lanterns and forks and with baskets on their backs to poke through the piles of rubbish which had been thrown out into the streets, searching for rags and bones, bottles and jars, hoping to find, and sometimes finding, an article more valuable before the rubbish wagons trundled along to cart the mounds away. And then, as the sun came up, bootblacks came out with scissors as well as brushes for they were as expert at clipping poodles as they were at polishing shoes; women who sold sweetmeats in the streets prepared their trays of cakes and chocolates, while soup and coffee vendors took up their places on the Pont Notre-Dame; *marchands de coco,* relics of the time of King Louis Philippe, wearing cocked hats and little bells, chopped up lemons and sticks of licorice to flavor the water they carried on their backs in highly polished ornamental tanks to offer for sale in goblets to thirsty passers-by; mechanics greased the wheels of the roundabouts in the Champs Elysees where gardeners watered the exotic flowers; and waiters scattered damp sand under the tables of cafes where clerks and laborers called for coffee and croisettes, brandy plums, absinthe or cheap Orleans wine as they streamed down on their way to work from the heights of Montmartre and La Chapelle, smoking clay pipes, toolbags slung on their backs and loaves of bread under their arms—masons in white jackets, locksmiths in blue overalls, tilers in blouses and small round caps, painters in long smocks swinging their pots, bricklayers with hods on their shoulders, chimney-sweepers harnessed to their barrows of soot.

After their *petit dejeuner* visitors from the country and foreign tourists emerged from their hotels, from the Hotel de Helder; the Hotel Louvre in the Place du Palais Royal which the enterprising Pereire brothers, Emile and Isaac, had built for the Paris Exhibition of 1855; from the even larger Grand Hotel on the Boulevard des Capucines which, with its 750 rooms was the largest in Europe; and from the Ambassade, the Ritz, and the Bristol which, patronized by the Prince of Wales who stayed there, ineffectively incognito, as the Duke of Lancaster, was to become the most fashionable of all.

The doors of the shops now opened, of the smaller, smarter boutiques whose prices varied in accordance with the apparent wealth or gullibility of their customers; of Denton's bookshop in the Palais-Royal where 6,000 copies of the Goncourt brothers' *La Lorette* had been sold in a single week in 1853; and of those recent phenomena, the large department stores, the Maison du Bon Marche, which had been founded by Norman Boucicaut in 1852, Chaucard's Louvre in the Rue de Rivoli and Jaluzot's Au Printemps on the Boulevard Haussmann. Their shopping done, mothers and nurses took their children and charges out to play with hoops and balls and wooden horses on wheels by the sparkling fountains in the gardens of the Tuileries, wearing billowing, brilliantly colored and intricately embroidered crinolines and flowered hats, while men walked past on their way to the Jockey Club, the Club de L'Union or Le Cercle Agricole, resplendent in shining silk hats, long, narrow-waisted coats, elaborate cravats and tight trousers with buttons down the seams.

By midday the boulevards were crowded with horse-drawn *imperiale* omnibuses, with phaetons and *voitures a laquais,* cockaded coachmen and footmen sitting on the boxes. Smaller equipages, fiacres, traps, landaus and tandems rattled down the Champs Elysees towards the Bois de Boulogne to parade around the lakes and along the Allee des Poteaux. Soon the green iron chairs beneath the striped awnings of the cafes and restaurants were occupied; and familiar faces could be seen at the Cafe de Cardinal on the corner of the Rue Richelieu, at Tortoni's on the Boulevard des Italiens, next door to the Restaurant de la Maison Doree, at the Cafe de Paris which was the favorite haunt of Eugene Sue, Heinrich Heine and Balzac, and at the Moulin Rouge, a smart restaurant on the Champs Elysees where "at the bottom of the garden, at all the windows on every floor, in the lighted depths of private rooms, just as in boxes at the theater, women's heads could be seen nodding left and right to former companions of their nights." In the evenings, as guests set out for fancy dress balls and private dinner parties and the cafe-concerts and the theaters began to fill, crowds collected outside the Theatre Francais to watch the fashionable and famous go into the House of Moliere.

Here it was that Sarah Bernhardt had decided to become an actress. She had been taken by her mother and three of her mother's friends—Regis Lavolie, a rich banker, Dumas and the Duc de Morny—to see a performance of Racine's *Britannicus*. She had found it so moving that she had burst into tears and then into sobs so loud that her mother blushed scarlet in embarrassment, other members of the audience had turned round calling "*Sh! Sh!*" and Lavolie had stalked out of the box in disgust, slamming the door behind him.

On their return to Julie Bernhardt's apartment, Sarah had been sent to bed in disgrace. But Dumas had kindly gone up with her and kissing her at her door, had whispered in her ear, "Goodnight, little star." Her chance of being a star had come in 1862 with her performance of *Iphigenie*. She had worked hard for the opportunity. With the influential help of the Duc de Morny, she had been granted an audience at the Conservatoire; then, having attended the classes there with enthusiastic assiduity, she had been taken on as a *pensionnaire* by the Comedie Francaise.

Overcome by stage fright, she gabbled her words throughout the first act, and although she recovered her confidence later on, neither audience nor critics were favorably impressed. Her subsequent performances were equally disappointing, and it was widely felt that the Comedie Francaise had been ill-advised to take her on in the first place. There was little regret when, after breaking her parasol over the head of the stage doorkeeper for some imagined slight and punching an elderly actress in the face during a violent quarrel, she was told to resign from the company. At least she could comfort herself with the thought that she had made a name for herself. Caricatures and stories about her appeared in the newspapers; and her mother's friend, Lavolie, had little difficulty in persuading the directors of the Gymnase, a theater which specialized in popular comedies, to give the now notorious young actress another chance. She did not flourish at the Gymnase either, though, and after one particularly disastrous performance, which reduced her to thoughts of suicide, she decided to follow Dumas' advice and go abroad for a time. According to her own account she went to Spain. But, since her own accounts were always flavored by a reckless indifference to truth, she may well have gone no further than Brussels. Certainly she returned to Paris pregnant by a Belgian aristocrat, the paternity of whose child she ascribed at various times to Leon Gambetta, Victor Hugo, General Boulanger and even to the infant Duke of Clarence who was, in fact, born a fortnight before his alleged progeny.

Within a few weeks of Maurice Bernhardt's birth, his mother went back to work, this time at the Porte-Saint-Martin, a theater renowned for its melodramas and *vaudevilles feeriques*. Here yet again she proved a disappointment. And it was not until—once more with the help of one of her mother's friends—she signed a contract at the Odeon, a national theater on the Left Bank near the Jardin du Luxembourg, that she made her mark at last. Here, in the leading female role in a revival of Dumas' *Kean,* she enjoyed her first unalloyed success. Thereafter triumph followed triumph. Her name on the playbills was sure to fill the theater. She became the darling of the Left Bank. After her portrayal of the minstrel boy

Zanetto in Francois Coppee's *Le Passant* in 1868, the Emperor's cousin, Princess Mathilde, arranged for a command performance at the Tuileries where she so impressed the Emperor himself that he gave her a splendid brooch blazing with diamonds. She moved into a large apartment in the Rue Auber; and here, in an untidy clutter of furniture and ornaments, over which turtles with gold-plated shells crawled to escape from barking dogs, she received an assortment of friends and lovers even more varied and distinguished than those who had paid court to her mother.

She entertained Leon Gambetta, then a young barrister and leading member of the political opposition, who was one day to become President of the Chamber of Deputies. She welcomed Princess Mathilde's brother, Prince Napoleon, like his sister a patron of literature and the arts, and a patron, too, of Cora Pearl, the saucy, irresistible English courtesan who was known to have presented herself to her admirers wearing nothing but a sprig of parsley. Sarah Bernhardt also welcomed Theophile Gautier, "*le bon Theo,*" whose praise of her art had done much to further her career. And, with particular pleasure, she opened her arms to Gautier's friend, George Sand, who, many years before, had left her husband, Baron Dudevant, to lead an independent, unconventional life in Paris, writing novels, wearing trousers, smoking incessantly, nursing Alfred de Musset through an illness before deserting him for his doctor, then going to live with Chopin. She was in her mid-sixties now, but working as hard as ever: Sarah Bernhardt appeared in two of her plays and grew to admire and to love her.

Both Gautier and George Sand were members of that coterie of writers and artists who, during these final years of the Second Empire, met regularly at Magny's, the restaurant in the Rue Contrescarpe-Dauphine which was run by Modeste Magny, an exceptionally gifted restaurateur from the Marne. George Sand had been one of his earliest customers, preferring his restaurant to the Pinson in the Rue de l'Ancienne-Comedie which she had previously patronized, despite the row made next door to Magny's by the performers and spectators at Aublin's *Les Folies Dauphine,* a *boui-boui* or music-hall known more familiarly as *Le Beuglant*

because of the bellowing sounds that burst from its windows.

George Sand had not, however, been present at the inauguration of the dining club at Magny's on November 22, 1862. On this Saturday evening among those present had been the once lively but now rather morose lithographer and caricaturist Gavarni, whose sketches of Parisian life had been one of the most notable features in the satirical paper, *Le Charivari;* Gavarni's friends and future biographers, the two inseparable brothers, Edmond and Jules de Goncourt, novelists, social historians, diarists and men of letters, who spoke alternately, the one elaborating, complementing and developing the remarks of the other; and the great critic, Sainte-Beuve, an ugly, fat little man with a black skull-cap on his bald head, now nearing the end of his life but seeming to enjoy it as much as in those earlier days when he had been the lover of Victor Hugo's wife and had dined in a private room every Saturday night at Magny's with other women friends. On later occasions these four had been joined by Gustave Flaubert, the robust though syphilitic author of *Madame Bovary* and *Salammbo;* by the philogist and historian, Ernest Renan whose influential and controversial *Vie de Jesus* cost him the professorship of Hebrew at the College de France; the towering, bearded Ivan Turgenev, out of favor with the rulers of his native Russia; and Hippolyte Taine, critic and philosopher, whose *Histoire de la litterature anglaise* had appeared in three volumes in 1862.

They dined in one of the seven private rooms on the first floor, served by the head waiter Charles Labran, who was to remain at Magny's until his master's death. And, as the Goncourts wrote in their journal after their first dinner there, they enjoyed "an exquisite meal, perfect in every respect, a meal such as [they] had thought impossible to obtain in a Paris restaurant." The *specialites de la maison* were *tournedos Rossini, chateaubriand, petites marmites, puree Magny* and *becasses a la Charles,* all of which the proprietor had contrived himself. Also exquisitely cooked at Magny's were *pieds de mouton a la poulette,* and *ecrevisses a la Bordelaise* which, as one customer said, "once you had begun eating there was no reason to stop, and you didn't stop either, unless there was a revolution or an earthquake."

With such dishes Magny gained for himself a special commendation in Adolphe

Joanne's guide to the restaurants of Paris which, dividing them all into six categories, considered only a few worthy of being listed in the first class. Apart from Magny's and Philippe's in the Rue Montorqueil, the knowledgeable *bon viveur* recommend Brebant's, haunt of the racing people from Longchamps and Chantilly; Vefour's for Rhenish carp, baked and stuffed and surrounded by soft roe; Ledoyen's for salmon with a green sauce the secret of which was unknown to other establishments; Aux Trois Freres Provencaux for cod with garlic; the Cafe Riche for *sole aux crevettes;* the Maison Doree for fillet steak, braised with tomatoes and mushrooms and served with "a veritable gravy of truffles"; and Bignon's for *barbue au vin rouge* and *filet Richelieu.* But though there were so few restaurants which Joanne could recommend without reserve, he calculated that there were 4,000 pot-houses which were "frequented only by workmen and coachmen." And even in these cheaper places the food was generally good and the service excellent, for in a city where prosperity had created an apparently insatiable demand for pleasure, those in search of it had learned to be discriminating.

"Civility appears to be the motive power of his life," an English visitor wrote of the Parisian waiter. "That wonderful fleetness with which he dashes through the cafe into the open air, and threads his way through rows of lounging customers at the green tables, carrying on the tops of his four fingers and thumb an immense pile of cups, liqueur glasses, bottles of iced water, and lumps of sugar . . . appears to be the noble effort of a chivalrous nature. Ask him for a light and he produces lucifers from any pocket. Although people are calling him or hissing to him in various directions, he finds time to light two or three lucifers and even to hold them till the fumes of the sulphur have passed away before he presents them to you . . . He is free with you; he has a light retort for any attempted joke; but he is never familiar—never rude . . . The reader who wishes to study the Parisian waiter in perfection, should choose a fine summer's night, and take his seat outside the rotunda in the Palais Royal about eight o'clock, in the midst of about 300 people, served by about eight waiters, who caper, loaded with crockery and newspapers with an activity that any Harlequin might envy."

There were numerous cafes in the Palais Royal, but mostly expensive and respectable. But for those who preferred less decorous establishments there were even more of these elsewhere. Paris, indeed, was a very *embarras de richesse* of cafes, cafe-concerts, taverns, *bouillons, cremeries, brasseries, pensions bourgeoises, assommoirs* and *estaminets* as well as brothels, *cabinets particuliers* and licentious dance-halls. One of the best known brothels was Farcy's where, in the drawing-room sprawling on red velvet divans around the floral-papered walls, the girls smiled and cooed and asked for drinks. One of the most expensive *cabinets particuliers* was the Grand Seize, an exotic private room at the Cafe Anglais hung with red wallpaper and gold hieroglyphics, furnished with gilt chairs and a crimson sofa, where Sarah Bernhardt was herself to be entertained by the Prince of Wales. And one of the most lively and wanton dance-halls was Mabille's in the Allee des Veuves where an orchestra of 50 played in a Chinese pavilion surrounded by artificial palm trees with gas globes hanging from the leaves; where, as a guidebook warned, "the limits of propriety [were] frequently passed"; and where parlormaids, *grisettes* and milliners could find men willing to pay them twenty francs for a night of pleasure, more than they could otherwise earn in a month.

In the summer of 1870 the carefree frivolity of the Second Empire came suddenly to a close. Napoleon III declared war on Prussia, and a few weeks later his army was crushingly defeated at Sedan. The confidence of the Parisians, who had never believed in the remotest possibility of such a catastrophe, was shattered overnight.

"Who can describe the consternation written on every face," wrote Edmond de Goncourt as his fellow citizens pondered on the consequences of the fall of the imperial government, "the sound of aimless steps pacing the streets at random, the anxious conversations of shopkeepers and *concierges* on their doorsteps, the crowds collecting at street-corners, the siege of the newspaper kiosks, the triple line of readers gathering around every gaslamp."

At news of the German army's approach, preparations for the expected siege of Paris gathered momentum. Mines were laid, woods chopped down, road blocks thrown up, road and river approaches obstructed, monuments protected by sandbags and boarding; and the capital's extensive defensive system of bastions, walls, moats and forts—which Adolphe Thiers had had constructed in 1840 but which had subsequently been neglected—was hastily restored and strengthened. Railway stations were converted into balloon factories or cannon-foundries, theaters into hospitals; couturiers' workshops began to make military uniforms, the Louvre to turn out armaments. Regular troops, marines and sailors marched into the city; conscripts and volunteers paraded through the streets; thousands of heavy guns were dragged out to the forest, while herds of cattle and sheep were driven into the Bois de Boulogne.

In the excitement of all this activity the morale of the Parisians rose. On September 13, a few days before the last mail-train left the city and the one remaining telegraph line to the west was cut, a review of the defenders was held by General Louis-Jules Trochu, president of the newly formed Government of National Defense, who galloped onto the scene to the rattle of drums and to shouts of *"Vive la France! Vive la Republique! Vive Trochu!"* Tens of thousands of soldiers lined the boulevards from the Place de la Bastille to the Arc de Triomphe. The National Guard, some in frock-coats, others in workmen's smocks, marched past to the strains of the *Marseillaise,* their rifles decorated with flowers and ribbons, children holding their fathers' hands.

Poets declaimed their verses; journalists issued proclamations; politicians harangued the crowds; priests preached sermons. Adelaide de Montgolfier, daughter of the great balloonist, watched the *Neptune,* the first postal balloon to leave Paris, soar into the sky above the Place Saint-Pierre in Montmartre, shouts of *"Vive la Republique!"* ringing in her ears, proud to think that her "dear father's invention [was] now proving of such great value to his country."

Enthusiasm was not matched, though, by achievement. Outside the city the French troops proved no match for the German invaders. Dejected and dispirited soldiers returned disconsolately from the front to the streets of Paris where already long queues were to be seen outside the butchers' shops as early as two o'clock in the morning and the restaurants started to serve beef that looked suspiciously like horse flesh.

Looking for scapegoats, the Parisians turned on foreigners, particularly on the English residents who were believed to share their Queen's sympathetic attitude towards Germany: *Les Nouvelles* proposed that the best way to settle the question as to whether the British were spies or not was to shoot the lot of them. "Anyone who did not speak French with purity was arrested," commented Trochu's aide-de-camp, Maurice d'Herisson. "Englishmen, Americans, Swedes, Spaniards and Alsatians were arrested alike. A similar fate befell all those who, either in dress or manner, betrayed anything unusual. Stammerers were arrested because they tried to speak too quickly; dumb people because they did not speak at all; and the deaf because they did not seem to understand what was said to them. The sewermen who emerged from the sewers were arrested because they spoke Piedmontese."

The people turned, too, on Trochu and his government whom they accused of not facing the crisis with sufficient determination. Demonstrations were held in the Place de la Concorde; marches made to the Hotel de Ville; demands presented for a *levee en masse* and a *sortie en masse,* the election of a Municipal Commune, the formation of a corps of Amazons, the manufacture of "guns, more guns and still more guns." At the end of October news reached the capital that Marshal Bazaine had surrendered Metz to the enemy and that Le Bourget, a village north of Paris which had been captured by the Prussians, had been retaken by them. There were also rumors that Leon Gambetta, who, with a basket of homing pigeons, had left Paris by balloon at the beginning of the month to join the elderly members of the Delegation of Tours, was inclining to their view that surrender was inevitable.

Incensed by all this, a crowd of about 15,000 demonstrators advanced on the Hotel de Ville, shouting "No armistice!" and "The Commune forever!" Several hundred of them burst inside the building, demanding the resignation of all the members of the Government of National Defense and calling out the names of men whom they wished to replace them. Their leaders—with Gustave Flourens, a revolutionary member of the National Guard, well to the fore—climbed onto the baize-covered table of the council-chamber and strode along it, trampling on papers and notebooks, knocking over inkstands and sandboxes, crushing pens

137

and pencils, their voices lost in the clangor of shouts, drums and trumpets, while General Trochu calmly smoked his cigar.

Trochu's apparent indifference to these agitators was justified: an energetic colleague, Ernest Picard, called upon the more constructive leaders of the National Guard for help, and a bourgeois battalion marched to the Government's rescue. While Flourens went into hiding, Parisians were asked to answer the following question in a plebiscite: "Does the population of Paris wish to maintain the powers of the Government of National Defense? *Oui ou Non?*" Overwhelmingly the answer was yes.

So Trochu continued in office; his forces remained on the defensive; and Paris grew more and more to resemble a beleaguered city. Many shops put up their shutters, having nothing to sell; others filled their windows with telescopes, knives, revolvers and brandyflasks. Fashionable clothes were no longer conspicuous on the boulevards: men wore makeshift uniforms, women their oldest dresses or nurses' aprons.

As Henry Labouchere, Paris correspondent of the London *Daily News,* recorded on November 15, Paris' mood now veered wildly "from the lowest depths of despair to the wildest confidence. Yesterday afternoon a pigeon arrived covered with blood, bearing on his tail a despatch from Gambetta, announcing that the Prussians had been driven out of Orleans . . . The despatch was read at the Mairies to large crowds, and in the cafes by enthusiasts who got up on the tables. I was in a shop when a person came in with it. Shopkeepers, assistants and customers immediately performed a war dance round a stove."

This festive mood was short-lived. People were soon complaining again about the National Guard, who performed very confidently on parade but showed little inclination to fight the enemy, and about General Trochu who, so one junior officer said, had associated so much with lawyers that he had become to resemble one himself: "He has dipped his pen in his scabbard and his sword in his inkstand, and when he finally attempts to draw the sword, he'll unsheath a penholder." Hopes were raised at the end of November by rumors of a great sortie involving 150,000 men who were to cross the Marne and occupy the enemy's positions at Champigny. But these hopes were dashed when the crowds,

which had gathered at Pont d'Austerlitz and along the Avenue du Trone, learned that the sortie had ended in tragic failure. Hard upon this reverse came news of the defeat of the Army of the Loire and the recapture of Orleans. Less than a fortnight later the spirits of the people were revived again by an optimistic message from Gambetta published in the *Journal Officiel,* only to be dampened soon afterwards by the failure of another sortie.

In common with most other theaters and many hotels, the Odeon was converted into a hospital. Assuming the responsibility for organizing it, Sarah Bernhardt rushed from one admirer to another, asking for supplies, obtaining brandy from Baron Rothschild, chocolate from Meunier, sardines from the rich grocer, Felix Potin, outside whose store in the Boulevard de Strasbourg long queues stood throughout the night. Acting as nurse as well as storekeeper, she dressed wounds, assisted at operations, carried food to the helpless and brandy to the dying; and as the weeks passed and the supplies of food grew ever more depleted, often went without meals herself so that the patients might be fed.

By the end of the year the shortage of food in Paris had become acute. Beef and mutton, at first severely rationed, now disappeared from the shops altogether. Cab-horses and race-horses were sold by the butchers instead, then cats, rats and dogs. Eels and gudgeons from the Seine fetched their weight in silver.

"People talk of nothing but what is eaten, can be eaten, or is there to be eaten [wrote Edmond de Goncourt]. Conversation has come down to this:

" 'You know, a fresh egg costs twenty-five sous.'

" 'It appears there's a fellow who buys up all the candles he can find, adds some coloring, and produces that fat which sells at such a price.'

" 'Mind you don't buy any coconut butter. It stinks a house out for three days at least.'

" 'I've had some dog chops, and found them really very tasty: they look just like mutton chops.'

" 'Who was it who told me he had eaten some kangaroo?' "

As well as kangaroo, the director of the zoo sold all manner of animals for slaughter—buffaloes and zebras, reindeer and camels, yaks and elephants. But these animals were soon consumed. And "failing meat," one commentator observed, "you cannot fall back on vegeta-

bles: a little turnip costs eight sous and you have to pay seven francs for a pound of onions. Nobody talks about butter any more, and every other sort of fat except candle-fat and axle-grease has disappeared too. As for the two staple items of the diet of the poor—potatoes and cheese—cheese is just a memory, and you have to have friends in high places to obtain potatoes at twenty francs a bushel. The greater part of Paris is living on coffee, wine and bread." And even bread, a hard black substance made principally of bran, rice and starch, was scarce.

Hunger was not the only privation. By the end of the year the temperature had fallen to twelve degrees below zero. While sentries froze to death, orders were given for the felling of six square miles of trees in the Bois de Boulogne and the Bois de Vincennes and along the city's boulevards. But the people could not wait: fences, trellises, benches and telegraph poles were cut up as well and dragged away to their homes.

To cold and hunger and the attendant sickness and disease was added the horror of bombardment. At first it was only the forts that were shelled. But at the beginning of January 1871, shells began also to burst in the city itself, mainly on the poorer houses on the Left Bank where the people bore the cannonade with stoic courage. "On every doorstep, women and children stand, half frightened, half inquisitive," wrote Edmond de Goncourt, "watching the medical orderlies going by, dressed in white smocks with red crosses on their arms and carrying stretchers, mattresses and pillows."

Before long most people grew quite accustomed to the bombing. Children, hearing an explosion, would say, "That was a shell," and then calmly continue with their game. And street urchins on seeing a well dressed person walk by, so Henry Labouchere observed, would cry out, "Flat! Flat! A shell—a shell—*a plat ventre!* Down on your faces!" "The man, gorgeous in fur, falls flat on the ground—perhaps in the gutter—and the Parisian urchin rejoices with exceeding great joy."

Despite all the hardships, Labouchere continued, the Parisians behaved with remarkable resignation. They criticized Trochu and the government endlessly, denouncing their mistakes and blunders; but, they made "no complaint about their miseries," accepting them "with an unpretending fortitude which no people in the world could surpass." By the end of January, however, it was clear that resistance could not much longer be maintained. Men and women were falling down dead in food queues; the death rate rose to almost 4,500 a week, many of these being children. "At every step," one survivor wrote, "you met an undertaker carrying a little deal coffin."

Edmond de Goncourt was struck by the deathly silence that had fallen over the city. You could no longer hear Paris living, he noted in his journal. Every face looked like that of a sick person or convalescent. You saw "nothing but thin, pallid features, faces as pale and yellow as horseflesh." One day a prostitute, splashing along behind him in the Rue Saint-Nicholas, called out pathetically, "Monsieur, will you come up to my room, for a piece of bread?"

On January 23, Jules Favre, the Foreign Minister, left Paris for the German headquarters at Versailles to open negotiations for surrender. "A tall, thin, stooping, miserable-looking lawyer," as his secretary described him, "with his wrinkled frock-coat and his white hair falling over his collar," he seemed no match for Count Bismarck, the robust, broad-chested Iron Chancellor, who received Favre in the tight, white tunic and yellow-banded cap of the White Cuirassiers. Yet Favre's apparent weakness, real dignity and "good old French manners" worked to his advantage. "It is very difficult for me to be as hard with him as I have to be," Bismarck told his wife. "The rascals know this, and consequently push him forward." The terms imposed upon them were, therefore, not as hard as the French had feared they might be. But they were nevertheless obliged to agree to the German army's ceremonial march into the capital. So, on Wednesday, March 1, German troops escorted by blaring bands and by cavalry with drawn swords, paraded through the Arc de Triomphe and down the Champs Elysees.

Parisians, their houses shuttered and their shops closed, were now in a bitter mood, harboring resentment not only against the Germans but also against the Government and the generals who, they felt, had failed them, as well as against the rich who, during the siege, had been able to pay for the food and warmth denied to others and who, now that it was over, had left for the country. There was resentment, too, against the provinces which, having escaped most of the horrors of the war, chose to elect a predominantly royalist assembly. In protest a *Federation Republicaine de la Garde Nationale* was formed; and insurgents established the Commune of Paris.

Civil war was now inevitable. On the orders of Adolphe Thiers, soon to be President of the Third Republic, an army of regulars was collected at Versailles under General MacMahon and marched into Paris. The subsequent slaughter was fearful. Prisoners taken by the Versailles forces were shot out of hand; in retaliation the Commune seized hostages, including the Archbishop of Paris and the Presiding Judge of the Court of Appeals, and executed them. In the Rue Haxo scores of other hostages, among them several priests, were shot by a frenzied crowd of men and women. Street battles raged and the pavements ran with blood; numerous public buildings were destroyed. The Palais des Tuileries and the Hotel de Ville, the Palais Royal and the Louvre, the Ministry of Finance and the Prefecture de Police were all set on fire. By the time the last defenders of the Commune had been shot down in the Pere Lachaise cemetery nearly 20,000 people, men, women and children, had lost their lives—more than the total number who had perished in the whole of France throughout the six years of the Revolution of 1789–95.

During the days of the Commune Bernhardt had left Paris to escape from the vindictive Prefect of Police whom she had much offended in the past by contemptuously returning to him a play he had written which she had said was "unworthy to touch let alone to read." But as soon as the troubles were over she returned to her apartment over which she splashed bottles full of her favorite scent to disperse the smell of smoke from the hill smoldering buildings on every side. Victor Hugo had also returned from exile in Guernsey to what he himself described as "an indescribable welcome" from fellow republicans who elected him a senator. Although he was now in his seventies his career as poet, novelist and dramatist was far from over; but it was in a play which he had written over 30 years before, *Ruy Blas,* that Bernhardt, as the Queen of Spain, was to achieve the greatest triumph she had yet enjoyed. After the first night Hugo knelt before her to kiss her hand; cheering crowds filled the Rue Vaugir-

ard; and a band of admiring young men unharnessed the horse of her carriage to drag it back themselves to her apartment, excitedly shouting "Make way for our Sarah!"

A few weeks later she was invited to return to the Theatre Francais. And here, in *Britannicus,* in Voltaire's *Zaire,* above all in Racine's *Phedre,* which some critics thought she played even more movingly than Rachel, she established herself as the most powerful dramatic actress of her time, mesmerizing her audiences, as Arthur Symons thought, "awakening the sense and sending the intelligence to sleep," interpreting her parts instinctively rather than intellectually with a kind of hypnotic fervor, and speaking in a voice in which, as Lytton Strachey said, "there was more than gold, there was thunder and lightning, there was heaven and hell."

As well as a great actress, Bernhardt also became known as a most outlandishly eccentric showman about whom stories—many invented, others that were not, yet seemed so—filled column after column in newspapers and magazines. Her apartment in the Rue de Rome and the house she later built on the corner of the Rue Fortury and the Avenue de Villiers, were furnished and decorated in the most bizarre manner, with a satin-lined rosewood coffin in which she sometimes slept and a canopied fur-strewn divan prominent amidst the medley of ill-matched chairs, tables, cupboards, carpets, a stuffed vulture, a leering skeleton and works of art of extraordinarily uneven quality. Visitors were likely to be accosted by an alarming variety of strange animals, wild cats, hawks, a baby tigress, a puma that ate Dumas *fils'* straw boater and a boa constrictor that devoured its owner's cushions.

They were also likely to meet many of the most famous and notorious people in Paris, from actors and actresses such as the lovable comedian Constant Coquelin whose creation of *Cyrano de Bergerac* was to become legendary, Sophie Croizette in whose company Bernhardt used to stuff herself with cakes and chocolates in Chiboust's *patisserie,* and the alluring Jean Mounet-Sully, to exotic aesthetes like Robert de Montesquiou and Oscar Wilde, the composer Gounod, Ferdinand de Lesseps and Louis Pasteur. She would hold court on her divan, Persian hangings and the leaves of jungle plants framing her intense, pale, quizzically seductive face, a vast Russian wolfhound sprawled by the fur hem of a dress raised slightly to reveal a pretty, provocative white-stockinged ankle. It was in this pose that one of her numerous lovers, the painter Georges Clairin, portrayed her in a picture which was the principle talking-point of the Academy's 1876 exhibition in the Salon d'Apollon in the Louvre.

Those interested more in art than in iconography, however, were discussing another exhibition that year, the second held by the so-called Impressionists. The growing dissatisfaction of these artists with academic teaching had been brought to a head in 1863 when an exhibition of works rejected by the Salon, including Manet's *Dejeuner sur l'herbe,* was ridiculed by traditionalists. Four of them, Renoir, Sisley, Bazille and Monet were fellow-students at the studio of Marc Charles Gabriel Gleyre. They remained friends after leaving Gleyre's studio and used to meet regularly at the Cafe de la Nouvelle-Athenes in Montmartre, where they were often joined by Pisarro, Cezanne, Degas, Manet and Berthe Morisot. In 1873, after works by several of these artists were turned away by the Salon, they decided to hold an exhibition of their own; and the next year they did so in the studio of Nadar, the aeronaut, caricaturist and photographer. One of the pictures shown was Manet's *Impression, soleil levant* which led a mocking journalist from *Le Charivari* to deride the whole movement as Impressionism, a term which the artists themselves accepted as applying to them all. For, although their school was never a homogeneous one with a jointly recognized purpose, they did share a common belief that painting and its techniques should not be restricted in the way that the Salon seemed to prescribe. "One does not paint a landscape, a seascape, a figure," Manet declared in a summary of the Impressionists' view: "one paints the impression of one hour of the day in a landscape, in a seascape, upon a figure." The Impressionists' exhibition of 1876 was followed by six others in which Caillebotte, Forain and the American exile, Mary Cassatt, also showed their work.

But none of them aroused any interest in Sarah Bernhardt. She far preferred the traditional style of Georges Clairin and the sweetly Romantic pictures of her Lesbian friend, Louise Abbema; and in her own watercolors and facile sculptures, which she occasionally exhibited at the Salon, she displayed no sign of

willingness to depart from the accepted Academy style. Discerning critics did not take her work seriously, agreeing with Rodin—whose masterpiece of 1877, *The Age of Bronze,* was condemned by Academicians as scandalous—that it was nothing but "old-fashioned tripe." Bernhardt, however, had one powerful apologist, a moody art critic, the first of whose great cycle of twenty *naturaliste* novels, *Les Rougon-Macquart,* had just been published. This was Emile Zola.

The Paris which Zola described in some of these novels was a far cry from the fashionable restaurants of the Boulevard des Italiens. It was a Paris where life was hard and the working day long, the Paris of the poor as depicted by Honore Daumier, a sad contrast to that of the elegant dandy as sketched by Constantin Guys. Here, in those mean streets northwest of the Gare du Nord, streets of crumbling, leaking tenement buildings and lodging-houses with rotting, rain-sodden shutters, scraggy hens scratched for worms between the pavements; colored streams of water poured from dye-works; butchers in bloodstained aprons stood before the doors of slaughter-houses; men dragged beds and mattresses to pawnshops from which they emerged to get drunk in wine shops, to eat six-sous meals in *bistingos* or to take home paper bags of chipped potatoes or cans of mussels; and, as the factory bells summoned their husbands to work, women carried their dirty clothes to the wash-house where, in steamy air, smelling of sweat and soda and bleach, they banged shirts and trousers against their washboards, their red arms bare to the shoulders, their skirts caught up to reveal darned stockings and heavy laced boots, shouting to each other above the din. This is the world of *L'Assommoir,* of Coupeau, the roofer, and Gervaise, the laundry-woman, and of their daughter, Nana, whose career Zola later unfolded in his great novel of 1880.

The year before *Nana* was published Bernhardt left Paris for the first of those foreign tours which were to make her as celebrated abroad as she was at home. She returned from America in 1881 at the age of 36 to find Zola the most discussed and widely read author in France. She also found herself far from popular with her fellow Parisians who were resentful of her having abandoned their theaters for more lucrative appearances overseas and who were assured by various hostile

journalists that she was becoming a prima donna of the most selfish, pretentious and avaricious kind. Her electrifying recitation of the *Marseillaise* at the end of a gala performance of the Opera on the glorious 14th of July, however, followed by a magnificent performance in Victorien Sardou's *Fedora*—whom she portrayed, in Maurice Baring's words, with "such tigerish passion and feline seduction which, whether it be good or bad art, nobody has been able to match since"—restored her to her former pre-eminence. She followed her Fedora with other equally brilliant performances—as Marguerite Gauthier in Dumas *fils' La Dame aux camelias,* as the Empress in Sardou's even more melodramatic *Theodora,* and as the heroine of Sardou's *Tosca.*

There were failures, too, though, and her private life was unhappy. Her sister, whom she loved dearly and had helped to bring up, died a drug addict. The Greek diplomat and would-be actor, the arrogant, selfish, compulsively satyric Aristide Damala, whom she found sexually enchanting and married, also became a morphine and cocaine addict, shamelessly injecting himself through his trouser leg in front of her friends, and further humiliating her by spending the money she gave him on other women before dying at the age of 34. Her former friend and colleague, Marie Colombier, of whom Manet painted a delightful portrait, revenged herself upon her for a professional slight by writing an obscene and libelous book, *The Memoirs of Sarah Barnum* which induced Bernhardt to burst upon the author in her apartment, brandishing a dagger in one hand and a riding crop in the other, committing a violent assault which furnished journalists and caricaturists with irresistible copy. Finally, Bernhardt's beloved son, as costly an expense as her husband, quarreled bitterly with his mother over the Dreyfus case and took himself off with his wife and daughter to the South of France where he remained for over a year, refusing to communicate with her.

Captain Alfred Dreyfus, a Jewish officer of unsullied reputation, was court-martialled in December 1894, found guilty of having passed military secrets to the German Embassy, and sentenced to life imprisonment on Devil's Island. It later appeared that the German's informant was not Dreyfus but another officer, Major Esterhazy. But the War Office suppressed this damaging discovery;

and, when Esterhazy was himself court-martialled, he was acquitted. The resultant uproar divided France into rival factions of furiously antagonistic *Dreyfusards* and *anti-Dreyfusards*. Sarah Bernhardt was as violent a champion of Dreyfus as her son was a denigrator of the "Jewish traitor." It is said that it was she who approached her friend Zola and persuaded him to write the celebrated letter, *J'Accuse,* to the President, denouncing the Army's disgraceful behavior. Certainly she proclaimed her sympathies loudly and publicly; professed her horror when Dreyfus, despite all the evidence, was found guilty after a fresh trial; and rejoiced when at last he was pardoned.

The quarrels over the Dreyfus affair were still raging when Bernhardt appeared as the Duc de Reichstadt in Edmond Rostand's *L'Aiglon* which night after night filled the large theater in the Place Chatelet that she had recently taken over at the age of 55 on a 25-year lease, restored and redecorated at immense expense, and renamed the Theatre Sarah Bernhardt. The play opened in March 1900 and was still running to packed houses in the summer when the Great Exhibition of that year filled Paris with visitors from all over the world.

This Exhibition was one of several which Paris had seen in Sarah Bernhardt's lifetime. The first had been in 1855 when a huge Palais de l'Industrie had been built beside the Champs Elysees and when Gustave Courbet had defiantly held a private exhibition of his work, entitled *Le Realisme,* immediately opposite the Palais des Beaux Arts where the more respectable paintings of Delacroix, Ingres, Vernet and Winterhalter had been shown. The next had been in 1867 when, in an immense brown and gold palace covering 40 acres on the Champ de Mars, the pictures of Jean Francois Millet had been displayed together with numerous marvels of modern science.

"A day at the Exhibition seems a mere hour," wrote Ludovic Halevy, who with Henri Meilhac wrote the libretto for Offenbach's *La Grande-Duchesse de Gerolstein* in which Hortense Schneider appeared at Varietes during the Exhibition's course. "How many things there are to see! . . . There are two miles or so of cafes and restaurants . . . You can eat and drink in every language . . . And the park round the palace, the houses from every land, the factories for glass-blowing and diamond-cutting, the bakery, the machine for making hats, and the machine for making shoes, and the machine for making soap . . . They make everything, these damned machines. I looked everywhere for the machines that turned out plays and novels. They are the only ones that are missing. They will be there at the next Exhibition."

The next Exhibition, the Universal Exhibition, had been held in 1878 to celebrate Paris' quick recovery from the horrors of the Commune. Another Palais de l'Industrie had appeared on the Champ de Mars, and Davioud's ornate palace on the Trocadero; and electric light had illuminated the Avenue de l'Opera. Eleven years later, another Universal Exhibition was held on the anniversary of the Revolution. And in that year visitors to Paris had their first sight of what was to become one of Paris' most familiar landmarks, the 300-meters-high iron tower constructed to the designs of Gustave Eiffel. And then in 1900 this new Universal Exhibition attracted over 50,000,000 visitors who visited the fine art shows in the new cast-iron halls by the Pont Alexandre III, who went for rides on the vast great wheel, and admired the immense metal bouquet glittering with electric lights near the Ecole Militaire.

Paris was now a modern city. Horse-drawn vehicles still trotted down the busy streets, but motor cars and electric trams were also to be seen, and the underground metropolitan railway was spreading fast beneath the pavements. *Haute couture* had become a large and thriving industry, enormously expanded since the days when the rich, following the example of the beautiful Empress Eugenie, had gone to the rooms in the Rue de la Paix where the Englishman, Charles Frederick Worth, held sway as the acknowledged arbiter of fashion. Now the firm founded by the banker Isadore Paquin and his wife alone employed nearly 3,000 people. Yet, for all the city's change and growth, its traditional pleasures remained unaltered. The essence of that Paris, to which King Edward VII made his famous and triumphant state visit in 1903, was the same as it had been when he was first captivated by its charm half a century earlier. The cafes of Montmartre, where Paul Verlaine had sat in slippered feet drinking hard until his death in 1896, were little different from those that the Goncourts had known a generation before; the performers at the Moulin Rouge, where La Goulue, plump and lascivious, and the pale, thin-legged Jane Avril kicked out their legs in the can-can, were as lively and exciting as Rigolette and Mogador and those other polka dancers at the Mabille in the days of Bernhardt's childhood. The brothels of the Rue des Moulins and Rue d'Amboise, where the ugly, crippled Comte de Toulouse-Lautrec sat closely observing the naked women through his pince-nez and portraying them with realistic sincerity, were much the same as those that Baudelaire had known at the time of the Second Empire.

When Toulouse-Lautrec died in 1901, Bernhardt was approaching her 57th birthday. But age meant nothing to her. She dismissed all thoughts of retirement, putting on play after play, some successful, others not, choosing them for the roles they offered her genius. In 1904 she was still "highly triumphant over time," in the words of Max Beerbohm, who was a professed "lover of Sarah's incomparable art," though he had derided her Hamlet which had made him wonder if she would next play Othello opposite the booming voiced Mounet-Sully as Desdemona. So little regard did Bernhardt pay to her age, in fact, that when she was 65 she took the leading role in Emile Moreau's *Proces de Jeanne d'Arc* in which she turned with serene confidence to the audience, when the Grand Inquisitor asked Joan her age, to answer in her still beautifully clear, silvery voice, *"Dix-neuf ans"* (19). Night after night the audience broke into rapturous applause.

Not long after the finish of this play's run the Great War broke out. Bernhardt announced her intention of remaining in Paris as she had done in 1870; but she was persuaded to leave by Clemenceau himself who told her that, as she was likely to be on a list of possible hostages, the Government did not want to be responsible for her safety.

She asked to be taken to the station by way of the Champs Elysees which she feared she might never see again. And as she drove into it she was amazed to come upon long lines of taxis, nose to tail and packed with soldiers, stretching as far as the eye could reach. These were the famous *Taxis de la Marne,* rushing troops to the front to reinforce the French 5th and 6th Armies which were making what was to prove a successful counterattack against the German forces on the River Marne.

Bernhardt had left Paris with her right leg in a plaster cast. She had injured it some time before, and by the time she reached the villa in the Bay of Arcachon where she was to stay, gangrene had set in. In February 1915 the leg was amputated in a hospital in Bordeaux. Yet even this did not destroy her determination to continue on the stage. By the end of the year she was back in Paris, appearing in Eugene Moraud's patriotic piece *Les Ca-thedrales,* balancing on one leg as she supported herself on the arm of a chair. She protested that she would carry on thus until she died, having herself strapped to the scenery if necessary. "Madame," she said to Queen Mary during a visit to England, "I shall die on the stage. It is my battlefield."

The prediction was almost fulfilled. On the night of a dress rehearsal of a play in which she was to appear with her old friend Lucien Guitry, his son Sacha and his daughter-in-law, Yvonne Printemps, she collapsed in a coma. Some weeks later, on May 26, 1923, her doctor opened a window of her house in the Boulevard Pereire and announced to the crowds below, "Messieurs, Madame Bernhardt is dead."

"Bernhardt is dead" one Parisian said, passing on the sad news to another. "How dark it seems all of a sudden."

'The White Man's Burden'? Imperial Wars in the 1890s

Lawrence James *looks at the mélange of racial theory, economic interest and Boys' Own 'derring-do' that fuelled European ambitions for a 'place in the sun'.*

Lawrence James

Lawrence James is the author of The Iron Duke: a military biography of the Duke of Wellington *(Weidenfeld and Nicholson, March 1992). He is currently working on a biography of Allenby and a general history of the British Empire.*

In the summer of 1900, Colonel James Willcocks led a small army of troops to Kumasi in what today is Ghana to fight the Asante King Prempe who had defied his new British overlords. During the march, Willcocks was approached by a village headman who claimed the Haussa soldiers had broken down his people's huts in their search for firewood and demanded compensation. Willcocks investigated the story, found it untrue and had its teller seized and brought before him. 'All he had to say', recalled Willcocks, 'was that I was his "good father", and I accordingly treated him as a good father does his child'. Like a naughty schoolboy whose mischief had been uncovered and punished by a firm but benign headmaster, the headman bore no grudges, later telling Willcocks he was a 'devilish fine fellow'.

This incident, and for that matter the campaign of which it formed a small part, are instructive, shedding light on contemporary attitudes towards empires and their subject races. Willcocks, a professional soldier with twenty years experience waging the small wars of empire, was proceeding against a native prince who had broken faith. His duplicity and that of the headman were reminders that those whom Kipling characterised as 'sullen, new caught peoples, half devil and half child' needed sharp lessons before they could be set along the road to moral and physical regeneration.

Lords of the earth? The Asante King Prempe and his mother making submission to the British expeditionary force – a *Graphic* illustration of 1896.

From *History Today*, August 1992, pp. 45-51. Reproduced by kind permission of History Today, Ltd., 83-84 Berwick Street, London W1V 3PJ, England.

Moreover, Willcocks revealed by his treatment of the headmen that he possessed that gift, claimed by many others like him, British and French, of a profound understanding of the native mind which enabled him to see through the fraud, treat its perpetrator appropriately and at the same time win his respect.

While readers today may be repelled by all that is implicit in this anecdote, their counterparts in the 1890s would have seen it as an amusing incident in the irresistible advance of European civilisation across Asia and Africa. This decade witnessed the heyday of self-confident, often self-congratulatory and always aggressive imperialism in which Britain, France, Germany, Italy, Japan and the United States conquered and annexed in the name of civilisation.

This unprecedented spate of expansion was seen as the culmination of a natural historical progression. Nations that had now reached what Cecil Rhodes believed was the highest state of civilisation were taking control over those which had lagged behind, or races, like the Asante, who were considered unfit to manage their own affairs. This process was inevitable and beneficial for all concerned. 'The future of Africa under any form of European tutelage must be better than the dark and evil nightmare of the past' concluded the *Dublin Review* after delegates to the 1885 Berlin Conference had sanctioned the continent's division among the European powers.

The work was soon underway in Africa and in some areas the results looked promising. Technical and cultural progress advanced side by side in the French Ivory Coast where a report of 1896 described the laying of telegraph and telephone lines through the bush. Most important was the spread of French taught in recently established schools where, allegedly, the pupils were proud to be mastering the language of their new rulers. Using their new tongue, they would learn, among other things, about the achievements and superiority of French civilisation and in time feel themselves a part of French culture.

Credit for the transformation of the Ivory Coast was given to a governor who was 'benevolent, fatherly and firm'. This model of enlightened imperialism had its equivalents elsewhere, although Frenchmen in general were dismissive of British civilisation, which they regarded as inferior to their own. For their part the British assumed the superiority of their own moral qualities which uniquely qualified them to govern. 'The British race', proclaimed Joseph Chamberlain, the future Colonial Secretary in 1885, was 'the greatest of governing races that the world has ever seen' and for this reason alone it was Britain's 'mission' to protect and enlarge her empire. In America, ardent imperialists followed a similar moral imperative; in 1900 Senator A. J. Beveridge announced that 'the civilisation of the world' was the God-given 'mission of our nation'. This was the opinion of Kipling, who believed in the brotherhood of all Anglo-Saxon nations. He aired the general view of their duty to uplift and civilise in his poem *The White Man's Burden,* which was an appeal to the American people after the annexation of the Philippines.

Those who shouldered the burden or undertook its French equivalent, the *'mission civilisatrice'* had first to win over the hearts and minds of subject races and persuade them that what was being done was to their ultimate advantage. Marshal Lyautey, a soldier-administrator who had developed his theories in Indo-China during the 1890s, favoured what he called displays of 'our care and welfare for their [the natives] moral and material interests'. 'It is', he wrote:

> . . .in the moral sphere, the most noble, the highest and the purest one, that the most worthy work of France and her tradition is associated with the destiny of Moroccans—not as a subject people—but as a people who are benefiting thanks to our Protectorate, from the fullness of their natural rights and the satisfaction of their moral needs.

These sentiments were echoed by Kipling who celebrated the conquest of the Sudan in 1898 with a poem whose theme was the British promise to build a university in Khartoum:

> They do not consider the Meaning of Things;
> They consult nor creed nor clan.
> Behold, they clap the slave on the back,
> And behold he ariseth a man!
> They terribly carpet the earth with dead,
> And before their cannon cool,
> They walk unarmed by twos and threes
> To call the living to school.

This was reassuring since nearly 11,000 Sudanese had been killed by artillery, machine-gun and rifle fire during the recent battle of Omdurman. Such blood-letting was unparalleled in a colonial war of this period, but it had been necessary, argued the *Daily Mail's* war correspondent, G. W. Steevens, to secure the 'downfall of the worst tyranny in the world' and to provide the Sudan with 'immunity from rape, torture and every extreme of misery'. His readers would have required no such reminder since the two-year campaign had been presented by the press as a contest between benign civilisation and brutal barbarism. The contrast was nicely shown in two *Daily Graphic* illustrations: a line drawing which portrayed a medical orderly tending a wounded Sudanese and a photograph of the bones of Jaalin tribesmen massacred at the orders of the Khalifa Abdullah.

And yet the Sudanese had fiercely resisted Kitchener's invasion. Wherever they went in the 1890s, the imperial powers had to overcome determined opposition before they could lay the foundations for their 'civilised' order. Even conquered people could display an alarming recidivism which some found inexplicable. Frederick Selous, colonist and big-game hunter, reflecting on the 1896 Ndebele uprising in Rhodesia, concluded that armchair imperialists were wrong to expect gratitude 'when we free a tribe of savages from what we consider a most oppressive and tyrannical form of government, overthrow the power of witchdoctors and take measures to safeguard life and property'. The evidence suggested not, and only the most condign chastisement, resolutely and repeatedly applied, would teach the natives 'the uselessness of rebelling against the white man'.

The dogma of the swift, annihilating response was outlined in forthright terms by General Sir Francis Younghusband who had spent much of the 1880s and 1890s putting it into practice:

> The moment there is a sign of revolt, mutiny or treachery, of which the symptoms not unusually are a swollen head, and a tendency to incivility, it is wise to hit the Oriental straight between the eyes, and to keep on hitting him thus, till he appreciates exactly what he is, and who is who.

Politicians, aware that the public could easily misunderstand the nature of these applications of main force, had to be more circumspect. Chamberlain told the Commons in 1895 that, 'expeditions, punitive or otherwise' were 'the only way we can establish peace between contending native tribes in Africa' and 'the only system of civilising and practically of developing the trade of Africa'. Like the nanny's smack or the caning delivered by the schoolmaster, war was a means of inducing the purblind or recalcitrant to accept what was best for their long-term interests.

The application of this simple doctrine revealed a gulf between the high-minded ideals of imperialism and the realities of empire-building. Columns of heavily-armed troops penetrated disaffected districts, chivvied rebels or resisters, burnt crops and villages and slaughtered or carried off livestock. Many found the work distasteful, others justified it on the grounds that barbarous methods were the only ones that would make a lasting impression on barbarous minds. One officer, in his published version of the mini-campaign fought against mutinous Sudanese askaris in Uganda in 1898–99, omitted details of the killing of the mutineers' families and was privately deeply ashamed of what he called a 'hateful' type of warfare. In French territories it took the form of the *razzia,* a systematic programme of destruction and looting designed to induce terror. During the suppression of the Maji Maji revolt of 1905–06 in German East Africa 75,000 died, nearly all the victims of an artificially created famine. Similar methods were employed by American troops in 1900 during the suppression *of* the Filipino revolt. Asked by a Senate investigating committee to defend the burning of villages, General Robert P. Hughes answered, 'These people are not civilised'.

Hughes' reprisals against the Filipinos had been the response to that most exasperating form of native resistance, guerrilla warfare. In conventional conflicts, imperial armies relied on overwhelming firepower and the all-too-common attachment of many Asian and African generals to the traditional tactic of the headlong charge, often by warriors who had convinced themselves that they had supernatural protection from bullets. On the way to relieve the Peking legations in 1900, Captain Jellicoe, then commander of a naval landing party, was amazed by the Boxer onrush:

Without any hesitation they charged a Maxim and were literally mown down— coming on at a jog trot and collapsing when hit. They often stopped a few yards off and went through gesticulations for rendering themselves immune from bullet wounds.

Nevertheless over-confident, neglectful or rash commanders could suffer defeats. The Italians were trounced at Adowa in 1896 by an Ethiopian army which, unusually, had a sprinkling of machine guns and modern artillery, and two small French columns were overwhelmed in southern Chad in 1898–99. The chances of such disasters occurring had been reduced by the Brussels agreement of 1890 by which the European powers banned the import of modern weaponry into Africa.

Climates, fevers and intestinal distempers caused more casualties than native weaponry, modern or antiquated. Three thousand men, a third of the army, died from diseases during the 1894–95 French campaign against the Hovas of Madagascar and only twenty-five from enemy action. Meticulous logistical planning prevented losses on this scale and, whenever possible, native troops and locally recruited auxiliaries were

deployed in torrid or febriferous regions. Jollre's detachment of 380 which captured Timbuktu in 1894 contained only twenty-eight Frenchmen. British campaigns in East and West Africa were fought by black troops, Sudanese mercenaries and Sikhs borrowed from the Indian army. White officers and NCOs always commanded and, as a precaution, manned machine guns which were the key to victory on the imperial battlefield. In 1905 there was one machine gun to every 130 men in the German army in East Africa, a far higher proportion than would have been considered necessary in Europe.

Black, Egyptian, Arab, Indian and Indo-Chinese troops did most of the donkey work in the imperial wars of the 1890s. Their European officers prided themselves in their skill in choosing those races and tribes who were the most warlike and responsive to training and discipline. Furthermore, many believed

through *baraka,* an interior charisma possessed by Muslim holy men that brought the owner luck and the reverence of others. British officers attributed their power of leadership to character, that amalgam of bravery, selflessness, adherence to duty, team spirit and prowess in games that had been instilled in them by the post-Arnoldian public schools. These institutions produced young men who were ideally suited to command and govern; in 1911 a Guards officer insisted that 'Public School spirit and public spirit are almost synonymous'.

It was not a sense of public duty alone that impelled young officers to seek service on imperial frontiers. Many were drawn to the colonies through a love for adventure, high rates of pay, an addiction for sport, especially shooting game, and the chance to make a name for themselves that would guarantee rapid promotion. 'When one once started on *safari*—i.e. the line of march in Africa, one never knows where it may lead to' wrote one subaltern during the 1898 Uganda campaign. For Kitchener, Haig, Joffre and Gallieni the path led to high command while others, like Wingate, Lugard and Lyautey stepped sideways and became high-ranking administrators.

All warrior preconsuls were unshaken in their belief that they were following a creed that was morally right. In many cases, they were impatient with political control exercised from afar by men ignorant of the day-to-day realities in areas where European power was still precarious. Some, particularly those anxious to make a career for themselves and win public attention, acted off their own bat or defied their political masters. In the early 1890s *commandant supérieur,* Louis Archinard, followed his own initiative and launched a series of offensives, including one against Timbuktu, that caused an exasperated official in Paris to complain about the 'State within a State' created in West Africa by a handful of disobedient officers. Lugard followed his own judgement rather than Chamberlain's and, in 1902, went ahead with preparations for a campaign in Northern Nigeria despite Colonial Office misgivings. Most famously, Rhodes engineered a *coup de main,* the Jameson Raid, against the Transvaal in 1895–96 in the belief that he was serving the best interests of the British Empire and with it the cause of civilisation in southern Africa which he believed would never be promoted by the Boers.

Co-option of the white Dominions into Britain's imperial mission was an important psychological element in the enterprise – this *Punch* cartoon of the famous 1897 Spithead Naval Review captures perfectly the sentiment, with the British lion taking the young cubs out for the 'proudest moment of my life'.

Brand loyalty: the mingling of empire derring-do and product promotion at the end of the Victorian era was one of the most visible expressions of the way imperialism penetrated popular culture – as in this Pattison's whisky advertisement touching, in questionable taste, on the victories of the Sudan campaign.

that their ability to command rested on inner qualities, unique to their race.

French colonial officers fancied that they established a rapport with their men

The Boer War in South Africa (above, a British heliograph crew in the field, 1899) excited unprecedented jingoism at home, though not necessarily with the troops. The British soldiers suffering heavy casualties and privations at the hands of the Boers, might well have had a sardonic word or two for the spectacle, left, of 'Art's Tribute to Arms' – an 'installation' to celebrate the relief of Mafeking prepared (complete with British lion and bust of Baden-Powell) by South Kensington Art Students.

26. 'White Man's Burden'?

The insubordination and temerity of these men were excused by their domestic partisans, particularly newspaper proprietors and editors. Imperial wars sold newspapers and weekly illustrated journals like the *Graphic*. The 1890s witnessed a rapid expansion of newspaper readership with the appearance of a new type of daily designed to attract the working and lower-middle class. Heavily reliant on a sensational style, the new press paid special attention to imperial wars which were given extensive coverage with front-line reports and pictures. Recent extensions of the international telegraph network now made it possible for the public to read up-to-the-minute news of wars, even in the most distant lands; details of the 1896 Rhodesia campaign took less than a day to reach London from Bulawayo. Soldiers welcomed war correspondents, but cautiously for they had an uncomfortable knack of exposing blunders. 'Remember I can make or mar you' one journalist warned an uncooperative young officer during a North-West Frontier campaign.

Press treatment of imperial wars was vivid. During July, 1896, *Daily Graphic* readers saw spirited line drawings of scenes of fighting in the Sudan and on-the-spot sketches of the bodies of murdered settlers in Rhodesia. Most satisfying for those who accepted the empire as an agent of civilisation was a pencil drawing of Muslim chiefs swearing on the Quran to renounce slavery, watched by Royal Niger Company officers.

Each imperial war produced a crop of instant books, either compiled by war correspondents or written by officers who had taken part, like Winston Churchill, whose account of the Malakand campaign was published in 1897. Much imperial literature was directed at the young, produced to encourage patriotism and give examples of the manly courage demanded of those who served the empire. G. A. Henty was the prolific master-wordsmith of this genre. His tales of imperial wars were fast moving, picaresque adventures in which every page is crammed with incident. Issues are presented starkly; in *With Buller in Natal* (1900), the Boers are dismissed as 'an ignorant race, a race almost without even the elements of civilisation, ignorant and brutal beyond any existing white community'. By contrast, Henty's young heroes combine 'pluck' with resourcefulness, a way with the natives and true sportsmanship.

3. INDUSTRY, IDEOLOGY, NATION-BUILDING, AND IMPERIALISM

Imperial lessons were taught in the schoolroom. In 1896 the *Practical Teacher* advocated regular lessons in elementary schools on the British Empire in which pupils would learn about the supremacy of the Royal Navy, the names of colonies and trade routes. Adults were reminded of such facts in advertisements; under a headline 'The Two Greatest Navies in the World', Players Navy Cut tobacco displayed the product together with the numbers of British warships and sailors. During the Boer War copywriters went wild and fighting men in khaki endorsed mustard, tobacco, cigarettes, beef extracts and patent cure-alls. This was an attempt to cash in on the enormous public excitement aroused by the war in South Africa. Its early and dramatic phases dominated newspapers (headlines included 'Koorn Spruit Ambush' and 'More Deeds of Derring-Do') and newsreel footage was shot of troops on campaign for showing in cinemas.

Later when the war resolved itself into a tedious anti-guerrilla campaign, public concern waned and the views of opponents of the war made some headway. During the 1890s there had been those, mainly on the left, who were apprehensive about imperialist principles and critical of the methods used in imperial wars. Reports of the fighting in Rhodesia and war artists' drawings of horsemen galloping down fleeing natives provoked Irish and radical MPs to make charges of inhumanity and there was disquiet about stories of Kitchener riding in triumph into a captured Sudanese town followed by emirs laden with chains. Other, equally distressful incidents like the use of firing squads carrying out the execution of captured rebels to test the effectiveness of different types of ammunition on the North-West Frontier in 1895 were deliberately kept secret for fear of public outcry. The public did hear, in 1902, of the trial and execution of Lieutenants Morant and Handcock for the multiple murders of Boer POWs, a crime which left one senior officer fearful that the Boer War would 'degenerate into pure savagery'. Sometimes the civilisers came close to embracing the very vices they were fighting to extirpate.

Imperial wars of the 1890s aroused great public interest, most of it emotional and transient. Disappointed and enraged Italians rioted when they heard the baleful news of Aduwa; New York theatre goers cheered the popular song *Unchain the Dogs of War* as American fleets sailed for Cuba and the Philippines; and the British public swung between mass despondency and delirium during the Boer War. There was exhilaration of another kind in Khartoum when nationalist Egyptian officers heard news of British defeats in South Africa in 1899 which seemed to them to mark an end to a decade of European invincibility. Indian nationalists likewise took heart from the news of Japan's victories over Russia in 1905.

Domestic patriotic hysteria never travelled to the imperial front line. A Scottish volunteer yeomanry man in South Africa noticed that soldiers never sang the jingoistic songs so popular at home. Another yeomanry man discovered in Cape Town a book kept to record the comings and goings of young patriots like himself. It contained one entry that read: 'Reason for Joining: Patriotic Fever; Reason for Leaving: Enteric Fever'. There was always a gap between rhetoric and reality in the imperial wars of civilisation against barbarism.

FOR FURTHER READING:

The best general account of this subject is V. J. Kiernan, *European Empires from Conquest to Collapse, 1815–1960* (Fontana); Winston Churchill's *The Malakand Field Force*, *My Early Life* and *The River War* and Richard Meinertzhagen's *Kenya Diary* (Eland books) give valuable insights. Something of the flavour of war in the 1890s can be gained from old copies of the *Graphic* and *Illustrated London News* and the mood of popular imperialism is reflected in the boys' stories of G. A. Henty and Captain Brereton which are still plentiful in second-hand bookshops.

Ecological Imperialism: The Biological Expansion of Europe, 900–1900

Alfred W. Crosby

Alfred W. Crosby, professor of American studies at the University of Texas at Austin, currently holds a Guggenheim grant and is doing research in Washington, D.C. This article is excerpted from the prologue, chapter 6, and the conclusion of Ecological Imperialism: The Biological Expansion of Europe, 900–1900, *which won the Emerson Award for 1987. The paperback version of this book is available from Cambridge University Press.*

EUROPEAN EMIGRANTS and their descendants are all over the place, which requires explanation.

It is more difficult to account for the distribution of this subdivision of the human species than that of any other. The locations of the others make an obvious kind of sense. All but a relative few of the members of the many varieties of Asians live in Asia. Black Africans live on three continents, but most of them are concentrated in their original latitudes, the tropics, facing each other across one ocean. Amerindians, with few exceptions, live in the Americas, and nearly every last Australian Aborigine dwells in Australia. Eskimos live in the circumpolar lands, and Melanesians, Polynesians, and Micronesians are scattered through the islands of only one ocean, albeit a large one.

All these peoples have expanded geographically—have committed acts of imperialism, if you will—but they have expanded into lands adjacent to or at least near to those in which they had already been living, or, in the case of the Pacific peoples, to the next island and then to the next after that, however many kilometers of water might lie between. Europeans, in contrast, seem to have leapfrogged around the globe.

Europeans, a division of Caucasians distinctive in their politics and technologies rather than in their physiques, live in large numbers and nearly solid blocks in northern Eurasia, from the Atlantic to the Pacific. They occupy much more territory there than they did a thousand or even five hundred years ago, but that is the part of the world in which they have lived throughout recorded history, and there they have expanded in the traditional way, into contiguous areas.

The Neo-Europes are intriguing for reasons other than the disharmony between their locations and the racial and cultural identity of most of their people.

They also compose the great majority in the populations of what I shall call the Neo-Europes, lands thousands of kilometers from Europe and from each other. Australia's population is almost all European in origin, and that of New Zealand is about nine-tenths European. In the Americas north of Mexico there are considerable minorities of Afro-Americans and *mestizos* (a convenient Spanish-American term I shall use to designate Amerindian and white mixtures), but over 80 percent of the inhabitants of this area are of European descent. In the Americas south of the Tropic of Capricorn the population is also dominantly white. The inhabitants of the "Deep South" in Brazil (Paraná, Santa Catarina, and Rio Grande do Sul) range between 85 and 95 percent European, and Uruguay, next door, is also approximately nine-tenths white. Some estimations put Argentina at about 90 percent and others at close to one 100 percent European. In contrast, Chile's people are only about one-third European; almost all the rest are *mestizo*.

But if we consider all the peoples of that vast wedge of the continent poleward of the Tropic of Capricorn, we see that the great majority are European. Even if we accept the highest estimations of *mestizo*, Afro-American, and Amerindian populations, more than three of every four Americans in the southern temperate zone are entirely of European ancestry.

The Neo-Europes are intriguing for reasons other than the disharmony between their locations and the racial and cultural identity of most of their people. These lands attract the attention—the unblinking envious gaze—of most of humanity because of their food surpluses. They compose the majority of those very few nations on this earth that consistently, decade after decade, export very large quantities of food.

In 1982, the total value of all agricultural exports in the world, of all agricultural products that crossed national borders, was $210 billion. Of this, Canada, the United States, Argentina, Uruguay, Australia, and New Zealand accounted for $64 billion, or a little over 30 percent, a total and a percentage that would be even higher if the exports of southern Brazil were added. The Neo-European share of exports of wheat, the most important crop in international commerce, was even greater. In 1982, $18 billion worth of wheat passed over national boundaries, of which the Neo-Europes exported about $13 billion.

In the same year, world exports of protein-rich soybeans, the most important new entry in international trade in foodstuffs since World War II, amounted to $7 billion. The United States and Canada accounted for $6.3 billion of this. In exports of fresh, chilled, and frozen beef and mutton, the Neo-Europes also lead the world, as well as in a number of other foodstuffs. Their share of the international trade in the world's most vitally important foods is much greater than the Middle East's share of petroleum exports.

3. INDUSTRY, IDEOLOGY, NATION-BUILDING, AND IMPERIALISM

The dominant role of the Neo-Europes in international trade in foodstuffs is not simply a matter of brute productivity. The Union of Soviet Socialist Republics usually leads the world in the production of wheat, oats, barley, rye, potatoes, milk, mutton, sugar, and several other food items. China outproduces every other nation in rice and millet, and it has the most pigs. In terms of productivity per unit of land, a number of nations outdo the Neo-Europes, whose farmers, small in number but great in technology, specialize in extensive rather than intensive cultivation. Per farmer, their productivity is awesome, but per hectare it is not so impressive. These regions lead the world in production of food *relative to the amount locally consumed,* or, to put it another way, in the production of surpluses for export. To cite an extreme example, in 1982 the United States produced only a minuscule percentage of the world's rice, but it accounted for one-fifth of all exports of that grain, more than any other nation.

The parts of the world that today in terms of population and culture are most like Europe are far away from Europe—indeed, they are across major oceans— and although they are similar in climate to Europe, they have indigenous floras and faunas different from those of Europe.

The Europeans' proclivity for migrating overseas is one of their most distinctive characteristics, and one that has had much to do with Neo-European agricultural productivity. Europeans were understandably slow to leave the security of their homelands. The populations of the Neo-Europes did not become as white as they are today until long after Cabot, Magellan, and other European navigators first came upon the new lands, or until many years after the first white settlers made their homes there. In 1800, North America, [defined, for purposes of this book, as the United States and Canada] after almost two centuries of successful European colonization, and though in many ways the most attractive of the Neo-Europes to Old World migrants, had a population of fewer than 5 million whites, plus about 1 million blacks. Southern South America, after more than two hundred years of European occupation, was an even worse laggard, having less than half a million whites. Australia had only 10,000, and New Zealand was still Maori country.

Then came the deluge. Between 1820 and 1930, well over 50 million Europeans

Perhaps European humans have triumphed because of their superiority in arms, organization, and fanaticism, but what in heaven's name is the reason that the sun never sets on the empire of the dandelion? Perhaps the success of European imperialism has a biological, an ecological, component.

migrated to the Neo-European lands overseas. That number amounts to approximately one-fifth of the entire population of Europe at the beginning of that period. Why such an enormous movement of peoples across such vast distances? Conditions in Europe provided a considerable push—population explosion and a resulting shortage of cultivable land, national rivalries, persecution of minorities—and the application of steam power to ocean and land travel certainly facilitated long distance migration.

But what was the nature of the Neo-European pull? The attractions were many, of course, and they varied from place to place in these new-found lands. But underlying them all, and coloring and shaping them in ways such that a reasonable man might be persuaded to invest capital and even the lives of his family in Neo-European adventures, were factors perhaps best described as biogeographical.

Let us begin by applying to the problem what I call the Dupin technique, after Edgar Allan Poe's detective, C. Auguste Dupin, who found the invaluable "Purloined Letter" not hidden in a bookbinding or a gimlet hole in a chair leg but out where everyone could see it in a letter rack. A description of the technique, a sort of corollary to Ockham's razor, goes like this: Ask simple questions, because the answers to complicated questions probably will be too complicated to test and, even worse, too fascinating to give up.

Where are the Neo-Europes? Geographically they are scattered, but they are in similar latitudes. They are all completely or at least two-thirds in the temperate zones, north and south, which is to say that they have roughly similar climates. The plants on which Europeans historically have depended for food and fiber, and the animals on which they have depended for food, fiber, power, leather, bone, and manure, tend to prosper in warm-to-cool climates with an annual precipitation of 50 to 150 centimeters. These conditions are characteristic of all the Neo-Europes, or at least of their fertile parts in which Europeans have

settled densely. One would expect an Englishman, Spaniard, or German to be attracted chiefly to places where wheat and cattle would do well, and that has indeed proved to be the case.

The Neo-Europes all lie primarily in temperate zones, but their native biotas are clearly different from one another and from the biota of northern Eurasia. The contrast becomes dramatically apparent if we look at some of their chief grazers and browsers of, say, a thousand years ago. European cattle, North American buffalos,* South American guanacos, Australian kangaroos, and New Zealand's three-meter-high moa birds (now, sadly, extinct) were not brethren under the pelt. The most closely related, the cattle and buffalos, were no better than very distant cousins; even the buffalo and its closest Old World counterpart, the rare European bison, are different species. European colonists sometimes found Neo-European flora and fauna exasperatingly bizarre. Mr. J. Martin in Australia in the 1830s complained that the "trees retained their leaves and shed their bark instead, the swans were black, the eagles white, the bees were stingless, some mammals had pockets, other laid eggs, it was warmest on the hills and coolest in the valleys [and] even the blackberries were red."**

There is a striking paradox here. The parts of the world that today in terms of population and culture are most like Europe are far away from Europe—indeed, they are across major oceans—and although they are similar in climate to Europe, they have indigenous floras and faunas different from those of Europe. The regions that today export more foodstuffs of European provenance— grains and meats—than any other lands on earth had no wheat, barley, rye, cattle, pigs, sheep, or goats whatsoever five hundred years ago.

The resolution of the paradox is simple to state, though difficult to explain. North America, southern South America, Australia, and New Zealand are far from Europe in distance but have climates similar to hers, and European flora and fauna, including human beings, can thrive in these regions if the competition is not too fierce. In general, the competition has been mild. On the pampa, Iberian horses and cattle have driven

---

*American buffalos are really bison (buffalos are ox-like animals that live in Asia and Africa), but pedantically accurate terminology in this context would only lead to confusion.

**Joseph M. Powell, *Environmental Management in Australia, 1788–1914* (Oxford University Press, 1976), 13–14.

back the guanaco and rhea; in North America, speakers of Indo-European languages have overwhelmed speakers of Algonkin and Muskhogean and other Amerindian languages; in the antipodes, the dandelions and house cats of the Old World have marched forward, and kangaroo grass and kiwis have retreated.

Why? Perhaps European humans have triumphed because of their superiority in arms, organization, and fanaticism, but what in heaven's name is the reason that the sun never sets on the empire of the dandelion? Perhaps the success of European imperialism has a biological, an ecological, component.

A Biogeographic Exception

Europeans can create Neo-European societies in the hot and humid tropics—indeed, they have done so—but the prerequisites are stiff. It is a valuable lesson in biogeography to examine them. Let us look at the early history of Queensland, the white and remarkably healthy state in tropical northeastern Australia. It had several special dispensations from fate, enabling it to become a Neo-Europe in an area quite as steamy as many where European colonies died of mildew, rot, and malaria. Ultimately, the problem of European settlements in the wet tropics was not the heat *per se* or the humidity *per se,* although these did contribute massively to the difficulties; the problem was contact with tropical humans, their servant organisms, and *attendant parasites,* micro and macro.

Queensland had as much moisture and warmth as an *Anopheles* or *Aëdes* mosquito or a tsetse fly or a hookworm or any other kind of worm could want, but it did not have a large population of indigenes and their animals and plants teeming with tiny malevolent occupants. The Queensland Aborigines were few in number, and therefore they had fewer kinds of parasitic organisms; they had no crops and only one animal, the dingo, to provide a medium for the evolution of germs and what have you to prey on immigrant plants and animals.

When the white invaders imported laborers to work their sugar plantations, they brought them in from the relatively healthy Pacific islands, not from the disease-ridden continents. The "kanakas," as these contract workers were called, did bring some tropical infections with them, as did the few Chinese who came and British soldiers from India, but all together they did not arrive with as rich a selection of pathogens and parasites as, for instance, the Africans carried to Brazil and the Caribbean.

Malaria established itself in Queensland, but not firmly. The government prohibited further immigration of nonwhites (for a variety of reasons, economic, humanitarian, and racist), greatly reducing the inflow of disease organisms, and the white Queenslanders accepted and applied the lessons of the sanitationist and bacteriological revolutions of the nineteenth and twentieth centuries to protect themselves, their livestock, and crops. Malaria faded away, and Queensland be-

---

An extraordinarily, perhaps frighteningly, large number of humans elsewhere in the world depend on the Neo-Europes for much of their food, and it appears that more and more will as world population increases.

---

came, as it remains, one of the healthiest areas on earth, inside or outside the torrid zone.

This has cost a great deal of money, which Australia, by one means or another, has supplied. Queensland's Neo-European society is not so artificial as the one the United States created in the Panama Canal Zone, but neither is life there so cool, comfortable, and easy as in southern and *temperate* Australia, where a reincarnated William Wordsworth could observe "the young lambs bound as to the tabor's sound," and in some locations he might be flimflammed into thinking himself home in the Lake Country.

Conclusion

An extraordinarily, perhaps frighteningly, large number of humans elsewhere in the world depend on the Neo-Europes for much of their food, and it appears that more and more will as world population increases. The trend is not a new one: Accelerating urbanization, industrialization, and population growth obliged Great Britain to give up hopes of autarchy nearly a century and a half ago, and in 1846 Britain repealed the Corn Law, lifting all duties on foreign grains. At the beginning of the next century, its farmers were producing only enough wheat to feed Britain for eight weeks annually; in both world wars, submarine blockade, constricting its access to the Neo-Europes, almost starved Britain into defeat. In the nineteenth century, a great deal of Britain's imported grain came from tsarist Russia, but many of the same demographic and economic factors that forced Britain to accept dependence

on others for food have since had their effect on communist Russia, and in the 1970s the USSR began to buy enormous quantities of grain from the Neo-Europes, and continues to do so. Increasingly, the Third World also turns to the Neo-Europes for food. Often in defiance of ideology and perhaps of good sense, more and more members of our species are becoming dependent on parts of the world far away where pale strangers grow food for sale. A very great many people are hostage to the possible effects of weather, pests, diseases, economic and political vagaries, and war in the Neo-Europes.

The responsibilities of the Neo-Europeans require unprecedented ecological and diplomatic sophistication: statesmanship in farm and embassy, plus greatness of spirit. One wonders if their comprehension of our world is equal to the challenge posed by the current state of our species and of the biosphere. It is an understanding formed by their own experience of one to four centuries of plenty, a unique episode in recorded history.

I do not claim that this plenty has been evenly distributed: The poor are poor in the Neo-Europes, and Langston Hughes's nagging question "What happens to a dream deferred?" still nags, but I do insist that the people of the Neo-Europes almost universally believe that great material affluence can and should be attained by everyone, particularly in matters of diet. In Christ's Palestine, the multiplication of the loaves and fishes was a miracle; in the Neo-Europes it is expected.

The responsibilities of the Neo-Europeans require unprecedented ecological and diplomatic sophistication: statesmanship in farm and embassy, plus greatness of spirit.

The Americas and Australasia have provided windfall advantages to humanity twice, once in the Paleolithic and again in the last half millennium. The profits from the first entry into these lesser divisions of Pangaea were largely used up in the first few thousand years of the Holocene.

Today we are drawing on the advantages accruing from second entry, but widespread erosion, diminishing fertility, and the swift growth in the numbers of people dependent on the productivity of Neo-European soils remind us that the profits are finite. We are in need of a flowering of ingenuity equal to that of the Neolithic or, lacking that, of wisdom.

Modernism and Total War: The Twentieth Century

The nineteenth century ended with high hopes for the future of Western civilization. Popular novelists foresaw air travel, television, visual telephones, sound recordings, interplanetary travel, and even the construction of a new continent in the Pacific. Technology would liberate those living in the twentieth century from most of their burdens, or so argued the futurists of the day. There were skeptics, of course: Mark Twain punctured the pious hypocrisies of fellow Occidentals who presumed that their Christianity and their technology demonstrated their superiority over the benighted heathens of the non-Western world. And a few observers questioned whether humankind would be any happier, even with all the material benefits the future promised.

Even before this glittering future could be realized, turn-of-the-century artists and thinkers brought forth an alternative vision of far greater originality. They set in motion a period of unprecedented cultural innovation and artistic experimentation, out of which emerged modern music, modern theater, modern literature, modern art, and modern architecture. Never before had there been so many cultural manifestos: Fauvism, Cubism, Futurism, and other avant-garde movements proclaimed themselves. In philosophy it was the age of pragmatism, positivism, and Bergsonism. On another intellectual frontier, Alfred Binet, Ivan Pavlov, and Sigmund Freud reformulated the premises of psychology. Advanced work in experimental science concentrated on rays, radioactivity, and the atom, setting the stage for Albert Einstein's abstract but unsettling theories.

Thus, in the years before the Great War, the West was able to point to unrivaled accomplishments. Aristocrats and the middle class were confident of the future because they were eminently satisfied with the present. Their general sense of well-being was captured by Osbert Sitwell in his autobiography:

Never has Europe been so prosperous and so gay. Never had the world gone so well for all classes of the community. . . . I remember from my childhood, what must have been a common experience with members of my generation, reading the Bible, and books of Greek, Roman, and English history, and reflecting how wonderful it was to think

that, with the growth of commerce and civilization, mass captivities and executions were things of the rabid past, and that never again would man be liable to persecution for his political or religious opinions. This belief, inculcated in the majority, led to an infinite sweetness in the air we breathed.

In light of subsequent events, all of this seems a great illusion. "Sarajevo: The End of Innocence" shows how such illusions contributed to the coming of war. Millions of lives were lost in the Great War, which was a showcase for the destructive force of Europe's vaunted technology. The war dashed the hopes of an entire generation and contributed to revolution in Russia, the breakup of the Ottoman Empire, the collapse of the international economy, and the emergence of totalitarian dictatorships. It finally played itself out in a second, even more devastating conflict.

"When the Red Storm Broke" provides an unusual perspective on the Russian Revolution. "How the Modern Middle East Map Came to Be Drawn" traces many current problems to the geopolitics of the World War I settlement. The articles by Charles Delzell and Nathan Stoltzfus explore fascism in Italy and Germany. "A People Under Terror" and "Night Witches, Snipers, and Laundresses" cover neglected aspects of life during World War II. The impact of Europe's second great war is conveyed in "1945" and "The War Europe Lost." "The August Revolution" and "Facts on File" deal with the demise of the Soviet Union.

Looking Ahead: Challenge Questions

How was it that the events at Sarajevo sparked a world war?

What were the major consequences of the two major wars of this century? Who were the real winners and losers?

How and why did the United States become involved in the Russian Revolution of 1917?

What were the three instances of successful domestic opposition to the policies of Hitler?

Why did Italians turn to Mussolini and Fascism? How did Italian Jews fare under Mussolini's regime?

What happened in August 1991 to finally undo the Soviet regime in Russia?

Sarajevo
The End of Innocence

After fifty years of explanations, it is still difficult to see why a political murder in a remote corner of the Balkans should have set off a war that changed the world forever

Edmund Stillman

A few minutes before eleven o'clock in the morning, Sunday, June 28, 1914, on the river embankment in Sarajevo, Gavrilo Princip shot the archduke Franz Ferdinand and brought a world crashing down.

After fifty years and so much pain, Sarajevo is worth a pilgrimage, but to go there is a disappointing and somehow unsettling experience: this dusty Balkan city in its bowl of dark and barren hills, is an unlikely setting for grand tragedy. Blood and suffering are endemic to the Balkans, but Sarajevo is so mean and poor. Why should an age have died *here?* Why did the double murder of an undistinguished archduke and his morganatic wife touch off a world war, when so many graver pretexts had somehow been accommodated—or ignored—in the preceding quarter-century? It was an act that no one clearly remembers today; indeed, its details were forgotten by the time the war it engendered was six months old. Nowadays, even in Sarajevo, few pilgrims search out the place where Princip stood that morning. Nearby, on the river embankment, only a dingy little museum commemorates the lives and passions of the seven tubercular boys (of whom Princip was only one) who plotted one small blow for freedom, but who brought on a universal catastrophe. Within the museum are faded photographs, a few pitiable relics of the conspirators, a fly-specked visitors' book. A single shabby attendant guards the memorials to a political passion that seems, well, naïve to our more cynical age. "Here, in this historic place," the modest inscription runs, "Gavrilo Princip was the initiator of liberty on the day of Saint Vitus, the 28th of June, 1914." That is all, and few visitors to present-day Yugoslavia stop to read it.

There is so much that goes unanswered, even though the facts of the case are so well known: how the failing Hapsburgs, impelled by an unlucky taste for adventure, had seized Bosnia and Herzegovina from the Turks and aggravated the racial imbalance of the Austro-Hungarian Empire; how the southern Slavs within the Empire felt themselves oppressed and increasingly demanded freedom; how the ambitious little hill kingdom of Serbia saw a chance to establish a South-Slavic hegemony over the Balkans; and how Czarist Russia, itself near ruin, plotted with its client Serbia to turn the Austro-Hungarian southern flank. But there is so much more that needs to be taken into account: how Franz Ferdinand, the aged emperor Franz Josef's nephew, became his heir by default (Crown Prince Rudolf had committed suicide at Mayerling; Uncle Maximilian, Napoleon III's pawn, had been executed in Mexico; Franz Ferdinand's father, a pilgrim to the Holy Land, had died—most improbably—from drinking the waters of the Jordan); how the new heir—stiff, autocratic, and unapproachable, but implausibly wed in irenic middle-class marriage to the not-quite-acceptable Sophie Chotek—sensed the danger to the Empire and proposed a policy that would have given his future Slav subjects most of what they demanded; how the Serbian nationalists were driven to panic, and how the secret society of jingoes known as "The Black Hand" plotted Franz Ferdinand's death; how seven boys were recruited to do the deed, and how one of them, Gavrilo Princip, on the morning of June 28, 1914, shot Franz Ferdinand and his Sophie dead.

But why the mindlessness of the war that followed, the blundering diplomacies and reckless plans that made disaster inevitable once hostilities broke out? It is all so grotesque: great and shattering consequences without proportionate causes. When the inferno of 1914–18 ended at last, the broken survivors asked themselves the same question, seeking to comprehend the terrible thing that had happened. To have endured the inferno without a justifying reason—to be forced to admit that a war of such terror and scope had been only a blind, insouciant madness—was intolerable; it was easier to think of it as an unworthy or a wrongful cause than as a ghastly, titanic joke on history. After the event Winston Churchill wrote: "But there was a strange temper in the air. Unsatisfied by material prosperity the nations turned restlessly towards strife internal or external. . . . Almost one might think the world wished to suffer." Yet if this opinion had been widely accepted, it would have been a judgment on human nature too terrible to endure. And so a new mythology of the war grew up—a postwar mythology of materialist cynicism almost as contrived as the wartime propaganda fictions of the "Beast of Berlin" or the wholesale slaughter of Belgian nuns. It embraced the myths of the munitions manufacturers who had plotted a war they were, in fact, helpless to control; of Machiavellian, imperialist diplomacies; of an ever-spiraling arms race, when in fact the naval race between England and Germany had, if anything, somewhat abated by 1914. But no single cause, or combination of such causes, will explain the First World War. Neither the Germans, the Austrians, the Russians, the French, the Italians, nor the British went to war to fulfill a grand ambition—to conquer Europe, or the world, or to promote an ideology. They did not even seek economic dominion through war. The somber truth is that Western civilization, for a hundred years without a major war and absorbed in a social and technological revolution—progress, in short—turned on itself in a paroxysm of slaughter.

On both sides the actual war aims, so far as they were articulated at all, were distressingly small. Merely to humiliate Serbia and to "avenge" a man whose death few particularly regretted, the Austro-Hungarian Empire began a war which cost it seven million casualties and destroyed its fabric: to prevent a senile Austria-Hungary from gaining a precarious (and inevitably short-lived) advantage in the poverty-stricken western Balkans, imperial Russia lost more than nine million men—killed, wounded, or taken prisoner. To support an ally, and to avoid the public humiliation and anxiety of canceling a mobilization order once issued, Germany lost almost two million dead, Alsace-Lorraine, a third of Poland, and its growing sphere of influence in Central Europe and the Middle East. England, to keep its word to Belgium, committed eight million men to the struggle, and lost nearly one million dead. France, to counter its German enemy and to avenge the peace treaty it had accepted in 1870, endured losses of 15 per cent of its population and initiated a process of political decline from which it may not yet have emerged.

This was the price of World War I. Two shots were fired in Sarajevo, and for more than four years thereafter half the world bled. At least ten million soldiers were killed, and twenty million were wounded or made prisoners. But the real legacy of the war was something less tangible—a quality of despair, a chaos, and a drift toward political barbarism that is with us to this day. We have not recovered yet.

In the summer of 1914 the armies marched out to Armageddon in their frogged tunics, red Zouave trousers, and gilded helmets. Five months later they were crouching in the mud, louse-ridden, half-starved, frozen, and bewildered by the enormity of it all. "Lost in the midst of two million madmen," the Frenchman Céline was to write of the war, "all of them heroes, at large and armed to the teeth! . . . sniping, plotting, flying, kneeling, digging, taking cover, wheeling, detonating, shut in on earth as in an asylum cell; intending to wreck everything in it, Germany, France, the whole world, every breathing thing; destroying, more ferocious than a pack of mad dogs and adoring their own madness (which no dog does), a hundred, a thousand times fiercer than a thousand dogs and so infinitely more vicious! . . . Clearly it seemed to me that I had embarked on a crusade that was nothing short of an apocalypse."

The savagery of the war and the incompetence of the military commanders quickly became a commonplace. The generals proved wholly unprepared for quick-firing artillery, machine guns, field entrenchments, railroad and motor transport; and the existence of a continuous front in place of the isolated battlefield of earlier centuries. They were helpless in the face of a combat too vast, too impersonal, too technical, and too deadly to comprehend. Quite aside from their intellectual shortcomings, one is struck by the poverty of their emotional response. Kill and kill was their motto. No one in command was daunted by the bloodletting, it seems. No more imaginative battle tactic could be devised than to push strength against strength—attacking the enemy's strongest point on the theory that one side's superior *élan* would ultimately yield up victory. Verdun in 1916 cost the French some 350,000 men and the Germans nearly as many: the German penetration was five miles, gained in a little more than three months. The Somme cost the Allies more than 600,000 casualties, the Germans almost half a million: the offensive gained a sector thirty miles wide and a maximum of seven deep in four and a half months.

That it was an insane waste of lives the combatants realized early, but no one knew what to do. The waste of honor, love, courage, and selfless devotion was the cruelest of all: at the first Battle of Ypres, in the opening days of the war, the young German schoolboy volunteers "came on like men possessed," a British historian records. They were sent in against picked battalions of British regulars who shot them to pieces on the slopes of Ypres with the trained rifle fire for which they were famous. The incident has gone down in German history as the *Kindermord von Ypern*—"The Slaughter of the Innocents at Ypres." No other phrase will do.

It was a strange world that died that summer of 1914. For ninety-nine years there had been peace in Europe: apart from the Crimean War, only eighteen months of all that time—according to Karl Polanyi—had been spent in desultory and petty European wars. Men apparently believed that peace was man's normal condition—and on those occasions when peace was momentarily broken, war was expected to be comprehensible and salutary, an ultimately useful Darwinian selection of the fittest to lead. To us, after the profuse horrors of mustard gas, trench warfare, Buchenwald, the Blitz, Coventry, and Hiroshima, to name only a few, this is incomprehensible naïveté. But that we have been disillusioned and awaked to our condition is due to the events of 1914–18.

In the nineteenth century the belief in progress—automatic progress—went deep. The American anthropologist Lewis Morgan had sounded a note of self-confident hope for the entire age when he said, in 1877, "Democracy in government, brotherhood in society, equality in rights and privileges, and universal education, foreshadow the next higher plane of society to which experience, intelligence and knowledge are steadily tending." The emphasis here was on *steadily:* nothing could stop the onward march of mankind.

And the progress was very real. The age that died in 1914 was a brilliant one—so extravagant in its intellectual and aesthetic endowments that we who have come after can hardly believe in its reality. It was a comfortable age—for a considerable minority, at least—but it was more than a matter of Sunday walks in the Wienerwald, or country-house living, or a good five-cent cigar. It was an imposing age in the sciences, in the arts, even in forms of government. Men had done much and had risen high in the hundred years that came to an end that summer. From Napoleon's downfall in 1815 to the outbreak of war in 1914, the trend had been up.

"As happy as God in France," even the Germans used to say. For France these were the years of the *belle époque*, when all the world's artists came there to learn: Picasso and Juan Gris from Spain,

4. MODERNISM AND TOTAL WAR

Chagall and Archipenko from Russia, Piet Mondrian from the Netherlands, Brancusi from Romania, Man Ray and Max Weber from America, Modigliani from Italy. All made up the "School of Paris," a name which meant nothing but that in this Paris of the *avant-guerre* the world of the arts was at home.

"Paris drank the talents of the world," wrote the poet-impresario of those years, Guillaume Apollinaire. Debussy, Ravel, and Stravinsky composed music there. Nijinsky and Diaghilev were raising the modern ballet to new heights of brilliance and creativity. The year 1913 was, as Roger Shattuck puts it in *The Banquet Years,* the *annus mirabilis* of French literature: Proust's *Du Côté de chez Swann,* Alain-Fournier's *Le Grand Meaulnes,* Appolinarre's *Alcools,* Roger Martin du Gard's *Jean Barnis,* Valéry Larbaud's *A. O. Barnabooth,* Péguy's *L'Argent,* Barrès's *La Colline inspirée,* and Colette's *L'Entrave* and *L'Envers du music-hall* appeared that year. "It is almost as if the war *had* to come in order to put an end to an extravaganza that could not have been sustained at this level." That was Paris.

Vienna was another great mongrel city that, like Paris, drank up talent—in this case the talents of a congeries of Austrians, Magyars, Czechs, Slovaks, Poles, Solvenes, Croats, Serbs, Jews, Turks, Transylvanians, and Gypsies. On Sunday mornings gentlemen strolled in the Prater ogling the cocottes; they rode the giant red Ferris wheel and looked out over the palaces and parks of the city; or they spent the morning at the coffeehouse, arguing pointlessly and interminably. It was a pleasure-loving city, but an intellectual one, too. The names of the men who walked Vienna's streets up to the eve of the war are stunning in their brilliance: Gustav Mahler, Sigmund Freud, Sandor Ferenczi, Ernst Mach, Béla Bartók, Rainer Maria Rilke, Franz Kafka, Robert Musil, Arthur Schnitzler, Hugo von Hofmannsthal, Richard Strauss, Stefan Zweig—these hardly begin to exhaust the list. (There were more sinister names, too. Adolf Hitler lived in Vienna between 1909 and 1913, an out-of-work, shabby *Bettgeher*—a daytime renter of other people's beds—absorbing the virulent anti-Semitism that charged the Viennese social atmosphere; so did Leon Trotsky, who spent his evenings listening contemptuously to the wranglings of the Social Democratic politicians at the Café Central.)

England was still gilded by the after-glow of the Edwardian Age: the British Empire straddled the earth, controlling more than a quarter of the surface of the globe. If the realities of trade had begun to shift, and if British industry and British naval supremacy were faced with a growing challenge from the United States and Hohenzollern Germany, the vast British overseas investments tended to hide the fact. England had its intellectual brilliance, too: These were the years of Hardy, Kipling, Shaw, Wells, the young D. H. Lawrence and the young Wyndham Lewis, Arnold Bennett, Gilbert Murray, A. E. Housman, H. H. Munro (Saki)—who would die in the war—and many others, like Rupert Brooke, Robert Graves, Siegfried Sassoon, and Wilfred Owen, who were as yet hardly known.

As for the Kaiser's Germany, it is melancholy to reflect that if Wilhelm II himself, that summer in 1914, had only waited—five years, ten years, or twenty— Germany might have had it all. But Wilhelm was shrewd, treacherous, and hysterical, a chronic bully whose mother had never loved him. His habitual style of discourse was the neurotic bluster of a small man who has had the bad luck to be called upon to stomp about in a giant's boots. Wilhelm II lived all his life in the shadow of "the Great Emperor," his grandfather Wilhelm I, who had created a united Greater Germany with the help of his brilliant chancellor, Prince Otto von Bismarck; he wanted to make the world stand in awe of him, but he did not know, precisely, how to go about it.

If only he could have been patient: Austria-Hungary was really a German satellite; the Balkans and the Middle East looked to Berlin; Germany's industrial hegemony on the continent was secure, and might soon have knocked Britain from her commanding place in the world's trade. By 1914, fourteen Germans had won Nobel Prizes in the sciences (by contrast, their nearest competitors, the French, had won only nine).

But the lesson is something more than a chapbook homily on patience. Wilhelm's personal anxiety merely expressed in microcosm the larger German anxiety about the nation's place in the world. Something strange lay beneath the stolid prosperity of the Hohenzollern Age—a surfeit with peace, a lust for violence, a belief in death, an ominous mystique of war. "Without war the world would quickly sink into materialism," the elder Von Moltke, chief of the German General Staff, had proclaimed

in 1880; and he, his nephew the younger Von Moltke, and the caste of Prussian militarists they represented could presumably save the world from that tawdry fate. But this belief in war was not a monopoly of the Right: even Thomas Mann, spokesman of German humanism, could ask, in 1914, "Is not war a purification, a liberation, an enormous hope?" adding complacently. "Is not peace an element in civil corruption?"

There had been peace in the world for too long. From Berlin, in the spring of 1914, Colonel House wrote to Woodrow Wilson: "The whole of Germany is charged with electricity. Everybody's nerves are tense. It only requires a spark to set the whole thing off." People were saying: "Better a horrible ending than a horror without end." In expressing this spirit of violence and disorientation, Germany was merely precocious. It expressed a universal European malaise.

The malaise was evident everywhere— in the new cults of political violence; in the new philosophies of men like Freud, Nietzsche, and Pareto, who stressed the unconscious and the irrational, and who exposed the lying pretentions of middle-class values and conventions; and in the sense of doom that permeated the avantgarde arts of the prewar years. Typical of this spirit of rebellion was the manifesto set forth in 1910 by the Italian Futurist painters: it declared that "all forms of imitation should be held in contempt and that all forms of originality glorified; that we should rebel against the tyranny of the words 'harmony' and 'good taste' . . . ; that a clean sweep be made of all stale and threadbare subject matter in order to express the vortex of modern life—a life of steel, pride, fever, and speed. . . ."

In England and France, as in Germany and Italy, the darker strain was there. When the war came, a glad Rupert Brooke intoned:

Now God be thanked Who has matched us with His hour.

A fever was over Paris as the spring of 1914 slipped into summer. Charles Péguy— Dreyfusard, Socialist, man of good will and reason, to his intellectual generation "the pure man"—had caught this other darker spirit as well. That spring he had written:

Heureux ceux qui sont morts dans les grandes batailles . . .

Happy are those who have died in great battles,
Lying on the ground before the face of God.

By September of that year he himself was dead.

No doubt we shall never understand it completely. What is absolutely clear about the outbreak of the First World War is that it was catastrophic: the hecatombs of dead, the appalling material waste, the destruction, and the pain of those four years tell us that. In our hearts we know that since that bootless, reckless, bloody adventure nothing has really come right again in the world. Democracy in government, brotherhood in society, equality in rights and privileges, universal educa-

tion—all those evidences of "the next higher plane of society" to which experience, intelligence, and knowledge seemed to be steadily tending—gave way to mass conscription and the central direction of war, the anonymity of the trenches, the calculated propaganda lie: in short, between 1914 and 1918 Europe evolved many of the brutal features of the modern totalitarian state. And twenty-one years after the last shot was fired in the First World War, a second war came: a war of even greater brutality, moral degradation, and purposeful evil, but one where the issues at last matched the scale on which men had, a quarter-century earlier, blindly chosen to fight. Here was a deadly justice. That such a war should be fought at all was the direct outcome of

the spiritual wasteland that the first war engendered.

Woodrow Wilson, greeting the Armistice, was able to proclaim to his fellow Americans that "everything" for which his countrymen had fought had been accomplished. He could assert that it was America's "fortunate duty to assist by example, by sober, friendly counsel, and by material aid in the establishment of a just democracy throughout the world."

But today we know that the poet Robert Graves more truly expressed the spirit of the nightmare from which the world awakened in 1918 when he wrote, "The news (of the Armistice] sent me out walking alone along the dyke above the marshes of Rhuddlan . . . cursing and sobbing and thinking of the dead."

When the Red Storm Broke

To a Russia in revolution, America sent rival groups of amateur diplomats. The calamitous results of their indecision still afflict us

William Harlan Hale

In the early days of November, 1917, a wiry, abbreviated man bearing on his face the expression of a determined ferret and in his pocket an important commission from President Woodrow Wilson, stopped off in London at the Savoy Hotel, then noisy with officers on leave from the western front and a banjo band straight from Dixie. He soon heard disconcerting news. "Vague word of a strange new Russian disturbance called Bolshevik" (so he was to recall in his memoirs) had begun to permeate London. "Petrograd became silent. Accounts from points outside Russia were murky and contradictory. The American Embassy was no better informed than others."

Among the least informed was the traveler himself, which was somewhat ironic, since he was momentarily on his way direct to Petrograd as a supposed expert on information, propaganda, and counterintelligence. The October Revolution was fought and won before Edgar Sisson, the special Petrograd representative of President Wilson's wartime Committee on Public Information, ever got wind of it.

Sisson, a minor and now forgotten actor who briefly blundered onto center stage in an erupting world, is interesting historically only as a symbol. He stands, so to speak, for the shortcomings of American diplomacy at one catastrophic moment. And further, he represents what could be called the Great Russo-American Reversal of 1917–18, which brought to an end our century-old friendly relations with a czarist empire remote from our interests but hitherto benevolent to our own republican growth. When social upheaval toppled the Autocrat of all the Russias in early 1917, the United States

believed that the old relations would continue as before, but the events of late 1917 doomed these simple hopes. When Red Russia threatened to leave the war against the Kaiser's Germany just after we had gotten into it, and next threatened to substitute for that war of nations a war of classes—to be fomented even inside America as well—the sudden reversal reached its climax. A few shattering months led to a total breakdown of communications between Russia and America, to the point where the two hitherto cordial peoples and governments on opposite sides of the globe grew so riddled with mutual fears and suspicion as to become all but incomprehensible to one another. From this situation, as everyone knows, we have never really recovered; the few intervals of *rapprochement* over the years have all turned out to be false dawns, and we still live under the sign of that darkness which descended between the two contrasting world powers in the bitter winter of 1917–18.

Did it have to happen—or happen as it did? Historians keep sifting the evidence, each through his own sieve. All agree that revolutionary Russia provided the challenge; what remains at issue is the shrewdness, the imagination, and the wisdom of America's response. In its upheaval, the far-off empire that we had so long looked upon as the legendary haven of the ikon and the muzhik suddenly swung into America's ken with a spectacle of total disorder and social threat. The shock was great, and a surprised and inexperienced America responded to it with its own spectacle of confusion and disorder, presented first of all right on the ground of Petrograd.

For it was there, even before the guns went off and snows and machine-gun nests clogged the wintry streets, that our troubles with the new Russia began. The

United States, a newcomer to great-power politics, had been content to choose, as the great majority of its emissaries, rank amateurs—in the form of deserving campaign contributors, political pensioners, and an occasional hungry intellectual seeking a paid-for existence overseas. When Russia erupted in such a violent and confusing way, we did not greatly change our manner of selecting diplomats; we simply sent more of them. The result was that America descended upon Petrograd with such a cloud of assorted troubleshooters, visiting firemen, adventurers, and idealists as had never before been seen in the relations between civilized states—each of them independent of the next, and all of them amateur. Therewith began a new stage of American diplomacy under threat of crisis—that of mass deployment abroad designed to conceal by sheer numbers underlying cross-purposes and indecision at home.

President Franklin D. Roosevelt, in the succeeding generation, was to prove himself a past master of this tactic of sending out multiple and often mutually contradictory emissaries, and then letting the pieces fall where they might; but President Wilson, fresh in the exercise of American world power, was the pioneer. Perhaps never before had one nation dispatched to another in times of the latter's travail such a mixed company of the unskilled and innocent, with so little knowledge and preparation for what lay ahead. Nor had so many American diplomats ever gone forth with such lack of concerted purpose. Ridden with rivalries and cross-purposes that added to the general misunderstandings now arising between the United States and Russia, these multiple envoys were no match for the monolithic Lenin and Trotsky, who knew precisely what they wanted; and the end result of a winter's tortuous efforts in Petrograd was the breakdown of relations that had existed between the two countries for over a century.

The "strange new disturbance" of which Sisson wrote, referring to the Bolsheviks, had been making itself felt for quite some time before his arrival there, and with increasing virulence for fully seven months—in fact, ever since the Czar's war-battered regime had collapsed in March, 1917, and given way to a Provisional government of republican reformists. But it had not as yet penetrated the consciousness of faraway Washington. Indeed, practically all America, then just entering upon its crusade against the Kaiser's autocratic Germany, had hailed the Czar's abdication as the removal of an autocratic incubus on our own side, and—upon receiving confident advice from our Embassy in Russia—had fully believed through the summer and into the fall of 1917 that such enlightened new leaders as Prince Lvov and Alexander Kerensky would democratize Russian institutions, rebuild fighting morale, and make of their nation a worthy partner of ours in a common cause. This was the dream; and here was one of its carriers, Sisson, chosen for his mission because of his stature as one of America's most astute journalists (editor of the *Cosmopolitan Magazine* and, before that, managing editor of *Collier's*), passing through London with little inkling of what had been occurring under the surface farther east and none at all as to where this was now about to lead.

On November 25, after making his way across a U-boat-infested North Sea and a wintry Scandinavia, he reached the Russian capital's Finland Station. There he found, as he bounced in his sleigh over the icy hummocks of the Liteiny Prospekt and turned down the Furshtatskaya to the American Embassy, a city of dim-lit streets, tight-shuttered windows, and long-coated, muffled figures with rifles warming themselves before wood fires at the intersections. These were no policemen of a friendly, Provisional Kerensky; these were the Red Guards of the Petrograd Soviet of V. I. Lenin, who had arrived at the Finland Station too (but half a year earlier than Sisson) and who, while the bemused American editor was traveling, had seized the capital and then all Russia as well. Almost overnight Kerensky had been toppled by the Bolshevik Revolution of October, 1917 (November, by the

Western calendar). Russia's ill-used armies were melting away, as the slogan "Peace, Bread, and Land" resounded through their ranks; banks, businesses, church properties, great estates were being seized. Moreover, the very day after Sisson arrived in Petrograd, bearing vague and now antiquated general instructions which he summed up as meaning "To be helpful to Russia in any practical way that might develop" and "To place before Russians the American viewpoint on the waging . . . of the war," Lenin's Commissar for Foreign Affairs, Leon Trotsky, formally appealed to the German high command for an armistice.

When Sisson took up quarters in the Embassy building—a low, sprawling monstrosity in a once-fashionable street, whose imitation-classical friezes, swollen balustrades, misbegotten balconies, and squashed-down mansard roof embodied the worst taste of the recent Romanov past—he found it stuffed to the rafters with a small army of assorted Americans as confused and at loose ends as he, and, moreover, at loggerheads with one another.

There were four other key and contrasting men at the core of the American official colony in Petrograd: the Ambassador, David R. Francis, an elderly St. Louis grain dealer and Democratic politician; William Boyce Thompson, a multimillionaire copper magnate, promoter, and flamboyant high-liver, who headed the American Red Cross Commission to Russia; Thompson's deputy, Raymond Robins, a fiery Chicago social reformer and Progressive party orator with Indian blood in his veins, who had made a fortune in the Alaska gold rush; and Brigadier General William V. Judson, military attaché—the only one of them who had had any previous experience of Russia or even of foreign service, having witnessed the Russo-Japanese War as a military observer. Of these, Ambassador Francis should have been, by virtue of his position, the dominant and controlling personality. That he was not—that he became in fact the very opposite—was due partly to his own shortcomings and partly to the Washington approach to appointments abroad that was both frivolous and chaotic.

In times past America had sent to Russia both some very good envoys and some very bad ones, the range extending all the way from the masterly John Quincy Adams and the scholarly An-

drew D. White to the alcoholic John Randolph, the notoriously corrupt Simon Cameron, and that boisterous showman from border Kentucky, Cassius M. Clay, who in President Lincoln's day liked to sport his pearl-handled bowie knife at the Czar's court. In this ill-assorted gallery, David R. Francis was not as outrageous as some who had preceded him; he was simply quaint and totally miscast for his job. A mayor of St. Louis back in the rough-and-tumble 1880's, and then governor of Missouri, he looked like a period piece out of those days, with his white mane, high stand-up collar, and thick gold watch chain; his tastes ran to long evenings of poker, and during the ten days that shook the world, he sometimes seemed to be concerned chiefly with maintaining his supply of bourbon and cigars. In the delicious portrait George F. Kennan paints of him in *Russia Leaves the War,* the author suspects that the legend of Francis' "portable cuspidor, with its clanking, foot-operated lid may have been apocryphal," but recounts the Ambassador's custom of accompanying his diplomatic dinners with records played on a squeaky gramophone behind a screen, with his Negro butler and confidant "interrupting the service at table from time to time to crank it," all to the astonishment of the guests.

Elderly as he was, the amiable grain dealer sent out by the Calvinist Woodrow Wilson was not too old to indulge his tastes in another direction—which resulted in one of the more grotesque indiscretions in the chronicles of American diplomacy. While the eyes of the world were focused apprehensively on the progress of Lenin's uprising, cables hurried between Washington and Petrograd on the subject of the American ambassador's relationship with a certain Mme. Matilda de Cram. This handsome lady had sought out Francis' acquaintance aboard ship while he was on his way without his family to his post, and subsequently became a constant visitor of his at the Embassy. It was understood that she was giving him French lessons. All might have been well, in the worldly environment of continental diplomacy, save that Mme. de Cram, the wife of a Russian officer, was strongly suspected by Russian authorities of being a German agent. She was also on the secret suspect list of the Inter-Allied Passport Agency. General Judson, who was particularly concerned about the proximity to coded messages and code books when in the Ambassador's private presence, finally confronted Francis with the stories going round about her—only to be told to mind his own business. Then someone at the Embassy directly informed the State Department, which took the extraordinary step of requesting Francis to discontinue his relationship with Mme. de Cram. To this Francis replied crustily that the lady in question hadn't visited him for quite some time. A second exchange took place; then the department, realizing that to remove Francis, a deserving Democrat, might produce a scandal, sent him a mollifying cable welcoming his information that Mme. de Cram's visits had ceased. End of episode—and whether she was in fact what she was suspected of being has never been substantiated.

While these intramural exchanges were going on, Lenin and Trotsky had entered upon somewhat more significant ones with the German high command at Brest-Litovsk. It was midwinter; they sought a separate peace and were about to dissolve the multiparty Constituent Assembly at Petrograd in order to establish a complete Bolshevik dictatorship over Russia. The Ambassador, however, who had rarely ventured out of his Embassy during the explosive days of November, made no personal contact with either of the new Russian chiefs. In this he was acting on instructions from Washington on December 6 to refrain from such contact—instructions which, however, were in effect just Francis talking to Francis, since they had been drafted in response to his own cabled advice, the burden of which over many months had been that he saw no point in talking with the Bolsheviks. They were a minority agitational group, he explained, and evidently not here to stay.

As time off from poker and Mme. de Cram allowed, Francis had kept informing the President and Secretary of State Robert Lansing of his satisfaction with the way matters in Russia were proceeding under Kerensky. Thus on May 31, 1917: "Kerensky is still continuing his inspection of the front, and is met everywhere with the greatest enthusiasm." "Enthusiasm," however, had been hardly the right word with which to describe the state of mind of Russia's sullen conscripts, then on the verge of throwing down their guns. Meanwhile the Ambas-

sador's private, conservative predilections had run much deeper; soon after Kerensky took power in March of 1917, Francis had written one of his chief deputies, Consul General Maddin Summers at Moscow (a Foreign Service professional who held high prestige in Francis' eyes because of his marriage into a highly connected czarist family), "I am much pleased to hear that the President of the [new] Ministry, [Prince] Lvov, is a first cousin of your mother-in-law and that other members of the Ministry are connected with your family. . . . I have been of the opinion that it would be unwise to attempt to establish a republican form of government in Russia just now, but if such men as these are put at the helm, it is possible they may be able to steer through the breakers . . ."

It seems never to have occurred to President Wilson that an envoy of such predilections might become a drawback in exploding Russia, and that he should be replaced. Instead, vaguely uneasy, Wilson had begun in the spring of 1917 to send out numbers of other missions, commissions, and individuals to strengthen Francis' and America's hand there—although none of these was responsible to the chief missionary on the ground.

Would Kerensky's Russia keep fighting the Germans? Wilson, whose lack of knowledge of that far country was as conspicuous as his command of political processes at home, had dispatched in May a nine-man fact-finding and goodwill committee headed by the venerable Republican ex-Secretary of State, Elihu Root. Mr. Root's mandate was simply to display to troubled Russia America's "sympathy and interest," and he was hardly an ideal choice: he had confessed before setting out that he expected to be "awfully bored" there, and after a month-long round of receptions and banquets with Provisional ministers, during which he and his fellow committeemen disdained contact with the emerging Left, he returned home to deliver a bland report saying that Russia was out of danger and could be relied on. Almost simultaneously, another American delegation descended upon Russia—also without invitation: a task force of eminent American railroad men, arriving to lend advice on how to strengthen the deposed Czar's floundering transportation system. The prospect of American dollar aid was invigorating to Kerensky's officials, but the presence of so many Americans at once was rather crushing

to their working hours and protocol. What next?

Next came the Red Cross Commission—and a group of men with more unusual designs under the cross of Geneva had never set foot from one nation into another. William Boyce Thompson, the squat, thickset victor of many a stock-market raid and Montana mining scheme, was one of many Americans anxious in the spring of 1917 to get into the war. As his biographer, Hermann Hagedorn, recalls:

His friends were already deep in [it] as field-marshals and ambassadors. Baruch, on the Council for National Defense, was wielding dictatorial power in the economic field. . . . Henry P. Davison [a partner of the house of Morgan], as head of the American Red Cross, was dramatizing the code of the Samaritan on an almost mythical scale. Thompson no longer found promotions and stock operations stimulating enough for his imagination. . . . The overthrow of the Czar startled and thrilled him. Russia would be the decisive factor in the war, he said. If Russia could be held firm, Germany would be defeated. If the Russian front broke—
. . .

So Thompson approached his friend Davison, then projecting a Red Cross relief mission to Russia, to propose that he himself go along on it—not, indeed, simply to help supervise the distribution of foodstuffs and blankets, but to enlarge its scope immensely, its goal to be nothing less than to shore up the Provisional regime. Thompson, whose means were as spacious as his dreams, offered to pay all costs of the mission himself! The proposal was dazzling, and no one seems quite to have sensed the implications of letting a private relief body mix in with high politics abroad. The President, casting about for at least some way of influencing the course of affairs in Russia, gave the scheme his blessing, and before midsummer a party of some twenty experts, all decked out for the occasion in military uniforms and sporting assimilated military titles, was on its way across the Pacific to Vladivostok.

Kerensky's people had let it be known that they did not see the need of an American Red Cross mission: their own hospitals and food supplies were adequate, thank you. Ambassador Francis also opposed it, fearing (quite rightly, as it turned out) that it would trespass on his own domain. Yet the caravan came on.

Before its departure, though, Davison startled Thompson—now "Colonel" Thompson—by including on the roster a Chicago Progressive friend of Theodore Roosevelt. Having refused to let the ex-President lead an infantry division in France, the Administration was trying to appease him.

"What! Raymond Robins, that uplifter, that Roosevelt shouter!" exploded Thompson on learning of the appointment. "What the hell is he doing on this mission?"

With Robins, there entered upon the stage a figure who was to prove the one brilliant, although short-lived, star in a cast of many-colored American principals in Russia. For principals they all were, each man regarding himself the direct representative of the President by virtue of blessing or laying-on of hands, and thus responsible first to the White House, second to his own conscience and beliefs, and to the ambassador on the spot not at all—a situation that President Wilson did nothing to resolve. The ebullient Thompson, setting himself up in high style in Petrograd and taking over the imperial box at the Opera, reported directly to Washington and did not even show the unhappy Francis his cables; thus, when Thompson donated a million rubles' worth of his own money to the moderate Social-Revolutionary party, Ambassador Francis learned of this startling American involvement only through the newspapers. Nor did General Judson, busily maneuvering in the revolutionary murk at the head of his own independent military mission, confide in the Ambassador; while Edgar Sisson too, a small man inflated by a sense of sovereign responsibility, was to write proudly of *his* mission to Petrograd, "I was not set to work under [Francis], and was independent of him, in powers and in funds."

In this chaos of unco-ordinated equals, the municipal reformer from Chicago was to stand out by the sheer intensity of his personality as America's strongest man on the scene. Although submerged in memory today, Raymond Robins was in 1917 a famous figure in the liberal camp at home. His physical presence itself was commanding: broad-shouldered, deep-chested, square-jawed, with intense, searching eyes and a rasping, emotional voice that could carry away whole convention halls of reformers. He had been the Progressive party's keynoter in 1916 and had run for the Senate. Yet there was something else in him,

too—a suggestion of mystical exultation that thrilled some followers and left others thinking him slightly unbalanced.

A "rough and ready evangelist," Sisson called him, and something of his passionate reformist spirit now communicated itself to Russia's far-left revolutionaries. They were not used to this: their own followers had been reared rigidly according to the gospel of St. Marx. Yet they were all still young in exercise of power, and not yet so calloused by it as to denounce every non-Marxist reformer as an enemy; and so, responding to the warmth and virility of Robins' presence, they saw in him a bridge—perhaps the only bridge—between their erupting Russia and the capitalist West. And Robins, whose experience was also limited but whose sympathies were broad, responded in kind. As his British friend and opposite number as London's special agent in Russia, R. H. Bruce Lockhart, was to remark,

[Robins] was an Indian chief with a Bible for his tomahawk . . . Yet, in spite of his sympathies for the underdog, he was a worshipper of great men . . . Strangely enough, Lenin was amused by the hero-worship, and of all foreigners Robins was the only man whom Lenin was always willing to see and who ever succeeded in imposing his personality on the unemotional Bolshevik leader.

So it happened that while David Francis remained closeted in the Furshtatskaya over cards, American initiative in dealing with the new rulers of Russia passed into the hands of this assimilated lieutenant colonel of the Red Cross.

All during the autumn of 1917, the unlikely combination of Thompson and Robins had worked together to succor the weakening Kerensky regime with money, foodstuffs, and propaganda placed in judiciously subsidized newspapers. But in mid-October Robins read the handwriting on Russia's wall and called for a change in our own response. The Provisional regime was doomed amid the rising cry of "Peace, Bread, and Land," he argued, unless Kerensky at once proceeded to distribute land to the peasants and launch other major social reforms. It should be America's new policy to exert pressure on all Russian moderates to move in this direction, he went on, if the Bolsheviks were not to take over at any moment and pull Russia out of the war altogether. Also, Robins thought it might

be a good idea at least to talk with these Bolshevik chieftains, size them up, and discover whether we could influence them all.

Then in October-November, the second and greater revolutionary storm in Russia broke out—just as Robins had predicted it would. The multimillionaire Thompson, finding himself in full agreement with his deputy's analysis, sped home to Washington to try to swing the Administration onto a new policy tack—only to find himself coolly rebuffed by Wilson, who was still reading David Francis' bland cables and who now refused to let himself be jolted. Meanwhile, in Petrograd, the headstrong Colonel Robins had taken it upon himself to approach Trotsky personally—and Lenin too.

In order to reach Trotsky, the Foreign Commissar of a regime the United States declined to recognize, Robins needed an intermediary. Soon he found one in the person of Alexander Gumberg, a squat, mournful-looking, shrewd Jewish Russo-American who had emigrated to the Bronx to become manager there of the Russian-language Socialist weekly, *Novy Mir*, to which Trotsky had contributed during his own American exile. Now returned to his old country to be close to his Socialist friends in action, Gumberg became Robins' personal aide—and threw open the Bolshevik leader's doors to him.

When Robins drove to the Smolny Institute in mid-November for his first meeting with Trotsky, he was still convinced, as were most of the other Americans in Petrograd, that the Commissar was in effect a German agent, bent on creating total upheaval in the Allied camp and on delivering a shattered Russia into the hands of Hindenburg and Ludendorff. When he came away, he had reversed his opinion. Trotsky, he later said, with the emotionalism typical of him, was indeed a " . . . son of a bitch, but the greatest Jew since Jesus Christ. If the German General Staff bought Trotsky, they bought a lemon."

"I won Trotsky," Robins recalled, "by putting my case absolutely on the square. By not hiding anything." He told Trotsky that he was there because he wanted to deal with those in power, that he wanted to maintain Red Cross activities in Russia, that he wanted to keep Russia in the war, and that he wanted to know plainly whether the Bolsheviks' sympathies were on the side of Germany or not. Trotsky, evidently astonished by this forthright approach, convinced his visitor that he was as anxious as Robins himself to keep vital war supplies out of the hands of the oncoming German legions, and on the spot worked out an arrangement with him to safeguard some essential stocks.

Soon after, though, Trotsky began commuting between the Smolny and the wintry waste of occupied Brest-Litovsk, in search of a separate peace with Germany—negotiations that, in Allied eyes, were an infamous betrayal. Could anything be salvaged from the wreckage? Robins still hoped so. It was now January, 1918, and there was no time to lose. At any moment the Germans, if sure of victory on their eastern front, might begin mounting a fresh onslaught in the west.

"We have started peace negotiations with the Germans," Trotsky told Robins flatly. "We have asked the Allies to join us in starting peace negotiations for the whole world, on a democratic basis—no forcible annexations, no punitive indemnities, and a full acceptance of the principle of the self-determination of all peoples. The Allies have refused to accept our invitation. We still hope, of course to compel them."

The Progressive gazed at the Commissar. "How?"

"By stirring up comrades in France and in England and in America to upset the policy of their governments by asserting their own revolutionary socialist will. . . . Germany will want a peace with annexations. *But we have these raw materials.* Germany needs them. If we can keep them away from Germany we have an argument in reserve, a big argument, perhaps a winning argument."

"I begin to see," said Robins.

The long-haired, bespectacled revolutionist ground on. "I want to keep them away, but you know our difficulties at the front. The front is in chaos. Send your officers, American officers, Allied officers, any officers you please. I will give them full authority to enforce the embargo against goods into Germany all along our whole front."

Which was it, then: were these new Russian masters sworn enemies of ours or still, despite all differences, potential allies against German domination? General Judson, after quiet talks on his own at the

Smolny, agreed with Robins: by recognizing them and showing them sympathy, we could keep Russia in the war and influence it in victory. (Back home, Thompson was saying to anyone who would listen, "Let's make them *our* Bolsheviks.") Ambassador Francis, on the other hand, after one brief moment of illumination in which he too agreed that we might do well to recognize the new rulers in order to revive Russia's role in the war, returned to regarding them as foes beyond the pale; and in late December he encouraged his consul general at Moscow, the aristocratically connected Maddin Summers, to send an emissary to make contact with the counterrevolutionary White russians gathering in the northern provinces—a move sure to bring about further enmity once the Soviets learned of it.

Very briefly, at the end of the year, a pale sun of possible Russo-American reconciliation rose over the wintry Neva. The Germans' territorial demands on Russia proved so outrageous that negotiations at Brest-Litovsk came near breaking down. On December 31, agog with excitement at the thought that Bolshevik Russia might yet resume the fight against Germany, Robins rushed to the Smolny to confront Trotsky. Then Trotsky asked him point-blank: What support could America give to Soviet Russia if it turned down the Germans' terms and thus re-entered the war? This, until the events of World War II, was perhaps the most formidable question asked of America in a crucial time—and Trotsky had to ask it of a man whom Francis described as a "wild Indian," and who could of course give him no authoritative answer.

One answer from the very summit did come, though, stimulated in part by another man on the spot: Edgar Sisson. Aware with Robins of the parlous state of American relations with Russia, Sisson on January 3 cabled his chief at the Committee on Public Information in Washington, George Creel, to propose that the President issue a statement on American war aims as against those of Germany, with particular reference to the latter's as revealed at Brest-Litovsk, "to . . . open up our opportunities for publicity and helpfulness" in Russia.

Just how directly the Sisson message influenced President Wilson remains a matter of dispute. Five days later, however, there emerged from the White house the famous statement known to

history as the "Fourteen Points," calling for many of the same principles in international settlement that Trotsky had aired to Robins. Sisson described its reception in Petrograd:

This time Lenin was back and we [*i.e.,* Sisson, Robins, and Gumberg, with a copy of the translation in hand] were able to get direct to him. It did not take one minute to convince him that the full message should go to Trotsky [who was then again at Brest-Litovsk] by direct wire. He grabbed the copy and sprinted for the telegraph office himself. . . . It was the first time either Robins or myself had met Lenin . . . Lenin, in appearance, might be the *bourgeois* mayor of a French town— short, sparsely bearded, a bronze man in hair and whiskers, small, shred eyes, round of face, smiling and genial when he desires to be. And this time he did. But he is the Wildest of the Wild Men of Russia . . . He welcomed the message . . . but he did not let us forget for a moment that he regarded it as coming not from a fellow thinker but from a just and tolerant class opponent.

Yet, while Wilson's Fourteen Points declaration momentarily re-inspirited the Bolsheviks in their idea of resistance, it was not followed up by any move of American recognition or aid, and thus did not affect the grim negotiations for Russian surrender and dismemberment now being resumed at Brest-Litovsk. (The Bolsheviks, for their part, had done their perverse best to reduce any chances of such aid by appropriating two million rubles for the use of their agents to foment world revolution— and publicizing this fact.) Trotsky, who reviled both the Germans and the Allies and who had no effective forces in hand to fight either, save through the deployment of ideas and slogans, hit upon the startling formula in the snows of Brest-Litovsk, "No peace and no war"— meaning that Russia was taking itself entirely out of the international community, refusing to fight, negotiate, or settle. Observers throughout the world were nonplused—none more so than our own in russia. Sisson, falling out with Robins, said he was sure now that Lenin and Trotsky were playing Germany's game, and he managed to acquire a stack of secret papers that in his opinion proved it. Robins, on the other hand, kept hoping that as Germany heightened its demands and backed them up with a march on Petrograd, a new fighting spirit among the Russians could yet be kindled—if only we recognized and aided their new chieftains. But his military ally, General Judson, had in the meantime been called home and shelved for "interfering" too much; and Ambassador Francis observed the final day of January, 1918, by breaking out a new stock of bourbon.

The Kaiser's hordes approached the capital, meeting no resistance. The Allied embassies burned their papers and fled to Vologda, a mud-ridden junction town on the railroad line to Archangel. On March 5 Robins had an extraordinary meeting with Lenin and Trotsky, then wavering between surrender and renewed resistance, and the three together drafted an inquiry to the United States government asking what kind of aid might be forthcoming if the Soviets refused to ratify the Brest-Litovsk treaty and resumed fighting. Nine days later Lenin confronted Robins again, just before entering the chamber of his All-Russian Congress of Workmen's, Soldiers', and Peasants' Deputies for the debate on the treaty. "Have you heard from your Government?" he asked.

"No, I've not heard yet."

"Has Lockhart heard from London?"

"Not yet," said Robins, and added, "Couldn't you prolong the debate?"

"The debate must take its course."

Two days later, a final confrontation at the Congress: once more Lenin asked Robins whether a reply had come from Washington. There had been none. Lenin turned away: "I shall now speak for the peace. It will be ratified."

Events thus moved quickly to their denouement. The Soviets ratified. Allied troops landed at Murmansk to protect war materials shipped there in aid of Russia from the West, and then to support White Russians against the regime. In America the sentiment for like armed intervention grew: the Bolsheviks, first dismissed as dim and distant agitators, now took on the image of world-wide ogres in cahoots with the Hun. Francis an ambassador without an embassy to perform, bestirred himself enough to order that any contacts with the Soviets by General Judson's remaining aides cease. In May, Robins was recalled; Secretary of State Lansing cut him off brusquely, and the President refused to see him. Sisson, for his part, had already slipped quietly out of Russia with his cache of documents purporting to show that Lenin and Trotsky were in the pay of Germany, and these were to be published amid great excitement under the seal of

the United States—though many experts, like Lockhart, later held them to be forgeries. In July, Francis himself packed up and left Vologda, thereby ending an American representation in Russia maintained ever since John Quincy Adams had arrived 109 years before; and in July, President Wilson agreed to American armed intervention on Russian soil (*see* "Where Ignorant Armies Clashed by Night," in the December, 1958, AMERICAN HERITAGE).

What had been undone on both sides was never fully to be repaired. As to the actors themselves, Robins, a lost soul, haunted the halls of Congress for a few years, trying to bring about recognition of the Soviets as a means of influencing them, and then dropped from sight. Sisson lived on to become a wizened minor propagandist in the Second World War, still buttonholing people to convince them of the authenticity of his documents. Francis, back in St. Louis with his gramophone, wrote a long book defending all he had done in Petrograd; Gumberg, a Socialist with a sure instinct for adaptation, became a highly paid executive in Wall Street; Trotsky, as everyone knows, met his end under the blow of an axe in Mexico City.

How the Modern Middle East Map Came to be Drawn

When the Ottoman Empire collapsed in 1918, the British created new borders (and rulers) to keep the peace and protect their interests

David Fromkin

Lawyer-historian David Fromkin is the author of a prizewinning book entitled A Peace to End All Peace.

The dictator of Iraq claimed—falsely—that until 1914 Kuwait had been administered from Iraq, that historically Kuwait was a part of Iraq, that the separation of Kuwait from Iraq was an arbitrary decision of Great Britain's after World War I. The year was 1961; the Iraqi dictator was Abdul-Karim Qasim; and the dispatch of British troops averted a threatened invasion.

Iraq, claiming that it had never recognized the British-drawn frontier with Kuwait, demanded full access to the Persian Gulf; and when Kuwait failed to agree, Iraqi tanks and infantry attacked Kuwait. The year was 1973; the Iraqi dictator was Ahmad Hasan al-Bakr; when other Arab states came to Kuwait's support, a deal was struck, Kuwait made a payment of money to Iraq, and the troops withdrew.

August 2, 1990. At 2 A.M. Iraqi forces swept across the Kuwaiti frontier. Iraq's dictator, Saddam Hussein, declared that the frontier between Iraq and Kuwait was invalid, a creation of the British after World War I, and that Kuwait really belonged to Iraq.

It was, of course, true, as one Iraqi dictator after another claimed, that the exact Iraq-Kuwait frontier was a line drawn on an empty map by a British civil servant in the early 1920s. But Kuwait began to emerge as an independent entity in the early 1700s—two centuries before Britain invented Iraq. Moreover, most other frontiers between states of the Mid-

dle East were also creations of the British (or the French). The map of the Arab Middle East was drawn by the victorious Allies when they took over these lands from the Ottoman Empire after World War I. By proposing to nullify that map, Saddam Hussein at a minimum was trying to turn the clock back by almost a century.

A hundred years ago, when Ottoman governors in Basra were futilely attempting to assert authority over the autonomous sheikdom of Kuwait, most of the Arabic-speaking Middle East was at least nominally part of the Ottoman Empire. It had been so for hundreds of years and would remain so until the end of World War I.

The Ottomans, a dynasty, not a nationality, were originally a band of Turkish warriors who first galloped onto the stage of history in the 13th century. By the early 20th century the Ottoman Empire, which once had stretched to the gates of Vienna, was shrinking rapidly, though it still ruled perhaps 20 million to 25 million people in the Middle East and elsewhere, comprising perhaps a dozen or more different nationalities. It was a ramshackle Muslim empire, held together by the glue of Islam, and the lot of its non-Muslim population (perhaps 5 million) was often unhappy and sometimes tragic.

In the year 1900, if you traveled from the United States to the Middle East, you might have landed in Egypt, part of the Ottoman Empire in name but in fact governed by British "advisers." The Egyptian Army was commanded by an English general, and the real ruler of the country was the British Agent and Consul-General—a position to which the

crusty Horatio Herbert Kitchener was appointed in 1911.

The center of your social life in all likelihood would have been the British enclave in Cairo, which possessed (wrote one of Lord Kitchener's aides) "all the narrowness and provincialism of an English garrison town." The social schedule of British officials and their families revolved around the balls given at each of the leading hotels in turn, six nights out of seven, and before dark, around the Turf Club and the Sporting Club on the island of El Gezira. Throughout Egypt, Turkish officials, Turkish police and a Turkish army were conspicuous by their absence. Outside British confines you found yourself not in a Turkish-speaking country but in an Arabic-speaking one. Following the advice of the *Baedeker,* you'd likely engage a dragoman—a translator and guide—of whom there were about 90 in Cairo ("all more or less intelligent and able, but scarcely a half of the number are trustworthy").

On leaving Egypt, if you turned north through the Holy Land and the Levant toward Anatolia, you finally would have encountered the reality of Ottoman government, however corrupt and inefficient, though many cities—Jerusalem (mostly Jewish), Damascus (mostly Arab) and Smyrna, now Izmir (mostly Greek)—were not at all Turkish in character or population.

Heading south by steamer down the Red Sea and around the enormous Arabian Peninsula was a very different matter. Nominally Ottoman, Arabia was in large part a vast, ungoverned desert wilderness through which roamed bedouin tribes knowing no law but their own. In those days Abdul Aziz ibn Saud, the youthful scion of deposed lords of most of the peninsula, was living in exile, dreaming of a return to reclaim his rights and establish his dominion. In the port towns on the Persian Gulf, ruling sheiks paid lip service to Ottoman rule but in fact their sheikdoms were protectorates of Great Britain. Not long after you passed Kuwait (see map) you reached Basra, in what is now Iraq, up a river formed by the union of the great Tigris and Euphrates.

A muddy, unhealthy port of heterogeneous population, Basra was then the capital of a province, largely Shiite Arab, ruled by an Ottoman governor. Well north of it, celebrated for archaeological sites like Babylon and Nippur, which drew tourists, lay Baghdad, then a heavily Jewish city (along with Jerusalem, one of the two great Jewish cities of Asia). Baghdad was the administrative center of an Ottoman province that was in large part Sunni Arab. Farther north still was a third Ottoman province, with a large population of Kurds. Taken together, the three roughly equaled the present area of Iraq.

Ottoman rule in some parts of the Middle East clearly was more imaginary than real. And even in those portions of the empire that Turkish governors did govern, the population was often too diverse to be governed effectively by a single regime. Yet the hold of the Turkish sultan on the empire's peoples lingered on. Indeed, had World War I not intervened, the Ottoman Empire might well have lasted many decades more.

In its origins, the war that would change the map of the Middle East had nothing to do with that region. How the Ottoman Empire came to be involved in the war at all—and lost it—and how the triumphant Allies found themselves in a position to redesign the Middle Eastern lands the Turks had ruled, is one of the most fascinating stories of the 20th century, rich in consequences that we are still struggling with today.

The story begins with one man, a tiny, vain, strutting man addicted to dramatic gestures and uniforms. He was Enver Pasha, and he mistook himself for a sort of Napoleon. Of modest origins, Enver, as a junior officer in the Ottoman Army, joined the Young Turks, a secret society that was plotting against the Ottoman regime. In 1913, Enver led a Young Turk raiding party that overthrew the government and killed the Minister of War. In 1914, at the age of 31, he became the

Ottoman Minister of War himself, married the niece of the sultan and moved into a palace.

As a new political figure Enver scored a major, instant success. The Young Turks for years had urgently sought a European ally that would promise to protect the Ottoman Empire against other European powers. Britain, France and Russia had each been approached and had refused; but on August 1, 1914, just as Germany was about to invade Belgium to begin World War I, Enver wangled a secret treaty with the kaiser pledging to protect the Ottoman domains.

Unaware of Enver's coup, and with war added to the equation, Britain and France began wooing Turkey too, while the Turks played off one side against the other. By autumn the German Army's plan to knock France out of the war in six weeks had failed. Needing help, Germany urged the Ottoman Empire to join the war by attacking Russia.

Though Enver's colleagues in the Turkish government were opposed to war, Enver had a different idea. To him the time seemed ripe: in the first month of the war German armies overwhelmingly turned back a Russian attack on East Prussia, and a collapse of the czar's armies appeared imminent. Seeing a

For years the real ruler of Egypt was Lord Kitchener, a general, whose main concern was for the Suez Canal.

Though he was blamed for Gallipoli, Winston Churchill was put in charge of reorganizing the entire Middle East.

chance to share in the spoils of a likely German victory over Russia, Enver entered into a private conspiracy with the German admiral commanding the powerful warship *Goeben* and its companion vessel, the *Breslau,* which had taken refuge in Turkish waters at the outset of hostilities.

During the last week of October, Enver secretly arranged for the *Goeben* and the *Breslau* to escape into the Black Sea and steam toward Russia. Flying the Ottoman flag, the Germans then opened fire on the Russian coast. Thinking themselves attacked by Turks, the Russians declared war. Russia's allies, Britain and France, thus found themselves at war with the Ottoman Empire too. By needlessly plunging the empire into war, Enver had put everything in the Middle East up for grabs. In that sense, he was the father of the modern Middle East. Had Enver never existed, the Turkish flag might even yet be flying—if only in some confederal way—over Beirut and Damascus, Baghdad and Jerusalem.

Great Britain had propped up the Ottoman Empire for generations as a buffer against Russian expansionism. Now, with Russia as Britain's shaky ally, once the war had been won and the Ottomans overthrown, the Allies would be able to reshape the entire Middle East. It would be one of those magic moments in history when fresh starts beckon and dreams become realities.

"What is to prevent the Jews having Palestine and restoring a real Judaea?" asked H. G. Wells, the British novelist, essayist and prophet of a rational future for mankind. The Greeks, the French and the Italians also had claims to Middle East territory. And naturally, in Cairo, Lord Kitchener's aides soon began to contemplate a future plan for an Arab world to be ruled by Egypt, which in turn would continue to be controlled by themselves.

At the time, the Allies already had their hands full with war against Germany on the Western Front. They resolved not to be distracted by the Middle East until later. The issues and ambitions there were too divisive. Hardly had the Ottoman Empire entered the war, however, when Enver stirred the pot again. He took personal command of the Ottoman Third Army on the Caucasus frontier and, in the dead of winter, launched a foolhardy attack against fortified positions on high ground. His offensive was hopeless, since it was both amateurishly planned and executed, but the czar's generals panicked anyway. The Russian government begged Lord Kitchener (now serving in London as Secretary of State for War) to stage a more or less instant diversionary action. The result was the Allied attack on the Dardanelles, the strait that eventually leads to Constantinople (now Istanbul).

Enver soon lost about 86,000 of his 100,000 men; the few, bloodied survivors straggled back through icy mountain passes. A German observer noted that Enver's army had "suffered a disaster which for rapidity and completeness is without parallel in military history." But nobody in the Russian government or high command bothered to tell the British that mounting a Dardanelles naval attack was no longer necessary. So on the morning of February 19, 1915, British ships fired the opening shots in what became a tragic campaign.

Initially, the British Navy seemed poised to take Constantinople, and Russia panicked again. What if the British, having occupied Constantinople, were to hold onto it? The 50 percent of Russia's export trade flowing through the strait would then do so only with British permission. Czar Nicholas II demanded immediate assurance that Constantinople would be Russia's in the postwar world. Fearing Russia might withdraw from the war, Britain and France agreed. In return, Russia offered to support British and French claims in other parts of the Middle East.

With that in mind, on April 8, 1915,

British camel unit jogs down the Jordan Valley; Prince Faisal and T. E. Lawrence often used camels in guerrilla raids on Turks.

the British Prime Minister appointed a committee to define Britain's postwar goals in the Middle East. It was a committee dominated by Lord Kitchener through his personal representative, 36-year-old Sir Mark Sykes, one of many remarkable characters, including Winston Churchill and T. E. Lawrence, to be involved in the remaking (and remapping) of the Middle East.

A restless soul who had moved from school to school as a child, Sykes left college without graduating, and thereafter never liked to stay long in one spot. A Tory Member of Parliament, before the war he had traveled widely in Asiatic Turkey, publishing accounts of his journeys. Sykes' views tended to be passionate but changeable, and his talent for clever exaggeration sometimes carried over into his politics.

As a traditional Tory he had regarded the sultan's domains as a useful buffer protecting Britain's road to India against Britain's imperial rivals, the czar chief among them. Only 15 months earlier, Sykes was warning the House of Commons that "the disappearance of the Ottoman Empire must be the first step towards the disappearance of our own." Yet between 1915 and 1919, he busily planned the dismantling of the Ottoman Empire.

The Allied attack on the Dardanelles ended with Gallipoli, a disaster told and retold in books and films. Neither that defeat, nor the darkest days of 1916–17, when it looked for a while as though the Allies might lose the war, stopped British planning about how to cut up the Turkish Middle East. Steadily but secretly Sykes worked on. As the fight to overthrow the Ottoman Empire grew more intense, the elements he had to take into account grew more complex.

It was clear that the British needed to maintain control over the Suez Canal, and all the rest of the route to their prized colonial possession, India. They needed to keep the Russians and Germans and Italians and French in check. Especially the French, who had claims on Syria. But with millions of men committed to trench warfare in Europe, they could not drain off forces for the Middle East. Instead, units of the British Indian Army along with other Commonwealth forces attacked in the east in what are now Iraq and Iran, occupying Basra, Baghdad and eventually Mosul. Meanwhile, Allied liaison officers, including notably T. E. Lawrence, began encouraging the smallish group of Arabian tribesmen following Emir (later King) Hussein of the Hejaz, who had rebelled against the Turks, to fight a guerrilla campaign against Turkish forces.

Throughout 1917, in and near the Hejaz area of Arabia (see map), the Arabs attacked the railway line that supported Turkish troops in Medina. The "Arab Revolt" had little military effect on the outcome of the war, yet the fighting brought to the fore, as British clients and potential Arab leaders, not only Hussein of the Hejaz, but two of his sons, Faisal and Abdullah. Both were deadly rivals of Ibn Saud, who by then had become a rising power in Arabia and a client of the British too.

British officials in Cairo deluded themselves and others into believing that the whole of the Arabic-speaking half of the Ottoman Empire might rise up and come over to the Allied side. When the time came, the Arab world did not follow the lead of Hussein, Abdullah and Faisal. But Arab aspirations and British gratitude began to loom large in British, and Arab, plans for the future. Sykes now felt he had to take Arab ambitions into account in his future planning, though he neglected those of Ibn Saud (father of today's Saudi king), who also deserved well of Britain.

By 1917 Sykes was also convinced that it was vital for the British war effort to win Jewish support against Germany, and that pledging support for Zionism could win it. That year his efforts and those of others resulted in the publication of a statement by Arthur James Balfour, the British Foreign Secretary, expressing Britain's support for the establishment of a Jewish national home in Palestine.

The year 1917 proved to be a turning point. In the wake of its revolution Russia pulled out of the war, but the entrance by the United States on the Allied side insured the Allies a victory—if they could hold on long enough for U.S. troops to arrive in force. In the Middle East, as British India consolidated its hold on areas that are now part of Iraq, Gen. Edmund Allenby's Egyptian-based British army began fighting its way north from Suez to Damascus. Lawrence and a force of Arab raiders captured the Red Sea port of Aqaba (near the point where Israel and Jordan now meet). Then, still other Arabs, with Faisal in command, moved north to harass the Turkish flank.

By October 1918, Allenby had taken Syria and Lebanon, and was poised to invade what is now Turkey. But there was no need to do so, because on October 31 the Ottoman Empire surrendered.

As the Peace Conference convened in Paris, in February 1919, Sykes, who had been rethinking Britain's design for the Middle East, suddenly fell ill and died. At first there was nobody to take his place as the British government's overall Middle East planner. Prime Minister David Lloyd George took personal charge in many Middle East matters. But more and more, as the months went by, Winston Churchill had begun to play a major role, gradually superseding the others.

Accordingly, early that year the ambitious 45-year-old politician was asked by the Prime Minister to serve as both War Minister and Air Minister. ("Of course," Lloyd George wrote Churchill, "there will be but one salary!") Maintaining the peace in the captured—and now occupied—Arab Middle East was among Churchill's new responsibilities.

Cheerful, controversial and belligerent, Churchill was not yet the revered figure who would so inspire his countrymen and the world in 1940. Haunted by the specter of a brilliant father, he had won fame and high office early, but was widely distrusted, in part for having switched political parties. Churchill's foresighted administration of the Admiralty in the summer of 1914 won universal praise, but then the botched Dardanelles campaign, perhaps unfairly, was blamed on him. As a Conservative newspaper put it, "we have watched his brilliant and erratic course in the confident expectation that sooner or later he would make a mess of anything he undertook." In making Churchill minister of both War and Air in 1919, Lloyd George was giving his protégé a try at a political comeback.

By the end of the war, everyone was so used to the bickering among the Allies about who was going to get what in the postwar Middle East that the alternative—nobody taking anything—simply didn't enter into the equation. Churchill was perhaps the only statesman to consider that possibility. He foresaw that many problems would arise from trying to impose a new political design on so troubled a region, and thought it unwise to make the attempt. Churchill argued, in fact, for simply retaining a reformed version of the Ottoman Empire. Nobody took him seriously.

After the war, a British army of a million men, the only cohesive military force in the region, briefly occupied the Middle East. Even as his real work began, however, Churchill was confronted with demands that the army, exhausted from years of war, be demobilized. He understood what meeting those demands meant. Relying on that army, Prime Minister Lloyd George had decided to keep the whole Arab Middle East under British influence; in the words he once used about Palestine: "We shall be there by conquest and shall remain." Now Churchill repeatedly warned that once British troops were withdrawn, Britain would not be able to impose its terms.

Lloyd George had predicted that it would take about a week to agree on the terms of peace to be imposed on the defeated Ottoman Empire. Instead it took nearly two years. By then, in Churchill's words, the British army of occupation had long since "melted

After the final surrender of the Turks, on October 31, 1918, the question was: How to administer the remains of the Ottoman Empire?

away," with the dire consequences he predicted.

In Egypt, demonstrations, strikes and riots broke out. In Arabia, Ibn Saud, though himself a British client, defeated and threatened to destroy Britain's protégé Hussein. In Turkey, the defeated Enver had long since fled the country to find refuge in Berlin. From there he journeyed to Russia, assumed leadership of Bukhara (in what is now the Uzbek Republic of the USSR) in its struggle for independence from Moscow, and was killed in battle against the Red Army of the Soviet Union in 1922. Turkish nationalists under the great Ottoman general Mustafa Kemal (later known as Kemal Ataturk) rebelled against the Allied-imposed treaty and later proclaimed the national state that is modern Turkey.

In Palestine, Arabs rioted against Jews. In what is now Saddam Hussein's Iraq, armed revolts by the tribes, sparked in the first instance by the imposition of taxes, caused thousands of casualties. "How much longer," the outraged London *Times* asked, "are valuable lives to be sacrificed in the vain endeavour to impose upon the Arab population an elaborate and expensive administration which they never asked for and do not want?"

By the end of 1920, Lloyd George's Middle East policy was under attack from all sides. Churchill, who had warned all along that peacetime Britain, in the grip of an economic collapse, had

neither the money, the troops, nor the will to coerce the Middle East, was proved right—and placed even more directly in charge. On New Year's Day 1921 he was appointed Colonial Secretary, and soon began to expand his powers, consolidating within his new department responsibility for all Britain's domains in Arabic-speaking Asia.

He assembled his staff by combing the government for its ablest and most experienced officials. The one offbeat appointment was T. E. Lawrence. A young American journalist and promoter named Lowell Thomas, roaming the Middle East in search of a story, had found Lawrence dressed in Arab robes, and proceeded to make him world-famous as "Lawrence of Arabia." A complex personality, Lawrence was chronically insubordinate, but Churchill admired all the wonderful stories he'd heard of Lawrence's wartime exploits.

Seeking to forge a working consensus among his staff in London and his men in the field, Churchill invited them all to a conference that opened in Cairo on March 12, 1921. During the ten-day session held in the Semiramis Hotel, about 40 experts were in attendance. "Everybody Middle East is here," wrote Lawrence.

Egypt was not on the agenda. Its fate was being settled separately by its new British proconsul, Lord Allenby. In 1922 he established it as an independent kingdom, still largely subject to British

Prime Minister Lloyd George (right) sought full control of the Middle East.

control under terms of a unilateral proclamation that neither Egypt's politicians nor its new king, Fuad, accepted.

All Britain's other wartime conquests—the lands now called Israel, the West Bank, Jordan and Iraq—were very much on the agenda, while the fate of Syria and Lebanon, which Britain had also conquered, was on everybody's mind. In the immediate aftermath of the war, it was control of Syria that had caused the most problems, as Lloyd George tried to keep it for Britain by placing it under the rule of Lawrence's comrade-in-arms, Prince Faisal, son of Hussein. After Syria declared its independence, the French fought back. Occupying all of Syria-Lebanon, they drove Faisal into exile. The French also devised a new frontier for Lebanon that invited eventual disaster, as would become evident in the 1970s and '80s. They refused to see that the Muslim population was deeply hostile to their rule.

Churchill, meanwhile, was confronted by constant Arab disturbances in Palestine. West of the Jordan River, where the Jewish population lived, Arabs fought against Jewish immigration, claiming—wrongly, as the future was to show—that the country was too barren to support more than its existing 600,000 inhabitants. Churchill rejected that view, and dealt with the Arab objections to a Jewish homeland by keeping—though redefining—Britain's commitment to Zionism. As he saw it, there was to be a

Early planning for postwar Middle East fell to Sir Mark Sykes, whose work grew in complexity as rival Allied and Arab claims evolved.

Jewish homeland in Palestine, but other homelands could exist there as well.

The 75 percent of Palestine east of the Jordan River (Transjordan, as it was called, until it became Jordan in 1950) was lawless. Lacking the troops to police it and wanting to avert additional causes of strife, Churchill decided to forbid Jews from settling there, temporarily at least.

Fittingly while still War and Air Minister, Churchill had devised a strategy for controlling the Middle East with a minimum number of British troops by using an economical combination of airpower and armored cars. But it would take time for the necessary units to be put in place. Meanwhile tribal fighting had to be contained somehow. As the Cairo conference met, news arrived that Abdullah, Faisal's brother, claiming to need "a change of air for his health," had left Arabia with a retinue of bedouin warriors and entered Transjordan. The British feared that Abdullah would attack French Syria and so give the French an excuse to invade Transjordan, as a first step toward taking over all Palestine.

As a temporary expedient Churchill appointed Abdullah as governor of a Transjordan to be administratively detached from the rest of Palestine. He charged him with keeping order by his prestige and with his own bedouin followers—at least until Britain's aircraft and armored cars were in place. This provisional solution has lasted for seven decades and so have the borders of Transjordan, now ruled over by Abdullah's grandson, Hussein, the Hashemite King of Jordan.

The appointment of Abdullah seemed to accomplish several objectives at once. It went partway toward paying what Lawrence and others told Churchill was Britain's wartime debt to the family of King Hussein, though Hussein himself was beyond help. Too stubborn to accept British advice, he was losing the battle for Arabia to his blood rival, Ibn Saud. Meanwhile Prince Faisal, Britain's preferred Arab ruler, remained in idle exile.

Other chief items on the Cairo agenda were the Ottoman territories running from the Persian Gulf to Turkey along the border of Persia, which make up present-day Iraq. Including what were suspected—but not proved—to be vast oil reserves, at a time when the value of oil was beginning to be understood, these territories had been the scene of the bloodiest postwar Arab uprisings against

Map shows the Middle East redrawn by the British as of 1922. Iraq has just been created out of three more or less incompatible Ottoman provinces. Part of Palestine has become Transjordan (today's Jordan), which is still ruled by one of Abdullah's descendants.

British rule. They caused so many difficulties of every sort that Churchill flirted with the idea of abandoning them entirely, but Lloyd George would have none of it. If the British left, the Prime Minister warned, in a year or two they might find that they had "handed over to the French and Americans some of the richest oil fields in the world."

As a matter of convenience, the British administered this troubled region as a unit, though it was composed of the three separate Ottoman provinces—Mosul, Baghdad and Basra, with their incompatible Kurdish, Assyrian Christian, Jewish, Sunni Muslim, and Shiite populations. In making it into a country, Churchill and his colleagues

found it convenient to continue treating it as a single unit. (One British planner was warned by an American missionary, "You are flying in the face of four millenniums of history . . .") The country was called Iraq—"the well-rooted country"—in order to give it a name that was Arabic. Faisal was placed on the throne by the British, and like his brother Abdullah in Transjordan, he was supposed to keep Iraq quiet until the British were ready to police it with aircraft and armored cars.

One of the leftover problems in 1921 was just how to protect Transjordan's new governor, Abdullah, and Iraq's new king, Faisal, against the fierce warriors of Ibn Saud. In August 1922 Ibn Saud's camel-cavalry forces invading Transjordan were stopped outside Amman by British airplanes and armored cars. Earlier that year, the British forced Ibn Saud to accept a settlement aimed at protecting Iraq. With this in mind, the British drew a frontier line that awarded Iraq a substantial amount of territory claimed by Ibn Saud for Arabia: all the land (in what is now Iraq) west of the Euphrates River, all the way to the Syrian frontier. To compensate Ibn Saud's kingdom (later known as Saudi Arabia) the British trans-

ferred to it rights to two-thirds of the territory of Kuwait, which had been essentially independent for about two centuries. These were valuable grazing lands, in which oil might exist too.

It is this frontier line between Iraq, Kuwait and Arabia, drawn by a British civil servant in 1922 to protect Iraq at the expense of Kuwait, that Iraq's Saddam Hussein denounced as invalid when he invaded.

In 1922, Churchill succeeded in map-

ping out the Arab Middle East along lines suitable to the needs of the British civilian and military administrations. T. E. Lawrence would later brag that he, Churchill and a few others had designed the modern Middle East over dinner. Seventy years later, in the tense deliberations and confrontations of half the world over the same area, the question is whether the peoples of the Middle East are willing or able to continue living with that design.

Remembering Mussolini

Charles F. Delzell

Charles F. Delzell, 68, is professor of history at Vanderbilt University. Born in Klamath Falls, Oregon, he received a B.S. from the University of Oregon (1941) and an M.A. (1943) and a Ph.D. (1951) from Stanford University. He is the author of Mussolini's Enemies: The Italian Anti-Fascist Resistance *(1961),* Italy in Modern Times *(1964), and* Italy in the 20th Century *(1980).*

After meeting Benito Mussolini in Rome in 1927, Winston Churchill, then a Conservative member of Parliament, said that had he been an Italian, he would have "wholeheartedly" supported the Fascist leader's "triumphant struggle against the bestial appetites and passions of Leninism." In 1940, however, when he was prime minister of an embattled Britain, Churchill called the *Duce* a "jackal," and blamed this "one man alone" for dragging Italy into World War II and disaster.

There have been few, if any, dictators of the Right or Left in our century whose rise to power owed more to the myopia of democratic statesmen and plain citizens. Mussolini's fall from power was as dramatic as his ascent, and the Fascist era merits our reflections today.

Many younger Americans may think of Mussolini only as actor Jack Oakie portrayed him in Charlie Chaplin's classic 1940 film, *The Great Dictator*: a rotund, strutting clown, who struck pompous poses from his Roman balcony and tried to upstage Adolf Hitler when they first met, in Venice in 1934.

Yet the caricature should not blind us to history. Perhaps the most sobering aspect of Benito Mussolini's career was how much applause he once enjoyed from highly respected intellectuals, journalists, and politicians, abroad and at home. Exasperated by Italy's fragile, fractious parliamentary democracy, worried about increasing popular unrest, and fearful of the Socialists' rising popularity, statesmen such as the Liberal Party leader Giovanni Giolitti and King Victor Emmanuel III welcomed Mussolini's advent to power in 1922. And the King supported him during most of the 21 years that the *Duce* ruled in Rome.

Mussolini's strong-man appeal—and that of the Fascism he espoused—grew out of the postwar disorder and economic hardship which reigned in Italy and much of Europe. It also stemmed in some measure from the fact that during the late 19th and early 20th centuries, Italy had been governed by squabbling legislators. By 1883, the year Mussolini was born, the various kingdoms and duchies on the Italian peninsula had only recently been unified under Victor Emmanuel II, King of Sardinia-Piedmont. "The patriotism of the Italians," as the 19th-century Neapolitan historian Luigi Blanch has observed, "is the love of a single town, not of a country; it is the feeling of a tribe, not of a nation."

Indeed, Italy was heir to long-embedded regional differences; these were aggravated by poor transportation and great disparities in education, wealth, and class. During the early 20th century, the church was powerful almost everywhere. And every corner of the country had its own traditions, customs, and dialect. The north-south contrasts were striking: At the turn of the century, for example, there were no primary schools in the south; in fact nearly 80 percent of all southerners were illiterate. Many peasants lived in a kind of Third World poverty, subject to drought, malaria, and the vagaries of absentee landlords.

The nation was politically fragmented too. In rural Italy, especially in the central "Red" Romagna region where Mussolini was born, anarchist-socialist ideas had spread rapidly. By the 1890s, a Marxist brand of socialism won favor among workers in northern Italy's new "industrial triangle." By 1919 Italy's Socialist Party—"revolutionary" and "revisionist" factions—held more seats than any other single party (though still not a majority) in the Parliament, thanks to the introduction of universal manhood suffrage and proportional representation. The Roman Catholic Church, meanwhile, was at odds not only with the Socialists but also with the kingdom of Italy itself. The kingdom had annexed the papal states of Rome and central Italy between 1861 and 1870, prompting Pope Pius IX to proclaim himself a "prisoner of the Vatican."

In the eyes of his early Fascist supporters, Benito Mussolini was the man who was restoring order and establishing national unity.

His origins were no more auspicious than Hitler's or Stalin's. He was born on July 29, 1883, into a poor but politically active household. His father, Alessandro Mussolini, was a blacksmith and an anarchist-socialist who helped organize a local group of the Socialist International, and who read aloud parts of *Das Kapital* to his family. Benito's mother, Rosa, was a pious Catholic schoolteacher who insisted that the family speak high Italian, rather than the Romagna dialect. Benito lived with his parents and a younger brother and sister in two rooms on the second floor of a small, shabby building outside of Predappio, about 50 miles southeast of Bologna. Two pictures hung on a wall in the parents' bedroom: one of the Virgin Mary and one of the Italian nationalist and anticlerical agitator Giuseppe Garibaldi. The parents named their eldest son not after a saint but after Benito Juarez, the Mexican revolutionary who had helped overthrow Santa Anna's dictatorship in 1855.

In his youth, Benito was moody at home and a bully at the Catholic boarding school he attended in nearby Faenza. Indeed, he was expelled after stabbing a fellow student with a knife and assaulting a priest who tried to discipline him. Benito was, nevertheless, an academic achiever; in 1901 he got his diploma from another school, in Forlimpopoli, and later became a part-time schoolteacher. At age 19, Mussolini left Italy for Switzerland ("that republic of sausages"), partly to avoid compulsory military service. "I was a bohemian in those days,"

From *The Wilson Quarterly*, Spring 1988, pp. 118-135. Copyright © 1988 by The Woodrow Wilson International Center for Scholars.

he later wrote. "I made my own rules and I did not keep even them."

CHANGING TUNES

At first, Mussolini lived a vagabond's life in Switzerland—moving from town to town, doing odd jobs to survive, sometimes sleeping in public lavatories and parks. But the young man's interest soon turned to politics. In 1903 Mussolini took up residence in Bern; he began contributing articles to socialist journals, organized a strike of masons, and fought a (harmless) pistol duel with a fellow socialist.

After wandering through Switzerland, France, and Germany, Mussolini returned to Italy to do his military service. In 1909 he decided to move to Italian-speaking Trento in Austria-Hungary. There he edited a weekly socialist newspaper, *L'Avvenire del Lavoratore* ("The Workers' Future"). Later, in Forlì, Italy, he edited another socialist weekly, *La Lotta di Classe* ("The Class Struggle"), and translated Pyotr Kropotkin's *Great French Revolution*. By 1910, displaying a natural talent, he was one of Italy's best-known socialist journalist-polemicists. That year he also began to live with Rachele Guidi, the 17-year-old daughter of a widow with whom Benito's father had lived after the death of his wife. Their civil marriage would not take place until 1915.

Mussolini's early commitment to socialism, or to any other *ism,* should not be taken too seriously, despite his passionate rhetoric. Mussolini would repeatedly demonstrate his willingness to change his political stance whenever it advanced his prospects. As a young man he read the works of Niccolò Machiavelli, Friedrich Nietzsche, Georges Sorel, and others. But he was mostly interested in ideas that he could appropriate for his own use. Like other Italian socialists, Mussolini at first condemned World War I as an "imperialist war." His country's involvement, he said, would constitute an "unpardonable crime." But after France's amazing survival at the Marne in September 1914, he reversed his position. In *Avanta!*, the Socialist Party newspaper that he then edited in Milan, he urged that Italy enter the conflict on the side of Britain and France. The Socialists promptly expelled him as a traitor.

FASCI DI COMBATTIMENTO

Now a maverick "national" socialist, Mussolini quickly founded his own newspaper in Milan, *Il Popolo d'Italia* ("The People of Italy"). The paper was financed, in part, by local industrialists. Slogans on the paper's masthead read: "Whoever has steel has bread" (from the French revolutionary Auguste Blanqui) and "The Revolution is an idea which has found bayonets!" (from Napoleon). When the government declared war on Austria-Hungary in May 1915, Mussolini hailed the event as "Italy's baptism as a great power" and "a culminating point in world history."

Mussolini's own role in the conflict—he was drafted in August 1915 and served in the Alps—would provide him with a lode of (mostly imaginary) stories about his heroics in combat. Never involved in any major battles, the young sergeant was injured on February 22, 1917, when a mortar accidentally exploded in his trench, spraying his backside with 44 pieces of shrapnel. After recovering, Mussolini returned to *Il Popolo,* where he pounded out fiery editorials in favor of the war effort and against bolshevism. He considered Lenin a "man of straw" and observed that "only a Tartar and Mongolian people could fall for such a program as his."

As time went on, Mussolini became increasingly nationalistic. Insisting upon Italy's "great imperial destiny," he demanded the annexation of the Austro-Hungarian territories where Italian was spoken, such as the port of Trieste, the Italian Tyrol, and most of Dalmatia. With strong business support, Mussolini changed the subtitle of *Il Popolo d'Italia* from "a socialist newspaper" to "the newspaper of combatants and producers." And in a speech in Rome in February 1918, Mussolini declared that Italy needed "a man who is ferocious and energetic enough to make a clean sweep, with the courage to punish without hesitation, particularly when the culprits are in high places."

Although Italy emerged as a victor in World War I, the conflict had wreaked havoc on Italian society. Some 650,000 soldiers had perished. Returning veterans swelled the ranks of the unemployed; nearly two million Italians found themselves out of work by the end of 1919. A wave of industrial strikes broke out in the north. Some workers, stirred by the news of the Bolshevik Revolution in Russia, urged a "dictatorship of the proletariat" for Italy. Meanwhile, in Rome, one feeble Liberal Party coalition government after another tried vainly to restore stability.

With the Great War at an end, and the fear of bolshevism widespread, Mussolini cast about for a new nationalist cause to lead. On March 23, 1919, he founded Italy's Fascist movement in a businessmen's club off Milan's Piazza San Sepolcro. His *Fasci di Combattimento* ("Fighting Fasces") took their name from the bundle of rods with protruding axe-blades that had been the symbol of authority and discipline in ancient Rome. About 120 people were present at the Milan meeting, including veterans of the *arditi,* a group of wartime shock troops. "We, the survivors who have returned," Mussolini wrote, "demand the right of governing Italy." The Fascists chose as their uniform the same black shirt Romagna laborers had favored.

Though Mussolini's Fascist movement was always anti-Marxist, anti-Liberal, and virulently nationalistic, it would endorse (and quickly drop) many causes. At first Mussolini called for a republic and universal suffrage, and criticized the Roman Catholic Church. Later, he would endorse the monarchy, render elections meaningless, and cozy up to the church. The Fascist movement attracted unemployed youths, frightened members of the bourgeoisie, industrialists, land-owners, and, especially, war veterans who believed that Italy, at the 1919 Paris peace conference, had not gained all of the territories she was due.

"When I came back from the war," Italo Balbo, a noted Fascist, would later recall, "I, like so many others, hated politics and politicians, who, it seemed to me, had betrayed the hopes of the fighting men and had inflicted on Italy a shameful peace. . . . Struggle, fight to return the country to Giolitti who had bartered every ideal? No. Better [to] deny everything, destroy everything in order to build everything up again from the bottom."

CUDGELS AND CASTOR OIL

The Fascist movement's ability to straddle, however awkwardly, Italy's conventional political divisions between Right and Left proved to be one of its greatest initial strengths. During the "Fascism of the First Hour," Mussolini's program did not differ much from that of the Socialists, except that the Fascists had favored Italy's wartime role and still praised it. But when the Fascist movement failed to elect even one of its candidates to Parliament in the November 1919 election, Mussolini decided to shift to the Right.

To win more support from Catholics, he muted his anticlerical rhetoric and said that Rome should subsidize churches and religious schools. The Liberal government's decision to withdraw troops from Albania, which they had occupied since 1914, Mussolini said, represented a "disgusting exhibition of national cowardice." Above all, Mussolini intensified his anti-Socialist rhetoric and berated the Liberal government for "doing nothing" when, in September 1920, metal workers in the north forcibly occupied the factories and set up Soviet-style workers' councils. The Fascists, Mussolini promised, would restore "law and order."

Mussolini's message won over many employers, who believed that the Fascists could keep militant labor at bay. Bands of Fascist thugs, known as *squadristi,* launched "punitive expeditions" against Socialist and Catholic leagues of laborers and farmworkers. They beat some members with cudgels and forced castor oil down their throats. By official count, the Fascists destroyed 120 labor union offices and murdered 243 persons between January and May of 1921.

The ruling Liberals were happy to look the other way. Local police officers even supplied the Blackshirt militias with weapons. And when Prime Minister Giovanni Giolitti called for new elections, to take place on May 15, 1921, he proposed to the Fascists that, following the election, they should join his constitutional bloc in Parliament. This time, Mussolini's Fascist Party would win 35 seats.

By 1922, Mussolini was impatient to seize power in what seemed more and more like a political vacuum. In October of that year, the Fascist party held a congress in Naples, where Mussolini and his colleagues drew up plans for a "March on Rome." Under the plan, Fascist militias would lead the march while Mussolini prudently remained close to the Swiss border in case the attempted coup d'état failed. "Either we are allowed to govern," Mussolini warned in a speech to the Fascist militiamen, "or we will seize power by marching on Rome" to "take by the throat the miserable political class that governs us."

TAKING POWER

The weak coalition government led by Luigi Facta knew that Mussolini was planning a coup, but at first the prime minister did not take the Fascists' intentions seriously. "I believe that the prospect of a March on Rome has faded away," Facta told the King. Nor were all of the Socialists eager to confront the Fascist threat. Indeed, some radical Marxists hoped that Mussolini's "reactionary buffoonery" would destroy both the Socialists and the Liberals, thus preparing the way for a genuine Communist revolution. For their part, the Liberals worried most about the Socialists, because of their anticapitalist ideology. Indeed, Liberals and Socialists were "as anxious to scuttle each other," as historian Denis Mack Smith has observed, "as to prevent a Fascist revolution."

The Fascists initiated the "March on Rome" on the night of October 27–28, 1922. The militias began taking over telephone exchanges and government offices. Luigi Facta wanted the King to declare a state of siege, but in the end no showdown occurred. Unconvinced that the army could or would defend Rome from the Fascists, or that the Liberals could provide effective leadership, Victor Emmanuel refused to sign a formal decree declaring a state of emergency. Instead, he telegraphed Mussolini, asking him to come to Rome to form a new government.

Boarding a train in Milan, Mussolini informed the stationmaster that he wanted to depart "exactly on time [because] from now on everything must function perfectly"—thereby giving rise to the myth that he made Italy's trains run on time. Upon his arrival in Rome, the *Duce* proceeded at once to the Palazzo del Quirinale. Still wearing a black shirt, he told the 53-year-old monarch (who had expected him to appear in formal dress): "I have come from the battlefield."

Thus, on October 31, 1922, at age 39, Mussolini became the youngest prime minister in Italy's short parliamentary history. With the Fascists holding only 35 seats in the 510-member Chamber of Deputies, he headed a cabinet of "national concentration" composed mostly of Liberals, socialist Democrats, and Catholic *Popolari.* In his first speech to the deputies, who gave him an overwhelming vote of confidence, he boasted: "I could have transformed this drab hall into a bivouac for my squads . . . I could

have formed a government exclusively of Fascists, but I chose not to, at least not for the present."

Despite the *Duce's* threats, many veteran politicians in Rome thought that, in time, they could co-opt Mussolini. Even Giovanni Giolitti and Antonio Salandra, the two senior members of the Liberal Party establishment favored Mussolini's ascension to power. Luigi Albertini, the editor of Milan's *Corriere della Sera* voiced his delight that Fascism had, above all, "saved Italy from the danger of Socialism."

Others were pleased that, finally, Italy enjoyed strong leadership, of whatever kind. "The heart of Fascism is the love of Italy," observed the Liberal senator and philosopher Benedetto Croce in January 1924. "Fascism is overcoming the traditional indifference of Italians to politics . . . and I value so highly the cure which Italy is undergoing from it that I rather hope the patient will not get up too soon from his bed and risk some grave relapse."

In Britain, France, and the United States, many conservatives also gave their blessings. The *New York Tribune* remarked that "the Fascisti movement is—in essentials—a reaction against degeneration through socialistic internationalism. It is rough in its methods, but the aims which it professes are tonic." Even the *New York Times* suggested that Mussolini's coup was of a "peculiar and relatively harmless type."

THE MATTEOTTI CRISIS

Now at the center of power, Mussolini increasingly became a solitary figure. During his first five years in office, the *Duce* lived alone in a small rented apartment; his wife Rachele remained in Milan, where she cared for their five children. He lived austerely, dined on vegetarian meals, and, partly to avoid irritating a gastric ulcer, eschewed alcohol and tobacco. (He once bragged of his "utter contempt for the lure of money.") An inveterate womanizer, Mussolini evinced little genuine affection for the opposite sex, or for people in general. "I have no friends," he once admitted to the German publicist Emil Ludwig, "first of all because of my temperament; secondly because of my views of human beings. That is why I avoid both intimacy and discussion."

Mussolini managed to project a more congenial image to the outside world. He contrived frequent "photo opportunities," posing at the controls of an airplane, grinning behind the wheel of a sports car, or taming a lion cub in its cage at the zoo. Many Americans saw him as an Italian Teddy Roosevelt—a stout-hearted advocate of the strenuous life.

But "image" was not enough. Eager to put more Fascists in Parliament, Mussolini called for an election, to take place on April 6, 1924. During the campaign and voting, the *squadristi* engaged in widespread intimidation. "When it is a matter of the Fatherland or of Fascism," Mussolini said on January 28, 1924, "we are ready to kill and die."

In the election, the Fascists claimed to have won 64.9 percent of the votes. But on May 30, Giacomo Matteotti, the widely respected leader of the Unitary Socialist Party, courageously stood up in Parliament to read a list of incidents in which Blackshirts had threatened voters and tampered with the ballot boxes. Fascist deputies, now in the majority, taunted him, yelling "Hireling!", "Traitor!", "Demagogue!". Ten days later, Fascist toughs who were closely linked to Mussolini's press office kidnapped Matteotti near his home in Rome, stabbed him, and then half buried his corpse in a grove outside the capital.

The assassination precipitated the most serious crisis of Mussolini's early days in power. Many Italians, after all, believed that Mussolini had at least incited, if not ordered, the murder. The anti-Fascist opposition—Socialists, Catholic *Popolari*, Republicans, and Constitutional Democrats—boycotted the Parliament, forming the "Aventine Secession." It was time for the King, they believed, to dismiss Mussolini and call for new elections.

But the ever-timid King, who was weary of the governments of the past, refused to intervene. Nor did the Vatican support the oppositionists. Pope Pius XI himself warned Italians against "cooperation with evil" (i.e. the Socialists) for "whatever reason of public welfare."

In a fit of wishful thinking, many foreign commentators did not blame Mussolini for the murder. They preferred to cite certain "gangster elements" among the Fascists. "The Matteotti incident," lamented the *New York Times* "is of a kind that may kill a movement by depriving it at one stroke of its moral content."

In Rome, Mussolini taunted his hapless, divided opponents during a speech in Parliament:

> But after all, gentlemen, what butterflies are we looking for under the arch of Titus? Well, I declare here before this assembly, before the Italian people, that I assume, I alone, the political, moral, historical responsibility for everything that has happened. . . .

By failing to oust Mussolini during the Matteotti crisis, his foes effectively entrenched the *Duce* as Italy's all-powerful leader.

On January 3, 1925, Mussolini launched a counter-offensive, announcing in an impassioned half-hour speech to Parliament that "force" was the "only solution" to the threat of disorder. Under a series of "exceptional decrees," Mussolini censored the press and outlawed all opposition parties, including the Socialists and Liberals. He replaced labor unions with Fascist syndicates. His Special Tribunal for the Defense of the State sentenced thousands of opposition activists (especially Communists and anarchists) either to long prison terms or to internal exile in the south. Youngsters were recruited by Fascist youth organizations—a future model for Germany's Hitler Youth—which stressed indoctrination and discipline, and exhorted them to "Believe! Obey! Fight!"

All the while, Mussolini continued to garner praise abroad. "Mussolini's dictatorship," observed the *Washington Post* in August, 1926, "evidently appeals to the Italian people. They needed a leader, and having found him they gladly confer power upon him."

GIVING ITALY BACK TO GOD

Mussolini called his regime the Totalitarian State: "Everything in the State, Nothing outside the State, Nothing Against the State!" But his "totalitarianism," harsh and noisy as it often was, was far less brutal than that of Stalin's Russia or Hitler's Germany—partly because the King retained control of the Italian Army and the right to dismiss the prime minister. Not until 1938 did the regime begin to discriminate against the nation's roughly 40,000 Jews; many would lose their jobs in government and academia. But Mussolini did not seek a "final solution" to Italy's "Jewish problem"—as the Germans did after they occupied northern Italy in September 1943.

On the economic front, Mussolini's "Corporative State" tried to foster "class conciliation." The regime set up parallel Fascist syndicates of employers and workers in various sectors of the economy. Labor courts settled disputes under a system of compulsory arbitration.

In 1933, the regime established the Institute for Industrial Reconstruction (IRI) as a holding company to shore up failing industries. State-subsidized (or "parastate") industrial organizations would soon furnish about 17 percent of all goods and services. To stimulate the economy, Mussolini built roads, sports stadiums,and government buildings. The government launched numerous programs for mothers and children and developed a land reclamation scheme, which was responsible for draining the Pontine Marshes near Rome. Mussolini initiated a much-publicized "battle for grain"; newsreel cameramen filmed him pitching straw, bare from the waist up. Perhaps most significantly, the *Duce* began an ill-fated effort to rebuild the nation's army, navy, and air force.

Despite Mussolini's promise to restore "the Augustan Empire," he generally failed to push Italy's backward economy forward. The regime's cartels sometimes hindered economic advance by discouraging innovation and modernization. The *Duce* demoralized workers by cutting wages, raising taxes, and banning strikes and other forms of protest. Even as the government took over industries and prepared for war, unemployment remained high. Fully half of those who did work were employed in agriculture. Italian families, meanwhile, were spending 50 percent of their incomes on food.

Mussolini, however, sought (and gained) amicable relations with the Catholic church by signing the Lateran Pacts with the Vatican in February 1929. The pacts created the State of Vatican City, within which the Pope would be sovereign. They established Roman Catholicism as Italy's state religion, bestowing on it extensive privileges and immunities. The *Duce*'s star soared throughout the Catholic world; devout Italian peasants flocked to church to pray for the man who had "given back God to Italy and Italy to God." Ignoring the suppression of civil liberties, Pope Pius XI referred to Mussolini as "a man whom Providence has caused to meet us" and sprinkled him with holy water.

GRABBING ETHIOPIA

By the late 1920s, the *Duce* had solidified support for his regime, both in Rome and abroad. Soon after entering the White House in 1933, Franklin D. Roosevelt wrote that he was "deeply impressed" by this "admirable Italian gentleman," who seemed intent upon "restoring Italy and seeking to prevent general European trouble."

Indeed, until the mid-1930s, Mussolini stayed (for the most part) out of foreign ventures. But great nations, Mussolini believed, could not be content with achievements at home. "For Fascism," as he wrote in the *Enciclopedia Italiana* in 1932, "the growth of empire . . . is an essential manifestation of vitality, and its opposite a sign of decadence. Peoples which are rising, or rising again after a period of decadence, are always imperialist: any renunciation is a sign of decay and death."

Mussolini would become increasingly obsessed with foreign conquests after January 1933, when Adolf Hitler became chancellor of Germany and soon won dictatorial powers. Although Mussolini and Hitler, as fellow Fascists, admired each other, their alliance would be marked by periodic fits of jealousy on the *Duce*'s part. Hitler, as biographer Joachim C. Fest has written, "aroused in Mussolini an inferiority complex for which he thereafter tried to compensate more and more by posturings, imperial actions, or the invoking of a vanished past."

Mussolini's first major "imperial action" would occur in Africa. The *Duce* had long coveted Emperor Haile Selassie's Ethiopia, which an Italian army had failed to conquer in 1896. On the morning of October 2, 1935, as 100,000 troops began moving across the Eritrea-Ethiopia border, Mussolini announced that "A great hour in the history of our country has struck . . . forty million Italians, a sworn community, will not let themselves be robbed of their place in the sun!"

Paralyzed by economic depression and public antiwar sentiment, Britain's Prime Minister Stanley Baldwin refused to intervene, despite the inherent threat to British colonies in Africa. The League of Nations denounced the Fascist aggression. However, lacking any coherent leadership or U.S. support, the League stopped short of closing the Suez Canal or imposing an oil embargo on Italy.

Either action, Mussolini said later, would have inflicted "an inconceivable disaster."

The barefooted Ethiopian levies were no match for Italy's Savoia bombers and mustard gas. The *Duce*'s pilot son, Vittorio, told journalists in Africa that the Ethiopian soldiers, when hit from the air, "exploded like red roses." Addis Ababa fell in May 1936. With this victory, Mussolini reached the pinnacle of his popularity at home. Speaking to an enormous crowd from his Palazzo Venezia balcony, the *Duce* declared that his "triumph over 50 nations" meant the "reappearance of the Empire upon the fated hills of Rome." Signs everywhere proclaimed *Il Duce ha sempre ragione* ("The leader is always right").

Emboldened by his Ethiopian success, Mussolini began to intervene elsewhere. He dispatched aircraft and some 70,000 "volunteers" to help Generalissimo Francisco Franco's Falangist insurgents in the Spanish Civil War. He pulled Italy out of the League of Nations and decided to line up with Hitler's Germany, which had already quit the League. Thus, in June 1936, Mussolini's 33-year-old foreign minister and son-in-law, Count Galeazzo Ciano, negotiated the Rome-Berlin Axis, which was expanded into a full-fledged military alliance, the "Pact of Steel," in May 1939. Both countries also established links with Japan through the Anti-Comintern pact. The *Duce* now belonged to what he called the "most formidable political and military combination that has ever existed."

HUMILIATIONS IN THE DESERT

Mussolini's military forces, however, could not be described as formidable. Lacking coal, iron, oil, and sufficient heavy industry, Italy's economy could not support a major war effort. The *Duce,* who spoke of "eight million bayonets," proved a better propagandist than military planner. On the eve of World War II, the Italian Army owned 1.3 million outdated rifles and even fewer bayonets; its tanks and artillery were obsolete. By June 1940, the Italian Navy boasted fast battleships and Western Europe's largest fleet of submarines. But it sadly lacked radar, echo-sounding equipment, and other new technologies. And Mussolini's admirals and generals were better known for their political loyalty than for professional competence.

When Hitler quickly annexed Austria in March 1938, and Czechoslovakia in

March 1939, Mussolini complained to Count Ciano: "The Italians will laugh at me. Every time Hitler occupies a country, he sends me a message." The *Duce,* ignoring Catholic sensibilities, ordered the invasion of Albania on Good Friday, April 7, 1939, bringing that backward Adriatic country into his empire.

When Germany invaded Poland on September 1, 1939, thereby launching World War II, Mussolini knew that Italy was not ready to fight. He initially adopted a position of "non-belligerency." The list of needed war supplies that the *Duce* requested from Berlin, noted Count Ciano, "is long enough to kill a bull." But as Hitler's Blitzkrieg brought Denmark, Norway, the Low Countries, and France to their knees in 1940, Mussolini decided he had little to lose, and perhaps some spoils to gain.

On June 10, 1940, without consulting either his cabinet or the Fascist Grand Council, Mussolini declared war on both France and Britain. In joining the conflict, Mussolini inadvertently let Hitler become the master of Italy's fate.

The Italian people soon felt the pain. The battlefield performance of Mussolini's armed forces reflected the homefront's lack of zeal. One debacle after another ensued. Under Field Marshal Rodolfo Graziani, Italy's much-touted armored brigades in Libya attacked the British in Egypt, hoping to capture the Suez Canal. But in the seesaw battles across the desert, as well as in naval engagements in the Mediterranean, the outnumbered British inflicted repeated humiliations on the Italians, who had to beg the Germans for help. By the end of 1941, the British had also shorn Mussolini of Italian Eritrea and Somalia, as well as Ethiopia, reinstating Haile Selassie as emperor.

THE KING SAYS GOOD-BYE

Italy's invasion of Greece, launched from Albania on October 28, 1940, did not fare much better. Saying he was "tired of acting as Hitler's tail-light," Mussolini launched the attack without notifying Berlin. The war against the Greeks, the *Duce* predicted would be little more than a "military promenade." But the Italians were bogged down in the mountains for months, until Hitler's spring 1941 invasion of the Balkans rescued Mussolini's lackluster legions. And

Italy's participation in Germany's 1941 invasion of the Soviet Union yielded few triumphs. Mussolini dispatched three infantry divisions and one cavalry division. At least half of the 240,000 Italian soldiers sent to the Eastern front never returned.

For Italy, the beginning of the end came on December 7, 1941, when the Japanese bombed Pearl Harbor, bringing the United States into the war against the Axis powers. Although Mussolini seemed delighted to be fighting "a country of Negroes and Jews," he knew that his regime was now in deep trouble.

Across the Mediterranean, in November 1942, General Dwight Eisenhower put Allied forces ashore in Morocco and Algeria. He began a push to meet Field Marshal Bernard Montgomery's British Eighth Army, which had already broken through Axis defenses at el-Alamein. The German *Afrika Korps* fought a tough delaying action. But when the North Africa campaign ended in May 1943, some 200,000 Italians had been taken prisoner; few had fought the Allies with much enthusiasm.

New bases in North Africa enabled Allied airmen to step up the bombing of Italian cities and rail centers, which left the nation's already hard-pressed economy in tatters. Tardily, the regime rationed food supplies and restricted the consumption of gas and coal. Despite wage and price controls, inflation soared, and a black market flourished. Ordinary Italians began to demonstrate their disaffection. In early 1943, public employees in Turin and Fiat workers in Milan went on strike. "In Italy," Mussolini would later write, "the oral repercussions of the American landing in Algiers were immediate and profound. Every enemy of Fascism promptly reared his ugly head. . . ."

By the time the Allies invaded Sicily on July 10, 1943, even those Italian politicians who had long enjoyed privileges and perquisites were fed up; plots were being hatched in Rome to oust Mussolini and turn over political power to King Victor Emmanuel. All this came to a head on the night of July 24–25, when the Fascist Grand Council met at the Palazzo Venezia to decide Mussolini's fate. Some Fascist councillors criticized the shaken dictator to his face for being too indecisive; others berated him for not ridding the government of incompetents. Nothing was working, they said, and the Germans in Italy, coping with Anglo-

American advances, regarded their sagging ally with contempt.

In a two-hour monologue, the *Duce* tried to defend himself saying that "this is the moment to tighten the reins and to assume the necessary responsibility. I shall have no difficulty in replacing men, in turning the screw, in bringing forces to bear not yet engaged." But the council adopted a resolution, which had been supported by Count Ciano, calling upon the King to take over the leadership of the nation.

The next afternoon, Mussolini went to the King's villa, hoping to bluff his way through the crisis. But the King had decided, at last, to separate himself from the Fascist regime. He quickly informed Mussolini that he had decided to set up a royal military government under the 71-year-old Army Marshal, Pietro Badoglio. "Then everything is finished," the *Duce* murmured. As the ex-dictator left the Villa Savoia, a *Carabiniere* officer motioned him into an ambulance, pretending this was necessary to avoid "a hostile crowd."

Mussolini was taken to a police barracks, unaware that he was under arrest. At 10:45 a government spokesman announced over the radio the formation of the new regime by the King and Badoglio. Jubilant crowds rushed into the streets to celebrate. But they were dismayed by Badoglio's statement that "the war continues"—a statement made to ward off German retaliation.

RESCUING THE DUCE

Marshal Badoglio placed the former *Duce* under guard. Later, he was transferred to a ski resort atop Gran Sasso, the tallest peak in central Italy. He remained there for almost a fortnight, while the new regime secretly negotiated an armistice with the Allies. The armistice was announced on September 8—even as American and British troops landed against stiff German resistance at Salerno, near Naples.

Thereafter, events moved swiftly. Anticipating Italy's' about-face, Hitler had dispatched strong *Wehrmacht* reinforcements across the Alps; the Germans were able quickly to disarm and intern the badly confused Italian troops. Fearing capture, the King and Badoglio fled Rome before dawn on September 9 to join the Allied forces in the south. Six weeks later the Badoglio government,

now installed in Bríndisi, declared war on Germany.

On September 12, 1943, Captain Otto Skorzeny, leading 90 German commandos in eight gliders and a small plane, landed outside the mountaintop hotel on Gran Sasso where the sickly *Duce* was still being kept. Skorzeny's men brushed aside the Italian guards, and took Mussolini to Munich, where Hitler met him. Henceforth, the *Duce* would be one of Hitler's lackeys, a "brutal friendship" as Mussolini put it.

The *Führer* ordered Mussolini to head up the new pro-Nazi Italian Social Republic (RSI) at Salò, in German-occupied northern Italy. The Italian Fascists would help the Nazis deport, and later exterminate, over 8,000 Jews. From Munich, Mussolini appealed by radio to his "faithful Blackshirts" to renew Axis solidarity, and purge the "royalist betrayers" of the regime.

But few Italians willingly backed the "Salò Republic." Instead, most hoped for a swift Allied victory. A determined minority even joined the partisans—the armed anti-German and anti-Fascist resistance—in northern Italy. But Mussolini did manage to punish the "traitors of July 25." In Verona, a special Fascist tribunal put on trial Mussolini's son-in-law, Count Ciano, and others in his party who had voted for "the elimination of its *Duce*." Rejecting the pleas of his daughter Edda, Mussolini decreed that Ciano and his co-conspirators be shot to death, and so they were, on January 11, 1944.

At last, in April 1945, the grinding Allied offensive, having reached northern Italy, overwhelmed the Germans, whose homeland was already collapsing under attack from East and West. At this point, Mussolini tried to save himself by negotiating with anti-Fascist resistance leaders in Milan. but when he learned that they insisted on an "unconditional surrender," he fled with several dozen companions to Lake Como, where he was joined by his mistress, Clara Petacci. From there, they planned to escape to Switzerland.

PER NECESSITA FAMILIALE

Unable to cross the border, Mussolini and his band decided to join a German truck convoy that was retreating toward Switzerland through the Italian Alps. But Italian partisans halted the convoy near Dongo. Ever the actor, Mussolini donned a German corporal's overcoat, a swastika-marked helmet, and dark glasses, and climbed into one of the trucks. But the partisans identified Mussolini, arrested him and his companions, and let the Germans proceed unmolested.

The next day, Walter Audisio, a Communist resistance chief from Milan, arrived, claiming he had orders to execute the *Duce* and 15 other Fascist fugitives. He summarily shot Mussolini and his mistress at the village of Giulino di Mezzegra on April 28. Their corpses were taken to Milan and strung up by the heels in Piazzale Loreto, where an infuriated mob repeatedly kicked and spat on the swinging cadavers.

Looking back on Mussolini's career, it might be said that he changed Italy more than he changed the Italians. Indeed, the *Duce* left behind a network of paved roads, reclamation projects, and a vast centralized bureaucracy. The IRI holding company and other para-state corporations that Mussolini founded still exist today; they account for the most inefficient 20 percent of the nation's economy.

But Mussolini convinced few Italians for long that Fascism was the wave of the future. To be sure, many had supported the *Duce* enthusiastically, especially from the time his regime signed the concordat with the Pope (1929) through the easy conquest of Ethiopia (1936). And a small neo-Fascist party, the *Movimento Sociale Italiano* (MSI), still wins roughly five percent of the popular vote in national elections today.

Most Italians quietly turned their backs on Mussolini once it became clear that he had engaged the nation in costly ventures that could not succeed. (More than 400,000 Italians lost their lives in World War II.) During the *Duce*'s foolish expeditions against the Greeks, the British, and the Soviets, many Italians considered themselves to be "half-Fascists," who had taken out their Fascist Party membership cards only *per necessità familiale* (for the good of the family).

On June 2, 1946, the first time that Italians got a chance to vote in a postwar election, they chose to oust the monarchy. They could not forgive King Victor Emmanuel for inviting Mussolini to take power, and for supporting the *Duce*'s imperial ambitions—even if they forgave themselves. The voters elected a constituent assembly, which drafted a new constitution for the republic, providing for a prime minister, a bicameral parliament, and a system of 20 regional governments.

Mussolini and his ideology proved influential beyond Italy's borders. As the world's first and perhaps most popular Fascist leader, he provided the model for other aspiring authoritarian rulers in Europe and Latin America who, for a time, would make fascism seem an attractive alternative to socialism, communism, or anarchy.

In Germany, Adolf Hitler called Mussolini's 1922 March on Rome "one of the turning points of history." The mere idea that such a march could be attempted, he said, "gave [Germany's National Socialists] an impetus." When Nazis did their outstretched arm salutes, or when Spanish Falangists cried "Franco! Franco! Franco!", they were mimicking their counterparts in Italy. Juan Perón, Argentina's president (1946–1955), echoed the sentiments of many another ambitious Latin strongman when he called Mussolini "the greatest man of our century."

Just before Mussolini came to power, Italians, like citizens of several troubled European societies after World War I, faced a choice—either muddling through disorder and economic disarray under often inept, yet essentially benevolent democratic regimes, or falling in line behind a decisive but brutal dictatorship. Italians chose the latter. They embraced the strong man's notions of a grand New Age. But Mussolini's intoxicating vision of Italy as a great power, they eventually discovered, was a disastrous delusion.

The Fascist era serves to remind Italians and others of something important: that national well-being may not come from charismatic leadership, revolutionary zeal, or military might. Indeed, Italy's peculiar greatness today may lie in its citizens' tolerance of regional and economic differences, in their ability to cope with the inefficiencies of democratic government, in their pragmatic acceptance of human foibles—and, most of all, in their appreciation of the rich texture of everyday life.

Resistance of the Heart in Nazi Germany

It complicates our received idea of totalitarianism to learn that there were successful protests in Nazi Germany. This is the story of three of them: protests that forced changes in policy, including, in one very special case, the release of Jews slated for the death camps

Nathan Stoltzfus

Nathan Stoltzfus is completing a doctoral dissertation in history at Harvard University. He is at work on a book about the Rosenstrasse protest of 1943.

On April 1, 1943, the American Legation in Bern sent this dispatch to Washington: "Action against Jewish wives and husbands on the part of the Gestapo . . . had to be discontinued some time ago because of the protest which such action aroused." The protest to which this dispatch referred had been a street demonstration a month earlier in Berlin. The demonstration was remarkable for the courage of the people who participated in it, for the sheer fact of its occurrence, and above all for its outcome. For it marked the single instance of group protest by Germans of the Third Reich in behalf of fellow citizens who were Jewish—and it worked. This article, which is based on more than two years of research and interviews in the former West and East Germanys, seeks to tell the story of that protest, and two others of other kinds. The story, known to only a few close students of the Third Reich, raises a question that goes far beyond it: If nonviolent mass protest by Aryan Germans worked in Berlin in 1943, could it have slowed or stopped the destruction of Germany Jewry?

That question, of course, is provocatively abstract. Whether or not it *could* have, history shows only that the mass of Germans either did nothing or supported the Nazi regime. It is important to say this at the outset of an article about why a handful of Germans protested.

ON THE ROSENSTRASSE

Until early 1943 the Nazi regime had exempted from the Final Solution Jews married to Aryans. But during a mass arrest of the last Jews in Berlin, beginning on February 27, 1943, a change was made. Unannounced, the SS burst into Berlin's factories at daybreak that Saturday morning and arrested all Jews. Simultaneously the local Gestapo, assisted by the municipal police, kidnapped Jews from their homes. Anyone on the streets wearing the Star of David was carted off without explanation and taken with other Jews to huge "collecting centers" in central Berlin, in preparation for large-scale deportations to Auschwitz.

This was the most brutal chapter of the expulsion of Jews from Berlin. The Gestapo referred to it simply as the *Judenschlussaktion* (final roundup of Jews). Meant to be a precedent-setting action against Jews married to Aryans, it employed special national forces. Reichsmarschall Hermann Göring converted the riding stable of his air force in central Berlin into a collecting center. Reichsführer-SS Heinrich Himmler participated in planning the action and made Adolf Eichmann's deputy, Rolf Günther, one of the three executive managers of it. Adolf Hitler himself authorized a two-day loan of the Leibstandarte Adolf Hitler, the SS division originally created for his personal protection. The Führer was reportedly offended that so many Jews still lived in Berlin, and Joseph Goebbels, as the Nazi Party regional director for greater Berlin, was determined to make the Reich capital *judenfrei* in time for the Führer's fifty-fourth birthday, in April.

Of the 10,000 Berlin Jews arrested in the Final Roundup, 8,000 were murdered at Auschwitz. The remaining 2,000 were to experience a different fate. These Jews, related by marriage to Aryan Germans, were locked up at Rosenstrasse 2–4, an administrative center of the Jewish community in the heart of Berlin. By the repellent racial logic of the Nazis, the leadership had reason to deport these Jews before all other Jews. The Aryan spouses, who were mostly women, hurried alone or in pairs to the Rosenstrasse, where they discovered a growing crowd. A protest broke out when the hundreds of women at the gate began calling out, "Give us our husbands back!" Day and night for a week they staged their protest, and the crowd grew larger.

On different occasions armed guards commanded, "Clear the streets or we'll shoot!" This sent the women scrambling into surrounding alleys and courtyards. But within minutes they began streaming out. Again and again they were scattered by threats of gunfire, and again and again they advanced, massed together, and called out for their husbands, who heard them and took hope.

The square, according to one witness, "was crammed with people, and the accusing, demanding cries of the women rose above the noise of the traffic like passionate avowals of a love strengthened by the bitterness of life." One protester described herself as feeling deep solidarity with those sharing her fate. Normally people were afraid to dissent, fearing denunciation, but in the square they knew they were among friends. A Gestapo man, impressed by the display, announced to the Jews, "They are calling for you out there. They want you to come back—this is Germany loyalty."

The headquarters of his section of the Gestapo was just around the corner, within earshot of the protesters. A few bursts from a machine gun could have emptied the square. But instead the Jews were released. Goebbels decided that the simplest way to end the protest was to give in to the protesters' demands. "A large number of people gathered and in part even took sides with the Jews," Goebbels complained in his diary on March 6. "I ordered the [Gestapo] not to continue Jewish evacuation at so critical a moment. We want to save that up for a couple of weeks. We can then go after it all the more thoroughly."

But the Jews married to Aryans remained. They survived the war, officially registered with the police, working in officially authorized jobs, and officially receiving food rations.

The protest by Aryan women on the Rosenstrasse was the culminating act of allegiance to their families. It followed naturally in a trajectory of acts of resistance to measures of the state intended to tear their husbands and children from them. The Nazis prohibited sexual relations between Aryans and Jews. *Rassenschande*—literally "racial shame"—was their name for this crime. In July of 1938 the government eased the divorce laws to enable Aryans married to Jews to end these incriminating unions. At the same time, many of them began receiving orders to appear at Gestapo offices, where they were pressured to divorce. A decree in October of 1941 went further. It made "friendly relations" of any kind with Jews punishable by imprisonment. A decree of 1942 made it a crime even to supply newspapers to Jews. Aryans married to Jews were forbidden to take civil-service jobs, were blocked in their work and professional careers, were given radically reduced rations yet were expected to work, were treated as pariahs by their neighbors, and were even forbidden to seek refuge in the same air-raid shelters as their neighbors. One woman, an Aryan married to a Jew, was told when she went to the Aryan air-raid shelter, "The air that you breathe out, we can't stand to breathe in." Yet, in the face of these immense legal and social pressures to abandon their spouses, about 93 percent of the Aryans married to Jews remained

married. The Rosenstrasse protest was just one more overt step in their battle of wills with the regime.

TOTALITARIAN POLITICS

The Rosenstrasse protest had powerful repercussions, reaching beyond March of 1943 and beyond Berlin. Goebbels reported in his diary on March 6 that by releasing Jews he was merely deferring deportations a few weeks, but on March 18 Himmler recorded in his telephone diary the decision reached after a conversation with the Gestapo chief, Heinrich Müller: "No deportation of privileged Jews [those related to Aryans]." About the same day twenty-five Jews from intermarriages who on March 6 had been sent from the Rosenstrasse camp to Auschwitz work camps were released. The Berlin Gestapo, not wanting to risk information leaks about Auschwitz, forced these twenty-five to sign statements that swore them to secrecy concerning their Auschwitz experiences, and on the basis of trumped-up charges of spying, spreading rumors, and breaking the rules of the concentration camp, they were then put under "protective custody" and sent to the Grossbeeren "work-education camp," near Berlin. Goebbels declared Berlin *judenfrei* on May 19. He was under pressure to get this done and apparently preferred lying to risking another protest.

On May 21 Rolf Günther responded to a question from the German police in Paris, who had been waiting to hear from headquarters about what to do with French Jews in intermarriages. The treatment of intermarriages cannot be resolved for foreign areas now, the deputy wrote, because it is not yet solved in the Reich. The policy for the Reich had to be applied first to Berlin, because about half the intermarried couples lived in Berlin, and because it was in keeping with the Nazi sense of propriety that precedents for the Reich were set in its capital.

Also on May 21 Himmler's deputy Ernst Kaltenbrunner issued a memorandum ordering the immediate release from concentration camps of all intermarried Jews except those interned on criminal charges. He turned to Himmler's order that every Jew be removed from the Reich by June 30, and listed four categories of Jews that had often been spared up until this point, including those considered irreplaceable by weapons industries. The first three categories were

now to be deported. But the fourth—Jews in intermarriages—was not: "I order expressly that Jewish intermarriage partners are in no case to be sent. There may also be protective custody arrests and deportations only when they have committed real offenses. In so far as Jewish intermarriage partners have been deported on general grounds [that is, strictly because of their Jewish identity] they are to be successively released."

On December 18, 1943, Himmler himself ordered the deportation of Jews whose Aryan spouses had died or divorced them. He decreed, however, that no such Jew would be deported if he or she had a child or children who might stir up unrest as a result.

Apparently the exemption of a German Jew from Nazi genocide depended on whether an Aryan somewhere in German society was likely to make problems for the Nazi regime by threatening both the secrecy surrounding the Final Solution and the high morale needed for waging war. (The longer and more total the war, the more the leadership feared public dissent and its deleterious effect on patriotism.) The salvation of a German Jew, it seems, depended not on marriage to an Aryan per se but on whether a German Aryan might care enough to risk career and possibly life itself by joining with National Socialism's victims, rather than with National Socialism.

The Nazi Party stressed that the source of its political power was the conscious decision of the people to support it. In *Mein Kampf*, Hitler wrote that mass popular support was the distinguishing characteristic of the Nazi Party, and by 1932 no other Weimar party was as successful at the polls as Hitler's. Once in power, the party maintained support by making concessions to the masses. The regime temporarily restricted imports for arms production in order to forgo food rationing, and retreated on plans to mobilize labor when workers protested and women refused to report to work. Even the destruction of Jews married to Aryans, it seems, had to come second to the needs of this internal politics.

THE CROSS OVER THE SWASTIKA

Catholic schools were the focus of Nazi efforts to usurp the place of traditional

Catholic leadership and dominate German Catholics through their own organizations. By late 1936 the Nazi dictatorship, impatient with the failure of the Church to abandon traditional Christian allegiance for the new Nazi faith, made a bold attempt to win the struggle for ideological domination by forcibly replacing Catholic symbols with Nazi ones. When the Nazi regional leader from Oldenburg, in Protestant northern Germany, issued a decree, on November 4, 1936, ordering the removal of crucifixes (and pictures of Luther) from public schools throughout his district, his action resulted in what secret police reports called a "storm of indignation" in the town of Cloppenburg, a Catholic enclave. Prelates of the area supported the protests "with all means," and cried that godless Bolshevism was threatening the fatherland. A special nine-day church service of entreaty and penance was held, church bells were rung in protest every evening, and families began holding their own devotional ceremonies at home. Children went to school wearing crucifixes around their necks; numerous protest commissions sprang up, demanding that officials rescind the decree; and church officials complained bitterly to the government. To the consternation of officials in Berlin, the "grave unrest" caused by the crucifix decree spread even into Nazi Party circles. Nazi administrators put office resources at the disposal of protest groups; the Nazi Women's Organization refused to carry out certain orders; even members of the Hitler Youth failed to cooperate.

On November 25 the Oldenburg leader called a meeting at a large auditorium in Cloppenburg to announce that the Nazis were backing down. Such a public announcement suggests that those in charge considered the problem to be widespread, and not to be solved merely by punishing organization leaders.

The police reported that Catholic activists were telling each other that "all regulations of the state would remain unsuccessful if the Catholic people stand together united." The clergy had begun to think of collective action as a tactic for resisting Nazi infringements on church traditions.

The success of what became known as the Spirit of Cloppenburg was an important precedent for a struggle in 1941, when Catholics again forced the retraction of a crucifix decree, this time in southern Germany, by using various forms of noncooperation and public protest. On April 23 of that year the Bavarian minister of education, Adolf Wagner, ordered that crucifixes be removed from his district, that the usual school prayer be dropped in favor of Nazi slogans or songs, and that by the end of the summer holidays Christian pictures be replaced by "pictures suited to the present time." When the local population—and many local functionaries—protested, Wagner stepped up his timetable. This only caused more protests. Two weeks later Wagner was forced to rescind the decree, but in the hope of saving face, he did so secretly.

The result was explosive civil disobedience by devout villagers which was "greater than at any previous time during the Third Reich in Bavaria," the historian Ian Kershaw wrote in his account of this region. Mothers of schoolchildren used a variety of tactics to mobilize popular opinion and noncooperation with the regime. Kershaw continued,

> The most frequent tactic used by the activist mothers was to send a delegation to the head teacher, the mayor, the local Party leader, and the [district magistrate], with a threat to remove their children from school until the crosses were replaced. In many instances a school strike began and successfully persuaded the local authorities that the time had come to bow to the pressure. . . . Any form of unwillingness to concede on the part of the local authorities led to demonstrations by angry groups or crowds of people, prominent among them the women of the village.

Other methods of resistance used in this "mother's revolt" included petitions threatening school strikes; criticism that while Germany fought "godless Bolshevism" in Russia, godlessness was rearing its head at home; and threats of resignation from the party and the women's organization. Exploiting their intimate link with the war front, women encouraged one another to write to their husbands about their struggle. The replies they received—recording their husbands' dismay and falling morale—were then used as ammunition in the fight for crosses. One wife claimed to have received a letter from her husband saying that the news had made him decide to stop concealing how horrible conditions at the front really were. According to Kershaw, women were prominent in this

civil disobedience because of their close ties to school and church. Once women took the initiative, others joined in their fight, on the Rosenstrasse as well as in these schools.

THE EUTHANASIA PROTEST

All roads to power start with the people, the Führer had written. In the interest of maintaining power, the Nazi dictatorship released Jews and rescinded crucifix decrees. Also responding to the force of popular opinion, Hitler ordered a stop to "euthanasia"—as the Nazis called the murder of the insane and deformed—by gassing. In nineteen months, from January of 1940 to August of 1941, euthanasia claimed some seventy thousand victims. But the doctors and bureaucrats grew careless: families of those murdered received two urns of ashes, persons who had long ago had appendectomies were reported to have died of appendicitis, and asylum staff members, tongues loosened at the local pub, let slip the tale of their ghastly work.

The purpose of Hitler's order was to stop public protests against euthanasia rather than euthanasia itself. In the final forty-four months of Nazi Germany euthanasia claimed an additional thirty thousand victims. The gassing of the insane and deformed stopped, but was replaced by a decentralized effort, more difficult to blame on the regime. Trustworthy doctors, nurses, and caretakers were told that it was not undesired to kill such people through overdoses of medication and starvation diets. Patients were fed potato peels, thistles, and dandelions. Suffered in the chill of poorly heated or unheated rooms, this fare led to death by intestinal catarrh, diarrhea, and lung infection—all "natural causes." Overdoses of medication, especially in combination with starvation rations and cold, also resulted in death only gradually, so that death could again be characterized as natural.

Another measure to minimize protests was the selection of victims without German families. Many of the thirty thousand later victims were not Germans but forced laborers from the east. They were the *Untermenschen,* racially inferior persons who, no longer fit for work after falling ill, or falling apart, were killed by starvation or poison. Many others of the later victims were orphans and juvenile delinquents in concentration camps—

Germans with no families or with very weak family ties. Without family members among the *Volk,* they had no voice among the *Volk,* and so would never occasion a protest.

Like the removals of crucifixes in 1936 and 1941, the euthanasia by gassing was stopped as a direct consequence of the force of popular opinion. But the fight against euthanasia was primarily conducted by religious leaders such as Catholic bishops, especially Clemens August von Galen. Unlike the crucifix protest, it was not expressed through direct action (the task of rescuing victims of euthanasia would have been formidable in comparison with replacing Hitler's visage with the cross). Collective civil disobedience was not important in the fight against euthanasia, nor were mass protests.

But the leaders who condemned euthanasia from the pulpit were effective only because they represented the public will. The regime was probably not much worried about a few letters from a bishop here or there: isolated individuals could be threatened into silence or imprisoned, and their letters could be burned. Von Galen was not executed, because the public loved and respected him. And he made public what the regime meant to keep secret.

Because popular opinion was powerful, the regime wished to carry out both euthanasia and the Final Solution behind the backs of the people (euphemisms for murder were just the outside veil of the regime's cover-up). Nazi policies for breeding a "racially pure" and plentiful German population meant the sterilization and destruction of *lebensunwerten Lebens,* "life unworthy of life." Racial hygiene, the cornerstone of Nazi politics, eventually began to threaten popular support, the cornerstone of Nazi power. Whereas the regime relied on public support, its totalitarian attempt to change Germany's racial composition through murder would elicit public wrath and social unrest—unless it could be carried out in secret.

German officials first acknowledged the existence of troublesome rumors about euthanasia in late 1940. When the party's local group leader in Bruckberg wondered how he could combat rumors that inmates of a nearby asylum were being killed, the party regional leader instructed him that it was better to say nothing at all than to draw attention to an action that the general populace would

denounce. In a letter to the Reich's Chancellor on March 4, 1941, Franz Schlegelberger, the acting Minister of Justice, warned that rumors were mounting because the boundaries of the murder program were unknown. Who was to be killed, and why? Fears mounted that euthanasia would extend to those injured in the war, old people incapable of working, and political opponents. Schlegelberger argued that the rumormongers could not be prosecuted, because this would only spread reports about the program, with consequent unrest. Trials held in secret would be just as problematic as public trials, the minister wrote, because the regime would still have to explain "the particular elements of offense [which] would unfurl the entire problem."

In July and August of 1941 Von Galen preached three blistering sermons from his pulpit in Münster-Westphalia against the lawless power of the Gestapo, warning his congregation that no one was safe from arbitrary arrest and punishment, and that, according to the logic of a program that sacrificed those who were of no obvious productive use to the war effort, the state could soon be administering euthanasia to wounded soldiers at the front as well as to cripples, the old, and the weak. Walter Tiessler, an official in the party chancellery, suggested to Goebbels that Von Galen be hanged. But Goebbels told Tiessler that only Hitler himself could condemn the bishop to die, and said, "If something against the bishop was done, one could forget about receiving support of the people of Münster for the rest of the war"—perhaps, he went on, even the population of the entire region of Westphalia. Many soldiers at the front derived their will to fight from their Catholic beliefs, and others less devout would be demoralized if their relatives at home lost their faith in Germany's cause. The soldiers' morale would understandably be undermined if a bishop were executed for warning that they, too, if wounded, might be targets of a state that killed all those it deemed useless.

As soon as Von Galen spoke out, he had public awareness on his side. If he were arrested, the public would know immediately both about his arrest and about the reason for it. Von Galen helped to form the opinion that protected him. He gave the many whispered fears about euthanasia public voice. Now that euthanasia was being publicly discussed, it had to be ended.

According to the writer Conor Cruise O'Brien, Hitler backed away from confrontation with the German churches "because he thought this was bad for the morale of Germany's armed forces." O'Brien concluded that the churches "might well have" forced the Nazi regime to stop the Holocaust if they had "spoken out against the persecution of the Jews with the same vigor as they had shown in the case of 'Euthanasia.' " The scholar J. P. Stern agrees. He writes that it "seems beyond any doubt that if the Churches had opposed the persecution of the Jews as they opposed the killing of the congenitally insane and sick, there would have been no 'Final Solution.' "

"US-ISM"

The civilian actions that forced state concessions in widely varying political circumstances and that represented a spectrum of threats to Nazi power shared certain fundamental qualities essential to their success. First, successful acts of noncooperation or protest at least appeared to have been undertaken collectively by an integral part of society, rather than demonstrating isolated disaffection. People were executed for offenses as minor as telling an anti-Nazi joke—when they acted individually.

Second, successful actions were nonviolent. Nonviolent actions avoided the appearance of treason and failed to legitimate the crushing violence of the Nazi regime. Police violence generally had the potential to be ineffective or counterproductive against broadly based opposition, rooted in social customs and traditions. If the protesters on the Rosenstrasse had come armed, the police would have *had* to shoot them, Leopold Gutterer, who was Joseph Goebbels's deputy from 1941 to 1944, told me in a recent interview. Gutterer also said that it was important that the protesters had acted for all to see, risking their lives, making public confessions of their loyalty to their families, rather than acting behind the back of the state, in the manner of traitors: "They were as persons there; anyone could recognize who they were; they demonstrated openly and risked their existence."

Third, then, opposition that succeeded in reversing Nazi policies was overt as well as broad-based and nonviolent. The state controlled the press and radio, but public noncooperation and direct action, rumors, public preaching, and open protest were all forms of communication difficult to control. Goebbels needed to clear the streets of protesters to stop others from getting the same idea, according to Gutterer. Publicly expressed opposition not only drew attention to secret programs and demonstrated dissent but also potentially transmitted knowledge about a politically powerful means of dissent. Certainly secrecy, rather than publicity, was a key condition for saving many Jews, including those hiding in the German underground. But in the incidents discussed here, public opposition led to the public reversal of the offensive decrees and programs.

Those on the Rosenstrasse who risked their lives for Jews did not express opposition to anti-Semitic policies per se. They displayed primarily what the late Primo Levi, a survivor of Auschwitz, called "selfishness extended to the person closest to you . . . us-ism." In most of the stories I have heard of Aryans who risked their lives for Jews to whom they were married, they withdrew to safety, one by one, the moment their loved ones were released. Their protests bring home to us the iron limits, the tragically narrow borders, of us-ism.

In his *Question of German Guilt,* Karl Jaspers argues that what we see in the crimes of the Nazis and in the silent complicity of the German people—as well, we might add, in the us-ism of the protesters—is "the human essence" in "its German form." That is a disquieting observation. While not absolving the Germans of guilt for the greatest crime in history, it leaves us squarely on the moral hook, reminding us of the inescapable responsibility of peoples for the conduct of their governments.

A People Under Terror

Italian Jews During World War II

Alexander Stille

We print below an excerpt from Benevolence and Betrayal,* *an extremely rich portrayal of the fate of the Italian Jews during the Second World War. By showing the varying fates of several Italian Jewish families, Alexander Stille, a gifted young writer of Italian descent, has provided a valuable record of a tragic experience.*

Mussolini's regime was at first relatively tolerant toward the Jews, some of whom declared themselves "loyal citizens." By 1938, however, under pressure from his ally Hitler, Mussolini announced a new set of "racial laws." During the war a large percentage of the Italian Jews were deported to concentration camps in Germany and Poland; only a few returned home. In the pages below, Stille traces the story of a Jewish family in the ghetto of Rome.

*This excerpt is printed with the kind permission of the author.—*EDS.

In Rome, the circle was closing rapidly on the Jews hiding throughout the city. The Italian puppet government installed a new chief of the Rome police, Pietro Caruso, who pursued the search for Jews with quickened vigor. In his first month on the job, February 1944, the number of Jews arrested in the city jumped from 29 to 141. And in March the number climbed further to 163.

The hopes of an immediate Allied victory had faded. Although they were only about sixty kilometers from Rome, American troops were bogged down for the winter in the treacherous moun-

---

Benevolence and Betrayal: Five Italian Jewish Families under Fascism, by Alexander Stille. New York: Summit Books, 1991. © 1991 by Alexander Stille.

tainous country at Cassino in a stand-off that seemed to last forever.

With the Germans settling in for a long occupation, many Italians began reconsidering their options. Hunger was rampant in the city. Hard-line Italian fascists crawled out from hiding and were on the ascendant; the temptation to make several thousand lire by selling Jews to the police became too much for some people.

Throughout those months the family of Enrico Di Veroli moved from house to house and convent to convent, staying a step or two ahead of the Germans and the neofascists. Having narrowly escaped arrest while staying at their relatives' house in Trastevere, the family went to stay in a convent near the Ponte Rotto. "After about ten days we had to escape from there because someone told the Germans that we were there. In this convent there were, along with Jews, a number of soldiers and officers who had escaped from the Italian army. The people in the convent tried to help us as much as possible but they had to send us away."

After leaving the convent in the middle of the night, the family found refuge with another former client of their store, who lived in Via Porta Settimiana. "They opened their house to us, they gave us their bedrooms. There's no way around it, the people of Rome opened their hearts to us. Some did it out of self-interest, but a lot of them out of pure generosity. What little they had, they shared with us. We were well there, we stayed a few months, but then one day my father saw some people being arrested right under the windows of the house and he became afraid."

Olga Di Verdi recalls that period as a string of adventures, escapes, and disasters. "After October 16, I began writing something down in my own fashion and my father said to me: 'What do you want

to write down? These are days you'll never forget as long as you live.' And so it's been."

From that hideaway, the family decided to find a place in another convent or monastery. Olga's brothers, Michele and Gianni, didn't like the idea of going into a monastery and, instead, left Rome to join the antifascist resistance. "I didn't want to go into any convent," says Michele, Enrico's son. "I didn't want to die like a mouse in a trap. The Germans raided some of the convents. If you have to die, better to die with rifle in hand. That's the way I am."

Michele and Gianni went to a partisan formation in the hills of Lazio led by Giorgio Costanzo. Their main task was to recover parachutes dropped by Allied aircraft and give aid to American and British paratroopers. "Every day, a new episode," Michele says. "We were constantly on the move, trying to avoid a round-up." Fighting alongside his brother, rather than being a source of comfort, Michele says, only made things worse. "It was a time of constant fear. To be at war with your own brother is the worst thing imaginable. What happens if your brother dies alongside of you? What do you do? Shoot yourself?"

The rest of the family—Enrico, his wife, Grazia, and their two younger daughters, Olga and Flora—found a place to stay in buildings connected to the parish church of San Benedetto. There, they met up with Attilio Di Veroli and his entire family of seven as well as Michele Di Veroli, son of Umberto, known as Monsieur Macaroni.

Not long after this reunion, on March 3 the church of San Benedetto was hit by an Allied bomb—one of the few that fell on Rome during the war. "I had gone out to get some bread, and as I was coming back I hear this explosion and a whole wing of the convent just collapsed," recalls Rosa Di Veroli. "Luckily, no one was killed. But they said: 'Everyone has to leave.' "

Michele Di Veroli was immediately able to find another place in a monastery but the other Di Verolis were not so lucky. "After the bombing, we wanted to stay in another convent but they wanted money, something like 200 lire a day, which we didn't have. Michele went and we had to move from here to there to try to save ourselves."

Having nowhere else to go, Rosa's family went with her uncle Enrico Di Veroli and his family to their store back in the ghetto for several days. So the ten of them lived in the two-room store with no kitchen, bathroom, or running water. "There was a concierge at a building nearby on Via Arenula who at night would bring us a bottle of water that we had to use for all our needs, for drinking, cooking, and washing," says Olga Di Veroli. "There were some friends who had a store nearby who would let us know when it was okay to go out and who brought us things that we needed."

But remaining in the ghetto at this point was untenable and the two families left and split up after four or five days. At the end of their resources, Rosa and her family found themselves back in the old Theater of Marcellus, the ancient amphitheatre just next to the ghetto where the Jews from the neighborhood had been rounded up on October 16 before being taken away in trucks. "We were sitting there in the ruins the whole day because we had nowhere else to go," Rosa remembers. "In the evening we would try to find somewhere to sleep, sometimes in the open air."

One day on the street, their father ran into an acquaintance whom he persuaded to take in his family for a while. "We ate bread and lettuce, which we dressed with the salty liquid that come from anchovy cans." To collect a few lire a day, Attilio Di Veroli had taken up his old itinerant life, making the round of the city's churches, collecting used furniture, fixing things, receiving an occasional handout. Because he was blind in one eye, he took his fifteen-year-old son Michele with him.

"One day we had an appointment to meet my father and brother at the Teatro Marcello and when he didn't show up we knew they had been taken," Rosa recalls. "It was the eighteenth of March 1944."

Although they do not know for sure, Rosa and her family suspect they were turned in by the seamstress with whom they were staying at the time. "It's only an idea; we have no proof," says Rosa. "But I never had a good feeling about that place. One morning when my sister and I were sleeping we heard the woman's little boy playing with a German soldier. And the morning my father was arrested the woman told us: 'Don't all go out together.' So my sisters, my mother, and I went out alone and we never saw my father and brother again; that's why we suspected her. That evening we were afraid to go back there. Luckily, we were able to find a place to stay in a convent near the Teatro Marcello.

"The next day, March 19, was a national holiday, the day of Saint Joseph. My sister, my older sister, Silvia, and I went to Via Tasso [the site of Gestapo headquarters] and I said: 'I am an Italian citizen; you have arrested my father and I want to bring him something.' 'Are you Jewish?' one of them asked. 'Yes,' I said. And they told me to go look in Regina Coeli prison. And we went there and brought him food. We brought him food every day. We were afraid, but we wanted to know and at that point I didn't care. I was always the most reckless of the family."

Every day after her father's arrest, Rosa would appear at Regina Coeli to bring him something to eat, something to supplement the meager prison rations. But on the morning of March 24, when she arrived at the prison gates, the guards told Rosa that her father and brother were no longer there and they had no idea where they had been taken.

Rosa, however, had her own suspicions. The previous day, March 23, 1944, a bomb had exploded in Via Rasella while a convoy of German soldiers was passing, killing thirty-two German soldiers. It had been set by partisans. Because the Germans were well known for their threat of killing ten Italians for every German murdered, the city trembled at the prospect of a massive retaliation.

"We knew the day of the attack at Via Rasella that they had taken some Jews," Rosa says. "We knew that for every German, ten people would be killed. But instead of killing 320, they killed more."

The story quickly circulated through the city that the Germans had taken a large group of Italians, mostly antifascists being held in the Rome prisons, to the Ardeatine Caves just outside the city. Chained together in groups of three, they were led into the caves, made to kneel down, and shot in the back of the head. When the killing was done—it took several hours—the Germans exploded dynamite at the caves' entrance to hide the evidence of their crime.

No one knew the names of the people who had been killed. Not long after the massacre, Rosa and her older sister, Silvia, ventured back into the ghetto area to get some bread. Although it was dangerous to return to the old Jewish quarter, the baker knew them there and made sure they got something to eat. As they were leaving, Rosa saw an old childhood friend, Celeste Di Porto, with whom she had gone to elementary school. Known as "Stella" (meaning "Star"), because of her beauty, Celeste was from another of the large, old ghetto families. During the German occupation, however, Celeste had become the city's most lethal German informant, turning in about fifty Jews from the ghetto. Standing on the bridge between the ghetto and Trastevere, she would finger people as they walked by. In this period, the beautiful dark-haired Celeste earned a new nickname: "La Pantera Nera," the Black Panther.

"I saw her and I thought, 'Mamma mia, if they get us?' It was enough for her to make a sign and they would have grabbed us. I got up my courage—I had been to school with her—and said: 'Ciao, Celeste, how are you? You, who know so much, do you know what's happened to my father and brother?' 'They're fine,' she said. 'They're with my cousin.' Silvia and I started walking off, when suddenly I hear her call me, 'Rosa.' And I said to myself: 'Oh, God, she's going to get me.' 'Listen,' she told me, 'stay out of sight for a few days.' And we went away."

To find out more about her father and brother, Rosa called her old employer (and distant cousin) Renato Di Veroli, who was hidden inside the Vatican City. "He had been able to see a list of the victims, and Attilio Di Veroli and Michele Di Veroli were on the list. He [Renato] had a brother named Attilio Di Veroli and thought it might be him. But I was sure it was my father.

"Celeste had said they were 'fine,' they were 'with her cousin,' and in fact they were with her cousin, dead at the Ardeatine Caves. A couple of days after the massacre I went out to the caves to look. I got a ride on a garbage truck. But I couldn't see a thing.

"It was dangerous to move around this way, but I had a certain strength that came from the fact that I didn't give a crap anymore. There were certain things that needed to be done."

Of the 335 men killed in the Ardeatine Caves, 77 were Jews, all of them, like Attilio and Michele Di Veroli, nonpolitical Jews who simply happened to be in the Rome prison at the time of the ambush. They served to round out the number so that the Germans could maintain their ten-to-one quota. Twenty-six of the Jews who died in the massacre are believed to have been turned in by the Black Panther.

Lazzaro Anticoli, a young street peddler arrested the morning of the massacre, managed to scribble a note before being dragged off to the caves: "If I never see my family again, it is the fault of that sellout Celeste Di Porto. Avenge me." According to Italian historian Silvio Bertoldi, Anticoli's name was added at the last minute, replacing that of Celeste Di Porto's brother. The Black Panther's own father was so deeply ashamed by his daughter's betrayal that he turned himself into the Germans and died in a concentration camp.

Among the Jews killed at the Ardeatine Caves was Aldo Finzi, former undersecretary of the interior and a member of the first Fascist Grand Council. Naturally, Finzi had been among the "discriminated" Jews, those granted exemptions for their patriotic contributions. But this counted little with the Germans. The majority of the victims, however, were ghetto Jews with typically Roman last names such as Di Consiglio, Di Veroli, Di Porto, and Funaro. The youngest was Rosa's little brother, Michele, who had celebrated his fifteenth birthday the month before his death.

"My mother continued to delude herself that they would come back, that there had been a mix-up, and maybe they had exchanged clothes and documents with other people," says Rosa. "She got this idea in her head."

Olga and Flora, together with their mother, moved into a convent of Philippian Sisters on Via Cicerone. Despite the dangers of the German occupation, the women continued to move freely about the city during the day. They wanted, especially, to remain in contact with Enrico Di Veroli, who was staying with friends. To stay locked in a room, with no news of the family, was more than they could bear.

Sometimes Enrico and his wife, Grazia, would walk arm in arm through the city.

With spring weather beginning to warm the city and Allied troops inching daily closer and closer to Rome, the future was beginning to look brighter. On the afternoon of April 25, 1944, Enrico Di Veroli was walking his wife back to the convent, when he heard someone call his name. "My mother, who was holding him by the arm, said she remembers feeling my father jump," Olga says. " 'Don't turn around,' my father said to her. 'Di Veroli, Di Veroli.' Finally, my father turned around and said: 'My name is Niccolata Rita' [the false name he was going by]. The man, who was with another guy, was a client of our store who had lost an arm in World War I. My father had loaned him a thousand lire. 'Enrico, don't play games with me. Don't you remember, you gave a thousand lire of merchandise on credit. I'm supposed to pay you back one hundred lire a day. See, here's your signature on this receipt.' My father said: 'That's okay, it can wait until the end of the war.' But the man said, 'You have to come with us.' My father said: 'Don't hurt me, I have a family.' 'What hurt? We're just taking you in for questioning.' "

As they dragged off Enrico Di Veroli, a fracas ensued. His wife was thrown to the ground, knocked unconscious, and lost several teeth. Luckily, several women who were watching the incident came to her aid. Because the melée occurred in front of the convent where the Di Verolis were staying, the women, without knowing where she lived, picked her off the pavement and carried her to the convent.

When Olga and her sister Flora returned that evening, they found their mother in a strange state. "She was laughing and laughing. My sister said: 'Look, how happy mother is. Maybe something has happened, maybe Silvia [their older sister] has been freed.' 'No,' I said, 'I don't think she's happy. She seems nervous.' We finally learned that my father had been arrested. We tried to shake Mama a bit, but we couldn't get her to stop laughing. So we went up to a woman hiding in the convent whom we knew to be Jewish, also. We explained what had happened, and said, 'My mother seems half-crazy.' The woman came and gave my mother a hard slap across the face. Mamma stopped laughing and started crying.

"That evening the Mother Superior came up to me and said, 'Listen, Carmela' (that was the false name I went under), 'you should have told me you

were Jewish.' I said: 'If you want us to go, we'll leave immediately.' 'No, it's not that, we just need to know so that if they were to come for you, we can take you down a secret passageway.' They were incredibly good and courteous to us. After that episode they even insisted on bringing us our meals in our room so that we would be seen as little in public as possible. They were afraid of informants."

After her father's arrest, Olga and her family developed contacts in the Rome prison that allowed them to keep up a clandestine correspondence. "We had a system of communication, slipping notes inside the clean laundry or inside the packages of food," Olga says. "Using the same method, he was able to send us back a couple of notes."

Particularly striking in Enrico Di Veroli's letters is the degree of concern for others at a time when he himself was in constant mortal danger.

May 15, 1944

Dear Grazina,
You cannot imagine how much pleasure I had receiving your letter of the 12th and in receiving goods news and knowing that you all are well.

I beg you not to worry, that I am well and I feel strong and full of courage because I have hope that all will end soon and we will be able to embrace one another in perfect health.

Although full of spelling and punctuation mistakes, the letters are written in a shrewdly constructed code in order to avoid identifying friends and relatives. At one point he writes: "I hope that Misses Michelina Rita and Gianna Rita study hard and never tire, succeed at their exams, and listen to the advice of Professor Resciude and pass their exams." The Misses "Michelina and Gianna Rita" are in fact his sons, Michele and Gianni; the last name "Rita" is the false name the family had been going under. The "Professor Resciude" to whom he refers was a fictional invention; although he spelled it incorrectly, the word "resciudde" in Judeo-romanesque dialect means "beat it" or "get lost"; so that by urging his sons to "study hard" and "listen to the advice of Professor Resciude" Enrico Di Veroli was telling them to lie low and stay out of sight.

His concerns run from the practical ("Don't send cooked meat, it goes bad, send hard-boiled eggs instead") to salutations to friends he has left behind: "Give my greetings to all those who ask of me. . . ." His most strongly desired wish is that his family write him immediately [adding a second "b" to the word "subito" (immediately) to stress its importance]: "I beg you to answer me immediately so that I can be at peace."

On May 20 the Allies finally broke the stalemate at Monte Cassino and began the final offensive that would soon culminate in the liberation of Rome. But the day after Cassino fell, the Germans loaded 281 Jews into a train headed for the detention camp at Fossoli. Prisoner number 175 on the list was Enrico Di Veroli.

Two weeks later, on June 4, when Rome was liberated, Enrico Di Veroli was at the transit camp in Fossoli, near Modena—an area that would have to wait another nine months for the end of the war. On June 16, from Fossoli, Enrico managed to get another letter to his wife, through a Catholic friend in Rome.

Written a few days before his deportation, this letter is much more full of foreboding: "Up till now I have been at Fossoli, and we do not know what fate awaits us." Nonetheless, he takes great pains to reassure his family and keep them from worrying: "I want you to know that I am well and that I am ready for whatever the future holds in store." And yet, at moments, he writes with the stoic concern of a man trying to wrap up his affairs and take leave of the world. "I beg you all to be good, calm and to always get along, and to take the best possible care of Mamma, to pick up the stuff from Sig. Riso and that of all the others . . . so that when I return I find all in good order, and if by some chance I should be delayed a bit not to despair and to remain calm."

Even at this late date, he does not appear to have grasped the full extent of the Germans' "final solution." Writing hopefully of his eldest daughter, Silvia, arrested with her husband and children on October 16, he says: "I have had news that Silvia and all the others are in Theresienstadt in Czechoslovakia and that we can write her through the International Red Cross."

One of Enrico Di Veroli's principal concerns is that the family find ways of thanking and repaying the Catholic friends who have helped them in this time of calamity. He explains how one friend, a certain Gasparini, went all the way from Rome to Fossoli in order to give him a thousand lire. "Be sure," he urges his family, "never to forget as long as you should live the great and good action of this man . . . in fact I beseech you as soon as you have received this letter to go and thank him and repay him all I owe him."

Ten days later, a convoy of roughly one thousand Jews left Fossoli for Auschwitz. Only 275 were admitted to the camp to work as laborers; the other 750—including Enrico Di Veroli—were gassed immediately. Out of the group of one thousand, only 32 would return after the war.

L ike his Uncle Attilio and Uncle Enrico and their families, Michele Di Veroli (Umberto's son) was forced to find a new hiding place after the bombing of the San Benedetto church.

"I moved to the Angelo Mai Institute [a religious institute belonging to the Catholic church], where about a hundred Jews were hiding. And from there I went to the Palazzo Laterense, through Monsignor Tercole, a friend of my father's. It was not easy to get into the Palazzo Laterense. Because my father had lots of Catholic friends I was always fortunate to be able to find hiding places in churches and convents. My Uncle Attilio had much more trouble.

"They needed to be certain about the people they let in to the Palazzo Laterense. Because there were a lot of important Italian soldiers and antifascists there, people who became important political figures after the liberation. They even had a radio transmitter there. This radio transmitted war news to the Americans and the English. I sometimes had to do guard duty at night on the roof because they were constantly watching out for a possible raid by the Germans the way they did at the basilica of Saint Paul's [which the Germans broke into, arresting numerous Jews and antifascists]."

Michele (Umberto's son) was posing as a Neapolitan student named Michele Capuiano who had been stranded in Rome behind the battle lines. "I had gotten the false documents through friends who knew someone in one of the government ministries. The people at the convent never tried to convert me. I can only say good things about the people there. They tried to help in every way possible.

In the convent at Via Cicerone after her father's arrest, Olga, her sister, and mother spent the remaining days of the German occupation listening to the artillery shells coming closer to Rome and trying to avoid a last minute capture.

Of the original nucleus of thirty-three Di Veroli family members—the four brothers and their children—some ten were either deported to Auschwitz or killed at the Ardeatine Caves. Giuditta and Silvia [sisters] were the only two to return. There were 353 Di Verolis listed in the 1938 census; 77 were deported during the German occupation, 8 returned. Not included in this total are the five grandchildren and the two sons-in-law who were also arrested and deported. Nor does it include the dozens of others cousins, aunts, uncles, cousins-once-and-twice removed on the maternal side of the family. The Di Verolis, however, were in no way exceptional. Out of the estimated eight thousand Jews present in Rome at the moment of the German occupation, about a fourth were captured. Of the 2,091 deportees, 1,067 were men, 743 were women, and 281 were children. Of the 2,091 deported, roughly one in twenty survived: 73 men and 28 women.

Night Witches, Snipers and Laundresses

In its desperate battle to fight off the advancing Germans, the Soviet Union called on its women to play as active and probably more wide-ranging a role as its men. John Erickson records the military and civilian efforts during the Great Patriotic War.

John Erickson

John Erickson is the director of the Centre for Defence Studies at the University of Edinburgh, and author of the forthcoming Blood, Bread and Steel: Soviet Society at War 1941–45 *for Yale University Press.*

As the Soviet regimental commander approached, the young girl sentry in oversize boots and overlong men's trousers guarding parked aircraft cried out in a mixture of panic and confusion: 'Would you please stop! Who goes there? I really must ask you to excuse me, I am going to shoot.' Years after that wartime· incident, senior pilot Guards Lieutenant Antonina Bondareva recalled in mock despair the hapless *naivetée* of the sentry. Yet in its own way it illustrates the enormous burden placed on all Soviet women, young and old alike, during the war years, a saga which has yet to be told in all its astonishing variety and harrowing individual detail. Tragedy abounds. I certainly recall hearing German veterans of the Eastern Front, tough and battle-tested, describe their numbed shock at coming upon dead Soviet women soldiers on the battlefield.

What is undoubtedly strange and not a little reprehensible is the lack of attention which not only Soviet historians but others have paid to this extraordinary dimension of the Soviet war effort, though much credit must go to Svetlana Meksievich for· carrying her tape-recorder around city, town and village to uncover firsthand evidence of the scale and scope of the wartime experience of Soviet women. A little later Valentina Galagan published *Ratnyi podvig zhenshchin v gody Velikoi Otechestvennoi volny* (1986), a rather more academic but nevertheless illuminating study of Soviet womanhood at war.

Writing in the *International Herald Tribune* on January 11th, 1990, under the impress of recent American operations in Panama, Edwin M. Yoder Jr. brought up the question of combat roles for women with an obvious *frisson de terreur,* fearful of what might transpire should it be affirmed that 'women are as expendable in war as men'. While the combat role, actual and potential, of women is a matter of great and growing controversy, wherein Soviet experience has a singular relevance, this should not wholly obscure deeper investigation by historians, sociologists, psychologists, indeed the medical profession, into the basic workings of the wartime 'home fronts' where, perhaps even more than battlefield performance, myth and reality collide and conflict quite violently, with the 'heroic image' yielding ultimately to the seemingly humdrum and the mundane.

Yet, paradoxically, the mundane hides drama all its own and screens dreadful anguish with so many profiles of coercion, conformity and choice inextricably bound up with the social consequences of total war and searing 'barbarisation'. Daily necessity looms large. For example, little of a 'heroic' image is conjured up by young Soviet wartime women soldiers finding themselves in front-line units unable to find suitable clothing for them, until the girls cut the bottoms out of kit-bags to provide makeshift skirts. What is gruesomely stark is that the women and young girls serving as 'front-line medics' with rifle battalions suffered losses second only to those of the fighting troops themselves; proportionately, losses among women at the front were heavier than among men—though exact figures are very hard to come by.

Certainly Soviet women were no strangers to 'defence duties' before the war. In 1927 War Commissar Voroshilov emphasised, as did many others, the need for women to train in order to participate actively in 'defence'. Nor were they strangers to backbreaking work, not merely domestic but in factories and on the land: at the beginning of 1940 women made up no less than 41 per cent of the labour force. The war brought them into both the factory and the front-line. No less than 800,000 women saw active service on the battlefronts, not just as nurses but as combat pilots, navigators, snipers, gunners, paratroops, tank crews, as front-line 'laundresses' in field bath/laundry units, cooks, sappers (the latter with a low-life expectancy clearing mines), while in a ghastly war of unparalleled barbarism women of all ages played a prominent role in the partisan movement.

Behind them (or beside them) women of the home front tended to what passed for the home fires, worked in munitions factories, enrolled as air-raid wardens, marched with the labour squads conscripted to dig anti-tank ditches, suffered

From *History Today,* July 1990, pp. 29-35. Reproduced by kind permission of History Today, Ltd., 83-84 Berwick Street, London W1V 3PJ, England.

in the frantic, improvised mass evacuations eastwards, with families split and dispersed, struggled desperately with the ghastly privations imposed by the siege of Leningrad (and elsewhere), vowing not to surrender. They also came latterly under punitive wartime legislation which 'militarised' labour, where absenteeism was equated with desertion and met with the ferocity of court-martial sentences or NKVD military tribunals. Absence without leave, even for hours, from a war-industry enterprise was punishable—and was punished—by five to eight years imprisonment. A certain Mrs Golubeva was sentenced in July 1944 to six years imprisonment for 'desertion' from her place of work. Locksmith Mrs Chadayeva was also found guilty of 'unauthorised absence' and was put before the military tribunal of the Upper-Volga Basin. The subsequent application of military disciplinary codes to workers in transport and communications (signals), though extra-legal, was draconian in both intent and practice.

Women turned miners, welders, machine operators, painters—like the 'special women's brigade' which, to speed the guns to the front, painted the artillery pieces on the flat-cars as they were trundled by rail to the war zone. History in its own right peeps out from time to time in these circumstances. The first ever woman engine driver in the Soviet Union was Maria Meksandrovna Arestova who took over the foot-plate in 1931 amidst much cheering and flag-waving. When war came, she drove special, highly dangerous 'flying column' trains up to the front, exposed to *Luftwaffe* strafing attacks aimed directly at the locomotive. Her husband acted as senior co-driver, and their wartime home was a heated goods-van housing their tiny son.

Severe, sustained and gruelling hardship fell on the women who worked the land. At the beginning of the war the Red Army stripped men, machines and horses from the collective farms, tractors turned into gun-tows, men mobilised for the infantry divisions leaving the farms literally powerless. To provide that power women were not infrequently harnessed to the ploughs, half a dozen at a time. Women formed special 'tractor brigades' to operate the few precious machines, and the combine-harvesters, learning not merely to drive but to coddle the machines in the absence of spare parts and a dearth of lubricants. Not until late in the

war were some new machines forthcoming but the 'battle for bread' was critically important. Suffice it to say that thanks to women labourers assisted by the very young and the elderly, Russia was at least fed, not grandly nor even satisfyingly, but fed.

The deterioration of conditions inflicted grim impoverishment. The State, the Party and the NKVD, rigorously enforced grain collections. Shortages were compounded by mistaken policies, while the army continued to drain off labour—including at least 1 million women. The land suffered the chaos of the evacuation of 1941, the ravages of German occupation and then the bouts of 're-collectivisation' as the Red Army recovered Soviet territory. The labour force continued to fall, down to 4 million men and 11 million women in 1943. For exhausting labour and fulfilling mandatory 'labour days', the peasant household received 'payment in kind' (if and when it was available)—200 grammes of grain, 100 grammes of potatoes (100 grammes = 4 ounces, in effect, one potato and a cupful of grain). Not a single tractor went to the farms between 1941–42. As 'militarisation' bit into the industrial labour force, on the land the penalties for failing to meet the 'labour days' requirement and the mandatory requisitions of grain meant the punitive hand of the NKVD—or a deadlier threat, taking away the vital 'private plots'.

The women fighting with the partisan movement or working with the underground resistance, faced the prospect of death or betrayal and arrest, the way to a martyrdom of torture beginning with the horrible 'Fascist manicure'. Though women and girls played a large part in the partisan movement, only one woman—Aleksandra Zakharova—became a commissar of a partisan unit, the 225th Gomel Region Partisan Regiment, the commissar being the heart of the units, entrusted with both party-political and military duties. For so many others fate and German rule with its forced deportations consigned them to the *Reich* as handmaidens to the *Herrenvolk,,* a slave-labour system for house, farm or factory which ripped families apart, igniting a passionate hatred of German domination, whatever the early promises which beguiled not a few in the first days of occupation.

Not only the advent of German rule but the huge, hastily improvised mass evacuation into the Soviet hinterland

early in the war brought fresh suffering. The flood of evacuees and a relocated labour force brought the near collapse of housing and transport and chaos in feeding arrangements. Factory canteens were clogged, and housing—always a chronic problem—became desperate as people poured into the Volga region, the Urals and Siberia. In September 1941, the government reacted to this mounting crisis, assigning 200 million rubles for housing in the east, setting up a separate commissariat for building programmes, but houses do not grow on trees. New factories were built at frantic speed in the east or were re-assembled after evacuation. Families dug earth shelters as 'homes' or used derelict barracks. In one giant tank factory 8,500 workers and their families lived in mere holes in the ground, or in 'worker settlements' which housed 15,000—yet had only six stand-pipes for water, no furniture and no fuel for heating (in a Siberian winter).

Wartime stringency bit most savagely in the Soviet Union. Sugar, jam, matches, knitwear and meat vanished from sight. Unbelievably ghastly conditions prevailed in Leningrad, ringed by German guns and troops, where the first deaths from starvation occurred in the late autumn of 1941. Here heroic myth and an unbearable reality met and fused, creating the unrelieved horror of a siege filled with medieval nightmares. Leningrad women produced vile jellies from sheep-gut as food: for baking, in the absence of any vegetable oils, an emulsion of sunflower oil, soap stock and cornflour was used. Everything remotely edible was used, even the scrapings of wallpaper paste. It is no exaggeration to say that not only did the Leningraders tighten their belts, they ate them.

Sieges proliferated. In Odessa, also besieged, women dished out the meagre water ration. In Moscow siege conditions prevailed for many months, with the breakdown of transport in the winter of 1941–42 bringing added hardship. Only 30 per cent of the meat ration and 34 per cent of the sugar ration was 'honoured'.

Not that rationing was new, bread rationing having been introduced in 1929 and rationing for grain, meat, herring and sugar in 1932; but in 1935 foodstuffs had came off the ration. Soviet women had to struggle anew, shuttling between home, factory, air-raid post, digging defensive positions, coping with differentiated rationing systems—'bread norms', between 800 grammes and 1.2 kilo per day for 'special categories' (miners, workers in heavy industry), industrial workers 500 grammes, the remainder 400 grammes, children and expectant mothers 3–400 grammes. Communal feeding lightened the burden a little, but for 'shopping' the house-wife had to go to the peasant *kolkhoz* markets, to buy but to pay: in 1942 a kilo of grain cost 53 roubles 80 kopek (1 rouble 88 kopek in 1940), a litre of milk 38 roubles (2 roubles in 1940), a kilo of mutton 196 roubles. It is to the credit of the Soviet trade unions that they worked strenuously to bring some order into factory supply committees, to organise communal feeding, to combat black-marketeering and to check on the illegal use of ration cards. In 1944 things eased somewhat with a freer sale of foodstuffs and some consumer goods, again at higher prices in the 'off-the-ration markets'— *kommercheskaya torgovlya*. Greater use of fish and a little more meat lifted some of the gloom, but we have yet to hear in full the saga of the indomitable Soviet housewife.

It was in 1942, the year of looming catastrophe as the German armies drove deeper and deeper, coiling round Stalingrad, that the State Defence Committee (the GKO) ordered mass mobilisation for Soviet women. Long before this the *Komsomol*, the Young Communist League, had been put on a war footing. Many young women volunteered for front-line duty, much to the consternation of the flustered, overworked mobilisation and recruiting centres the military commissariats (*voenkoms*). Infused with genuine patriotic fervour and urged on by the sights and sounds of universal destruction about them, the young marched to war and to a massacre of the innocents which scythed down the seventeen to twenty-one year olds.

Very often it became a question of the 'long and the short and the tall' in this muster of young women—'lined up by height, Polina Nazdrecheva heard the officer say "And who is this Thumbelina? What are you going to do here? Perhaps you had better go back to your mum and grow a bit bigger".' This same 'Thumbelina' duly went on to become a highly-decorated front-line veteran. Thousands of Thumbelinas went to war.

Junior Lieutenant Aleksandra Boiko graduated from the Chelyabinsk Armoured Technical School with her husband and proceeded to become the commander of an JS-122 (Joseph Stalin-122) heavy tank, the sole woman Red Army commander of a heavy tank, with her husband acting as driver-mechanic. However, other girls crewed the medium T-34 tanks. Machines also dominated the lives of women on the land, the precious, ageing, quirky temperamental tractors— 'Work was hard. We slept three or four hours a day. For a long time we warmed up the engines with naked flames, strictly against the rules . . . lubricants and fuel were rationed. You answered with your head for every drop just as for every melted bearing.' The same women and girls in the 'tractor brigades' also donated large sums from their wages to the Soviet Defence Fund, which over four years reached the staggering total of 94.5 billion roubles, the sum of donations, proffered wages and gifts, women surrendering jewellery of considerable value, not least diamonds worth thousands.

Dry as they are, statistics furnish a certain illumination. The young women of the Young Communist League, the *Komsomol*, provided 43,662 of their members to the Red Army in 1942, with 8,683 at the front and 34,979 in the various military districts. In a matter of two years those figures had shot up to 247,551 at the front, 85,921 in the districts. Both within and without the *Komsomol* women and girls played an increasingly important role in the anti-aircraft defences, crewing the guns and operating passive defences—more than 300,000 women all told. As for that distinction between 'young girl' and 'woman soldier', while it may be hard to describe it faithfully, the Red Army had its own way—cutting off the girls' plaits, the sign and symbol of the advance into military womanhood (with many a quiet tear shed).

As he war drew on and as casualties mounted, 'women-soldiers' appeared in greater numbers in the Red Army's front-line divisions, with an average of 2–3,500 in each army. In 1944 on the 1st Belorussian Front, about to smash into the formidable Army Group Centre, some 3,000 women served with the front's armies. In January 1944, in the offensive to relieve Leningrad, 22,000 women served at the front. More than 20,000 women served on the 2nd Belorussian Front (3,636 officers, 5,081 sergeants). The Soviet navy mustered 25,000 women. The partisan movement directly involved at least 100,000 women, including the woman doctor enticed with a literal 'sweetener' (the chocolate is-sued to paratroops) to go for parachute training and drop behind the lines. Women provided 41 per cent of the Red Army's doctors and 43 per cent of front-line medical personnel who, working under fire, brought in not only the wounded but also their weapons. 'I was my mother's darling and had never left the city before being appointed junior medical officer at a mortar battery. Well, what I went through . . .', a far from uncommon comment from a Soviet woman doctor.

By my own reckoning, to produce yet another statistic, some eighty-eight women were awarded the highest Soviet decoration, Hero of the Soviet Union—drawn from pilots, scouts, partisans, machine-gunners, snipers, tommy-gunners, tank crews, medical assistants, nurses, radio operators. Soviet woman served in some of the most dangerous operational roles and not a few famous names abound as a consequence, especially amongst the pilots, navigators, mechanics and armourers of the all-women 46th Guards Taman Women's Air Regiment ('Taman' being a battle honour), flying their 'swallows' (the *Lastochki*), wooden U-2 biplanes (like Tiger Moths), unarmed until 1944, when they acquired a defensive machine-gun.

Carrying out low-level bombing and strafing attacks, flying largely by night and stirring up the German defences, wearied German troops nicknamed these women fliers the 'night witches'. But again a heavy toll was exacted and strain told on the survivors. 'After a mission an aircraft stayed on the ground for a few minutes and then was back in the air. Imagine how our girl armourers worked! During those few minutes they had to load the bomb racks with four bombs— 400 kilos—by hand . . . the body reorganised itself to the extent that we ceased to be women throughout the war . . . we had no female functions at all. We all smoked . . . I smoked too, it made you feel a little calmer.' Thus Alexandra Semyonova Popova, combat pilot who flew 365 missions, her last over Berlin in 1945.

Red Army women snipers established a special place for themselves but their fate too was often pitiful. One captured German officer, astounded by the fact so many of his men had been killed by head wounds only, asked to see the marksman who was so deadly with a rifle. The Soviet commander could not oblige him, for the 'marksman', girl sniper Sasha

Shlyakova had just been killed in a sniper duel, betrayed by her sole concession to femininity, a red scarf.

The doyenne of Red Army women snipers, all graduates of sniper school, was Nina Pavlovna Petrova, who was forty-eight when she first went to the front, notched up 122 kills and, as an instructor to Red Army men, became 'the sniper's Mum', teaching her trade. She died in a truck crash in February 1945. Less dramatic but equally spine-chilling were the duties of the women Red Army sappers in field engineering companies like that commanded by Lieutenant Stanislava Volkov. When the Soviet general bellowed for the sapper commander to report, he brushed aside a grubby, dishevelled, grime-streaked girl soldier, only to be told that he was indeed looking at the platoon commander, none other. She duly cleared the mines for his advancing tanks.

All fell rightly heir to decorations and awards, all save the laundresses, tubbing, scrubbing and rubbing away in field laundries with the thunder of the battlefield rolling about them. Organised into detachments, with their own political officers, including one famously formidable laundresses' commissar, they finally got campaign medals and justifiably so, for as Aleksandra Mishutina said, 'if a soldier is to fight well, he must be clothed, shod, fed, his clothes must be washed . . .' And the Red Army did fight well.

With the coming of victory, or the prospect of it, relief came mixed with sadness. The liberated areas were devastated, houses burned, gutted, mined, schools ruined, orphans in need of care and mothering. Anti-epidemic measures were sorely needed, the campaign against tuberculosis intensified and the 350,000 infectious cases in the liberated areas treated. Housewives did what they could in towns and villages turned into moonscapes by German demolition squads in full retreat, dynamiting and booby-trapping. Wartime ruination pulverised 1,170 towns, 70,000 villages and 7 million dwellings.

While the housewives sought some normality, post-war life for the front-line women proved to be harsh and unyielding. Many hoped to return from the front as 'marriageable girls', only to see themselves prematurely aged and grey-haired. Those badly wounded hid themselves and their infirmities, like the legless lady who shunned the world, mangled as she had been on the battlefield. Others lived as best they might with persistent traumas or, like one grandmother, never spoke of her days at war.

There is much yet to be learned of Soviet women at war, much which would tell us a great deal more not only about individual behaviour, motivation, morale, response to maximum stress and the mechanisms of the family but also more about the fundamental nature of Soviet society, its past, present and possible future.

In sum, the investigation of Soviet women at war is not an excursion into 'heroic imagery' but specifically, even clinically, an evaluation of heroism in all its forms, the dramatic, the self-sacrificing, the compassionate and, so very far from being least, the plain, dogged, dutiful humdrum—embracing the washerwoman and the machine-gunner alike.

FOR FURTHER READING:

There is no standard work either in English or in Russian which deals with Soviet women at war. Svetlana Alekseivech, *War's Unwomanly Face* (Progress, Moscow, 1988) is a translation of *U voiny—ne zhenskoe litso* . . . V. Ya. Galagan's *Ratnyi podvig zhenshchin v gody Velikoi Otechestvennoi voiny* (The martial feat of women in the Great Patriotic War) was published in Kiev in 1986. On Soviet women bomber and fighter pilots, there is a popular memoir, M. P. Chechneva, *Nebo ostaetsya nashim* (The sky stayed ours) (Moscow, 1976) of which there are some partial translations. Harrison Salisbury, *The Siege of Leningrad* (London 1986), has much graphic detail about life under siege, while the English-language *Soviet Soldier,* has scattered material—see No. 1 (1990), on military traffic policewoman Karima Gaifutdinova and Junior Sergeant Lidiya Spivak, also a woman MP.

1945

Ryszard Kapuściński

*Ryszard Kapuściński, the Polish journalist
and writer, is the author of* Shah of Shahs
*(Harcourt Brace Jovanovich). Born in 1932,
he now lives in Warsaw. This essay was
translated by Klara Glowczewski.*

TODAY, when I go back in memory
to those years, I realize, not without
a certain surprise, that I remember better the beginning rather than the end of
the war. The beginning is clearly fixed
for me in time and place. I can easily re-
create its image because it has retained
all its coloring and emotional intensity.
It begins with my suddenly noticing
one day, in the clear azure sky of the
end of summer (and the sky in September 1939 was marvelously blue, without
a single cloud), somewhere very, very
high up, 12 glimmering silver points.
The entire bright, lofty dome of sky is
filled with a hollow, monotonous hum,
of a kind I've never heard before. I'm
seven years old, I'm standing in a
meadow, and staring at the points barely, barely moving across the sky.

Suddenly, nearby, at the edge of the
forest, there's a tremendous roar. I hear
bombs exploding with an infernal rack-
et. (That these are bombs I will learn
later, for at this moment I still don't
know that there is such a thing as a
bomb, the very concept is foreign to
me, a child from the sticks who doesn't
yet know about the radio or the movies,
doesn't know how to read or write, and
also hasn't heard of war and lethal
weapons.) I see gigantic fountains of
earth spraying upward. I want to run

toward this extraordinary spectacle; it
astounds and fascinates me. I have no
war experiences yet and cannot relate
into a single chain of causes and effects
these glistening silver airplanes, the
roar of the bombs, the plumes of earth
flying up to the height of trees, and my
imminent death. So I start to run toward the forest, in the direction of the
falling and exploding bombs. But a
hand grabs me from behind and throws
me to the ground. Stay down, I hear my
mother's trembling voice, don't move.
And I remember that my mother, pressing me to her, is saying something that
I don't yet know exists, whose meaning
I don't understand, and about which I
want to ask her: *that way is death.*

It's night and I'm sleepy, but I'm not
allowed to sleep. We have to leave, run
away. Where to, I don't know; but I do
understand that flight has suddenly become some kind of higher necessity,
some new form of life, because everyone is running away. All highways,
roads, even country paths, are jammed
with wagons, carts, and bicycles, with
bundles, suitcases, bags, buckets, with
terrified, helplessly wandering people.
Some are running away to the east, others to the west, north, south; they run
in all directions, circle, fall from exhaustion, sleep for a moment, then, summoning the rest of their strength, begin
anew their aimless journey. I must hold
my younger sister firmly by the hand.
We mustn't get lost, my mother warns;
but even without her telling me, I
sense that the world has suddenly become dangerous, foreign, and evil,
that one must be on one's guard.

I'm walking with my sister beside a
wagon. It's a simple ladder wagon,
lined with hay, and high up on the hay,
on a cotton sheet, lies my grandfather.
He cannot move; he is paralyzed. When
an air raid begins, the entire patiently
trudging and now suddenly panicked
throng dives into ditches, burrows into
bushes, drops down into the potato
fields. Only the wagon on which my
grandfather lies remains on the deserted road. He sees the airplanes flying at
him, sees them violently dip and take
aim at the abandoned wagon, sees the
fire of the weapons aboard, hears the
roar of the engines passing over his
head. When the planes disappear we
return to the wagon and my mother
wipes my grandfather's perspiring face.
Sometimes there are air raids several
times a day. After each one, perspira-
tion pours from my grandfather's
gaunt, tired face.

WE'RE entering an increasingly
gloomy landscape. There's smoke
on the horizon. We pass by deserted
villages, solitary, burned-out houses.
We pass battlefields strewn with abandoned war equipment, bombarded railway stations, overturned cars. It smells
of gun powder, and of burning, decom-
posing meat. Carcasses of horses are
everywhere. The horse—a large, defenseless animal—doesn't know how to
hide; during a bombardment it stands
motionless, waiting for death. There are
dead horses at every step, right in the
road, by the side in the ditch, further
away in the field. They're lying with
their legs up in the air, taunting the

world with their hooves. I don't see any dead people, for these are buried quickly; only horses, everywhere—black, bay, piebald, chestnut, as if this were not a people's war but a war of horses, as if it were they who waged among themselves a fight to the death, as if they were its only victims.

A hard, freezing winter comes. If people are badly off, they feel more keenly the chill of the environment, the cold is more piercing. For those who live in normal conditions, winter is but another season, a waiting for the spring, but for the poor and the unfortunate, it is a disaster, a catastrophe. And that first winter of the war was truly severe. In our apartment the stoves are cold, and a white, hoary frost covers the walls. There's nothing with which to heat the oven; we cannot buy fuel, and we cannot risk stealing it. For the theft of coal—death; for the theft of wood—death. Human life is now worth next to nothing: a lump of coal, a bit of wood.

WE HAVE nothing to eat. My mother stands for hours at the window; I can see her fixed stare. One can see people staring out into the street from many windows, as if they were counting on something, waiting for something. I roam around the backyards with a gang of boys; it's something between play and searching for something to eat. Sometimes the smell of cooking will come wafting through a door. Then one of my friends, Waldek, sticks his nose into the crack and hurriedly, feverishly, inhales the smell, stroking his stomach as if he were sitting at a richly laden table.

One day we hear that they'll be giving out candy in a store near the marketplace. Immediately we make a line— a long queue of cold and hungry children. It's afternoon, dusk is approaching. We stand in the frost all evening, all night, and the following day. We stand huddled together, hugging one another for warmth. Finally they open the store. But instead of candy each of us receives an empty metal container that once held some fruit drops (what happened to the candy, who took it, I don't know). Weak, numb from the cold, yet at this moment happy, I carry my booty home. It's valuable, because on the inside wall of the can there remains a residue of sugar. My mother heats some water and pours it into the can. We have a hot, sweet drink: our only nourishment in several days.

Then we're on the road again, traveling from Polesie, from our town Pińsk, west, because there, my mother says, in a village near Warsaw, is our father. He was on the front, was captured, escaped, and is now teaching in a small country school. Today, when we who during the war were children reminisce about that time and say "father," or "mother," we forget, because of the gravity of those words, that our mothers were young women and our fathers young men, that they desired each other very much, missed each other very much, wanted to be with each other. My mother, too, was a young woman then, so she sold everything she had in the house, rented a wagon, and we set out in search of my father. We found him by accident. As we were passing through a village called Sieraków, my mother suddenly cried out to a man crossing the street: Dziudek! It was my father.

From that day on we lived together in a tiny room without light or water. When it grew dark we went to sleep, for there wasn't even a candle. Hunger followed us here from Pińsk. I was constantly looking for something to eat, a crust of bread, a carrot, anything. One day my father, having no other choice, said in class: children, anyone who wants to come to school tomorrow must bring one potato. He didn't know how to trade, didn't know how to do business, he had no salary, so he realized he had only this one option. Some children brought a half, even a quarter. A whole potato was a great treasure.

NEAR MY village is a forest, and in this forest, near a settlement called Palmira, is a clearing. SS men carry out executions there. At first they shoot only at night, and we are awakened by hollow-sounding machine-gun volleys, repeated at even intervals. Later they also do it in daytime. They bring the condemned in covered, dark green trucks, and at the end of the convoy in an open truck rides the firing squad. Those from the squad are always in long coats, as if a long belted coat were an indispensable prop of the murder ritual. When a convoy passes, we, a group of country children, watch, hidden among the roadside bushes. In a moment, behind the cover of trees, something we are forbidden to look at will begin to happen. I can feel my flesh tingling, can feel myself trembling all over. With bated breath we wait for the volleys of gunfire. There they are. Then we hear individual shots. After a time the convoy returns to Warsaw. At the end, in the open truck, ride the SS men from the firing squad, smoking cigarettes and talking.

At night the partisans come. I can see their faces, pressed to the glass, as they appear suddenly at the window. I look at them as they sit at the table, always moved by the same thought: they can die today, they are as if marked by death. Of course we could all perish, but they boldly embrace that possibility, meet it face-on. They came once, as always, at night. It was autumn and raining. They spoke in whispers with my mother. (I hadn't seen my father in a month and wouldn't until the end of the war; he had gone into hiding.) We had to get dressed quickly and leave. There was a roundup in the area, and entire villages were being deported to the camps. We were to go to Warsaw, to a designated hideout. It was my first time in a big city, the first time I saw a trolley car, tall, multistoried buildings, rows of large stores. How we later found ourselves in the country again, I don't remember. It was some new village, on the other side of the Vistula. I remember only walking again next to a wagon and hearing the sand of a warm, country road sifting through the wheels' wooden spokes.

THROUGHOUT the entire war I dream of a pair of shoes. *To have shoes.* But how to get them? What did I have to do to have shoes? In the summer I walk barefoot and the soles of my feet are tough as leather. At the beginning of the war my father made me some shoes out of felt, but he's not a shoemaker and they look ill-shaped; besides, I've grown, and they're already too tight. I dream of strong, massive shoes with taps, shoes that make a loud, distinct sound as they strike the pavement. The fashion then was for boots. They were a symbol of masculinity, of strength. I could stare for hours at a pair of good-looking boots. I liked the luster of the leather, I liked to listen to its crunch. But it wasn't just a matter of the beauty of a good pair of shoes, of comfort. A good strong shoe was a symbol of prestige and power, a symbol of rule. A poor, torn shoe was a sign of degradation, the mark of a man stripped of all dignity, condemned to a subhuman existence. Having a good pair of shoes meant being strong, or simply *being*. But in those years all my dream shoes, which I encountered in the streets and roads, passed me by indifferently. I was left (thinking that I would remain thus forever) in my heavy wooden clogs covered with black tarpaulin, to which I tried, unsuccessfully, with the help of some greasy stuff, to impart a bit of luster.

In 1944 I became an altar boy. My priest was the chaplain of a field hospital. Rows of camouflaged tents stood hidden in a pine forest on the left bank of the Vistula. During the Warsaw uprising, and then later, when the January offensive began, there was feverish, exhausting activity here. From the front, which thundered and smoked nearby, arrived speeding ambulances bringing the wounded, who were often unconscious, piled up in haste and confusion one on top of the other, as if they were sacks of grain (only sacks dripping blood). The orderlies, themselves already half-dead with exhaustion, took out the wounded and laid them on the grass. Then, with a rubber hose, they sprayed them with a strong jet of cold water. Whichever of the wounded began to show signs of life they carried into the tent that housed the operating room. (In front of it, right on the ground, there was each day a fresh heap of amputated arms and legs.) Whoever did not move again they carried to an enormous grave at the back of the hospital. It was there, over that boundless tomb, that I stood for hours on end beside the priest, holding his breviary and aspersorium. I repeated after him the prayer for the dead. "Amen," hundreds of times a day, "Amen," in haste, for somewhere nearby, beyond the forest, the machine of death was working overtime. Until finally, one day, it grew empty and quiet. The rush of ambulances ceased, the tents disappeared (the hospital moved west), and in the forest only crosses remained.

And after? Now, as I write these pages for a book about my war years (a book I'll probably never write), I'm thinking about how its final pages would look, its end, its epilogue. What would it say about the end of the great war? Nothing, I think. I mean nothing definitive, nothing that would close the subject once and for all. Because in a certain but essential sense the war did not end for me in 1945, or even soon thereafter. In many ways something of it endures even today, because for those who live through it, war never, finally, ends. There is an African belief that someone really dies only when the last of those who knew and remembered him die, that someone (or something) ceases to exist when all bearers of memory leave this world. Something like this also happens with war.

Those who live through a war never free themselves from it. It remains within them like some sort of mental hump, a painful growth which even that excellent surgeon, time, will be unable to remove. Listen to a gathering of survivors, around a table, in the evening. It doesn't matter what they start out talking about. There can be a thousand beginnings, but there will be one end: remembering the war. These people, even in changed, peacetime circumstances, think in terms of its images, superimpose them on every new reality, with which they can no longer fully identify because that reality is of the present and they are possessed by the past, the constant returning to what they lived through and how they managed to live through it. Their thinking is an obsessively repeated retrospection.

BUT what does it mean to think in wartime images? It means seeing everything as existing in a state of extreme tension, as breathing cruelty and dread. For wartime reality is a world of extreme, Manichaean reduction, which erases all intermediate hues, gentle, warm, and limits everything to a sharp, aggressive counterpoint, to black and white, to the primordial struggle of two forces—good and evil. Nothing else on the battlefield! Only the good, in other words, us, and the bad, meaning everything that stands in our way, which appears to us, and which we lump into the sinister category of evil. The wartime image is saturated with the atmosphere of force, a physical, material, crackling, smoking, frequently erupting force, constantly attacking someone, brutally expressed in every gesture, in the sound of every footstep striking the pavement, of a rifle butt striking a skull. Force is the only criterion of value: only the strong counts, his reason, his shout, his fist—because conflict is resolved not through compromise, but by destroying the opponent. All this takes place in a climate of intensified emotion, exaltation, fury, passion, in which we feel constantly stunned, deafened, and— above all—threatened. We move about in a world full of hateful glances and clenched jaws, full of gestures and voices that terrify.

I thought for a long time that was the only world, that was how it looked, how life looked. For the war years coincided with my childhood and then with the start of maturity, of first understanding, of the birth of consciousness. It seemed to me that war, not peace, was the natural state, even the only state, the only form of existence; that roundups and executions, lies and shouts, contempt and hatred, were part of the natural and immemorial order of things, the content of life, the essence of being. So when the guns suddenly fell silent, when the roar of exploding bombs died away and suddenly there was quiet, I was astonished by it. I didn't know what it meant, what it was. I think that a grown-up, hearing this quiet, could say: hell is over. Finally peace has returned. But I did not remember what peace was. I was too young for that; when the war ended hell was all I knew.

THE YEARS passed, yet the war constantly reminded us of its presence. I lived in a city reduced to ashes, I climbed mountains of rubble, roved through a labyrinth of ruins. The school to which I went had no floors, no windows, no doors; everything had gone up in flames. We had no books, no notebooks. I still had no shoes. War as affliction, as want, as hardship, went on. I still had no home. The return home from the front is the most keenly felt symbol of war's end. *Tutti a casa!* But I could not go home, because what had been my home was now abroad, in another country. Once, after class, we were playing soccer in a nearby field. One of my friends, chasing the ball, ventured into some bushes. There was a terrible bang; we were thrown to the ground. He died from a mine that had been left there. War was still laying traps for us, it refused to surrender. Its victims hobbled along the streets leaning on wooden crutches, waved empty arm sleeves in the wind. Those who survived it, it tormented by night, reminding them of itself in bad dreams.

But war continued for us above all because of the fact that for five years it had shaped our young characters, our psyche, our mentality. It had tried to deform and ruin us, setting the worst examples, compelling us to ignominious behavior, letting loose the basest emotions. "War," wrote in those years the Polish philosopher Boleslaw Miciński, "warps not only the souls of those who try to oppose the invader." Yes, to come out of the war meant to cleanse oneself internally, and above all to cleanse oneself of hatred. But how many really tried? And how many were successful? It was a process, in any event, exhausting and long, which could not take place overnight; the wounds from that conflagration, the psychological and moral wounds, were truly deep.

When there's talk of 1945 . . . I'm irritated by the phrase one often hears in reference to it: the joy of victory. What joy? So many people died. Millions of bodies were buried. Thousands lost arms and legs, lost sight and hearing, lost sanity. Each death is a misfortune. No, the end of every war is sad: yes, we survived, but at what a cost! War is proof that man, as a thinking and feeling being, failed the test, let himself down, was defeated.

When there's talk of 1945 . . . some-time in the summer of that very year, my aunt, who through some miracle survived the Warsaw uprising, brought out to us in the country her son Andrzej, born during the uprising. Today he is a 40-year-old man. When I look at him I think—how long ago all that was! How many generations have already been born who have no idea what war is! But those who survived should bear witness. Bear witness in the name of those who fell by their side, and often in their place. Bear witness about what the camps were, the extermination of the Jews, the destruction of Warsaw and Wroclaw. Is this easy? No. We who survived know how difficult it is to convey the truth about it to those for whom, happily, it is an unfamiliar experience. We know how language fails us, words fail us; how all that, at bottom, cannot be conveyed; how often we feel helpless. (Once someone said to me in Chicago: "They took him to Auschwitz? But why did he agree? Why didn't he get a lawyer?")

Still, despite these difficulties and limitations, of which we must be aware, we should speak. Because talking about all that does not divide but unites, allows us to establish threads of understanding, threads of community. The dead admonish us. They transmitted something important to us, and we must be responsible. To the degree that we are able, we should oppose everything that could again give rise to war, to crime, to catastrophe. Because we who have survived war know how it begins, whence it comes. We know that it comes not only from bombs and rockets. We know that it comes also, perhaps above all, from fanaticism and from pride, from stupidity and from contempt, from ignorance and from hatred. That it feeds on all that, that on that and from that it grows.

When there's talk of 1945 . . . I think of those who were no longer there.

When there's talk of 1945 . . .

Wild passions have gone to sleep
And rash acts;
Love of God, love of man,
Quietly revives in us.
                                    —J.W. Goethe, *Faust*

If only. If only.

The War Europe Lost

Ronald Steel

September 1939. For a few a searing memory. For most a dim recollection or a date in a history book. The Luftwaffe spreading death and destruction from the air, Hitler's Panzer divisions slicing through a hapless Poland. Britain and France, having refused a year earlier to help a defensible country, Czechoslovakia, come to the aid of an indefensible one. World War II is under way.

Forty years have passed, and yet the event has not been put into perspective. We are still uncertain as to what it means. Young Germans, not even born when the war began, are only now learning the truths that their elders preferred not to think about, learning of the Holocaust from a commercial television program. The evil that was once unspeakable has now become historic and, judging from the current spate of books and films about Hitler, dramatically entertaining.

Unlike World War I, which was fought entirely in Europe and whose consequences were largely confined there, the second war was truly a world war, one that undermined the authority of the vanquished European states and broke their imperial hold on the colonial world. In this sense the consequences of the war were at least as great, perhaps greater, outside Europe as within. A world centered on Europe and defined in terms of it—the "Near East," the "Far East," the "New World"—shifted in perspective as Europe's hold on its colonies and clients was broken.

The demise, or at least the precipitous decline, of Europe itself as a power center and arbiter of the world's destiny was an event few could have predicted. Hitler's attempt to unify the continent in a Pax Germanica had cataclysmic consequences. It made Europe the instrument of the two victorious flanking powers, America and Russia, and destroyed the political and moral authority of the European state system. Europe, having been the predatory power, became the quarry, the object of others' diplomacy rather than the prime mover. One of the great unintended effects—and surely one of the most ironic—of World War II was to end the hegemony of Europe in the very act of trying to assert it.

Europe may rise again as a political power. But it will be in very different form. And such revival can find its impetus only in an attempt to regain what has so incontestably been lost—lost not only to America and Russia, but, as hardly needs to be underlined, to colonial areas Europe once held in thrall. This condition has become so accepted that few anymore think it remarkable that the value of the pound sterling should be dependent on Arab deposits in British banks.

Although Europe indeed lost much as a result of World War II, it gained a great deal—perhaps even more on balance. It gained liberation from its own colonies; liberation from the costly and often bloody pursuit of empire; liberation from the deadly rivalries of a state system perpetually out of balance because a unified Germany was simply too big and too powerful to contain. One of the few happy results of the war was the division of Germany, a division that solved the problem, temporarily at least, of how it would be possible to create a European balance Germany would neither dominate nor try to overturn. This development, most Germans would agree, has been as desirable for them as for their neighbors. It has provided an answer to the dilemma first posed a century ago when Bismarck created a Reich under Prussian dominance. What was achieved by the sword in 1870 was undone by the sword in 1945.

Thus it can be said that the result of World War II, unintended though it may have been, was to save Europe from itself. Europe, as a political entity, lost the war it had brought on itself. America and Russia expanded to a global scale in quest of a balance that was no longer possible to maintain within Europe itself. The successor powers, America and Russia, not only gained control over Europe, but to protect their newfound role also developed a vested interest in the continued division of Europe. A divided Europe is of no harm to either superpower. A unified Europe, either allied to one of them or standing between them, represents an enormous and potentially threatening change in the world political balance.

Thus, looking back from the perspective of 40 years, we can see World War II not only as a human tragedy, as all wars are, but as a political lesson. The war itself resulted from the attempt to resolve the German question. This problem had been left hanging ever since the Treaty of Versailles 20 years earlier, in 1919. World War I, for all its carnage, resolved nothing. It neither gave Germany the mastery of Europe, as the Kaiser and his generals hoped, nor removed Germany's power to seek that mastery once again. It could be argued that, if the United States had not entered the European war in 1917, the Allies would have been obliged to agree to a compromise peace giving Germany hegemony over Eastern Europe. Such a compromise in turn probably would have allowed Kerensky's parliamentary regime to have survived in Russia and avoided the conditions within Germany that allowed Hitler to come to power in 1933.

A concern with the European power balance is what brought the United States into the Second World War, as into the first one. That concern was twofold, although we tend to forget the second part. It was, first, that Europe not fall under the control of an aggressive power hostile to the United States; and, second,

4. MODERNISM AND TOTAL WAR

that Europe not be dominated by *any* single power. The reason for the second concern is simply that a unified Europe with a single political will inevitably would have needs and ambitions different from, and even hostile to, those of the United States.

The sadistic brutality and maniacal racial practices of Nazi Germany gave a moral patina, so far as Britain and America were concerned, to what was essentially a dynastic conflict. The United States, like Britain, was not drawn into World War II because it found Nazi evil insupportable. Had Hitler confined his genocide within the German frontiers fixed at Versailles, the democratic nations would have done no more to stop him than they did to stop his latter-day admirer, Idi Amin. Rather it was his attempt to overturn the European balance by force, to gain control of the continent, that brought Britain and France, and ultimately the United States and Russia, into belated alliance against him.

Thus it is worth remembering that the last European war, whose 40th anniversary we note this fall, was not about freedom versus slavery, but about more mundane considerations of the balance of power. The character of the Nazi regime, appalling and inhuman though it was, was not the question at issue. The question was whether that regime should be allowed to impose its authority by force of arms upon all of Europe. When that objective moved from the abstract to the verge of attainment, the United States set up the conditions by which it was drawn into the European war.

It is well to remember anniversaries like the current one, but there is danger in overdrawing or misunderstanding their significance. World War II is not the cold war. Soviet Russia is not Nazi Germany. Angola is not republican Spain. History does not repeat itself. The person who overlearns its "lessons" is condemned to relive its chastisements. Conditions change, and so do alliances. If, as Palmerston said, nations have no allies, only interests, the definition of those interests changes with time and circumstance.

What happened on the plains of Poland 40 years ago represented the last attempt to resolve the German problem within a strictly European context. It was a "world" war only as a result of its unintended consequences. That situation cannot recur because Europe has lost the mastery of its fate—precisely as a result of that war for the mastery of Europe. The slogans of World War II—"appeasement," "isolation," "neutrality"—are of no more value today than that war's antiquated tanks and Flying Fortresses.

196

The August Revolution

Martin Malia

The new Russian Revolution of August 1991 has now won out over the heritage of the first Russian Revolution of October 1917. Begun in 1989 with the emergence of a democratic opposition to communism led by Andrei Sakharov and launched into the broad light of day with Boris Yeltsin's election as Russian president last June, this revolution reached a climax in the popular explosion ignited by the failed August coup. The Leninist regime born of the successful October coup seventy-four years earlier collapsed within three days. To paraphrase Marx on the coup of Louis Napoleon, the "Soviet experiment," begun in tragedy, thus ended in farce: with Yanayev substituting for Lenin, Yazov for Trotsky—and Gorbachev for Kerensky. But the present drama also produced a tough new hero, Yeltsin, who together with his colleagues might, this time, bring about a happier ending.*

The ambiguous words "reform" and "perestroika" should now be retired from our vocabulary. For the reform communism of the past six years was only a preliminary to what was needed to make it possible for Russia to "return to Europe" and to become again a "normal" society—an unambiguous and revolutionary break with communism. This is as true now for Russia as it was for Poland, East Germany, Czechoslovakia, and Hungary before the anti-Communist revolutions of 1989. (It is precisely because Communist power has survived under the label "social democracy" in Romania, Bulgaria, and Serbia that the political situation is still so unpromising in all these countries.) Thus, the former Soviet Union this summer has, at last, made the exit from communism that

most of Eastern Europe accomplished in the autumn of 1989.

But release from the Marxist burden in Russia is of much greater moment than its earlier end in Eastern Europe. Russia, after all, is the homeland of Lenin and the archetype of Communist regimes throughout the world. It's demise in Moscow means its eventual demise everywhere: it requires no great powers of prophecy to predict that the remaining Leninist lands, from the China Seas to the Caribbean, will follow suit before very long.

The liberation of Russia from communism is momentous in still another sense. For the former Soviet Union was not just another "authoritarianism" or military despotism. It was in its time the world's principal source of Orwellian totalitarianism, a regime that, as Václav Havel has said, "justifiably gave the world nightmares." Its once ruling party is now characterized openly by the Russian Parliament as a "criminal enterprise."

Thus the revolution of August 1991 is not just another twentieth-century revolution; it is, in Hegelian terms, "world-historical": the greatest international turning point since 1945, and, even, in a sense, since 1917. For the world war that began in 1914 marked the start of what turned out to be a seventy-five years of global turbulence and troubles, characterized by a pattern in which the violence of war has shaded into the violence of revolution. The October Revolution was the first fruit of the disaster of 1914. Fascism and Nazism were the second. And World War II was the culmination of the century's tragedy. The cold war, finally, together with the Communist revolutions in the third world, was the long, lugubrious aftermath of the second global conflict. The anti-Communist revolutions between 1989 and 1991 have brought our violent century to a close, neither with a whimper nor with the long-feared bang.

Although this outcome clearly calls for sober analysis of the staggering problems and the certain dangers ahead, there have been too few moments of hope in Russia's tragic history to pass this one carelessly by. The present moment calls for celebration along with the Russians, just as we celebrated with the East Europeans after the fall of the Berlin Wall in 1989. The peoples of the former Soviet Union are expecting an expression of democratic solidarity deriving from the Western humanistic principles that many of them greatly admire. It is such shared principles that led Sergei Stankevich, the deputy mayor of Moscow, to warn against "witch hunts" of deposed Communists and Yeltsin to call on the population to refrain from converting "euphoria" into "vindictiveness."

A Western sense of solidarity is the more justified because the capacity for democratic participation is far from being a prominent feature of Russian history. Indeed, the land of the knout, the pogrom, and the autocracy of Ivan the Terrible has long been held to be incapable of civilized self-government; and the Lenin-Stalin regime has accordingly often been viewed as Russia's destiny. But, of course, this view is a stereotype; the predominance of despotism in Russian history has in fact been alleviated for extended periods. From the Great Reforms of Aleksandr II in the 1860s to the constitutional experiment with the Duma between 1905 and 1914, Russia had a growing European-style liberal movement, alongside the eventually victorious revolutionary one. Indeed, in the October general strike of 1905—which called for a constitution, not socialism—the Russian people demonstrated remarkable capacity for mass democratic action, though this capacity was later perverted by the Bolsheviks amid the chaos of 1917. Yet the Russian case of aborted democracy is hardly unique: other, more mature, major nations of Europe were also hijacked by

---

*See author's earlier article, "A New Russian Revolution?" in *The New York Review,* July 18, 1991.

ideological adventurers in the turmoil that followed the Great War.

The leaders of the Russian democratic movement are quite aware of both the negative and positive aspects of the national heritage; and it is the latter that emerged triumphant in the unprecedented elections of last June and the new Russian Revolution that followed. If the negative aspects eventually recur, as they may, it is to be hoped that Russian democratic forces will know how to deal with them. The problem of the moment, however, is the urgent and staggering one of liquidating once and for all the disastrous heritage of October 1917.

In the hindsight of late August, it is clear that the coup was a blessing in disguise. Indeed, it was the ideal catalyst for rapidly bringing about a collapse of the Soviet Union's old regime. That it was attempted at all discredited both the people and the political forces that were behind it. And that it failed galvanized the left and accelerated the anti-Communist revolution enormously. It also occurred in the nick of time: for the economic situation is now so disastrous that any more weeks wasted before the winter on the continuing deadlock over reforms might well have proved catastrophic.

Without the coup, the democratic forces who were led by Yeltsin, Gavriil Popov, the mayor of Moscow, and Anatoli Sobchak, the mayor of Leningrad, all elected last June, would have had to chip away for months at the Party's resistance to genuine economic change. This was the lot of the Poles in the months after their electoral breakthrough of June 1989. Indeed, the Poles to this day are burdened with a Sejm whose members are two thirds Communist or from Communist puppet parties because this was the agreement signed at the Round Table of February 1989, when Solidarity still had to share power with the Party.

Thus, there are times when a sharp revolutionary break can be preferable to evolutionary progress. The Moscow August was one of them. It cleared the air of indecision and dissipated the ambiguities hovering over Russia since 1989.

Though there is still much that remains murky about the botched coup, certain facts are clear. Its origins go back to the fall of 1990, when Gorbachev reneged on his August agreement with Yeltsin and rejected the 500-Day Plan worked out by Stanislav Shatalin and Grigori Yavlinsky. He then veered to the right—and toward the very officials, and the forces behind them, that made up the future junta.

Gorbachev rejected the 500-Day Plan when he belatedly realized that introducing a market system and privatizing state enterprises would inevitably destroy the Party's monopoly of power. True, he had abandoned the constitutionally defined "leading role of the Party" in March 1990. He apparently did so, however, because after the collapse of Eastern Europe he could no longer formally insist on the Party having this role in Russia; nevertheless, his actions reveal that he intended to preserve the Party's primacy in practice, because, as he has often said, this was his genuine Leninist conviction. At the same time it became clear to him that the 500-Day Plan's provisions for devolution of economic power to the republics would mean the de facto dissolution of the Union. And the "indestructible Union," as the first two words of the Soviet anthem put it, was also a matter of deep principle for Gorbachev, as his behavior has demonstrated.

But Gorbachev was not alone in being alarmed by the Plan's consequences for the integrity of the Union and by the demands for sovereignty being made in nearly all the republics. He was joined in his fears by most of the Soviet establishment, from the Party apparat, to the upper echelons of the army and the KGB, to the military-industrial complex, which controlled nearly half the country's economy and probably employed one third of its work force. And representatives of these interests had always made up the majority of Gorbachev's entourage. Eduard Shevardnadze and Aleksandr Yakovlev, though highly visible internationally, had always been the two lone liberals in the Soviet high command. Moreover, the other liberals who until 1989 had followed the General Secretary were now in the democratic opposition and gravitating toward Yeltsin, Popov, and Sobchak, all of whom had quit the Party during the summer of 1990.

The first signs of hard-line pressure on Gorbachev came in September 1990 when mysterious army maneuvers around Moscow were widely interpreted as a warning to him to change direction. In October, after stormy meetings with leaders of the military-industrial complex, Gorbachev in effect backed out of the 500-Day Plan by proclaiming that he would leave the matter to the Soviet Parliament. In November, after meeting with a group of about one thousand army officers, he replaced his liberal interior minister, Vadim Bakatin, with the former KGB general Boris Pugo; in December, he replaced the tepid Nikolai Ryzhkov as prime minister with Valentin Pavlov, a "command-administrative" economist deeply hostile to radical reforms. It is this accumulation of events, as well as signs of impending crackdown in the Baltic republics, that produced Shevardnadze's dramatic, and at the time enigmatic, resignation at the end of the year.

Gorbachev's motives in making his autumn move to the right are not far to seek. It is commonplace of political commentary in such Soviet liberal publications as *Moscow News* and *Commercant* that Gorbachev is a brilliant tactician who lacks a strategy. Or, more precisely, once his original strategy of reform communism had led to a dead end in 1989, he fell back on empty tactical maneuvering. Tacking now to the left, now to the right, and forever playing one side against the other, he sought to remain indispensable to each yet beholden to neither. He seems to have clung to a Micawberish hope that something would turn up, most likely in the form of foreign aid. It is yet another commonplace of Soviet commentary that by the Twenty-Eighth Party Congress in the summer of 1990, Gorbachev had undermined any possibility of forming a cohesive coalition of the forces of the center. This came about because his indecision estranged his Politburo allies, Shevardnadze and Yakovlev, who stood for the center in the country at large. Since perestroika had previously alienated the conservatives led by Yegor Ligachev, he was thus estranged from both his flanks, and so wound up suspended in midair over an abyss.

But sheer opportunism and a drive for personal survival cannot account for Gorbachev's policies. Genuine principle was involved—that is, the preservation of Party unity, socialist "property," and the Union. It was indeed to save all this, though in a modernized and more open form, that he had embarked on the gamble of perestroika and limited democratization in the first place.

During the winter of 1991 the "creeping *coup d'état*" launched during the previous autumn gathered momentum with the violent attacks against the Baltic States during January, and then with the brief assignment of soldiers to patrol the Moscow streets in February. (For people with long memories, this succession of measures recalled General Jaruzelski's step-by-step autumn buildup to his coup of December 13, 1981.)

But other developments that seemed simply bizarre at the time now make sense. Prime Minister Pavlov claimed before Parliament in January that Western aid to the Soviet Union was designed to destabilize and destroy Soviet socialism. And shortly after this speech, the government confiscated all bills larger than fifty rubles ostensibly to reduce the monetary excess, but perhaps in fact as a preparation for "command-administrative" shock therapy to remedy the country's now desperate economic crisis. In another speech in parliament at about the same time, the KGB chief, Vladimir Kryuchkov, accused the CIA of using promarket propaganda to destroy Soviet socialism. In retrospect, it seems that a program of rigid state controls was being devised to accompany and justify the military and police actions that had already begun.

At the end of this winter of gathering gloom Yeltsin demanded Gorbachev's resignation, indeed even calling for a "declaration of war" against the President, statements that at the time seemed comparable in their wildness to those of Pavlov and Kryuchkov. Once again in retrospect, however, it is clear that Yeltsin anticipated that both he and Russia's precarious new sovereignty would be the next victims of the advancing crackdown. He understood from long experience that such was the mode of operation of the Communist Party-state which, in Zbigniew Brzezinksi's phrase, was a "conspiracy in power."

For the coup that eventually took place, for all its ineffectual planning, was not a mere "right-wing" plot of isolated conspirators. Its leaders came from Gorbachev's own cabinet, and had all been appointed by him. Moreover, it had behind it the central institutions of the Soviet system: the Party, the planning bureaus, the police, and the army command, together with their respective nomenklaturas.

In March, these forces moved toward what they apparently thought would be the culmination of their winter campaign. Their strategy was expressed in the Party's efforts to impeach Yeltsin, their most lucid and powerful opponent, by using a Communist plurality in the Russian Parliament to unseat him as its chairman. This very public move was thwarted by Yeltsin's mobilization on March 28 of several hundred thousand Muscovites in the streets in direct defiance of Gorbachev's ban against demonstrations, a ban reinforced with 50,000 troops. Yeltsin's bold counterthrust was accompanied by strikes, from the Siberian coal mines to the Byelorussian factories, which, among other things, called for Gorbachev's resignation.

But what went almost unnoticed at the time was that, on March 7, Gorbachev had appointed a National Security Council composed of, among others, Vice-President Gennadi Yanayev, Prime Minister Pavlov, Foreign Minister Aleksandr Besmertniykh, and Valeri Boldin, the chief of staff of Gorbachev's personal cabinet. None of these officials opposed the August coup, and most of them turned up on its general staff. And before the attempt to impeach Yeltsin failed, they no doubt expected to complete their creeping winter coup in late March or April. But the term "coup," whether for this period or for August, is not really the right word; for the members of this group in fact came from the Soviet establishment, and therefore they could always declare a "legal" state of emergency.

They were foiled, however, not only because Yeltsin and his followers beat them back, but also because, in response to this development, Gorbachev once again changed sides and started acting like a democrat himself. He did so, no doubt, because the embrace of the right was becoming uncomfortably tight. He may also have feared that once he had signed a declaration of emergency he might no longer be needed by his own government. But he must also have seen that Yeltsin and the liberals were now the stronger party, and it was they therefore that had to be appeased. The result was what amounted to Gorbachev's capitulation to the left in the "Nine Plus One" Agreement of April 23, in which he abandoned his previous unshakable commitment to preserving the Union and

accepted the idea of real autonomy for the republics.

This flip-flop could only have infuriated the "right," that is, Gorbachev's own government. And we know, in fact, that at the Central Committee meeting that took place immediately after the "Nine Plus One" accord there was a move to unseat Gorbachev, with the intention of replacing him with Anatoli Lukyanov, Gorbachev's old Moscow University classmate, longtime right-hand man, chairman of the Supreme Soviet, and thus second in line to the succession after Vice-President Yanayev. But Gorbachev beat back this attempt, partly by arguing that the "Nine Plus One" accord was his new instrument for saving the Union, but even more by daring the Party to accept his resignation in the knowledge that they would not defy the principle of Party unity in the face of an external threat. Gorbachev survived, but this was his last successful tack, his final, and quite Pyrrhic, victory. For after this, who could trust him, right or left? He was like Aleksandr Kerensky before the October 1917 coup, who had first alienated the left by putting down the Bolshevik July days and then the right by arresting General Kornilov for allegedly preparing an August Putsch. Gorbachev was seen as a traitor both to his fellow Communists and to his more recent democratic allies: suspended in midair, he was without a base or a constituency.

From this point on the denouement of perestroika would be swift. In the June elections, the victory of Yeltsin and the liberals clearly showed that the Communists had the support only of a minority in Russia. The hitherto latent situation of dual power in the country was now clear-cut, and just as clearly weighted to the left.

Confronted with this development, the leaders of the Soviet establishment panicked; and their panic explains another bizarre incident that was inadequately appreciated at the time. In late June Pavlov went before the Supreme Soviet and demanded that decree powers normally held by the president be transferred to himself. At the same time Yazov, Kryuchkov, and Pugo told a closed session of the legislature that the country was faced with imminent disaster; they clearly implied that Gorbachev was personally responsible for failing to deal with it, indeed guilty of having provoked it. By way of response, Gorbachev went before parliament and harangued the delegates into refusing to accept Pavlov's demands that he be stripped of his powers.

The weakness of this response is astounding. Any head of state with real power would simply have fired Pavlov and his allies for insubordination verging on sedition. That he did not do so shows that Gorbachev was no longer in control, indeed that the Soviet Union did not in fact have a coherent government, and that this situation probably went back to December and to the warning issued by Shevardnadze. Again, a parallel can be drawn with the impotent government of Kerensky during the last months before the October Revolution. Indeed, one is even reminded of the last months of Nicholas II, when he was unable to react either to the assassination of his protégé Rasputin or respond when the Duma accused the Empress and his ministers of treason.

But Gorbachev, no more than his predecessors did, seemed not to have understood the situation, and so went through the motions of government as if he were still in charge. Under continuing pressure from Yeltsin, he pursued his leftward tack by agreeing in late July to yet another draft of the Union treaty, a version that came near to dissolving the Union by giving very strong powers to the republics, conceding to them even the powers to collect taxes and to turn over only a share to the central government. At the same time, he returned home from the meeting with Bush and the other Western leaders in London with no "grand bargain," not even a petty one. Then, in a final bravura performance before another meeting of the Central Committee, he produced a new Party platform, which jettisoned Marxism-Leninism in favor of a vague "humane and democratic socialism," as if this deathbed conversion of the Party by verbal formula would make a difference to the country. Finally, he got the Central Committee to vote to hold a Party Congress in December, in order to buy a few more months before the issue of deposing him could be "constitutionally" raised. From subsequent events we can easily imagine the rage and desperation of the right-wing forces he himself had appointed. At this juncture, in early August, Gorbachev went to the Crimea on vacation.

In his absence, the already existing general staff of the coup moved to act. The full details will not be known until after the coming trials of the surviving guilty parties and the investigations that have already started. But in the immediate wake of August, enough became known, especially through the none-too-veiled accusations of Shevardnadze and Yakovlev, for us to surmise plausibly what happened. Lukyanov is generally thought to have been the "ideologue" of the plot, because he believed that only a state of emergency could stave off the collapse of the Party, the economy, and the Union. In his eyes Gorbachev had repeatedly proved himself incapable of any such resolute action. But Lukyanov did not actually joint the future junta, and the task of organization fell to Oleg Baklanov, first deputy chairman of the Defense Council, i.e., of the military-industrial complex and therefore the senior Communist official in charge of the arms industry. In so doing, the plotters, according to reports in the Soviet press, were encouraged by the belief that Gorbachev, after Yeltsin had refused by phone to attend a meeting of the Federation Council, might now wish to back out of the new Union treaty, then scheduled for signing on Tuesday, August 20.

With such grounds for hope of a new flip-flop, Lukyanov, Baklanov, Kruychkov, and Yazov, on August 18, pressed Gorbachev to take action. Baklanov and Valentin Varennikov, the commander of the Soviet army's land forces, and Valeri Boldin of Gorbachev's personal cabinet, visited him in the Crimea after his phones had been cut off. They put to him an ultimatum—either sign their declaration of a state of emergency or give way to Vice-President Yanayev. Gorbachev apparently replied, in what he later called his counter-ultimatum, that he would agree to a state of emergency if it were first approved "constitutionally" by the Supreme Soviet. Since such a course would reveal the plans for declaring an emergency, this was in fact saying no, but in typically Gorbachev fashion, without doing so directly. So the top members of the government, pressed by the pending Tuesday deadline for the Union treaty's signing, and with their preparations for a coup already underway, dispensed with the direct "constitutional" path. They fell back instead on a more oblique one. They declared the president to be incapacitated, thus put-

ting Yanayev as vice-president in charge and so able to establish "legally" a State Committee of Emergency.

But why did the plot fizzle so farcically? We know that the resistance of Yeltsin in rallying the Moscow democrats was the main cause of the defeat. But for this to work so effectively, the Soviet establishment—the cabinet, the Party leadership, the three high officers of the KGB, and the Army—had to be capable of ineptitude and miscalculation on a Homeric scale. As Yeltsin revealed on August 25, the members of a special KGB unit that the plotters relied on to arrest him and other leaders, and to take over the Russian Parliament building, refused to follow orders. Their loyalties had not been ascertained in advance.

In part such misjudgments may be explained by haste and improvisation; but even more they showed how out of touch with Soviet reality were the leaders of a system now parasitic on the population and irrelevant to the country's real needs. With their own careers at stake, all that these people were fighting for was the preservation of the Party, state "property," and the Union—which Gorbachev himself had been trying to preserve in his more sophisticated manner. Unable to grasp the popularity of Yeltsin and the democratic movement, believing them to be powerless because they had no armed forces officially at their disposal, the members of the Soviet establishment thought it would be enough to secure Moscow militarily and then send out orders to the rest of the country through the state and Party apparats. In other words, their models were the intra-government coups that had deposed Khrushchev in 1964, and Beria in 1953.

The plotters thus took nomilitary measures outside Moscow, Leningrad, and the Baltic States, and for the rest of the country they relied on the regular officer corps to obey them. But the armed forces, a majority of whom had voted for Yeltsin, were divided, and after the refusal of the special KGB units to attack, they refused to move, and the plan to secure Moscow failed. The plotters also neglected to call on the independent right-wing group, Soyuz, led by Colonel Viktor Alksnis. They even botched the mobilization of the Party out of a desire to exclude the deputy general secretary, Vladimir Ivachko, who was thought unreliable. This meant that the Central

Committee Secretariat did not immediately support the coup after the Emergency Committee's televised press conference.

These delays on Monday the 19th made it possible for Yeltsin to mobilize the Moscow public by the 20th, and so bring about the collapse of the coup on the 21st. Thus what had begun as a coup within the Party was transformed under the new democratic conditions created by a revived Russian civil society into a genuine and world-historical revolution.

But the decisive element in this outcome was that the system was too far gone in corruption and decay to be able to defend itself under any circumstances. To measure this decay two historical comparisons are apposite. The first is with General Jaruzelski's almost flawlessly executed imposition of martial law of December 1981, at a time when both the Moscow and Warsaw regimes still had sinew and nerve. The second is with the Russian Imperial government, which by 1914 was hardly in flourishing health, but which still had to undergo three years of a bloody and futile war before it fell apart in February 1917. That an ostensibly advanced industrial nation and major international power should collapse without any shock of large-scale military defeat, after forty-five years of peace, and essentially from internal causes, is unheard of in modern history.

One of the advantages of Yeltsin and his supporters was that, unlike the Soviet establishment, they knew that the system was already only a husk. Moreover, since their brush with near doom during the winter, they were ready to act on this knowledge, and abolish the system, if ever the occasion presented itself. And many Russians, awakened and educated by the six years of perestroika, and exasperated both by the deepening crisis and by the clear ineptitude of the regime, were at last prepared to support vigorous action by the democratic leadership.

So the long-suffering population in the capital rallied to Yeltsin on the second day of the coup. By the end of the week the border republics, and even the Russian provincial heartland, hitherto the bastion of the right, began to dismantle the Party network. And they did so in large part spontaneously, without direction from the new leadership. The Dzerzhinsky monument was toppled, the red flag was replaced by the tricolor of

the Provisional Government of 1917, the Lenin statues came down, and Yeltsin's "White House," so called because of its actual color and because of admiration for the American political system, displaced the crenellated Kremlin both as the symbol and the real power of the emerging new order.

Russia thus had carried out a revolution similar to that of February 1917, except in one crucial respect: this time there was a coherent and popular provisional government prepared to take over. If there was any "coup" in Moscow this August, it is that of the skillful organization with which Yeltsin and the anti-Communists picked up the pieces both from the junta and from Gorbachev.

The decisiveness and the intelligence with which they moved throughout the week suggested that they had thought matters through beforehand, and even had a program and a group of qualified people ready to fill the anticipated void.

First they had prepared a political position. On Monday, August 19, when the Soviet cabinet with only one dissenting voice endorsed the coup, and while the Central Committee Secretariat simply remained silent, Yeltsin, together with Popov, Stankevich, and Sobchak publicly called for resistance. Yet they did not move to take power themselves; they called instead for the restoration of Gorbachev as the "legitimate" president, both to ensure continuity of state power and to give constitutional legitimacy to their own de facto exercise of that power. Admittedly, Soviet "constitutionality" is not worth a great deal because it derives from the Party, not the people. Still, this fig leaf of legitimacy was useful, both domestically and internationally, in the heat of the crisis. At the same time, Yeltsin dispatched the Russian foreign minister, Andrei Kosyrev, to Paris with authority to establish a provisional government in exile if things went badly.

When it turned out that the coup had failed, and Gorbachev had returned to Moscow, his restored legitimacy was liberally used by Yeltsin and his new majority in the Russian Parliament (the compromised right wing had simply decamped) to validate on national television a series of decrees that Yeltsin had issued during the interregnum, including one suspending the Communist party throughout the Russian Republic. This display of revolutionary authority has

disturbed a number of people in the West. But would it have been prudent and responsible for the still unarmed democratic forces to have left such dangerous adversaries unchallenged and unaccused, with the high command of the KGB and the Army intact? The same goes for the suspension of *Pravda,* which is not simply a newspaper but is essentially an instrument of the Party, conforming to Lenin's dictum that "a newspaper is a collective agitator and a collective organizer." Many on *Pravda*'s staff are indeed genuine journalists; but *Pravda* as an institution predictably used its enormous resources to publish the plotters' program for suppressing the democratically elected Russian leadership. Taking account of this, the Moscow liberals applauded Yeltsin's decree to suspend its publication. *Pravda*'s reporters, however, may soon reorganize the paper on their own, as the journalists of *Izvestia* have now done.

But more important than these dramatic signals that times had changed were the two main policies of the new provisional government. The first was to destroy the institutional power of the Party in every aspect of Soviet life: the state apparatus and local government, all the economic enterprises, the Army, the KGB—everywhere. For the Party was not a party at all; it was the hidden but real force behind the formal power in every Soviet institution. It exercised this power through a nationwide network of Party cells connected to the central national authority and, until glasnost, its policies were coordinated by a ubiquitous agitprop.

This omnipresent organization, moreover, commanded everything yet produced nothing, and so lived like a parasite on the body of the nation. This is why it has long been called by many citizens a "criminal organization" and a "mafia," and why, since perestroika, the groups that make up Russian civil society have taken up the discarded Western term "totalitarianism" to describe it. This is also why Yeltsin and his democratic allies took as their most important task the dismantling of their tentacular enemy. And this is why, finally, they moved so swiftly against it, in the heat of the crisis, without much attention to due process for an organization whose "dictatorship" had always been based on the denial of all law and on the use of terror. For they wished to leave the Party apparatus no time to recoup and hang on, as happened, for example, in Romania after the revolutionary crisis had passed.

Once again, to judge from the rapid cascade of anti-Party decrees, this program most probably had been thought through in advance. No doubt there is something residually Leninist in this process, as well as in the liberals' willingness to ride the wave of temporary near-anarchy to produce a new order. The Party education of most of the democratic leaders no doubt taught them something about the radical manipulation of power. But again, there is a crucial difference from 1917: whereas the Bolsheviks sought to stimulate and deepen the anarchy as the "creative" expression of class struggle, the new Russian revolutionaries are now seeking to contain and calm it, so as to give their fragile democracy a chance. And insofar as the present leadership made use of the popular explosion, it was because the monolithic nature of their adversary left them no choice but to dissolve all its structures whenever the opportunity arose to do so. In such a situation, the fiction of Soviet "legitimacy" made possible by Gorbachev's acceptance of Yeltsin's decrees was obviously a cover; yet it provided a useful facade of continuity. The question now facing Yeltsin and his colleagues is how long they can go on using Gorbachev, who is in effect their hostage, to give legitimacy to the interim government, while preparing for new elections and negotiating new arrangements with the increasingly independent republics.

The second main goal of the new government's policy was the systematic replacement of the old nomenklatura by young, liberal, and Westernizing professionals, who would take charge of all main sectors of the national life. Often organized in teams that were first formed as part of Yeltsin's entourage last summer, they almost immediately started to put the Moscow "White House's" program of radically transforming the economy into action.

The most urgent problem facing them is a completely unprecedented economic disaster whose full dimensions are still not adequately appreciated in the West: the USSR had a negative growth rate of 6 percent in 1990; and a negative growth rate of 17 percent for 1991 is estimated by the PlanEcon organization in Washington. In the worst year of the American

Great Depression, 1929–1930, the drop in economic growth was 9 percent. Moreover, Soviet transport, communications, and other infrastructure are collapsing, and most Soviet capital stock is obsolete and will have to be replaced if the country is to be integrated into the competitive world market.

To attack this problem, Yeltsin told Gorbachev to appoint a special committee under Ivan Silayev, the Russian prime minister, and composed, among others, of Grigori Yavlinsky, one of the designers of the 500-Day Plan, and Arkadi Volsky, head of a major association of private and state-owned enterprises. Their mission is to put an end to the previous regime's equivocations about moving toward a market system and privatizing the economy, and to plunge ahead, while the new government has the country's confidence, with "shock therapy" on the Polish model, which is in fact their inspiration.

But to make the ruined Soviet economy more businesslike, this team will have to purge large numbers of the country's managers who are too incompetent, too compromised, and too politically minded to adapt themselves to an entrepreneurial system. The aim of the planned firings, as Yeltsin and his associates have clearly said, is not a witch hunt, though part of the population, feeling swindled by seventy years of Communist fraud, would want Nuremberg-style justice. The basic approach of the economic reforms, as Yavlinsky and his group conceive them, will be to set nonpolitical, professional standards for running all economic institutions and to put the process of de-Communizing the economy on a functional basis, in which people would be judged by technical ability, not their political past. Two overriding practical considerations account for this policy in addition to ethical ones: many of the country's highly trained and competent personnel were in the Party, which only a few years ago had nineteen million members; and it would be folly to create legions of enemies who felt they had no choice but to organize a resistance.

The same policy of functional de-Communization and professionalization is to be applied in virtually all the other spheres of Russia's once wholly politicized life. The two other most important spheres are the Army and the KGB. Gorbachev, on his return

from the Crimea, in one of the many signs that he badly misunderstood the new situation, appointed Marshal Mikhail Moiseyev to replace Yazov, and a faceless KGB bureaucrat to replace Kryuchkov—that is, two near duplicates of their predecessors. Yeltsin immediately made him annul these actions and appoint instead, Yevgeni Shaposhnikov, aged forty-nine, as Minister of Defense, and Vadim Bakatin, Pugo's liberal-minded predecessor at the Interior, as head of the KGB. Between them, the Defense Ministry and the KGB have control over still another great potential danger in the current semi-chaotic situation, the huge Soviet stock of nuclear weapons dispersed over several republics. The keys and codes to this arsenal are now in the hands of Yeltsin's men, though Gorbachev is nominally in charge along with them. The mission of Shaposhnikov and Bakatin is to carry out an extensive purge of their respective institutions, to permanently reduce the size of both, to dissolve the existing Party cells, and to put their departments under the control of a soon-to-be-elected new state authority.

The same goes for the Party itself, but in this case, since the Party's central function was to assert political authority over the rest of society in the sacred name of "building socialism," depoliticizing the Party will mean dissolving it, so far as public sponsorship of it is concerned. Again, Gorbachev was called upon as general secretary to announce the plans for dissolution, by which the Party's extensive holdings, its presses and newspapers, its dachas and private hospitals, were transferred by decree to the state. All this does not mean that the Party has been banned. If convinced Marxist-Leninists want to get together to form a political association—that is, a normal party—they are free to do so under existing Soviet and Russian law.

By the end of August, President Gorbachev was also being called upon to preside over the liquidation of the pseudo-Union, together with the constitution he had granted it in 1989, both of which also had been emanations of, in fact spurious democratic fronts for, the Party. For the Soviet Federation has in fact always been a unitary state, held together by force that was papered over with the lie that the purely formal self-government allowed to the republics was in some sense real. It is partly in reaction to this lie that the nationalities problem has assumed such virulence since the conflict between

Armenians and Azerbaijanis at Nagorny-Karabakh erupted in 1988. For the same reason, beginning with Lithuania's declaration of independence in March 1990, a number of the republics have taken the lead in breaking up the Soviet Union itself.

The republics have been crucial in breaking up the Soviet political system as well, for several of them, first of all Lithuania, introduced elections by universal suffrage, both for Parliament and for president. They had done so in response to what they felt to be the fraudulent "democratization" of the Congress of Peoples' Deputies which Gorbachev convened in 1989 with a rigged suffrage. That body had been created by the Politburo so as to produce a "legislature" of reform Communists and their allies outside the Party who were to act as Gorbachev's counterweight to the recalcitrant main-line Party. Approximately a third of the seats were reserved for the Party itself, others for various "social organizations," and only a third for delegates to be elected by general suffrage. The Lithuanians walked out on this charade at the first gathering of the Congress in 1989 and went home to introduce universal suffrage. Lithuania's declaration of independence then set in motion the Russian sovereignty movement, and Yeltsin imitated Vytautis Landsbergis's strategy by using a direct presidential election to gain a legitimacy in Russia that Gorbachev did not have.

To be sure, national independence and universal suffrage are not automatically guarantees of democracy, of respect for minority rights, and of the humane toleration of difference. Zviad Gamsakhurdia the recently elected but highly authoritarian president of now independent Georgia, is an alarming example, for he has attacked ethnic minorities in Georgia and arrested political opponents. Who knows what other republics may have in store for their own minorities, including their resident Russian populations.

A prominent case in point is the eleven million Russians in the eastern Ukraine, whom Yeltsin feels obligated to protect, and whose territory the Ukrainians could not accept abandoning. On August 29 leaders of the two republics seemed sufficiently aware of the potential danger of such conflicts to have signed, in Kiev, a provisional economic and military alliance. This agreement might eventually become the basis of a new, loose post-Soviet confederation, and of a common post-Soviet economic sphere, which some of the smaller and more peripheral republics could then join.

Nevertheless, in the modern world there is only one basis for democratic legitimacy: "universal, equal, secret and direct suffrage," in the formula of the Russian Kadets, or Constitutional Democrats, in 1905. It was for this, not for revolutionary socialism, that the workers made the October general strike. It is to this formula that the present interim government, which is also the de facto government of whatever remains of the "Union," has made clear its intention to return, at every level from the top down. And early in September a last Congress of Peoples' Deputies is likely to finish the task of liquidating the old Soviet order by dissolving that final vestige of perestroika and by providing for prompt and genuinely democratic elections.

For the starkest fact of the Russian Revolution of 1991 is that virtually nothing remained of the old Leninist system. No basic Communist institutions have proved salvageable for a "normal" society. In the August Revolution much of the population, as if by a sudden joint decision, refused "to live according to the lie," in Aleksandr Solzhenitsyn's famous summons, and the entire once-intimidating structure dissolved in days. So out of a total system came total collapse.

The great question now is how one sixth of the world's land surface, with its three hundred million inhabitants, will re-emerge, as Solzhenitsyn put it, "from under the rubble." The rest of the planet, almost as much as Russia itself has a world-historical stake in the outcome.

Facts on File

Paul Quinn-Judge

Paul Quinn-Judge is Moscow correspondent of The Boston Globe.

On December 15, 1988, a few days after Mikhail Gorbachev won the hearts of the West with his speech to the United Nations in New York, the Soviet Communist Party leadership met to upgrade the bugging of Western journalists. The Secretariat was presented with a top secret memorandum signed by Alexander Kapto, deputy head of the Central Committee's Ideology Department, urging that it modernize the resources available to Glavlit, the official censors. The modernization was needed in order to tap into new Western computers and faxes. "Without the corresponding renewal of its technical base, the special service [of Glavlit] will not be able to fully undertake its assigned functions," the document warned. The Secretariat unanimously backed the appeal. Other leaders who signed off on the document include Alexander Yakovlev, the most respected and daring of the Gorbachevites.

Glavlit's request comes from the Special File, the personal archives of Communist Party leaders—their own repository for the secrets they cherished or perhaps feared the most, and which were never intended to see the light of day. (The documents have not been published yet in Russia: a small selection of them was made available to me recently by a person working on the archives.)

The Yeltsin administration is working through the file, preparing to release a careful selection of the material. So far officials have come up with information on a wide variety of unsavory dealings, from Soviet support of terrorists to links with the extreme nationalist Vladimir Zhirinovsky. This research is motivated by a desire to destroy the Communist Party and expose Gorbachev once and for all. Yeltsin and his aides are convinced that the now-banned Communist Party could yet provide a powerful base for an authoritarian movement that would try to restore the old regime. And they are obsessed with the idea that Gorbachev might somehow make a comeback. Yeltsin supporters feel that a hearing by Russia's constitutional court on the legality of the ban, now scheduled for July, will decide the Party's future.

A few weeks ago Yeltsin's aides began to assemble the material for the prosecution. Gennady Burbulis, Russia's secretary of state and probably Yeltsin's closest associate, called in a small group of specialists, gave them piles of documents from the Special File—tens if not hundreds of thousands of documents, dating back at least to the '20s—and told them to get working.

"It's a small world," one of the specialists said later. "Burbulis has been given Suslov's office." Mikhail Suslov, ideology chief under Leonid Brezhnev and Yuri Andropov, was one of the last Stalinists, a grim, stooped figure sometimes known as the Grand Inquisitor. The specialists were told that there were some documents the administration has no intention of releasing. The archives contained material on arms supplies to the IRA, one of Burbulis's colleagues said, but they would not release the documents for fear of reprisals against Russian diplomats. And to avoid embarrassing an ally, they would not be making available documents on KGB financial support for Indira Gandhi and other members of her family, including her son Rajiv.

Some documents provide proof that the Soviets did indeed give active support to terrorists in the 1970s. Another, dated August 28, 1969, and stamped top secret, shows Andropov demurely telling Brezhnev that the KGB has the capacity to turn out "up to 20,000 Muslims" in an anti-American demonstration outside the U.S. Embassy in New Delhi. Others, however, show how recently—even under Gorbachev—the Soviet Union was still the military aggressor. They report the massive flow of weaponry that was still being provided to Afghanistan in 1990—96,000 rifles, tactical rockets, and a promise of MIG-29s the following year.

Certainly the guiltiest secret that has turned up so far concerns the top leadership's knowledge of direct links with and support for one of the busiest terrorist groups of the 1970s, the Popular Front for the Liberation of Palestine. The paper trail starts in 1974. A two-page memorandum from Andropov to Brezhnev, dated April 23, reveals that since 1968 the KGB had been working with Wadia Haddad, a member of the Political Bureau and head of the Foreign Operations department of the Popular Front for the Liberation of Palestine. The key words—Haddad's name, his function, the country involved—were all added by hand in spaces left blank in the original typewritten version. "During a meeting in April of this year with the KGB resident in Lebanon, Wadia Haddad laid out the PFLP's long-term program of sabotage and terrorism," the letter says.

The program included "actions against U.S. and Israeli personnel in third countries" aimed at obtaining "reliable information about the plans and intentions of the USA and Israel." It also called for "sabotage and terrorist activities on the territory of Israel." The PFLP was planning a series of "special operations," including several aimed at oil storage facilities in Saudi Arabia, the Persian Gulf, and Hong Kong, Andropov told Brezhnev. Haddad was asking for "certain forms of special technical resources" necessary for sabotage operations. "Inform comrades Suslov, Podgorny, Kosygin, Grechko, Gromyko," says a note in an unknown but authoritative hand, running diagonally at the top of the page. Podgorny at the time was president, Kosygin premier, Grechko defense minister, and Gromyko, as ever, minister of foreign affairs.

A one-page letter dated May 16, 1975, informed Brezhnev that fifty-three automatic rifles, fifty pistols—"ten of them fitted with silencers"—and 34,000 rounds of ammunition had been delivered at night, by dead drop, off the coast of Aden. The weapons were of foreign origin, Andropov said, and only Haddad knew where they came from. A drop had been made "in conference with a decision of the Central Committee of the CPSU." Haddad, an early pioneer of the plane hijack, is said to have had links with a wide network of terrorist organizations, including the Baader-Meinhof group and the Japanese Red Army. Six months after he received the KGB weapons, he is said by Israeli sources to

have masterminded the attack on OPEC headquarters in Vienna. He died in East Germany in 1978.

The revelations that have emerged so far about the Gorbachev era show a leader clearly cooperating with Party hard-liners. Take an appeal from the new, reformist German Party chief Gregor Gysi to Gorbachev in March 1991. The Wall was already down, and Gysi's Party was reduced to a rump of true believers. But the German Party's archives had been taken over by the Kohl government, and Gysi was desperate. The files should either be returned to their rightful owners or destroyed, he told a senior Soviet official, Valentin Falin. Publication would be a catastrophe: the archives provided details of financial aid given to illegal Communist parties by the East Germans. The document noted that Gorbachev had once urged Helmut Kohl not to publish the archives. Could he not raise the subject again in a few days' time, when Foreign Minister Hans-Dietrich Genscher vis-

ited? There is also evidence that in January 1990 Gorbachev authorized secretly loaning the remnants of the Polish Party more than a million dollars.

The leaking of all this explosive material is no accident. Yeltsin has made it clear that he bitterly objects to the way Gorbachev continues to speak out on domestic politics. The Special File papers may well be a way to shut Gorbachev up. It's not inconceivable that Yeltsin will offer Gorbachev a deal: political silence in return for the nonpublication of some of the more embarrassing documents. If this does not happen, we are probably destined to see a steady stream of revelations over the next few months that will bespatter a number of respected former leaders such as Yaklovlev and Shevardnadze. More importantly, Yeltsin's political lieutenants, who have never hidden their contempt for Gorbachev, will be given the freedom to dig out the documents that depict the last Soviet leader's compromises, improvisation, and cover-ups as he lurched toward August 1991.

Conclusion:
The Human Prospect

From the perspective of the 1990s, the West contemplates the year 2000 and the turn of another century. This time the prospects for disillusionment seem slight, for there is little optimism about the current or future prospects of Western civilization. Indeed, with the development of nuclear weapons and intercontinental missiles, we are forced to consider the possibility that our civilization might destroy itself in an instant. Of course, like our ancestors a century ago, we can point to continued progress, particularly in science and technology. But, unlike our predecessors, we are attuned to the potential for the unforeseen disruptions and disasters that can accompany such innovation.

Our ambivalence about technology is paralleled by our growing recognition that we can no longer depend upon an unlimited upward spiral of economic growth. In the course of this century, other dreams have eluded us, including the hope that we could create a just and equal society through drastic and rapid social reorganization. Most of the great revolutionary promises of the age have not been kept. Nor do we continue to believe very fervently that the elimination of repressive social and moral taboos will produce an era of freedom and self-realization. By now virtually all areas of human conduct have been demystified (and trivialized), but confusion rather than liberation seems to be the immediate result. Finally, modernism, that great artistic and intellectual movement of the century's early years, has exhausted itself. For decades, as one commentator observes, the avant-garde had "pushed back frontiers of form, structure, and tonality until there was no structure left to topple." Now we find ourselves in the so-called post-modern condition, "a kind of unregulated marketplace of realities in which all manner of belief systems are offered for public consumption." Old beliefs and new are in a continuous process of redefinition. Under the circumstances, as Walter Truett Anderson comments in *Reality Isn't What It Used to Be*, our world cannot be defined by what it is, only by what it has just ceased to be.

These developments have contributed to an uncommon degree of self-consciousness in our culture. Seldom in any era have people been so apprehensive about the future of civilization and the prospects for humanity. The articles in this concluding section convey some current concerns. Several, including "Jihad vs. McWorld" and "Return of the *Volksgeist*," focus particularly on the widespread reversion to tribalization, a trend that is manifest in the ever-increasing conflicts that pit culture against culture, religion against religion, ethnic group against ethnic group. These tensions are often aggravated by the unprecedented mass migrations of our time, a topic covered in "Europe's Muslims" and "Global Boat People." "World City-States of the Future" contends that the nation-state system will not survive in a tribalized world and will give way to regional city-states. "The Fall and Rise of French" suggests that a global culture may yet be possible, for in Africa and elsewhere a widely-shared language has somewhat countered tribalism. The volume concludes with Thomas Sowell's speculations about the prospects for Western civilization.

Looking Ahead: Challenge Questions

"Jihad vs. McWorld" outlines two possible scenarios for the world in the immediate future. Based on current developments in Western civilization and the world at large, which scenario seems most likely? Can you imagine (and defend with facts and trends) other scenarios?

What is the status of Muslims in Europe?

What does futurist Riccardo Petrella have in mind when he says that we are entering a "postnational" era that will somewhat resemble "prenational" times?

What will be the short-term and long-term consequences of the unprecedented and ongoing mass migration of peoples from the poorer to the richer parts of the world?

How might Johann Gottfried Herder, whose ideas are summarized in "Return of the Volksgeist," react to the issues raised in "Jihad vs. McWorld" and "The Fall and Rise of French"?

What, according to Thomas Sowell, are Western civilization's major accomplishments and shortcomings? What, in his opinion, are its future prospects?

Unit 5

Jihad vs. McWorld

The two axial principles of our age—tribalism and globalism—clash at every point except one: they may both be threatening to democracy

Benjamin R. Barber

Benjamin R. Barber is the Whitman Professor of Political Science at Rutgers University. Barber's most recent books are Strong Democracy *(1984),* The Conquest of Politics *(1988), and* An Aristocracy of Everyone.

Just beyond the horizon of current events lie two possible political figures—both bleak, neither democratic. The first is a retribalization of large swaths of humankind by war and bloodshed: a threatened Lebanonization of national states in which culture is pitted against culture, people against people, tribe against tribe—a Jihad in the name of a hundred narrowly conceived faiths against every kind of interdependence, every kind of artificial social cooperation and civic mutuality. The second is being borne in on us by the onrush of economic and ecological forces that demand integration and uniformity and that mesmerize the world with fast music, fast computers, and fast food—with MTV, Macintosh, and McDonald's, pressing nations into one commercially homogenous global network: one McWorld tied together by technology, ecology, communications, and commerce. The planet is falling precipitately apart and coming reluctantly together at the very same moment.

These two tendencies are sometimes visible in the same countries at the same instant: thus Yugoslavia, clamoring just recently to join the New Europe, is exploding into fragments; India is trying to live up to its reputation as the world's largest integral democracy while powerful new fundamentalist parties like the Hindu nationalist Bharatiya Janata Party, along with nationalist assassins, are im-

periling its hard-won unity. States are breaking up or joining up: the Soviet Union has disappeared almost overnight, its parts forming new unions with one another or with like-minded nationalities in neighboring states. The old interwar national state based on territory and political sovereignty looks to be a mere transitional development.

The tendencies of what I am here calling the forces of Jihad and the forces of McWorld operate with equal strength in opposite directions, the one driven by parochial hatreds, the other by universalizing markets, the one re-creating ancient subnational and ethnic borders from within, the other making national borders porous from without. They have one thing in common: neither offers much hope to citizens looking for practical ways to govern themselves democratically. If the global future is to put Jihad's centrifugal whirlwind against McWorld's centripetal black hole, the outcome is unlikely to be democratic—or so I will argue.

MCWORLD, OR THE GLOBALIZATION OF POLITICS

Four imperatives make up the dynamic of McWorld: a market imperative, a resource imperative, an information-technology imperative, and an ecological imperative. By shrinking the world and diminishing the salience of national borders, these imperatives have in combination achieved a considerable victory over factiousness and particularism, and not least of all over their most virulent traditional form—nationalism. It is the realists who are now Europeans, the utopians who dream nostalgically of a resurgent England or Germany, perhaps even a resurgent Wales or Saxony. Yesterday's

wishful cry for one world has yielded to the reality of McWorld.

The market imperative. Marxist and Leninist theories of imperialism assumed that the quest for ever-expanding markets would in time compel nation-based capitalist economies to push against national boundaries in search of an international economic imperium. Whatever else has happened to the scientistic predictions of Marxism, in this domain they have proved farsighted. All national economies are now vulnerable to the inroads of larger, transnational markets within which trade is free, currencies are convertible, access to banking is open, and contracts are enforceable under law. In Europe, Asia, Africa, the South Pacific, and the Americas such markets are eroding national sovereignty and giving rise to entities—international banks, trade associations, transnational lobbies like OPEC and Greenpeace, world news services like CNN and the BBC, and multinational corporations that increasingly lack a meaningful national identity—that neither reflect nor respect nationhood as an organizing or regulative principle.

The market imperative has also reinforced the quest for international peace and stability, requisites of an efficient international economy. Markets are enemies of parochialism, isolation, fractiousness, war. Market psychology attenuates the psychology of ideological and religious cleavages and assumes a concord among producers and consumers—categories that ill fit narrowly conceived national or religious cultures. Shopping has little tolerance for blue laws, whether dictated by pub-closing British paternalism, Sabbath-observing Jewish Orthodox fundamentalism, or no-Sunday-liquor-sales Massachusetts puritanism. In the context of common markets, international law ceases to be a vision of justice and becomes a workaday framework for getting things done—enforcing contracts, ensuring that governments abide by deals, regulating trade and currency relations, and so forth.

Common markets demand a common language, as well as a common currency, and they produce common behaviors of the kind bred by cosmopolitan city life everywhere. Commercial pilots, computer programmers, international bankers, media specialists, oil riggers, entertainment celebrities, ecology experts, demographers, accountants, professors, athletes—these compose a new breed of men and women for whom religion, culture, and nationality can seem only marginal elements in a working identity. Although sociologists of everyday life will no doubt continue to distinguish a Japanese from an American mode, shopping has a common signature throughout the world. Cynics might even say that some of the recent revolutions in Eastern Europe have had as their true goal not liberty and the right to vote but well-paying jobs and the right to shop (although the vote is proving easier to acquire than consumer goods). The market imperative is, then, plenty powerful; but, notwithstanding some of the claims made for "democratic capitalism," it is not identical with the democratic imperative.

The resource imperative. Democrats once dreamed of societies whose political autonomy rested firmly on economic independence. The Athenians idealized what they called autarky, and tried for a while to create a way of life simple and austere enough to make the polis genuinely self-sufficient. To be free meant to be independent of any other community or polis. Not even the Athenians were able to achieve autarky, however: human nature, it turns out, is dependency. By the time of Pericles, Athenian politics was inextricably bound up with a flowering empire held together by naval power and commerce—an empire that, even as it appeared to enhance Athenian might, ate away at Athenian independence and autarky. Master and slave, it turned out, were bound together by mutual insufficiency.

The dream of autarky briefly engrossed nineteenth-century America as well, for the underpopulated, endlessly bountiful land, the cornucopia of natural resources, and the natural barriers of a continent walled in by two great seas led many to believe that America could be a world unto itself. Given this past, it has been harder for Americans than for most to accept the inevitability of interdependence. But the rapid depletion of resources even in a country like ours, where they once seemed inexhaustible, and the maldistribution of arable soil and mineral resources on the planet, leave even the wealthiest societies ever more resource-dependent and many other nations in permanently desperate straits.

Every nation, it turns out, needs something another nation has; some nations have almost nothing they need.

The information-technology imperative. Enlightenment science and the technologies derived from it are inherently universalizing. They entail a quest for descriptive principles of general application, a search for universal solutions to particular problems, and an unswerving embrace of objectivity and impartiality.

Scientific progress embodies and depends on open communication, a common discourse rooted in rationality, collaboration, and an easy and regular flow and exchange of information. Such ideals can be hypocritical covers for power-mongering by elites, and they may be shown to be wanting in many other ways, but they are entailed by the very idea of science and they make science and globalization practical allies.

Business, banking, and commerce all depend on information flow and are facilitated by new communication technologies. The hardware of these technologies tends to be systemic and integrated—computer, television, cable, satellite, laser, fiber-optic, and microchip technologies combining to create a vast interactive communications and information network that can potentially give every person on earth access to every other person, and make every datum, every byte, available to every set of eyes. If the automobile was, as George Ball once said (when he gave his blessing to a Fiat factory in the Soviet Union during the Cold War), "an ideology on four wheels," then electronic telecommunication and information systems are an ideology at 186,000 miles per second—which makes for a very small planet in a very big hurry. Individual cultures speak particular languages; commerce and science increasingly speak English; the whole world speaks logarithms and binary mathematics.

Moreover, the pursuit of science and technology asks for, even compels, open societies. Satellite footprints do not respect national borders; telephone wires penetrate the most closed societies. With photocopying and then fax machines having infiltrated Soviet universities and *samizdat* literary circles in the eighties, and computer modems having multiplied like rabbits in communism's bureaucratic warrens thereafter, *glasnost* could not be far behind. In their social requisites, secrecy and science are enemies.

The new technology's software is perhaps even more globalizing than its hardware. The information arm of international commerce's sprawling body reaches out and touches distinct nations and parochial cultures, and gives them a common face chiseled in Hollywood, on Madison Avenue, and in Silicon Valley. Throughout the 1980s one of the most-watched television programs in South Africa was *The Cosby Show.* The demise of apartheid was already in production. Exhibitors at the 1991 Cannes film festival expressed growing anxiety over the "homogenization" and "Americanization" of the global film industry when, for the third year running, American films dominated the awards ceremonies. America has dominated the world's popular culture for much longer, and much more decisively. In November of 1991 Switzerland's once insular culture boasted best-seller lists featuring *Terminator 2* as the No. 1 movie, *Scarlett* as the No. 1 book, and Prince's *Diamonds and Pearls* as the No. 1 record album. No wonder the Japanese are buying Hollywood film studios even faster than Americans are buying Japanese television sets. This kind of software supremacy may in the long term be far more important than hardware superiority, because culture has become more potent than armaments. What is the power of the Pentagon compared with Disneyland? Can the Sixth Fleet keep up with CNN? McDonald's in Moscow and Coke in China will do more to create a global culture than military colonization ever could. It is less the goods than the brand names that do the work, for they convey life-style images that alter perception and challenge behavior. They make up the seductive software of McWorld's common (at times much too common) soul.

Yet in all this high-tech commercial world there is nothing that looks particularly democratic. It lends itself to surveillance as well as liberty, to new forms of manipulation and covert control as well as new kinds of participation, to skewed, unjust market outcomes as well as greater productivity. The consumer society and the open society are not quite synonymous. Capitalism and democracy have a relationship, but it is something less than a marriage. An efficient free market after all requires that consumers be free to vote their dollars on competing goods, not that citizens be free to vote their values and beliefs on competing political candidates and programs. The free market flourished in junta-run Chile, in military-governed Taiwan and Korea, and, earlier, in a variety of autocratic European empires as well as their colonial possessions.

The ecological imperative. The impact of globalization on ecology is a cliché even to world leaders who ignore it. We know well enough that the German forests can be destroyed by Swiss and Italians driving gas-guzzlers fueled by leaded gas. We also know that the planet can be asphyxiated by greenhouse gases because Brazilian farmers want to be part of the twentieth century and are burning down tropical rain forests to clear a little land to plough, and because Indonesians make a living out of converting their lush jungle into toothpicks for fastidious Japanese diners, upsetting the delicate oxygen balance and in effect puncturing our global lungs. Yet this ecological consciousness has meant not only greater awareness but also greater inequality, as modernized nations try to slam the door behind them, saying to developing nations, "The world cannot afford *your* modernization; ours has wrung it dry!"

Each of the four imperatives just cited is transnational, transideological, and transcultural. Each applies impartially to Catholics, Jews, Muslims, Hindus, and Buddhists; to democrats and totalitarians; to capitalists and socialists. The Enlightenment dream of a universal rational society has to a remarkable degree been realized—but in a form that is commercialized, homogenized, depoliticized, bureaucratized, and, of course, radically incomplete, for the movement toward McWorld is in competition with forces of global breakdown, national dissolution, and centrifugal corruption. These forces, working in the opposite direction, are the essence of what I call Jihad.

JIHAD, OR THE LEBANONIZATION OF THE WORLD

OPEC, the World Bank, the United Nations, the International Red Cross, the multinational corporation . . . there are

scores of institutions that reflect globalization. But they often appear as ineffective reactors to the world's real actors: national states and, to an ever greater degree, subnational factions in permanent rebellion against uniformity and integration—even the kind represented by universal law and justice. The headlines feature these players regularly: they are cultures, not countries; parts, not wholes; sects, not religions; rebellious factions and dissenting minorities at war not just with globalism but with the traditional nation-state. Kurds, Basques, Puerto Ricans, Ossetians, East Timoreans, Quebecois, the Catholics of Northern Ireland, Abkhasians, Kurile Islander Japanese, the Zulus of Inkatha, Catalonians, Tamils, and, of course, Palestinians—people without countries, inhabiting nations not their own, seeking smaller worlds within borders that will seal them off from modernity.

A powerful irony is at work here. Nationalism was once a force of integration and unification, a movement aimed at bringing together disparate clans, tribes, and cultural fragments under new, assimilationist flags. But as Ortega y Gasset noted more than sixty years ago, having won its victories, nationalism changed its strategy. In the 1920s, and again today, it is more often a reactionary and divisive force, pulverizing the very nations it once helped cement together. The force that creates nations is "inclusive," Ortega wrote in *The Revolt of the Masses.* "In periods of consolidation, nationalism has a positive value, and is a lofty standard. But in Europe everything is more than consolidated, and nationalism is nothing but a mania. . . ."

This mania has left the post-Cold War world smoldering with hot wars; the international scene is little more unified than it was at the end of the Great War, in Ortega's own time. There were more than thirty wars in progress last year, most of them ethnic, racial, tribal, or religious in character, and the list of unsafe regions doesn't seem to be getting any shorter. Some new world order!

The aim of many of these small-scale wars is to redraw boundaries, to implode states and resecure parochial identities: to escape McWorld's dully insistent imperatives. The mood is that of Jihad: war not as an instrument of policy but as an emblem of identity, an expression of community, an end in itself. Even where there is no shooting war, there is fractiousness, secession, and the quest for ever smaller communities. Add to the list

of dangerous countries those at risk: In Switzerland and Spain, Jurassian and Basque separatists still argue the virtues of ancient identities, sometimes in the language of bombs. Hyperdisintegration in the former Soviet Union may well continue unabated—not just a Ukraine independent from the Soviet Union but a Bessarabian Ukraine independent from the Ukrainian republic; not just Russia severed from the defunct union but Tatarstan severed from Russia. Yugoslavia makes even the disunited, ex-Soviet, nonsocialist republics that were once the Soviet Union look integrated, its sectarian fatherlands springing up within factional motherlands like weeds within weeds within weeds. Kurdish independence would threaten the territorial integrity of four Middle Eastern nations. Well before the current cataclysm Soviet Georgia made a claim for autonomy from the Soviet Union, only to be faced with its Ossetians (164,000 in a republic of 5.5 million) demanding their own self-determination within Georgia. The Abkhasian minority in Georgia has followed suit. Even the good will established by Canada's once promising Meech Lake protocols is in danger, with Francophone Quebec again threatening the dissolution of the federation. In South Africa the emergence from apartheid was hardly achieved when friction between Inkatha's Zulus and the African National Congress's tribally identified members threatened to replace Europeans' racism with an indigenous tribal war after thirty years of attempted integration using the colonial language (English) as a unifier, Nigeria is now playing with the idea of linguistic multiculturalism—which could mean the cultural breakup of the nation into hundreds of tribal fragments. Even Saddam Hussein has benefited from the threat of internal Jihad, having used renewed tribal and religious warfare to turn last season's mortal enemies into reluctant allies of an Iraqi nationhood that he nearly destroyed.

The passing of communism has torn away the thin veneer of internationalism (workers of the world unite!) to reveal ethnic prejudices that are not only ugly and deep-seated but increasingly murderous. Europe's old scourge, anti-Semitism, is back with a vengeance, but it is only one of many antagonisms. It appears all too easy to throw the historical gears into reverse and pass from a Communist dictatorship back into a tribal state.

Among the tribes, religion is also a battlefield. ("Jihad" is a rich word whose generic meaning is "struggle"—usually the struggle of the soul to avert evil. Strictly applied to religious war, it is used only in reference to battles where the faith is under assault, or battles against a government that denies the practice of Islam. My use here is rhetorical, but does follow both journalistic practice and history.) Remember the Thirty Years War? Whatever forms of Enlightenment universalism might once have come to grace such historically related forms of monotheism as Judaism, Christianity, and Islam, in many of their modern incarnations they are parochial rather than cosmopolitan, angry rather than loving, proselytizing rather than ecumenical, zealous rather than rationalist, sectarian rather than deistic, ethnocentric rather than universalizing. As a result, like the new forms of hypernationalism, the new expressions of religious fundamentalism are fractious and pulverizing, never integrating. This is religion as the Crusaders knew it: a battle to the death for souls that if not saved will be forever lost.

The atmospherics of Jihad have resulted in a breakdown of civility in the name of identity, of comity in the name of community. International relations have sometimes taken on the aspect of gang war—cultural turf battles featuring tribal factions that were supposed to be sublimated as integral parts of large national, economic, postcolonial, and constitutional entities.

THE DARKENING FUTURE OF DEMOCRACY

These rather melodramatic tableaux vivants do not tell the whole story, however. For all their defects, Jihad and McWorld have their attractions. Yet, to repeat and insist, the attractions are unrelated to democracy. Neither McWorld nor Jihad is remotely democratic in impulse. Neither needs democracy; neither promotes democracy.

McWorld does manage to look pretty seductive in a world obsessed with Jihad. It delivers peace, prosperity, and relative unity—if at the cost of independence, community, and identity (which is generally based on difference). The primary political values required by the global market are order and tranquillity, and freedom—as in the phrases "free trade,"

"free press," and "free love." Human rights are needed to a degree, but not citizenship or participation—and no more social justice and equality than are necessary to promote efficient economic production and consumption. Multinational corporations sometimes seem to prefer doing business with local oligarchs, inasmuch as they can take confidence from dealing with the boss on all crucial matters. Despots who slaughter their own populations are no problem, so long as they leave markets in place and refrain from making war on their neighbors (Saddam Hussein's fatal mistake). In trading partners, predictability is of more value than justice.

The Eastern European revolutions that seemed to arise out of concern for global democratic values quickly deteriorated into a stampede in the general direction of free markets and their ubiquitous, television-promoted shopping malls. East Germany's Neues Forum, that courageous gathering of intellectuals, students, and workers which overturned the Stalinist regime in Berlin in 1989, lasted only six months in Germany's mini-version of McWorld. Then it gave way to money and markets and monopolies from the West. By the time of the first all-German elections, it could scarcely manage to secure three percent of the vote. Elsewhere there is growing evidence that *glasnost* will go and *perestroika*—defined as privatization and an opening of markets to Western bidders—will stay. So understandably anxious are the new rulers of Eastern Europe and whatever entities are forged from the residues of the Soviet Union to gain access to credit and markets and technology—McWorld's flourishing new currencies—that they have shown themselves willing to trade away democratic prospects in pursuit of them: not just old totalitarian ideologies and command-economy production models but some possible indigenous experiments with a third way between capitalism and socialism, such as economic cooperatives and employee stock-ownership plans, both of which have their ardent supporters in the East.

Jihad delivers a different set of virtues: a vibrant local identity, a sense of community, solidarity among kinsmen, neighbors, and countrymen, narrowly conceived. But it also guarantees parochialism and is grounded in exclusion. Solidarity is secured through war against outsiders. And solidarity often means obedience to a hierarchy in governance,

fanaticism in beliefs, and the obliteration of individual selves in the name of the group. Deference to leaders and intolerance toward outsiders (and toward "enemies within") are hallmarks of tribalism—hardly the attitudes required for the cultivation of new democratic women and men capable of governing themselves. Where new democratic experiments have been conducted in retribalizing societies, in both Europe and the Third World, the result has often been anarchy, repression, persecution, and the coming of new, noncommunist forms of very old kinds of despotism. During the past year, Havel's velvet revolution in Czechoslovakia was imperiled by partisans of "Czechland" and of Slovakia as independent entities. India seemed little less rent by Sikh, Hindu, Muslim, and Tamil infighting than it was immediately after the British pulled out, more than forty years ago.

To the extent that either McWorld or Jihad has a *natural* politics, it has turned out to be more of an antipolitics. For McWorld, it is the antipolitics of globalism: bureaucratic, technocratic, and meritocratic, focused (as Marx predicted it would be) on the administration of things—with people, however, among the chief things to be administered. In its politico-economic imperatives McWorld has been guided by laissez-faire market principles that privilege efficiency, productivity, and beneficence at the expense of civic liberty and self-government.

For Jihad, the antipolitics of tribalization has been explicitly antidemocratic: one-party dictatorship, government by military junta, theocratic fundamentalism—often associated with a version of the *Führerprinzip* that empowers an individual to rule on behalf of a people. Even the government of India, struggling for decades to model democracy for a people who will soon number a billion, longs for great leaders; and for every Mahatma Gandhi, Indira Gandhi, or Rajiv Gandhi taken from them by zealous assassins, the Indians appear to seek a replacement who will deliver them from the lengthy travail of their freedom.

THE CONFEDERAL OPTION

How can democracy be secured and spread in a world whose primary tendencies are at best indifferent to it (McWorld) and at worst deeply antithetical to it (Jihad)? My guess is that globalization will eventually vanquish retribalization.

5. THE HUMAN PROSPECT

The ethos of material "civilization" has not yet encountered an obstacle it has been unable to thrust aside. Ortega may have grasped in the 1920s a clue to our own future in the coming millennium.

Everyone sees the need of a new principle of life. But as always happens in similar crises—some people attempt to save the situation by an artificial intensification of the very principle which has led to decay. This is the meaning of the "nationalist" outburst of recent years. . . . things have always gone that way. The last flare, the longest; the last sigh, the deepest. On the very eve of their disappearance there is an intensification of frontiers—military and economic.

Jihad may be a last deep sigh before the eternal yawn of McWorld. On the other hand, Ortega was not exactly prescient; his prophecy of peace and internationalism came just before blitzkrieg, world war, and the Holocaust tore the old order to bits. Yet democracy is how we remonstrate with reality, the rebuke our aspirations offer to history. And if retribalization is inhospitable to democracy, there is nonetheless a form of democratic government that can accommodate parochialism and communitarianism, one that can even save them from their defects and make them more tolerant and participatory: decentralized participatory democracy. And if McWorld is indifferent to democracy, there is nonetheless a form of democratic government that suits global markets passably well—representative government in its federal or, better still, confederal variation.

With its concern for accountability, the protection of minorities, and the universal rule of law, a confederalized representative system would serve the political needs of McWorld as well as oligarchic bureaucratism or meritocratic elitism is currently doing. As we are already beginning to see, many nations may survive in the long term only as confederations that afford local regions smaller than "nations" extensive jurisdiction. Recommended reading for democrats of the twenty-first century is not the U.S. Constitution or the French Declaration of Rights of Man and Citizen but the Articles of Confederation, that suddenly pertinent document that stitched together the thirteen American colonies into what then seemed a too loose confederation of independent states but now appears a new form of political realism, as veterans of Yeltsin's new Russia and the new Europe created at Maastricht will attest.

By the same token, the participatory and direct form of democracy that engages citizens in civic activity and civic judgment and goes well beyond just voting and accountability—the system I have called "strong democracy"—suits the political needs of decentralized communities as well as theocratic and nationalist party dictatorships have done. Local neighborhoods need not be democratic, but they can be. Real democracy has flourished in diminutive settings: the spirit of liberty, Tocqueville said, is local. Participatory democracy, if not naturally apposite to tribalism, has an undeniable attractiveness under conditions of parochialism.

Democracy in any of these variations will, however, continue to be obstructed by the undemocratic and antidemocratic trends toward uniformitarian globalism and intolerant retribalization which I have portrayed here. For democracy to persist in our brave new McWorld, we will have to commit acts of conscious political will—a possibility, but hardly a probability, under these conditions. Political will requires much more than the quick fix of the transfer of institutions. Like technology transfer, institution transfer rests on foolish assumptions about a uniform world of the kind that once fired the imagination of colonial administrators. Spread English justice to the colonies by exporting wigs. Let an East Indian trading company act as the vanguard to Britain's free parliamentary institutions. Today's well-intentioned quickfixers in the National Endowment for Democracy and the Kennedy School of Government, in the unions and foundations and universities zealously nurturing contacts in Eastern Europe and the Third World, are hoping to democratize by long distance. Post Bulgaria a parliament by first-class mail. Fed Ex the Bill of Rights to Sri Lanka. Cable Cambodia some common law.

Yet Eastern Europe has already demonstrated that importing free political parties, parliaments, and presses cannot establish a democratic civil society; imposing a free market may even have the opposite effect. Democracy grows from the bottom up and cannot be imposed from the top down. Civil society has to be built from the inside out. The institutional superstructure comes last. Poland may become democratic, but then again it may heed the Pope, and prefer to found its politics on its Catholicism, with uncertain consequences for democracy. Bulgaria may become democratic, but it may prefer tribal war. The former Soviet Union may become a democratic confederation, or it may just grow into an anarchic and weak conglomeration of markets for other nations' goods and services.

Democrats need to seek out indigenous democratic impulses. There is always a desire for self-government, always some expression of participation, accountability, consent, and representation, even in traditional hierarchical societies. These need to be identified, tapped, modified, and incorporated into new democratic practices with an indigenous flavor. The tortoises among the democratizers may ultimately outlive or outpace the hares, for they will have the time and patience to explore conditions along the way, and to adapt their gait to changing circumstances. Tragically, democracy in a hurry often looks something like France in 1794 or China in 1989.

It certainly seems possible that the most attractive democratic ideal in the face of the brutal realities of Jihad and the dull realities of McWorld will be a confederal union of semi-autonomous communities smaller than nation-states, tied together into regional economic associations and markets larger than nation-states—participatory and self-determining in local matters at the bottom, representative and accountable at the top. The nation-state would play a diminished role, and sovereignty would lose some of its political potency. The Green movement adage "Think globally, act locally" would actually come to describe the conduct of politics.

This vision reflects only an ideal, however—one that is not terribly likely to be realized. Freedom, Jean-Jacques Rousseau once wrote, is a food easy to eat but hard to digest. Still, democracy has always played itself out against the odds. And democracy remains both a form of coherence as binding as McWorld and a secular faith potentially as inspiring as Jihad.

Europe's Muslims

Anthony Hartley

Anthony Hartley is editor of Encounter.

During the weekend of July 14–15, 1990, a conference, called together by the Muslim Institute—a body representing some of the more fervent Muslims residing in Britain—met in London. The director, Dr. Kalim Siddiqui, a controversial figure, presented to the meeting a document entitled "The Muslim Manifesto—A Strategy for Survival." The purpose of this document was to provide "a common text defining the Muslim situation in Britain. It also seeks to provide a framework for a healthy growth of all parts of the community as well as a common Muslim identity and purpose." By implicitly describing Muslims in Britain as a threatened species, the subtitle of the Manifesto set its tone, and Dr. Siddiqui's speech introducing it was equally uncompromising:

> We are an autonomous community, capable of setting our own goals and priorities in domestic and foreign relationships.

And still more forcefully:

> We are sick and tired of headmasters and teachers discriminating against our children. We are sick and tired of being told to "free" our women from "slavery." Our women will never be available to become sex slaves of the West. Our message to our tormentors is short and simple—get off our backs.

The Manifesto exhorts British Muslims to practice their religion and obey its laws. It calls for the establishment of a Council and General Assembly of British Muslims and rejects the idea of integration into British society. Finally, it contains an "agenda" for British Muslims—a list of subjects likely to be of importance to them in the future. These include a new legal status for Islam in Britain, including an extension of the law on blasphemy, Islamic proselytism in Britain, Islamic schools, and the possibility of an Islamic university.

The Muslim Institute is believed to be under Iranian influence (indeed, Dr. Siddiqui has acknowledged his own "special relationship" with Iran), and it might be doubted whether its followers are the majority or even a considerable proportion of British Muslims. The Manifesto has been attacked by Dr. Hesham el Essawy, head of the Islamic Society for Religious Tolerance, as being likely to play into the hands of "racists." Moreover, its excitable rhetoric has to be taken with a pinch of salt. Does Dr. Siddiqui really want to give up his vote in British elections, which is what his attitude would seem to imply? Nonetheless, there is little doubt that some of the questions raised in the Manifesto accurately reflect areas of friction between Muslim immigrants and the society which they have adopted—particularly in matters concerning religious observance, education, and sexual morality. Muslim parents fear that their authority over their children will wane as their children encounter, at school or through the media, the norms of Western life. Undoubtedly, this is a potentially explosive sociological situation—Islam's religious content makes it that—and it is hardly surprising that it should lead to reactions that are over emotional or appear to bring British Muslims into conflict with society at large.

One such incident was brought about by the publication of Salman Rushdie's novel, *The Satanic Verses,* in which Islam and the Prophet were satirized in a manner offensive to Muslims. After the Ayatollah Khomeini's sentence *(fatwa)* condemning Rushdie to death and the burning of his book by Bradford Muslims, it was Dr. Siddiqui who, at a meeting of Muslims in Manchester, asked those of his audience who approved the *fatwa* to raise their hands. Most did so.

The episode was followed by calls for Dr. Siddiqui's prosecution for incitement to violence, but the matter was allowed to drop.

The Rushdie affair, accompanied as it was by bombings of bookshops, drew the attention of the British political class and educated public to the problems and paradoxes accompanying the existence of a substantial Muslim minority in their midst. At the same time it began to be apparent that Britain was not alone in such difficulties. A steady flow of immigration from the Indian subcontinent, Malaysia, the Middle East, and Africa, both north and south of the Sahara, is affecting all European countries. This movement has been caused by the desire for a higher standard of living on the part of the immigrants and by Europe's need for cheap labor.

In the 1980s, however, with unemployment running at higher levels in Western Europe and the prospect of East Germans replacing Turkish *gastarbeiter* (migrant workers) in the Federal Republic of Germany, increasing restrictions have been placed on immigration and work permits. No doubt, however, this movement of population still continues, since control is hard to exercise and will probably become still more difficult when frontier checks between European Community states diminish further after 1992. (France, Germany, and Benelux have already abolished them.)[1]

THE MAIN CONCENTRATIONS

Muslim communities in European countries differ in numbers, countries of origin, and types of employment. Likewise their impact on the host societies has varied according to the traditions and the political and legal structures of the countries concerned. Different local situations have engendered diverging political and social aspirations. Institutions offer differing levels of opportunities for Muslims to fit into communities, and conflicts can arise over a wide range of issues.

In Britain, the number of Muslims is variously estimated as between 1 million and 1.5 million; though, in the absence of any religious census and the fact that many have arrived illegally, there is no accurate count. They come mostly from the Indian subcontinent (Bangladesh, India, and Pakistan), but there are also East African Asians, Arabs, Malaysians, and Nigerians. The majority have collected in the centers of northern industrial cities (Birmingham, Leeds, Bradford) and in the East End of London in the garment districts once occupied by Jewish immigrants. Their jobs are mostly unskilled, though, surprisingly, there is also a higher proportion of Muslims in professional occupations than is the case with the population as a whole: based on 1981 census figures, 15.4 percent of Muslim men had managerial jobs (national figure, 6.5 percent).

These communities are served by some 600 mosques, the most important of which have been built with donations from the Middle East. Saudi Arabia appears to be the largest donor and has also exercised considerable influence on the appointment of Imams (prayer leaders). The next largest donor is Libya. The mosques, in addition to their religious function, organize Koranic teaching for children (i.e., instruction in Arabic for Urdu-speaking Asians) and generally act as a center for the communities in which they are located.

One characteristic of the status of British Muslims, which is significantly different from what is to be found in other European countries, is the fact that, since most of them were originally immigrants from Commonwealth countries, they are citizens and have the right to vote in local and national elections. This has far-reaching consequences. Despite what "The Muslim Manifesto" may say, these Muslims are integrated into British political life, and a number of them hold political office—something that gives them considerable potential leverage to realize specific objectives. The practical results of this and the issues it raises for British politicians will be discussed later.

In France, as might be expected given its geographical position and historic ties with the Maghreb, there is a still larger Muslim population: estimated to be between 2.5 and 3 million. These are mostly Algerians, Moroccans, and Tunisians, but there are also some Turks and an increasing number of Muslim Africans from countries like Senegal, Mali, and Niger. The Muslim communities are concentrated in the industrial areas of France, particularly in the north and in the suburbs of Paris. There are well over a thousand mosques or "prayer rooms" where Islam is practiced. Around these, and often as part of the struggle to obtain a place of worship on housing estates or in factories, have grown Muslim groupings, whose general aim is to improve the immigrants' lot. Sometimes these have merged into wider social or political movements such as "SOS Racisme" or the "March of the *beurs* (Arabs)," whose effect has been to end temporarily the isolation of Muslim communities and bring them into French political life. Since many Muslims work in factories—especially in the big automobile plants around Paris—strikes in those industries have been accompanied by efforts on the part of the communist Confederation Générale du Travail to organize Muslim workers, while making accusations that the leaders of a rival "company" union had broken the Ramadan fast.

Most French Muslims do not have the right to vote, though this is changing as young people, born in France, grow up as French citizens. This gradual formation of a Muslim electorate will facilitate the acceptance of demands voiced by the Muslim community—as, for example, the letter sent by the Union islamique en France to headmasters asking for an end to mixed classes. But the integration of Muslims into French political life will be a slow process and one which must involve a greater degree of cultural integration than would be welcomed by many Muslims. The controversy about the three Muslim girls in the town of Creil who wore head-scarves to school, thereby offending against the cherished principles of the *école laïque,* shows how difficult it is for a secular state to deal with Islamic activism. (The controversy ended with the minister of education, Liónel Jespin, a Socialist, giving way—much to the dismay of partisans of secular education and a unitary state.)

French Muslims have looked with some envy toward Belgium, which has given its Muslim community a distinct legal status by creating a Supreme Council for the Muslim religion. Recently, France's interior minister, Pierre Joxe, took the first step toward a similar solution by establishing an advisory council whose task will be to prepare the regulations for a consultative council of the Muslim community. Such a body would at least help the French government ascertain what Muslims really want. At present, in a medley of competing sects and rival influences from Muslim states, their aspirations remain problematic.

In what was until recently West Germany, according to the *Islam-Archives-Deutschland,* there are 1.9 million Muslims. Of these the great majority are Turkish (1.4 million) with considerable numbers of Arabs (130,000) and Bosnian Muslims (100,000). They have at their disposal nearly 900 mosques. Again, most of them live in the industrial areas of big cities or in city centers—the Kreuzberg area of West Berlin is the best known of these districts of Turkish settlement. These immigrants have the status of migrant workers; they do heavy or menial manual work, and are, to a considerable degree, at the mercy of economic circumstances (which now include competition of labor from the East). Some of them by now have wives and families with them. There are also close ties with families in their homelands. Remittances back to Turkey ran at DM 3.35 billion a year between 1981 and 1984. Relations with immigrants in matters such as education and social services are the responsibility of the regions (*Länder*), which work out their own solutions to problems. The Senate of West Berlin, for example, agreed with the Turkish government to pay for two hours of Islamic instruction per week for Turkish children.[2]

The Muslim workers in Germany have no vote and little political power. Though some 50,000 of them have become German citizens, this process is only at its beginning and goes ahead slowly. A considerable part of the Muslim community is drawn together by the Islamic Council for the Federal Republic. Most political activity among German Muslims, however, reflects the political attitudes of their country of origin. In the liberal atmosphere of the Federal Republic, Turkish Islamic zealots can find more tolerance and freedom of expression for their views than exist in Turkey itself. The *süleymanci* movement, for instance, a politico-religious party arising from a mystical confraternity of a type familiar in Turkish Islam, thrives in Germany, but is frowned on by the Turkish state.

Italy is also a host country for many Muslims, most of them from the other side of the Mediterranean—Egypt, Libya, Morocco, and Tunisia. Since the great majority of these are illegal immigrants—the use of tourist visas to enter the country is widespread among intending immigrants—figures are uncertain, but the Italian authorities put the number at 1.7 million. Their installation does not seem to have caused much trouble, though there is a growing movement behind the slogan "Jobs for Italians first!" However, in southern Italy and Sicily there have always been interchanges with North Africa, and so far the only notable crisis—apart from the incidence of assassinations inseparable from the pursuit of Middle Eastern politics in European capitals—has been worry as to whether the building of a mosque in Rome infringed the Lateran Treaty. Apart from the four major concentrations, Belgium and the Netherlands also have significant Muslim minorities. In Belgium they number 200,000 North Africans and Turks; in the Netherlands, there are 285,000 Turks, Moroccans, and Surinamese.

MUSLIM DEMANDS

As this brief overview indicates, the considerable Muslim community in Western Europe contains much diversity—above all in countries of origin and political status—but its peculiar requirements, as it inserts itself into Western industrial society, and, hence, the difficulties that arise between it and its hosts, are not dissimilar. These concern the practice of Islam, the bringing up of families in the Islamic faith, and anxiety lest social conditions in Europe should undermine Muslim morality and separate child from parent.

All over Europe Muslims have demanded places to pray at work, in workers' hostels, and on housing estates; the provision of *Halal* food (food that accords with the prescriptions laid down in the Koran) in canteens and schools; time off to celebrate Muslim holidays (the two great festivals *Aid al kabir* and *Aid al saghir)*; and the right to attend the mosque on Friday.

Many of these requirements are not easy to meet. The Ramadan fast—which involves not eating from sunrise to sunset for a whole month—may diminish the physical capacity of workers doing heavy manual labor, and absences during the day to pray are not easily compatible with the rhythms of modern industrial production. Islamic burial, which requires a corpse to be laid on its side facing Mecca, is difficult to arrange in crowded urban cemeteries. Young Muslims, during their life in Western society, are liable to encounter—and perhaps even acquire a taste for—alcohol, tobacco, and "unclean" food. For religious Muslims, everyday life in European cities is full of temptations that can lure the young away from Islam.

This preoccupation with the possible secularization of young Muslims is, of course, at its most sensitive when it comes to public education. It is no accident that a clash between Muslims and the French state should have taken place in this precise area. The surrender by the French minister of education to the girls of Creil is highly significant, a breach in French educational doctrine which was never conceded to France's Catholics. Moreover, it was a recognition of the principle of female segregation which runs contrary to that of equality of the sexes, now so firmly and, one might say in some cases, so fanatically established in the Western consciousness and practice.

Demands about schools put forward by Muslim parents in Britain include the adoption of Islamic dress by girls, segregated swimming and physical education classes, *Halal* food to be provided at school meals, the availability of "prayer rooms," and time off for visits to the mosque and Islamic festivals. It is at the mosque that children will receive their Koranic instruction. There is also deep disquiet among Muslims about sex education in schools, particularly about homosexuality. Similar demands were contained in the letter to French headmasters mentioned previously.

However, the situations in Britain and France differ in an essential respect. In France such decisions depend on the minister of education who rules a centralized school system. In Britain they are the responsibility of the local authorities. Moreover, a new British education act has given parents greater power over schools and introduced the possibility, if they so desire, of a school "opting out" of the local authority system. In a heavily Muslim area, therefore, the possibility now exists of Muslim governors and parents controlling the school and changing its workings in accordance with their own needs and beliefs. Private Muslim schools have also appeared and are seeking government grants in the same way that Anglicans, Catholics, and Jews have done before them.

Such possibilities pose difficult questions of principle for any British government. How can Whitehall refuse to Muslim schools subsidies which it gives to other religious groups? Why should a Muslim private school not become "grant-aided"? In state schools with a majority of Muslim pupils what is to happen to the non-Muslim minority? The rise of a specifically Muslim educational sector would institutionalize and perpetuate a barrier between Muslim immigrants and the rest of society which government policy has hitherto sought to overcome. To which it could be, and has been, answered that the discipline inculcated by Islam is a valuable asset for a country and that it is better for Muslim youth to be subjected to traditional forces of social control than to be left to its own devices. If Muslims do not want to integrate into Western societies, should they be forced to do so?

Here the responses given in Britain and France might be very different, reflecting very different conceptions of the state and its functions. It is significant that, in its dealings with the Muslim community over education, the French state was forced to abandon a general principle. In Britain, on the other hand, a looser structure of administration creates dilemmas which, though acute, remain local. But, whatever the response of the host country, immigrants who, for religious reasons, wish to remain distinct from the mass of the population pose one particularly fundamental problem: that of allegiance.

LOYAL TO WHOM?

One aspect of the Muslim communities in Western Europe which must be disquieting to governments is the influence exercised on them by Muslim states and sects in Asia and Africa. This is more fundamental than a mere importation of murderous feuding onto the streets of European cities, though this admittedly gives a good deal of trouble to police forces. Religious and political movements originating in Islamic countries from Malaysia to the Maghreb are also reflected in Muslim communities in Europe. The channels through which such influences travel are not well known. New immigrants, broadcasts, films, books, newspapers, tapes, videos, Imams sent out to man newly constructed mosques—messages from the Islamic world come in a variety of guises. (Western security services, lacking Arabic- or Urdu-speaking officers, are, it appears, none too well informed even about the content of the addresses given in the mosques.) However these channels work, the existence of such ties seems certain, as the evolution of opinion and political events in the Muslim world have their repercussions in Europe.

Sometimes there is a clear institutional channel of influence. In France, for instance, the Great Mosque in Paris is now directly under the control of the Algerian government, following a long and complicated dispute about who should appoint its rector. For a long time after Algerian independence, the mosque had remained under the leadership of Si Hamza Boubakeur, a nominee of the French government in its imperial days. Now, however, he has been replaced by Cheikh Abbas, an official of the Algerian Ministry of Education. His tenure has seen a reconciliation between the Algerian state and the associations of *harkis* in France as well as the "re-islamization" of the latter.[3] Backed by a number of Muslim communities, the Great Mosque has intervened on numerous issues affecting Muslims in France: custody of children in divorce cases concerning mixed marriages, immigration laws, relations between young Muslims and the police, etc. In other words, as Gilles Kepel, the foremost authority on Muslims in France, points out in *Les Banlieu l'Islam,* an institution under the aegis of Algiers is playing a part in France's political life—a part that may become more considerable as more French Muslims attain French citizenship.

Similarly, in Great Britain, appointments to the Central London Mosque have been influenced by Saudi Arabia, with results that were felt during the Rushdie affair. In his book, *A Satanic Affair: Salman Rushdie and the Rage of Islam* , Malise Ruthven, a well-informed observer sympathetic to Islam, comments:

Dr. al Ghamdi and his colleagues in the Union of Mosques Organisation and the Islamic Council of Europe simultaneously contrived to inflame Muslim opinion and to alienate important sections of the British public by their ill-informed and overheated response to Rushdie's book. Instead of explaining to the Muslim community that their

decision to settle in Britain had placed them outside the "protection" of *Dar al Islam* and the writ of the *Shari'a* law, they lent their authority to a campaign which they and their British advisors ought to have known would lead nowhere, since Rushdie had broken no British law.

It is certainty a paradox that Muslim institutions should become a conduit for influence exercised by those who care little for civil order in Britain. Ruthven adds:

Given that the Islamic community is now an established part of the British population, the wisdom of allowing British Muslim institutions to be run by foreign-funded appointees possessing inadequate knowledge of British culture, law or institutions must be questioned.

A rather different type of influence has been that exerted by the example of the Iranian Islamic Revolution. In France, this was followed by an intense agitation excited by followers of the Ayatollah Khomeini. Among Muslim students in the mosques and Koranic schools, work of missionary endeavor and proselytism has gone forward. According to Kepel, the appeal of the Iranian model to young Muslims is clear:

. . . the humiliation inflicted on the "arrogant" American superpower is a sign: the Western dominance of the universe is not irreversible, battle "in the name of God" can end in tangible earthly success.

The effect of the Iranian Islamic Revolution has been a heightening of Muslim consciousness in Western countries, whose effects range from assassinations and demonstrations to the founding of youth movements and a new impetus given to the building of mosques and the preaching of the Prophet's message. The influence exercised by Saudi money has been replaced by the far more fiery message from Tehran. That message is anti-Western, hostile to modern industrial society in Europe and the United States, and opposed to the integration of Muslims into it.

In Britain, outside sectarian influences played a major part in the inception of the Rushdie affair. Muslims in the United Kingdom seem to have been alerted to the implications of *The Satanic Verses* when the book was banned in India in October 1988 because of the danger of intercommunal riots. In November, the chairman of the Council for Mosques in

Bradford, Sher Azam, wrote to the prime minister to protest against the book's publication. Earlier, the Islamic Foundation of Leicester had published its own protest. In this case the impulsion seems to have come from Muslim activists of the Jamaat-i-Islami, a highly politicized reforming sect based in India with links to the Muslim brotherhood in the Middle East. British Muslim reactions to the Rushdie affair were also affected by other events in the Indian subcontinent: the tense state of Muslim opinion in India following a court decision allowing Hindus access to a shrine on whose site a mosque had been built, and feelings among strict Muslims in Pakistan following the choice of a woman, Benazir Bhutto, as prime minister. By the beginning of 1989 an agitation among British Muslims was already under way. This was to be symbolized and given wide publicity by the burning of Rushdie's book at a Bradford demonstration in January. It was only in February that the Ayatollah Khomeini issued his *fatwa* condemning Rushdie as well as those associated with the book's publication and distribution.

The effect of the *fatwa,* apart from putting Salman Rushdie's life in real danger, was to create an obstacle in the path of any reconciliation between Iran and Western countries, which was presumably the intention of the radicals who had submitted the case to the Ayatollah for his judgement. Thus what was to become a difficult political problem in Britain was affected by political opportunism in Iran and Pakistan, and by the reactions of the Muslim minority in India. At present, though relations between Britain and Iran appear to be improving, it looks as if Rushdie will remain a virtual prisoner for the foreseeable future, as the agitation against his book by British Muslims continues. In Mr. Ruthven's words, "The goal of social integration has become significantly more distant for a community whose thrift and industriousness had made it likely to prosper in the free market conditions created by Thatcherism."

THE MULTICULTURAL TRAP

Two series of consequences stemming from the presence of Muslim communities in Europe—the insertion of Islamic beliefs and mores into a modern industrial setting and the influence exercised by the Muslim world on European countries—converge in the Rushdie affair. Out of it, however, emerges another problem: the status of religion in a secular society. In the April–June 1990 issue of *Political Quarterly*, Tariq Modood, a Muslim writer, identifies this point as the most salient feature of the Rushdie case:

The Rushdie affair is not about the life of Salman Rushdie nor freedom of expression, let alone Islamic fundamentalism or book-burning or Iranian interference in British affairs. The issue is of the rights of non-European religious and cultural minorities in the context of a secular hegemony.

For anyone brought up in an Erastian—not to say agnostic—Western tradition, however, such a statement begs more questions than it answers. In fact, it appears—as an attempt to obscure issues such as law and order and freedom of speech in an impenetrable smokescreen, in which the only discernible feature is the emotive reference to the "rights" of "non-European religious and cultural minorities." But do these include the right to pursue individual citizens with death threats? And is the evolution of European society toward tolerance over three hundred years to go for nothing? In the sixteenth century anyone taking part in a desecration of the sacraments, such as was recently performed by gay activists in the Catholic cathedral of New York, would have met a lingering and painful death. Nowadays, whatever disgust may be felt concerning such actions, no one is about to burn the perpetrators. In Britain the blasphemy law is a rusty instrument, one rarely used in recent years, and prosecutions under it would probably be thrown out by juries. Now, liberals, opposed to any restriction on the right to publish, find themselves faced with Muslim demands for an extension of that law to protect Islam from insult. Their reply has been to demand the removal of the blasphemy law from the statute book—but this would hardly satisfy Muslims, even though it would put them on an equal footing with their Christian brethren. Indeed, on this and other issues (including religious education in the schools) there have recently been signs of an incipient alliance between British Muslims and some fundamentalist Christians.[4]

Faced with such choices, British liberal opinion has split. Intellectuals are pulled one way by their traditional attachment to free speech and another by

their more recently acquired belief in the virtues of a "multicultural" society. That those, toward whom they have done their best to recommend a rational tolerance, should suddenly display violently illiberal feelings strikes at the very heart of a meliorist tradition that descends from the Enlightenment. Of course, their favorable view of a "multicultural" society depended on picking and choosing among the cultural elements composing it. Such phenomena as the infliction of the death penalty for apostasy or the social subjection of women were not considered as being "rich" or "exciting," and it came as a shock to find that Islam had to be accepted as a whole. The Rushdie episode has been part of the dissolution of the liberal consensus in Britain, and it may have served a useful purpose if it brings home the message that "multiculturalism" is only possible if it means embracing the (to modern European eyes) bad features of alien cultures as well as the good. The phrase itself is a hypocritical way of avoiding this conclusion.

France and other European countries have not yet had their Rushdie. But sooner or later a similar incident will almost certainly set off much the same train of events. The problem of Muslim communities is now posed for European governments and peoples. Is Islam to be given a special status, which carries with it immunity from criticism, let alone satire? Are the children of Muslim immigrants to integrate fully into the societies which their parents have chosen? Clearly it must be the aim of religious leaders, taking the view they do of Western behavior, to prevent this, to guard their young people with a ring fence of prohibitions and exhortations. But can they reasonably expect that the secular states in which they find themselves will aid them in this task? Can they also expect that, if tensions continue—which seems probable—Western countries will go on allowing preachers in mosques to indulge themselves in violent and abusive rhetoric? Can Islam expect to be above the law or to apply its own laws in European societies?

For what the spokesmen for Islamic communities in Europe appear to be demanding are additional rights over and above those they receive as citizens of their adopted countries. Dr. Siddiqui, for example, does not contemplate abandoning his right to vote in British elections. Nonetheless he wants other privileges which express the separateness of his

community as Muslims. The girls of Creil are not leaving France's school system; in effect they have imposed their own terms on it. But this claim to a "special position" in European society could cut both ways. If Muslims succeed in remaining "apart" in, say, the same way in which British merchants in India during the eighteenth century were "apart," then they will find that there will be positions in society to which their sons and daughters cannot aspire. One man's "apartness," after all, quickly evolves into another man's discrimination.

APPLY THE LAW

In fact, it is likely that, were they to be let alone, European Muslims would resolve the tensions between them and their hosts by practical compromises and the application of common sense as to what is acceptable under Western law and what is not. It might be thought that it is perfectly legitimate for Muslims to seek the right to pray during their work day, but that rioting and calls for the death of individuals in the name of Islam are not acceptable. After all, even "The Muslim Manifesto" acknowledges that Muslims must obey the laws of the non-Muslim state in which they live. But compromise is undermined by constant calls from outside bodies for a purer and more intransigent Islam and by the waves of fanaticism which arrive from the Middle East.

There are conclusions to be drawn from the present situation:

First, European countries already have considerable Muslim communities. These are likely to grow and to acquire greater political influence as immigrants and their children become citizens of the states in which they are domiciled.

Second, these communities, in so far as they can be judged by their political spokesmen, appear not to be taking the path of integration trodden by other types of immigrants. Their Islamic identity carries with it beliefs and practices that separate them from their adopted societies. Their demand, therefore, is for a special status, privileges additional to the ordinary rights of European citizens.

Third, European societies are finding it hard to resist such a demand. Indeed, there have already been occasions when host societies have had to abandon their prevailing social norms and defer to the customs of Islam, even when these run contrary to cherished beliefs (e.g., on the equality of women).

And fourth, these Muslim communities have also become a conduit through which movements of opinion in the Islamic world are conveyed into the host country. The governments of Muslim countries and the leaders of Islamic religious sects can, therefore, to a certain extent, exert influence on European societies.[5]

For the host governments in Europe, therefore, there is only one course to pursue. While displaying sympathy for Islam as a great religion and doing their best to ensure that Muslims find the conditions necessary for the practice of their faith, they must also insist that their laws be observed and that public order not be endangered by ecclesiastical oratory. The complexities of the Islamic settlement in Europe are, after all, not going to go away. Indeed, it is likely that the numbers of Muslim immigrants will increase as instability in the Middle East and poverty in Africa drive migrants across the Mediterranean. Nor will the ties between Europe and the heartlands of Islam be cut; it may be expected that the European Muslims will continue to be influenced by messages from their home countries for a long time to come. All this is a reaction to past and present humiliations. But European countries will not for long take on a penitential stance about their past imperial dealings with Islam, nor will they forever make allowances for wounded religious sensibilities. The application of law is their only answer to the paradoxes of Muslim expansion and renewal. If the European Muslims get no more and no less than that, they will not have done badly.

NOTES

1. It is interesting—and perhaps indicative of trouble to come—that France should recently have protested to Bonn about what seemed to be German encouragement for the emigration to France of surplus Turkish workers.

2. This agreement, however, has led to a paradoxical form of religious instruction. Since the teachers are supplied by the Turkish government and Kemalism has made Turkey a secular state, this course in Islamic studies largely consists of the repetition of phrases like "My fatherland is Turkey. I love Turkey more than my life." See Tomas Gerholm and Yngve Georg Lithman, eds., *The New Islamic Presence in Western Europe* (London: Mansell, 1988).

3. The *harkis* are Algerians who fought for France during the Algerian war and had to leave the country when it became independent.

4. See S. P. D. Green, "Beyond the Satanic Verses," *Encounter* (June, 1990).

5. The latest instance of this, which may serve as a postscript to this article, is the reaction of British Muslims to the annexation of Kuwait. Both the Muslim Institute and the more moderate Association of British Muslims have denounced the presence of American forces in Saudi Arabia as "blasphemy" and a "desecration of these holy places." It is true that some voices have also attacked the Iraqi invasion, but the United States has drawn the most fire from British Muslims. See the *Independent on Sunday,* August 19, 1990. A non-Muslim reaction has been an arson attempt at the Saddam Hussein Mosque in Birmingham.

World City-States
of the Future

Riccardo Petrella

Head of the Forecasting and Assessment of Science and Technology (FAST) division of the European Community, Riccardo Petrella is responsible for providing a futurist perspective to the Eurocrats in Brussels. Here he discusses the emergence of city-state economics in the new world order.

The new world order taking shape is not the one imagined by obsolete statesman of the cold-war era. Rather than an order of nation-states weighing in on a new global balance of power, an archipelago of technologically highly developed city-regions—or mass-consumer *technopoles*—is evolving. These city-regions are linked together by transnational business firms that bypass the traditional nation-state framework in their ceaseless pursuit of new customers, as well as by thousands of local and transnational Non-Governmental Organizations that are active in the promotion of customer protection and citizens rights.

If present trends continue, for better or for worse, by the middle of the next century nation-states such as Germany, Italy, Denmark, the United States, and Japan will no longer be the most relevant socio-economic entities and the ultimate political configuration. Though the nation-state entity will not disappear, *national identities* and cultures will survive or new ones will emerge. Areas like Orange County, Osaka, the Lyon region, or the new Ruhrgebiete will acquire predominant socio-economic and political status. Already within Europe, a new web of cooperative programs has mushroomed between Barcelona, Lyon, Milan, Strasbourg, and Stuttgart—all without passing through a national hierarchy of capitals or central ministries. Lyon,

which already is home to Europe's largest intercity airport, recently established direct service to and from the U.S.

Evidence shows a strong movement toward the emergence in the next few decades of a Europe of city-regions.

At the world level, the real decision-making powers of the future, it appears, will be a network of transnational companies in alliance with city-regional governments. Today the decision-making powers are already the networks of transnational companies, with the support of declining nation-state governments.

High-Tech Hanseatic League On a global scale, this new order will resemble the flourishing fourteenth- and fifteenth-century European economy, which was governed by the Hanseatic cities and intercity alliances that hosted trading guilds and their networking merchants. The postnational economic geography of the future will look very much like that of prenational times.

The postnational economic geography of the future will look very much like that of prenational times.

As the urbanist John Friedmann has sketched it, today's global economy is principally organized through a system of some thirty world-city regions—nodes of the world capitalist system. These are London, New York, Tokyo, Toronto, Chicago, San Francisco, Los Angeles, Houston, and Miami; Mexico City and Sao Paulo; Seoul, Taipei, Hong Kong, Singapore, and Bangkok; Paris, Zurich, Vienna, Milan, Madrid, and more or less the whole of Holland [Randstadt].

This trend toward a new Hanseatic phase of the world economy, with its multiplication of interfirm consortia and networks between U.S., Japanese, and European firms—especially in high technology—has been intensified by the *triadic approach* to development. This business strategy, backed up by government policies, is based on the idea that in order to remain competitive, any internationally oriented firm or economy must be present simultaneously in the largest, creasingly integrated, consumer market comprising America, Japan, and Europe. Kenichi Ohmae, the Japanese management guru calls this the "global-insider" strategy; Sony's Akio Morita calls it "global localization."

The aim of such a strategy is to attain global technological and industrial supremacy by capturing the allegiance of those with the means to be consumers; that is, about seven hundred to eight hundred million people worldwide.

I call this approach "myopic utilitarian opportunism" because it excludes—save for the tiny fraction of elites in such world cities as Sao Paulo, Mexico City, and Hong Kong, or in places like Caracas, Cairo, and Bombay—any concern with development among what, by the year 2020 will be the world's other seven billion-plus inhabitants. Even if sixty to eighty million Indians, for example, were linked to the prosperous archipelago of the privileged territories fifty years hence, ten times as many Indians would be excluded. And, estimates suggest, by the year 2020, more than twenty megacities in the poor world, with populations of twenty-five million each, will appear.

Obviously, committing the vast majority of the world's population to a global underclass is not only unjust but unsustainable in a well-armed world that is

From *New Perspectives Quarterly*, Fall 1991, pp. 59-64. Copyright © 1991 by the Center for the Study of Democratic Institutions.

ecologically interdependent and exposed to unstoppable waves of mass migration.

Absent a strategy to use science and technology constructively in the global interest—rather than in the competitive interest of becoming Number One—the future, I fear, will be characterized by a prosperous network of transnational firms and revitalized capitals of innovation that will grow dynamically together in what is basically a G-7 club, leaving behind the great mass of humanity that doesn't qualify as customers.

Committing the vast majority of the world's population to a global underclass is not only unjust but unsustainable in a well-armed world that is ecologically interdependent and exposed to unstoppable waves of mass migration.

By absurdly redefining humanity as *customers,* the population of the planet in such a new world order would be conveniently reduced from an order of eight to one! Imagine how this *order* would redraw the world map: on one side we would see a dynamic, tightly linked, fast-developing archipelago of technopoles comprising less than one-eighth of the world's population; on the other side would be a vast, disconnected and disintegrating wasteland which is home to seven out of every eight inhabitants of the earth.

Everyday, this disarticulated world—what Alvin Toffler refers to as the growing gap between the fast and slow worlds—is being formed before our eyes. As universities are closing all across Africa, every week the European Community, Japan, and the U.S. (as well as Korea) are building new research parks and university facilities. As new *airtropolises* are being constructed in Japan and Singapore, and a new High Speed Train network is developing in Western Europe, the transportation infrastructure in Africa is worse than it was ten years ago, and is continuing to deteriorate. While Mercedes and Mitsubishi are joining up to capture world markets, famine and malnutrition are catching up with

millions in sub-Saharan Africa. The EC budget for one research program—the Esprit microelectronics consortium—is fourteen times the total EC aid to the entire continent of Latin America.

Triadic Techno-Nationalism When Europeans, Americans, and Japanese talk about globalization, they always seem to talk as if the world beyond their borders didn't exist. And they increasingly tend to speak about each other in the terminology of *technonationalism* or *technological patriotism.*

People are told they are soldiers in an open technological war; that their countries are fighting for survival; that they must be more and more skilled and educated if they want to find and keep a job. They are told that their future is linked with the mastery and use of high-tech products and systems, combined with good management and new organizational models. Productivity, efficiency, effectiveness, flexibility, reliability, and quality are the new by-words in the vocabulary of commercial war. Individuals and masses of people have been promoted from the *factors of production,* as they were known during the industrial age, to *human resources.*

Commercial performance has become the whole point of national policy under the triadic approach; it has become the primary objective of national ingenuity and action. Over the past twenty years, the ideology of competitiveness, based on technological innovation and nourished by scientific advance, has overshadowed all other objectives.

In Europe this has meant that national priority in the development of science and technology has been given to measures that favor and facilitate successful integration of domestic firms into triadic consortia and networks.

Not surprisingly, such an approach favors the most developed regions of the EC, where the potential and capability to compete in the global markets are considerably more developed. The robotics industry in Italy is a good example.

The production of robots and their diffusion into Italian manufacturing are characterized by strong regional inequalities between the north and south of that country, with the southern region participating to a very modest degree in this new technology. The intensification of triadic power will thus largely benefit the already developed urban regions of London, Frankfurt, Paris, and Zurich; it will mean little for Naples or Sicily. For Italy

the same applies to the development of financial services. And, naturally, to the extent serious competition remains between countries in Europe, the worse the consequences for regional development.

Moreover, this intensification of triadic power will exacerbate the already growing *democratic deficit* of the new Europe. Though European integration is scheduled for 1992, the formal mechanics of representative democracy have yet to be adjusted from the national level to the European level.

Perhaps more importantly, though, the rise of the new high-tech Hanseatic network has eroded the basis of democracy that was associated with the development of the nation-state. Territorial accountability has been radically diminished. City councils may spend weeks debating the allocation of $200,000 for housing rehabilitation, while the British financial houses transfer $120 billion from one market to another within minutes, fundamentally affecting the currency balances, exchange rates and terms of industrial finance. Where's the democracy?

Globalization Process The globalization of technological innovation is not a new phenomenon. The chemical industry (particularly pharmaceuticals), the steel industry, and car manufacturing have been globally organized for decades. A few examples: Through joint ventures, personnel exchanges, cross-licensing research, and production partnerships, or through shares of ownership, Chrysler is linked to Mitsubishi, Samsung, and Fiat as well as Volkswagen; GM is linked to Toyota, Isuzu, and Suzuki; Ford is linked to Mazda and BMW; Nissan is linked to Volkswagen as well as Daewoo; and Mitsubishi with Hyundai.

The intensification of triadic power will exacerbate the already growing democratic deficit of the new Europe.

Globalization today is accelerating at the heart of the technological revolution—in semiconductors and computers, robots, telecommunications, and biotechnology. There is increasing integration, cooperation, and strategic links between multinationals, who are in turn allied with local manufacturers. Such alliances, for example, link Motorola with Nippon Electric Company and, in turn, to Hitachi; Nippon Telephone and Telegraph is linked to IBM as well as to Mitsui and Hitachi; Sony is linked to RCA; the Swedish Ericsson company to Honeywell and Sperry; Ricoh is tied to Rockwell.

In the electronics industry, strategic partnerships have been established between Hitachi and Hewlett-Packard, between Fujitsu and Texas Instruments, and between Siemens and Intel.

Many factors are pushing this globalization—high R&D costs that must be shared, the limited pool of high-quality skilled scientists and engineers, and the multinational corporate system itself, which requires telecommunications, organized research, coordinated production, and financial infrastructure on a global scale.

The triadic approach, if it remains dominant, will result in so widening the gap between the privileged archipelago and the sea of impoverished peoples that the whole world system will be at risk.

In fifteen to twenty years time many believe that there will remain only eight to ten large world consortia in telecommunications, five to eight in the automobile industry, three to five in tire manufacturers, and so on.

The presence of these global companies, with their global markets and quests for advanced communication infrastructures and socio-cultural services, is reshaping the functions, the internal organization, and the image of cities for better and for worse. As hosts to corporate divisions, universities, research labs, and sophisticated consumers—as well as large pools of low-wage labor, often immigrants—cities have become the real loci of the innovation process.

Alternatives to the Triadic Approach
Rather than going global, one alternative to the widely shared triadic strategy gaining appeal as 1992 approaches is "going European in an open world economy." In this way, Europe as a whole could pay more attention to its internal

regional inequalities as a matter of policy—gaining scales of efficiency by sharing R&D and joint projects, like the successful Airbus—and to the definition and implementation of the proper conditions for a new European social contract.

However, the absence of a large enough internal market (purchasing power in the East is still paltry) and—more significantly—the weakness of European common socio-economic projects limit the possibilities for European firms to develop strategic capabilities strong enough to take on their world competitors. Since economic globalization, driven by the market, is happening much faster than the politically managed economic integration of Europe, European firms risk remaining prisoners of a vicious, limiting circle if they chose *going European* only.

There is yet another, in my view preferable, option of global common development. Aware of the pernicious influence of the competitiveness metaphor and of the long-standing dangerous effects of the war for triadic power the most highlighted and inspired sectors of society from Europe, the U.S., and Japan should give priority to science and technological development—not in order to compete for global leadership of a market of seven hundred million people, but to seek development for the entire eight billion inhabitants of the planet fifty years from now.

The triadic approach, if it remains dominant, will result in so widening the gap between the privileged archipelago and the sea of impoverished peoples that the whole world system will be at risk. Moreover, the competitive triadic approach also is the least effective way of using global resources, particularly the opportunities associated with science and technology, because their chosen challenges primarily concern how to find new products for the market rather than how to resolve the most pressing problems of humanity.

Obviously, competition between economic powers is not going to stop. It would be naive to expect such a thing. But, its importance can be lessened and brought into greater balance with the logic of cooperation organized around projects that focus on reversing the disintegration of Africa, Arab countries, Latin America, or the Indian subcontinent and linking them to the fast world.

By order of priority, the first effort should be to meet basic food and health needs, and to hold back the desertifica-

tion and reclaim lands for agriculture; then meet basic food and health needs; then put in place a telecommunications and transportation infrastructure.

In the coming year, several Japanese, U.S., and European intellectuals and scientists, including myself, will make an appeal to the G-7 to promote scientific and technological cooperation for Latin America and Africa on precisely these matters.

We have an enormous capacity at the world level to solve the problems I have described. It is only a matter of the willful use of science and technology for another purpose than serving the imperatives of market competition.

NPO But can technology alone make development happen? Isn't it more a matter of culture and mentality?
Riccardo Petrella I don't think the impoverished of Africa, Latin America, or the Arab world are structurally unable to develop, although temporary cultural conditions may be negative in this respect.

After all, seventy years ago it would have been said of Koreans that they didn't have the mentality to develop. Look at them now.
NPO But South Korea has a kind of Protestant-Confucian culture that is conducive to the kind of work ethic, order, and accumulation required for capitalist development.

For better and for worse, one doesn't see the same cultural mentality, say, in Islamic Africa.

We must accept that the eight billion people of our future will be an enormously rich taxonomy of cultural variety.

Petrella True, they have been increasingly unable to cope with the G-7-type of development that dominates today. But it is of course also true that the mentality of building a great civilization was nonexistent in Europe during Islam's glory days of the thirteenth century. One can hardly say that they are culturally incapable of inventing technological solutions their problems.

5. THE HUMAN PROSPECT

Your question raises an important point, however. Although the triadic competitive model does not admit to it, especially in the wake of communism's collapse, there *can* be another concept of development. There is no single *best* model.

As long as we don't incorporate a diversity of paths to technological development into our own conceptions, we will in fact create the conditions that prevent development alternatives from arising.

This is why *geocultural* strategies for common global development, stressing diversity, are every bit as important as geopolitical conceptions of balance of power were in the old world order.

We must accept that the eight billion people of our future will be an enormously rich taxonomy of cultural variety.

For example, the diversity of religious imagination will make an enormous difference in the path new technological developments will take. Catholic Europeans and Americans, for instance, morally sanction genetic engineering or experimentation on animal embryos, but draw the line of scientific intervention at the human embryo. By contrast, Japan's mix of Buddhism and Shintoism sees life and death as a seamless whole, precluding them from conceiving the fracture between life and death as the West does.

So, the transfer of organs is inconceivable to them. In Shintoism, body and nature are pure and whole; life and death are continuous. Therefore, any kind of genetic engineering or manipulation of genes that transform the purity of nature is not permitted.

Geoculturally speaking, then, the map of our unfolding world must be extremely differentiated.

The utilitarian, opportunistic approach of triadic competition to development does not recognize the value of diversity and human needs and rights. It only recognizes the uniform, though segmented, customer.

Global Boat People

Andries Van Agt

The European Community's Ambassador to the U.S., Andries van Agt was Prime Minister of the Netherlands from 1976–1979.

Though history is punctuated by tales of migration—not just quests for a better life, but also conquests, crusades, and colonization—the current global movement of people from South to North and from East to West is developing into a problem of immense proportions.

The contemporary notion of *migrant* is all-inclusive, and embraces a far wider group than the refugees to whom even the United Nations Convention of 1951 applies. That convention applies only to those that have left their country because of a "well-founded fear of persecution" for reasons of race, religion or nationality; or because they belong to a particular social group; or because of their political convictions.

The broader concept includes people leaving their home country for reasons other than fear of persecution. And it also includes those who have fled their homes and become displaced within the boundaries of their own state.

Of course, not every migrant poses a problem. Many are resettled, able to earn a decent living for themselves and their family, and to contribute in one way or another to the economy and society of their new-found land. However, many others are not so lucky. They find themselves facing the worst conceivable living conditions and becoming a burden—either culturally, financially, or both—for the host country.

Size of the Problem There are now some 15 million refugees that meet the strict criteria of the UN convention—as compared to 2.5 million in 1970. Even more disturbing, the International Labor Organization estimates that the total number of legal and illegal economic migrants could be as high as 100 million.

Applications for asylum in the traditional asylum-granting regions of North America and Europe have gone up from 25,000 per year in the early seventies to some 600,000 per year today. Needless to say, not all applicants pass the test. Only a little more than 3 percent of these applicants are eventually recognized as political refugees under the UN Convention.

The United States still takes in as many immigrants—political refugees and others—annually as all others put together: about three quarters of a million each year. The number of illegal aliens residing in the U.S.—many of whom are from Mexico, which is by far the largest net exporter of migrants in the world—is estimated to be more than 10 million.

As far as Western Europe is concerned, the potential for migration from the neighboring countries to this land of milk and honey is breath-taking.

Australia and Canada are next in line as recipient countries, followed by, of all places, Saudi Arabia and the Ivory Coast.

As far as Western Europe is concerned, the potential for migration from the neighboring countries to this land of milk and honey is breath-taking: Today, some 400 million people live between the Oder-Neisse and the Bering Strait; some 150 million people live in North Africa, including Egypt; and some 170 million live in West Asia, including Turkey but excluding Iran.

The Causes of Migration The causes of migration are well known, ranging from persecution and violations of human rights to warfare, economic deprivation, and environmental degradation, to any number of problems exacerbated by rapid population growth.

Today most wars are being waged in the developing world. All told, there are thirty-eight internal wars going on right now. The Horn of Africa epitomizes the problem: Almost 700,000 Ethiopians have taken refuge in Sudan; almost 400,000 Sudanese in Ethiopia. Some 600,000 Ethiopians have fled to Somalia, and more than 300,000 Somalians to Ethiopia.

Though this list is far from complete, civil wars and ethnic strife have also been hitting Angola, Mozambique, Afghanistan, Cambodia, Vietnam, Sri Lanka, Nicaragua, and El Salvador.

Countries in the Northern Hemisphere carry a considerable amount of responsibility for this state of affairs. In quite a few cases, armed clashes are rooted in the legacy of colonization: arbitrary borders and artificially created nation-states. Furthermore, there is the impact of the East-West cold war, which prompted arms exports and the eventual militarization of numerous developing countries.

Though there has been migration all over the world since time immemorial, the information revolution and the transportation revolution have greatly accelerated migration.

Due to the information revolution, people are much better informed than ever before on living conditions in other regions of the world. This knowledge inevitably increases the desire and willingness to escape misery and suffering at home.

Additionally, the means of transportation now provide access to the islands of affluence or, at least, to places where life is somewhat kinder and gentler.

Environmental Refugees There is also another class of refugees: those who

The New Breed of Global Refugee

In the decades ahead, the mass uncontrolled movement of refugees across the globe will be one of the principal threats to international security. Today, an explosion of *poverty refugees* fleeing the destitution of their homelands far exceeds the number of *traditional refugees* fleeing persecution and war.

Unlike the few thousand refugees that had to be resettled after the Hungarian uprising of 1956, for example, today scores of millions are trying to survive by negotiating the chasm between the rich and poor nations.

After years of demanding open borders and the free movement of people in the context of the cold war, the relatively well-to-do West must not now build a new Berlin Wall of visa restrictions to keep out poor migrants. Unless we seek to alleviate the source of their misery through development assistance, we surely risk inviting a new kind of global violence. That violence will be born of despair and could well be carried out with the chemical or nuclear weapons so easily accessible today.

In short, the current dimensions of the world refugee problem demand a redefinition of the issue in terms of security, not charity alone.

Go to the Source of the Problem
Undoubtedly, as the disparities between wealth and poverty grow on a world scale at the same time as political regimes like those in Eastern Europe liberalize, the flow of new refugees will swell even further.

While it may be as understandable that people try to escape from poverty as that they flee political persecution—indeed, it may be more dangerous to life and health to be forced to return to conditions of poverty than repression—it is quite impossible to absorb the new refugees through the usual means of asylum. Already the limits of psychological, if not physical, saturation are being reached by countries that have traditionally granted asylum.

As can be clearly seen in the case of the Vietnamese who fled to Hong Kong in the hopes of moving on to America or Europe, it is much more difficult now than it was twenty or even ten years ago to find a third country for refugees.

Therefore, I am convinced, as we move toward the next century, that the only viable course is to maintain the formal distinction between traditional political refugees and the new economic refugees. But just as persecution and oppression have to be met by the opportunity for asylum, the response to migration for economic reasons must be met by development aid to the poverty-stricken nations.

Unfortunately, because the flood of poverty refugees is now so great, one of our major problems is determining just who has fled for reasons of persecution, as opposed to poverty, and thus deserves traditional asylum. In many instances we don't even have the opportunity to conduct interviews with those who are fleeing; boatloads of Vietnamese are callously pushed back out to sea in many Southeast Asian countries. In such circumstances, no one is helped.

For this reason, the UN High Commission for Refugees is prepared to assist the return of refugees voluntarily to their countries of origin. The recent repatriation of more than forty-three thousand Namibians, thirty thousand Salvadorans and Nicaraguans and some one hundred thousand refugees from Pakistan to Afghanistan shows that voluntary return is possible, at least in these circumstances related to civil strife.

Our current program to voluntarily return Vietnamese *boat people* to Vietnam may serve as a model for the future. The effort is proving effective both in stemming the outflow of poverty refugees and inspiring others to return. Fewer are leaving Vietnam and more are going back.

First, we make reliable information available about the real consequences of leaving. Many have believed they could board a boat in Vietnam and land in Florida or California. In reality, many have ended up living on shelves in Hong Kong camps.

Second, under the auspices of the UN-HCR, we direct economic assistance toward the regions in Vietnam that are sources for most emigration.

Finally, we monitor the returnees to assist wherever possible in their re-integration into the life of their country.

Now that the ideological and military conflict between East and West has diminished, we have a rare opportunity to recast the resources and responsibilities of international organizations to meet new realities. By redefining the new problem of poverty refugees in the context of security, and vigorously addressing the root cause of the mass movement of peoples across the globe, we have a real chance to avoid the violent conflagration that otherwise awaits us.

Thorvald Stoltenberg
The United Nations High Commissioner for Refugees from 1989–90 and currently Norway's Minister of Foreign Affairs.

---

become displaced in their homelands due to environmental disasters such as the destruction of forests, erosion of arable land and desertification, water pollution, droughts, and floods.

By the early eighties, more than 1.5 billion hectares of cropland were irretrievably lost to the deserts, impacting more than 250 million people. Each year desertification and erosion take away 6 to 7 million hectares of cropland; floods and salinization another 1 or 2 million hectares.

The UN Environmental Program estimates the current number of environmental refugees at five hundred million. By the turn of the century their number could reach 1 billion. Moreover, these environmental crises have produced a mass exodus of former peasants, partly to still-usable regions and partly to the already overcrowded cities. The UN forecasts that by the middle of the next century about half of the world population will be living in urban areas.

Migration to Western Europe The wealthier part of Europe is now faced with two immigration flows: one from the South, in particular North Africa and the Middle East, and another from the East.

Migration from the South and South-East has been flowing into Europe for a number of years. Both France and Germany are said to harbor some 5 million legally residing aliens each, and the U.K. some 3.5 million. More than half of all these legal immigrants are non-European. And it is fair to estimate that the number of illegal aliens in these countries is many times higher.

As the economic gap between North and South grows along with an exploding population—the populations of Morocco, Algeria, and Tunisia are expected to double over the next thirty years—the pressure to further open Europe's door will grow.

Though there has been migration all over the world since time immemorial, the information revolution and the transportation revolution have greatly accelerated migration.

Mindful of the fact that the deprived will cross the sea in massive numbers unless their economies are boosted rapidly and vigorously, the European Community decided last year to triple its aid to the Southern Mediterranean Rim.

Spain and Italy, supported by France, are now advocating the creation of a conference on security and cooperation for the Mediterranean, modelled on the Helsinki structure. This should provide a framework and an incentive for development cooperation in various forms—including technology and know-how transfer—and it should result in more market access for countries south of the Mediterranean.

Growing Backlash Against Migrants
All opinion polls, as well as several key election results, have underscored a growing reluctance—even outright hostility—in Western Europe toward accepting more immigrants from Africa and Asia.

Additionally, one cannot but fear that the images of Khadafi, Khomeini, and Saddam Hussein, and the impact of the Rushdie affair, will only serve to consolidate existing biases toward migration from the Muslim world.

But objections to admitting more immigrants do not hold: These immigrants don't really endanger the survival of European culture, and they don't steal jobs. In fact, they mostly fill jobs less

favored by Europeans and, on balance, they contribute to the host countries' economies. People readily ignore the fact that their own ancestors had to go abroad by the millions no more than a century ago to find a decent living. Indeed, by the end of the nineteenth century, 30 million Italians had sought refuge outside their homeland.

The greatest concern at the moment, however, is immigration from Eastern Europe and the Soviet Union. From the early seventies to the mid-eighties no more than 100,000 people per year migrated from Eastern to Western Europe. As of 1989 that number has risen to nearly 1.5 million.

In the event of a collapse of Eastern European economies, or even a dramatic downward turn, unemployment in some Eastern European states and in the Soviet Union could rise to 50 percent for those between fifteen and twenty-five years of age. A recent study by Morgan Stanley Investment Bank concludes that unemployment could hit 14 million people in the Eastern European states and 30 to 40 million people in the Soviet Union within three years.

As for the Soviet Union, there is a worst-case scenario, not completely out of touch with reality, in which economic downfall and ecological degradation—alongside ethnic tensions and secessionist pressures—could spark a mass exodus toward the West. The Soviet State Labor Committee itself has estimated that 6 million Soviet workers could leave the USSR looking for work in the West. Even Eastern European countries fear this deluge. Czechoslovakia and Poland have already introduced restrictions on visits from the Soviet Union.

An Appropriate EC Response The EC is in the process of completing its *Single Market 1992,* which is designed to realize the free movement of goods, services, capital, and persons. At this late stage of integration, however, the free movement of persons has grown into a most thorny and sensitive issue due to new concerns about mass immigration.

Only two years after the fall of the Berlin Wall, there is, understandably, a tendency to erect higher outer walls to Europe in order to help EC member states overcome their reluctance to abolish all internal frontier controls. Western European countries are sharpening visa

restrictions, including invitation requirements. Some states have developed mechanisms that would put return tickets and cash into the hands of entrants. Strict obligations are going to be imposed on airlines and other transportation companies. Experiments are already underway—without much success—that offer return premiums for aliens already legally admitted.

Western European countries are sharpening visa restrictions, including invitation requirements.

In the end, however, efforts aimed solely at restricting immigration are bound to fail unless the prosperity gaps between North and South, and between East and West, are narrowed.

There are two critical areas in which it is necessary to act in order to begin closing the gap. First, the Uruguay Round of the GATT—that grand multilateral undertaking designed to open markets, diminish subsidies, and foster international trade and investment—must be completed. Trade restrictions in the highly industrialized countries discourage making investments in Eastern Europe, the Soviet Union, the Maghreb, and elsewhere in the poorer world. Without such investments, these economies cannot possibly rise to their feet.

Additionally, inasmuch as political considerations may not be sufficient yet to urge us to do so, enlightened self-interest should prompt the West, and certainly the Europeans, to come to the rescue of the people presently living in the former Soviet Union. Germany's rescue of its own countrymen, as well as its generous aid to the Soviet Union, should set a guiding example for all the West.

Western Europeans who dreamed about a common European home cannot now abandon the vision because it has become possible to realize it. The prosperous Western world must recognize that isles of affluence cannot harbor the Noah's Arc of the blessed. In the end, global apartheid is not sustainable.

Return of the *Volksgeist*

Isaiah Berlin

Perhaps the West's foremost political philosopher, Sir Isaiah Berlin is a fellow at All Soul's College, Oxford. Born in Riga, Latvia in 1909, he is author of Karl Marx, The Age of Enlightenment, Four Essays on Liberty, *and* Vico and Herder. *A selection of Sir Isaiah's essays, entitled* The Crooked Timber of History: Chapters in the History of Ideas, *was published in 1991.*

NPQ According to Harold Isaacs, author of *Idols of the Tribe*, today we are witnessing a "convulsive ingathering" of nations. Open ethnic warfare rages in Yugoslavia. The Soviet Union has been rent asunder by resurgent nationalist republics.

The new world order built from the rubble of the Berlin Wall has already gone the way of the Tower of Babel. What are the origins of nationalism? Whence this ingathering storm?

Isaiah Berlin The Tower of Babel was meant to be unitary in character; a single great building, reaching to the skies, with one language for everybody.

The Lord didn't like it.

There is, I have been told, an excellent Hebrew prayer to be uttered when seeing a monster: "Blessed be the Lord our God, who introducest variety amongst Thy creatures." We can only be happy to have seen the Soviet Tower of Babel collapse into ruin, dangerous as some of the consequences may turn out to be—I mean, a bitter clash of nationalisms. But, unfortunately, that would be nothing new.

In our modern age, nationalism is not resurgent; it never died. Neither did racism. They are the most powerful movements in the world today, cutting across many social systems.

None of the great thinkers of the nineteenth century predicted this. Saint-Simon predicted the importance of industrialists and bankers. Fourier, who understood that if glass was made unbreakable there could be no business for the glazier, grasped the contradictions of capitalism. Karl Burchhardt predicted the mil-

itary–industrial complex. Not very much of what Marx predicted turned out to be true, but the vitally important insight that technology transforms culture. Big Business and class conflicts are among its results.

They all thought that the imperial regime of the great states was the central problem of the twentieth century. Once these tyrannical conglomerations—the British Empire, the Austro-Hungarian Empire, the Russian Empire—were, together with colonialism, destroyed, the peoples under their heels would live peacefully together and realize their destiny in a productive and creative manner. Well, they were mistaken.

Although most liberal philosophers of the nineteenth century opposed the cruel exploitation of the *dark masses* by imperialism, in no case did any of them think that black, Indian, or Asian men could ever have states, parliaments, or armies—they were completely Eurocentric.

That, I suspect, changed with the Russo-Japanese war of 1904. The fact that an Asiatic nation defeated a great European power must have produced an electric shock in the minds of many Indians, Africans, and others, and given a great fillip to the idea of anti-imperialist self-assertion and national independence. In the twentieth century, no left-wing movement succeeded in Asia or Africa—in Indo-China, Egypt, Algeria, Syria, or Iraq—unless it went arm in arm with nationalist feeling.

Non-aggressive nationalism is another story entirely. I trace the beginning of that idea to the highly influential eighteenth-century German poet and philosopher Johann Gottfried Herder.

Herder virtually invented the idea of belonging. He believed that just as people need to eat and drink, to have security and freedom of movement, so too they need to belong to a group. Deprived of this, they felt cut off, lonely, diminished, unhappy. Nostalgia, Herder said, was the noblest of all pains. To be human meant to be able to feel at home somewhere, with your own kind.

Each group, according to Herder, has its own *Volksgeist*, or *Nationalgeist*—a set of customs and a lifestyle, a way of

perceiving and behaving that is of value solely because it is their own. The whole of cultural life is shaped from within the particular stream of tradition that comes of collective historical experience shared only by members of the group.

Thus one could not, for example, fully understand the great Scandinavian sagas unless one had oneself experienced (as he did on his voyage to England) a great tempest in the North Sea.

Herder's idea of the nation was deeply nonaggressive. All he wanted was cultural self-determination. He denied the superiority of one people over another. Anyone who proclaimed it was saying something false. Herder believed in a variety of national cultures, all of which could, in his view, peacefully coexist.

Each culture was equal in value and deserved its place in the sun. The villains of history for Herder were the great conquerors such as Alexander the Great, Caesar, or Charlemagne, because they stamped out native cultures. He did not live to see the full effects of Napoleon's victories—but since they undermined the dominion of the Holy Roman Empire, he might have forgiven him.

Only what was unique had true value. This is why Herder also opposed the French universalists of the Enlightenment. For him there were few timeless truths: time and place and social life—what came to be called civil society—were everything.

NPQ Of course, Herder's *Volksgeist* became the Third Reich.

And today, the Serbian *Volksgeist* is at war with the Croatian *Volksgeist,* the Armenians and the Azeris have long been at it, and, among the Georgians and Russians—and even the Ukrainians and the Russians—passions are stirring.

What transforms the aspiration of cultural self-determination into nationalist aggression?

Berlin I have written elsewhere that a wounded *Volksgeist,* so to speak, is like a bent twig, forced down so severely that when released, it lashes back with fury. Nationalism, at least in the West, is created by wounds inflicted by stress. As for Eastern Europe and the former So-

From *New Perspectives Quarterly*, Fall 1991, pp. 4-10. Copyright © 1991 by the Center for the Study of Democratic Institutions.

viet empire, they seem today to be one vast, open wound. After years of oppression and humiliation, there is liable to occur a violent counter-reaction, an outburst of national pride, often aggressive self-assertion, by liberated nations and their leaders.

Although I am not allowed to say this to German historians, I believe that Louis XIV was principally responsible for the beginnings of German nationalism in the seventeenth century. While the rest of Europe—Italy, England, Spain, the Low Countries, above all France—experienced a magnificent renaissance in art and thought, political and military power, Germany, after the age of Dürer, Grünewald, and Reuchlin, became with the exception of architecture, a relative backwater. The Germans tended to be looked down upon by the French as provincials, simple, slightly comical, beer-drinking yokels, literate but ungifted.

At first, there was naturally much imitation of the French, but later, as always, there was a reaction. The pietists asked, "Why not be ourselves? Why imitate foreigners? Let the French have their royal courts, their salons, worldly abbés, soldiers, poets, painters, their empty glory. It's all dross. Nothing matters save a man's relation to his own soul, to God, to true values, which are of the spirit, the inner life, Christian truth."

By the 1670s a pietist national counter movement was under way; this was the spiritual movement in which Kant, Herder, Hamann, the sages of East Prussia, grew up. The pietist attitude was, "We don't require what Paris offers. It is all but worthless. Only inner freedom, purity of the soul, matter." It was a grand form of sour grapes.

That is when nationalist self-assertion begins. By 1720 Thomasius, a minor German thinker, dared to give university lectures in his own tongue, in German, instead of Latin. That was a major departure.

The corresponding consequences of the deeper German humiliations—from the Napoleonic wars to the Treaty of Versailles—are only too obvious.

Today Georgians, Armenians and the rest are trying to recover their submerged pasts, pushed into the background by the huge Russian imperial power. Persecuted under Stalin, Armenian and Georgian literature survived: Isakian and Yashvili were gifted poets; Pasternak's translations of Vaz Pshavela and Tabidze are wonderful reading—but

when Ribbentrop went to see Stalin in 1939, he presented him with a German translation of the twelfth-century Georgian epic *The Knight in the Tiger Skin* by Rustaveli. Who, in the West, knew of later masterpieces?

Sooner or later, the backlash comes with irrepressible force. People tire of being spat upon, ordered about by a superior nation, a superior class, or a superior anyone. Sooner or later they ask the nationalist questions: "Why do we have to obey them. What right have they . . .?" "What about Us?" "Why can't we . . .?"

NPQ All these bent twigs in revolt may have finally overturned the ideological world order. The explosion of the Soviet system may be the last act of deconstruction of the Enlightenment ideals of unity, universality, and liberal rationalism. That's all finito now.

Berlin I think that that is true.
And Russia is an appropriate place to illuminate the misapprehensions of the *lumiéres*.

Most Russian westernizers who followed the eighteenth-century French thinkers admired them because they stood up to the church, stood up to reactionary tendencies, stood up to fate. Voltaire and Rousseau were heroes because they enlisted reason, and the right to freedom, against reaction.

But even the radical writer, Alexander Herzen, my hero, never accepted, for example, Condorcet's claims to knowable, timeless truths. He thought the idea of continuous progress an illusion, and protested against the new idolatries, the substitute for human sacrifice—abstractions, like the universal class, or the infallible party, or the march of history; the victimization of the present for the sake of an unknowable—future, that would lead to some harmonious solution.

Herzen regarded any dedication to abstract unity and universality with great suspicion. For him, England was England, France was France, Russia was Russia. The differences neither could nor should be flattened out. The ends of life were life itself.

For Herzen, as for Herder and the eighteenth century Italian philosopher Giambattista Vico, cultures were incommensurable. It follows, though they do not spell it out, that the pursuit of total harmony, or the perfect state, is a fallacy, and sometimes a fatal one.

Of course, nobody believed in univer-

sality more than the Marxists: Lenin, Trotsky, and the others who triumphed saw themselves as disciples of the Enlightenment thinkers, corrected and brought up to date by Marx.

If one were to defend the general record of communism, which neither you nor I would be willing to do, it would have to be defended on the basis that Stalin may have murdered forty- million people—but at least he kept nationalism down and prevented the ethnic babel from anarchically asserting its ambitions. Of course, Stalin did keep it—and everything else—down but he didn't kill it. As soon as the stone was rolled away from the grave it rose again with a vengeance.

NPQ Herder was a *horizontal critic,* if you will, of the French *lumiéres* because he believed in the singularity of all cultures. Giambattista Vico also opposed the Enlightenment idea of universality but from a *vertical,* or historical, perspective.

As you have written, he believed each successive culture was incommensurable with others.

Berlin Both rejected the Enlightenment idea that man, in every country at every time, had identical values. For them, as for me, the plurality of cultures is irreducible.

NPQ Does the final breakup of communist totalitarianism, a creature of the ideal of universality, suggest that we are living out the final years of the last modern century?

Berlin I accept that, almost. The ideal of universality, so deeply perverted that it would utterly horrify the eighteenth-century philosophers who expounded it, evidently lives on in some form in the remote reaches of Europe's influence: China, Vietnam, North Korea, Cuba.

NPQ One can only imagine how differently the twentieth century would have turned out had Vico and Herder prevailed rather than the French philosophers, or Hegel and Marx; if the local soul had not been overrun by the world soul. We might have had a century of cultural pluralism instead of totalitarianism.

Berlin How could that have happened? Universalism in the eighteenth century was the doctrine of the top nation, France. So everyone tried to emulate its brilliant culture.

Perhaps it is much more the rise of the natural sciences, with the emphasis on universal laws, and nature as an organism or a machine, and the imitation of scientific methods in other spheres, which dominated all thinking.

Fuelled by these ideas, the nineteenth-century explosion of technology and economic development isolated the intellectual stream deriving from such non-quantitative—indeed, qualitative—thinkers as Vico and Herder.

The temper of the times is illustrated in a story told in one of Jacob Talmon's books. He writes of two Czech schoolmasters talking with each other around the early 1800s. "We're probably the last people in the world to speak Czech," they said to each other. "Our language is at an end. Inevitably, we'll all speak German here in Central Europe, and probably the Balkans. We're the last survivors of our native culture."

Of course, such survivors are today in the saddle in many lands.

NPQ What political structure can possibly accommodate this new age of cultural self-determination, preserve liberty, and perhaps stem some of the impending bloodshed?

Berlin Cultural self-determination without a political framework is precisely the issue now, and not only for the East. Spain has the Basques and Catalans; Britain has Northern Ireland; Canada the Quebecois; Belgium has the Flemings; Israel the Arabs, and so on. Whoever in the past would have dreamed of Breton nationalism or a Scottish national party?

Idealists like Herder evidently didn't consider this problem. He merely hated the Austro-Hungarian Empire for politically welding together incompatible elements.

In Eastern Europe they really do seem to loath each other: Romanians hate the Hungarians and Hungarians have for years disliked the Czechs in a way the Bretons can't pretend to hate the French. It is a phenomenon of a different order. Only the Irish are like that in the West.

Only in America have a variety of ethnic groups retained their own original cultures, and nobody seems to mind. The Italians, Poles, Jews, and Koreans have their own newspapers, books, and I am told, TV programs.

NPQ Perhaps when immigrants forsake their soil, they leave behind the passionate edge of their *Volksgeist* as well.

Yet even in America, a new multicultural movement has emerged in academia that seeks to stress not what is common but what is not in the curriculum.

Berlin Yes, I know. Black studies, Puerto Rican studies, and the rest.

I suppose this too is a bent twig revolt of minorities that feel disadvantaged in the context of American polyethnicity.

Polyethnicity was not Herder's idea. He didn't urge the Germans to study Dutch, or German students to study the culture of the Portuguese.

In Herder, there is nothing about race and nothing about blood. He only spoke about soil, language, common memories, and customs. His central point, as a Montenegrin friend once said to me, is that loneliness is not just absence of others but far more living among people who do not understand what you are saying; they can truly understand only if they belong to a community where communication is effortless, almost instinctive.

Herder looked unkindly on the cultural friction generated in Vienna, where many nationalities were crammed into the same narrow space. It produced men of genius, but with a deeply neurotic element in a good many of them—one need only think of Gustav Mahler, Ludwig Wittgenstein, Karl Kraus, Arnold Schoenberg, Stefan Zweig, and the birth of psychoanalysis in this largely Jewish—particularly defenseless—society.

All that tremendous collision of not very compatible cultures—Slavs, Italians, Germans, Jews—unleashed a great deal of creativity. This was a different kind of cultural expression from that of an earlier Vienna, that of Mozart or Haydn or Schubert.

NPQ In grappling with the separatist Quebecois, Pierre Trudeau often invoked Lord Acton. He felt that wherever political boundaries coincided with ethnic ones, chauvinism, xenophobia, and racism inevitably threatened liberty.

Only individual constitutional rights—equal citizenship rights for all, despite ethnicity—in a federal republic could protect minorities and individuals. "The theory of nationality," Trudeau quoted Acton as saying, "is a retrograde step in history."

Berlin Lord Acton was a noble figure, and I agree with him. Yet we have to admit that, despite Trudeau's efforts, the Quebecois are still seeking independence.

In the grand scale of things, one has to consider that, despite royal and clerical

monopolies of power and authority, the Middle Ages were, in some ways, more civilized than the deeply disturbed nineteenth—and worse still, our own terrible century, with widespread violence, chauvinism, and in the end mass destruction in racial, and Stalin's political, holocausts. Of course, there were ethnic frictions in the Middle Ages, and persecution of Jews and heretics, but nationalism as such didn't exist. The wars were dynastic. What existed was the universal church and a common Latin language.

We can't turn history back. Yet I do not wish to abandon the belief that a world that is a reasonably peaceful coat of many colors, each portion of which develops its own distinct cultural identity and is tolerant of others, is not a utopian dream.

NPQ But of what common thread can such a coat be spun?

In a universe of autonomous cultural worlds, each in its own orbit, where is the sun that keeps the various planets from colliding with the others?

Berlin The idea of a center can lead to cultural imperialism again.

In Herder's universe, you didn't need a sun. His cultures were not planets, but stars that didn't collide. I admit that at the end of the twentieth century, there is little historical evidence for the realizability of such a vision.

At eighty-two, I've lived through virtually the entire century. I have no doubt that it is the worst century that Europe has ever had.

Nothing has been more horrible for our civilization. In my life, more dreadful things occurred than at any other time in history. Worse even than the days of the Huns.

One can only hope that after the peoples get exhausted from fighting, the bloody tide will subside. Unless tourniquets can be applied to stop the hemorrhaging, and bandages to the wounds so that they can slowly heal, even if they leave scars, we're in for the continuation of a very bad time.

The only nations about which one need not wring one's hands are the sated nations, unwounded or healed, such as the liberal democracies of North America, Western Europe, Australia, New Zealand, and one hopes, Japan.

NPQ Perhaps the two futures will live, decoupled, side by side. A civilization of the soil, so to speak, and a civilization of the satellite.

Instead of the violent splintering of nations, the sated nations will become a small world after all, with the passions of blood and soil drained away by homogenizing consumerism and mass entertainment.

Perhaps that is the price of peaceful integration. As Milan Kundera has recently written, frivolous cultures are anthropologically incapable of war. But they are also incapable of producing Picassos.

Berlin As for that, I don't believe that only tragic events and wounds can create genius. In Central Europe, Kafka and Rilke bore wounds. But neither Racine not Moliére not Pushkin nor Tolstoy—unlike Dostoyevsky—bore deep wounds. And Goethe seems completely free from them. The fate of the Russian poets of our century is another, gloomier, story.

Without doubt, uniformity may increase under the pressure of technology, as is already happening with the Americanization of Europe. A great many people hate it, but it clearly can't be stopped.

As we discussed, it is possible, as in the Austro-Hungarian Empire, to have political and economic uniformity, but cultural variety.

That is what I ultimately visualize. A degree of uniformity in the sated nations, combined with a pleasing degree of peaceful variety in the rest of the world. I admit that the present trend is in the opposite direction: sharp, sometimes aggressive, self-assertion on the part of some very minor human groups.

NPQ What about the emergence of a new set of common values—ecological rights and human rights—that can to some degree unite all these erupting cultures without cramping their style?

Berlin At the present, there don't seem to be accepted minimum values that can keep the world straight. Let us hope, one day, that a large minimum of common values, such as the ones you mention, will be accepted. Otherwise we are bound to go under.

Unless there is a minimum of shared values that can preserve the peace, no decent societies can survive.

NPQ The liberal dream of cosmopolitanism, even in the sated world, is not on the agenda as far as you are concerned?

Berlin Like Herder, I regard cosmopolitanism as empty. People can't develop unless they belong to a culture. Even if they rebel against it and transform it entirely, they still belong to a stream of tradition. New streams can be created—in the West, by Christianity, or Luther, or the Renaissance, or the Romantic movement—but in the end they derive from a single river, an underlying central tradition, which, sometimes in radically altered forms, survives.

But if the streams dried up, as, for instance, where men and women are not products of a culture, where they don't have kith and kin and feel closer to some people than others, where there is no native language—that would lead to a tremendous desiccation of everything that is human.

NPQ So, for you, Vico and Herder, the apostles of cultural pluralism, are the philosophers of the future?

Berlin Yes, in the sense that we are all affected by a variety of values to some degree. From the Greeks and the Hebrews to the Christian Middle Ages to the Renaissance and the Enlightenment of the seventeenth and eighteenth centuries, unity was the great virtue. Truth is one, many is error.

Variety is a new virtue, brought to us by the Romantic movement, of which Herder and Vico, whom I regard as the prophets of variety, were an important part. After that, variety, pluralism (which entails the possibility of many incompatible ideals that attract human devotion), sincerity (not necessarily leading to truth or goodness)—all these are thought to be virtues. Once pluralism of ways of life is accepted, and there can be mutual esteem between different, uncombinable outlooks, it is difficult to suppose that all this can be flattened—*gleichgeschaltet*—by some huge, crushing jackboot.

On this score, let me make a prophecy for the twenty-fifth century.

Aldous Huxley's *Brave New World* could perhaps be established, in part as an irresistible response to the endless ethnic violence and nationalist rivalry at the turn of the millennium.

Under this system everyone would be clothed and fed. All would live under one roof, following one single pattern of existence.

But, sooner or later, somebody will rebel, somebody will cry for room. Not only will people revolt against totalitarianism, but against an all-embracing, well-meaning, benign system as well.

The first terrible fellow to kick over the traces will be burned alive. But other trouble-makers will be sure to follow.

If there is anything I'm certain about, after living for so long, it is that people must sooner or later rebel against uniformity and attempts at global solutions of any sort.

The Reformation was such a rebellion against claims to universal authority. The domination of the vast territories of the Roman Empire collapsed in due course. So, too, the Austro-Hungarian Empire. The sun set on the British Empire. And now the Soviet empire.

There is a Russian story about a sultan who decided to punish one of his wives for some misdeed and ordered her sealed up, with her son, in a barrel with little holes for air. The sultan set them afloat at sea to perish.

After several days the son said to the mother, "I can't bear being so cramped. I want to stretch." "You can't," she responded, "you'll push out the bottom, and we'll drown."

Several days later, the son protested again, "I long for room." The mother said, "For God's sake don't do it, we'll drown." The son then said, "So be it, I must stretch out, just once, and then let it come." He got his moment of freedom, and perished.

The Russian radical Herzen, whom I greatly admire, applied this to the condition of the Russian people. They were bound to strike out for freedom—no matter what came after.

NPQ In Herder's day, we might have been unable to grasp the masterpiece of a Scandinavian saga without experiencing a North Sea tempest, but today, through MTV, teenagers from Beijing to Moscow to Los Angeles can share the same thrill of watching a Madonna concert. What can cultural self-determination mean in such an age?

Berlin All the same—past differences take their toll: The spectacles through which the young of Bangkok and Valparaiso see Madonna are not the same. The many languages of the islands of Polynesia and Micronesia are said to be totally unlike each other; this is also true of the Caucasus. If you think that all this will one day give way to one universal language—not just for learned purposes or politics or business, but to convey emotional nuances, to express inner lives—then I suppose what you suggest could happen: this would not be one culture, but the death of culture. I am glad to be as old as I am.

The Fall And Rise of French

Alors! The world has 5 times as many French speakers as it did 100 years ago. Africa will have more than half the total in the next century. Right now the Sun King's language is battling English and German for a place in the new Europe's sun. Can 260 million Francophones be wrong?

George Tombs and Angéline Fournier

George Tombs and Angéline Fournier are a husband-and-wife team who have traveled widely exploring the subject of La Francophonie. They are the authors of a forthcoming book on Quebec and contributing editors of a Canadian monthly in French, Cité Libre.

"When people talk of the decline of French, I see a decline of culture more than of language," said Thierry de Beaucé, who was long the French Foreign Office specialist most directly concerned with what is happening to French around the world. "The lack of great minds in literature upsets me much more than hearing a few new Anglo-Saxon words crop up in our language."

Is the influence of French shrinking worldwide, or is it growing? It all depends on whom you talk to. But the question is being asked by many anxious Francophones—French speakers—at a time when English is making gains just about everywhere.

In a recent book, Beaucé came up with a startling analysis of the fall and rise of French: In the 21st century, over half the world's Francophones will be in Africa. Last summer Beaucé was put in charge of African affairs at the Elysée, President Mitterrand's office. This prestigious appointment confirms France's intention of developing ever closer relations with French-speaking Africa.

"The language will become, for the most part, a Franco-African and Franco-Arabic language," Beaucé predicted. "The French of luxury and elegance will become the language of people who are hungry. The language of Latin superiority will become the means of expression of Muslim and animist civilizations. What a surprising turn of events!"

Surprising indeed, since French used to be the guiding light of diplomacy, science, and international culture. It stunned all of Europe with its brilliance, just as the Sun King, Louis XIV had done.

Decline had set in by World War I. The humiliations of Nazi occupation in World War II and the postwar meltdown of the French empire were the *coups de grâce.*

The language never seemed to recover, although its lingering glory stirs hearts to this day.

To an English-speaking person, this attention to language might seem excessive. But in the French hierarchy of prestige, people like Thierry de Beaucé who are extremely articulate are always put at the top—more than people who have money. Language is a source of authority, a perishable quality.

"One of the things which does make French political life more interesting than in other countries, even when it isn't exciting substantively, is that people are literate," commented Stanley Hoffmann, director of Harvard's Center for European Studies. "You can't be a distinguished president if you can't spend an hour on television talking about Baudelaire or Maupassant."

Worldwide some 260 million people know or have studied French, according to a recent estimate by the Agency of Cultural and Technical Cooperation (ACCT). That's five times the number of Francophones a century ago. The forty French-speaking countries together are known as La Francophonie, a loose political grouping a little like the British Commonwealth of Nations. The ACCT, based in Paris, is La Francophonie's official organization.

"Le francien"—the dialect of Île-de-France, the region around Paris—set the standard from the 16th century onward. But, since the 1970s, many other dialects and accents have become more widely accepted.

"There are real differences in the way French is used around the world," said Jean-Louis Roy, the Canadian secretary-general of the ACCT. "People everywhere create words relating to their own experience, whether in Europe or sub-Saharan Africa. Also, if you speak Bambara or Arabic, your French will be colored by the fact your mother tongue is different. But the general meaning of words is a common heritage."

French-speaking *Québécois* like Roy proudly defend their language. Americans have long been fascinated by French. Brazilians are lining up in droves to learn it. The language of higher learning in Senegal, Tunisia, and many other countries is still French. It has survived the communist deepfreeze of Romania, which may be home to 4 million Francophones today. Even in former French Indochina it is staging a modest comeback.

French is above all the proud creation of one country—France itself, one of the world's cultural superpowers. And it is taken very seriously.

"Just yesterday I received a delegation of Cambodians who spoke my language," said François Léotard, France's former minister of culture, a leading opposition member of the National Assembly and a possible contender for the presidency in 1995. "It all goes to show that French is not just the private property of my country: It is a language of *fraternité*—of brotherhood—among nations."

Can France maintain a double role as a leading star of Europe and the world capital of the French-speaking community? After all, post-imperial Britain went through a long period of soul-searching, and it plays a stronger role in Europe today than in the Commonwealth.

France clearly wants to have it both ways. It organizes regular Franco-African summits of heads of state and contributes a whopping 10% of all foreign aid given by the Organization for Economic Cooperation and Development (OECD). The "end of empire" hasn't put a stop to the use of French military forces abroad, whether in Zaire's Katanga province, in Chad, or in Lebanon (as the first peacekeepers there in 1982).

The countries on the receiving end of all this attention sometimes develop what could be called "post-colonial dependence syndrome," a slavish imitation of the grandeur that was France. The most extreme example would surely be Jean Bedel Bokassa. In 1977 he crowned himself "emperor" of the Central African Republic in order to become a new Napoleon for Africa.

Could it be that La Francophonie is merely a new name for an old empire?

Beaucé is frank. "That attitude is a mistake, because it leads nowhere. It's a sort of defensive, rearguard view, and that's why, very often in France, La Francophonie is so sniveling. We have to get beyond that."

Yet the influential newsmagazine Jeune Afrique once suggested, tongue in cheek, that Paris had a fair claim to being "the capital of the third world." It has been home to such revolutionaries-in-exile as Ayatollah Khomeini, and to developing-world news media like Jeune Afrique. Wealthy and working-class neighborhoods alike have become multicultural, and Paris banks have cashed in on the flight of developing-world capital.

Léotard doesn't believe in neo-colonialism any more than Beaucé. But he maintains: "It wasn't just products that built America's or Britain's world empire, it was language. French people should understand that our language opens up relations that aren't just cultural."

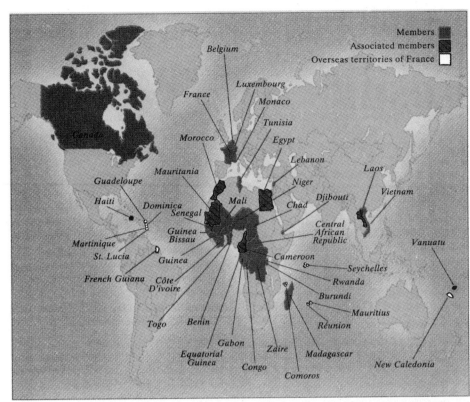

Agency of Cultural and Technical Cooperation: Paris-based official organization of French-speaking world, La Francophonie.

While French engineering companies and arms merchants remain active throughout La Francophonie, the commercial partnership with ex-colonies is still relatively minor. France's trade with the European Community is four times greater than with ACCT members. And 80% of its trade with ACCT member states or participating governments is accounted for by just four countries: Belgium, Luxembourg, Switzerland, and Canada. Which leaves only 20% for the ACCT's developing-world members.

Behind the passion and bravado of France lurks a fear that Anglo-American civilization is breaking down the last defenses of French in Europe itself. The Pasteur Institute is a world leader in AIDS research. (Its scientists have won eight Nobel prizes in various fields.) It caused a political furor when it decided to publish its annals in English only. In 1990 the Mitterrand government intervened in order to protect French as a language of scientific research.

Back in 1958 Jacques Tati's film masterpiece "Mon Oncle" poked fun at the fate that a plastic, pragmatic America reserved for a charmingly archaic France. Today even Mickey Mouse seems to have more chic than old Cyrano de Bergerac

has flair. Or at least that's the way many French people feel.

"All but one of the French theme parks built in recent years have already gone out of business," said the chairman of a large French construction group. "But Euro-Disneyland near Paris will be a huge success. Why? Because it is superbly organized, and it is American."

London is also nibbling away at the prerogatives of Paris. The language of work and communication of the European Community used to be French until Britain joined. Ever since, English has tended to supplant French. But the two languages may not be locked in a struggle for supremacy, not anymore.

"It's true that there is fierce competition in Europe between English, French, and German," said Stanley Hoffmann. "But I don't think any single language will predominate. The unification of Germany creates a new imbalance, and German will be very important for trade and for eastern Europe."

One of the objectives of La Francophonie is to develop an appreciation for French as a universal language. But the hodgepodge of some 40 states around the world with a common tradition of using French suffers from a structural disadvantage. Unlike Brazil or Hispanic America, the Francophone community is not massive. Nor does it run in a broad swath across whole continents, the way the Arabic-speaking world does. Instead, La Francophonie is an archipelago, a spattering of lonely islands around the globe, most of them former colonies or protectorates of Belgium and France.

The Arabic cries of schoolchildren at play drifted up to the apartment balcony, as Halina ben Amor took in the view of Tunis at dusk. She is a leading figure in Tunisia's women's movement, and a former diplomat and French teacher.

"I was born in 1929," she said. "In the days of the protectorate, people of my generation learned French as our mother tongue. I had to recite a line from the Lavisse school manual, which was printed in France. *'Nos ancêtres, les Gaulois,'* it read, 'Our ancestors, the Gauls.' It still makes me laugh because my grandparents were likely Berbers!"

Like many other Tunisian women, she began to study Arabic at age 12. That made entry into the workaday world after independence all the more challenging.

"French is a practical language for Tunisians, who have their own language, Arabic," according to Rashid Idriss, president of the Association of International Studies in Tunis and a former ambassador to both the United States and the United Nations. "It is a language for science and for communications with other countries, and we don't have any complexes about that. We see it as normal that we use another language than ours."

In neighboring Algeria, however, French is officially frowned upon. The 1 million dead of Algeria's 1954–62 war to wrest independence from Paris have not been forgotten. Islamic fundamentalism today associates French with anti-Islamic values.

In the early 1960s Habib Bourguiba and Léopold Senghor, the fathers of independence in Tunisia and Senegal, realized that decolonization offered the challenge of how to maintain the French language, which was too valuable an asset to be discarded. They gave a new impetus to La Francophonie, with a helping hand from Charles de Gaulle. "The General" was always looking for ways to counter "Anglo-Saxon" influence in any case.

The French president's historic *"Vive le Québec libre!"*—"long live free Quebec!"—from the balcony of Montreal City Hall in 1967 reflected his passionate interest in defending "French America." In Montreal he articulated a powerful idea: that French conveys universal values, what he called "the common conception of life and human relations which is ours, and which is expressed by our language."

But it wasn't until the Paris, Quebec City, and Dakar (Senegal) summits in the 1980s that La Francophonie really got going as a political institution. A further summit scheduled for November 1991 in Kinshasa was moved to Paris owing to the opposition of some ACCT members, Belgium and Canada among them, to Zaire's dictator Mobutu Sese Seko.

Today La Francophonie offers interesting avenues for North-South dialogue and cooperation. The ACCT has set up TV5, an international satellite TV network in French, pooling productions from North and South alike.

In addition, the agency is working hard at promoting French in artistic creation, education, and high technology. Computer-assisted translation is a priority. Senghor University, an international institution for African development, has just been set up in Alexandria, Egypt. The purely fun part of La Francophonie is music festivals with participants from five continents.

According to Jean-Louis Roy, the reason for joining forces is clear. "In terms of cultural productions, scientific research, and audio-visual production, we need to cooperate with our partners. Quebec alone, France alone, Senegal alone, Madagascar alone are too small to develop individual markets for their products."

Roy is the second *Québécois* to run the ACCT since its inception in 1970. The former African colonies of France and Belgium prefer a Canadian at the helm, since Canada has no history of empire. The provincial government of Quebec has used the agency as leverage to develop its own independent international presence, occasionally putting it at loggerheads with Ottawa. At the same time, Quebec has aggressively promoted its French character within its borders, establishing French as the sole official language in 1974.

France's most visible agency to promote French is doubtless the Alliance Française (AF), a state-supported but independent network of centers and libraries, until recently under the authority of Thierry de Beaucé. It offers course in French language and civilization to 300,000 students worldwide, half of them in Latin America.

In Rio de Janeiro the AF has its biggest center of all, with 14,000 students. "People are attracted by the modernity of France, but there is also a strong tradition in Brazil, going back to the 19th century, of turning toward France," said Pierre Rivron, AF delegate-general in Rio.

"We also have a sector we're developing in Rio and São Paulo, of French courses offered to companies. If the number of students is anything to go by, the decline of French is not visible in Latin America."

Nobody can deny that La Francophonie exists as a linguistic community, embracing places like France, Tunisia, Quebec, perhaps even Rio de Janeiro. Where people differ is in their assessment of the official institution, the ACCT.

"I don't think La Francophonie is important except for politicians and mostly civil servants," said Jean Paré, the publisher of L'actualité, a Montreal newsmagazine. "It's just not important for people like me in the media, or writers."

The ACCT is an institution suffering from its own peculiar tunnel vision. It maintains that a majority of Francophones in the world today are in neither Europe nor America. This sounds both generous and comforting, and jibes with the view that French is well represented in every part of the globe.

If one takes a closer look at official ACCT figures, the picture is quite different. About two-thirds of the 105 million people who have a real mastery of French, using it on a regular basis, live in Europe and Canada, places with low birthrates. The rest of La Francophonie is made up of bilingual communities speaking first their own language, then French.

Counts of Francophones around the world reveal a similar narrow vision. When the magazine Géo (like a French National Geographic) put out a lavish special issue on La Francophonie, it celebrated the existence of 35,000 French-speakers in Djibouti, 1,800 in Equatorial Guinea, and even 300 on the Caribbean island of Dominica. But the 1.6 million bilingual Canadians, whose mother tongue is not French but have learned it nevertheless, was simply ignored.

And just how Francophone are the countries of "Francophone Africa"? Roy admits that only 10% of their population really know the language.

Stanley Hoffmann at Harvard expresses some ambivalence about the idea of La Francophonie: "Actually the percentage of people on the globe who speak French as their principal language is declining. European populations generally do not grow as fast as the newly independent countries. The reservoir of French-speakers would be even smaller if North Africa took measures to make Arabic the language of teaching and reduce French there."

Judging by the example of English, the importance of a language depends on how much economic and political power is wielded by the people who speak it.

Still, defenders of La Francophonie like to point out that several great 20th-century authors have elected to write in French, their second language: the American Julian Green, the Romanian Eugene Ionesco, the Moroccan Tahar ben Jalloun, and the late Irishman Samuel Beckett.

As Blaise Pascal wrote in the 17th century, "The heart has its reasons, which reason knows nothing of." Which is another way of saying, *"Vive la différence!"*

Whither Western Civilization?

Achievements and Prospects

Thomas Sowell

Mr. Sowell is a Senior Fellow at the Hoover Institution.

There are many reasons to enumerate and reflect upon the achievements of Western civilization, other than a parochial vanity. For several centuries now, Western civilization has been the dominant civilization on this planet, so that its fate is intertwined with the fate of human beings around the world, whether they live in Western or non-Western societies. The products of Western civilization, from the sophisticated technology of air travel to various flavors of carbonated drinks, can be found in the most remote and non-Western regions of the world. More important, the ideas and ideals of Western civilization are in the minds and hearts of people of non-Western races with non-Western traditions. Perhaps the most dramatic examples were the throngs of Chinese people who risked their lives in Tiananmen Square for Western concepts of freedom and democracy.

Unfortunately, even to speak of the achievements of Western civilization goes against the grain of the intellectual fashions of our time. Both Western and non-Western intellectuals tend to judge and condemn the West, not by comparison with the achievements and shortcomings of alternative cultures and traditions, but by comparison with standards of perfection which all things human must inevitably fail. Such attitudes of sweeping, corrosive, and incessant condemnation from within are among the principal dangers to the survival of Western civilization.

WESTERN CIVILIZATION AS GLOBAL CIVILIZATION

Western civilization today no longer means simply the civilization of Europe, where it originated. Transplants of this civilization in the Western Hemisphere, Australia, and New Zealand are among its most vigorous elements, and its leadership and survival in a nuclear age depend crucially on the United States of America. The cultural penumbra of Western civilization reaches even farther. Its science and technology are today also the science and technology of Japan. Its languages span the globe and provide a common medium of communication among peoples whose respective mother tongues are incomprehensible to one another. Pilots speak to control towers in English around the world, even if they are Japanese pilots speaking to an Egyptian control tower. English is spoken by a billion people of all races—more people than speak any other language.

Much of the global sweep of Western civilization today, as its critics are quick to point out, is a product of conquest over the past five centuries and of the enslavement of millions of human beings torn from their homelands. Tragically, the horrors of war, subjugation, enslavement, plunder, and devastation are the common heritage of all mankind, on every continent, and in *every* civilization—Western and non-Western. Conquerors and tyrants whose very names struck fear into every heart have come from every region of the globe and have come in every color and countenance found among the human species. What has been peculiar to the West has not been its participation in the common sins and agonies of the human race but its special ways of trying to cope with those sins and agonies—the philosophy, religion, and government of Western civilization, which provided the intellectual and moral foundation on which rise the benefits of freedom, of science, and the material well-being of hundreds of millions of humans around the world.

Western civilization has not always been in the forefront of world civilizations, though it clearly has been for the past two or three centuries. A thousand years ago, China was far more advanced than Europe. As late as the sixteenth century, China had the highest standard of living in the world. There were Chinese dynasties before there was a Roman Empire—indeed, before Rome itself was founded. Confucius had died before Plato and Socrates were born. The Chinese empire had cities of more than a million inhabitants each, at a time when the largest city in Europe contained only fifty thousand people. Even after the emergence of classical Greek and Roman civilization, the evolution of Christianity from its Judaic background, and the rise and fall of the Roman Empire over a period of several centuries, Western civilization was still just one of the great civilizations of the world—not yet preeminent. As late as the Middle Ages, Russian rulers were vassals of the Mongol conquerors, to whom they paid tribute. The Ottoman Empire also penetrated deep into Europe, conquering the Balkans and holding them in subjugation for centuries. As late as the sixteenth century, Ottoman armies were at the gates of Vienna. The organization, science, technology, and scholarship of the Ottoman Empire were comparable to those of Europe, and its military forces won victory after victory against European nations. But, from the seventeenth century on, the tide turned decisively in favor of Western civilization—technologically, militarily, economically, and politically. More than anything else, Western civilization became the free world.

Historically, freedom was a very long time developing in the West, though it developed here earlier and more fully than in any other mass civilization. It has been less than a thousand years since the Magna Charta, yet that document exem-

From *Current*, September 1991, pp. 18-25. Excerpt from "Western Civilization: Achievements and Prospects," by Thomas Sowell, *The World & I*, May 1991, pp. 585-603. Copyright © 1991 by Thomas Sowell. Reprinted by permission of the author.

plified a crucially distinctive idea with deep roots in the Western tradition—the idea that the *law* is supreme and not the ruler. Whatever controversies may rage among scholars and polemicists as to the immediate effect or social bias of the Magna Charta, what has made it a landmark in the development of human freedom is that it established the supremacy of law—what has also been called "the rule of law" or "a government of laws and not of men."

THE RULE OF LAW

Like so many of the blessings of Western civilization that we so easily take for granted, the idea of the rule of law is radically different from the principles on which other great civilizations were founded. Even late in the twentieth century, many people in other cultures around the world found it incomprehensible that a president of the United States could be forced out of office on charges that he violated the law. Within Western civilization itself, it is little more than 300 years (not long as history is measured) since Louis XIV said, "I am the state." Yet, even then, the idea so conflicted with Western notions as to be worth remembering. Neither Genghis Khan nor Sultan Süleyman of the Ottoman Empire would have found it necessary to remind anyone that his *word* was the supreme law—and if anyone did need reminding, that reminder would be in blood and not in words. The West itself has of course also had rulers who were above any law—Hitler and Stalin being the most notorious examples, though unfortunately not the only examples. The West itself has not always lived up to Western ideals. The point here is that those ideals were distinct from the ideals of other great civilizations and, ultimately, they have made the West different in reality.

The rule of law—the principle that the law is supreme and that rulers are subject to it—goes far back into Roman times. The Emperor Julian once fined himself ten pounds of gold for a minor transgression and, in the words of Edward Gibbon, "embraced this public occasion of declaring to the world that he was subject, like the rest of his fellow-citizens, to the laws." Roman emperors in general were among the most flagrant violators of this principle, but the principle outlived the emperors and the empire—and ultimately the principle triumphed. The

Magna Charta was only one landmark on the road to that triumph. The Constitution of the United States was another.

Other great civilizations might have traditions or religions to which the ruler was at least nominally subject, but no human being was authorized to disobey, oppose, or nullify the edicts of the ruler, as appellate courts under the U.S. Constitution can nullify the edicts of presidents or Congress. In the great Chinese dynasties, for example, as a scholar has noted:

> Chinese law was always merely an instrument of government; it was not thought to have divine sanction, nor was it considered an inviolable constitution. It was part of, and inseparable from, routine administration. There were no provisions limiting state authority, and there was no church or independent judiciary before which the state could legally be called to account.

In the Ottoman Empire, the supremacy of the ruler was likewise subject to no constraint. According to Lord Kinross' classic study of the Ottoman Empire, a fifteenth-century sultan "who was known to have ambivalent sexual tastes sent a Eunuch to the house of Notaras, demanding that he supply his good-looking fourteen-year-old son for the Sultan's pleasure." Notaras, a Christian, chose instead that he and his son would be beheaded—but that was the only alternative. There was no law higher than the sultan's command. The rule of law seems like such a mundane phrase, but without it, freedom and human dignity are in deadly peril. It is, perhaps, Western civilization's greatest gift to the world.

The rule of law, the supremacy of law, a government of laws and not of men—different ways of saying the same thing—is not a result of words written on pieces of paper. The Magna Charta was not accepted because King John thought it was a good idea but because the amount of military power lined up against him by his barons left him no choice. *Power offset by power* has remained the key to freedom through the rule of law. When the Constitution of the United States was crafted, the separation of powers was the heart and soul of it. The ability of each branch of government to impede or nullify the powers of the other branches means that there is no individual with supreme power.

What is to prevent whoever controls the military—the ultimate power of brute

force—from imposing his will on the other branches of government and on the people at large? This has in fact happened in a number of Third World countries that received their independence after the Second World War, even though many of these countries copied the institutions of Western democracy—in some cases, right down to the powdered wigs of lawyers and judges in the British legal tradition. What they could not copy, however, were the centuries of history, distilled into the traditions that make free institutions viable. In a society where such traditions are deeply imbedded in the moral fiber of its people, no ruler can issue orders to violate the Constitution with any assurance that his officers or troops will obey—and if they do not obey, he may be facing not only the end of his power but imprisonment and disgrace as well. Behind the institutions of freedom are the traditions of freedom that give those institutions strength. Both are among the highest achievements of Western civilization.

SLAVERY AS AN INSTITUTION

Freedom has many dimensions and we so often take them all for granted that we find it almost inconceivable that other places and other times could have seen things so much differently. To virtually anyone raised in modern Western civilization, it is painful to realize that the evil and inhuman institution of slavery has existed in civilizations on every continent inhabited by human beings. Slavery existed for untold thousands of years in China. It existed in the Western Hemisphere long before Columbus' ships ever appeared on the horizon. Africa, Europe, the Middle East—it was virtually everywhere. The eastern European peoples known as Slavs were for centuries slaves—and their name provided the basis for the word. Ten million Africans were shipped as slaves to the Western Hemisphere but fourteen million were sent as slaves to the Islamic countries of the Middle East and North Africa. The sweeping scope and long history of slavery make it entirely possible that most of the peoples on this planet today are descendants of slaves, from one time or place or another.

What is even more incomprehensible to us today than the magnitude and endurance of slavery is that it aroused little, if any, moral concern in most parts of the world. A few offered moral apologies for it but in many places the institution was so widely accepted that no apologies were considered necessary. Only very late in the history of the world's great civilizations did a major moral revulsion against slavery begin. It began in the West.

Those who spearheaded the organized effort to abolish the slave trade were British evangelical Christians. The worldwide abolition of slavery was a long, arduous, and costly struggle—partly because of opposition within Western civilization but much more so because the non-Western world (Asia, Africa, and especially the Arab world) bitterly resisted abolition of this institution, around which their own economies were often built. For more than a half a century, British warships patrolled the waters off the coast of West Africa, capturing slave ships and setting the slaves free in Sierra Leone. It would be difficult, if not impossible, to find in history another example of a great nation committing such resources, for so many decades, for a cause which would gain it neither money nor territory.

The next phase of the struggle was to abolish slavery itself. This abolition first took place in the British Empire in 1834. Within sixty years, slavery was abolished in country after country, throughout the Western Hemisphere. A worldwide institution, untold thousands of years old, was gone from three of the five inhabited continents (North America, South America, and Europe)—all in less than a century. What doomed slavery was that all of Western civilization had finally turned against it.

Other civilizations still retained slavery for generations after it was abolished in Europe and in European offshoot societies around the world. In African societies where the enslavement of other Africans had been going on for centuries before the white man came, there was bitter resistance to the increasing pressures from European nations for an end to the slave trade and an end to slavery itself. Among the Arabs, opposition was the most determined. Even czarist Russia, a despotic government by Western standards, forced the abolition of slavery in Central Asia over the opposition of its Central Asian subjects, who evaded the prohibition, when they dared not defy it.

With slavery, as in other areas, the West has not been immune to the sins that have disgraced the human species

around the world for centuries. But what was different about Western civilization was the way it attempted to cope with the sins that have plagued mankind. It is only the fact that the peoples of Western nations share all the shortcomings and evils of other peoples that makes their experience relevant to the rest of humanity and their example an encouragement to others. This is especially true of the United States, which has very few indigenous people and is populated by the peoples of other lands. It is the American traditions and American institutions that keep us free, not our individual virtues or our individual wisdom.

MATERIAL PROSPERITY

While freedom has been the highest achievement of Western civilization, material prosperity has been its most visible achievement. Stark as the contrast is today between an affluent, Western way of life and the grim poverty of many Third World countries, it has been just a few centuries since the masses of people in Europe lived on a level not very different from that found today among the masses in many parts of the Third World. In Scotland, at the beginning of the seventeenth century, people were still using farming implements as primitive as those in ancient Mesopotamia and it was common for ordinary people to live in unventilated, shantylike homes, homes shared with their animals and abounding with vermin. There were somewhat higher standards of living in England and on parts of the European continent but Ireland, southern Italy, and parts of eastern Europe were not better off. As late as the eighteenth century, visitors to Edinburgh found it worth mentioning that the inhabitants of that city no longer disposed of their sewage by throwing it out the windows—which had been a source of considerable unhappiness to passersby, even when warnings were shouted.

What changed all this? No great invention or discovery remade the economies of Europe or of European offshoot societies overseas. Instead, a gradual but persistent economic improvement continued over the years, with occasional setbacks, but building incrementally a new economic world of greater abundance. Here and there the wonders of science and technology gave Western civilization railroads, steamboats, electric lights, radio, and eventually the abil-

ity to fly. But the world did not stagnate between great inventions. Progress was virtually continuous and only cumulatively did it become dramatic. It was the wide diffusion of skills rather than the occasional outbursts of genius that was crucial. It was the spread of those skills from one Western nation to another that marked the rise of Western civilization to preeminence in the world, and the diffusion of its products that spread the benefits to non-Western regions of the globe as well.

England, for centuries lagging behind the economic and cultural progress of continental Europe, became in the eighteenth century the spearhead of economic development in Europe and the world. Englishmen introduced railroads to the world, not only by the example of railroad building in their own country, but also by themselves building and manning the first railroads in Germany, Argentina, India, Russia, Kenya, and Malaya—among other places. The steam engine was of course crucial to the railroad, and revolutionized industry and transport in general. For the first time in human history, man could *manufacture his own power* and was no longer dependent on his own muscles, or the muscles of animals, or on the spontaneous forces of nature (such as wind or water power) to get massive amounts of work done.

The modern technology of iron and steel making, on which a whole spectrum of industrial activities depends, also originated in the British Isles. Britain likewise spearheaded the development of the modern textile industry, supplying not only the major inventions but also initially the managers and skilled workers needed to train foreign workmen to operate British-made machinery in Russia, China, India, Mexico, and Brazil. In short, British know-how and British capital were transplanted and took root around the world—in Asia, Africa, and Latin America, as well as in such offshoots of British civilization as the United States, Canada, and Australia.

Once set loose in the world, the skills and technology acquired a life of their own, traveling unfettered, and flourishing wherever the social climate was favorable. While Englishmen had to install industrial equipment in Germany and teach the Germans how to use it, this knowledge was not merely absorbed but improved. By the last decade of the nineteenth century, Germany overtook Great Britain in the production of steel—

and by 1913 German steel output was double that of Britain. Across the Atlantic, the United States took the industrial technology in which the British had pioneered and developed it to become the leading industrial nation in the world. In 1870, Britain produced 32 percent of all the manufactured goods in the world, followed by the United States at 23 percent and Germany at 13 percent. By 1913, however, Britain's relative share of the world's growing supply of manufactured goods was down to 14 percent—exceeded by Germany at 16 percent and by the United States at 36 percent. Far away in Asia, Japan was already busy acquiring Western science and technology, though its own rise to prominence in the international economy was still decades away.

Why some countries and cultures seized upon the leading development in Western civilization and others did not is a question that may never be fully answered. It was certainly not due to "objective, material conditions" as some Marxist or other predestination theorists would have us believe. The industrial revolution did begin in a country (Britain) rich in coal and iron ore, among other natural resources used in industry. But one of the most spectacular current examples of high-technology industrialization is Japan, which is almost totally lacking in natural resources, while countries with rich natural resources (such as Mexico) are often lagging in economic and technological developments.

THE THIRD WORLD AND WESTERN CIVILIZATION

Different responses to the leading scientific, technological, political, and moral developments in the West have not been confined to those nations or cultures within Western civilization itself. Much of the ethnic strife within newly independent Third World countries is between groups who seized the benefits of Western civilization to differing degrees during the colonial era and achieved differing levels of progress and prosperity as a result. In Nigeria, for example, the Muslim northern region did not want Christian missionary schools established in their area. Therefore the majority of Nigerians, who lived in the northern region, did not receive the exposure to Western education received by the Yoruba

and Ibo peoples of southern Nigeria. The Ibos, a weaker, poorer tribe in a less productive part of the country, were especially avid for Western education and Western ways. The net results, after two or three generations of British rule in Nigeria, were dramatic inequalities, now favoring southern Nigerians.

As of 1926, there were more than 138,000 Nigerian children in primary school, of whom only about five thousand were in northern Nigeria, where most Nigerians lived. In the middle of the twentieth century, as Nigeria was moving toward independence, there were a total of 160 physicians in the country—only one of whom was from the north. In the army, three-quarters of the riflemen were from the north but four-fifths of the commissioned officers were from the south. As late as 1965, half of the officer corps were from the Ibo minority. Within northern Nigeria itself, at one time most of the factory workers, merchants, and civil servants were from the south. The envy and resentments this generated—especially when inflamed by ambitious political leaders—led eventually to bloodbaths in the streets, in which thirty thousand Ibos were slaughtered by raging mobs in northern Nigeria. Surviving Ibos struggled back to their region of origin in southeastern Nigeria, which tried to secede from Nigeria to form the independent nation of Biafra. A million more lives were lost in the civil war that followed.

American missionary schools were established on the northern tip of the island of Ceylon, off the eastern coast of India, during the era of British colonial rule. This happened to be a region inhabited by the Tamil minority who, like the Ibos of Nigeria, lived in an agriculturally less productive part of the country and who were also eager to seize upon Western education as a way to improve their otherwise limited prospects in life.

By contrast, the Sinhalese majority, who had rich, fertile land, had no such sense of urgency about Western education and their Buddhist leaders were not anxious to see them attend schools run by Western Christian missionaries. With the passing years, the Tamil minority—about 15 percent of the population—became over-represented among those in the educated professions. By 1921, 44 percent of all doctors in Ceylon were Tamils, compared with 34 percent who were from the Sinhalese majority (the rest being members of other minority

groups). Even in later years, after education became more widespread, the historical head start of the Tamils was evident in their continued over-representation in high-level professions. As of 1948, on the eve of Ceylon's becoming the independent nation of Sri Lanka, the Tamils were still 40 percent of all engineers and 46 percent of all accountants.

Until this time, Ceylon or Sri Lanka was widely known for having some of the most harmonious relations anywhere among its various ethnic, linguistic, and religious groups. Inequality alone was not enough to cause polarization—but all it needed was one skilled demagogue to whip up group against group. This happened in the 1956 election campaign and Sri Lanka has never been the same. Mob violence of Sinhalese against Tamils erupted again and again over the years, as a country once held up as a model of harmonious intergroup relations saw Sinhalese mobs capture Tamils at random and burn them alive in the streets.

Fortunately, not all intergroup inequalities among groups with differing exposure to Western culture have led to such dramatic and ghastly consequences. But such inequalities have been widespread, from India to Sierra Leone to Latin America. Those indigenous peoples who happened to be located where Western imperial powers established schools, colonial capitals, industry, or port facilities have tended to acquire decisive advantages over those in the hinterlands, and these advantages have persisted long after the Western powers have withdrawn and the former colony has become independent. There is a special irony to this pattern, for many intellectuals—both Western and non-Western—depict the Third World as exploited by the West, its poverty caused by the West, and Western prosperity as being extracted from the colonized nations. In reality, the poorest people in the Third World have typically been those with the least contact with Western civilization, while those who have achieved prosperity and leadership have been those most able and willing to absorb what Western civilization has had to offer.

Much has been said about the prospects of a decline of Western civilization, its eclipse by other, rising civilizations or its institutions and values succumbing to forces within the West with radically different ideas and goals. If there were some better world likely to be created by some new civilization replacing that of the West on the world stage, our fondness for what is familiar to us might have to compete for our loyalties with a broader concern for the happiness and progress of the whole human race. But no such conflict exists. There is no higher and nobler civilization standing in the wings. The alternative political and economic systems contending with Western democracy have little attractive power for the peoples of the world and in some cases have difficulty preventing their own citizens from fleeing to the West.

THE SURVIVAL OF WESTERN CIVILIZATION

With all its achievements, what are the prospects of survival for Western civilization? The external military danger is only one of the threats to the survival of Western civilization. Signs of internal degeneration are both numerous and dangerous: declining educational standards, the disintegration of families, drug addiction, and violent crimes are just some of the more obvious signs. Will such things alone destroy a society and a civilization? Perhaps not. But the internal and external threats are not wholly separate today, any more than they were in the days of the decline and fall of the Roman Empire. Internal demoralization of a free people cannot help affecting the confidence and zeal with which they are prepared to defend themselves—or the resignation with which some are willing to accept other systems that seem only marginally different from what they have.

In the Roman Empire, as in much of Western civilization today, there was a growing class of people who would not work but instead lived off the government. Today, healthy-looking young beggars are as common in Paris as they are in the streets of New York or San Francisco. The economic drain of such people may be overshadowed by the social demoralization they represent and which they contribute to in others.

THE TREASON OF INTELLECTUALS

Much more active agents of demoralization are the intelligentsia, including the media, schoolteachers, and academics. Despite some welcome exceptions, these classes tend generally to take an adversary stance toward Western civilization.

Sins and tragedies common to the human race around the world are discussed as if they were peculiarities of "our society." Slavery is only one of these indictments of Western civilization. *Colonialism* or *imperialism* to the intelligentsia mean, almost exclusively, Western colonialism or Western imperialism, even though non-Western countries had empires long before the West and even though the West has been abandoning most of its former empires since World War II. The only empire that has expanded overseas in the postwar era is the Soviet empire, often using Cuban troops to suppress any uprising against unpopular communist regimes in Africa.

Double standards have become almost too common to notice. No matter how many billions of dollars Americans or other Westerners donate to humanitarian causes, at home or overseas, they are still called selfish and materialistic, while other countries are called spiritual and high-principled, on the strength of their words, unsupported by deeds. Representatives of foreign countries, where racial or ethnic clashes have killed more people in a week than such clashes have killed in the United States over the past half-century, nevertheless, lecture Americans on the subject.

Why intellectuals have so often repudiated their own country and civilization in the West is a large question on which there are many theories. Perhaps it is precisely the freedom of the common man—including his ability to ignore intellectuals and live as he chooses—that has made intellectuals look so favorably on so many foreign despotisms that impose a master blueprint from the top down. These despotisms to which many leading Western intellectuals gave praise have included both imperial Russia and China and communist Russia and China. Intellectuals have romanticized despots from Robespierre to Stalin and Castro. But they have not favored *all* despots; the principal difference between those despots who have been praised by intellectuals and those that have not been is that despots with a master plan to remake the common man in a predetermined image have had the intellectuals' support. Ordinary, garden-variety despots seeking power and money, but leaving the common man alone to live as he pleases, have not had the support of the intelligentsia. Intellectuals supported Castro but not Batista, though Castro was more of a despot. Similarly, they supported Mao Tse-tung

but not Chiang Kaishek, Lenin but not Czar Nicholas. It is hard to deny Edmund Burke's observation, two hundred years ago, that intellectuals like theories more than people. And they support those who promote social theories. . . .

FREE MARKETS

The success of free market policies in the 1980s in the United States has spread the idea of free markets, not only to countries like Britain under Margaret Thatcher but also to left-wing and socialist governments in France, Australia, and New Zealand. Behind these practical political results have been a growing number of free market intellectuals. Friedrich Hayek once said that he was optimistic for the future because he was virtually alone when he wrote *The Road to Serfdom* in 1944. Now there are such intellectual giants as Milton Friedman and organizations—think tanks—springing up across the United States, in Britain, Jamaica, Hong Kong, Peru, Australia, and New Zealand. The political Left remains still dominant among intellectuals but today, at least, there is a struggle going on to save the basic values and institutions of Western civilization. Moreover, it is a struggle that can be won.

While millions of refugees from all parts of the world have flooded into Western democratic nations over the past half-century or more, some have come from totalitarian countries within Europe—first from Nazi Germany and its satellites and subjugated nations during the 1930s and 1940s, and now from the Soviet bloc. Russia has always been only partly a Western nation, whether under the czars or under the communists. It is not primarily a question of geography, though more of that country lies in Asia than in Europe. Nor is it a matter of racial composition, for people of European origin are about as high a proportion of the Soviet population as of the population of the United States. Russia has always been a fringe member of Western civilization in the deeper sense that the West's greatest achievements—freedom, democracy, and material prosperity—have come to the Russian empire (for that is what it still is) slowly, incompletely, and with a lag, if at all.

Nazi Germany likewise illustrates the fact that some of the greatest dangers to the survival of Western civilization can come from within Europe itself. Had

Hitler triumphed, nothing that we would recognize as Western civilization would have survived—not freedom, certainly not democracy, nor any of the other humane or spiritual achievements we call Western civilization. It is doubtful how long even material progress could have continued under suffocating economic controls by the Nazi state.

Western civilization today is endangered primarily from within the West—ideologically by Marxism, militarily by the Soviet bloc, morally and socially by degeneration within Western democratic nations. Let us look first at the external dangers and then at the internal dangers. Finally, let us console ourselves with a few hopeful signs that all may not be lost, though the hour is late and the outcome still uncertain.

Shortly after the end of the Second World War, Winston Churchill said: "There was never a war in all history easier to prevent than the war which has just desolated such great areas of the globe." How could the leaders of the Western democracies have failed to prevent a war that was preventable—a war in which forty million human beings lost their lives? They failed by operating on assumptions very much like our assumptions today and following policies very much like the policies of Western democracies in our time.

THE ILLUSION OF PACIFISM

One of the fundamental assumptions of the Western democracies throughout the period between the two world wars was that military weapons were the problem and that international treaties to reduce weapons were the answer. Strong pacifist movements and pacifist sentiments existed throughout the West, in the wake of the terrible carnage and devastation of the First World War. The shadow of that war hung over a whole generation, much as the grim shadow of Vietnam has hung over a generation of Americans. The determination to avoid another war is not only understandable but highly laudable. What was tragic was that the policies chosen led directly into another—and even worse—World War. At the heart of those policies was the assumption that disarmament treaties meant peace and that building a military deterrent meant war. Then, as now, maintaining and modernizing military forces sufficient to deter potential aggressors was called an

"arms race"—something to be avoided at almost any cost.

If the theory that disarmament and international treaties mean peace were correct, there would never have been a Second World War. The two decades leading up to that war were filled with disarmament agreements and international peace treaties—perhaps more so than any other two decades in the history of the world. This long string of ineffective treaties began with the Treaty of Versailles that ended the First World War. That treaty severely limited the military forces Germany would be permitted to have, did not allow those forces to be stationed in Germany's Rhineland, and forbade the Germans from having military conscription. Those were the peace terms imposed by the victors on the vanquished.

Almost immediately after the war, new international disarmament agreements and treaties were signed among all the leading powers of the world, including not only large and small nations in Europe but also the United States and Japan. The 1920s saw the Washington Naval Agreement of 1922, the Kellog-Briand Pact, and the Locarno Pact, among others. The 1930s saw the Lausanne Conference of 1932, later an agreement between Britain and Germany limiting each side's naval forces, the Munich agreement of 1938, and the nonaggression pact of 1939 between Nazi Germany and the Soviet Union. Added to all this, and often part of the process, were repeated visits of heads of states, to establish "personal contacts" as British Prime Minister Neville Chamberlain repeatedly called them. Heads of state had met before to work out international agreements, as at Versailles in 1919 or at the Congress of Vienna in 1815. But now there were repeated, almost incessant meetings, supplemented by public exchanges of letters between heads of state. . . .

Why did all these efforts for peace end so tragically in war? Fundamentally, it was because international peace, like domestic freedom, depends on a *balance* between opposing forces. Both pacifist movements and disarmament treaties had completely asymmetrical effects on democratic nations and totalitarian powers. Pacifist movements operate freely and pacifist sentiments influence foreign policy only in democratic nations. They weaken the ability of democratic nations to maintain sufficient military forces to balance those of totalitarian nations. Dis-

armament treaties are likewise asymmetrical. It is much easier for a totalitarian government to maintain secrecy when it cheats on a disarmament treaty, even when the treaty itself is evenhanded. In addition, the political pressures are on democratic leaders to sign an agreement, which will be regarded as a "success," while returning home empty-handed from an international meeting will be considered a "failure." The actual specific terms of an agreement are likely to be known and their implications understood by far fewer people than those who measured "success" or "failure" by whether or not a treaty was signed. A totalitarian government, which does not have to meet the same pressures and potential public criticism at home, is in a much better position to hold out for favorable terms before signing. . . .

History need not inevitably repeat itself. Recent changes within the Soviet bloc may be matched by changes in their foreign policy as well. It is much too early to know how real or how lasting any of these changes are. But it is worth looking back at what preceded these changes. It was Ronald Reagan's insistence on matching the Soviet nuclear buildup in Europe with new American missiles in Europe, pointed at the Soviet Union. While many in the media decried the futility of a new "arms race," declaring that the Soviet Union would match everything we did, round after round, the Soviets themselves understood that they did not have the unlimited resources implied by that argument. In fact, the stresses of maintaining their existing military forces were being felt economically and politically.

Now that a show of strength and resolve has brought some pullbacks by the Soviets and some hope of better future relations, the cry is already heard, in Congress and elsewhere, that we should cut back our military forces, as they are no longer so necessary. This attitude is painfully similar to the attitude that developed after the discovery of a polio vaccine, which led to sharp reductions in the incidence of that disease. When there was less polio, fewer people felt a need to get vaccinated—with the result that more people were needlessly afflicted by polio. Now that military deterrence has produced beneficial results, unilateral cutbacks seem dangerously similar to the polio fallacy. Reductions in military forces on both sides can be mutually beneficial if they mean a balance of power—but *not* if they mean simply maintenance of Soviet military superiority at a price the Soviet bloc economies can afford.

Military superiority matters, even if a shot is never fired. "Power wins, not by being used but by being there," someone once said. The implicit threat of military power provides the framework within which all sorts of political and economic decisions are made, all over the world. The Soviets have not invested such huge resources in military weaponry for no reason—and certainly not for defensive reasons. Whether the current pause in their overseas expansionism will last probably depends on how long the resistance of the West will last.

Index

Abdullah, 168
Act of 1729, 95
Adolphus, Gustavus, of Sweden, 6, 7
Agency of Cultural and Technical Cooperation, 230, 231, 232
Alexander I, 80
Algarotti, Francesco, 107–108
Alger, Horatio, 121
Algeria, 216
Allenby, Edmund, 167
Andropov, Yuri, 204–205
Arabia, 168
Arabian Peninsula, 164
architecture, Russian, 29, 30, 31
art: French, and public image of Louis XIV, 25–27; Russian, 29, 30, 31, 32
Asante, 143–144
astronomy, development of, 40–46
August Revolution, in Russia, 197–203
Augustus the Strong, of Saxony, 8
Austria, 12, 80; emergence of, as Great Power, 6–11; in World War I, 154–157
automatons, 65

Baghdad, 165
Baker, A. B., 48
balance of power, European, 7, 196
Balfour, George, 54
Basra, 165
Beaucé, Thierry de, 230, 231
Belgium, 154, 155
belle époque, 155–156
Bentham, Jeremy, 122, 125
Berlin, Isaiah, 226–229
Bernhardt, Sarah, 134–142
biogeography, 151
Boer War, 147–148
Bolsheviks, 82, 158–163
Bonaparte, Napoleon, see Napoleon (Bonaparte)
bourgeoisie, theory of Engels on proletariat and, 111–118
Brahe, Tycho, 41, 42
Brezhnev, Leonid, 204–205
Brooke, Rupert, 156–157
Burke, Edmund, 71, 80, 89–90

Calvinism, 35
Canada, Quebec and, 228, 230
Capital (Marx), 114, 118
Caribbean, 53; sugar plantations in, 22–24
Catholicism, 6, 179–180, 181
Charles I, of England, 35
Charles II, of England, 7, 20, 34, 68
Charles XII, of Sweden, 8
Chartism, 111, 112, 119
chemistry, Lavoisier as founder of modern, 84
childhood, commercialization of, in eighteenth-century Great Britain, 62–66
China, 234, 235
Chladni, Ernst F. F., 108–109
Churchill, Winston, 154, 167–169, 170, 239
classical liberalism, John Stuart Mill and, 125–128
climate change, origins of Western environmentalism and theories of, 53–54, 55
Clive, Robert, 70–71
Colbert, Jean-Baptiste, 25, 27
Cold War, 196

colonialism: imperial wars of Great Britain in, 143–148; West Indian sugar plantations and, 22–24
Commerson, Philibert, 52
communism, 82, 111, 112, 114–115, 117
Condition of the Working Class in England (Engels), 111–118
Conduitt, John, 47
conservationism, origins of Western, 51–55
Copernicus, Nicolaus, 40–42, 44
Constitution, Montesquieu as godfather to American, 75–78
Corn Laws, British, 111, 119, 151
cottage industry, see domestic system
Czechoslovakia, 195

Darwin, Charles, 54, 119, 123
de Tocqueville, Alexis, 79, 80, 81, 82
Denmark, 8, 18, 19
despotic power, vs. infrastructural power, 15
diplomacy: origin of modern, 9; U.S.–Soviet, during Russian Revolution, 158–163
domestic system, and factory system in nineteenth-century Great Britain, 100–106
Drake, Francis, 12

East India Company, 13, 18, 35, 52, 53, 54, 67–74, 125
ecological imperialism, 149–151
education, European Muslims and, 215
educational toys, in eighteenth-century Great Britain, 62–66
Egypt, 164, 168
electromagnetic radiation, kinds of, 43
Elizabeth I, of England, 68
Emile (Rousseau), 57, 88, 90
Engels, Friedrich, 111–118
Enlightenment, 84; birth of public opinion in, 56–60
Enver Pasha, 165–166
environment, globalization and, 210
environmental refugees, 223–224
environmentalism, origins of Western, 51–55
Essay Concerning Human Understanding, An (Locke), 33, 34, 36, 37
Europeans, biological expansion of, 149–151
euthanasia, dissent in Nazi Germany over, 180–181

Faisal, 169–170
Federalist, 76, 77
Ferdinand, Franz, 154
Fielding, Henry, 96–97
Fifth Republic, of France, 82
Fontenelle, Bernard Le Bovier de, 47
Fourier, Jean-Baptiste-Joseph, 110
France, 12, 20, 21, 70, 77, 112, 144, 227; emergence of, as Great Power, 6–11; Muslims in, 214, 215, 216; origins of environmentalism and, 52–53; public image control by Louis XIV and, 25–27; public opinion and, 56, 57–58, 59–60; revolution in, 77–78, 79–82, 83–87, 88, 90, 91
Francis, David R., 159, 160–161, 163
free markets: globalization and, 209–210; Western civilization and, 238–239
Freemasonry, 58–59

French language, growth in numbers of people speaking, 230–233

Galileo (Galilei), 42–43, 44, 83
Garibaldi, Giuseppe, 129–133
Garve, Christian, 60
Gauss, Carl Friedrich, 108
George, David Lloyd, 167, 168
George III, of England, 12, 79
Germain, Sophie, 107–110
Germany, 6, 7, 21, 29, 35, 111–112, 150, 215, 227, 236–237; dissent in Nazi, 178–182
gin, in eighteenth-century Great Britain, 93–97
Gin Acts, in eighteenth-century Great Britain, 95, 96, 97
globalization, 208–210, 220–221
Glorious Revolution of 1688, 8, 14, 21, 33, 79
Gorbachev, Mikhail, 198–200, 201, 202, 203, 204, 205
Great Britain, 76–77, 79, 80, 81–82, 111, 112, 150, 151, 236–237; breakup of Ottoman Empire and, 164–170; colonialism and, 143–148; commercialization of childhood in eighteenth-century, 62–66; cottage industry and factory system in, 100–106; East India Company and, 13, 18, 35, 52, 53, 54, 67–74, 125; emergence of, as Great Power, 6–11, 12–16; gin in eighteenth-century, 93–97; Muslim in, 213, 214, 215, 216–217; origins of environmentalism and, 52, 53–55; trade rivalry of, with Dutch, 17–21, 67–74
Great Powers, emergence of, 6–11
guillotine, 78, 82, 83
Gysi, Gregor, 205

Haddad, Wadia, 204–205
Hales, Stephen, 53
Hamilton, Alexander, 76, 77, 78
Hanseatic League, 18, 19, 219–222
Hapsburg family, 6, 154
heliocentric universe, theory of, 42–43
Helvétius, 76
Henry VIII, of England, 35
Henty, G. A., 147
Herder, Johann Gottfried, 226, 227, 228, 229
Herschel, William, 45
Herzen, Alexander, 227
high-tech Hanseatic cities, 219–222
Hogarth, William, 96, 97
Hohenzollern family, 8, 156
Hughes, Robert P., 145
Hugo, Victor, 79, 139
human rights, 88
Humboldt, Alexander von, 53
Hungary, 8; in World War I, 154–157

immigration, 223–225
industrial revolution, in Great Britain, 100–106
information-technology, globalization and, 209–210
infrastructural power, vs. despotic power, 15
intellectuals, treason of, and Western civilization, 238
Iran, 216
Iraq, 164, 165

Italy, 9, 18, 19, 29, 215; Jews in, during World War II, 183–186; Giuseppe Garibaldi and, 129–133; Benito Mussolini and, 171–177

Jacobin Club, 77–78, 81, 82
James II, of England, 33
Jefferson, Thomas, 33
Jews: in Italy during World War II, 183–186; dissent in Nazi Germany and, 178–179, 182
jigsaw puzzle, invention of, 65

Kerensky, Alexander, 159, 160, 161, 195
Kings Hill Forest Act, 53
Kuwait, 164, 165

Lacépède, comte de, 84
Lagrange, Joseph-Louis, 107, 108, 109, 110
Lalande, Joseph-Jérôme, 108
L'Ambassadeur et ses fonctions (Wicquefort), 9–10
language, growth of people speaking French and, 230–233
Lavoisier, Antoine, 83–87
law, in Western civilization, 235
Lawrence, T. E., 160
Legendre, Adrien-Marie, 108, 110
Lenin, V. I., 81, 117, 159, 160, 161, 162, 163
Léotard, François, 230–231
Letter Concerning Toleration (Locke), 33, 36–37
liberty: John Locke and, 33–37; John Stuart Mill and, 119, 125–128; Montesquieu and, 76–77
literature: for British children in eighteenth century, 62–66; French, 26, 156; Russian, 29
Little Pretty Pocket-Book (Newbery), 63–64
Locke, John, 33–37, 62, 126
Louis XIV, of France, 7, 8, 10, 15, 65, 75, 227; public image control by, 25–28
Louis XVI, of France, 83, 90
Louis-Phillippe, of France, 80, 81, 82
Luddite movement, 101, 104
Luftwaffe, 195
Luther, Martin, 40
Lyell, Charles, 54

Madison, James, 33, 76, 77, 78
Magna Charta, 234–235
Marx, Karl, 81, 82, 125, 161; Engels and, 112–113, 114–115, 116
mathematics, Sophie Germain and women in, 107–110
Mauritius, 52–53
media, public image of Louis XIV and, 25–27
mercury, neurological basis of abnormal behavior of Isaac Newton, 49–50
metric system, invention of, 86
Middle East, 164–170
migration, 223; causes of, 223; Western Europe and, 224–225
Mill, John Stuart, 119, 125–128
Moguls, 68–69, 70, 71
Montesquieu, 33; as godfather of American Constitution, 75–78
Moscow Baroque, 29, 30, 31
"Muslim Manifesto—A Strategy for Survival, The" (Siddiqui), 213, 217–218
Muslims, in Europe, 213–218

Mussolini, Benito, 171–177
"myopic utilitarian opportunism" approach, city-states of future and, 219

Napoleon (Bonaparte), 82
Napoleon III, 81, 134, 154
nationalism, 226–229
Nazi Germany, dissent in, 178–182
Neo-Europes, 149–151
Netherlands, 6, 7, 8, 52; Great Britain and, 12, 17–21, 67–74
neurology, abnormal behavior of Isaac Newton and, 47–50
Newbery, John, 63–64
Newton, Isaac, 36, 43–44, 45, 63; abnormal behavior of, 47–50
Nigeria, 237
nuclear weapons, 101

Origin of Species, The (Darwin), 54
Ortega y Gasset, José, 210
Ottoman Empire, 234, 235; breakup of, after World War I, 164–170
outwork system, see domestic system

pacifism, 239–240
Pasha, Enver, 165–166
Persian Letters, The (Montesquieu), 75
Peter the Great, of Russia, 8, 9, 29, 31, 32
Petrella, Riccardo, 221–222
philosophes, 76
physiocracy, French conservationism and, 52
pietists, 227
playing cards, educational, 65
Poisson, Simeon-Denis, 109, 110
Poivre, Pierre, 52
Popular Front for the Liberation of Palestine (PFLP), 204–205
Portugal, 18, 68, 80
poverty refugees, 224
Prempe, 143, 144
proletariat, theory of Engels on, 111–118
Principles of Geology (Lyell), 54
property, Locke's theory on, 33, 34
protests, in Nazi Germany, 178–182
proto industrialization, 101, 102
Prussia, 6–11, 12, 14, 83, 195
Ptolemy, Claudius, 40, 41
public image, control of, by Louis XIV, 25–28
public opinion, 56–61
Puritanism, 35

Quebec, 228, 230

raj, British, 67, 72, 73
refugees, 223–225; environmental, 223–224; poverty, 224
Reign of Terror, 83, 84, 86
religion, as cause of war, 6, 7
renaissance, in seventeenth-century Russia, 29–32
Revolt of the Masses, The (Ortega y Gasset), 210
ritual, 25
Robespierre, 78, 80, 82
Robins, Raymond, 161–162, 163
Romanticism, 79, 125
Roosevelt, Franklin D., 158
Rousseau, Jean-Jacques, 33, 57, 58, 77, 80, 82, 88, 90
Rushdie, Salman, 213, 216–217
Russia, 18, 81, 82, 165–166, 197–203; emergence of, as Great Power, 6–11;

relations of, with U.S. during Russian Revolution, 158–163; seventeenth-century renaissance in, 29n32; *see also,* Soviet Union
Ruthven, Malise, 216

Satanic Verses, The (Rushdie), 213, 216–217
Saudi Arabia, 216
Second Empire, of France, 82
Self-Help (Smiles), 119–124
separation of powers, in American government, 77, 235
Serbs, 154, 155
Siddiqui, Kalim, 213, 217–218
Sir Isaac Newton's Philosophy Explain'd for the Use of the Ladies (Algarotti), 107–108
Sisson, Edgar, 158, 159, 161, 162
slavery: West Indian sugar plantations and, 22–24; Western civilization and, 235–236
Smiles, Samuel, 119–124
Smith, Adam, 122–123, 126
social Darwinism, 123
socialism, 82, 111
Soviet Union: end of, 197–203; secret files of, 204–205
Spain, 6, 18, 19, 21, 80, 150
Spirit of the Laws, The (Montesquieu), 76
St. Pierre, Bernardin de, 52
St. Vincent, 53
Stephenson, George, 119, 124
Stirner, Max, 114
sugar plantations, slavery in West Indian, 22–24
Sweden, 7, 8, 14, 29
Sykes, Mark, 166, 167

technology, globalization and, 209–210
technopoles, 219–220
telescope, invention of, 44–45
terrorism, support of, by Soviet Union, 204–205
textile industry, British, in nineteenth century, 100–106
Third World, Western civilization and, 237–238
Thirty Years' War, 6, 7, 18
Thompson, William Boyce, 160–161
Tippling Act of 1751, 97
toys, educational, in eighteenth-century Great Britain, 62–66
trade rivalry, Anglo-Dutch, 17–21, 67–74
triadic approach, city-states of future and, 219–222
Trotsky, Leon, 81, 159, 160, 161–162, 163
Trudeau, Pierre, 228
Turkey, 6, 7, 18, 19, 154; *see also,* Ottoman Empire
Two Treatises of Government (Locke), 33, 34
Tycho (Brahe), 41, 42

United States, 223; American Revolution and, 75; Constitution of, 75–78; relation of, with Soviet Union during Russian Revolution, 158–163
Uranus, discovery of, 45
utilitarianism, John Stuart Mill and, 125–128

Versailles Treaty, 195
Vichy France, 82
Vico, Giambattista, 227, 229

Vindication of the Rights of Women (Wollstonecraft), 88, 89, 90, 91, 92
Volksgeist, 226–229
Voltaire, 57, 76

Walpole, Robert, 93, 95, 96
Washington, George, 72, 73
West India, 53; sugar plantations in, 22–24
Western Europe, migration and, 223, 224–225
Westfall, Richard S., 47
Wicquefort, Abram de, 9–10

Wilhelm II, of Germany, 156
Wilkes, John, 93
Willcocks, James, 143–144
William III, of Netherlands, 8, 21
William and Mary, of England, 33, 34, 35
Wilson, J. Spotswood, 54
Wilson, James Fox, 53–54
Wilson, Woodrow, 157; Russia and, 158, 160, 161, 162
Witherspoon, John, 77
Wollstonecraft, Mary, 88–92
women: in nineteenth-century British textile industry, 102, 103; rights of, 88–92, 127; role of, in Soviet Union during World War II, 187–190
World War I, 81, 141, 154–157, 158, 162, 164–170, 195
World War II, 161, 178–182, 183–186, 191–194, 195–196

Yeltsin, Boris, 197, 198, 199, 201, 202, 203, 204, 205
Young Hegelians, 112, 114, 117
Younghusband, Francis, 144

Zedong, Mao, 82
Zola, Emile, 140

Credits/ Acknowledgments

Cover design by Charles Vitelli

1. The Age of Power
Facing overview—The Dover Pictorial Archives Series. 17—Rijksmuseum/Yale University Press. 20—Rijksmuseum. 21—British Museum.

2. Rationalism, Enlightenment, and Revolution
Facing overview—National Gallery of Art. 41—Peabody Museum, Harvard University. 42—The Bettmann Archive. 43—National Aeronautics and Space Administration. 68—Bowring Cartographic. 69, 70, 71 (top)—Larry Burrows Collection. 71 (bottom)—National Portrait Gallery, London. 94 (both)—By courtesy of the Trustees of the British Museum. 95 (both), 96—Mansell Collection.

3. Industry, ideology, Nation-building, Imperialism
Facing overview—National Archives. 100—From *The Textile Manufactures of Great Britain,* by George Dood, London, 1844. 102 (top)—From *Book of English Trades,* London, 1804; (bottom) From *Cotton Manufactures in Great Britain,* by Edward Baines, London, 1833. 103 (left top and bottom)—From *The Book of English Trades;* (right top) From *Penny Magazine,* November 1944. 104-106—Mansell Collection. 109—Courtesy of The History of Science Collection, Cornell University Library; photograph by Robert Prochnow. 110—Graphic by Laurie Grace. 120—Mansell Collection. 122—*Punch,* November 1858. 123—*Punch,* October 1858. 129, 131 (both)—Mansell Collection. 143—By courtesy of Lawrence James. 145—Mansell Collection. 146 (top)—HT Archives; (bottom) By courtesy of Lawrence James. 147 (top)—By courtesy of Lawrence James; (bottom) Mansell Collection.

4. Modernism and Total War
Facing overview—The Library of Congress. 165—The Bettmann Archive; The Illustrated London News Picture Library. 166, 167—The Illustrated London News Picture Library. 168—UPI/Bettmann; The Illustrated London News Picture Library. 169—Bowring Cartographic.

5. The Human Prospect
Facing overview—United Nations photo by John Isaac. 231—Dave Herring in *World Monitor,* The Christian Science Monitor Monthly. Copyright © 1992 by TCSPS.

ANNUAL EDITIONS ARTICLE REVIEW FORM

■ NAME: _____ DATE: _____

■ TITLE AND NUMBER OF ARTICLE: _____

■ BRIEFLY STATE THE MAIN IDEA OF THIS ARTICLE: _____

_____

_____

_____

_____

■ LIST THREE IMPORTANT FACTS THAT THE AUTHOR USES TO SUPPORT THE MAIN IDEA:

_____

_____

_____

_____

_____

_____

■ WHAT INFORMATION OR IDEAS DISCUSSED IN THIS ARTICLE ARE ALSO DISCUSSED IN YOUR TEXTBOOK OR OTHER READING YOU HAVE DONE? LIST THE TEXTBOOK CHAPTERS AND PAGE NUMBERS:

_____

_____

_____

_____

_____

_____

■ LIST ANY EXAMPLES OF BIAS OR FAULTY REASONING THAT YOU FOUND IN THE ARTICLE:

_____

_____

_____

_____

_____

■ LIST ANY NEW TERMS/CONCEPTS THAT WERE DISCUSSED IN THE ARTICLE AND WRITE A SHORT DEFINITION:

_____

_____

_____

_____

_____

*Your instructor may require you to use this Annual Editions Article Review Form in any number of ways:
for articles that are assigned, for extra credit, as a tool to assist in developing assigned papers, or simply
for your own reference. Even if it is not required, we encourage you to photocopy and use this page;
you'll find that reflecting on the articles will greatly enhance the information from your text.

We Want Your Advice

ANNUAL EDITIONS:
WESTERN CIVILIZATION, Volume II
Article Rating Form

Annual Editions revisions depend on two major opinion sources: one is our Advisory Board, listed in the front of this volume, which works with us in scanning the thousands of articles published in the public press each year; the other is you—the person actually using the book. Please help us and the users of the next edition by completing the prepaid article rating form on this page and returning it to us. Thank you.

Here is an opportunity for you to have direct input into the next revision of this volume. We would like you to rate each of the 45 articles listed below, using the following scale:

1. **Excellent: should definitely be retained**
2. **Above average: should probably be retained**
3. **Below average: should probably be deleted**
4. **Poor: should definitely be deleted**

Your ratings will play a vital part in the next revision. So please mail this prepaid form to us just as soon as you complete it.
Thanks for your help!

Rating	Article	Rating	Article
	1. The Emergence of the Great Powers		23. John Stuart Mill and Liberty
	2. War, Money, and the English State		24. Giuseppe Garibaldi
	3. Competing Cousins: Anglo-Dutch Trade Rivalry		25. Sarah Bernhardt's Paris
	4. The High Price of Sugar		26. 'The White Man's Burden'?: Imperial Wars of the 1890s
	5. The Fabrication of Louis XIV		27. Ecological Imperialism: The Biological Expansion of Europe, 900–1900
	6. The 17th-Century 'Renaissance' in Russia		28. Sarajevo: The End of Innocence
	7. Locke and Liberty		29. When the Red Storm Broke
	8. From Astronomy to Astrophysics		30. How the Modern Middle East Map Came to Be Drawn
	9. Newton's Madness		31. Remembering Mussolini
	10. Origins of Western Environmentalism		32. Resistance of the Heart in Nazi Germany
	11. The Birth of Public Opinion		33. A People Under Terror: Italian Jews During World War II
	12. The Commercialization of Childhood		34. Night Witches, Snipers, and Laundresses
	13. A Whole Subcontinent Was Picked Up Without Half Trying		35. 1945
	14. The Godfather of the American Constitution		36. The War Europe Lost
	15. The French Revolution in the Minds of Men		37. The August Revolution
	16. The Passion of Antoine Lavoisier		38. Facts on File
	17. The First Feminist		39. Jihad vs. McWorld
	18. Gin and Georgian London		40. Europe's Muslims
	19. Cottage Industry and the Factory System		41. World City-States of the Future
	20. Sophie Germain		42. Global Boat People
	21. Engels in Manchester: Inventing the Proletariat		43. Return of the *Volksgeist*
	22. Samuel Smiles: The Gospel of Self-Help		44. The Fall and Rise of French
			45. Whither Western Civilization?

(Continued on next page)

ABOUT YOU

Name_____ Date_____
Are you a teacher? ☐ Or student? ☐
Your School Name _____
Department _____
Address _____
City _____ State _____ Zip _____
School Telephone # _____

YOUR COMMENTS ARE IMPORTANT TO US!

Please fill in the following information:

For which course did you use this book? _____
Did you use a text with this Annual Edition? ☐ yes ☐ no
The title of the text? _____
What are your general reactions to the Annual Editions concept?

Have you read any particular articles recently that you think should be included in the next edition?

Are there any articles you feel should be replaced in the next edition? Why?

Are there other areas that you feel would utilize an Annual Edition?

May we contact you for editorial input?

May we quote you from above?

ANNUAL EDITIONS: WESTERN CIVILIZATION, Volume II, 7th Edition

BUSINESS REPLY MAIL

First Class   Permit No. 84   Guilford, CT

Postage will be paid by addressee

The Dushkin Publishing Group, Inc.
Sluice Dock
DPG **Guilford, Connecticut 06437**

No Postage
Necessary
if Mailed
in the
United States